THE *Babe*

Edited by Bill Nowlin and Glen Sparks

Associate editors Carl Reichers and Len Levin

Introduction by Jane Leavy

Society for American Baseball Research, Inc.
Phoenix, AZ

THE BABE
Edited by Bill Nowlin and Glen Sparks
Associate editors Carl Reichers and Len Levin
Introduction by Jane Leavy

Copyright © 2019 Society for American Baseball Research, Inc.
All rights reserved. Reproduction in whole or in part without permission is prohibited.
ISBN 978-1-970159-16-5
(Ebook ISBN 978-1-970159-17-2)

Cover photograph by Leslie Jones, courtesy of the Boston Public Library.
Book design: Rachael Sullivan
Society for American Baseball Research
Cronkite School at ASU
555 N. Central Ave. #416
Phoenix, AZ 85004
Phone: (602) 496-1460
Web: www.sabr.org
Facebook: Society for American Baseball Research
Twitter: @SABR

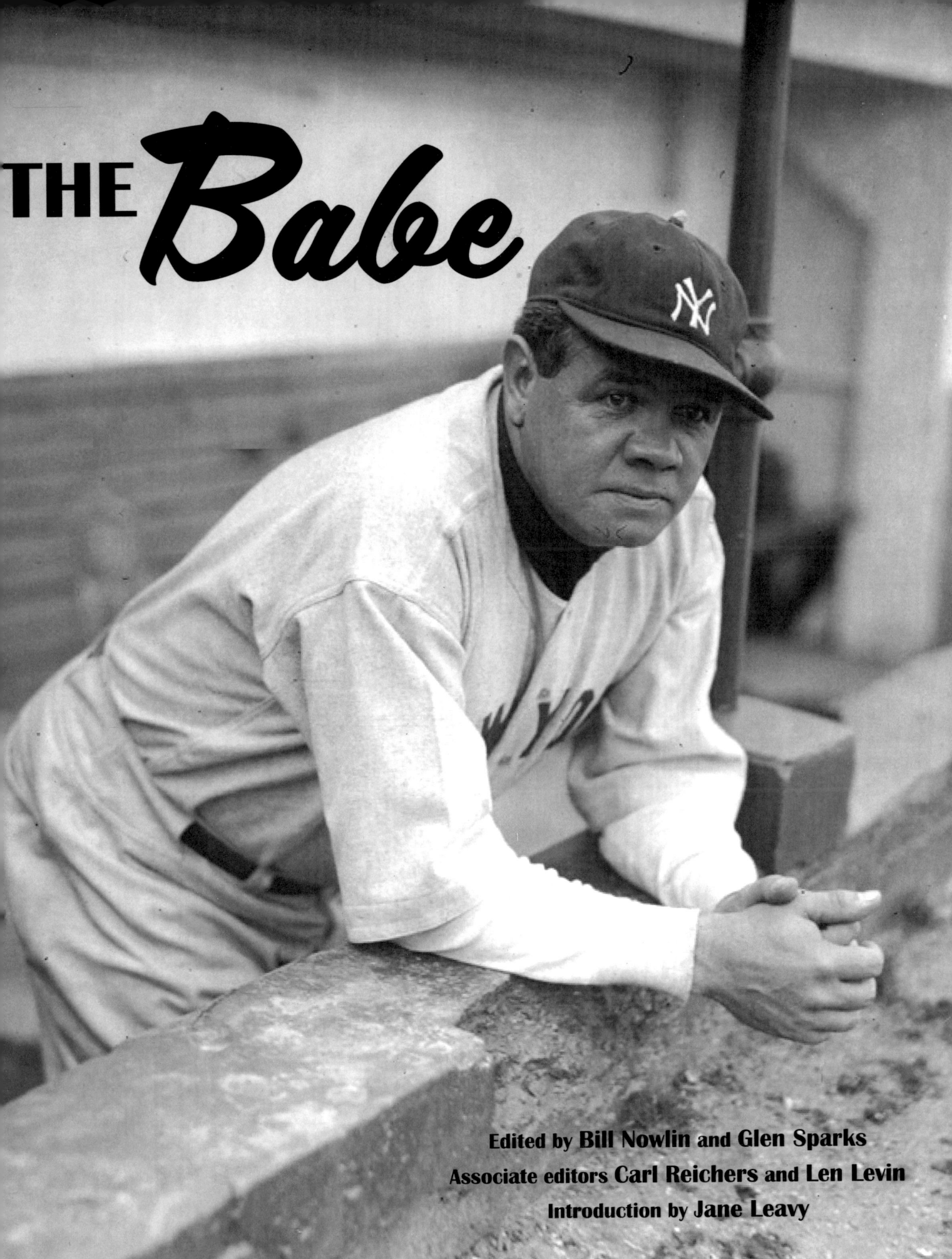

THE Babe

Edited by Bill Nowlin and Glen Sparks
Associate editors Carl Reichers and Len Levin
Introduction by Jane Leavy

TABLE OF CONTENTS

    Introduction   Jane Leavy..7

1. *George Herman "Babe" Ruth*   Allan Wood...9
2. *Babe – A Baseball Nickname*   Bill Nowlin...19
3. *How "Ruthian" Was Babe Ruth?*   Mike Huber..21
4. *Cool Babe Ruth Facts*   Allan Wood..24
5. *The Home Runs That Changed Everything*
    Hot Springs Historic Baseball Trail Research Team:
    Mark Blaeuer, Mike Dugan, Don Duren, Bill Jenkinson, and Tim Reid......................35
6. *Showdown: Babe Ruth's Rebellious Barnstorming Tour*   T.S. Flynn.................39
7. *Babe Ruth in Minnesota*   Stew Thornley..45
8. *Babe Ruth Visits Louisville*   Harry Rothgerber......................................49
9. *The Babe Comes North*   David McDonald...57
10. *The Babe's Canadian Connections*   David McDonald.................................61
11. *Babe Ruth and Baseball Diplomacy*   Robert K. Fitts..................................65
12. *Cigars, Horses, and A Couple of Homers: The Bambino's Experience in Cuba*
    Reynaldo Cruz and Bill Nowlin..70
13. *Babe Ruth and Cricket*   Glen Sparks..75
14. *Sale of the Century: The Yankees Bought Babe Ruth for Nothing*
    Michael Haupert..79
15. *The Mystery of Jackie Mitchell and Babe Ruth*   Leslie Heaphy....................82
16. *Babe Ruth and Lou Gehrig*   Tara Krieger..85
17. *Babe Ruth and Ownership: Not A Match Made in Heaven*   Gary A. Sarnoff.....97
18. *Babe Ruth and the Boston Braves before Opening Day 1935*
    Carolyn Fuchs and Wayne Soini, with Herb Crehan...104
19. *Babe Ruth's National League "Career" 28 Games with the 1935 Boston Braves*
    Saul Wisnia...108
20. *U. S. Presidents and The Babe*   Curt Smith..113

21. *The Babe: In Person and Onscreen* Rob Edelman 122
22. *Babe Ruth Characterizations – and Caricatures* Rob Edelman 126
23. *To the Rescue: Brother Matthias* Brian (Chip) Martin 130
24. *Babe Ruth: A Man of Simple Faith* Gabriel B. Costa 133
25. *Babe Ruth's Final Legacy to the Kids* Alan Cohen 137
26. *The Babe's Final Personal Appearance* Steve Smith 141
27. *Even Against HOF Hurlers, Ruth Was King of Swing* Ed Gruver 143
28. *The Babe as a Pitcher* Pete Palmer 147
29. *Babe Ruth Stealing Home* Bill Nowlin 150
30. *715* Allan Wood 153

SELECTED BABE RUTH BALLGAMES

31. *July 11, 1914: Babe Ruth Debuts* Joe Schuster 159
32. *October 2, 1914: A Sign of So Many Swats to Come:*
    Ruth Doubles For First Time as Red Sox Rout Yankees Mark S. Sternman 162
33. *May 6, 1915: Red Sox Pitcher Babe Ruth Hits First Career Home Run But Suffers*
    Loss to Yankees in 13th Inning Mike Huber 165
34. *May 20, 1916: Babe Ruth Replaced While Throwing a No-Hitter* Bill Nowlin 168
35. *June 13, 1916: Red-Hot Ruth On a Tear Against the Browns* James Forr 171
36. *August 15, 1916: Ruth Outlasts Johnson in 13 Innings* Jack Zerby 173
37. *October 9, 1916: Red Sox Win Game Two on a Loaned Diamond;*
    Babe Ruth Goes the Distance in 14 Cecilia Tan and Bill Nowlin 176
38. *May 6, 1918: The Babe Makes His First Start As A Position Player* Glen Sparks 179
39. *September 5, 1918: Babe Ruth Tosses Shutout as Patriotism*
    Prevails in Opening of Fall Classic Mike Huber 182
40. *April 18, 1919: Ruth Hits Six Home Runs in Six At-Bats* Jimmy Keenan 185
41. *May 20, 1919: Babe Ruth's First Grand Slam* Skip Nipper 188
42. *July 5, 1919: Athletics Prevail Despite A Pair of Long Balls by Babe Ruth*
    Rock Hoffman 191
43. *July 29, 1919: Babe's Blast Ties American League Record as Boston Goes Down Swinging*
    Nathan Bierma 193

44. *September 20, 1919: The Babe's Walk-Off Round-Tripper Ties Season Home Run Record*
Gregory H. Wolf..196

45. *September 24, 1919: Babe Ruth Passes Ned Williamson's Homer Mark*
Glen Sparks...199

46. *May 1, 1920: Babe Ruth's First Yankee Home Run is a "Colossal Clout" Against Red Sox*
Mike Huber..202

47. *July 9, 1920: Bambino Homers on Babe Ruth Day at the Polo Grounds*
Stew Thornley..204

48. *July 19, 1920: Babe Ruth Knocks Two Home Runs to Move Record over 30*
Tim Rask..207

49. *September 24, 1920 (1): Ruth Smacks 50th HR*   Paul Hofmann..........................210

50. *September 24, 1920 (2): ...and then 51*   Paul Hofmann......................................213

51. *September 29, 1920: Ruth Hits Number 54*   James Forr..216

52. *June 13, 1921: Ruth's Yanks Knock Out Cobb's Tigers*
T.S. Flynn..219

53. *July 15, 1921: Ruth's 138th Career Home Runs Ties Roger Connor's Big-League Record*
Gregory H. Wolf..222

54. *July 18, 1921: Babe Ruth's 560-ft Homer Against Tigers Sets Career Record*
Mike Huber..225

55. *September 15, 1921: #55*   Paul E. Doutrich..227

56. *October 9, 1921: An Injured Babe Wallops His First World Series Home Run While Shufflin' Phil Steals the Show*   Gregory H. Wolf..230

57. *October 10, 1921: Yankees Win 3-1 and Regain Series Lead*   Kevin Larkin..........233

58. *May 25, 1922: Ruth's Ejection Costs Him Yankees Captaincy*   Mike Lynch..........236

59. *April 18, 1923: Yankee Stadium Grand Opening Hints at Franchise's Dynastic Future*
Frederick C. Bush..239

60. *July 5, 1924: Babe Hit the Wall, and The Wall Won*   Chad Osborne....................242

61. *June 1, 1925: Babe Ruth Returns from "Bellyache Heard 'Round the World"*
Josh Berk..245

62. *September 24, 1925: Babe Ruth Beats White Sox with Extra-inning Walkoff Grand Slam*
Mike Huber..248

63. *October 6, 1926: Babe Ruth First to Hit Three Homers in World Series Game*
Mark S. Sternman..250

64. *October 10, 1926: The Babe's World Series Gamble*   Paul E. Doutrich..................253

65. *August 16, 1927: Ruth and the Roof*   John Gabcik..256

66. *September 29, 1927: Babe Ruth Hits Grand Slam in Two Consecutive Games*
Thomas J. Brown Jr...259

67. *September 30, 1927: Babe Ruth Hits Record 60th Home Run*   Kevin Larkin...............262

68. *October 9, 1928: The Sultan of Swat Smacks Three Homers to Sink the Cardinals*
Richard Cuicchi...264

69. *August 7, 1929: Bambino On Fire*   Thomas E. Schott......................................267

70. *August 11, 1929: Babe Hits 500th Home Run*   Chad Osborne..............................269

71. *October 1, 1932: The Babe Calls His Shot...Or Does He?*   Gary A. Sarnoff..................272

72. *July 6, 1933: A Dream Realized*   Lyle Spatz..275

73. *October 1, 1933: Lefty Ruth All Right In Final Mound Appearance*   Ed Gruver.............278

74. *July 13, 1934: The Babe Bashes 700th Career Home Run*   Kevin Larkin....................281

75. *May 25, 1935: Ruth Smashes Three Homers in Final Hurrah*   Jack Zerby...................284

76. *May 30, 1935: Babe Ruth Plays His Last Game*   Thomas J. Brown Jr....................287

77. *From Boston to Bushwick: The Big Bam Takes One Last Bow in 1935*
Frederick C. Bush..290

78. *June 19, 1938: Ruth Makes His Coaching Debut for the Dodgers*   Glen Sparks.....................292

79. *July 4, 1939: Lou Gehrig Appreciation Day: Ruth and Gehrig End Feud*
Paul Hofmann...295

80. *April 27, 1947: Babe Ruth Day*   Joe Schuster..298

81. *June 13, 1948: Babe Ruth Makes Final Visit to Yankee Stadium*   Glen Sparks.................301

82. *Contributors*..304

The Babe

I reached Michael Haupert in his car as he was driving home to Wisconsin from his annual trip to Cooperstown. My email in-box tells me the date was May 22, 2015. Tom Shieber, senior curator at the Hall of Fame, had told me Mike, a professor of economics at the University of Wisconsin-La Crosse, was the go-to guy on Babe Ruth, the Yankees, and the economic underpinnings of the Evil Empire.

Fifteen years earlier, on a previous research trip to Cooperstown, Mike had discovered a motherlode of Yankee financial data in unopened boxes in a climate-controlled storage room at the Hall of Fame, where they had languished since 1973 when a team employee offered them to the head librarian in advance of the renovation of Yankee Stadium. The boxes contained 24 years of accounting books and team ledgers from Jacob Ruppert's tenure as owner. The current owner, George M. Steinbrenner III, had deemed them superfluous.

Mike, executive director of the Economic History Association, and beleaguered Cubs fan, quickly understood their value: they offered a peek inside the inner workings of the most successful professional sports team in American history, a heaping portion of the forbidden financial fruit that baseball ownership had managed so effectively to keep to themselves through decades of hegemony. The closely kept figures showed how much they made, and how little they spent on player salaries; how much they charged their players for use of the pinstriped uniforms and how much they paid private investigators to follow them out of uniform. They revealed how much Ruppert agreed to pay Red Sox owner Harry Frazee for Babe Ruth in December 1919—$100,000, not the $125,000 reported by the *New York Times* at the time of the sale—and how much they profited from the acquisition. That would be a whopping $12.6 million in net profits adjusted for inflation. Or $20 for each dollar they had invested in the Babe.

Mike had been dissecting the numbers ever since, creating with his economist's regressions a transformative accounting of the economics of baseball. But he only had half the story. The owners' side.

What he lacked, I had found a month earlier in a report put together by Ruth's agent, the indefatigable Christy Walsh, the original "Jerry Maguire," whose efforts on Ruth's behalf and revolutionary plan for marketing and promoting him as an entertainer had long since been lost to history. "FINAL REPORT For Mr. GEORGE H. 'BABE' RUTH From CHRISTY WALSH 1921-1938."

Sequestered in a faded lime green binder, in the home of Ruth's granddaughter Linda Ruth Tosetti, the pages revealed every dime the Babe earned for barnstorming, vaudeville, endorsements, personal appearances, movies, and radio broadcasts arranged during 14 years of Christy Walsh Management. The total of $447,392.07—what Walsh called "by product money" equals $124,603,370 in 2016 dollars. The document was proof positive that my operating theory—and the basis for my book—was correct. Ruth and Walsh had created a financial template for every millionaire and multimillionaire celebrity athlete who succeeded him—in time and dollars. They had created a blueprint for how to be wealthy and famous in a new America.

But absent what Mike knew, I couldn't establish the fiscal magnitude of "The Big Fella." Couldn't demonstrate how he began to rectify the imbalance of financial power between players and owners.

I reached Mike by phone that fine May day in his car somewhere outside Cleveland. We talked all the way through Indiana and into Chicago.

He got off the line only because he had to negotiate the traffic en route to Wrigley Field.

When he hung up, I knew for sure—and for the first time—that I could write the book I had set out to create. Needless to say, his chapter "Sale of the Century: The Yankees Bought Babe Ruth for Nothing" in this volume *The Babe* was the first I read and most enjoyed. He didn't confess the deal he had made with the Hall of Fame until he came to visit me this summer: they had given him a microfilm copy of the Ruppert files in exchange for a promise that he would share the information with researchers like me. He had to talk to me.

"Yeah, but not across state lines," Mike pointed out.

His discovery in the climate-controlled vault in Cooperstown—and my discovery of Mike—is an object lesson in writing history. What we think we know, we often don't. What we think is certain, is not. What we think is the complete story hasn't been written.

Within these pages, I found anecdotes I had not heard, details I lacked the space to include, stories I couldn't get. Pete Palmer's analytic assessment of Ruth's greatness as a pitcher comes to mind. Robert Fitts' account of Ruth's triumphant tour of Japan in the fall of 1934, at the end of his tenure with the Yankees, includes this lovely, salient detail on the fascination with all things Bambino: "One old man brought a pair of high-powered binoculars, amusing himself and neighboring fans by focusing on the Bambino's famous broad nose, making his nostrils fill the lens."

Steve Smith's account of "The Babe's Final Personal Appearance" in Minneapolis in the summer of 1948, based on a story in the *Minneapolis Star and Tribune* that I hadn't seen, touched me as much as the less detailed wire service story I relied on in my book.

In his last public appearance, carried on the radio, which was a figment of scientific imagination when Ruth was a Boston Red Sox rookie in 1914, he was interviewed by an 11-year-old boy named Johnny Ross, dubbed Minneapolis's "biggest sports enthusiast." Johnny was blind. Ruth, who would be dead two months later from nasal pharyngeal cancer, could barely talk.

Johnny: How are you, Babe?

Babe: I don't feel so good. I have a very bad throat and my head aches.

Johnny: Who's your favorite ball team?

Babe: I think I'll have to stick with the Yanks. They'll win the American League pennant.

Johnny: I know they say the time you called your homer was your biggest thrill, but was it?

Babe: Johnny, I think the time I pitched 29 consecutives innings without giving up a run.

Johnny: Would you sooner pitch or play the outfield?

Babe: I'd like to be in there every day. That's how much I like to play.

With that Johnny, who was sitting in the Babe's lap, ran out of things to ask. Ruth put his arm around the boy and said, "I think both of us are out of words, Johnny."

Spent, he canceled the remainder of his tour and went home, his place in the history books more secure than the life he still clung to.

History isn't finite—at least not where Ruth is concerned. The Babe always has more to give. He still generates more interest, more material, and more astonishment than anyone else who ever played the game. And that may be the best definition of his greatness.

— Jane Leavy, Truro, Massachusetts, August 21, 2019

George Herman "Babe" Ruth

By Allan Wood

Babe Ruth, October 22, 1930.
Leslie Jones photo, courtesy of the Boston Public Library.

During his five full seasons with the Boston Red Sox, Babe Ruth established himself as one of the premier left-handed pitchers in the game, began his historic transformation from moundsman to slugging outfielder, and was part of three World Series championship teams. After he was sold to the New York Yankees in December 1919, his eye-popping batting performances over the next few seasons helped usher in a new era of long-distance hitting and high scoring, effectively bringing down the curtain on the Deadball Era.

George Herman Ruth was born to George Ruth and Catherine Schamberger on February 6, 1895, in his mother's parents' house at 216 Emory Street, in Baltimore, Maryland. With his father working long hours in his saloon and his mother often in poor health, Little George (as he was known) spent his days unsupervised on the waterfront streets and docks, committing petty theft and vandalism. Hanging out in his father's bar, he stole money from the till, drained the last drops from old beer glasses, and developed a taste for chewing tobacco. He was only six years old.

Shortly after his seventh birthday, the Ruths petitioned the Baltimore courts to declare Little George "incorrigible" and sent him to live at St. Mary's Industrial School, on the outskirts of the city. The boy's initial stay at St. Mary's lasted only four weeks before his parents brought him home for the first of several attempted reconciliations; his long-term residence at St. Mary's actually began in 1904. But it was during that first stay that George met Brother Matthias.

"He taught me to read and write and he taught me the difference between right and wrong," Ruth said of the Canadian-born priest. "He was the father I needed and the greatest man I've ever known."[1] Brother Matthias also spent many afternoons tossing a worn-out baseball in the air and swatting it out to the boys. Little George watched, bug-eyed. "I had never seen anything like that in my life," he recalled. "I think I was born as a hitter the first day I ever saw him hit a baseball."[2] The impressionable youngster imitated Matthias's hitting style—gripping the bat tightly down at the knobbed end, taking a big swing at the ball—as well as his way of running with quick, tiny steps.

When asked in 1918 about playing baseball at St. Mary's, Ruth said he had little difficulty anywhere on the field. "Sometimes I pitched. Sometimes I caught, and frequently I played the outfield and infield. It was all the same to me. All I wanted was to play. I didn't care much where."[3] In one St. Mary's game in 1913, Ruth, then 18 years old, caught, played third base (even though he threw left-handed), and pitched, striking out six men, and collecting a double, a triple, and a home run. That summer, he was allowed to pitch with local amateur and semipro teams on weekends. Impressed with his performances, Jack Dunn signed Ruth to his minor-league Baltimore Orioles club the following February.

Although he was a bumpkin with minimal social skills, at camp in South Carolina Ruth quickly distinguished himself on the diamond. That spring, the Orioles played several major league teams. In two outings against the Phillies, Ruth faced 29 batters and allowed only six hits and two unearned runs. The next week, he threw a complete game victory over the Philadelphia Athletics, winners of three of the last four World Series. Short on cash that summer, Dunn sold Ruth to the Boston Red Sox.

On July 11, 1914, less than five months after leaving St. Mary's, Babe made his debut at Fenway Park: he pitched seven innings against Cleveland and received credit for a 4-3 win. After being hit hard by Detroit in his second outing, Ruth rode the bench until he was demoted to the minor leagues in mid-August, where he helped the Providence Grays capture the International League pennant. Ruth returned to Boston for the final week of the 1914 season. On October 2, he pitched a complete game victory over the Yankees and doubled for his first major-league hit.

Babe spent the winter in Baltimore with his new wife, Boston waitress Helen Woodford, and in 1915, he stuck with the big club. Ruth slumped early in the season, in part because of excessive carousing with fellow pitcher Dutch Leonard, and a broken toe—sustained by kicking the bench in frustration after being intentionally walked—kept him out of the rotation for two weeks. But when he returned, he shined, winning three complete games in a span of nine days in June. Between June 1 and September 2, Ruth was 13-1 and ended the season 18-8.

In 1916, Ruth won 23 games and posted a league-leading 1.75 ERA. He also threw nine shutouts—an American League record for left-handed pitchers that still stands (it was tied in 1978 by the Yankees' Ron Guidry). In Game Two of the World Series, Ruth pitched all 14 innings, beating the Brooklyn Dodgers, 2-1. Boston topped Brooklyn in the series four games to one.

Ruth's success went straight to his head in 1917, and he began arguing with umpires about their strike zone judgment. Facing Washington on June 23, Ruth walked the first Senators batter on four pitches. Feeling squeezed by home plate umpire Brick Owens, Ruth stormed off the mound and punched Owens in the head. After Ruth was ejected, Ernie Shore came in to relieve. The baserunner was thrown out trying to steal and Shore retired the next 26 batters. Ruth got off lightly with a 10-day suspension and a $100 fine. He ended the year with a 24-13 record, completing 35 of his 38 starts, with six shutouts and an ERA of 2.01.

Although Ruth didn't play every day until May 1918, the idea of putting him in the regular lineup was first mentioned in the press during his rookie season. Calling Babe "one of the best natural sluggers ever in the game," Washington sportswriter Paul Eaton thought Ruth "might even be more valuable in some regular position than he is on the slab—a free suggestion for Manager [Bill] Carrigan."[4] The *Boston Post* reported that summer that Babe "cherishes the hope that he may someday be the leading slugger of the country."[5]

In 1915, Ruth batted .315 and topped the Red Sox with four home runs. Braggo Roth led the AL with seven homers, but he had 384 at-bats compared to Babe's 92. Ruth didn't have enough at-bats to qualify, but his .576 slugging percentage was higher than the official leaders in the American League (Jack Fournier .491), the National League (Gavvy Cravath .510), and the Federal League (Benny Kauff .509).

With the Red Sox offense sputtering after the sale of Tris Speaker in 1916, the suggestion to play Ruth every day was renewed when he tied a record with a home run in three consecutive games. Ruth hated the helpless feeling of sitting on the bench between pitching assignments, and believed he could be a better hitter if given more opportunity. In mid-season, with all three Boston outfielders in slumps, Carrigan was reportedly ready to give Babe a shot, but it never happened.[6] Ruth finished the 1917 season at .325, easily the highest average on the team. Left fielder Duffy Lewis topped the regulars at .302; no one else hit above .265. Giving Ruth an everyday job remained nothing more than an entertaining game of "what if"—until 1918.

The previous summer, the United States had entered the Great War; many players had enlisted or accepted war-related jobs before the season began. Trying to strengthen the Red Sox offense, about two weeks into the season, manager Ed Barrow, after discussions with right fielder and team captain Harry

Hooper, penciled Ruth into the lineup. The move came only a few days after a Boston paper reported that team owner Harry Frazee had refused an offer of $100,000 for Ruth. "It is ridiculous to talk about it," Frazee said. "Ruth is our Big Ace. He's the most talked of, most sought for, most colorful ball player in the game."[7] Later reports revealed that the offer had come from the Yankees.[8]

On May 6, 1918, in the Polo Grounds against the Yankees, Ruth played first base and batted sixth. It was the first time he had appeared in a game other than as a pitcher or pinch-hitter and the first time he batted in any spot other than ninth. Ruth went 2-for-4, including a two-run home run. At that point, five of Ruth's 11 career home runs had come in New York. The *Boston Post*'s Paul Shannon began his game story, "Babe Ruth still remains the hitting idol of the Polo Grounds."[9]

The next day, against the Senators, Ruth was bumped up to fourth in the lineup—and he hit another home run—where he stayed for most of the season. Barrow also wanted Ruth to continue pitching, but Babe, enjoying the notoriety his hitting was generating, often feigned exhaustion or a sore arm to avoid the mound.[10] The two men argued about Ruth's playing time for several weeks. Finally, after one heated exchange in early July, Ruth quit the team. He returned a few days later and, after renegotiating his contract with Frazee to include some hitting-related bonuses, patched up his disagreements with Barrow.

"I don't think a man can pitch in his regular turn, and play every other game at some other position, and keep that pace year after year," Ruth said. "I can do it this season all right, and not feel it, for I am young and strong and don't mind the work. But I wouldn't guarantee to do it for many seasons."[11] Ruth then began what is likely the greatest nine- or ten-week stretch of play in baseball history. From mid-July to early September 1918, Ruth pitched every fourth day, and played either left field, center field, or first base on the other days. Ruth's double duty was not unique during the Deadball Era—a handful of players had done both—but his level of success was (and remains) unprecedented.[12] In one 10-game stretch at Fenway, Ruth hit .469 (15-for-32) and slugged .969 with four singles, six doubles, and five triples. He was remarkably adept at first base, his favorite position. On the mound, he allowed more than two runs only once in his last ten starts. The Colossus, as Babe was known in Boston, maintained his status as a top pitcher while simultaneously becoming the game's greatest hitter.

Ruth's performance led the Red Sox to the American League pennant, in a season cut short by the owners, partially because of dwindling attendance. All draft-age men were under government order to either enlist or take war-related employment—in shipyards or munitions factories, for example—which led to paltry turnouts of less than 1,000 for many afternoon games that summer.

Ruth opened the World Series on September 5 against the Chicago Cubs with a 1-0 shutout. He pitched well in Game Four, despite having bruised his left hand during some horseplay on the train back to Boston, and his double drove in what turned out to be the winning runs. Those performances, together with his extra-inning outing in 1916, gave Ruth a record of 29 2/3 consecutive scoreless World Series innings, one of the records Ruth always said he was most proud of.[13] His streak was finally broken by Whitey Ford of the Yankees in the 1960s.

While with the Red Sox, Ruth often arranged for busloads of orphans to visit his farm in Sudbury for a day-long picnic and ball game, making sure each kid left with a glove and autographed baseball. When the Red Sox were at home, Ruth would arrive at Fenway Park early on Saturday mornings to help the vendors—mostly boys in their early teens—bag peanuts for the upcoming week's games.

"He'd race with us to see who could bag the most," recalled Tom Foley, who was 14 years old in 1918. (Ruth was barely out of his teens himself.) "He'd talk a blue streak the whole time, telling us to be good boys and play baseball, because there was good money in it. He thought that if we worked hard enough, we could be as good as he was. But we knew better than that. He'd stay about an hour. When we finished, he'd pull out a $20 bill and throw it on the table and say 'Have a good time, kids.' We'd split it up, and each go home with an extra half-dollar or dollar depending on how many of us were there. Babe Ruth was an angel to us."[14]

To management, however, Ruth was a headache. His continued inability—or outright refusal—to adhere to the team's curfew earned him several suspensions and his non-stop salary demands infuriated Frazee. The Red Sox owner had spoken publicly about possibly trading Ruth before the 1919 season, when Babe was holding out for double his existing salary and threatening to become a boxer. However, Ruth and Frazee came to terms and the Babe's hitting made headlines across the country all season long. He played 110 games in left field, belted a record 29 home runs, and led the major leagues in slugging percentage (.657), on-base percentage (.456), runs scored (103), RBIs (113), and total bases (284). He also drove in or scored one-third of Boston's runs. But while Ruth also won nine games on the mound, the rest of the staff fell victim to injuries and the defending champs finished in the second division with a 66-71 record.

The sale of Ruth to the Yankees was announced after New Year's 1920 and although it was big news, public opinion in

Boston was divided. Many fans were aghast that such a talent would be cast off, while others, including many former players, insisted that a cohesive team (as opposed to one egomaniac plus everyone else) was the key to success.[15]

"While Ruth, without question, is the greatest hitter that the game has ever seen, he is likewise one of the most selfish and inconsiderate men that ever wore a baseball uniform," Frazee explained. "Had he possessed the right disposition, had he been willing to take orders and work for the good of the club like the other men on the team, I would never have dared let him go."[16] And despite Ruth's record-setting (and attention-grabbing) 29 home runs, the Red Sox had finished in sixth place. Frazee considered the long balls "more spectacular than useful."[17]

He also intimated that the Yankees were taking a gamble on Ruth. It was a statement he would be later ridiculed for, but at the time the Yankees felt the same way. The amount paid ($125,000) was astronomical, Ruth ate and drank excessively, frequented prostitutes, and had been involved in several car accidents. It would have surprised no one if, for whatever reason, Ruth was out of baseball in a year or two.

Amidst this speculation over his future, on February 28, 1920, Babe Ruth left Boston and boarded a train for New York, on his way to spring training in Florida. He was still just 25 years old.

* * *

Babe Ruth arrived in New York City at the best possible time for his outsized hitting and hedonistic lifestyle. It was the Roaring Twenties, the Jazz Age, a time of individualism, more progressive social and sexual attitudes, and a greater emphasis on the pursuit of pleasure. (Prohibition, instituted in 1920, had no effect whatsoever.) Sportswriter Westbrook Pegler called it "the Era of Wonderful Nonsense."[18]

It was also a time when "trick pitches" – the emeryball, the spitter, and various ways of scuffing the ball—were outlawed. Both leagues began using a better quality (i.e., livelier) baseball. Ruth thrived—and over time, so did the players in both leagues.

The Babe got off to a slow start in 1920. He was in spring training for nearly three weeks before he crushed his first home run. Ruth also jumped into the stands to fight a fan who had called him "a big piece of cheese" (probably not a direct quote).[19] While tracking a fly ball during an exhibition game in Miami, Ruth ran into a palm tree in center field and was knocked unconscious.

After a disappointing April, in which he missed time due to a strained right knee, Ruth began May with home runs in consecutive games against the Red Sox. He went on to set a major league record for the month with 11 homers. That record lasted less than 30 days, when he smacked 13 long balls in June. He tied his own single-season record of 29 home runs—set the previous year with Boston—on July 16. Two weeks later, he had 37.

He finished the year with the unfathomable total of 54 home runs. He outhomered 14 of the other 15 major league teams. The AL runner-up was George Sisler, with 19; Cy Williams needed only 15 to top the National League. Ruth hit 14.6% of the American League's 369 home runs. For Barry Bonds to outdistance his peers in 2001 (when he set a new single-season mark of 73 home runs) as Ruth did in 1920, Bonds would have needed to hit 431 homers. In addition to this stunning display of power, Ruth was fourth in batting average at .376. His slugging percentage of .847 stood for more than 80 years—until Bonds reached .863 in 2001.

Ruth's arrival in New York began a stretch of offensive dominance the game will likely never see again. In the 12 seasons between 1920 and 1931, Ruth led the AL in slugging 11 times, home runs 10 times, walks nine times, on-base percentage eight times, and runs scored seven times. His batting average topped .350 eight times. In exactly half of those 12 seasons, he batted over .370. (Ruth once said that if he shortened his swing and tried to hit singles, he'd hit .600.[20])

Ruth's effect on the national game was nothing short of revolutionary. Leigh Montville, author of *The Big Bam*, wrote that Ruth's teammates reacted with the same sense of wonder as everyone else in America. "They never had seen anything like it. The game they had learned was being changed in front of their faces."[21]

Ruth also starred in a short movie entitled *Headin' Home*, which was filmed in Fort Lee, New Jersey. The plot, such as it was, starred Babe as a country bumpkin who makes good in big league ball—not exactly playing against type. According to *Variety*, "It couldn't hold the interest of anyone for five seconds if it were not for the presence of Ruth."[22] Babe often returned to the Polo Grounds after a morning of filming still wearing his movie makeup and mascara, much to the annoyance of manager Miller Huggins.[23]

During his final season in Boston, Ruth played most of his games in left field. When he joined the Yankees, and began playing his home games at the Polo Grounds, he played all three outfield positions. In 1920, Ruth started 84 games in right, 31 in left, and 25 in center. The following season, he was almost exclusively used in left, starting 132 of 150 games; he didn't play even one inning in right field. Once the Yankees moved into their own stadium in the Bronx, Ruth generally played right field at home and left field on the road. Although the Babe is remembered as mainly a right fielder, he started nearly as many games in left (1,040) during his career as he did in right (1,122).[24]

Ruth quickly became one of the most famous people in the country. On Yankees road trips, people with no interest in baseball traveled hundreds of miles to get a glimpse of the Babe. He was cheered wildly in every park—for rival fans, if Ruth smacked one out of the park, it hardly seemed to matter what the final score was.

Sunday baseball became legal in New York in 1919 and the fan base changed forever. Women and children came out regularly to the park. One of Ruth's most enduring nicknames—the Bambino—came from the Italian fans in the upper Manhattan neighborhood around the Polo Grounds.

Everyone wanted to know as much about Ruth as possible. The New York papers (more than 15 English-language dailies) began devoting more and more space to the Babe's exploits. Nothing was too trivial. According to sportswriter Tom Meany, if Ruth was seen "taking an aspirin, it was practically a scoop for the writer who saw him reach for the sedative."[25] Marshall Hunt was hired by the *Daily News* to write about the Babe—and only the Babe—365 days a year.[26]

"There was no such thing as no news with the Babe. ... The Speed Graphic, the newspaper photographer's camera of choice, loved his broad face with its flat nose and tiny eyes, loved his absolutely unique look, features put together in a hurry, an out-of-focus bulldog, no veneer or sanding involved. This was a face that soon was instantly recognizable, seen again and again ... The Babe was an incorrigible, wondrous part of everyone's family. ... He was the life of everybody's party. ... Laughing but earnest men in fedoras and off-the-rack suits, sportswriters, watched the sun rise and fall on his big head and were moved to grand statements. They typed the legend into place, adding layer upon layer of adjectives until often the man in the middle couldn't even be seen."[27]

In the 1920s, these giddy sportswriters were coming up with nicknames for Ruth nearly every day. His Boston nickname—the Colossus—morphed into the Colossus of Clout. From there, a seemingly endless—and often silly—list emerged: the Wizard of Wham, the Maharajah of Mash, the Rajah of Rap, the Caliph of Clout, the Sultan of Swat, the Behemoth of Bash, the Bazoo of Bang, the Potentate of Pow, the Wali of Wallop, the Prince of Pounders, and on and on.

His own name became a nickname, bestowed on someone who was the best in his or her field: the Babe Ruth of Surfing, the Babe Ruth of Bowling, the Babe Ruth of Poker. His last name became an adjective: "Ruthian," defined as "colossal, dramatic, prodigious, magnificent; with great power."[28] His teammates usually called him "Jidge" (for George).

The Yankees finished the 1920 season in third place with a 95-59 record, only three games behind Cleveland. It was their best showing in 10 years. They followed that up in 1921 by winning 98 games and their first-ever pennant. And somehow Ruth may have actually had a better year at the plate than he did in 1920. His batting average improved slightly (.376 to .378), and while his OBP (.532 to .512) and slugging (.847 to .846) dipped slightly, he drove in 168 runs and hit a career-high 16 triples. (According to manager Huggins, Ruth was the second-fastest player on the team.[29]) He also broke his own single-season home run record—for the third consecutive year—with 59. On July 18, Ruth became the game's career home run leader, hitting his 139th homer, passing Roger Connor. Ruth also set new season records for runs scored (177), extra base hits (119), and total bases (457) – three achievements that no player has yet matched.

Ruth also pitched in two games. On June 13, he allowed four runs in five innings. He also hit two home runs that day and finished the game in center field as the Yankees won, 13-8.

In September 1921, Ruth underwent three hours of tests at Columbia University to determine his athletic and psychological capabilities. Sportswriter Hugh Fullerton wrote up the findings for *Popular Science Monthly*:

> "The tests revealed the fact that Ruth is 90 per cent efficient compared with a human average of 60 per cent. That his eyes are about 12 per cent faster than those of the average human being. That his ears function at least 10 per cent faster than those of the ordinary man. That his nerves are steadier than those of 499 out of 500 persons. That in attention and quickness of perception he rated one and a half times above the human average. That in intelligence, as demonstrated by the quickness and accuracy of understanding, he is approximately 10 per cent above normal."[30]

The psychologists also discovered that Ruth did not breathe during his entire swing. They stated that if he kept breathing while swinging, he could generate even more power.

The Yankees faced their co-tenants in the Polo Grounds, the New York Giants, in the 1921 World Series. Ruth cut his left arm (which then became infected) during a slide in the second game and wrenched his knee in the fifth game. Babe made only one pinch-hitting appearance in the final three contests. The Yankees won the first two games, but the Giants took the best-of-nine series, five games to three.

After the World Series, Ruth and some other Yankees went on a barnstorming tour to earn extra money. This was in violation of the National Commission's 1911 edict that players on the two pennant-winning teams could not barnstorm after the World Series—enacted, perhaps, to preserve the integrity of the World Series or to limit the players' total income. Kenesaw Mountain Landis, newly installed as the game's first commissioner, suspended Ruth and fellow outfielder Bob Meusel for the first six weeks of the season, and fined them each $3,362—the amount of their 1921 World Series share.

When Ruth returned to the lineup on May 20, he was also named as the team's captain, succeeding Hal Chase (1912) and Roger Peckinpaugh (1914-21). The honor lasted less than one week. Ruth was again slow to get his bat started and after five games, he was hitting .095 and being booed.

On May 25, he was thrown out trying to stretch a single into a double and, furious at the call, threw dirt in umpire George Hildebrand's face. On his way towards the dugout, he spied a heckler and jumped into the stands, ready to fight. The fan ran away and Ruth ended up standing on the dugout roof, screaming, "Come on down and fight! Anyone who wants to fight, come down on the field!"[31] Ruth was fined $200 and was replaced as captain by shortstop Everett Scott.

Babe was also suspended for three days in mid-June for his part in an obscenity-laced tirade against umpire Bill Dinneen. When Ruth got the news the following day, he challenged Dinneen to a fist fight—and the suspension was increased to five days.[32] In the wake of the suspensions, Ruth made an effort to check his temper. On June 26, as some of his teammates argued with Dinneen, Babe merely sat down in the outfield grass and watched.[33]

Ruth played in only 110 games in 1922. His batting average dropped to .315, but he led the league with a .672 slugging percentage and his OBP of .434 was fourth-best.

The Yankees and the Giants met in the World Series for the second straight year. After a three-year experiment as a best-of-nine, the series was back to being a best-of-seven, where it has remained to the present day. The Giants swept the Yankees in five games (Game Two ended in a tie due to darkness). Ruth went 2-for-17.

The Yankees left the Polo Grounds and began 1923 in their own ballpark, directly across the Harlem River in the borough of the Bronx. Yankee Stadium was dubbed the House that Ruth Built, but with its short right-field porch, a more appropriate title might be the House Built for Ruth. Babe returned to his battering ways with a vengeance. He hit .393—if only four of his 317 outs had fallen for hits, he would have batted .400—and hit 41 home runs. Harry Heilmann of the Tigers led the AL with a .403 average.

The Yankees won their third straight pennant, finishing 16 games ahead of the Tigers. And for the third straight year, the World Series was an all-New York affair. This time, it was the Yankees, after losing two of the first three games, who prevailed. Ruth went 7-for-19 in the Series, with three home runs. However, all three came at the Polo Grounds. Giants' outfielder Casey Stengel hit the first World Series home run at Yankee Stadium.

Ruth won his only batting title in 1924, easily topping the AL at .378—almost 20 points higher than Charlie Jamieson's .359. Babe hit 46 home runs and tied for second with 124 RBIs. His .739 slugging percentage was more than 200 points higher than runner-ups Harry Heilmann and Ken Williams (both at .533). However, the Yankees finished in second place, two games behind the Washington Senators.

In 1925, the Yankees fell all the way to seventh, 69-85, 28 1/2 games out of first place. It was a bad year from the start. Ruth showed up for spring training at 256 pounds and went on to have the worst year of his career. He hit .290/.393/.543 (batting/on-base/slugging), with 25 home runs and a paltry 67 RBIs. This was also the year Ruth suffered what W.O. McGeehan of the *New York Tribune* famously called "The Bellyache Heard 'Round the World."[34] Ruth fell ill during the team's spring training exhibition tour. The initial story was that Ruth had eaten too many hot dogs, and the *New York Evening Journal* ran a photo of Ruth with 12 numbered franks superimposed on his stomach.[35]

However, it was clearly more serious than indigestion or a matter of Ruth being "run down and [having] low blood pressure," as the Yankees' team doctor claimed.[36] On April 17, Ruth had minor surgery for what doctors termed an "intestinal abscess"[37] and he did not return to the Yankees lineup until June. Several teammates hinted it might have been a sexually-transmitted disease; one teammate said it wasn't a bellyache, "it was something a bit lower."[38]

Whatever it was, it didn't cramp Ruth's style. Babe was staying out all night more often than not and by the end of the season, he was a physical wreck. In mid-December, Ruth realized if he wanted to continue playing ball into his thirties, he needed to do something different. He showed up at Artie McGovern's gymnasium on East 42nd Street in Manhattan, a well-known gym used by New York's rich and famous.[39]

Ruth committed himself to McGovern's strict regimen of exercise, diet, and rest. Six weeks later, by the time he was ready to head south for spring training, Ruth had lost 44 pounds and shed almost nine inches from his waistline.[40]

The Babe still had plenty of fun, obviously, but he never let himself get seriously out of shape again. As Robert Creamer wrote in *Babe: The Legend Comes to Life*, "From 1926 through 1931, as he aged from thirty-two to thirty-seven, Ruth put on the finest sustained display of hitting that baseball has ever seen. During those six seasons, he averaged 50 home runs a year, 155 runs batted in and 147 runs scored; he batted .354. … From the ashes of 1925, Babe Ruth rose like a rocket."[41]

As Ruth rose, so did the Yankees. The Bombers went from seventh place to first, winning 91 games and the 1926 pennant. Ruth batted .372/.516/.737, with 47 home runs (runner-up Al Simmons had 19), and drove in 153 (36 more than his nearest challenger). The Yankees were also boosted by the great play of two rookie infielders: second baseman Tony Lazzeri and shortstop Mark Koenig. First baseman Lou Gehrig, in his second full season at age 22, led the league with 20 triples and 83 extra-base hits—one more than Ruth.

In Game Four of the World Series against the St. Louis Cardinals, Ruth belted three home runs. It was the first time he had ever hit three in one game—and it was the first time that had been done in a World Series game. This was also the game before which Ruth allegedly promised to hit a home run for 11-year-old hospital patient Johnny Sylvester.

The 1926 Series came down to a deciding seventh game at Yankee Stadium. New York trailed 3-2 in the bottom of the ninth inning, when Ruth walked with two outs. Bob Meusel was facing Grover Cleveland Alexander when Ruth took off for second. He was thrown out trying to steal—ending the game and the World Series.

The 1927 Yankees are often talked about as the greatest team in baseball history. New York finished with a 110-44 record, winning the league by a whopping 19 games and sweeping the Pittsburgh Pirates in the World Series. They scored 976 runs, 131 more than second-best Detroit.

Ruth's fabled 60 home runs—which he had become obsessed with since hitting 59 six years earlier—captured the headlines, but Gehrig, at age 24, had a better season. He outhit Ruth (.373 to .356) and nearly matched him in on-base percentage (.474 to .486), and slugging (.765 to .772). Gehrig had more extra base hits (117 to 97), total bases (447 to 417), and RBIs (173 to 165). He led the major leagues in doubles, RBIs, and total bases and was second in the American League in triples, home runs, hits, and batting average.

The Yankees won nine fewer games in 1928, but their 101-53 record was still good enough for a third straight pennant. Ruth batted only .323, but his 54 home runs helped him lead the major leagues in slugging at .709. The Yankees used only three pitchers as they swept the Cardinals in the World Series. Ruth batted .625 (10-for-16), with three doubles, three home runs, and a 1.375 slugging percentage. Gehrig hit .545 (6-for-11) and slugged 1.727.

In January 1929, Babe's first wife, Helen, died in a house fire in Watertown, Massachusetts. At the time, Helen was living with Edward Kinder, a dentist, and while the deed on the house listed Helen and Kinder as husband and wife, they were not, in fact, married. (Babe and Helen had never officially divorced.) Ruth was devastated by the news. At the funeral, he wept uncontrollably.[42]

Babe married Claire Hodgson on April 17. The following day, the Yankees—with numbers on the back of their uniforms for the first time—opened the season against the Red Sox. Babe, wearing his new #3, whacked a first-inning home run to left field and doffed his cap to Claire as he rounded the bases.

On August 11 in Cleveland, Ruth hit the 500th home run of his career. The *New York World* called it "a symbol of American greatness."[43] The man who retrieved the homer got two signed baseballs and, after posing for a photo with Ruth, the Babe slipped him a $20 bill.[44]

Miller Huggins passed away suddenly near the end of the 1929 season—and Babe lobbied for the manager's job for 1930. (Ruth would drop hints about wanting to manage for the next four years, but the Yankees never seriously considered it.) Ruth also asked for his salary to be increased to $100,000—this coming a few months after Black Tuesday and the start of what became the Great Depression. He ended up signing a two-year deal for $80,000 per season. With exhibition game receipts, movie shorts, personal appearances, and endorsements, Ruth probably earned close to $200,000 in 1930.

By the end of June 1930, Ruth was ahead of his 60-homer pace of 1927, but injuries slowed him down and he finished with 49.

The Yankees were an offensive juggernaut. In both 1930 and 1931, they scored more than 1,000 runs—an average of nearly seven runs per game. But it was the Philadelphia Athletics who won the pennant in 1929, 1930, and 1931 behind the big bats of Jimmie Foxx and Al Simmons and the pitching of Lefty Grove.

In 1931, at age 36, Ruth had one of his finest seasons. He hit .373/.495/.700, with 46 home runs, 162 RBIs, 128 walks and 149 runs scored.

Ruth made his final trip to the World Series in 1932. Amazingly, in the seven-year reign of Ruth and Gehrig from 1929-1935, the Yankees won only one pennant. Gehrig (.349/.451/.621, 34 HR, 151 RBIs) and Ruth (.341/.489/.661, 41 HR, 137 RBIs) were ably assisted by Lazzeri, Bill Dickey, Ben Chapman and

Earle Combs. However, it was Jimmie Foxx of the A's who led the league in home runs (58).

The Yankees swept the Chicago Cubs in the 1932 World Series, giving them wins in 12 straight World Series games. It was during the third game—October 1 at Wrigley Field—that Ruth added to his legend. The game was tied 4-4 when Ruth stepped in against Cubs starter Charlie Root with one out in the fifth inning. Ruth had already hit a three-run homer and flied to deep right, and the Cubs' bench-jockeying was at a fever pitch.

Everyone agrees that as Root threw two called strikes to Ruth, the Babe held up one and two fingers. What exactly happened before Root threw his 2-2 pitch will never be definitively known. The legend says Ruth pointed towards the center field bleachers, indicating that was where he was going to hit the next pitch. Or he may have been saying "I've still got one strike left." Or he was jawing with the hecklers in the Cubs' dugout.

Either way, Ruth swung and belted the ball to deep center field—one of the longest home runs seen at Wrigley—for his second home run of the afternoon. He laughed as he jogged around the bases, pointing and jeering at the Cubs dugout.

Of the many game stories written that afternoon, only one (Westbrook Pegler) mentioned Ruth "calling his shot."[45] Within two or three days, however, writers who had initially made no reference to Ruth's theatrics – and even a few who had not been in attendance at the park – were offering their own recollections. And thus a legend was born.[46] A 16mm home movie of the at-bat surfaced in 1999. The grainy film does show Ruth pointing his arm, but it's impossible to determine exactly what he is doing.

Root maintained that Ruth "did not point at the fence before he swung. If he had made a gesture like that, well, anybody who knows me knows that Ruth would have ended up on his ass."[47] As for the Babe, when asked whether he had really pointed to the bleachers, he smiled and said, "It's in the papers, isn't it?"[48]

It was Ruth's last trip to the World Series. He played on seven World Series champions: four with the Yankees (1923, 1927, 1928, 1932), and three with the Red Sox (1915, 1916, 1918). He was also on the losing side of three World Series teams with New York (1921, 1922, 1926).

1933 was Ruth's 20th season in major league baseball. He batted only .301 with 34 home runs, though he still led both leagues in walks. One of the season's highlights was the inaugural All-Star Game, played at Comiskey Field in Chicago. Ruth hit the game's first home run. He also robbed Chick Hafey of a home run in the eighth inning, to preserve the AL's 4-2 win.

The Yankees finished seven games behind the Senators and, in an effort to boost attendance for the last home game of the year, announced that Ruth would pitch against the Red Sox. The 39-year-old outfielder held the Red Sox without a run for five innings. With a 6-0 lead, he stumbled in the sixth, allowing a walk, five singles, and four runs. The Yankees held on to win, 6-5. Although Ruth prepared for the start by throwing batting practice for weeks, the complete game took its toll. He couldn't so much as comb his hair with his left arm for about a week.[49]

Ruth took a $17,000 pay cut in 1934. His $35,000 contract was still the highest in the game, but it was his lowest salary since 1921. On July 13, in Detroit, Babe hit his 700th career home run. (At that point, only two players had hit even 300 home runs: Lou Gehrig (314) and Rogers Hornsby (301).) Four days later, Ruth drew his 2,000th walk.

In August, during the Yankees' final trip to Fenway, a record crowd of 48,000 turned out on a Sunday afternoon, assuming it would be Ruth's last appearance in Boston. The fans cheered everything Ruth did. When he grounded out in his final at-bat, he was given a long, standing ovation. "Do you know that some of them cried when I left the field?" Ruth said afterwards. "And if you wanna know the truth, I cried too."[50]

On the other hand, on September 24, for what was rumored to be his final home game in a Yankees uniform, only 2,000 fans showed up. Babe played only one inning, being replaced by a pinch-runner after drawing a walk. He ended the year with a .288 batting average.

During the off-season, Ruth agreed to travel with an all-star team to Japan. In arranging for a passport, he discovered that his date of birth was February 6, 1895. He had always believed he was born on February 7, 1894.[51] He was actually a year younger than he had thought.

Yankees owner Jacob Ruppert, not wanting Ruth to return in any capacity in 1935, worked out a secret deal with Boston Braves owner Emil Fuchs. Fuchs would offer Ruth a contract that included the titles of "assistant manager" and "vice president."[52] Ruth loved the idea and when he informed Ruppert, the Yankee owner said he wouldn't stand in Ruth's way. At spring training in 1935, Ruth learned that the Yankees had already assigned his #3 to George Selkirk. They were also using his locker to store firewood.[53]

Ruth ended up playing in 28 games for the Braves, batting .181. The one bright spot came on May 25 in Pittsburgh. Ruth belted the final three home runs of his career, and drove in six runs. Career home run #714 disappeared over the right field roof—the longest home run ever hit at Forbes Field.

Many of the hitting records Ruth once held have been broken, but what cements Babe's status as the best to ever play the game is the combination of hitting for average, hitting with power, and his work on the mound. In addition to his batting exploits, Ruth also pitched in 163 games, with a record of 94-46 and a career ERA of 2.28 (12th-best in the modern era, since 1900). For 71 years, he was also the unlikely answer to a great trivia question: Who is the only major leaguer to pitch in at least 10 seasons and have a winning record in all of them? Ruth had winning records in 10 seasons: 1914-1921, 1930 and 1933. Andy Pettitte now holds the record at 13 seasons (1995-2007).

Ruth retired to a life of golf, fishing, bowling, and public appearances. In November 1946, he checked into French Hospital on 29th Street in Manhattan, complaining of headaches and pain above his left eye. It was cancer, though the newspapers never printed the word.

Babe Ruth Day was held at Yankee Stadium (and every other major league park) the following April. A crowd of 58,339 was there and many of them, players as well as fans, were shocked at how frail and shrunken the mighty Babe had become.

Ruth was in and out of the hospital for the next year. He returned to the Bronx one more time, on June 13, 1948, a rainy, cold day. Yankee Stadium was celebrating its 25th anniversary and Babe's #3 was being retired. Ruth was back in the hospital 11 days later. The cancer had spread to his liver, lungs, and kidneys. He knew he was dying.

Babe Ruth died at 8:01 p.m. on August 16, 1948. He was 53 years old. He is buried at the Gate of Heaven Cemetery in Valhalla, New York, next to his second wife Claire, who died in 1976.

Leigh Montville, author of *The Big Bam*, called Ruth "the patron saint of American possibility … The fascination with his career and life continues. He is a bombastic, sloppy hero from our bombastic sloppy history, origins undetermined, a folk tale of American success."[54]

The New York Times began its obituary: "Probably nowhere in all the imaginative field of fiction could one find a career more dramatic and bizarre than that portrayed in real life by George Herman Ruth."[55]

Sources

In addition to the sources cited in the Notes, the author also consulted Baseball-Reference.com.

Notes

1 Allan Wood, *Babe Ruth and the 1918 Red Sox* (San Jose, California: Writers Club Press, 2001), 55.

2 Ibid.

3 George Herman Ruth, *Babe Ruth's Own Book of Baseball* (New York: G.P. Putnam's Sons, 1928; Lincoln: University of Nebraska Press, Bison Books, 1992), 5-6.

4 Paul W. Eaton, *Sporting Life*, August 7, 1915.

5 "Talking It Over In The Dugout At Fenway Park," *Boston Post*, August 15, 1915.

6 The *Boston Globe* of June 12, 1916 reported: "Some one of these days Babe Ruth may become an outfielder. [Manager Bill] Carrigan, [pitcher Vean] Gregg and others think that with the proper training, the Baltimore slugger should make a whale of a player for the outer garden." The next day, the *Boston American* reported, "Babe is such a great hitter that Bill wants to have him in the lineup daily if possible. So fans at home don't be a bit surprised if Ruth soon becomes one of the Red Sox outfielders." Paul Shannon wrote in the *Boston Herald*, "[If] the batting of certain parties does not improve, big Babe Ruth may soon be a fixture in the Boston outfield." As quoted in Kerry Keene, Raymond Sinibaldi and David Hickey. *The Babe in Red Stockings: An In-Depth Chronicle of Babe Ruth with the Boston Red Sox 1914-1919* (Champaign, Illinois: Sagamore Publishing, 1997), 81.

7 Burt Whitman, "Frazee Rejects $100,000 Offer For Pitcher Ruth," *Boston Herald and Journal*, April 30, 1918.

8 "Frazee States Col. Ruppert Offered $150,000 For Ruth," *Boston Herald and Journal*, May 29, 1918. Frazee: "I think the New York man showed good judgment in making such a big offer. Ruth already is mighty popular in New York, and just think what he would mean to the Yankees if he were playing for them every day and hitting those long ones at the left field bleachers and the right field grandstand!"

9 Glenn Stout, *The Selling of the Babe: The Deal That Changed Baseball and Created a Legend* (New York: Thomas Dunne Books, 2016), 52.

10 Wood, 144, 146-147.

11 F.C. Lane, "The Season's Sensation," *Baseball Magazine*, October 1918: 472.

12 Wood, 204-206. Several players had both pitched and played in the field before Ruth, but none of them were as talented or successful. Guy Hecker pitched, played the outfield, and spent time at first base from 1882-90. In 1884, he won 52 games for the Louisville Colonels (American Association) and had a 1.80 ERA. Hecker was rarely among the league's top hitters, but his .341 average in 1886 won the batting title. Washington Senators pitcher Al Orth pulled double duty for several seasons, but when he led the American League in wins and complete games in 1906, he played only one game in the outfield. Doc White of the Chicago White Sox led the American League in 1907 with 27 wins, but appeared on the mound in all but two of his 48 games. In 1909, when he truly divided his time, he batted only .234 (although his on-base average was .347) and was 11-9 with a 1.72 ERA. Doc Crandall played second base and pitched for the St. Louis Terriers of the Federal League in 1914, leading his team in batting average (.309) and tying for the lead in wins (13). The following year, as a pitcher and pinch-hitter, Crandall won 21 games and batted .284.

13 Robert W. Creamer, *Babe: The Legend Comes To Life* (New York: Simon and Schuster, 1974), 177.

14 Interviews with Allan Wood, July 22, 1995, October 30, 1995, and January 5, 1997. Allan Wood, "Someone Can Recall Red Sox Title," *Baseball America*, March 6, 1997.

15 Fred Tenney and Hugh Duffy, former members of the Boston Beaneaters (National League), supported the deal. Tenney: "I agree with Frazee for he knows his business best. … No ball player is indispensable to a team." Duffy: "Star players do not make a winning team. Players of ordinary ability working for the interest of the club are greater factors in the winning machine than the individual." Johnny Keenan, leader of Boston's Royal Rooters: "It will be impossible to replace the strength Ruth gave to the Red Sox. The Batterer is a wonderful player and the fact that he loves the game and plays with his all to win makes him a tremendous asset to a club." (*New York Times*,

January 7, 1920: 22.) Orville Dennison, a fan living in Cambridge, wrote to the *Boston Globe*: "Many sane followers of baseball claim that there is no player in the game who is worth paying $100,000 for, and that if the Boston club obtained such a sum, it is the gainer." (Wood, 352.) Frazee: "[B]aseball fans pay to see games won and championships achieved. They soon tire of circus attractions. And this is just what Ruth has become." (Stout, 190.) Ed Cunningham of the *Boston Herald* noted that while Ruth "is of a class of ball players that flashes across the firmament once in a great while … Stars generally are temperamental. This goes for baseball and the stage. They often have to be handled with kid gloves. Frazee has carefully considered the Ruth angle … Boston fans undoubtedly will be up in arms but they should reserve judgment until they see how it works out." Ed Cunningham, "Red Sox Sell Babe Ruth to Yanks for More than $100,000," *Boston Herald*, January 6, 1920: 18.

16 "Babe Ruth Accepts Terms Of Yankees," *New York Times*, January 7, 1920: 22.

17 Wood, 352.

18 Kal Wagenheim, *Babe Ruth: His Life and Legend* (New York: Praeger Publishers, 1974), 62.

19 Leigh Montville, *The Big Bam: The Life and Times of Babe Ruth* (New York: Doubleday, 2006), 111.

20 During the 1946 World Series, Ruth watched the St. Louis Cardinals employ a drastic shift against Ted Williams of the Boston Red Sox. Ruth told sportswriter Frank Graham: "They did that to me in the American League one year. I could have hit .600 that year slicing singles to left." Mark Gallagher, *The Yankee Encyclopedia* (6th Edition) (Champaign, Illinois: Sports Publishing LLC, 2003), 206.

21 Montville, 114.

22 *Variety*, September 24, 1920.

23 Marshall Smelser, *The Life That Ruth Built* (New York: Random House, 1975), 201.

24 Ruth's fielding statistics can be found at Baseball Reference (https://www.baseball-reference.com/players/r/ruthba01.shtml#all_standard_fielding).

25 Tom Meany, *Babe Ruth: The Big Moments of the Big Fellow* (New York: A.S. Barnes and Company, 1947), 84.

26 Montville, 167-71.

27 Montville, 159-60.

28 Paul Dickson, *The New Dickson Baseball Dictionary* (New York: Harcourt Brace & Company, 1999), 424.

29 Glenn Stout and Richard A. Johnson. *Yankees Century: 100 Years of New York Yankees Baseball* (Boston: Houghton Mifflin Company, 2002), 99.

30 Hugh Fullerton, "Why Babe Ruth is Greatest Home Run Hitter," *Popular Science Monthly*, October 1921. (The magazine's cover promised: "Babe Ruth's Home Run Secrets Solved by Science.")

31 Creamer, 258.

32 Creamer, 261.

33 Creamer, 262.

34 Montville, 203.

35 Wagenheim, 140. The caption read: "Notice how snugly they nestle in the vast cavern of his interior."

36 Montville, 203.

37 Stout and Johnson, 112.

38 Wagenheim, 140.

39 Montville, 216-18.

40 Montville, 218-21.

41 Creamer, 301.

42 Montville, 282-84.

43 Wagenheim, 196.

44 Montville, 293.

45 Creamer, 364, 367-68.

46 Stout and Johnson, 153.

47 Creamer, 366-67.

48 Creamer, 368. In *The Big Bam*, Leigh Montville writes: "He called shots all the time. He loved to create situations. It was for other people to determine what they meant. … He challenged his entire environment. Whipped up all parties, then made them shut up. The specifics might be hazy, but the general story was not wrong." (312) The next day, Cubs starter Guy Bush, facing Ruth in the top of first inning, with men on first and second and no outs, drilled the Babe with a first-pitch fastball. Montville adds: "*Something* out of the ordinary [had] happened." (313)

49 Montville, 322.

50 Montville, 327.

51 Ibid.

52 Montville, 337-38.

53 Montville, 339.

54 Montville, 13.

55 Murray Schumach, "Babe Ruth, Baseball's Greatest Star and Idol of Children, Had a Career Both Dramatic and Bizarre," *New York Times*, August 17, 1948: 14. "A creation of the times, he seemed to embody all the qualities that a sport-loving nation demanded of its outstanding hero. … Ruth [was] a figure unprecedented in American life. A born showman off the field and a marvelous performer on it, he had an amazing flair for doing the spectacular at the most dramatic moment."

Babe – A Baseball Nickname

George Herman Ruth did have other nicknames than Babe — "Jidge," for instance, and was given some other monikers such as "The Sultan of Swat."

But he was more widely known as Babe Ruth than by his real name.

He was far from the only player, before or since, known as Babe. A quick perusal finds these prior Babes:

Babe Adams (1906-26)

Babe Borton (1912-16)

Babe Danzig (1909)

Babe Doty (1890)

Babe Towne (1906)

And Dan Sherman, who started in 1914 – the same year as Mr. Ruth – and also attracted the nickname Babe.

Some Babes who overlapped or followed, include:

Babe Ellison (1916-20)

Babe Pinelli (1918-27)

Babe Twombly (1920-21)

Ollie Klee (1925)

Babe Herman (1926-45)

Babe Ganzel (1927-28)

Elliot Bigelow (1929)

Babe Phelps (1931-42)

Babe with young boy, a "mascot" – 1922.
Bain News Service. *Courtesy of Library of Congress.*

Ed Linke (1933-38)

Babe Dahlgren (1935-46)

Babe Young (1936-48)

Babe Barna (1937-43)

Woody Davis (1938)

Phil Marchildon (1940-50)

Russ Meers (1941-47)

Ed Butka (1943-44)

Ed Klieman (1943-50)

Babe Martin (1944-53)

Del Wilber (1946-54)

Mario Picone (1947-54)

Babe Birrer (1955-58)

Tex Nelson (1955-57)

Phil Roof (1961-77)

It seems that around a half-century ago, the nickname Babe went out of fashion.

Baseball-Reference.com lists nine Negro Leagues players nicknamed Babe, as well as more than 40 minor leaguers and seven "other players and scouts."

There were, of course, variants. Ted Williams was known as "The Kid." There are more players with "Kid" as their nickname, or part of their nickname, than there are Babes.

— Bill Nowlin

How "Ruthian" was Babe Ruth?

By Mike Huber

The ultimate comparison of sluggers in baseball occurs when a player is linked to George Herman "Babe" Ruth. Ruth is arguably the greatest player to ever swing a bat. His nicknames include The Bambino, Sultan of Swat, Big Bam, Behemoth of Bust, Colossus of Clout, and Maharajah of Mash. There is an old saying in sabermetrical studies: If you conduct a sabermetrical analysis of the greatest players in baseball history and Babe Ruth does not come out at or near the top, something's wrong with your study.

Besides his prowess at the plate, Ruth was a great pitcher. Had he spent his playing time only on the mound, he still might have been elected to the Hall of Fame. He never had a losing season. He had a .671 career winning percentage (94-46, which places him 12th in major-league history on the career list) and a lifetime earned-run average of 2.28. He led all American League hurlers in 1916 with a 1.75 mark in 40 starts, including nine shutouts, and completed 107 of 147 starts. Ruth's World Series record was 3-0, with two complete games, a shutout, and a 0.87 ERA. He also set the pitching record of 29⅔ consecutive scoreless innings in the World Series – a record Ruth held for 43 seasons.[1]

Let's concentrate on hitting, though. How dominant was The Babe with a bat in his hands? In 1918, the 23-year-old Ruth split time between mound duties (winning 13 of 20 decisions) and being a position player for the Boston Red Sox. He played 59 games in the outfield and 13 more at first base. In 317 at-bats, he clubbed 11 home runs to tie Tillie Walker for tops in the

The New York Yankees' Babe Ruth gazes towards the right field stands after hitting a ball in front of an unknown Boston Red Sox catcher and unknown umpire at Fenway Park. 1933-34. *Leslie Jones photo, courtesy of the Boston Public Library.*

American League. Walker, an outfielder with the Philadelphia Athletics, needed 414 at-bats to get the same number. A year later Ruth smacked 29 homers to lead both leagues, setting a new record for home runs in a single season, breaking Ned Williamson's 1884 record of 27. Second-most in 1919 was Gavvy Cravath, who hit 12 for the Philadelphia Phillies. In 1920, his first season with the New York Yankees, Ruth became the first batter in history to hit 30, 40, and then 50 home runs in a season, when he clouted 54 round-trippers. Second place that year in the American League was future Hall of Famer George Sisler (29); in the National League, the leader was Cy Williams (15).

What makes Ruth's 1920 totals more impressive is the fact that he hit more home runs than every other *team* in the American League (meaning his 54 were more than the totals of each and every other AL team); Ruth also out-homered all but one National League squad. In his career, Ruth out-homered 90 teams, including four ties. Further, he single-handedly out-homered *pairs of teams* 18 times. Not too many players can claim to have out-homered an entire team, and the last time this was somewhat possible was during World War II, when the Chicago White Sox hit a paltry 33 home runs in 1943, 23 home runs in 1944, and 22 in 1945.[2]

Roger Connor was an infielder for the New York Giants and St. Louis Cardinals who played from 1880 to 1897. Connor hit 138 home runs in his career. Ruth had 108 total at the end of the 1920 campaign, and he had been an everyday player for only two seasons.

In the bottom of the eighth inning in a July 19, 1921, contest at Detroit's Navin Field, Ruth sent a Bert Cole pitch over the fence at the deepest part of the ballpark. The historic shot officially measured a distance of 560 feet, giving Ruth his 36th home run of the season and the 139th of his career,[3] passing Connor. Ruth, of course, continued to add to his home-run total. He hit 23 more round-trippers in 1921, setting a new season high of 59, breaking his own record of 54 set the season before. His career total continued to increase over the next 14 seasons, finally settling on 714 in 1935. That record stood until 1974, when Hank Aaron hit his 715th. Ruth had owned the career home-run record for 53 seasons.

Ruth led the majors in home runs 11 times. (In 1930 he hit 49 homers to lead the AL, but Chicago Cubs slugger Hack Wilson smacked 56 to lead both leagues.) In the first All-Star Game, in 1933, the 38-year-old Ruth hit the very first home run in the midsummer classic's history.

Ruth was a consistent batter. He batted .343 with 271 home runs with none on base and .352 with 274 homers with men on (not in scoring position); with runners in scoring position, Ruth hit .351 with 146 home runs. He batted .315 in games in which he pitched. He slugged .698 at home and .682 away.

The Babe finished his career at the top of most offensive categories. In 2,503 games he posted a .342 batting average, 10th best in history. His career RBI mark of 2,214 stood for 40 years (also broken by Aaron). In 1922 he overtook Dan Brouthers for the highest career slugging percentage (.696). That number eventually settled to .690 (remember, Ruth played until 1935), but it still, almost 100 years later, leads all batters for a career level. Ruth's single-season slugging mark of .847 held the top spot from 1920 until 2001, when Barry Bonds posted an .863 slugging percentage.

Using recent statistics, Ruth's career numbers still show dominance. His lifetime Offensive Wins Above Replacement (WAR) is 154.3, a mark that has stood at the top since he surpassed Ty Cobb's 151.2 career number in 1933. The Offensive WAR career list names the best of the best. After Ruth and Cobb come Barry Bonds (143.7), Willie Mays (136.8), and Hank Aaron (132.4). Rounding out the top 10 are Ted Williams (126.4), Stan Musial (124.8), Tris Speaker (124.2), Honus Wagner (123.3), and Rogers Hornsby (121.8). Regarding his contemporaries, Ruth led the majors in Offensive WAR in seven seasons, finished second five times, and made the the top 10 list in every season from 1918 to 1933.

The Bambino's on-base percentage of .4739 ranks second all-time, behind Ted Williams's .4817, which means that Ruth's 1.1636 OPS is tops, and might be tops for a long time to come.[4] Ruth did not have the luxury of being a designated hitter, a rule change adopted by the American League in 1973. He played every day, averaging 140 games per season from 1919 through 1933. Toss in 10 postseasons (all in the World Series) in which he averaged .326 and hit 15 home runs, and Ruth showed he could perform at the highest level anytime, against any opponent.

Beyond the statistics, can we scientifically measure how dominant Ruth was as a home-run hitter? In the October 1921 edition of *Popular Science Monthly*, researchers at Columbia University in New York City hooked up Ruth to apparatus after apparatus and "analyzed his brain, his eye, his ear, his muscles; studied how these worked together, reassembled him, and announced the exact reasons for his supremacy as a batter and a ballplayer."[5] This was after his phenomenal 1921 season. One test required Ruth to put a stylus in three holes on a triangular-shaped board in consecutive order. He did it 132 times in one minute. Another test required him to press a telegraph key when a light flashed. He responded more than 10 percent quicker than the average man. According to the article, "the tests revealed the fact that Ruth is 90 per cent efficient compared with a human average of 60 per cent. [Ruth's] eyes are about 12 per cent faster than those of the average human being. [His] ears function at least 10 per cent faster than those of the ordinary man. [His] nerves are steadier than those of 499 out of 500 persons. In intelligence, as demonstrated by quickness and accuracy of understanding, he is approximately 10 per cent above normal."[6] The researchers used results from their tests to explain Ruth's superiority. Then, in a surprise, they revealed that he could be even better than his 59-home-run self in 1921. Ruth evidently held his breath while hitting, and "for that reason, he is not getting the maximum force into his batting."[7] The report concluded that by "dissecting the 'home run king' [the researchers] discovered brain instead of bone, and showed how little mere luck, or even mere hitting strength, has to do with Ruth's phenomenal record."[8]

Some critics might say that Ruth never played at night, never played against African-Americans, never had to battle jet lag, etc. However, Ruth had a reputation for playing hard, both on the field and off it. He still had to hit the ball where they ain't when he stepped into the batter's box, no matter who the opponent was or what he had done the night before. And his success, far and away above those who played before him, with him, and after him, is why we define baseball dominance as Ruthian.

Sources

In addition to the sources mentioned in the Notes, the author consulted baseball-reference.com and retrosheet.org.

Notes

1. Ruth remains second only to Whitey Ford's 33⅔ scoreless-innings streak.
2. Rudy York led the AL with 34 home runs in 1943. Vern Stephens led the AL with 24 home runs in 1945. Bill Nicholson led NL with 33 in 1944 and Mel Ott had 26. Tommy Holmes led the NL with 28 in 1945 and Chuck Workman hit 25.
3. See baseball-reference.com:8080/players/event_hr.cgi?id=ruthba01&t=b for a log of Ruth's 714 career home runs.
4. As of the beginning of the 2019 season, Mike Trout's career OPS mark is .9913. The next active player is Joey Votto, 18th on the career list, with a .9536 career OPS.
5. Hugh Fullerton, "Why Babe Ruth Is Greatest Home-Run Hitter," *Popular Science Monthly*, October 1921, Vol. 99, No. 4: 19.
6. Ibid.
7. Ibid.
8. Ibid.

Cool Babe Ruth Facts

Compiled by Allan Wood

I've spent years looking at Babe Ruth's career statistics – both for research and for pleasure – and I have come to the inescapable conclusion that the man considered by many as the greatest player in the history of baseball is *underrated*.

The more I have learned about Ruth – both on and off the diamond – the more unbelievable and improbable each portion of his life has seemed. Boston sportswriter Burt Whitman felt the same way, writing in July 1918: "The more I see of Babe and his heroic hitting the more he seems a figure out of mythology." (I can only wonder what Whitman thought during the early 1920s.)

The following statistics (taken from Baseball Reference) show Ruth's utter dominance and a ridiculously high level of consistency.

New York Yankee Babe Ruth strikes a batting pose at Fenway Park. 1931-34.
Leslie Jones photo, courtesy of the Boston Public Library.

The Babe

Babe Ruth – Career Splits

	AVG	OBP	SLG	OPS
Career	**.342**	**.474**	**.690**	**1.164**
Right-Handed Pitchers	.344	.465	.687	1.152
Left-Handed Pitchers	.324	.460	.668	1.128
Home	.346	.483	.698	1.181
Away	.338	.466	.682	1.148
First Half	.343	.479	.697	1.176
Second Half	.341	.469	.682	1.152
April	.322	.452	.638	1.089
May	.329	.465	.702	1.168
June	.353	.497	.710	1.207
July	.364	.490	.712	1.202
August	.333	.469	.665	1.134
September/October	.334	.453	.679	1.132
Left Fielder	.322	.445	.653	1.097
Right Fielder	.350	.476	.702	1.179
Batting Third	.345	.481	.703	1.184
Batting Fourth	.341	.472	.695	1.167
With 0 outs	.355	.472	.718	1.191
With 1 out	.340	.459	.696	1.155
With 2 outs	.323	.461	.635	1.096
Bases Empty	.336	.453	.696	1.149
Men on Base	.341	.473	.667	1.140
Runners in Scoring Position	.347	.479	.677	1.156
2 outs, Runners in Scoring Position	.327	.470	.630	1.099
Late & Close	.339	.491	.713	1.204
Team Ahead	.353	.474	.737	1.211
Team Behind	.341	.458	.656	1.113
Within 1 run	.329	.469	.646	1.115
Within 2 runs	.331	.466	.664	1.130
Within 3 runs	.331	.462	.661	1.123
Within 4 runs	.334	.462	.670	1.132
More than 4 runs	.362	.471	.746	1.218
High Leverage	.324	.461	.626	1.086
Medium Leverage	.340	.473	.678	1.151
Low Leverage	.343	.458	.707	1.165
Starting Pitcher	.337	.461	.669	1.131
Relief Pitchers	.342	.472	.722	1.194
Power Pitchers	.323	.462	.654	1.115
Finesse Pitchers	.373	.483	.756	1.239
Flyball Pitchers	.336	.464	.698	1.162
Groundball Pitchers	.347	.469	.669	1.137
Starting Pitcher, 1st PA	.315	.456	.612	1.068

	AVG	OBP	SLG	OPS
Starting Pitcher, 2nd PA	.332	.463	.628	1.091
Starting Pitcher, 3rd PA	.346	.462	.727	1.188
Starting Pitcher, 4th PA	.365	.467	.735	1.202
Relief Pitcher, 1st PA	.336	.470	.704	1.174
Relief Pitcher, 2nd PA	.354	.491	.799	1.290
Relief Pitcher, 3rd+ PA	.350	.437	.670	1.107
Innings 1-3	.327	.464	.634	1.098
Innings 4-6	.330	.454	.677	1.131
Innings 7-9	.366	.475	.751	1.225
Extra Innings (only 70 PA)	.265	.463	.633	1.095
Boston Red Sox	.337	.464	.683	1.147
Chicago White Sox	.340	.470	.681	1.151
Cleveland Indians	.354	.507	.686	1.193
Detroit Tigers	.338	.477	.744	1.221
New York Yankees	.337	.438	.663	1.100
Philadelphia Athletics	.352	.479	.703	1.181
St. Louis Browns	.351	.484	.673	1.157
Washington Senators	.332	.446	.676	1.122
Teams Over .500	.352	.483	.704	1.187
Teams Below .500	.330	.463	.672	1.134
Fenway Park (Red Sox)	.323	.440	.583	1.024
Comiskey Park (White Sox)	.309	.442	.611	1.053
League Park (Cleveland)	.372	.528	.728	1.257
Navin Field (Tigers)	.332	.479	.735	1.215
Polo Grounds (Yankees)	.365	.497	.828	1.324
Yankee Stadium (Yankees)	.349	.487	.697	1.183
Shibe Park (Athletics)	.357	.472	.753	1.225
Sportsman's Park (Browns)	.342	.470	.696	1.166
Griffith Stadium (Senators)	.332	.435	.637	1.072

Babe Ruth — OPS By Months

	April	May	June	July	August	Sept./Oct.	Season	AL Rank	All-Time Rank
1918	1.033	1.284	1.007	.931	.782	.933	.968	1st	
1919	1.234	.844	1.167	1.113	1.146	1.239	1.114	1st	#74
1920	.508	1.384	1.540	1.581	1.188	1.394	1.382	1st	#3
1921	1.467	1.154	1.537	1.327	1.507	1.237	1.356	1st	#5
1922		.642	1.173	1.071	1.209	1.174	1.104	1st	#84
1923	1.243	1.254	1.139	1.436	1.435	1.291	1.313	1st	#6
1924	1.170	1.335	1.150	1.441	1.283	1.014	1.252	1st	#12
1925			.767	1.010	.724	1.151	.936	DNQ	
1926	1.253	1.312	1.435	1.036	1.298	1.205	1.253	1st	#11
1927	1.095	1.247	1.339	1.342	1.063	1.364	1.258	1st	#9
1928	1.067	1.547	1.046	1.226	1.114	.922	1.172	1st	#31
1929	.688	1.063	1.465	1.229	1.230	1.012	1.130	1st	#59
1930	1.018	1.412	1.477	.996	1.304	1.047	1.225	1st	#15
1931	1.314	1.314	1.228	1.135	1.113	1.199	1.195	1st	#23
1932	1.263	.993	1.034	1.294	1.341	.820	1.150	2nd	#45
1933	1.181	.911	1.081	1.134	.687	1.223	1.024	3rd	#298
1934	1.024	1.044	.844	1.136	.901	.955	.986	5th	
1935 (NL)	.921	.715					.789	DNQ	
Career	1.089	1.168	1.207	1.202	1.134	1.132	1.164	1st	#1

Statistics begin with 1918 because that is the first season Ruth ceased being a full-time pitcher and began playing every day.
DNQ: Did Not Qualify (not enough plate appearances to be listed among league leaders)

September 1925 to August 1932: Ruth posted an OPS over .900 in 41 of 42 consecutive months, over eight seasons. In the lone month his OPS was below .900 (April 1929), he played in only 10 games. It was, of course, a momentarily slip. Ruth batted .371/.457/.736 over the next two months.

1919-1934 (16 seasons): In nearly half of the months that Ruth was a full-time outfielder for the Red Sox and Yankees (44 of 93, 47.3%), his OPS topped 1.200, including 13 months over 1.400.

Babe Ruth – OPS Against American League Teams

	Red Sox	Browns	White Sox	Cleveland	Tigers	Senators	Athletics	Yankees
1918		1.038	.757	.962	.888	1.239	.827	1.126
1919		1.052	1.032	1.162	1.134	1.005	1.197	1.177
1920	1.453	1.371	1.616	1.336	1.424	1.193	1.296	
1921	1.220	1.448	1.082	1.720	1.387	1.251	1.430	
1922	1.363	.811	1.356	1.037	1.171	.558	1.548	
1923	1.209	1.429	1.331	1.201	1.260	1.306	1.445	
1924	.980	1.183	1.493	1.319	1.265	1.033	1.530	
1925	1.070	1.023	.737	.866	1.155	.602	1.067	
1926	1.313	1.426	1.159	1.230	1.169	1.377	1.091	
1927	1.325	1.305	1.188	1.384	1.162	1.285	1.152	
1928	.925	.830	1.333	1.093	1.508	1.440	1.148	
1929	1.085	1.075	1.063	1.328	1.585	1.084	.834	
1930	1.208	1.145	1.118	1.188	1.358	1.241	1.334	
1931	1.152	1.269	1.419	1.211	.960	1.081	1.249	
1932	.918	1.129	.848	1.758	1.230	1.068	1.110	
1933	1.062	.808	1.123	.940	1.047	1.137	1.018	
1934	.916	1.128	1.015	.729	.802	1.071	1.241	
Career	1.147	1.157	1.151	1.193	1.221	1.122	1.181	1.100

1920: Ruth's lowest on-base and slugging percentages against any team came against the Senators. Yet his .473 on-base percentage would have finished third in the American League and his .720 slugging percentage was at least 88 points higher than any other player in the major leagues.

1922: Ruth had a .605 on-base percentage against the Red Sox, reaching base 26 times (12 hits, 14 walks) in 43 plate appearances. Ruth also batted .400 (20-for-50) against the Athletics, with 7 singles, 3 doubles, 1 triple, and 9 home runs.

1929: Ruth's OPS against the Tigers was 1.585, with 18 of his 28 hits going for extra bases.

Babe Ruth – OPS (Various Splits)

	vs LHP	vs RHP	Home	Away	Wins	Losses	No One On	Men On	RISP
1918	.882	.988	.955	.977	1.003	.915	N/A	N/A	N/A
1919	1.032	1.142	1.088	1.136	1.203	1.029	N/A	N/A	N/A
1920	1.500	1.343	1.535	1.260	1.531	1.110	N/A	N/A	N/A
1921	1.141	1.430	1.470	1.251	1.445	1.192	N/A	N/A	N/A
1922	1.139	1.094	1.002	1.197	1.315	.733	N/A	N/A	N/A
1923	1.203	1.358	1.377	1.255	1.376	1.176	N/A	N/A	N/A
1924	1.142	1.311	1.267	1.237	1.369	1.073	N/A	N/A	N/A
1925	.913	1.028	.902	.979	1.037	.848	1.057	.887	1.037
1926	1.086	1.224	1.238	1.267	1.391	1.023	1.102	1.235	1.236
1927	1.204	1.270	1.268	1.249	1.415	.870	1.264	1.239	1.228
1928	1.208	1.217	1.188	1.157	1.245	1.029	1.341	1.098	1.304
1929	1.136	1.012	1.106	1.148	1.366	.809	.926	1.171	1.212
1930	1.145	1.257	1.293	1.164	1.351	1.058	1.336	1.122	1.156
1931	1.180	1.236	1.152	1.238	1.397	.866	1.208	1.236	1.171
1932	1.292	1.102	1.089	1.217	1.251	.902	1.048	1.251	1.073
1933	1.120	.981	1.152	.911	1.186	.799	1.024	1.023	.944
1934	.958	.995	1.051	.913	1.071	.863	1.022	.957	1.041
1935 (NL)	.944	1.045	.952	.690	.933	.723	.937	1.100	1.333
Career	1.152	1.128	1.181	1.148	1.297	.952	1.149	1.140	1.156

	0 out	1 out	2 out	Innings 1-3	Innings 4-6	Innings 7-9
1925	.872	1.040	.991	.796	1.054	1.143
1926	1.092	1.185	1.244	1.292	.990	1.216
1927	1.279	1.247	1.229	1.287	1.122	1.303
1928	1.356	1.278	1.021	1.034	1.220	1.428
1929	1.121	1.057	.964	.997	1.061	1.109
1930	1.302	1.140	1.251	1.175	1.218	1.361
1931	1.447	1.060	1.224	1.165	1.383	1.156
1932	1.153	1.234	1.080	.980	1.318	1.233
1933	1.148	1.126	.826	.997	.937	1.148
1934	.954	.987	1.010	1.045	.898	1.001
1935 (NL)	.850	1.366	.667	1.115	1.019	.778
Total (11 Seasons)	1.191	1.155	1.096	1.098	1.131	1.225

Data for these splits not available for seasons before 1925.

Ruth would have had to go 0-for-1,501 for his career OPS of 1.164 to fall below 1.000.

Only 25 players in history finished their careers with a slugging percentage over .550. Ruth would have had to go 0-for-2,135 for his career slugging percentage to fall below .550.

Barry Bonds has the fifth-best slugging percentage of all-time (.607). To unseat Ruth's .690 slugging percentage from the number-1 spot, Bonds would have had to hit 247 consecutive home runs. Conversely, Ruth would have had to go 0-for-1,147 for his slugging percentage to drop below Bonds' .607.

Ruth still holds the record for the most extra-base hits in a season, with 119, in 1921 (44 doubles, 16 triples, 59 home runs).

Ruth is the all-time leader in Isolated Power (.348), which measures how many extra bases a player averages per at-bat (roughly, slugging percentage minus batting average). Mark McGwire is second, at .325.

Ruth holds the single-season record for total bases, with 457, in 1921.

Only 11 players in history have had even one season with an OPS+ of 206 or better. That is Ruth's career average.

In 1923, Babe Ruth reached base by hit, walk, or hit by pitch 379 times, which remains the all-time record.

	Year	TB	1B	2B	3B	HR	BB	HBP
Babe Ruth	1923	379	106	45	13	41	170	4
Barry Bonds	2004	376	60	27	3	45	232	9
Billy Hamilton	1894	362	181	25	15	4	128	9
Ted Williams	1949	358	109	39	3	43	162	2
Barry Bonds	2002	356	70	31	2	46	198	9
Babe Ruth	1921	353	85	44	16	59	145	4
Babe Ruth	1924	346	108	39	7	46	142	4
Ted Williams	1947	345	100	40	9	32	162	2

Ruth had seven seasons with at least a .350 batting average, .480 on-base percentage, and .730 slugging percentage. Everyone else in baseball history – nearly 20,000 players – has combined for five such seasons.

	AVG	OBP	SLG
Babe Ruth, 1920:	.376	.532	.847
Babe Ruth, 1921:	.378	.512	.846
Babe Ruth, 1923:	.393	.545	.764
Babe Ruth, 1924:	.378	.513	.739
Babe Ruth, 1926:	.372	.516	.737
Babe Ruth, 1927:	.356	.486	.772
Babe Ruth, 1930:	.359	.493	.732
Rogers Hornsby, 1925:	.403	.489	.756
Ted Williams, 1941:	.406	.553	.735
Ted Williams, 1957:	.388	.526	.731
Barry Bonds, 2002:	.370	.582	.799
Barry Bonds, 2004:	.362	.609	.812

Note: Ted Williams did it at ages 22 and 38.)

Ruth had three seasons with at least a .375 batting average, .500 on-base percentage, and .750 slugging percentage.

	AVG	OBP	SLG
Babe Ruth, 1920:	.376	.532	.847
Babe Ruth, 1921:	.378	.512	.846
Babe Ruth, 1923:	.393	.545	.764

No other player in history has had even one season with those averages. In fact, only four other players have ever had a season with any two of those benchmarks.

.375 batting average and .500 on-base percentage

	AVG	OBP	SLG
Rogers Hornsby, 1924:	.424	.507	.696
Ted Williams, 1941:	.406	.553	.735
Ted Williams, 1957:	.388	.526	.731

.375 batting average and .750 slugging percentage

	AVG	OBP	SLG
Rogers Hornsby, 1925:	.403	.489	.756

.500 on-base percentage and .750 slugging percentage

	AVG	OBP	SLG
Barry Bonds, 2001:	.328	.515	.863
Barry Bonds, 2002:	.370	.582	.799
Barry Bonds, 2004:	.362	.609	.812

Babe Ruth had six seasons with an OPS over 1.250. Only two other players in history have had even one season.

Babe Ruth
1920: 1.379
1921: 1.359
1923: 1.309
1924: 1.252

The Babe

1926: 1.253
1927: 1.258

Barry Bonds
2001: 1.379
2002: 1.381
2003: 1.278
2004: 1.422

Ted Williams
1941: 1.287
1957: 1.257

Ruth holds eight of the top 17 spots on the Best Single-Season OPS+ list (1901-2018). The only three players with more than one season in the Top 20:

Babe Ruth   8 (1919, 1920, 1921, 1923, 1924, 1926, 1927, 1931)
Barry Bonds   4 (2001, 2002, 2003, 2004)
Ted Williams   2 (1941, 1957)

Bonds' top nine seasons: 1st, 2nd, 3rd, 9th, 30th (tied), 37th, 90th (tied), 90th (tied), 122nd (tied). Ruth's top nine seasons: 4th, 5th, 6th, 10th (tied), 10th (tied), 14th (tied), 16th, 17th, 23rd.

In 276 games from May 11, 1920, to October 2, 1921, Ruth batted .388.

In 250 games from April 30, 1923, to August 8, 1924, Ruth batted .402.

On August 30, 1923, Ruth's batting average was .405. He finished the season at .393. Just four more hits – one additional hit every six weeks – would have given him a .400 average. Ruth's OPS dropped below 1.120 on only three days (May 13, 14, 16). Ruth's on-base percentage never dropped below .484, and it was above .500 on all but eight days (all between May 14-22).

In 162 games from July 24, 1927, to July 30, 1928, Ruth hit 71 home runs.

Babe Ruth never went more than two games in his entire career without a hit or a walk. He had 21 two-game "slumps," although two games cannot honestly be called a slump. If you exclude his seasons as a full-time pitcher, games in which he pinch-hit or came into the game after it had begun, and games shorter than nine innings, he had 14 such instances. From September 21, 1928, to July 31, 1934 – a span of 786 games over seven seasons – Ruth had back-to-back games with no hits and no walks only twice.

Ruth is the only player in history to hit grand slams in consecutive games on two occasions.

September 27, 1927, off Lefty Grove (Athletics)

September 29, 1927, off Paul Hopkins (Senators)

August 6, 1929 (G2), off Bobby Burke (Senators)
August 7, 1929, (G1) off Howard Ehmke (Athletics)

Ruth is the only player to hit three home runs in a postseason game twice (1926 World Series, Game Four; 1928 World Series, Game Four).

Ruth hit 259 home runs in the original Yankee Stadium. Only Mickey Mantle hit more (266), but he needed six more years (18 seasons to Ruth's 12).

When Ruth played his last game for the Yankees in 1934, he had hit 28.3 percent of all home runs in Yankees history.

Hank Aaron hit 41 more home runs than Ruth (755) but needed 3,318 more plate appearances. Barry Bonds hit 48 more home runs than Ruth (762), but needed 1,983 more plate appearances.

In the five seasons from 1919 to 1923, only 11 players hit more than 50 home runs. Ruth led the pack with 218.

HOME RUNS, 1919-1923 (5 SEASONS)
Babe Ruth   218
Cy Williams   109
Ken Williams   108
Rogers Hornsby   97
Tillie Walker   89
Harry Heilmann   75
High Pockets Kelly 68

The average American League team (excluding Ruth's team in each season) hit 238 home runs over those five seasons.

In 10 World Series, Ruth batted .326, slugged .744, hit 15 home runs ... and pitched 31 innings (including two complete games and one shutout) with an 0.87 ERA.

Ruth played five positions during his career: right field (1,130 games), left field (1,048 games), pitcher (163 games), center field (74 games), and first base (32 games). Two other players have logged at least 70 games both on the mound and in the outfield – Blondie Purcell and George Van Haltren – but their careers were spent mostly in the 1880s and 1890s. Since the formation of the American League in 1901, Ruth is the only one.

1920 AND 1921

Ruth's first season in New York started slowly. In 1920 he was batting .210 and slugging only .371 after 18 games. But on May 11 everything clicked. Ruth batted .403 (average)/.564 (on-base)/.924 (slugging) (1.488 OPS) for the rest of the season, reaching base in 121 of 124 games. Over the entire season, there were 33 games in which Ruth did not get a hit, but his on-base percentage in those games was still .328, thanks to 42 walks.

Ruth finished the 1920 season with 54 home runs, out-homering all but two major-league teams. The Phillies hit 64 and the Yankees (minus Ruth's total) hit 61.

The original Yankee Stadium was known as the House That Ruth Built, but the Babe must have been sad to say goodbye to the Polo Grounds. In 1920 he slugged .990 at his home park in Upper Manhattan. More than two-thirds of his hits went for extra bases (56 of 81, 69%) and he hit more home runs (29) than singles (25). In 1921, Ruth slugged .926 at home, with 63 of his 103 hits (61%) going for extra bases, including 32 home runs.

Over the 1920 and 1921 seasons, Ruth slugged .847. On the list of players with at least 600 plate appearances over those two seasons, Rogers Hornsby (at number 2, .599) was closer to number 105 than he was to number 1.

In 1920-21, Ruth hit 113 home runs, 74 more than his former team (the Red Sox) hit in those two seasons (39).

On June 11-14, 1921, the Yankees swept a four-game series at home against the Tigers. Ruth, at that time playing center field, went 8-for-12, with two doubles and six home runs (28 total bases). He scored nine runs and drove in 12. He drew six walks and struck out only once in 18 plate appearances. (He made exactly one out in each game.) Ruth's OPS in those four games was 3.111. He also stole a base ... and he pitched five innings in the third game of the series and picked up the win. Ruth hit more home runs in those four games than any Red Sox batter hit in the entire 1921 season. Ruth's 59 homers that year set a new single-season record – a record he had broken for the third consecutive year.

STREAKS

Over a period of 90 games in 1920 (May 11 to August 14), Ruth batted .427/.584/.986 (1.570 OPS), with 40 home runs and only 45 strikeouts. His entire career is filled with similar hot streaks – some shorter, some longer, sometimes several of them in one season. The following is only a sampling.

June 1 to July 31, 1920 (63 games): .445/.596/.965 (1.561 OPS); more than twice as many walks (73) as strikeouts (36).

June 9-16, 1921 (eight-game hitting streak): .577/.703/1.538 (2.241 OPS); 15-for-26, with 4 singles, 4 doubles, and 7 home runs; on base 26 times in eight games (15 hits and 11 walks), with only 5 strikeouts.

July 28 to August 25, 1921 (career-best 26-game hitting streak): .483/.610/1.045 (1.655 OPS); 43-for-89, with 8 doubles, 3 triples, and 12 home runs; 35 runs scored, 39 RBI, 29 walks, 10 strikeouts.

May 15 to June 4, 1923 (19 games): .420/.565/.928 (1.493 OPS).

June 30 to July 19, 1923 (22 games): .468/.596/.861 (1.457 OPS).

July 7 to September 1, 1923 (51 games): .460/.585/.864 (1.449 OPS); more extra-base hits (35) than strikeouts (26) (15 doubles, 4 triples, 16 home runs).

July 27 to August 30, 1923 (29 games): .500/.624/.940 (1.564 OPS); 50-for-100, 13 doubles, 9 home runs; 32 runs scored, 32 RBIs, 31 walks. (The Yankees somehow went only 15-14.)

July 6 to August 8, 1924 (37 games): .507/.595/1.022 (1.617 OPS); 97 hits and walks in 165 plate appearances. (This period included hitting streaks of 17 and 12 games.)

May 5-20, 1926 (14 games): 16-for-46 (.348), 4 singles, 1 double, and 11 home runs.

August 26 to September 13, 1927 (18 games): 22-for-70, only a .314 average, but .929 slugging, with 5 singles and 17 extra-base hits, including 12 home runs.

September 6 to October 1, 1927 (last 24 games of season): .393/.491/.978 (1.468 OPS); 35-for-89, 16 home runs, 40 RBIs.

May 1-29, 1928 (27 games): .424/.562/1.000 (1.562 OPS); 14 home runs. (The Yankees won 23 of the 27 games.)

June 21 (Game 2) to August 17, 1929 (52 games): .403/.498/.874 (1.372 OPS); 23 home runs and 70 RBIs.

May 21-24, 1930 (six games): .522/.621/1.565 (2.186 OPS); 12-for-23, with 8 home runs and 18 RBIs.

July 3 to August 28, 1932 (52 games): .427/.577/.805 (1.381 OPS).

July 28 to August 28, 1932 (30 games): .459/.616/.929 (1.545 OPS).

PITCHING

Ruth finished his playing career with a 2.28 ERA in 1,221⅓ innings pitched. Since Ruth's last game on the mound, in 1933, only one pitcher has thrown as many innings with a lower ERA: Mariano Rivera, 2.21 ERA in 1,283⅔ innings.

While Ruth was rewriting the record book as a hitter for the Yankees – and for almost three decades after he retired – he also held the record for most consecutive scoreless innings pitched in the World Series (29⅔, eventually broken in 1961 by Whitey Ford).

Ruth is the only player who pitched in at least 10 seasons and had a winning record in all of them. Andy Pettitte of the Yankees would have held the record at 13 seasons if he had retired after 2007. But Pettitte kept pitching and went 14-14 in 2008.

Ruth was a full-time pitcher for only three seasons (1915-17). He burst on the scene at age 20 as one of the best pitchers in baseball. In those three seasons, Ruth's 2.02 ERA was third lowest, behind Pete Alexander (1.54) and Walter Johnson (1.88). Ruth was also third in wins (65) and tied for third in shutouts (16) and fourth in complete games (74) and strikeouts (410).

At the same time, Ruth was far and away the best hitting pitcher in the majors. For those three years, only four pitchers had a batting average higher than .250, and only one hit better than .268: that was Ruth, at .302. He led all pitchers in hits (106, seven more than Walter Johnson, despite having 68 fewer at-bats), runs scored (48, six more than Johnson), home runs (9, nearly double Claude Hendrix's total of 5), RBIs (50, 11 more than Johnson), and walks (31, one more than Lefty Tyler). Ruth was tied with Johnson with 21 doubles and second in triples (7, two fewer than Johnson).

Among American League left-handers in the 1910s with at least 1,000 innings, Ruth had the lowest ERA (2.19), the highest winning percentage (.659), and was tied for fourth in shutouts.

It's difficult to compare the statistics of the Deadball Era, which ended 100 years ago, to the performances of modern pitchers. ERA+ is a statistic that adjusts a pitcher's ERA to both the ballpark and the league. An ERA+ of 100 is league average. An ERA+ of 110 is 10 percent better than league average.

Clayton Kershaw led the National League with a 2.31 ERA in 2017. His ERA+ was 179, also tops in the NL. Back in 1917, Fred Anderson of the Giants had an ERA+ of 177 and an ERA was 1.44. So a 2.31 ERA in 2017 was slightly better than a 1.44 ERA in 1917.

The following list includes pitchers whose career ERA+ is somewhat similar to Ruth's 125 ERA+ with the Red Sox. (Ruth made five spot starts for the Yankees during his 15 seasons in New York, lowering his overall ERA+ to 122.) All eight of the retired pitchers on this list are in the Hall of Fame.

CAREER ERA+

Sandy Koufax	131
Max Scherzer	130
Tom Seaver	127
Bob Gibson	127
John Smoltz	125
Babe Ruth	125
Jim Palmer	125
Zack Greinke	123
Bob Feller	122
Jon Lester	122
Warren Spahn	119
Nolan Ryan	112

The career ERA+ of the three active pitchers are through the end of the 2018 season. These numbers will likely drop as the players get older. Ruth never experienced that particular decline, of course, but he also stopped pitching for the Red Sox when he was only 24 years old.

Using Baseball Reference's Play Index, I searched for pitchers since 1901 with an ERA+ of at least 120 over their first five seasons (pitching a minimum of 700 innings) and whose fifth season was no later than their age-23 season.

There are 12 pitchers besides Ruth that fit the bill.

	ERA+	YEARS	AGE	GMS	IP	W	L	ERA
Walter Johnson	148	1907-11	19-23	175	1355.1	82	78	1.77
Bob Feller	140	1936-40	17-21	161	1105.1	82	41	3.19
Christy Mathewson	138	1901-04	20-23	168	1354.2	97	59	2.21
Clayton Kershaw	135	2008-11	20-23	118	716.1	47	28	2.88
Dwight Gooden	134	1984-88	19-23	158	1172.2	91	35	2.62
Bert Blyleven	134	1970-74	19-23	181	1335.2	80	75	2.74
Frank Tanana	131	1973-77	19-23	142	1082.0	66	49	2.69
Babe Ruth	129	1914-18	19-23	141	1057.0	80	41	2.09
Bret Saberhagen	126	1984-87	20-23	133	806.0	55	39	3.39
Felix Hernandez	125	2005-09	19-23	138	905.0	58	41	3.45

Gary Nolan
    123   1967-71   19-23   144   980.2   61   42   2.98

Dennis Eckersley
    123   1975-78   20-23   138   901.2   60   40   3.15

Vida Blue
    122   1969-73   19-23   119   807.1   53   28   2.74

Half of the 12 other pitchers are in the Hall of Fame (Johnson, Feller, Mathewson, Blyleven, Eckersley) or will be (Kershaw).

A FEW PITCHING STREAKS, TOO

July 13 to October 6, 1915: 17 games, 15 starts, 1.67 ERA, 0.994 WHIP, 83 hits allowed (76 singles), .198 opponents average, .148 opponents slugging.

August 12 to September 29, 1916: 15 games, 12 starts, 9 complete games; 0.76 ERA, 0.943 WHIP, 117⅔ innings, 10 earned runs, 73 hits allowed (66 singles), .181 opponents average, .149 opponents slugging.

July 11 to September 29, 1917: 21 games, 18 starts, 18 complete games, 2 saves; 1.46 ERA in 166⅔ innings, .192 opponents average, .243 opponents slugging.

July 5 to August 31, 1918: 11 starts, 10 complete games, 1.76 ERA, 0.918 WHIP, .184 opponents average, .178 opponents slugging.

September 2, 1915, to June 13, 1917 (66 games): Over 494⅔ innings and 1,979 batters, Ruth did not allow a home run. He hit three homers as a batter during that period, though.

For most of his career (15 seasons), Ruth did not wear a uniform number. He wore number 3 for only his final six seasons in New York. Ruth never wore the Yankees' famous interlocking NY logo. It didn't become a permanent part of the team's jerseys until after Ruth left the team.

In 1936, the year after Ruth's retirement, the Hall of Fame inducted its first five players (Ty Cobb, Honus Wagner, Walter Johnson, Christy Mathewson, and Ruth). Ruth received 95.1 percent of votes; 11 of the 226 voters left him off their ballots.

The Home Runs That Changed Everything

How Babe Ruth's Home Runs at Hot Springs, Arkansas, in March of 1918 Changed the Game of Baseball Forever

By the Hot Springs Historic Baseball Trail Research Team: Mark Blaeuer, Mike Dugan, Don Duren, Bill Jenkinson, and Tim Reid

---

"I saw it all happen, from beginning to end. But sometimes I still can't believe what I saw. This 19-year-old kid, crude, poorly educated, only lightly brushed by the social veneer we call civilization, gradually transformed into the idol of American youth and the symbol of baseball the world over – a man loved by more people and with an intensity of feeling that perhaps has never been equaled before or since."

Babe Ruth's Red Sox teammate Harry Hooper [1]

***

Hercules Meets Hot Springs

Babe Ruth first arrived in Hot Springs, Arkansas, on March 6, 1915, a rookie pitcher for the Boston Red Sox. As was their custom, the Red Sox lodged at the Majestic Hotel, one of the town's preeminent spa hotels. Babe was immediately smitten with Hot Springs, then regarded as "the Mecca of professional base ball players."[2] It was the most exotic place he had ever seen. The warm baths, mountain vistas, golf courses, horse races, and attractive women seemed like a dream. Until 1914, his world had been mostly limited to the waterfront streets of Baltimore or the inside of St. Mary's Industrial School for Boys.[3]

Twenty-year-old Babe Ruth was an unstoppable force of nature. The 6-foot-2-inch, rock-hard, 200-pound juggernaut hit the ball harder, pitched better, hiked with more stamina, and ate more food than anyone in town. Pitching in an intrasquad game on March 23, 1915, Ruth belted a savage line-drive home run to right-center field that left witnesses in disbelief. Despite Boston's talent-laden pitching staff, Ruth earned a place in their starting rotation, eventually winning 18 games as a rookie.[4]

The Red Sox returned to Hot Springs in 1916 and 1917, and Babe Ruth kept getting better. He won 23 games and led the league with a spectacular 1.75 ERA in 1916. The next year he led the majors with 35 complete games, posting a stellar 2.01

ERA. Over the course of those two seasons, the southpaw from Baltimore amassed an imposing total of 650 innings pitched. During those first three years (1915-1917), he also belted nine home runs. Everyone knew Babe could hit, but his greatness as a pitcher virtually assured that he remained on the mound. But then, larger events intervened.[5]

With the Great War raging in Europe, many big-league players joined the conflict. That included Red Sox player-manager Jack Barry. Accordingly, owner Harry Frazee signed former International League President Ed Barrow to take over as manager. Barrow was an intelligent, competent man, but he was also humorless and unimaginative. Barrow believed converting Babe Ruth to a position player in 1918 would have made him "the laughingstock of baseball."[6]

The Wizard of Whittington

> *"Every ball player in the park said it was the longest drive they had ever seen … soaring over the street and a wide duck pond, finally finding a resting place in the Ozark Hills."*
>
> *Edward Martin,* Boston Globe[7]

> *"Before the echo of the crash had died away the horsehide had dropped somewhere in the vicinity of South Hot Springs. … The sphere cleared the fence by about 200 feet and dropped in the pond beside the Alligator Farm, while the spectators yelled with amazement. …"*
>
> *Paul Shannon,* Boston Post [8]

Babe left Boston by train for Arkansas on March 9, 1918. He was in peak physical condition after spending the winter with his wife in a remote cottage in rural Sudbury, Massachusetts. He chopped wood all winter, and vigorously engaged in various winter sports and activities.[9]

During his first week of practice in Hot Springs, Ed Barrow worked all his pitchers hard, making them hike over mountains, shag fly balls, and take infield practice. Barrow had already decided that big-league teams carried too many pitchers, and he wanted his hurlers in optimum shape to handle the increased workload. Yet, in those early stages, Ruth had looked comfortable at first base, and, as usual, had clubbed several batting-practice homers.[10]

So when regular first baseman Dick Hoblitzell was not ready to play in the opening exhibition game, Barrow inserted the 23-year-old Bambino into his position. The game was played at Whittington Park on March 17 against the Brooklyn Dodgers (aka Robins). It was the first time Ruth ever played against a major-league team in any position other than pitcher.[11]

Left: Babe Ruth on the mound at Majestic Park in Hot Springs, Arkansas, during his first spring with the Red Sox. March 1915. *Right:* Babe and first wife, Helen, at the Happy Hollow Amusement Park in Hot Springs. Behind Helen is Edna Bancroft, wife of Hall of Fame shortstop Dave Bancroft. March 1921. *Image editing by Tim Reid III of ltr3designs*

Batting in the fourth inning, Babe lined a mammoth shot to deep left-center field that landed in a distant woodpile, enabling Ruth to easily circle the bases. Two innings later, Babe did even better. This time he unloaded a drive to right-center field that passed so far over the fence that it landed across the street in the Arkansas Alligator Farm, a well-known tourist attraction. The blow was so amazing that even the Dodgers stood up and cheered. None of them had ever seen anybody hit a baseball with such astonishing force. It was surely the longest home run ever hit, and *may* even have been the first to land over 500 feet on the fly.[12]

Six days later, on March 23, Babe wowed the crowd at the newly built Army training center, Camp Pike, in North Little Rock, launching out five home runs in a batting exhibition. The troops loved him.[13]

Word of these remarkable events quickly circulated around the baseball community, and everyone wondered if they would ever be reprised. The very next day, Saturday, March 24, the Red Sox again faced the Dodgers at Whittington Park. Barrow started Carl Mays on the mound but had to use Babe Ruth in right field due to the ongoing manpower shortage. Again, Ruth was in the field more due to chance than actual design, and, again, he took advantage.[14]

In the third inning, he smashed another tremendous home run to right-center field, a grand slam that cleared a pond just to the right of the same Alligator Farm. Stunning the crowd, Babe had launched this drive even farther than the second St. Patrick's Day blast. Without question, it flew well over 500 feet.[15]

The Babe

Polo Grounds Potentate

"Babe Ruth could hit a ball so hard, and so far, that it was sometimes impossible to believe your eyes. We used to absolutely marvel at his hits. Tremendous wallops. You can't imagine the balls he hit."

Opposing pitcher and teammate Sad Sam Jones[16]

Despite his inconceivable display of slugging power in Hot Springs, when the regular season opened at Fenway Park on April 15, Babe was the starting pitcher, hurling a masterful four-hitter against the Athletics. Three weeks later, though, he swatted two jaw-dropping home runs against the Yankees at the Polo Grounds, one on May 4, one on May 6. Before hitting the first, he hit a rocket-shot foul into the right-field upper deck. Additionally, Babe slammed three homer-length fouls during that same game, as well as a 440-foot double to the exit gate in deep right-center.[17]

Baseball writer and historian Fred Lieb described Ruth's phenomenal power and intimidating impact in this way:

> *"[Despite the] soggy, lifeless ball of 1918 [Ruth] chilled [the] blood of pitchers ... rocket[ing] home runs out of stadiums [and, on May 8] going 5 for 5, with three doubles and a triple."*[18]

Babe's superhuman performances in New York left an indelible impression on fans, press, and, perhaps most important of all, Yankees co-owner Jacob Ruppert, who witnessed it from his owner's box, usually, if not always, with Harry Frazee sitting by his side. Ruppert offered to buy Ruth from the Red Sox in 1918, but Frazee refused. It took a drastic change of financial circumstances for Frazee, Ruppert's deep pockets, and the help of Yankees co-owner Cap Huston before Frazee agreed to sell Ruth, and other Red Sox stars to the Yankees, in what infamously became reviled in Boston as the "Rape of the Red Sox."[19]

New York fans were in awe of Ruth. As Paul Shannon of the *Boston Post* reported, Ruth was "the hitting idol of the Polo Grounds." As sensational a pitcher as Babe was for the Red Sox, it was his breathtaking shows of unimaginable slugging against the Yankees that resulted in his becoming a Yankee himself. The die was cast.[20]

***

The Great, Powerful, and Beloved Babe Ruth

"Every so often some superman appears who follows no set rule, who flouts accepted theories, who throws science itself to the winds and hews out a rough path for himself by the sheer weight of his own unequaled talents. Such a man is Babe Ruth in the batting world and his influence on the whole system of batting employed in the major leagues is clear as crystal."

Baseball writer F.C. Lane[21]

"Don't tell me about Ruth. I've seen what he did to people; fans driving miles in open wagons through the prairies of Oklahoma to see him in exhibition games as we headed north in the spring. Kids, men, women, worshippers all, hoping to get his name on a torn, dirty piece of paper, or hoping for a grunt of recognition when they said 'Hi Ya, Babe.' He never let them down, not once. He was the greatest crowd pleaser of them all."

Babe's Red Sox and Yankee teammate Waite Hoyt[22]

Those moonshots at Whittington Park in March of 1918 had initiated a series of occurrences nobody could control. Even "Simon Legree" Barrow was no match for the inevitability of Babe's herculean power at the plate, nor for his popularity with the fans. So awesome was his slugging that Babe rarely appeared on a major-league mound again after his years with the Red Sox, pitching only five regular-season games during his 14 years with the Yankees, (1920-1934), the winning pitcher in every one.[23]

Babe basically gave up pitching after his years with Boston, but he did not give up Hot Springs.

He often returned for preseason conditioning and fun during the Roaring Twenties and beyond.

He took the baths, hiked the trails, bet the ponies, enjoyed the nightlife, and played a lot of golf.

What he did in regular seasons, however, is what made him the most famous and beloved sports figure in American history. He revolutionized the game of baseball with the unprecedented number and splendor of his home runs, a mind-boggling 659 of them with the Yankees.

Beginning in March of 1918 in Hot Springs, Arkansas, Babe changed baseball forever.[24]

***

Special thanks and dedication to Steve Arrison,

Creator of the Hot Springs Historic Baseball Trail

Notes

1. Lawrence S. Ritter, *The Glory of Their Times* (New York: Macmillan Company, 1966), 137.

2. Jay Jennings, "When Baseball Sprang for Hot Springs," *Sports Illustrated,* March 22, 1993.

3. "Majestic Hotel," in *Encyclopedia of Arkansas History & Culture,* encyclopediaofarkansas.net/encyclopedia/entry-detail.aspx?entryID=8351, accessed December 3, 2018; Jay Jennings, "When Baseball Sprang for Hot Springs"; Brother Gilbert, C.F.X., *Young Babe Ruth: His Early Life and Baseball Career, from the Memoirs of a Xaverian Brother* (Jefferson, North Carolina: McFarland & Co., 1999), 1-4; Robert W. Creamer, *Babe: The Legend Comes to Life* (New York: Simon & Schuster, 1974), 27-33; Kal Wagenheim, *Babe Ruth: His Life and Legend* (Boca Raton, Florida: "Florida Atlantic University Digital Library, 1999), 10-14, 30.

4. T.H. Murnane, "Babe Ruth's Home Run Drive Is His Undoing*,"* Boston Globe*,* March 24, 1915; Allan Wood, *Babe Ruth and the 1918 Red Sox* (Lincoln, Nebraska: Writers Club Press, 2000), 77.

5. Babe Ruth Central: "Babe Ruth's Pitching Stats," baberuthcentral.com/babe-ruth-statistics/babes-ruthsfull-baseballstatistics/babes-ruths-pitching-stats/, accessed December 3, 2018; Bill Jenkinson, "Where Pitchers Became Legends," Hot Springs Historic Baseball Trail, hotspringsbaseballtrail.com/untold-stories/hot-springs-where-pitchers-became-legends/, accessed December 3, 2018.

6. "15 Red Sox Enlisted," *Brooklyn Daily Eagle*, March 18, 1918; Creamer, 152; Babe Ruth, *The Babe Ruth Story,* as told to Bob Considine (New York: E.P. Dutton & Co., 1972, 14th reprinting), 60.

7. Edward Martin, "Babe's Crash Good for Four Sox Runs," *Boston Globe*, March 25, 1918.

8. Paul Shannon, "Ruth Smashes Up Hopes of Dodgers," *Boston Post*, March 25, 1918.

9. Edward Martin, "Ruth Here to Talk Salary with Frazee," *Boston Globe*, January 10, 1918; Mel Webb, "Babe Ruth, of the Red Sox, Spending Winter Among the Pines," *Boston Globe*, January 20, 1918; Paul Shannon, "Red Sox Given First Workout," *Boston Post*, March 13, 1918; Paul Shannon "'Rainbow Ball' Marks Practice," *Boston Post*, March 14, 1918; Bill Jenkinson, *The Year Babe Ruth Hit 104 Home Runs* (New York: Carroll & Graf, 2007), 24-27.

10. Wood, 15; Wagenheim, 36-37.

11. Wood, 15, 16.

12. Literature and ephemera provided by June Koffi, David Diakow, and Mark Levine, of the Brooklyn Central Library's Collections, Biography, and Sports departments, respectively; Brooklyn, New York, December 2018; Paul Shannon, "Red Sox Hammer Dodgers," *Boston Post*, March 17, 1918; "Superbas Helpless Against the Swatting of Babe Ruth," *Brooklyn Daily Eagle*, March 18, 1918.

13. Leigh Montville, *The Big Bam* (New York: Random House, 2006), 105, 106.

14. Edward Martin, "Babe Ruth a Star of First Magnitude," *Boston Globe*, March 25, 1918; Paul Shannon, "Ruth Smashes Up Hopes of Dodgers," *Boston Post*, March 25, 1918.

15. Tim Reid and L.T. Reid, III, "Baseball's First Five-Hundred Foot Home Run/Diagrams of Babe Ruth's Historic Hot Springs Home Runs of 1918," firstfivehundredfoothomerun.jimdo.com/home-run-diagrams/, accessed December 3, 2018.

16. Ritter, 230, 232.

17. W.J. MacBeth, "Russell Outpitches Ruth, Humbles Red Sox Clan 5 to 4," *New York Tribune*, May 7, 1918; Frederick G. Leib, "Murderers' Row Batters Red Sox," *New York Sun*, May 7, 1918; W.J. MacBeth, "Ping Bodie Brings Glory to Yankee Escutcheon," *New York Tribune*, May 7, 1918; "Babe Ruth's Fine Clouting Stunt," *Bridgeport Times and Evening Farmer*, May 7, 1918.

18. Marshall Smelser, *The Life That Ruth Built* (New York: Quadrangle/New York Times Book Co., 1975), 98.

19. Michael T. Lynch, *Harry Frazee, Ban Johnson, and the Feud That Nearly Destroyed the American League* (Jefferson, North Carolina: McFarland & Company, 2008), 84; Frederick G. Lieb, *The Boston Red Sox* (Carbondale: Southern Illinois University Press, 2003), 178.

20. Ruth, 82-83; Paul Shannon, *Boston Post*, May 6, 1918; "Sox Vanquish Yanks, 7 to 3," *Boston Herald*, June 25, 1918; Wood, 39.

21. John E. Dreifort, Editor, *Baseball History from Outside the Lines: A Reader* (Lincoln: University of Nebraska Press, 2001), 125.

22. "Waite Hoyt Remembers the Babe," baseballhall.org/discover-more/stories/short-stops/waite-hoytremembers-babe-ruth, accessed December 3, 2018.

23. Hardball Times, "Babe Ruth, the New York Pitcher," tht.fangraphs.com/babe-ruth-the-new-york-pitcher/.

24. "Babe Ruth's Last Visit to Hot Springs," hotspringsbaseballtrail.com/untold-stories/babe-ruths-last-visit-hot-springs/, accessed December 3, 2018; Baseball Reference, "Babe Ruth, Summary of 714 Home Runs," baseball-reference.com/players/event_hr.fcgi?id=ruthba01&t=b; "100 Greatest Baseball Players," Baseball Almanac, baseball-almanac.com/legendary/lisab100.shtml, accessed December 3, 2018; "The 40 Most Important People in Baseball History," *The Sporting News*, sportingnews.com/us/mlb/news/most-important-influential-people-in-mlb-baseball-history-list-players-owners-general-managers/1uga2utsurjcc19cwjmsz47apr, accessed December 3, 2018; Seth Everett, "Babe Ruth Awarded Presidential Medal of Freedom," *Forbes*, November 19, 2018, forbes.com/sites/setheverett/2018/11/19/babe-ruth-awarded-presidential-medal-offreedom/#3f1ea0004913.

Showdown: Babe Ruth's Rebellious Barnstorming Tour

By T. S. Flynn

A day after the New York Yankees lost the 1921 World Series to their landlords, the New York Giants, the squad gathered at the Polo Grounds to divide $87,756.67, the losers' share of the postseason proceeds. During the meeting, each player also received a letter signed by Commissioner Kenesaw Mountain Landis reiterating Article IV, Section 8(b) of the rules governing Organized Baseball: "Both teams that contest in the world's series are required to disband immediately after its close and the members thereof are forbidden to participate as individuals or as a team in exhibition games during the year in which the world's championship was decided."[1] On that same morning, an item had appeared in the *Bridgewater* (New Jersey) *Courier-News*: "Carl Mays' All Stars – with 'Babe' Ruth and probably [Bob] Shawkey, [Bill] Piercy, [Wally] Schang and other Yankees – are booked to play the Meadowbrooks in Newark tomorrow afternoon."[2] Ruth was under contract to play in 17 additional exhibitions during the fall and early winter of 1921, headlining a tour originating in New York and Pennsylvania before moving westward to locales including Oklahoma, Missouri, Texas, and Utah.

The World Series had been a disappointing conclusion to The Babe's spectacular regular season, his second with the Yanks. He broke Roger Connor's career record of 138 home runs on July 18 – a record since 1897 – when he blasted a 560-foot shot at Detroit, his 36th round-tripper of 1921.[3] He finished the season leading all of baseball with 59 home runs (breaking his own record of 54, set in 1920), 12.9 WAR, 1.359 OPS, 177 runs, and 457 total bases (79 more than runner-up Rogers Hornsby).

Ruth had revolutionized baseball, altering the game with his prodigious power and personality, and it was widely believed that he'd end his spectacular season by carrying his club to its first World Series championship. But the Yankees lost the best-of-nine series to the Giants in eight games. An infected boil on Ruth's elbow limited his participation to the first five games and one desperate pinch-hitting appearance in the bottom of the ninth inning of the final game. He grounded out to first. Two outs later, both the Series and Ruth's two-year, $40,000 contract with the Yankees ended. He intended to negotiate a new contract during the offseason, but first he planned to make some dough plying his trade in small towns across America.

The Newark exhibition was canceled when Schang and Mays bowed out, unwilling to test Landis's resolve. Ruth, unswayed, phoned the commissioner to discuss his offseason plans. "He's an obstinate man," the Babe said when asked about the call. "He hung up on me twice."[4] Ruth insisted he'd play as planned the following day, October 16, in Buffalo. He and teammates Bill Piercy and Bob Meusel, along with former teammate and roommate Tom Sheehan, were scheduled to compete against a squad calling themselves the Polish Nationals. As was customary on tours such as this, local semipros would fill out the rogue Yankees' roster.

Fundamentally, Ruth considered the barnstorming ban unfair. Players on third- and fourth-place teams were allowed to tour despite receiving World Series shares, he argued, and although the rule had been on the books for years, its enforcement was uneven. When Ruth and other Red Sox barnstormed after the 1916 World Series, their punishment had been individual fines of $100. When World Series participants barnstormed in 1919 and 1920, the leagues took no action.[5] But Landis was uninterested in debating the rule's history or fairness in 1921. "The rule was drawn up some time ago and applies only to teams which take part in a world's series. It is a rule and as such must be enforced," the commissioner insisted.[6] "If the Babe defies the order, it will be a personal issue between Ruth and me to determine which man is the bigger in baseball."[7]

Riding a wave of popularity and emboldened by the support of most big-league owners following his lifetime banishment of the 1919 Black Sox, Landis saw Ruth's rising popularity as a threat to the balance of power in the game. Kansas City sportswriter Alport Hager claimed, "No living American – or dead either, for that matter – has received more publicity than Babe Ruth, unless it be our presidents and possibly 'Billy' Sunday. There is not a 'burg' in the country from coast to coast, a mining town in Alaska or a hamlet in Canada, where his name is unknown. The Cuban school boys, where the game is popular, know more about Ruth than they do of Cuba Libre."[8]

Less well known was the origin of the barnstorming ban and the central role Cuba played in its establishment. In December of 1910 the Detroit Tigers and the World Series champion Philadelphia Athletics (with notable exceptions manager Connie Mack, second baseman Eddie Collins, and third baseman Home Run Baker) toured Cuba and played exhibition games against Havana and the defending island champions, Almendares. Upon learning of the trip, American League President Ban Johnson said, "I was not in favor of the Athletics tour to Cuba, but the news did not reach me in time to ask them not to go through with it. You see, for the world's series games we ask raised prices from the fans, because this is the most important of all games. Then for the champions to put themselves on display in exhibition clashes does not quite appeal to me. The Athletics, by defeating the Cubs, are supreme in baseball, but, being off their stride now as a result of the long layoff, these Cubans probably will beat and outplay them. The Athletics can gain nothing by winning and it would certainly injure their standing to be beaten."[9] And beaten they were. The A's lost the first game

BABE RUTH COMING ad, *Buffalo Courier*, October 15, 1921: 8

on the tour to Detroit, 6-2, before playing each Cuban team five times. The Mackless Men won just four of those games, going 2-3 against each Cuban squad.[10]

While Johnson, and later Landis, publicly expressed concern for the integrity of the World Series as the reason behind the barnstorming ban, the public and press were unconvinced. News reports from the 1910 Athletics tour made clear that the depleted roster affected the outcome of the games, and fans didn't confuse the results of exhibitions with sanctioned championship contests.

During the escalation of The Babe's barnstorming brouhaha of 1921, John B. Foster, writing for the *Washington Evening Star*, suggested another reason for the prohibition: "The rule against barnstorming by world series contestants was passed because certain players in the past met objectionable characters and engaged with them on the diamond to the detriment of base ball. The players have not always been careful what they have done. They have gone into games with ineligible players, with players of outlaw leagues and with negro teams, which doesn't find favor with the owners."[11] In fact, the 1910 Havana club that took three of five from the A's was "an exclusively negro team ... native Cuban with the exception of three or four American negroes, secured from the crack Leland Giants, of Chicago [Grant Johnson, Pop Lloyd, Pete Hill, and Bruce Petway]."[12] Likewise, Almendares was "practically an exclusively native team, but two or three of its men [were] white Cubans."[13]

Organized Baseball's opposition to barnstorming became codified in the American League in 1910, shortly after the Athletics and Tigers returned from their tour. In 1916 the rule was expanded to cover both leagues. Players who toured during the offseason often earned more income from barnstorming than from their regular-season salaries, thereby calling into question the market value for their services. By 1921 Organized Baseball had already weathered three attempts by players to unionize (1885, 1900, and 1912),[14] and conditions were ripe for another effort. "[Babe

Fate of Swatting Babe Hangs on Word of Itinerant Judge

Fate of Swatting Babe headline, *Minneapolis Star Tribune*, October 18, 1921: 16

Ruth's 1921 outlaw tour] lends credence to the fact that a new baseball players' organization is in the making, and that Ruth, Meusel, and the others have been selected as the rebels to make the fight for the men against the existing powers in the game."[15]

His demands ignored, Landis confronted the perceived threat with the full power of his office, contacting Organized Baseball operators across the country and warning them not to open their ballparks to Ruth or any other ineligible players during the off-season. Any team failing to comply would face a season-long suspension.

Local promoters and Ruth's tour managers, Connie Savage and Charles W. Lynch, scrambled to find a suitable replacement venue in Buffalo. With just hours to spare, the game was moved to Legionnaire Park, a venue ill-equipped for a large crowd. Many fans stayed home, but the teams still played. "Piercy pitched, Meusel played at shortstop, Sheehan covered right field and Babe decorated first base," his elbow still heavily bandaged.[16] Ruth and Meusel hit back-to-back home runs in the sixth inning, and the barnstormers won the contest, 4-3.[17]

Landis spent the day traveling from New York to his office in Chicago. After the game, Ruth told local newspapermen, "I am doing this with full knowledge of what it may mean and am not worrying about the consequences. I believe I am right, and that it is time a move of this kind was made for the ball players. The interests of organized base ball are served when a man gives them full effort and carries out every phase of his contract for the season's period. When the bell rings after the world series why should I or any other player be kept from earning money?"[18]

The money at issue was significant. Ruth and the other barnstorming Yankees were promised a big payday for the Buffalo game, "but when the scene shifted to a sandlot field, Babe's $4500 guarantee faded. Babe probably didn't have much more than carfare when the day's work was over."[19]

"Back in Chicago, [Landis] said he had a number of questions to attend to before the matter of the great swatter's defiance of his order concerning exhibition games."[20] Ruth and his teammates continued the tour, beginning with games in the New York towns of Elmira (October 17) and Jamestown (October 18).

Yankees owners Jacob Ruppert and Tillinghast Huston issued a statement to the press: "It is regrettable that the rule ... has been violated so defiantly by some of the Yankee players. Judge Landis has no alternative but to meet the situation firmly."[21] The commissioner's hard line had escalated the situation and created a dilemma. Suspending Ruth for the 1922 season – or even for a significant portion of it – would deal a serious financial loss to Ruppert and Huston, two of the commissioner's "staunchest supporters."[22]

Ruth responded to the escalating public-relations battle with his most effective weapons: his popularity and baseball skills. He dazzled fans in Elmira with a pair of home runs and exhibited charitable largesse when he insisted that hundreds of "small boys hanging wistfully around the outside of the park [be] let in" free of charge.[23] After leading his club to a 6-0 victory, The Sultan of Swat addressed the barnstorming hullabaloo: "I know I am right and Landis is wrong and that we will fight it out. I think the trouble with Landis is that he is getting a little too big headed over his job."[24] When asked what he'd do in the event of a long suspension, Ruth laid out his plan: "I will continue to play baseball next year, that's a cinch. If I organize my own team, however, it won't be a team of outlaws. By that I mean players who have been thrown out of the game for gambling and things like that. I won't have anything to do with those former Chicago White Sox players who were mixed up in that world series scandal. But my team would be formed of good, clean fellows, players who are straight, but who have jumped from the American League."[25]

The next day, the barnstormers played through persistent rain in Jamestown, winning 14-10. "The game was played on the Coloron grounds on the shore of Chataqua [sic] Lake, and for the first time in history the ball was knocked into the lake, Ruth doing the trick during an exhibition of batting which preceded the game. During the game Ruth got a couple of two-baggers, but failed to get a home run."[26] Before departing for Warren, Pennsylvania, where the barnstormers were scheduled to play the following afternoon, Ruth reasserted that he was right in his fight with Organized Baseball. "He cited the case of George Sisler, of the St. Louis Browns, who is now said to be playing ball in the west. 'Sisler shared in third club money … but he is not molested by Judge Landis. Meusel, Piercy, and Sheehan are going to stick with me and we are going right along with our schedule until early in November, when I begin a vaudeville engagement at Mount Vernon, N.Y.'"[27]

On the fourth day of the tour, Babe Ruth's All-Stars defeated the Warren Independents, 5-3, in front of 2,000 fans. Ruth hit a home run and even pitched an inning but, heeding the advice of Christy Walsh, "the manager of a syndicate handling his writings," he refused to discuss the Landis matter after the game.[28]

Hornell, New York, hosted the fifth exhibition of the tour, on October 20. After breakfast in the small town, Ruth hired a car to drive him to St. Ann's Cemetery to visit the grave of Tommy Padgett, with whom he had roomed and played ball at St. Mary's Industrial School for Boys, in Baltimore. Padgett signed with the Class-D Hornell Green Sox in 1914 shortly before Ruth signed to play for the Double-A Baltimore Orioles. Padgett's baseball career lasted two seasons. He enlisted in the Army at the outbreak of the Great War and was wounded while serving overseas. Upon recovery, he returned to Hornell and found work as a railroad brakeman. During his third day on the job Padgett fell between two freight-train cars "and was cut to pieces." Ruth spent 30 minutes at his fallen pal's gravesite.

Besides promising the proceeds of the day's game (above the guarantee), The Bambino pledged 20 percent of his personal share to the local children's home.[29] The weather didn't cooperate. "Hours of rain converted the diamond into a sea of mud in which the big Bambino floundered and slipped and fell. Only three innings were played, and Ruth was permitted to bat half a dozen times. He didn't knock a single pitch out of the infield, but Bob Meusel cracked one over the race track fence, breaking a record that had stood for ten years."[30] To assuage the large crowd that had rousingly welcomed the ballplayers to Hornell, Ruth spoke at a local theater that evening, giving "a brief talk on baseball in general."[31] He said the Yankees would have won the World Series if his arm had been healthy, but he declined to comment on the showdown with Landis, other than to announce that the barnstorming tour would end in two weeks.[32]

After spending the night in Hornell, the rogue Yanks planned to cross back into Pennsylvania, where they were scheduled to play a team of semipros from the Inter-County League at Scranton's Athletic Park on Friday, October 21. As with the first five games of the tour, the price of admission would be $1. Rumors had appeared in newspapers around the country that Landis would impose a long suspension for Ruth, perhaps as lengthy as a full season. Promoters, in turn, proposed a yearlong barnstorming tour or a third major league for Babe to call home,[33] promising the star as much as $1,000 per day.[34] The financial outlook for the current tour was less promising. The *Burlington* (Vermont) *Daily News* reported, "From pretty good authority, we learn that Babe Ruth's Stars have not been packing 'em along the line thus far. The attendance for the first three days was reported to have been about 1,500 a game at $1 a head. The actual paid attendance at one of the games was 1,102 persons. … Unless the Babe can draw an average attendance of at least 2,000 at $1 each, it is impossible to see where the Ruth tour will weather things financially. He will be barred from the real parks in cities represented in organized baseball, and the kerosene oil circuit will not come across a dollar a smash."[35]

After his theater appearance in Hornell, The Babe spoke by phone with Huston. The Yankees co-owner "pointed out to Ruth the consequences of his actions and told him that the New York American League Club, by losing Ruth's services during part of next season, would be the real sufferer in the controversy."[36] Ruth did not want to hurt the club or his teammates, and he indicated a willingness to cancel the tour after the next day's game in Scranton. The hassles associated with the unavailability of minor-league ballparks and the increasingly bad weather probably influenced the decision. It was a good time to cut the tour's compounding losses and prepare for his vaudeville engagement.

BASEBALL Athletic Park Scranton ad, *Scranton Republican*, October 17, 1921: 14

Huston, delighted by Ruth's acquiescence, arrived in Scranton by train the next morning and checked into the Hotel Casey at about 9 o'clock. "Ruth, at the head of a delegation of one dozen men – players on his outlaw team and men he carried along in building up his outlaw organization – reached Scranton at 10:15. They immediately went to the Hotel Casey, where a short time after registering Ruth left the party and went to the room occupied by Colonel Huston. … The conference [to arrange for the cancellation of the tour] lasted close to one hour, after which Ruth dressed for the ball game at Athletic Park, and Colonel Huston prepared for his return to New York."[37] The barnstormers lost on the field that afternoon, falling to Scranton's Inter-County team, 8-6, their first defeat of the tour. Ruth and Meusel spent the evening with their Yankees teammates Mike McNally and Wally Schang, Cleveland Indians catcher Steve O'Neill, and featherweight boxing champion Johnny Kilbane. The athletes "made merry at a quiet dinner held in honor of the home run king."[38]

On the morning of October 22, Ruth met with the sporting editor of the *Scranton Republican* to officially announce the cancellation of the tour. He declined to address the details of the confab with Huston, saying only that the tour had ended and that the other barnstorming players supported the decision. "Asked whether he 'surrendered to organized baseball, the home run king answered that he wouldn't exactly call it 'surrendering.'"[39] At 3:47 P.M., Ruth departed Scranton on a train bound for his home in New York City.[40]

In a syndicated newspaper column published on October 24, Ruth wrote, "The best argument I heard at Scranton the other day as to why I should abandon barnstorming was that 'Wise men change their minds, fools never.' I never expect to be in Solomon's class, but I am glad that Col. Huston prevented me from getting in the other classification. ... The reason I started barnstorming was to do something, according to my way of thinking, that would help baseball players as a whole. The reason I stopped was to show my appreciation of Col. Ruppert and Col. Huston, who brought me to New York at an enormous expense and who have treated me fair and square ever since." Ruth added that he had "nothing but the highest regard and respect for [Landis] and the difficult position he holds."[41]

Landis remained silent on the matter for more than a month. Finally, on December 5, he suspended Ruth and Meusel from Opening Day to May 20. Besides forfeiting six weeks of the season, the two Yankees were ordered to return their World Series shares. Since Sheehan and Piercy hadn't been on the Yankees' World Series roster, they received no punishment for participating in the tour.[42] On December 20 Piercy was traded to the Red Sox with Rip Collins, Roger Peckinpaugh, Jack Quinn, and $100,000 for Bullet Joe Bush, Sad Sam Jones, and Everett Scott. Sheehan pitched in St. Paul in 1922, earning 26 of the Saints' 107 regular-season wins.

Fans petitioned Landis throughout the winter, begging him to rescind or shorten the suspensions for Ruth and Meusel, but Landis remained obstinately silent on the matter throughout the winter. Ruth quit the vaudeville tour early, in February, and traveled to Hot Springs, Arkansas, to relax for two weeks before joining the Yankees spring-training camp in New Orleans.[43] Huston met The Bambino in Hot Springs and they quickly came to agreement on Babe's new $52,000 annual contract. In late March Landis arranged to meet with Ruth in New Orleans. After emerging from their hourlong meeting, Landis told the press he'd make a statement after the Yankees' exhibition game that afternoon. With expectations raised, a flock of newsmen gathered for the announcement. John Kieran reported, "The Judge cleared his throat, gave a tug to the front of his coat amid a silence like that which reigns in the depths of northern forests, he snapped out: 'I have nothing whatever to add to my former statement.'"[44]

Attempting to offset the financial impact of the Babe's suspension, the Yankees embarked on a preseason exhibition tour of Texas, attracting "huge crowds from Galveston to San Antonio to Dallas."[45] Landis had won the barnstorming battle with Ruth, but American League attendance figures for April and May of 1922 proved that Ruth was the bigger man in baseball. Fans bought fewer than half the tickets to Yankees games at home and on the road than they had in 1921.[46] Landis continued to rule the game with a heavy hand and an appetite for photo opportunities. Before officially ending their suspensions, the commissioner required formal applications for reinstatement from Ruth and Meusel. Finally, on May 20, 1922, the two chastened Yanks returned to the game and were welcomed by 40,000 fans at the Polo Grounds. Legendary sportswriter Heywood Broun compared Ruth's return to that of the Prodigal Son. He was gifted not with a fatted calf but a silver bat, silver cup, and a floral wreath in the shape of a baseball diamond.[47]

Sources

In addition to the sources identified in the Notes, the author consulted Baseball-Reference.com and Retrosheet.org.

Notes

1. "Giants and Yankees Warned Against Barnstorming Trips," *New York Tribune*, October 15, 1921: 14.

2. "Mays and Ruth in Newark," *Bridgewater* (New Jersey) *Courier-News*, October 14, 1921: 12.

3. Mike Huber, "July 18, 1921: Babe Ruth's 560-Foot Blast Against Tigers Sets Career Home Run Record," sabr.org/gamesproj/game/july-18-1921-babe-ruth-s-560-foot-blast-against-tigers-sets-career-home-run-record

4. "Babe Ruth and Pals Defy Landis, Play Proscribed Buffalo Game," *Buffalo Morning Express*, October 17, 1921: 1.

5. Edmund F. Wehrle, *Breaking Babe Ruth: Baseball's Campaign Against Its Biggest Star* (Columbia: University of Missouri Press, 2018), 75.

6. "Babe Ruth to Play at Buffalo Despite Judge Landis' Edict," *Morning Call* (Allentown, Pennsylvania), October 16, 1921: 15.

7. "Baseball Row in Its Climax Hits Buffalo," *Buffalo Morning Express*, October 16, 1921: 59.

8. Alport Hager, "Playing the Game," *Kansan* (Kansas City, Kansas), October 16, 1921: 27.

9. "No Barnstorming to Be Permitted," *Daily Times* (Davenport, Iowa), December 1, 1910: 8.

10. "Baseball Gets Big Boom in Cuba," *Central New Jersey Home News* (New Brunswick), December 21, 1910: 7.

11. John B. Foster, "Public Sympathy is with Athlete," *Washington Evening Star*, October 18, 1921: 24.

12. Cesar Brioso, personal interview, citing *Cuban Baseball: A Statistical History, 1878-1961* by Jorge S. Figueredo (Jefferson, North Carolina: McFarland & Company, 2003).

13. Joe S. Jackson, "Boston Nationals on List of Spring Visitors Here," *Washington Post*, December 8, 1910: 8.

14. "History of the Major League Baseball Players Association," mlbpa.org/history, 2014.

15. "Ruth's Rebellion Is Seen as Big New War," *Philadelphia Inquirer*, October 18, 1921: 16.

16. "Ruth Is Fighting Organized Baseball, Not Judge Landis," *Buffalo Commercial*, October 17, 1921: 6.

17. Ibid.

18. "Flouts Ban of Judge on Playing Exhibitions," *Washington Evening Star*, October 17, 1921: 26.

19. "Ruth Is Fighting Organized Baseball, Not Judge Landis."

20. "Ruth's Rebellion Is Seen as Big New War."

21. "Landis to Let 'Gravitation' Attend to Ruth," *Chicago Tribune*, October 18, 1921: 17.

22. Damon Runyon, "Fate of Swatting Babe Hangs on Word of Itinerant Judge," *Star Tribune* (Minneapolis, Minnesota), October 18, 1921: 16.

23. "Ruth Plays at Elmira," *Pittsburgh Post Gazette*, October 18, 1921: 11.

24. Ibid.

25. "Ruth Threatens to Organize His Own Baseball Team," *Mt. Vernon Register News* (Illinois), October 18, 1921: 1.

26. "I Don't Care, Says Ruth, Just Like Eva Tanguay," *Baltimore Sun*, October 19, 1921: 11.

27. Ibid.

28. "Ruth's Stars Defeat Warren," *Pittsburgh Daily Post*, October 20, 1921: 10.

29. "Big Bambino Places Wreath on Mound of Boyhood Pal," *Buffalo Enquirer*, October 20, 1921: 6.

30. "Ruth Blames Sore Arm for Yank's Defeat," *Buffalo Commercial*, October 21, 1921: 6.

31. "Rain Prevents Ruth Contest," *Elmira Star-Gazette*, October 21, 1921: 19.

32. "Ruth Blames Sore Arm for Yank's Defeat."

33. "Third Big League in Making Says Report Movie Men Are Behind Project," *Oregon Daily Journal* (Portland), October 22, 1921: 8.

34. "Bait Babe Ruth With Huge Sum of $250,000." *Burlington* (Vermont) *Daily News*, October 22, 1921: 8.

35. Ibid.

36. Babe Ruth Repents; Quits Exhibitions," *New York Times*, October 22, 1921: 16.

37. "'Babe' Ruth Ends Baseball Revolt," *Scranton Republican*, October 22, 1921: 15.

38. Ibid.

39. "Babe Ruth Ends His Revolt Breaking Up Barnstorming Troupe," *Scranton Republican*, October 22, 1921: 1.

40. Ibid.

41. Babe Ruth "Wanted to Help Players," *Pittsburgh Press*, October 24, 1921: 19.

42. Leigh Montville, *The Big Bam* (New York: Doubleday, 2006), 145.

43. Montville, 146.

44. Wehrle, 82.

45. Ibid.

46. Wehrle, 83.

47. Wehrle, 83-84.

Babe Ruth in Minnesota

By Stew Thornley

Babe Ruth was drawn to Minnesota by baseball, but – as was the case with Ted Williams, who later challenged Ruth for the title of greatest hitter ever – the outdoors and nonbaseball opportunities in the state also attracted him.

After the World Series in 1921, Ruth and a pair of New York Yankees teammates, including Bob Meusel, went on a barnstorming tour. The excursion violated a prohibition on barnstorming by World Series participants and resulted in the players being suspended to start the 1922 season.

Restrictions on postseason touring were loosened, and, as the Yankees battled for the American League pennant again, Ruth planned another barnstorming trip that would bring him to Minnesota. One report had Ruth and Meusel, along with pitcher Joe Bush, coming to the central part of the state, from which Bush hailed. The trio discussed visiting the Brainerd Lakes area. (Bush was known in those parts as the Brainerd Meteor.) "If they can't make the duck hunting, they will be here to get a deer or moose," wrote the *Brainerd Dispatch*.[1]

That trip didn't happen, but reports soon emerged that Ruth and Meusel would play in Minneapolis on Sunday, October 15, and then head the next day to Sleepy Eye, a city in the south-central part of the state. Plans changed on this itinerary, as well, but it was Minneapolis that was left out, not the smaller city. The 1922 World Series ended on Sunday, October 8 (the New York Giants knocked off the Yankees in five games), and Ruth and Meusel began a Western tour with a game in central Iowa the following Friday.[2] Over the weekend, they played games in Lincoln[3] and Omaha, Nebraska. Then they took off to keep their date in Sleepy Eye, even though the journey demanded that they detour from their next day's destination, which was Sioux Falls, South Dakota.

How they settled on Sleepy Eye is still a mystery,[4] but Ruth and Meusel arrived by train in nearby Mankato the morning of Monday, October 16. An auto took them to Sleepy Eye, and they stopped at the Berg Hotel, where a crowd had gathered. The Sleepy Eye band gave a concert at a downtown intersection at 1:00 P.M. and then marched to the ballpark, where additional bleachers had been built. They weren't needed as the cold weather kept the attendance to under 1,000. Those who showed up got their money's worth as Ruth hit two long home runs in the game,[5] one a grand slam, as his squad beat Meusel's team 9-7 in a game called after 5½ innings. Ruth finished the game on the mound, retiring all three batters he faced, two on strikeouts, in the top of the sixth.

The Knights of Columbus held a reception that evening at St. Mary's School. Ruth said he hoped to include Sleepy Eye in his travels the next year[6] before he and Meusel boarded a train to South Dakota and eventually to Denver, where their tour ended on October 29.[7]

Ruth never returned to Sleepy Eye, but he and Meusel went back in Minnesota two years later. At the same time, while the New York Yankees were wrapping up their 1924 season – with a second-place finish to Washington – the Minneapolis Millers of the American Association were closing out a disappointing season. The Millers' rival, the St. Paul Saints, had won the pennant and were heading to the Little World Series, but a pair of Minneapolis boxing promoters were able to secure an appearance by Ruth at Nicollet Park, the Millers' home.[8] The date was set for October 14, and Meusel would be with Ruth again on a tour that would take them to the Pacific Coast.

Ruth played for the Odd Fellows, the city's amateur champions, and knocked a pair of home runs that cleared Nicollet Avenue beyond the right-field fence. He added a pair of singles, outdoing Meusel, who was held hitless while playing for a local all-star team assembled as the Odd Fellows' opponents.

The crowd was only around 3,000, but there were enough over-enthusiastic young fans to stop the game in the eighth inning by coming onto the field and swarming Ruth. "Try as Babe did, he couldn't get the kids off the field," wrote Charles Johnson in the *Minneapolis Star*. "They became so thick that Ruth couldn't get away. The kids didn't want anything (in) particular. They just wanted to be close to him. He's their idol. Babe grabbed the lone bat that the souvenir hunters left him and made a bee line for the gate with the kids after him."[9]

Ruth's appearances in Minnesota were to this point confined to postseason barnstorming, but the entire Yankees team came to St. Paul for a midseason exhibition game against the Saints at Lexington Park on June 16, 1926. Two years before, as part of his 1924 excursion, Ruth had planned to toss baseballs to fans from the *Minneapolis Tribune* building but canceled because of safety concerns.[10] In St. Paul, however, Ruth went through with the event, signing and then hurling autographed baseballs out a window of the *Pioneer Press and Dispatch* building in downtown St. Paul to a huge crowd gathered on the street. He then went to Lexington Park and put on a show in batting practice. That is all the fans got, though, as the game itself was rained out. "Every one of us is not only sorry but sore because we didn't get to play today," said Ruth, who promised to return and make up the game at the end of the regular season.[11]

It wasn't until the following season that the Yankees and Saints made up their rained-out game, but Ruth, by himself, came to Minnesota for a variety of nonbaseball activities in late October of 1926. Vaudeville was the main reason for his visit as large newspaper ads touted his appearances at the Pantages Theatre in downtown Minneapolis with such enticements as "See the Battering Bambino Unfold His Bag of Batting Tricks."[12]

Bob Meusel and Babe Ruth at Sleepy Eye, Minnesota, October 16, 1922.
Photograph taken at the Sleepy Eye ballpark by Stew Thornley.

Ruth also purchased a nonresident hunting license on Saturday, October 31, with an invitation by the Minneapolis police chief to go duck hunting the next day and a plan to delay this excursion long enough to meet Queen Marie of Rumania at the Minneapolis Institute of Art as she made a nine-hour stopover in the Twin Cities.[13] During his week in town, Ruth also worked in visits to the Shriners Hospital for Crippled Children, the Catholic Boys' Home, and a sanitarium for youngsters with tuberculosis at Glen Lake, just outside the Twin Cities. In addition, Ruth found time to work out with the Minnesota Gophers football team[14] and also visit St. Mary's Hospital to see Joe Boland, a player from Notre Dame who had broken his leg in a game against the Gophers three weeks earlier.[15]

The following summer the entire Yankees Murderers' Row returned to St. Paul for an exhibition game. The Yankees beat the Saints, 9-8, on Wednesday, July 20, 1927. Although neither Ruth, who went on to set a single-season record with 60 home runs that season, nor Lou Gehrig, cleared the fence at Lexington Park, the pair "spilled nearly a quart of ink autographing baseballs and score cards for small boys" before the game, according to the *St. Paul Pioneer Press*.[16]

Nearly 15,000 fans enjoyed the show, although the crowd dropped by at least one when 42-year-old John Kulasivig dropped dead of a heart attack after reportedly yelling, "Hit it over the fence, Babe."[17]

Ruth appreciated the hospitality he received during his visits to the state, and that played a role in his agreeing to interrupt his "first vacation in 21 years" in 1935. Ruth had retired as a player that spring. That summer, he agreed to play in the annual game of the Minneapolis and St. Paul police departments. During his 1926 postseason vaudeville tour in Minneapolis, Police Chief Frank Brunskill had made Ruth an honorary member of the department.[18]

On Sunday, September 1, 1935, Ruth played half a game at Nicollet Park with the police teams. He only hit a double, but *Minneapolis Tribune* reporter Bob Beebe wrote, "[H]e gave the fans an idea of how he can sock a baseball by walloping a dozen or so out of the park in a batting exhibition that preceded the actual contest. One of them was a terrific clout that cleared the fence in deep left center with plenty to spare."[19]

One of Ruth's unfulfilled desires was managing. Unable to land a job as skipper in the major leagues, he decided to prove himself in the minors and told people he might like to manage the St. Paul Saints in 1941. He remained frustrated when the Saints instead hired Ralph "Red" Kress, who had been a popular figure in the area when he played for the Millers in 1937.[20]

Ruth always seemed to enjoy his travels to Minnesota, starting with that first trip in 1922.[21] After playing in front of 700 fans on a cold day in Sleepy Eye, Ruth called those who turned out "the most loyal fans he had ever seen," according to the local newspaper. "He said that in New York not ten people would attend a game in the face of such a cold, snowy day."[22]

Randy Krzmarzick, a columnist and baseball historian in Sleepy Eye, has researched Ruth's 1922 appearance there. "I think it's likely the town did make an impression," he said. "We'd like to think so."[23]

Footnote

Ruth's final trip to Minnesota was Tuesday night, June 22, 1948, one of his last public appearances. He had flown in from South Dakota on a national tour to promote junior baseball. Before a battery of microphones at the Radisson Hotel in Minneapolis, Ruth was interviewed by 11-year-old Johnny Ross, who had lost his eyesight a few years before. "How are you, Babe?" asked Johnny. "I don't feel so good," replied Ruth. "I have a very bad throat and my head aches."[24]

Five years later, Ross played football and wrestled for Marshall High School in Minneapolis. In 1953 he was the state wrestling champion at 120 pounds.[25]

Ruth returned to New York on Wednesday and by the next day was in the hospital, where he spent most of the remaining six-and-a-half weeks of his life. According to Robert W. Creamer in *Babe: The Legend Comes to Life,* Ruth flew to Baltimore for a charity game, which was rained out. On July 26, he attended the premiere of *The Babe Ruth Story.* Ruth left early and returned to the hospital. He never left the hospital again.[26]

Notes

1. "Bush, Ruth and Meusel May Come Here: Trio of Baseball Stars Enthused with Our Region: Plan Hunting in Brainerd Lake Region after the World's Series," *Brainerd Dispatch,* September 25, 1922: 1.

2. "Ruth and Meusel to Play at Perry on Friday, Oct. 13," *Des Moines Sunday Register,* October 1, 1922: 2S. The first stop on a Western tour by Ruth and Meusel was in Perry, Iowa, northwest of Des Moines. Sec Taylor reported in the October 14, 1922, *Des Moines Register* that Ruth's Perry team beat Pella (with Meusel) 12-3 with Meusel hitting a home run and Ruth two triples. Taylor wrote that the "cool weather, high wind and dust that blew across the field in clouds" kept the crowd to only 800 and that promoters lost money on the game.

3. The *Lincoln Star* of October 13, 1922 (page 9) has an ad for appearances by Meusel and Ruth at charitable institutions in Lincoln to distribute candy on National Candy Day and for a game at Landis Field in the afternoon.

4. The selection of Sleepy Eye as a stop has been a topic of research by local historians, including Randy Krzmarzick. An article in the October 10, 1922, *Minneapolis Star* (page 8) states that the ball game was staged by the local unit of the American Legion. Krzmarzick believes the Knights of Columbus (of which Ruth was a member) may also have been involved and that Ruth may have been attracted by the St. Mary's School (the same name as the industrial school he attended in Baltimore). See foxsports.com/north/video/299603523964.

5. One of the home-run balls still exists, according to a Minneapolis television station report: kare11.com/article/news/local/land-of-10000-stories/babe-ruth-home-run-ball-turns-up-with-104-year-old-minnesotan/35072475. Eleven-year-old Len Youngman corralled one of Ruth's home runs and years later gave it to his grandson. Youngman turned 107 on March 27, 2018.

6. "'Babe' Hits Two Homers in Game Here Monday," *Sleepy Eye Herald-Dispatch,* October 19, 1922: 1.

7. *Lincoln State Journal,* Monday, October 30, 1922: 9.

8. "Babe Ruth to Play at Nicollet Park on October 14 or 15," *Minneapolis Star,* October 1, 1924: 10.

9. Charles Johnson, "Kids Break Up Ruth's Ball Game; Souvenir Hunters Have Big Day," *Minneapolis Star,* October 15, 1924: 11. Other reports suggest that the game had already been called by darkness by the time the fans swarmed onto the field.

10. "Ruth Appears at Tribune Today; Ball Tossing Is Eliminated," *Minneapolis Tribune,* October 14, 1924: 15.

11. "'Babe' Ruth Regretfully Leaves St. Paul, Promising to Return September 28 if Yankees Grab Pennant," *St. Paul Pioneer Press,* June 17, 1926: 1. Ruth and the Yankees said they would come back if they won the pennant since their regular season would

conclude September 26 while the National League season wasn't scheduled to conclude for another three days.

12 "Babe Ruth 'The Swat King' Now Appearing at Pantages," *Minneapolis Tribune,* October 31, 1926: Art Section, 7.

13 "Ruth, King of Swat, Delays Hunting to Greet Queen Marie," October 30, 1926: 1.

14 "Babe Ruth Visits Boland, Injured Notre Dame Star," *Minneapolis Tribune,* November 2, 1926: 21.

15 "Babe Ruth Works Out with Gophers; Tackles Joesting," *Minneapolis Journal,* November 2, 1926: 26.

16 "Ruth, Gehrig Find Pen Mightier Than Bat to Thrill Boys Here," *St. Paul Pioneer Press,* July 21, 1927: 1.

17 "Winona Man Drops Dead," *St. Paul Pioneer Press,* July 21, 1927: 1.

18 "Babe Ruth to Take Part in Police Tilt at Nicollet," *Minneapolis Tribune,* August 1, 1935: 16.

19 Bob Beebe, "13,000 Fans Watch Ruth in Police Game at Nicollet," *Minneapolis Tribune,* September 2, 1935: 14.

20 "Ruth to Manage Saints???" *St. Paul Pioneer Press,* September 22, 1940: Second Section, 1.

21 How many times Ruth came to Minnesota is unclear. The Nanibijou Lodge in Grand Marais, Minnesota, on the north shore of Lake Superior about halfway between Duluth and the Canadian border, claims Ruth and celebrities Jack Dempsey and Ring Lardner as charter members of the lodge when it opened in 1929: naniboujou.com. There is no mention of any of these celebrities in the *Cook Herald* (the newspaper for Cook County, where Grand Marais is) in the late 1920s.

22 "'Babe' Hits Two Homers in Game Here Monday," *Sleepy Eye Herald-Dispatch,* October 19, 1922: 1.

23 "Remembering Babe Ruth's Visit Sleepy Eye, Minn.," narrated by Tom Hanneman, Fox Sports North, July 8, 2014, foxsports.com/north/video/299603523964.

24 Joe Hendrickson, "Interview We Won't Forget," *Minneapolis Tribune,* June 23, 1948: 20.

25 Dan Stoneking, "Marshall-U," *Star Tribune* (Minneapolis), May 28, 1982: 1D.

26 Robert W. Creamer, *Babe: The Legend Comes to Life* (New York: Simon & Schuster, 1974), 423-424.

Babe Ruth Visits Louisville

By Harry Rothgerber

Louisville, Kentucky, has a wide array of historical credentials on its baseball résumé: charter member of the National League; the infamous scandal of 1876; 10-year member of the major-league American Association, followed by eight more years in the National League; home of Pete Browning; birthplace of Hillerich & Bradsby Company's Louisville Slugger bats; home of Louisville Slugger Museum & Factory; site of Honus Wagner's rookie year; Eclipse Park, Parkway Field, Cardinal Stadium; home of Pee Wee Reese; the Colonels' minor-league success in the American Association and IL; the million-fans Redbirds attendance record; current Louisville Bats; and Louisville Slugger Field, to list the highlights.

Add to that résumé the following credit: an age-old and ongoing love affair with Babe Ruth. In his lifetime he visited Louisville on at least five occasions for a variety of reasons: barnstorming money; loyalty to the Xaverian Brothers who raised him; presidential politics; golf with Bud Hillerich's PowerBilt clubs; and raising money for storm relief. His presence in the city was always appreciated and respected by the locals.

A closer examination of those visits begins by looking back almost 100 years ago.

August 15, 1921 – Colonels 3, Yankees 1

With much anticipation and great fanfare, the New York Yankees arrived by train at Louisville's Union Station at 7:35 A.M., and

Parkway Field, with the iconic Ralston Purina grain silos visible past the right field wall, was the site of benefit game between the Bustin' Babes and Larrupin' Lous in 1928. Ruth and Gehrig are flanked by some of the top local amateur ballplayers from Epps Cola and Beck's Lunch who comprised their teams. *Used with permission of Louisville Slugger Museum & Factory.*

Babe Ruth began a day of whirlwind activity.[1] A former teacher at Baltimore's St. Mary's Industrial School, where Ruth was raised, was instrumental in arranging this visit by his now-famous pupil.

In 1917, Brother Benjamin Burke, C.F.X., a member of the Catholic religious order of teachers known as the Xaverian Brothers, had become principal of St. Xavier's College (now St. Xavier High School) in Louisville.[2] It appears that, with Ruth's support, he worked for two years to persuade both leagues involved to reschedule games so that the Yankees could arrange a midseason visit.[3] In 1925 Brother Ben, as Ruth called him, would return to Baltimore and become St. Mary's superintendent, always maintaining a close friendship with Ruth.[4]

The local council of the Knights of Columbus, the international Catholic fraternal organization, quickly whisked Ruth and the Yankees away for a mini-tour of the city for the rest of the morning, followed by a stop at noon at the Louisville Industrial School, a residential placement for dependent, delinquent, and orphaned children.[5] This facility was part of the local House of Refuge,[6] a combination reformatory/orphanage that appears to have been similar to St. Mary's. Dressed in a suit and tie, Ruth took part in a "pitching contest" and was struck out by Edward Miner, one of the young wards there.[7]

The 3:00 P.M. exhibition game at Eclipse Park between the Yankees and the Louisville Colonels featured two first-place ballclubs – the Yankees led the American League as the result of Cleveland's loss to the White Sox the day before, and the Colonels owned a three-game lead over Minneapolis in the American Association.[8]

In conjunction with this event, the Hillerich & Bradsby Company purchased a newspaper advertisement titled "Babe Ruth's Bat a Louisville Slugger," noting that "Ruth's bat is 36 inches long and weighs 47 ounces." Accompanied by a photo of him, the ad copy read, "Like most Famous Sluggers of the national game, Ruth uses exclusively bats made by the Hillerich & Bradsby Co. He has found that Louisville SLUGGER bats have the spring, balance and driving power needed to slug them over the fence."[9]

On a partly cloudy day with a high of 78 degrees, Louisvillians jammed Eclipse Park for the event. Reserved seats had been sold out for days; temporary stands had been put up to seat the overflow patrons; and more people were allowed to stand in a roped area in the deep outfield, just behind the outfielders. Eventually, 12,081 fans were counted in attendance in a ballpark that had 7,500 seating capacity, with virtually every man wearing a straw bowler and dark suit, in the style of the day.[10] Before the game, Colonels player-manager Joe McCarthy – the same future Hall of Famer who would deftly manage the Bronx Bombers from 1931 to 1946 – accepted a silver loving cup from a local sporting-goods company.[11] It is likely that this is the first time that Ruth laid eyes on the so-called "bush-leaguer" who would become his manager in a mere 10 years.

As for the game itself, the two teams engaged in an underwhelming struggle, with the Colonels faithful exulting in a 3-1 victory. The news headlines captured much of the story: "Colonels Triumph Over Yankees Before Record Crowd" and "Babe Ruth Fails to Hit in Four Times Up; Strikes Out Twice."[12]

For the Colonels, left fielder Roy Massey was the batting hero, going 2-for-4 with three RBIs, while catcher Fred Hofmann scored the only run for the Yankees in the ninth on a double followed by an error.[13] Outfielder Ruth played first base, and many of the New York regulars were given the day off, as second-stringers dominated the lineup.[14]

Although Kentucky native Carl Mays had been expected to pitch for the visitors, he did not play.[15] Colonels pitchers Ernie Koob, Tommy Estell, and Tommy "The Windmill" Long held their opponents to only three hits, with Long striking out Ruth to end the game.[16] Ruth swung at all three pitches in an attempt to propel another ball out of the park as he had already done 44 times against AL pitching.[17]

After the game, which lasted only 1 hour and 22 minutes, Ruth had no time to rest. At 6:30 P.M. he appeared at St. Xavier's Park in a contest at which all boys under 16 years old were invited. Ruth, himself a member of the Knights of Columbus, took 24 baseballs autographed by the grand knight of the local council and batted them into the assembled group of lads who scrambled for the valued souvenirs. To continue his day of frenetic activity, he was honored at an evening dinner that the Knights sponsored.

At the conclusion of dinner, Brother Benjamin and the Knights accompanied the major leaguers to the train station, and the Yankees traveled 115 miles north to Indianapolis for an exhibition the next day. Meanwhile, the Colonels departed for Milwaukee and an exhausting 31-day stint on the road.

In the following days, a number of letters to the editor appeared in the newspaper. One angry fan commented, "It was a rotten game on the visitors' side. … I did not want to pay out my money to see a big tub like Babe Ruth stand up to the plate and put up a stall like he did Monday, especially the last time at bat. I expect he thought everybody paid their money just to look at his big frame, but I did not for one. …"[18] In response, another fan wrote, "… any baseball fan who was there knows that he saw a sure enough, hard fought baseball game, and not a one-sided contest by any means. This game was anybody's until the last man was out in the ninth. … Messrs. Huston and Ruppert are willing to pay him fifty thousand dollars per year for displaying his 'big frame.'"[19] Finally, a Louisvillian concluded, "I confess I was disappointed with Monday's game, but I thoroughly enjoyed the batting practice."[20]

In a later accounting of the profits of the day, the Yankees received $4,436.15, the Colonels received $2,436.15 and St. Xavier's was given $2,000.[21]

Season's end saw the Yankees win the AL pennant but lose the World Series to the Giants. Ruth amassed astounding numbers, including 59 homers and a .378 batting average. "Brainy" Joe McCarthy's Colonels, later described as "unquestionably one of the most powerful Louisville teams ever assembled," won the American Association pennant and then shocked Jack Dunn's dominant Baltimore Orioles by a margin of five games to three in the Junior World Series.[22]

June 2, 1924 – Colonels 7, Yankees 6

Babe Ruth, now firmly established as the nation's leading athlete-personality, led the defending world champions into town for their second Louisville appearance. Two days earlier, in the second game of a doubleheader, he had been knocked unconscious in a collision with Yankees second baseman Ernie Johnson. In typical Ruthian style, he recovered to homer later in the game.[23]

However, a native Kentuckian on the Yankees roster also attracted attention. Right fielder Earle Combs had graduated from Eastern Kentucky State Teachers College in 1921 and taught school until the Colonels signed the college slugger in 1922. After two stupendous years at the plate – batting .344 and .380 – the popular player known as the Kentucky Colonel was signed by the Yankees and had a superb start in his first season.[24] A future Hall of Famer, Combs would spend 12 seasons with the New Yorkers, mainly as a leadoff center fielder.

Once again the city rolled out the red carpet for the major leaguers, but a different venue awaited the two teams. Eclipse Park, wooden home of the Colonels for 21 years, had been destroyed by fire in November 1922.[25] The team's new ballpark was Parkway Field, a concrete and steel structure built in only 63 days and opened on May 1, 1923. It would be the home venue until 1957.[26]

The first-place Yankees arrived from New York by train at 11:45 A.M. As Ruth alighted from the train dressed in a "somberly blue striped suit" for his official welcome, he encountered a group of Confederate veterans on their way to a reunion in Memphis. They cheered him, and a photograph memorialized their chance meeting. After a hurried shave and lunch, he was taken to the ballpark, accompanied by a parade of cars, for the 3:00 game.[27]

Similar to three years earlier, there was extraordinary fan interest in the game, with some people clinging to telephone poles for a view. Before the game a Knights of Columbus official delivered an armload of roses to Combs and a silver service to Ruth, who, in turn, gave prizes to six youngsters who had triumphed in a local track and field event. Although Ruth was unable to visit St. Xavier's on this trip, the St. Xavier junior team players watched the game as special invitees.[28]

As for the game, the crowd of 9,986 received a daily double of excitement: The home team came from behind for a victory, and Ruth blasted a ninth-inning right-center-field homer that many believed to be the longest ball ever hit out of the ballpark.[29] It landed in a gas station on the corner of Shipp and Eastern Parkway, well over 500 feet away.[30] His other plate appearances resulted in a foul out to the catcher; a fielder's choice; a single and a groundout. Earle Combs also went 2-for-5, including a double, to please the home folks. Colonels pitchers Ernie Koob and Tommy Estell continued their mastery of the visitors.

Ruth's day was far from over when the game concluded after 1 hour and 28 minutes. First, he was off to the downtown Sutcliffe's sporting goods store where he handed out yellow mini-bats to more than a thousand youngsters who had earned a free ticket to the game by enlisting a new subscriber to the daily *Courier-Journal*.[31] After that, an unusual assignment beckoned: He journeyed a few blocks to the offices of the newspaper and joined sports editor Bruce Dudley in the composing room, where Ruth assisted in designing the following day's sports stories and pages.[32] In a late-night interview, he commented, "If I am any judge of a ball player, Combs will be a super star."[33]

Combs too was busy after the game – but at a different sporting-goods store. It was Earle Combs Day at Roe-O'Connor's, where an Earle Combs mini-bat was distributed to each customer, and the Yankee himself was on hand to give a free rule book to each child.[34]

By 11:00 P.M., Ruth was on a train for Chicago, where he was scheduled for an X-ray of the rib that he hurt earlier in the week.[35] Whatever that result, he led the Yankees to a 6-3 victory over the White Sox the next day, going 2-for-3 with two RBIs and a run scored.[36] Meanwhile, the Colonels left for the next day's league game in Columbus.[37]

Although the Louisville men won 91 games that season, they finished in third place in the American Association and failed to make the playoffs. The Yankees won 89 games and finished in second place in the AL, two behind Washington.

October 24, 1928 – Bustin' Babes 13, Larrupin' Lous 12

On September 17, 1928, the deadly Okeechobee hurricane struck Florida at West Palm Beach, leaving a trail of death and destruction. As a result, the *Courier-Journal* and the *Louisville Times* engineered a postseason visit by Ruth and Lou Gehrig to benefit the Red Cross Florida Storm Relief Fund.[38] Two weeks earlier, the Yankees had completed a four-game sweep of the St. Louis Cardinals in the World Series.

Ruth was scheduled to play first base for the Bustin' Babes – actually Epps Kola, the top amateur team in the city – while Gehrig would perform with the Beck's Lunch team, renamed the Larrupin' Lous for the occasion.[39]

A busy day awaited. At 1:40 A.M., the train carrying the two Yankees arrived in town from Columbus, Ohio, site of their previous day's game. Rising at 8:00 A.M., they were given a brief tour of the downtown area, including a stop at St. Xavier High School.[40] There, Ruth immediately recognized Prefect of Studies Brother Bernard, one of his former teachers at St. Mary's.[41] Brother Bernard was quoted as saying, "George, my boy, you certainly have grown into a fine, big fellow since the days when you came romping into my classroom. …" To which Ruth replied, "Yes, brother, I guess I have changed quite a bit, but you haven't. … Although it has been years since I saw you, I recognized you the minute I walked through the door."[42] Ruth addressed the St. X students, an event that was later memorialized in the school's yearbook.[43] The sportswriter Christy Walsh – Ruth and Gehrig's agent – was also there.[44]

After stops at City Hall and the Hillerich & Bradsby Company, maker of their Louisville Slugger bats – where Ruth persuaded owner John A. "Bud" Hillerich to give him a new set of golf clubs[45] — the two stars ate breakfast at the Kentucky Hotel, with Ruth ordering two of everything "except beans."[46] At noon, they were guests of the Kiwanis Club for lunch. Then they were driven to Parkway Field for the 2:00 game.

A paid crowd of 3,270 – distinctly fewer than in previous years – made their way to the ballpark in clear weather and 62 degrees.[47] Schoolchildren with a note from their parents were excused by the Board of Education to attend the game.[48] Ruth's team won a 13-12 decision as he slammed two home runs – including one inside-the-park – two doubles, and a single, while Gehrig clubbed one homer and a single. The two Yankees each pitched the last three innings for their respective teams.

A shortage of baseballs almost caused an early finish to the exhibition. Nine dozen baseballs were on hand at the start of the game, but by the eighth inning, all but one had been used. After the last one was fouled into the stands, a young fan had to be "induced" to give it back so that the game could go on.[49] (Babe had been prescient in this regard. A subheadline in the newspaper the day before read, "Babe Asks for 120 Baseballs – Slugger Thinks He and Lou Need That Many in City Game."[50])

With the game over in 1 hour and 50 minutes, Ruth and Gehrig, after eating, still had political commitments to fulfill. In the downtown Jefferson County Armory, a popular assembly place, Ruth addressed a packed house and extolled the virtues of his friend New York Governor Al Smith, who was the Democratic nominee in the coming presidential election.[51] After he finished his impassioned speech ("Don't forget what the Yanks did to Philadelphia when all the experts said the Yanks were through. …") and sat down, his chair broke under him. However, disaster was averted when he grabbed a railing and prevented himself from falling off the speaker platform.[52] John W. Davis, the Democratic nominee for president four years earlier, spoke after him. ("I agree with Democracy's best batsman. …")[53]

Ruth, joined by Gehrig, then walked a block to the auditorium of the historic Seelbach Hotel and spoke to a meeting of the Kentucky Young Men's Democratic League.[54] Although they had declined an invitation to take part in the Kentucky State Fox Hunt, it was still quite a hectic day for the two stars, described as "skilled fox hunters who seldom pass up an opportunity to indulge in one of their favorite pastimes."[55]

In any event, the gate receipts enriched the Storm Relief Fund by $500; Ruth said that he had never autographed that many balls during a single day;[56] and the two Yanks left by train to participate in a similar exhibition in Dayton, Ohio, the following day.[57]

April 4, 1932 – Yankees 9, Colonels 6

Eleven months after his retirement, Ruth attended the Kentucky Derby as a guest of his friend, Louisville bat-maker Bud Hillerich. Note the famous Twin Spires of Churchill Downs in the background. Barely visible in this view are the bandaged forefinger and thumb which Ruth contrived to deter autograph-seekers.
Courtesy of Churchill Downs Racetrack

This game marked the triumphant return to Louisville of a key member of the Yankee team – Joe McCarthy, in his second year as manager. He had spent 10 seasons with the Colonels, including seven at the helm, during which he won two pennants and one Junior World Series and had the team mostly in contention. Hired by the Cubs after the 1925 season, Marse Joe, as he came to be known, had yet to win a major-league World Series, although his Cubs won the 1929 NL pennant. His former player Bruno Betzel now managed the Colonels.

This exhibition game was a preseason affair, with both teams playing their way north after spring training. A day earlier, Colonels pitching held the visiting Cincinnati Reds to five hits in a 5-3 Louisville victory, while the New Yorkers trounced the Memphis Chicks, 17-4, after which they immediately left on a train for the Derby City.[58]

Despite their second-place American League finish in 1931, Ruth, Gehrig, and Combs still generated excitement wherever they played. The crowd that awaited their arrival at Central Station by the Ohio River was disappointed to learn that the Yankees had instead arrived at Union Station on Broadway, then proceeded to the nearby Kentucky Hotel.[59]

Prior to the afternoon game, Ruth made an appearance at a noon assembly at St. Xavier High School, where his old friend Brother Benjamin had once again become principal in 1931.[60] When St. X freshman Joe Wells addressed the Yankees slugger as "Mr. Ruth," he recalled what happened next: "… And with that, he shot back at me and said, 'You call me "Babe,"' and then he and Brother, they were laughing. They got a kick out of it. … So, anyway, we got off half a day, and most of us went out to Parkway Field to see the game. …"[61]

Before the game McCarthy took the field to an ovation from the 5,810 fans in attendance and was presented with a gold baseball manufactured by local jeweler Albert Grall.[62] Izzy Goodman, McCarthy's friend and former King of the Colonel Boosters, ended the pregame activities by giving him a large garland of roses.[63]

Although the April day was pleasant with a temperature of 73 at game's end, the fielding in the two-hour game was ugly. The hometown team outhit the visitors 14-11, but the Colonels also managed to make seven errors (to the Yankees' two), leading to a 9-6 New York victory. Gehrig and Combs went hitless in a combined 11 trips to the plate, but Ruth singled and doubled in five plate appearances, driving in three runs. Yankees right fielder Ben Chapman was a home run short of the cycle while pitcher Gordon Rhodes, relieved by Ivy Paul Andrews, picked up the victory. The Colonels hurlers Clyde Hatter (who took the loss), Archie McKain, and Eldon McLean gave up only one hit – a single –in the final four innings.[64]

Destinations were varied. In the short term, the Yankees headed 106 miles to Cincinnati for their exhibition against the Reds the next day, while the Colonels awaited the Chicago White Sox for games on April 5 and 6. In six months Ruth would be bound for his historic "called shot" game against the Cubs, helping the Yankees capture another World Series – the first of seven for manager McCarthy, who had been dismissed by the Cubs management two years earlier.

April 29 to May 2, 1936 – The Kentucky Derby

Instead of baseball bats, golf clubs were in Babe Ruth's hands during his next visit to Louisville. Upon arriving at 11:33 A.M. on Wednesday of Derby Week with his wife, Claire, and daughter, Julia, Ruth said, "I've been waiting 20 years for a chance to see the Kentucky Derby, and here I am."[65] The 62nd running of the "greatest two minutes in sport" was three days away.

Eleven months after his final appearance as a player, Ruth was in town as the guest of John A. "Bud" Hillerich, the man who transformed his father's woodworking company into one that manufactured the bats used and endorsed by the Yankees slugger.[66] They had been friendly for some years: In 1918, Ruth sent a thank-you note to Hillerich after the latter paid him a $100 endorsement fee to place his signatures on Louisville Slugger bats;[67] 15 years later, Ruth personally invited Hillerich to attend a dinner he gave at the New York Athletic Club to celebrate the All-American Board of Baseball writers who helped select Ruth's annual "All-American teams."[68] Then in October 1934, Hillerich and his wife, Rose, had accompanied 14 major-league players and their families, including Babe, Claire, and Julia, on their trip to Japan, where the "Babe Ruth and Lou Gehrig All-Stars" went 17-0.[69] After the series, Bud and Rose joined the Ruths, Lefty and June Gomez, and a few others as they continued their trip around the world, visiting Java, Bali, Egypt, Venice, Paris, St. Moritz, and London.[70] Expanding his PowerBilt golf-club line, Hillerich provided Ruth and other players with free clubs for offseason play in Florida.[71] No doubt personal bonds were formed over the years due to these connections.

Two hours after stepping off the train and checking into his suite at the Kentucky Hotel, Ruth was playing 18 holes at Audubon Country Club, where Ward Hillerich, Bud's son, was three-time defending club champion. Ruth's partner in the best-ball competition was Bobby Craigs, the club professional and a future member of the Kentucky Golf Hall of Fame. Hillerich was paired with Wild Bill Mehlhorn, a noted touring professional who had 20 wins on the PGA tour.[72]

Ruth was passionate about golf, and he played quite frequently.[73] For example, during the 1932 offseason, he played well at the West Coast Open tournament, leading the amateurs.[74] His powerful swing and marvelous hand/eye coordination served him well on the golf course.

However, Ruth and his partner were bested by Hillerich's team, 3 and 2, on that first day at Audubon, despite his drive that went 300 yards on the fourth hole. Individual scores were also kept, and Ruth shot an 84. One observer said, "The Babe cracks the ball like a willowy kid despite the tremendous depth and breadth of his chest and shoulders." Ruth called for a rematch, vowing to do better now that he had played the course.[75]

Before play began the next day, Ruth was made an honorary member of the Kentucky Association of Left-Handed Golfers.[76] On the course, the public had been invited to what he called "a grudge match," and, in front of a gallery of spectators, he improved his score to 80, with his team winning, 1-up. Amazingly, he had been allowed a six-stroke handicap![77]

Setting his golf clubs aside on Derby Eve, Ruth was invited by Bud Hillerich to be his guest at a different sporting event, and he spent the evening at the boxing matches in the downtown Armory.[78] Refereed by boxing legend Jack Dempsey – also now retired – the 10-round, nontitle main event pitted Barney Ross, the world welterweight champion, from Chicago, against Chuck Woods from Detroit, ranked sixth in that division. Ruth joined a crowd of 4,118 and saw Ross manhandle Woods, knocking him out in the fifth round.[79]

Other celebrities were present that night; in fact, the largest ovation was not directed at Ruth – he finished third in that comparison, behind crowd favorite Dempsey and Joe E. Brown, the popular wide-mouthed comic film star. All three were invited into the ring prior to the main event to briefly address the crowd, and they were involved in a bit of tomfoolery with each other.[80]

Another significant Kentucky personality was present that evening – A.B. "Happy" Chandler, then early in his first term as governor, who brought 50 of his political friends with him.[81] That evening may have been the beginning of the friendship that was forged between Ruth and Chandler, who became commissioner of baseball in 1945. In that future capacity, Chandler was a tearful visitor to a cancer-ravaged Ruth in the hospital; proclaimed April 27, 1947, to be Babe Ruth Day in every Organized Baseball ballpark; and was a speaker on that very day in Yankee Stadium when Ruth personally appeared.[82]

On a partly sunny, 78-degree Derby Day, Ruth and his wife shared a box out in the open with their host, Bud Hillerich; the Dempseys were seated not far away.[83] Ruth had a history of being besieged by autograph seekers when he came to Louisville; he remembered the vast numbers of baseballs that he autographed when he was in town in 1928.[84] He handled that possibility in unique Ruthian manner, according to Bud's son Junie: Before going to the track, Ruth put a bandage on his right thumb and forefinger and told autograph hounds that he hurt his hand in the elevator the night before.[85] Photographs support that story and the inference that left-handed-batting Ruth signed with his right hand.[86]

That wasn't the only trickery he perpetrated that day – he put one over on his wife, too. Well-known for the fiscal responsibility that she brought to their marriage, Claire kept a close eye on his betting. Babe wanted to place a $5,000 wager on the odds-on favorite, Brevity, and he did so by sneaking away from Claire before they went to the Downs and calling his bookmaker in New York.

Ruth didn't leave his seat all day except for a brief time to place a legal parimutuel wager on Brevity, and Claire was happy with his apparently responsible behavior. After Brevity finished second in the big race to Bold Venture, a 20-to-1 longshot, she became suspicious and questioned Babe about whether he had bet on the race. He confessed that he did, and he showed her the $10 ticket. Claire was very delighted – as was the bookie back home.[87]

Afterword

It appears that Babe never returned to the Derby City after that stay, but his memory lived on at Hillerich & Bradsby. Their advertising manager Jack McGrath recalled, "Ruth was an easy guy to please with bats. … Ruth seldom broke a bat, but he bought more of our bats than any ballplayer that ever lived. He gave so many away."[88] As a mark of his personal friendship with Bud Hillerich, Ruth always posed with the familiar H&B "Louisville Slugger" trademark logo showing on the bat he was holding.

Three months prior to Ruth's death at the age of 53 in August 1948, it was reported that he would possibly return to Parkway Field in July as the guest of Bruce Dudley, then president of the Colonels, in conjunction with an American Legion baseball tournament.[89] He and Dudley were longtime friends from the days when the latter was the sports editor of the *Courier-Journal* and would accompany the youthful winners of Ruth's All-American Contest to meet the Babe in person.[90] In light of the serious nature of Ruth's medical condition, such a Louisville visit was wishful thinking at best.

Louisville's love for Babe Ruth, begun almost 100 years ago, continues to this day. One of the most viewed items at popular Louisville Slugger Museum & Factory is a bat that he used during one of his baseball-bashing seasons. He carved 21 notches on it

– one for each home run he hit.[91] Outside of the factory/museum rests the world's largest baseball bat. Made of steel, it weighs 68,000 pounds and reaches 120 feet into the sky. According to curator Chris Meiman, "The Big Bat is an exact-scale replica of Babe Ruth's R43 Louisville Slugger bat."[92]

Notes

1. " 'Full House' To Greet Baseball's Champion Slugger Today," *Louisville Courier-Journal*, August 15, 1921: 6.

2. Brother John Joseph Sterne, *Growing in Excellence: The Story, Spirit and Tradition of Saint Xavier* (Louisville: ikonographics, Inc., 1989), 93.

3. "Full House."

4. Brother Gilbert, C.F.X.; edited by Harry Rothgerber, *Young Babe Ruth: His Early Life and Baseball Career* (Jefferson, North Carolina: McFarland and Co., Inc., 1999), 184-185. "Ruby's Report," *Louisville Courier-Journal*, April 5, 1940: 39. "Brother Benjamin Greeted as Principal at St. Xavier," *Louisville Courier-Journal*, August 25, 1931: 4.

5. *The Encyclopedia of Louisville*, s.v. "Orphanages," 679-681.

6. Ibid.

7. "Even Mighty 'Babe' Is 'Struck Out,' " *Louisville Courier-Journal*, August 16, 1921: 3.

8. "Full House."

9. Ibid.

10. "Full House"; Bruce Dudley, "Babe Ruth and Earle Combs Strut Stuff at Ball Park Today," *Louisville Courier-Journal*, June 2, 1924: 9. "Colonels Triumph Over Yankees Before Record Ball Crowd," *Louisville Courier-Journal*, August 16, 1921: 6. "Ruby's Report," *Louisville Courier-Journal*, January 31, 1946: 17.

11. "Colonels Triumph": 6, 7.

12. "Colonels Triumph": 6.

13. Ibid.

14. Ibid.

15. "Full House." "Colonels Triumph": 6.

16. "Colonels Triumph": 6,7.

17. Ibid.

18. A Constant Reader, "Monday's Baseball Game," Point of View column, *Louisville Courier-Journal*, August 18, 1921: 4.

19. R.J.H., "Pro-Ruth #2," Point of View Column, *Louisville Courier-Journal*, August 20, 1921: 4.

20. A Local Fan, "Pro-Ruth #3," Point of View Column, *Louisville Courier-Journal*, August 20, 1921: 4.

21. "Profitable Day for Yankees," *Louisville Courier-Journal*, August 18, 1921: 7.

22. Philip Von Borries, *The Louisville Baseball Almanac* (Charleston, South Carolina: History Press, 2010), 51.

23. "Yanks Break Even With Phillies; Babe Knocked Out, Then Gets Homer," *Louisville Courier-Journal*, June 1, 1924: 60.

24. Richard B. Lutz, "Earle Combs: Louisville Colonel and Gentleman," *A Celebration of Louisville Baseball in the Major and Minor Leagues* (Pittsburgh: Matthews Printing, 1997); Dudley, "Babe Ruth and Earle Combs."

25. Anne Jewell, *Baseball in Louisville* (Charleston, South Carolina: Arcadia Publishing, 2006), 36.

26. Jewell, 39, 60-61.

27. "10,000 Cheer Babe Ruth as Ball Sails Over Parkway Field Fence," *Louisville Courier-Journal*, June 3, 1924: 1, 3; "It Was a Perfect Day! Ruth Hit Homer and Colonels Won," *Louisville Courier-Journal*, June 3, 1924: 9.

28. "St. Xavier Cubs Win Tenth Straight," *Louisville Courier-Journal*, June 1, 1924: 59.

29. Bruce Dudley, "Mighty Babe Crashes Longest Hit in Louisville Baseball History," *Louisville Courier-Journal*, June 3, 1924: 9.

30. "Men With Louisville Ties Made Strong Impact on Career of Ruth," *Louisville Courier-Journal*, August 17, 1948: 15.

31. Dudley, "Babe Ruth and Earle Combs Strut Stuff," 10. "10,000 Cheer," 3.

32. " 'King of Swat' Will Appear at Parkway Field This Afternoon," *Louisville Courier-Journal*, June 2, 1924: 1. "10,000 Cheer": 1, 3.

33. "It Was a Perfect Day": 9. This is the earliest use of the term "super star" that the author has found.

34. "Earl [*sic*] Combs Day at Roe-O-Connor's Monday," *Louisville Courier-Journal*, June 1, 1924: 62.

35. "10,000 Cheer": 1.

36. "Yanks Combine Own Hits With Errors of White Sox to Capture First, 6-3," *Louisville Courier-Journal*, June 4, 1924: 7.

37. Dudley, "Babe Ruth and Earle Combs Strut Stuff," 10.

38. "Ruth, Gehrig to Come Here From Columbus for Contest," *Louisville Courier-Journal*, October 23, 1928: 13.

39. Ibid.

40. "Ruth and Gehrig to Exhibit at Parkway Field Today," *Louisville Courier-Journal*, October 24, 1928: 13.

41. "Former Teacher Greets Babe," *Louisville Times*, October 25, 1928: 1.

42. Ibid.

43. Senior Class of St. Xavier High School, *The Tiger*, 1934, 45.

44. Sterne, 105.

45. Tommy Fitzgerald, "Ruth Set Autographing Mark Here; Teams Beg Back Last of 108 Balls!" *Louisville Courier-Journal*, August 18, 1948: 17.

46. Pete Johnson, "Babe Asks for 120 Baseballs," *Louisville Times*, October 24, 1928: 1.

47. "Ruth and Gehrig Delight 3,270 Baseball Admirers Here," *Louisville Courier-Journal*, October 25, 1928: 17.

48. "Ruth and Gehrig to Exhibit": 14.

49. "Ruth and Gehrig Delight": 18.

50. Pete Johnson.

51. " 'Babe' Declares 'Al' Has Earned Victory," *Louisville Courier-Journal*, October 25, 1928: 1.

52. " 'Babe' Declares": 2.

53. " 'Babe' Declares": 1.

54. " 'Babe' Declares": 2.

55. "Ruth, Gehrig to Come Here From Columbus": 13.

56. "Ruth and Gehrig Delight": 17-18.

57. "Babe, Lou in Dayton After Showing Here," *Louisville Times*, October 25, 1928: 2.

58 "Colonels Beat Reds by 5-3 and Are Ready for Yankees," *Louisville Courier-Journal*, April 4, 1932: 8, 9.

59 "Marse Joe's Yankees Here, Play Colonels," *Louisville Times*, April 4, 1932: 1.

60 Bruce Dudley, "Colonels Outhit Yankees but Lose on Errors by 9 to 6," *Louisville Courier-Journal*, April 5, 1932: 11.

61 Joe Wells, tape-recorded interview, September 8, 1997.

62 Bruce Dudley, "Colonels Outhit Yankees": 11.

63 Ibid.; Jewell, 45.

64 Bruce Dudley, "Colonels Outhit Yankees": 11.

65 "Ruth, Here for Derby, Exults in His Freedom," *Louisville Courier-Journal*, April 30, 1936: 45.

66 Tommy Fitzgerald, "More People Fooled at 1936 Derby by Ruth Than by Bold Venture," *Louisville Courier-Journal*, August 19, 1948: 19.

67 David Magee and Philip Shirley, *Sweet Spot: 125 Years of Baseball and the Louisville Slugger* (Chicago: Triumph Books, 2009), 45.

68 "Ruth Asks Hillerich to Baseball Banquet," *Louisville Courier-Journal*, December 16, 1933: 10.

69 Magee and Shirley, 56-57.

70 Magee and Shirley, 57.

71 Magee and Shirley, 54.

72 Earl Ruby, "Audubon Championship," The Foreground Column, *Louisville Courier-Journal*, July 15, 1936: 14. Jack Harrison, "A Scorecard That Was Worth Keeping," *Louisville Eccentric Observer*, August 9, 2000: 22.

73 Robert W. Creamer, *Babe: The Legend Comes to Life* (New York: Fireside Books, 1974), 407-408.

74 "Burke Is Leader," *Louisville Courier-Journal*, February 28, 1932: 33.

75 "Ruth, Here for Derby," 47. Earl Ruby, "A Tip a Day," *Louisville Courier-Journal*, May 1, 1936: 27. Harrison: 22.

76 Earl Ruby, "Babe a Portsider," *Louisville Courier-Journal*, April 30, 1936: 46.

77 Harrison: 22.

78 "Ross-Woods May Draw Top Crowd," *Louisville Courier-Journal*, May 1, 1936: 27.

79 Heggy Dent, "Ross Knocks Out Woods With Shower of Blows in the Fifth," *Louisville Courier-Journal*, May 2, 1936: 13.

80 Dent: 14.

81 "Ross-Woods May Draw Top Crowd": 27.

82 Marshall Smelser, *The Life That Ruth Built: A Biography* (New York: Bison Books, 1993), 533-535.

83 Ulric Bell, "Favorites of Fortune Try Lucky Fling," *Louisville Courier-Journal*, May 3, 1936: 7.

84 Tommy Fitzgerald, "Ruth Set Autographing Mark Here," 17. "Ruth and Gehrig Delight," 18.

85 Tommy Fitzgerald, "More People Fooled at 1936 Derby": 19.

86 Ibid.

87 Ibid.

88 Ibid.

89 "Dudley May Be Host to Babe Ruth," Ruby's Report, *Louisville Courier-Journal*, May 21, 1948: 45.

90 Ibid.

91 Tommy Fitzgerald, "More People Fooled at 1936 Derby," 19. Email Interview with Louisville Slugger Museum & Factory curator and exhibits director Chris Meiman, July-August 2018.

92 Email Interview with LSMF curator Chris Meiman, August 2018.

The Babe Comes North

By David McDonald

Parc Dupuis, Hull, Quebec. October 15, 1928. L. to r., unidentified in striped tie; Peter St. Pierre, umpire; Gehrig; Hull mayor Théo Lambert (wearing Lou's cap); Ruth (with Lambert's size 7 1/8 bowler perched precariously on his prodigious melon); Gene Coderre (umpire). *From Lambert estate. Courtesy of Heritage Auctions.*

"Don't tell me about Ruth; I've seen what he did to people. ... I've seen them: kids, men, women, worshipers all, hoping to get his famous name on a torn, dirty piece of paper, or hoping to get a grunt of recognition when they said, 'H'ya, Babe.' He never let them down; not once! He was the greatest crowd pleaser of them all."

– Waite Hoyt [1]

Just six days after winning the 1928 World Series, Babe Ruth and Lou Gehrig stepped off a train at Union Station in Ottawa, Ontario, the Canadian capital. It was a Monday noontime in mid-October, and some 500 fans, many of them boys conspicuously absent from school, milled expectantly in the concourse.

Suddenly the two greatest players on the greatest team in baseball came through the gate. For all the attention he attracted, the younger one, a handsome, Columbia University-educated 25-year-old, who would one day screen-test for the role of Tarzan, might have been a railway clerk on his way to lunch. Every eye in the place was locked on his companion, a beaming, pug-faced 33-year-old in a brown suit, brown overcoat, and a brown felt hat.

The crowd engulfed him, slapping him on the back, yelling "Hurrah for The Babe."[2] Despite his 6-feet-2-inches and 217 pounds, Ruth moved with a surprising nimbleness, hailing knots of kids with a scattershot "Howdy, bud," as he made his way through the hall.[3] Breaking stride for an instant, he centered out one small boy on the fringes of the mob for a cheery "Hello." The boy went popeyed and almost fell over.[4] The biggest kid on the continent had spoken to him.

One reporter found Ruth "far from the phlegmatic type many imagine. … He had a cheery word for everybody and, while he is perhaps one of the most pestered people in the world, he stands the often trying adulation of the sport mob with great patience and takes zest in everything and everybody, particularly the youngsters."[5] In fact, one of the first things Ruth had done when he arrived was to dash off a wire to the superintendent of the Ottawa Boys' Club, with his best wishes for the organization.

The Murderers' Row Yankees, hit hard by illness and injury, had won 13 fewer games in 1928 than they had the previous season. Ruth, hobbled by a charley horse and other ailments, had seen his average dip from .356 to .323, and his home runs from an iconic 60 to a mere league-leading 54. Gehrig's average had held steady, but his home-run total had plummeted, from 47 to 27.

It was just enough to carry the Yankees to their third straight American League pennant, by 2½ games over the Philadelphia Athletics. In the Series, they would be up against the St. Louis Cardinals, a team featuring six future Hall of Fame players and a Hall of Fame manager.

It was no contest. Ruth batted .625 (10-for-16), with three home runs, all coming in the fourth and final game. "The able Ruth, heralded as a cripple, pounded the crack St. Louis hurlers as if they were but Class 'C' pitchers in a bad slump," the *Ottawa Journal* reported.[6] Gehrig, for his part, batted .545 with 4 home runs and 9 runs batted in. Sweep, Yankees. Babe and Lou each pocketed a winner's share of $5,531.97. Now it was time to make some real dough.

Star players could make as much or more with a postseason barnstorming tour as they could in an entire major-league season. Ruth, for one, had barnstormed practically every fall since 1916, when he was still a member of the Boston Red Sox. Given his prodigious appetite for flivvers, floozies, stogies, hooch, and weenies, the postseason appearances had become something of a financial necessity.

In 1927 Ruth had recruited rising superstar Gehrig and embarked on a 21-game "Bustin' Babes and Larrupin' Lous" odyssey, from Providence, Rhode Island, to San Diego, California. Playing with and against mostly amateur and semiprofessional squads, the pair drew some 220,000 fans. Ruth netted about $70,000 from the tour, the equivalent of his annual Yankees' salary. Gehrig received a flat $10,000, which was $2,000 more than he'd earned during a regular season in which he had batted .373 and driven in 173 runs.

The 1928 World Series wrapped up on October 9. Five days later, Ruth and Gehrig kicked off their second Bustin' Babes and Larrupin' Lous tour in Montreal, where they lined up with Ahuntsic, champion of the racially integrated, semipro Ligue de la Cité (City League), against Chappie Johnson's All-Stars,[77] an all-black team from the same circuit. Before the game, they staged a home-run derby, swatting pitch after pitch out of the park to the delight of a crowd of between 14,000 and 16,000.

The game ended – as these games frequently did – with the fans flooding onto the field in the bottom of the eighth to celebrate a Gehrig home run that gave Ahuntsic an 8-6 lead. Ruth, who had last pitched in the majors in 1920, tossed the final three innings for the win, but at the plate managed only a pair of singles and a walk.

Arriving in Ottawa the next day, Babe and Lou repaired to a first-floor suite at the landmark Château Laurier hotel, just across the Rideau Canal from Canada's Parliament Buildings. Ruth invited local newsmen to hang out as he and Gehrig prepared

Babe in Hull, Quebec, Broadside, October 1928.
From the estate of former Hull mayor Théo Lambert.
Courtesy of Heritage Auctions.

for their game later that afternoon in Hull, Quebec, the city on the north side of the Ottawa River opposite the capital.

Inevitably, having landed in a political town, Babe was pressed for his thoughts on the upcoming US presidential election. He was an Al Smith supporter, he said, referring to the anti-Prohibitionist Democratic governor of New York, but conceded that Smith had "a tough fight ahead of him."[8]

Gehrig's political opinions, if any, went unrecorded.

> *"I know that as long as I was following Ruth to the plate I could have stood on my head and no one would have known the difference."*
>
> – Lou Gehrig[9]

While the reticent Gehrig did his best to blend in with the wallpaper, The Babe held court. "Tell the boys we are both glad to be here, even for such a short visit," he said, "and at Dupuis Park this afternoon we will try and provide our share of the entertainment."[10]

Asked how he was feeling, Ruth said, "I bet I can't even throw a ball today, that arm of mine is so sore."[11] Was he going to pitch in Hull? "You bet your life I'm not," he guffawed, adding that he had also signed 18 dozen baseballs as part of the Montreal appearance.[12]

"Babe Ready for Hull Swatfest,"[13] reported the *Ottawa Citizen*, while the *Ottawa Journal* colorfully stated the obvious: "The thousands who are likely to crowd the park will want to see Lou and Babe whang the apple over the car tracks."[14]

For a 3 o'clock game on a Monday afternoon in the middle of October, more than 3,000 spectators paid a dollar apiece – 50 cents for kids – to see Ruth, in his black Bustin' Babes uniform (which, one reporter quipped, "showed his figure to advantage"[15]) and Gehrig, in his Larrupin' Lous whites, do some heavy whanging. Ahuntsic and an integrated all-star team from the Montreal City League made up the supporting cast. The promoters had brought five dozen baseballs so there would be a ready supply for the pregame home-run exhibition and autograph session.

On this day, Ruth and Gehrig swapped their usual positions. Babe shifted to first base to give his sore wing a rest, a move that would also give him the chance to engage in nonstop banter with the fans. Lou started in left field, then came in to pitch the last two innings.

A swatfest it wasn't. Neither slugger could make solid contact against the All-Stars' pitcher, from the Guybourg club of the Montreal City League. He was identified in the box scores as Guillaume, but his real name was Ralph Williams, nicknamed Bill. One of the top hurlers in the province, Williams was a 35-year-old right-hander with a baffling array of deliveries – overhand, side-arm, underhand. Guillaume was the gallicized *nom de guerre* he assumed when he played for francophone teams.[16]

After the match, there were grumblings from fans about Guillaume's perceived failure, whether dictated by nervousness or competitive pride, to groove some of his offerings to the Yankee sluggers. For eight innings, he held Babe and Lou not just homerless but hitless. One reporter would liken the disappointing spectacle to "a performance of Hamlet without the Dane."[17]

The All-Stars, bolstered by some local athletic royalty – future Hockey Hall of Famers Frankie Boucher, star center of the Stanley Cup champion New York Rangers, and his brother George, an Ottawa Senators defenseman – led 1-0. George belted a double off Gehrig and robbed Ruth with a one-handed stab up against the center-field scoreboard.

Ahuntsic tied the game in the seventh, when Gehrig reached base on an infield error and later scored. Then in the eighth, Ruth finally got hold of one, doubling to drive in two and break the 1-1 tie. Gehrig followed with a fly out, stranding Babe at second. With that the kids in the stands, unable to restrain themselves any longer, poured onto the field, bringing the game to an early end.

"Over the fence they came in hundreds," the *Citizen* reported, and The Babe was engulfed by "a milling, shouting, worshipping mob of youngsters who clamored for handshakes, autographs and what have you in general."[18] The what-have-yous included Ruth's Bustin' Babes cap and both sluggers' bats, which were borne off like religious relics.

Babe and Lou eventually managed to jostle their way to the parking lot. They drove away, a swarm of kids pursuing their car through the streets of Hull.

Back in Ottawa, they boarded an 11 P.M. train at Union Station. Next stop: Buffalo.

Notes

1 John Tullius, *I'd Rather Be a Yankee: An Oral History of America's Most Loved and Most Hated Baseball Team* (New York: Macmillan, 1986), 40.

2 "Big Crowd Welcomes Ruth and Gehrig to Ottawa; Babe Is for Al; Monarch of the Diamond Is in Ottawa with His Larruping Team-Mate; May Go Fishing Up the Gatineau," *Ottawa Journal*, October 15, 1928.

3 "Babe Ready for Hull Swatfest," *Ottawa Citizen*, October 15, 1928.

4 *Ottawa Journal*, October 15, 1928.

5 "Home Run Twins Perform Here Monday; Great Babe Ruth and Gehrig, Heroes of 1928 World Series, to Be in Action (at) Dupuis Park; Stars of New York Yankees' Triumph Over St. Louis Cardinals in World Series Will Exhibit Their Prowess with the Bat Before Ottawa and Hull Fans, Will Line Up with Two Teams Selected from Montreal

Semi-Pro Ranks. Yankee Pair Set Up String of Records with Home Run Drives Against Cardinals," *Ottawa Citizen,* October 12, 1928.

6 *Salt Lake City Tribune*, October 10, 1928.

7 ⁷A.k.a. the Chappies, owned and managed by former Negro Leagues star George "Chappie" Johnson Jr., a native of Bellaire, Ohio. The Chappies played in the Montreal City League in the late '20s and early '30s.

8 *Ottawa Journal*, October 15, 1928. Rarely reluctant to share his political opinions, Ruth nevertheless failed to cast a ballot in 1928 or in other presidential election until 1944.

9 Tom Meany, *Baseball's Greatest Players* (New York: Grosset & Dunlap, 1953), 99.

10 *Ottawa Citizen,* October 15, 1928.

11 Ibid.

12 Ibid.

13 Ibid.

14 Baz O'Meara, "Sport Facts and Fancies," *Ottawa Journal,* October 15, 1928.

15 "Ruth and Gehrig Failed to Hammer Out Keenly Awaited Circuit Wallops, Disappoint Three Thousand Fans; Young Admirers Rush Twain Off Field and Break Up Game – Ruth Good Showman – Geo. Boucher Stars with Circus Catch of Ruth's Hit," *Ottawa Journal*, October 16, 1928.

16 Bert Williams, 92-year-old son of Ralph Williams, telephone interview with author., December 17, 2009. Ralph Williams, a.k.a Guillaume, once told his son that facing Ruth and Gehrig "was the best thing he ever did."

17 *Ottawa Journal*, October 16, 1928.

18 "Ruth and Gehrig Thrill Crowd in Exhibition Game at Dupuis; Home Run Kings Play Before Huge Throng on Hull Diamond. Neither Lou nor Babe Blast Any Long Balls Out of the Park During Contest, but Show Prowess at Long Distance Hitting in Batting Practice. Ruth's Double Wins Game for Ahuntsic Team. Youngsters Terminate Game in 8th, Nearly Mobbing Babe and Lou," *Ottawa Citizen*, October 16, 1928.

The Babe's Canadian Connections

By David McDonald

"Something about Canada seemed to agree with him ... on an intriguing psychological level. He spent years telling people all sorts of odd fibs about his supposed Canadian connections."

—David Giddens, CBC Sports[1]

Given that he was a notoriously unreliable witness to his own life, the inconsistencies and the discrepancies in the Babe's telling of it are hardly surprising. While some of the purported connections between Ruth and Canada don't pan out, the country was a recurring setting and its people enthusiastic supporting players in the Babe Ruth story. Here are some of the highlights:

1902. Dispatched to St. Mary's Industrial School for Orphans, Delinquent, Incorrigible and Wayward Boys, in his native Baltimore, 7-year-old George Herman Ruth Jr. was taken under the wing of the school's hulking assistant athletic director and prefect of discipline, the Xaverian layman Brother Matthias.

Matthias's real name was Martin Boutilier,[2] and he had come to Baltimore from the coal-mining town of Lingan, on Nova Scotia's Cape Breton Island.

Ruth later described Matthias as "the father I needed"[3] and "the greatest man I've ever known."[4] It was the 6-foot-4, 225-pound Cape Bretoner (some sources list him at 6-feet-6 and up to 300 pounds) who mesmerized the young Ruth with his ability to

In support of the Canadian war effort, Ruth flew to Halifax, Nova Scotia, in the summer of 1942 to take part in the opening of the Royal Canadian Navy's Wanderers Grounds recreational facility. *Courtesy of David McDonald.*

hit towering fungoes during practices. "I think I was born as a hitter the first day I ever saw him hit a baseball," Babe said.[5]

July 9, 1914. Boston Red Sox owner Joe Lannin acquired Ruth, along with fellow pitcher Ernie Shore and catcher Ben Egan, from cash-strapped Baltimore Orioles owner Jack Dunn for a reported $25,000.

Lannin, from Lac-Beauport, Quebec, was a character from the pages of a Horatio Alger novel. Orphaned in his early teens, he set out to seek his fortune in the United States. Arriving in Boston in 1880 – legend has it, on foot – Lannin started out as a bellhop. Eventually he made a small fortune in commodities and real estate. In 1913 he bought a 50 percent share in the Red Sox.

Lannin's teams won World Series in 1915 and 1916. But the pressures of baseball, even winning baseball, proved overwhelming for the transplanted Quebecker. "I am too much of a fan to be an owner and it was interfering with my health," he told the *New York Times*.[6] In 1917 he sold his interest in the club to Harry Frazee, later vilified as the man who sold Ruth to the Yankees. Lannin is a member of the Canadian Baseball Hall of Fame.

July 11, 1914. Nineteen-year-old Babe Ruth's first day in Boston was an eventful one. In the morning, by most accounts, he stopped for breakfast at a diner called Landers Coffee Shop and took a fancy to a young waitress, Helen Woodford. In the afternoon, he started his first major-league game, where the first batter he faced was Cleveland Naps left fielder Jack Graney. Graney, from St. Thomas, Ontario, singled but Ruth recovered to pitch seven solid innings in a 4-3 win.

Graney played his entire 14-year career with Cleveland. In 1932 he became the first ex-major leaguer to become a play-by-play announcer, as the radio voice of the Indians. He is a member of the Canadian Baseball Hall of Fame.

September 5, 1914. Sent down to the International League Providence Grays, Ruth threw a one-hit shutout and hit his first – and only – minor-league home run. It was a three-run shot and came in the sixth inning of a 9-0 victory over the Maple Leafs at Hanlan's Point Stadium in Toronto.

October 17, 1914. After a courtship of less than two months, Ruth, 19, married his favorite waitress, Helen Woodford. Press reports variously stated they had married in Providence, Rhode Island, or in Boston. To add to the confusion, Babe would tell some people that Helen (like Brother Matthias) was a Nova Scotian, while, on her marriage-license application, Helen herself claimed to be from Galveston, Texas. By the time of Babe's first passport application, in 1920, Galveston would morph into El Paso. None of this was true.

The uncertainty about Helen's origins and the location of their wedding probably began as a subterfuge to obscure the fact she was still a few days shy of her 18th birthday when they got hitched. The facts are these: Helen was born Mary Ellen Woodford in Boston on October 20, 1896. (Why she and Babe wouldn't have waited another three days to marry legally remains a mystery.) Helen was the third of nine children of Michael and Johanna Woodford, immigrants, not from Nova Scotia as is sometimes stated, but from Newfoundland.[7] And Babe and Helen were married in Ellicott City, Maryland – or, as Ruth would later remember on Grantland Rice's radio show, in a place called "Elkton."[8]

October 1923. Ruth and pitcher Herb Pennock celebrated the Yankees' first World Series win with a hunting trip to "the big-game territory of the Miramichi, New Brunswick, where the moose run wild."[9] Oddly, their choice of a hunting companion was coach Hughie Jennings of the Series-losing Giants.

October 20, 1925. An ailing Babe, still struggling to bounce back from "the bellyache heard 'round the world,"[10] returned to New Brunswick on another moose-hunting expedition, this time in the company of fellow ballplayers Bob Shawkey, Eddie Collins, Joe Bush, Muddy Ruel, and Benny Bengough. Their camp, on the Tobique River in the northwest of the province, was located 40 miles deep into the bush. Babe managed the first 15 miles of the trek on foot but finished it on horseback.

Three weeks later, according to Shawkey, a revitalized Ruth hiked the entire 40 miles back to the nearest railway station without a word of complaint. Nevertheless, when Babe reported to a New York gym in early December, he tipped the scales at 254 pounds. His trainer, Artie McGovern, melodramatically pronounced Babe "as near to being a total loss as any patient I have ever had under my care,"[11] thereby setting the stage for a demonstration of his own miraculous abilities as a fitness guru.

October 17, 1926. A week after losing the Series to Pete Alexander and the St. Louis Cardinals, Ruth, along with Yankees teammate Urban Shocker, popped up in Montreal on the fourth stop of a postseason barnstorming tour. Babe was guaranteed a

The Babe, in civvies, takes a few cuts during a timeout in the middle a game between Royal Canadian Navy teams from Halifax and Toronto, at the opening ceremony for the Wanderers Grounds recreation facility in Halifax, August 1, 1942. *Courtesy of David McDonald.*

minimum of $3,000 for a cold, gray afternoon's work. He did not disappoint.

Suiting up for Guybourg against Montreal City League rival Beaurivage. Babe belted two home runs. The first came off Shocker, while the second, a game-winning rocket off Chicago White Sox prospect Paddy Galkin, reportedly traveled more than 600 feet. The blow came just five days after another Bunyanesque blast, one estimated by witnesses at Artillery Park in Wilkes-Barre, Pennsylvania, to have traveled 650 feet.

When a pregame slugging exhibition was added in, the Montreal moonshot became the Babe's 36th dinger of the day, and it brought the festivities to a sudden halt "because the management had no more spheres."[12] Ruth, with three innings of hitless relief, was also the winning pitcher.

November 1926. Ruth headlined for a week at the Pantages Theater in Vancouver, British Columbia, on a bill touted as the "The King of Swat and five other big acts."[13] The B.C. appearance was one stop on a highly lucrative vaudeville tour, for which the Babe took in "a cool 100,000 smacks for 12 weeks of cavorting before Alex's footlights."[14] It was almost twice Ruth's annual baseball salary and, on a weekly basis, eclipsed the earnings of vaudeville's biggest stars, including W.C. Fields, Al Jolson, and Fanny Brice.

The 20-minute "act," repeated four times a day, began with some film clips of the Babe in action, followed by a few jokes, a fictionalized and highly sanitized rendition of his life story, a swing demonstration, and an on-stage autograph session. Later on the tour, teammate Mark Koenig would pronounce Ruth's set "boring as hell."[15] Vancouver audiences were too spellbound to notice.[16]

October 1928. Ruth and Lou Gehrig brought their Bustin' Babes and Larrupin' Lous postseason tour to Montreal and Ottawa-Hull. (See the accompanying article, "The Babe Comes North.")

October 19, 1934. Ruth, then 39 and soon to be an ex-Yankee, returned to Vancouver as the star attraction of Connie Mack's All-Americans. The squad, featuring seven future Hall of Famers and polyglot backup catcher and future spy Moe Berg, was en route to Japan for a 16-game postseason tour.

In Vancouver, they were slated to play against a local semipro club, but with the rain pounding down, the players anticipated a relaxing evening. The Babe was even photographed in his hotel suite wearing striped pajamas and a garish bathrobe, smoking his pipe and digesting a roast-duck dinner. But when word reached the hotel that 3,000 fans were arriving at the ballpark demanding to see their idols in action, Ruth reportedly rallied

Joseph Lannin, Red Sox owner. *The Sporting News Archives, Public Domain.*

the troops. "If these people can take the weather, so can we," he said. "We're gonna give 'em a ball game."[17]

Ruth and company headed to the field, the outfield of which was described as a "rice paddy,"[18] the infield "a mud pit."[19] Gehrig appeared on field wearing rubber boots and holding an umbrella. But when the umpires tried to call the game after six innings, Ruth insisted on playing it to a soggy conclusion. The teams played to a 2-2 tie. The next day Babe and the All-Americans boarded the Canadian Pacific liner Empress of Japan for the 12-day voyage to Yokohama.

April 16, 1935. George "Twinkletoes" Selkirk, a native of Huntsville, Ontario, took over the most challenging position in baseball – post-Ruth right field in Yankee Stadium on Opening Day. Adding to the pressure, Selkirk took the field wearing Babe's iconic number 3 and batting in his old number 3 slot in the Yankees order. Still, he managed one of only two Yankee safeties in a 1-0 loss to Wes Ferrell and the Red Sox.

Over the next eight seasons, Twinkletoes would run up numbers that, while hardly Ruthian, were nevertheless fairly impressive. For his career, he batted .290/.400/.483 with a 127 OPS+ and 108 home runs. He won five World Series and appeared in two All-Star Games. Selkirk is another member of the Canadian Baseball Hall of Fame.

July 1936. Ruth, recently inducted into the National Baseball Hall of Fame's inaugural class, visited the coal town of Westville,

Nova Scotia, at the invitation of a local doctor he had met in New York. It was one of many post-retirement trips Babe made to the home province of his mentor, Brother Matthias.

Prior to a ballgame featuring the hometown Miners, the Babe took a few cuts and swatted a ball over the center-field fence. He also spent some time salmon fishing in the St. Mary's River, playing golf in Halifax, Digby, and Pictou, and knocking back a few crustaceans at the Pictou County Lobster Festival.

October 1937. Ruth's fall hunting trip to Nova Scotia was documented in *Outdoor Life* magazine: "He is a snapshooter, as quick as lightning, and he can drill a tomato can at 60 yards."[20]

Back in New York, Babe rolled off the ship from Yarmouth in his Stutz Bearcat, three deer carcasses strapped to the fenders and a 250-pound black bear slumped in the rumble seat. His next stop was a charity golf match on Long Island before 10,000 spectators.

August 1, 1942. Ruth flew to wartime Nova Scotia and appeared at the opening of a Royal Canadian Navy recreation complex in Halifax. A game between local seamen and personnel stationed in Toronto was interrupted so Babe could put on a hitting display. Local legend had it he homered on every swing. In truth, Ruth, now 47 and wearing street shoes and a cream-colored suit, failed to knock a single ball out of the park. The 5,000 in attendance had to be satisfied with the dozen or so autographed baseballs Babe tossed into the crowd. One is still in the collection of the Nova Scotia Sport Hall of Fame.

Notes

1   David Giddens, "Babe Ruth; Made in Canada?" cbc.ca/sportslongform/entry/babe-ruth-made-in-canada, June 13, 2017.

2   A number of Ruth chroniclers, including Leigh Montville, Marty Appel, Allan Wood, and Wilborn Hampton, give Matthias's birth name as "Boutlier," but in his home county, the name is invariably Boutilier. According to *Nova Scotia Vital Records, 1763-1957*, Martin Boutilier was born in Bridgeport, Nova Scotia, on July 11, 1872.

3   Paul MacDougall, "The Man Who Inspired the Babe," *Cape Breton Post*, August 22, 2014.

4   Robert Creamer, *Babe: The Legend Comes to Life* (New York: Fireside Books, 1992), 37.

5   Creamer, 35.

6   Quoted by David L. Fleitz, *The Irish in Baseball: An Early History*. (Jefferson, North Carolina, and London: McFarland and Company, 2009), 176.

7   Newfoundland didn't become a province of Canada until 1949. In Michael and Johanna Woodford's day it was a British colony.

8   Fred Shoken, "Babe Ruth's Marriage to Helen Woodford," familysearch.org/photos/artifacts/24940973?p=9153286&returnLabel=Mary%20E%20(Helen)%20Woodford%20(K8TQ-WMX)&returnUrl=https%3A%2F%2Fwww.familysearch.org%2Ftree%2Fperson%2Fmemories%2FK8TQ-WMX.

9   "20 Yankees Each Receive $6,160.46," *New York Times,* October 17, 1923: 6.

10 A popular take on W.O. McGeehan's original line: "It is not remarkable that the stomach ache of Babe Ruth was heard around the world." From "A Demigod Has Indigestion," *New York Herald Tribune*, April 11, 1925.

11 Quoted by Leigh Montville, *The Big Bam: The Life and Times of Babe Ruth* (New York: Doubleday, 2006), 218.

12 "Ruth, By Losing 36 Baseballs, Breaks Up Game in Montreal," *New York Times*, October 18, 1926: 27.

13 Advertisement, *Vancouver Morning Star*, November 30, 1926.

14 *Vancouver Sun*, November 29, 1926. Quoted by John Mackie, "This Day in History," *Vancouver Sun*, November 29, 2012. "Alex" is vaudeville impresario Alexander Pantages.

15 Quoted by Harvey Frommer, *Five O'Clock Lightning: Babe Ruth, Lou Gehrig, and the Greatest Baseball Team in History, the 1927 New York Yankees* (Lanham, Maryland: Taylor Trade Publishing, 2008), 12.

16 "His every word and action riveted the attention of all and the big fellow, who is baseball's greatest star, pleased the folks equally as much as his four ply clouts satisfy the fans who throng in thousands to watch him work on the diamond. Babe bats 1.000 in the footlight personality league and his 20-minute act is all too short." "Babe 'Scores' at Pantages," *Vancouver Sun*, November 30, 1926.

17 Tom Hawthorn, "The Day Babe Ruth Played in Vancouver's Rain," *The Tyee*, October 21, 2014. thetyee.ca/News/2014/10/21/Babe-Ruth-Played-in-Vancouver/.

18 Ibid.

19 Ibid.

20 Bob Edge, "Babe's in the Woods," *Outdoor Life*, March 1938.

Babe Ruth and Baseball Diplomacy

By Robert K. Fitts

Ruth posing with fans aboard Canadian Pacific liner *Empress of Japan*; on voyage from Vancouver, British Columbia, to Yokohama, Japan. October 1934. *Courtesy of David McDonald.*

The American ambassador to Japan stretched out his long legs and put the final touches on the speech to welcome the All American baseball team to the Land of the Rising Sun. Although the ambassador, Joseph Grew, was probably pleased with it, it read like most of his speeches – banal and pompous. "I am a 'fan' myself, decidedly so, and you may be sure that it is to me a great privilege, and it gives me one of those good old-time thrills that I used to get in exuberant youth, to find myself on the same platform with some of the doughty warriors whose names and valiant achievements have been just as familiar as those of the old Greek heroes of whom I learned at school but who could never quite compete in my youthful estimation with our own heroes of the diamond." At least it was short and ended with an appropriate message of goodwill. "I am confident that the result of your visit here will be a further contribution to the ideal of mutual understanding, mutual respect, and mutual friendship between our two countries…"[1]

In November 1934 Japanese-American mutual understanding, respect, and friendship needed a boost. The two nations were slipping toward war as they vied for control over China and naval supremacy in the Pacific. Politically, Japan was in turmoil. The Japanese had enjoyed a form of democracy and rapid modernization under the rule of the Meiji and Taisho emperors. Yet, as Japan's power grew, so did its nationalism. A growing minority felt that Japan should take its place among the world powers by expanding its military and colonizing its neighbors. Ultranationalist societies began assassinating liberal politicians and members of the free press. By the early 1930s, the civilian government could no longer control elements of the military. In 1931 nationalistic officers engineered the invasion of Manchuria and twice plotted to overthrow the government. Japan had recently withdrawn from the League of Nations and was now threatening to withdraw from the Washington Naval Treaty, which limited the size of the major powers' navies. War between the United States and Japan seemed inevitable.

On November 2 thousands of flag-waving, screaming fans lined the piers of Yokohama to welcome the All Americans to Japan. The team was one of the greatest squads ever assembled – Babe Ruth, Lou Gehrig, Connie Mack, Jimmie Foxx, Earl Averill, Charlie Gehringer, Lefty Gomez, Lefty O'Doul, and a gaggle of lesser-known stars, including a journeyman catcher named Moe Berg, who would eventually become an operative for the OSS, the forerunner of the CIA. After ceremonies and interviews, a train whisked the players to Tokyo for what a reporter called "the wildest motor parade in history."[2]

Hundreds of thousands packed the sidewalks, spilling into the streets, blocking traffic and trolleys. "Banzai! Banzai Babe Ruth!" they screamed. Reveling in the attention, the Bambino grabbed American and Japanese flags from the crowd and waved one in each hand as he stood in the rear of the limousine. Confetti and streamers showered the procession. Finally, the crowd surged forward, breaking police lines. They ran to Ruth, surrounding the limousine, climbing the bumpers, eager to touch. Ruth grinned, gave another hefty banzai and shook the outstretched hands – thousands of them.

"Tokyo Gives Ruth Royal Welcome," blared the *New York Times* on November 3. The Associated Press article, picked up by newspapers across the globe, continued, "The Babe's big bulk today blotted out such unimportant things as international squabbles over oil and navies." Many observers considered the all-stars' joyous reception proof that the two countries' differences could be reconciled.[3]

The 1934 tour, however, began not as a diplomatic mission but as a publicity stunt to attract readers to the *Yomiuri Shimbun*. Owner Matsutaro Shoriki believed he could increase sales by sponsoring a team of major-league all-stars and covering the event in his newspaper. Realizing the tour's potential to improve relations, both the governments of the United States and Japan quickly backed the idea.

The American players understood the importance of the trip. The night before the All Americans departed for Japan, Connie Mack called a meeting in his Vancouver hotel room. In a quiet, serious voice, the Philadelphia Athletics owner-manager explained that during this trip they would be more than baseball players, they would be ambassadors. Their behavior, both on and off the field, would reflect not only on themselves, but on major-league baseball and their country. Every player must promise to always try his best; to be friendly and sincere toward the tour hosts; to teach the Japanese players; and to be nice to the fans and always be respectful. "If you cannot keep this promise," Mack continued, "please leave this room and you can go wherever you want." Nobody stirred. Ruth, sitting in the front row, raised his right hand and swore that he would follow the rules. The others followed.[4]

The tour began with two games at Tokyo's Meiji Jingu Stadium, where thousands camped overnight to secure the best general-admission seats. It soon became apparent that the fans had not come to root on their countrymen but to see the major leaguers, and especially the Babe, hit home runs. The crowd followed the Babe's every move. A reporter stated, "[T]he fans went crazy each time Ruth did anything – smiled, sneezed, or dropped a ball." One old man brought a pair of high-powered binoculars, amusing himself and neighboring fans by focusing on the Bambino's famous broad nose, making his nostrils fill the lens.[5]

Another fan had a novel plan. He worked in a textile factory designing kimono and undergarment patterns. He would sit as close as possible to the field and study the Bambino's face. He would memorize every feature, every wrinkle. Then, he would return to the factory and create a pattern of the Babe's face for a new line of Babe Ruth underwear. He would become rich, he was certain.[6]

Over the next four weeks, the All Americans played 18 exhibition games against a Japanese all-star team called All Nippon. They visited the northern cities of Sendai and Hakodate in Hokkaido; the industrial cities of Yokohama, Nagoya, and Osaka; the ancient capital of Kyoto; Kokura on the southern island of Kyushu; and, of course, Tokyo.

More than 450,000 people attended the games and hundreds of thousands more waited outside ballparks and hotels just to glimpse the major leaguers. The young All Nippon team was usually no match for the All Americans. The Americans swept the Japanese by a combined score of 181 to 36. But in two games, they came close to toppling the mighty major leaguers. On November 20 in the small town of Shizuoka at the base of Mount Fuji, 17-year-old Eiji Sawamura recorded 11 straight outs, including consecutive strikeouts of Gehringer, Ruth, Gehrig, and Foxx, before the Bambino broke up his no-hitter. The shutout continued until Gehrig homered in the seventh to give the Americans a 1-0 victory. The game would make Sawamura a national hero, and today the annual award for the best pitcher is named in his honor. In the following contest, the Japanese once again nearly upset the Americans, entering the bottom of the eighth with a 5-3 lead before several poor decisions by the Japanese manager cost them the game.

Sotaro Suzuki, an unidentified All Nippon player, Lou Gehrig, Hisanori Karuta, and Babe Ruth. *Courtesy of Yoko Suzuki.*

Everywhere, Ruth was the center of attention. His face dominated the tour's advertising poster, the cover of magazines, newspapers, and baseball cards produced especially for the series.

The Babe's major-league career was nearly over. His knees were shot, he had put on weight, and had hit .288 with 22 home runs during the '34 season – his lowest batting average since 1916 and his fewest home runs since 1918. Before leaving the United States, he had agreed to part ways with the Yankees. But the Japanese fans' enthusiasm made him feel like a young man. His bat responded as he led the tournament in batting average, home runs, RBIs, and runs scored.

The Japanese besieged the Bambino for autographs. A reporter noted that he "autographed everything held before him, hundreds of baseballs, handkerchiefs, menus, plain sheets of paper, hats, caps, neckties, shirts, every conceivable article thrust at him in feverish excitement."[7] Ruth told Ambassador Grew that he signed between four dozen and five dozen balls each day while in Japan. In the beginning, he responded to all salutations with the only Japanese word he knew, "Banzai!"[8]

During the games, the Babe clowned around. When playing first base, he would stand on the bag and then pantomime the height difference between the smaller Japanese runners and himself. The fans loved it. When he missed a pitch during batting practice, he would twist around in a circle and sometimes fall over to get a laugh. In the second game, after his fly ball was caught against the wall, he looked up at the disappointed crowd, "pointed his finger up into the air [to show] that the ball was too high, wrung his hands to show his disappointment that it wasn't a homer" as the fans "roared" with laughter.[9]

Perhaps the highlight of the Bambino's showboating came on a rainy day in the southern city of Kokura. The rain had turned the field to mud, prompting Ruth and others to play in rubber boots. At one point, the Babe borrowed an umbrella from a fan and huddled under it while playing first base. Few, however, know of the other interesting event that occurred during the game. In the fifth inning, with the bases loaded, a 3-and-0 count, and 5-foot-1, 116-pound Shinji Hamazaki on the mound, the Babe stepped out of the batter's box and pointed to the outfield bleachers. Unlike his famed 1932 Called Shot, there was no doubt about Ruth's intentions this time. Sure enough, the Sultan of Swat crushed the next pitch over the right-field wall and onto the roof of an adjacent building, shattering its clay roofing tiles.[10]

Between the games, the All Americans attended banquets, visited cultural sites, and made public appearances. Nearly all the events emphasized the countries' mutual bond of baseball. Ruth became the team's spokesman, spreading messages of international tolerance and goodwill. Grew noted in his diary, "[A]ll Japan has gone wild over him. He is a great deal more effective Ambassador than I could ever be."[11]

On December 2 thousands of flag-waving fans crowded on to the train platform at Tokyo's Ueno Station to say adieu. "Goodbye, Goodbye!" they shouted as Ruth sniffled and yelled "Sayonara, Sayonara! Banzai Japan!" As the train readied for departure, the crowd quieted to hear the Babe's final speech, "I don't know how to show my appreciation, but if I have a chance I will come back," he concluded.[12] The train took the players to Kobe, where they boarded the Empress of Canada for the homeward journey.

Many on both sides of the Pacific declared the tour a diplomatic coup. Connie Mack summed up the consensus that the trip did "more for the better understanding between Japanese and Americans than all the diplomatic exchanges ever accomplished."[13] Similar claims of baseball's social importance had been around the game even longer than Mack. Nineteenth-century proponents endowed baseball with the almost supernatural abilities to indoctrinate the values of democracy, "civilize savages," and even initiate world peace.[14] By the 1930s, however, a more modest goal for international baseball emerged – mutual respect and friendship.

Initially, the 1934 trip seemed to accomplish these objectives. The intense Stateside media coverage allowed millions of fans in the United States to view the Japanese through the All American players' eyes. Newspapers, magazines, newsreels, and radio reports depicted thousands of Japanese waving the American flag and cheering wildly for Babe Ruth and other American heroes. Americans heard the ballplayers' glowing descriptions of Japan and its friendly inhabitants. The *Chicago Tribune* summarized, "Reports from Japan … reveal the Japanese people in an animated state of great good will toward the

Babe Ruth with Japanese students wearing Koshien jerseys. *Courtesy of Yoko Suzuki.*

United States."[15] These reports were the most favorable press the Japanese had received for some time.

Many news stories focused on the Babe's extraordinary success as a diplomat. "Babe, the Ambassador – Ruth Makes Japan Go American," proclaimed *The Sporting News*. It continued, "The stars and stripes have not been much in evidence in Japan within recent years, because of various diplomatic and political aspects, but Babe Ruth, by one visit to Nippon has changed all of that, for the Ginza – Tokyo's Broadway – broke out with a rash of Red, White, and Blue when the Bambino and his American League Stars came to town. … We believe that the recent trip to the Orient of baseball's finest has served to delay, if not prevent, any possible conflict. We like to believe that countries having such a common interest in a great sport would rather fight it out on the diamond than on the battle field."[16]

Ambassador Grew wrote, "their visit to Japan has been an unqualified success. … I told Babe Ruth that while he was here, there were two American Ambassadors to Japan, he and I. Certainly he and Connie Mack and the rest of the team did an immense amount of good towards the development of Japanese-American friendship … at least among certain sections of the people."[17]

Unfortunately, it was the other portion of the Japanese population that would be the problem.

On the morning of February 22, 1935, when *Yomiuri* owner Matsutaro Shoriki arrived at work, Katsusuke Nagasaki was waiting. Nicknamed "The Newspaper Thug," Nagasaki served as enforcer for the ultra-rightwing War Gods Society. As Shoriki began to climb the stairs into the building, Nagasaki strode forward, pulled a short samurai sword from beneath his coat, and swung for the neck. Fortunately, his aim was off and rather than decapitating the newspaperman, Shoriki fell forward with a large gash in the back of his head. He would survive. Later that day, Nagasaki walked into a local police station and gave a detailed confession. The primary reason for the assassination: Shoriki had defiled the memory of the Meiji Emperor by allowing Babe Ruth and his team of American all-stars to play in the stadium named in the ruler's honor.[18]

In July 1937 Japan invaded China. Whatever hope there had been for reconciling the United States and Japan vanished. Ultimately, the two countries' love for baseball could not overcome Japan's desire for regional dominance.

The Babe was lounging in his Manhattan apartment when he learned of the attack on Pearl Harbor. For him, Pearl Harbor was a personal betrayal. Cursing the double-crossing SOBs, he heaved open the living room window that looked out over Riverside Drive to the Hudson River. His wife, Claire, had decorated the room with souvenirs from the Asian tour – porcelain vases and plates, exquisite dolls, and various sundries. The Babe stormed to the mantle, grabbed a vase and tossed it out the window. It crashed on the street below. Other souvenirs followed as Ruth kept up a tirade about the Japanese. Claire rushed around the room, gathering up the most valuable items before they joined the pile on Riverside Drive.[19]

The Sultan of Swat knew how to take revenge. Using the same charisma that made him an idol in Japan, he threw himself into

The 32-page program from the 1934 tour of Japan. *Courtesy Robert Edward Auctions.*

the war effort, raising money to defeat the Japanese and their allies. One of Ruth's many biographers noted, "Ruth in his late forties had become a patriotic symbol, ranking not far below the flag and the bald eagle."[20] But Ruth's role as a symbol was not limited to the United States. In Japan, the jovial, overweight, self-indulgent demigod of baseball, so welcomed in 1934, had become a symbol of American decadence. On March 3, 1944, the *New York Times* published a description of Japanese infantry screaming, "To hell with Babe Ruth!" as they charged to their deaths in the South Pacific. The Babe's response was classic Ruth, "I hope every Jap that mentions my name gets shot – and to hell with all Japs anyway!" The day after the *Times* article, Ruth took to the streets to raise money for the Red Cross, telling reporters that he was spurred on by the Japanese war cry.[21]

By the time of his death in 1948, Ruth and the Japanese had reconciled. Faced with the daunting task of reuniting the nations after World War II, the American occupying forces emphasized the countries' shared love of baseball. On April 27, 1947, the Japan Pro Baseball League joined major-league baseball in celebrating Babe Ruth Day. Over the following decades, Ruth was immortalized with statues and plaques, as well as baseball cards, biographies, and magazines. Each year, hundreds of Japanese make the pilgrimage to the Babe Ruth Museum in Baltimore. Even today, more than eight decades after his visit to the Land of the Rising Sun, the Babe remains a symbol of the game that binds our two nations together.

Notes

1. Joseph Grew, Houghton Library, Harvard University, Joseph Grew Diaries and Scrapbook, 948-49.
2. *Cleveland Press*, November 23, 1934: 44.
3. *New York Times*, November 3, 1934: 2.
4. Sotaro Suzuki, *Unofficial History of Japanese Professional Baseball* (Tokyo: Baseball Magazine, 1976), 180-81.
5. *Yakyukai* 25 (no 3), 1935, 184.
6. *Yomiuri Shimbun*, November 6, 1934: 6.
7. *Cleveland Press*, November 23, 1934: 44.
8. Joseph Grew, Diaries and Scrapbook, November 16, 1934, 2122.
9. *Japan Times*, November 6, 1934, 6.
10. Osamu Mihara, *My Baseball Life* (Tokyo: Toshuppan, 1947).
11. Joseph Grew, Diaries and Scrapbook, November 6, 1934.
12. *Yomiuri Shimbun*, December 2, 1934.
13. *The Sporting News*, January 17, 1935: 4.
14. Robert Elias, *The Empire Strikes Out* (New York: New Press, 2000), 21-22.
15. *Chicago Tribune,* November 12, 1934: 14.
16. *The Sporting News,* January 3, 1935: 4.
17. Joseph Grew to Kenesaw Mountain Landis, Grew Diaries and Scrapbook.
18. Robert Fitts, *Banzai Babe Ruth* (Lincoln: University of Nebraska Press, 2012), 235-39.
19. Julia Ruth Stevens, telephone interview with author, November 7, 2007.
20. Marshall Smelser, *The Life That Ruth Built* (Lincoln: University of Nebraska Press, 1975), 526.
21. *New York Times*, March 3, 1944: 2; March 5, 1944: 37.

Cigars, Horses, and a Couple of Homers: The Bambino's Experience in Cuba

By Reynaldo Cruz and Bill Nowlin

Dedicated to the memory of Peter C. Bjarkman

Havana served for many years as something of a playground for the idle wealthy of the United States, as often as not those of New York, particularly during the Prohibition years (1920-1933), when alcohol was banned in by an amendment to the US Constitution. It was a major tourist mecca and attracted a large number of American entertainers, gamblers, gangsters, and businessmen prepared to exploit the Cuban citizenry and make as much money as they could.

That very first year of Prohibition – the 18th Amendment was ratified in January 1919 and went into effect one year later – Babe Ruth was in his first year at a member of the Yankees, and he hit a previously unfathomable 54 home runs (more than any other entire team in the major leagues save the Phillies, who hit 64 as a team.)[1]

As motion-picture newsreels became a widely available form of entertainment and information, Ruth and many other figures in sports, from baseball to boxing, and in other realms from music to the movies, were becoming true national celebrities. John McGraw's New York Giants had already been booked to play a number of postseason exhibition games in Cuba. But "[w]ith money to spare and ambitions that knew no limits, Cuban impresarios wanted to cash in on the new phenomenon and invited the Babe to display his talents as a Giant at Almendares Park."[2]

Cuba was at the time living in a period known as the "Vacas Gordas" (Fat Cows), mainly helped by the postwar boom reached with the sale of sugar, highly priced worldwide. This enabled Cuban entrepreneur Abel Linares to hire the slugger so that he could play nine games with the New York Giants, offering him an almost staggering 2,000 US dollars per game.[3] His salary for the full 1920 season is believed to have been $20,000. At the time, the Cuban peso and the US dollar had an exchange rate of one-for-one.

The Bambino's exploits were very well known in Cuba already, and his presence in the games (most of them to be played in the new Moderno Almendares Park) would definitely draw a lot of fans to the game, even though they would mostly be cheering against him and the Giants.[4]

Bilingual pamphlet The Bambino Visits Cuba 1920 by Yuyo Ruiz. *Courtesy of Jane Leavy.*

It wasn't just coincidence that the Giants of the day often played preseason games in Havana. John McGraw owned the Oriental Racetrack there, in partnership with team owner Horace Stoneham. He'd first visited the island when it was still a Spanish colony, in 1890. The Oriental Racetrack property also embraced a restaurant, a small hotel called the Cuban American Jockey Club, and a casino.[5] The property was acquired during October 1919, the very month that gambling interests corrupted a number of the Chicago "Black Sox" into throwing the 1919 World Series.

Ruth reportedly lost most of the money he was paid while "gambling at jai alai and other games."[6]

The Giants departed by train from New York's Penn Station on October 12 and arrived in Havana by ship from Key West on October 15, staying at the Hotel Plaza, just in time to play the "American Series" from October 16 through November 28.

Ruth himself didn't arrive until October 29, in time to play the ninth game in the series the following day. He came with his first wife, Helen, and they also stayed at the Hotel Plaza, across from Parque Central in Havana, at the corner of Zulueta and Neptuno. Nearly 100 years later, the Plaza still serves as a hotel and has a plaque outside of the room where the Ruths stayed. The Babe also visited the famous Sloppy Joe's Bar, opened in 1917, a block away from the hotel – the bar holds pictures of the famous people who have visited it, including Hall of Famer Ted Williams.

The costs of travel and accommodations for the Ruths were covered by Linares. The fee paid to Ruth to play was reportedly more than all of his teammates combined.[7]

Ruth's first game was on October 30. Research done by Cuban researcher and historian Jose Antonio "Tony" Perez in the pages of the Havana newspaper *El Mundo* indicates that Ruth played center field and doubled and tripled in the game, won by the Giants over Habana, 4-3. The losing pitcher was Oscar Tuero; both Jose Acosta and Lefty Stewart worked in relief. The winning pitcher was Pol Perritt.

Ruth's second game saw Rosy Ryan of the Giants shut out Almendares, 3-0, on October 31. Ruth singled and tripled off Emilio Palmero. In the sixth inning, Palmero struck out the Babe on three consecutive fastballs. When he got back to the bench, a very impressed Ruth reportedly proclaimed, "Where did the Cubans find that guy? He could pitch for any team."[8]

After two days off – Ruth was reportedly engaged with Havana's nightlife – Moderno Almendares Park witnessed the Giants' third victory, when Perritt again subdued Habana on November 3, holding them to one run and five hits, while Acosta and Tuero surrendered seven runs and nine hits; Acosta bore the loss.) Each team made two errors, and it happened to be Ruth's worst day at the plate; he was struck out by Acosta in all three at-bats, although he got on base a fourth time and scored one run.

On November 4 it was Almendares again. The Giants prevailed in a slugfest, 10-8. Each team had 14 hits and made three errors. Ryan got the win and Palmero bore the loss. Ruth was 2-for-3 at the plate, with a single and a double, and also pitched an uneventful inning.

The November 6 game was a remarkable one. Ruth played first base and again pitched briefly. He was 0-for-3. The real story, though, was provided by another Hall of Famer. "Cuban slugger Cristobal Torriente had stolen [Ruth's] thunder by clouting three mammoth round-trippers in a memorable afternoon" – one of the homers reportedly hit off Babe Ruth, who pitched briefly in that game.[9] Torriente was voted into Cooperstown in 2006. The summary of his career on the Hall of Fame website begins: "'The Black Babe Ruth' was the nickname Torriente acquired in the fall of 1920. ... Torriente outhit and out-homered Ruth in the series."[10]

Torriente later played several years for the Chicago American Giants (and a final season with the Detroit Stars) of the Negro National League. After the November 6 game, he was presented with 400 cigars, a gold watch, and 103 pesos in cash collected on the field during the day.

The Havana newspaper *El Día* presciently reported, "Yesterday, Cristobal Torriente elevated himself to the greatest heights of glory and popularity. His hitting will enter Cuban baseball history as one of its most brilliant pages."

Gonzalez Echevarria's account was more sanguine than Figueredo's. The score was indisputably 11-4 in Almendares' favor, but he readily confesses, "I was genuinely sad to discover that the facts did not quite square with the myth." As he reports, "The story goes that on this day Torriente outdueled Ruth by blasting three home runs, while the American idol could only muster one. The facts are as follows: Babe Ruth did not get a hit that day, and while Torriente got three homers and a double, the homers were against Highpockets Kelly, the Giant first baseman, who had pitched one game in relief three seasons earlier. The double was against the Babe himself, who had taken the mound for an inning as a stunt. … The inescapable truth is that Torriente's feat was accomplished against a first baseman and a former pitcher and in a kind of holiday spirit – almost a carnival atmosphere. Furthermore, it is not clear from contemporary accounts if Torriente's homers actually went over the far-flung fences of Almendares Park. All three went to left or left-center, where the dimensions [are] each six hundred feet, but the only thing the newspaper story says is that the balls went over the fielders' head."[11] Some of the Giants, according to *Diario de la Marina* sportswriter Ramon S. Mendoza, were *descompuestos* (politely suggesting they appeared to be hung over thanks to excess alcohol consumption.) Catcher Earl Smith, for instance, had four passed balls in the game.

Peter Bjarkman endorses this conclusion, in effect underscoring the same research: "A local press account cited by González Echevarría suggests that Giants pitchers were not taking most of the games on the tour very seriously, were in truth lobbing 'batting practice tosses' at the Almendares hitters, and were at any rate probably on the day of Torriente's heroics still feeling the effects of excessive partying the previous night."[12]

Much of the partying was undoubtedly done at McGraw's casino. Of the "American Series," Charles Alexander wrote, "For once McGraw didn't seem to take baseball seriously. The major-leaguers won most of the time, lost a few, and had plenty of fun at McGraw's and Stoneham's racetrack and casino. Playing before big crowds, the ballplayers did well financially, most of all Ruth. At least until the croupiers and assorted con artists got through with him, by which time he had little left of the $20,000 or so he'd gained from the trip."[13] One contemporary report, a lengthy summary in *The Sporting News,* said Ruth had lost $35,000 at the race track and that "the Cubans also stung him hard in a big crap game, and he returned to the States solely because he was broke."[14]

The next day, on November 7, Ruth was 2-for-3 – both hits were singles – against Stewart of Habana. Ruth was back in center field, where he played for the remainder of the games.

His first home run came during a 6-5 loss to Almendares on November 8, an inside-the-park home run. He was "safe at the plate by inches."[15]

Gonzalez Echeverria says that *Diario de la Marina*'s Mendoza reported the ball "went to the corner between the end of 'sol' and the center-field wall or scoreboard" and "may well have been the longest homer ever hit at Almendares Park; a rough estimate would be about 550 feet."[16]

There were then three days off. On November 12 the two teams played to a 3-3, eight-inning tie game, which was called due to darkness. Ruth was 0-for-4.

On the 14th the Babe collected his second home run, against Almendares in a 7-3 Giants win. He was 1-for-2. This one perhaps cleared the fence; Tony Perez, historian Dr. Oscar Fernandez, and longtime SABR member Ismael Sene have all told Reynaldo Cruz that one of Ruth's homers cleared the fence and it was the only homer to clear the fence in the whole series.

New York was outmatched by Adolfo Luque's Almendares team but beat Habana handily. Seventeen games in all were played, with New York posting records vs. Almendares of 2-4 (with three ties), and vs. Habana of 6-1 (with one tie.) There was one game played against an All-Cubans team, which ended in a 2-2 tie.[17]

The contingent moved to Santiago de Cuba, where Juan Lageyre paid the Bambino $3,000 for two games in Cuba Park of the eastern city. However, most of the Giants team sat out the game, and The Sultan of Swat made up a "Babe Ruth" team with Rosy Ryan and himself, along with a group of Cubans. They were whitewashed, 4-0, by Pablo Guillen (a pitcher who never played professionally and had a slow ball) and the Santiago team, which scored all of its runs in the third inning. Playing first base, Ruth went 1-for-3. According to the local newspaper in Santiago, Guillen struck out Ruth three times in a row.[18]

His stay in Santiago de Cuba was not as rewarding as he had anticipated. He bet on the horses at Oriental Park, gambling at jai alai matches and in casinos as well, in the night and in the mornings as well. He lost all his money betting and returned to Havana with only 40 cents in his wallet.[19]

Linares himself was understood to have made $40,000 in profits on the tour and to have "elevated Cuban baseball…to a new prominence."[20]

The *New York Times* summarized Ruth's reception in Cuba: "They liked the Babe down there in the land of tobacco, sugar and skimmed milk. He was greeted with uproarious applause constantly, although his prowess as a slugger was seldom on display. He made only two of his far-famed circuit smashes in the whole series."[21]

The Sporting News quoted Ruth as saying the fences in the Havana ballpark "are not made for home runs," though noting that Torriente had hit three in one game. The paper wrote, "The Babe hit a lot of mighty drives but the fielders played in the next county for him and gathered the most of them in. Two homers were all he got in the ten games he played as a member of the Giants." Ruth stayed on, having signed a new contract to play in 10 more games with a Cuban team.[22]

Ruth was less than politically correct when he declaimed on the ballparks in Cuba: "Oh, they're punk. The fence is four blocks from home plate, and them greasers expect you to knock it over every time." About the country in general, he said, "It's a great place. … The kids used to chase me all over the island calling me Bobbie Ruth." But he added, disparagingly, of Torriente in particular, "Them greasers are punk ball players. Only a few of them are any good. This guy they calls after me because he made a few homers is as black as a ton and a half of coal in a dark cellar. I guess I'll go back to Cuba next winter."[23]

The *Washington Post* reported that, despite just the two home runs, Ruth had hit for a .345 average, with three triples, three doubles, and two singles, and scored five runs. He struck out six times.[24] Figures compiled by Jose Antonio Perez agree, crediting him with 11 RBIs, 11 walks, two stolen bases, and one sacrifice bunt.[25]

In late November, Ruth wrote to Miller Huggins from Havana that he hoped for an even better regular season in 1921 than he had enjoyed in 1920. He noted that he had missed a number of games in 1920 but that by playing winter ball in Cuba he would be in "perfect trim" and that, furthermore, he wasn't going to mess with acting in motion pictures: "I am fully convinced that my batting eye was injured by the strong light of the movie studio, and I'm not going to let those fellows cheat me out of any more home runs."[26] However he may have prepared for the 1921 season, it paid off. He played in almost every game and hit 59 home runs.

Ruth visited Cuba only that one time to play baseball. Andres Pascual says he returned in 1921 to "engage in what would become a dangerous hobby for him: the horse races in Oriental Park."[27]

Sources

Thanks to Tony Perez for compiling figures on the 1920 visit of the New York Giants – and Ruth – to Cuba. Thanks to Jane Leavy for loaning the pamphlet "The Bambino Visits Cuba."

In addition to the sources cited in the Notes, the authors also consulted a number of biographies of Babe Ruth, including:

Creamer, Robert. *Babe: The Legend Comes to Life* (New York: Simon & Schuster, 1992).

Leavy, Jane. *The Big Fella* (New York: HarperCollins, 2018).

Montville, Leigh. *The Big Bam* (New York: Doubleday, 2006).

Wehrle, Edmund F. *Breaking Babe Ruth* (Columbia: University of Missouri Press, 2018).

Notes

1. The 29 home runs he had hit for the Boston Red Sox in 1919 had already set the major-league record and Ruth's 54 had nearly doubled that.

2. Roberto Gonzalez Echeverria, *The Pride of Havana: A History of Cuban Baseball* (New York: Oxford University Press, 1999), 158. Promoters from Cuba visited Ruth in August, and in early September signed him to play postseason games on the island. See "Want Ruth in Cuba," *New York Times*, August 7, 1920: 6, and "Ruth Signs Contract for Series in Havana," *Chicago Tribune*, September 9, 1920: 19.

3. Gonzalez Echeverria, 160. The average net *annual* income for US citizens filing tax returns in 1920 was $3,269.40. See Treasury Department, United States Internal Revenue, Statistics of Income from Return of Net Income for 1920 (Washington: Government Printing Office, 1922), 2. In Cuba, it was less, but perhaps not as much less as some might think. In 1929, it was reported to be 41 percent of the US total (and thus higher than states like Mississippi and South Carolina.) See Marianne Ward (Loyola College) and John Devereux (Queens College CUNY), "The Road Not Taken: Pre-Revolutionary Cuban Living Standards in Comparative Perspective," 30–31, cited at econweb.umd.edu/~davis/eventpapers/CUBA.pdf.

4. The park was located where Havana's National Bus Station is in 2019. The first Almendares Park, property of the Zaldo family, was located a few blocks away from the second. There is sometimes confusion over whether Ruth played in the first or the second. The first Almendares Park hosted the Cincinnati Reds, the New York Giants, and the Detroit Tigers. Cooperstown Hall of Famer Jose Mendez Baez cemented his fame in that ballpark. The Almendares Park in question, where Ruth played, has perhaps this visit and Cristobal Torriente's exploits as the most attractive historical fact.

5. Charles C. Alexander, *John McGraw* (New York: Penguin Books, 1988), 216.

6. Gonzalez Echeverria, 162.

7. Yuyo Ruiz, "The Bambino Visits Cuba 1920," undated pamphlet self-published by the author in San Juan, Puerto Rico, 14.

8. Ibid.

9. Figueredo, 134.

10. baseballhall.org/hall-of-famers/torriente-cristobal, accessed October 14, 2018.

11. Gonzalez Echeverria, 161. The author notes that most home runs in the ballpark were inside-the-park home runs.

12. Peter Bjarkman, "Cristóbal Torriente," SABR BioProject, https://sabr.org/bioproj/person/1755c43c

13 Alexander, 227. In the aftermath of the 1919 World Series scandal, Commissioner Kenesaw M. Landis forced McGraw and Stoneham to divest their interests in the Havana casino, which they did in July 1921. See Alexander, 229.

14 "Ruth Plays Role of Innocent Abroad on His Visit to Cuba," *The Sporting News*, January 13, 1921: 6. The story also said Ruth had lost $35,000 in a film venture and was accompanied by a photograph of the Babe under the caption "No Hero of Finance."

15 "Giants Back from Havana," *The Sporting News*, December 2, 1920: 3.

16 Gonzalez Echeverria, 162.

17 Gonzalez Echeverria, 136. The players on the Giants team were Earl Smith (C), Frank Snyder (C/OF), George Kelly (1B/P), Larry Doyle (2B), Frank Frisch (3B), Dave Bancroft (SS), George Burns (OF), Ross Youngs (OF), Babe Ruth (OF/1B/P), Jesse Barnes (OF/P), Pol Perritt (P), and Rosy Ryan (P).

18 Ruiz, 23.

19 Andres Pascual, "Babe Ruth in Santiago de Cuba," seamheads.com, November 1, 2011. seamheads.com/blog/2011/11/01/ruth-en-santiago-de-cuba-babe-ruth-in-santiago-de-cuba/.

20 Ruiz, 21.

21 "Giants Back Home from Cuban Trip," *New York Times*, November 20, 1920: 20.

22 "Giants Back from Havana."

23 "Ruth Plays Role of Innocent Abroad on His Visit to Cuba."

24 "Ruth Falls Short on Clouts in Cuba," *Washington Post*, November 19, 1920: 12.

25 The box scores do not include bases on balls or runs batted in, so it is impossible to know for sure how many Ruth had of either.

26 "Ruth Writes of His Hopes," *The Sporting News*, December 2, 1920: 8.

27 Andres Pascual.

Babe Ruth and Cricket

By Glen Sparks

Babe Ruth turned his cricket bat into a broken, splintered mess. Baseball's great home-run hitter had just smashed an hour's worth of bowling (cricket's term for "pitching"). He whacked balls all over a "subterranean" field near the Thames River in London. Alan Fairfax, formerly a top Australian player, coached Ruth and marveled at his pupil's bountiful swing. "I wish I could have him for a fortnight," Fairfax declared. "I could make one of the world's greatest batsmen out of him."[1]

Babe took his cuts in February of 1935, near the end of a worldwide tour. Just a few months earlier, he completed his 21st season in the major leagues, and his 15th campaign – most of them glorious – as a Yankee. He claimed 708 home runs, the all-time mark by a long shot, and led the majors in that category 12 times. Fans and sportswriters called him the Big Bam, the Sultan of Swat, and the Maharaja of Mash. He was near the end of his playing career.

All sorts of rumors swirled around Ruth's future after he hit 22 homers for the '34 Yanks. He said for several years that he longed to manage a big-league ballclub. Many critics said the hard-living Ruth could barely manage himself. How could he manage others? Some wanted to give him a chance. Maybe. According to one rumor, former Yankees co-owner Col. T.L Huston hoped to buy the Brooklyn Dodgers and hire Babe as skipper. Huston called the rumor "absolutely authentic." He continued: "I have no desire to ventilate the affairs of the Brooklyn club, as we have always been friends. I believe Babe Ruth would make as efficient a manager as any of the present major league managers and would throw away no more games than they do."[2] Also, the House of David, a religious society and traveling band of talented baseball players, reportedly offered Ruth a $35,000 contract. The Babe wouldn't have to grow a beard, unlike others on the House roster. "We'll take him with a naked face, so the folks will know it's really Babe Ruth," according to one House veteran.[3]

In the fall of 1934, Ruth joined a team of American League All-Stars for an offseason tour of Japan. The group, led by Philadelphia Athletics owner and manager Connie Mack, included Lou Gehrig, Jimmie Foxx, Charlie Gehringer, and others. "I ran the ball team on the field," Ruth contended.[4] It was a goodwill venture during a time of increasing tension between the two nations. Babe invited his wife, Claire, and older daughter, Julia, 18. Younger daughter Dorothy, 13 years old, stayed at home with relatives. Dorothy brooded over the slight. Supposedly, Julia went along as a way to celebrate her recent high-school graduation. Dorothy scoffed. "Well, if that trip was a graduation present, then Julia graduated about 15 times in five years," Dorothy wrote in *My Dad, The Babe*, published in 1988.[5]

Mack told the players during a meeting that they must maintain their best behavior. Ruth, prone to misbehavior, sat in the front row and promised to obey the rules. It would be worth the Bambino's while. Supposedly, Mack had some interest in hiring Ruth as the next Athletics manager. Baseball's Great

Tactician would turn 72 on December 22. Maybe it was time for a man born in the first full year of the US Civil War to hang up his straw hat, plus his managerial outfit of suit and tie, and hire a younger man.

The *Empress of Japan* left Vancouver, British Columbia, on October 20, 1934, all-stars aboard, and took several days to cross the Pacific Ocean. Long enough for Ruth and Gehrig to get on each other's nerves. The longtime teammates, former fishing buddies, and friendly rivals during an exhibition tour – the Larrupin' Lous and Bustin' Babes played a series of games after the 1927 World Series – had fallen out of favor with each other. Maybe the whole fuss began over a crack that Gehrig's mother, Christina, made a year earlier about how the Ruths dressed Dorothy in hand-me-downs. Julia, meanwhile, dressed in style. Ruth told Gehrig that Christina should mind her own business. Well, those were next to fighting words. The Iron Horse, then and there, just about quit speaking to the Babe.[6]

At one point Gehrig, according to Leigh Montville in *The Big Bam*, walked into Ruth's stateroom and saw his tipsy bride talking with the Babe. What else had gone on? Lou was furious. He knew all about the reputation of one George Herman Ruth. Eleanor Gehrig, though, wrote in *My Luke and I* that Claire Ruth had offered the invitation. Babe sat in the room "like a Buddha figure, cross-legged and surrounded by an empire of caviar and champagne."[7] Eleanor joined the party. She left two hours later and with the ship's horn bursting out a signal for a body overboard. A frantic Lou Gehrig could not find his wife. He worried that she had fallen into the deep. "The only place Lou had never thought to check out was Babe Ruth's cabin."[8]

Yes, Ruth and Eleanor knew one another. Eleanor grew up in Chicago. She played poker and smoked cigarettes in public (gasp!) and liked a stiff drink. She loved to attend parties. "Before she had known, Gehrig, she had known the Babe," Montville wrote. In fact, Eleanor and Lou met at a "free-flowing" party that Babe had hosted in his Chicago hotel suite.[9] Not long after the ship-wide search for Eleanor had ended, Ruth knocked on the couple's door; he wanted to be friends. "But my unforgiving husband turned his back. … Their feud, their ridiculous new feud, didn't diminish the team's performance when it came to baseball; we simply went our separate ways."[10] The rift lasted for years, until a dying Gehrig stood for an ovation at Yankee Stadium one final time, on July 4, 1939. Ruth and the Iron Horse embraced in front of 61,808 fans.

The all-stars arrived in Japan none too soon. The major leaguers played 18 exhibition games against Japanese teams, mostly college squads, and trounced the competition by a combined score of 181-36. Ruth gave the competition a so-so rating. "I was surprised by their high-class fielding and the ability of some of their pitchers," Ruth wrote in his autobiography. "But they couldn't hit a lick."[11]

The final scores didn't matter. Japanese baseball fans loved Ruth. Of course, they had heard all about the legendary ballplayer. They wanted him to hit home runs. They yelled for their hurlers to throw pitches that Ruth could launch into the sky and circle the bases to even more applause. They shouted, "Banzai Babe Ruth!," imploring him to live a thousand years, and ran toward the stocky baseball legend. Ruth, of course, loved the attention and waved US and Japanese flags. Nearly a half-million fans watched the action in Tokyo and other cities. The Babe signed autographs, posed for pictures, and earned plenty of laughs. He took exaggerated swings at times and made jokes about the height differences between the smaller Japanese players and himself. Ruth even borrowed an umbrella and held it high while he played first base one soggy day. The crowd loved the Babe's antics. Ruth loved them back. The players took lots of pictures. Moe Berg, an Ivy League-educated, weak-hitting catcher, took more than the others. He didn't take many tourist snapshots. He focused on pictures that showed Japanese industrial and military might. "He had been recruited by the OSS (Office of Strategic Services, forerunner of the CIA) as an American spy," Montville wrote in *The Big Bam*.[12]

After the tour, most of the players boarded a ship and made the return trip across the Pacific Ocean. Ruth and his family, along with the Gehrigs and a few other couples, kept trotting the globe. (The Ruths and Gehrigs took different ships. Probably a good idea.) The Ruths stopped off in Java and Bali. Babe didn't like the women, who chewed a red tobacco that stained their teeth. "They are billed as the most beautiful women in the world," said Ruth.[13] The ship sailed into the Red Sea, through the Suez Canal, and, finally, to the Mediterranean Sea.

The stayover in Paris disheartened Babe. No one knew him. The man who could draw a crowd almost anywhere, who could attract hero worshippers, photographers, and reporters in big cities and small towns, who boasted maybe the most famous face in the world, walked as a stranger in the fabled City of Light, a place he called "not much of a town."[14] No one recognized him as he strolled down the famed Champs-Elysees. Even the American boys living in Paris didn't play baseball. "Imagine an American kid not knowing how to swing a bat," Ruth said.[15] He probably shuddered at the very idea. Ruth did talk to one reporter in Paris about his future as a big-league skipper. He probably could have had the Cleveland Indians job or the Red Sox gig. He also mentioned the Athletics and the Braves. "One thing, though, if I can't manage a club, I'll quit," he insisted.[16] (Mack already had nixed the idea of hiring Ruth as skipper. It had nothing to do with possible shenanigans between Babe and Eleanor Gehrig, it seems. Mack didn't like the way Mrs. Ruth ordered her husband around while aboard ship. "If I gave the job to him, she would be managing the team in a month," Mack said.[17] There went that opportunity. (Mack, a part-owner of the Athletics, stayed on as skipper through the 1950 season. He retired at the age of 88.)

Paul Gallico wrote a column on Ruth's international adventures. He began it by informing his readers, "George Herman Ruth doesn't like Paris. He does not like the French." Supposedly, Ruth had "ten-thousand well-chosen words" on why he loathed the place. Gallico did not print the diatribe. He boiled it down to Ruth saying, "I do not think the French care much about baseball,' and hence, were probably not much concerned about Le Gros Bebe when he was in Paris."[18]

Ruth's mood brightened as he headed to the Swiss Alps and the St. Moritz resort. A reporter asked Babe if he could ski. Well, what a silly question to ask a real-life action figure. "Can I ski?" an incredulous Ruth responded, hardly believing the question. "I'm a champ at that game." He called his try at bobsledding the "the biggest thrill of his life."[19] Yes, bigger even than smashing three home runs in Game Four of the 1926 World Series or hitting 60 home runs in 1927. "I would like to quote his rich and racy language on that trip, but I cannot," Gallico wrote. "It seemed that all he could do was hold on, hold his breath and let the world go by." Moving fast. That's what Ruth did best. Also, "Babe on skis must have been a magnificent and eye-filling picture."[20]

Next stop, London. The Ruths flew across the English Channel, from Le Bourget to Croydon. They spent about 10 days in England. No, Ruth said, he still had no job as a manager. "But I would like one," he added.[21] (Col. Huston had decided, on the advice of his wife, not to buy the Dodgers, thus eliminating another possible managerial gig for Ruth. The Colonel, a gentleman farmer in Georgia, told reporters, "Mrs. Huston spoke her piece. Her tone and manner of saying it implied an indisputable authority." She said, 'You are not going to buy any ball club. You are going to stick to your cows.'"[22])

Ruth liked London. People there knew him. They ran up to him. They gave him the proper attention that he – The Sultan of Swat – felt he deserved. Like giving him cricket lessons. Babe put on the requisite leg pads and took his swings. He liked the game but not the salary. Top cricket players earned about $40 a week, a paltry sum for a home-run king. Ruth laughed when a few cricketers insisted that top bowlers could throw as hard as major-league pitchers like Walter Johnson, aka "The Big Train." Babe called that "blame foolishness." The cricketers said they would ask Harold Larwood, one of the game's most intimidating bowlers, to come down from his Birmingham home in the English Midlands and throw a few Ruth's way. The Babe hoped that more scientific instruments might be used, but he was game to get into the box against Larwood. "Anybody who thinks this Larwood fellow throws a faster ball than Walter Johnson used to throw past me can have my money."[23]

Alas, the great matchup between cricket bowler and baseball batter never happened. And more's the pity. Larwood couldn't make the trip down to London. John Lardner insisted that the sports world missed quite a battle. Lardner called Larwood "one of the most interesting athletes in England." He liked to bowl inside, dusting off his opponents and keeping them nervous. Hitting a batter is not against the rules in cricket, and Larwood, a part-time miner, bruised plenty of them. In a match against Australia, he hit the opposing batsmen "hard and profusely. He hit nearly all of them, playing no favorites."[24] Maybe Ruth would have taken exception to Larwood's high, hard ones.

Some cricketers swore that a top batsman could crush a ball 600 feet. Ruth didn't believe that claim. The Maharajah took a few more swings. "Whack! Whack!" He said, "I wish they would let me use a bat as wide as this in baseball. I'd be good for five more years."[25] Later, while sitting in his pajamas and smoking a cigar at the swanky Savoy Hotel, he answered claims that cricket requires more skill than baseball. Ruth broke into loud laughter. "Skill! A game? Why cricket's not a game at all. It's a tea party. It seems to me all they do is hold the bat and let the ball roll against it. Still, I don't want to criticize. I guess they enjoy it, or they wouldn't do it so much."[26] The British probably loved that comment.

Ruth played some golf in London and plunked himself in the process. He stood on a rooftop in front of the press corps and teed off a shot into the midtown air, taking aim at the nearby Thames. The ball smacked into a parapet that encircled the roof and ricocheted toward Ruth, thumping him in the chest. The energized drive "nearly went right on through him."[27]

Hamilton asked Ruth whether there existed a "yellow peril," i.e., did Japan pose an imminent threat to the United States. Babe, put into the role of amateur statesman, deflected the question. ("Warlike? Hell, they don't look warlike.") Instead, he once again complimented the Japanese for their great love of America's national pastime. "Man, they're just crazy about baseball. They play baseball before breakfast!" Ruth said he might yet hit a few more home runs in the big leagues. "But not many, I guess. After all, I'm 40 years old. I can't expect to play forever."[28] Finally, Ruth spoke to someone on the telephone – a hotel employee? – who assured him that the ballplayer's packing trunks – which he hadn't seen since leaving Japan – would be in Southampton before his ship, the Manhattan, left port the next day. "Boy, they better be!" Ruth bellowed.

The Manhattan arrived in New York City on February 20. A band greeted Ruth and serenaded him with a rendition of "Take Me Out to the Ball Game." Babe had traveled more than 21,000 miles in his four-month stay from home. It was the first real vacation he ever had, Claire Ruth said. Babe told the writers "It was great" and "I wouldn't do it again for $100,000."[29] Ruth played one more year as a player. The Boston Braves had purchased his contract from the Yankees, also naming him "assistant manager" and "vice president." Ruth smacked six home runs, hit .181 in 72 at-bats, and retired in late May. He never managed a big-league team.

Notes

1. Gayle Talbot (Associated Press), "Babe Busts a Bat Showing English What Is Cricket," *New York Daily News*, February 10, 1935: 197.
2. United Press, "Col. Huston Seeks Dodgers and Babe," *Paducah* (Kentucky) *Sun-Democrat*, November 2, 1934: 12.
3. "House of David Offers Babe Ruth $35,000 to Play," *Fresno* (California) *Bee*, November 2, 1934: 21.
4. Babe Ruth and Bob Considine, *The Babe Ruth Story* (New York: Signet, 1992), 203.
5. Dorothy Ruth Pirone and Chris Martens, *My Dad, the Babe* (Boston: Quinlan Press, 1988), 113.
6. Leigh Montville, *The Big Bam: The Life and Times of Babe Ruth* (New York: Doubleday, 2006), 332.
7. Eleanor Gehrig and Joseph Durso, *My Luke and I* (New York: Thomas Y. Crowell, 1976), 190.
8. Ibid.
9. Montville, 332.
10. Ibid.
11. Ruth and Considine, 203.
12. Montville, 334.
13. Montville, 335.
14. Jane Leavy, *The Big Fella: Babe Ruth and the World He Created* (New York: HarperCollins, 2018), 414.
15. Robert Creamer, *Babe: The Legend Comes to Life* (New York: Simon & Schuster, 1974), 381.
16. Creamer, 381.
17. Montville, 333.
18. Paul Gallico, "The Babe Doesn't Like Paris," *St Louis Star and Times*, February 23, 1935: 7.
19. Creamer, 381.
20. Gallico: 7.
21. Associated Press, "Babe Ruth Flies to London to Celebrate Uncertain Birthday," *Philadelphia Inquirer*, February 8, 1935: 15.
22. Associated Press, "Mrs. Huston Says 'No,'" *Allentown* (Pennsylvania) *Morning Call*, November 21, 1934: 20.
23. Associated Press, "Babe Ruth Breaks Bat Playing Cricket, Then Stirs Up Controversy," *Calgary* (Alberta) *Herald*, February 12, 1935: 7.
24. John Lardner, "Babe Misses Match with Ace of Cricket," *Lincoln* (Nebraska) *Journal Star*, February 13, 1935: 11.
25. Talbot, "Babe Busts a Bat."
26. M.H. Hamilton, "Cricket Is No Game, Says Mr. Babe Ruth," *Windsor* (Ontario) *Star*, February 28, 1935: 22.
27. Associated Press, "Golf Ball Nearly Drills Babe Ruth," *Brooklyn Daily Eagle*, February 25, 1935: 9.
28. Hamilton.
29. Montville, 336.

Sale of the Century: The Yankees Bought Babe Ruth for Nothing

By Michael Haupert

On January 5, 1920, the New York Yankees announced that they had purchased the contract of Babe Ruth from the Boston Red Sox. The next morning's *New York Times* erroneously reported the sale price as $125,000. The actual purchase price was $100,000, payable in four annual installments of $25,000 at 6 percent interest. New York had made the first payment on December 19, 1919. Including interest, the Yankees paid $108,375 for Babe Ruth. Or so it appeared.

Any serious baseball fan would agree that the Yankees got the best of that bargain. Indeed, as research has shown, New York earned an astounding financial return on Ruth.[1] When The Babe left Boston for the Bronx, he already was a two-time American League home-run champion. Ruth bashed a major-league-record 29 homers in 1919, a mark he would eventually shatter.

Not surprisingly, Red Sox fans have cursed Harry Frazee's name for a century over that sale. But what if they knew all the details surrounding this transaction? Details that reveal just how sweet the deal really was for New York. It turns out that Harry Frazee, a theatrical agent and producer, actually paid Yankees co-owner Jacob Ruppert to take Ruth off his hands.

New York Yankee Babe Ruth in dugout at Fenway Park. 1933.
Leslie Jones photo, courtesy of the Boston Public Library.

Two parts of the deal led to this unfortunate (for Red Sox fans) outcome. The first one involved the three-year contract at $10,000 per season that Ruth had signed before the 1919 season. The second involved a loan. Both issues were known at the time, though the specifics were not. And as they say, the devil is in those details.

Even before the sale took place, Ruth had been making noise about wanting to renegotiate his contract. When the sale was announced, Ruth renewed his demands for a new deal and also called for a share of the sale price. While he did not get the latter, he did get the former. Anticipating just such a demand from Ruth, the Yankees had made provisions with the Red Sox to cover a salary increase.

Fearing their new ballplayer might threaten to hold out, the Yanks negotiated to have the Sox pay half of any salary increase or bonus that New York offered to Ruth for the duration of the deal, up to $5,000 per year. Indeed, the Yankees agreed to raise Ruth's compensation to $20,000 per year for the remaining two years. Because of this agreement, the Yankees actually paid Ruth only $15,000 per year through 1921, with the Red Sox reimbursing the Yankees for $5,000 each of the two years. Technically, the Yankees structured Ruth's new salary as the same $10,000 base salary, with another $10,000 in bonuses each year.

Considering this salary-sharing agreement, the Red Sox, in effect, returned $10,000 of the purchase price for Ruth to the Yankees, who in turn passed it on to Ruth in the form of higher compensation. Since it was the Yankees, and not the Red Sox, who negotiated this new contract with Ruth, the Yankees had to pay for it. Savvy negotiating by Ruppert got the Red Sox to chip in, effectively reducing the purchase price for Ruth from a total (with interest) of $108,375 to $98,375. But that was only small change compared to the impact of the loan.

When news of the sale first broke, there were reports that the deal was more complicated than the simple cash transaction announced by Colonel Ruppert.[2] Rumors began to crop up about a second part to the deal: a loan from the Yankees to Frazee in an amount ranging between $300,000 and $400,000. In this case, the rumors proved to be true. On May 25, 1920, Ruppert made a personal loan to Frazee for $300,000, with Fenway Park as collateral. Because Frazee owned the Red Sox and Ruppert owned half of the Yankees, and the collateral for the loan was Fenway Park, it was very much a part of the Ruth transaction.

The original terms of that loan called for Ruppert to lend the funds at 7 percent per year, with interest to be paid semiannually for five years. At the end of that time, Frazee would repay the $300,000 or forfeit the rights to the Fenway Park mortgage, allowing Ruppert to dispose of the park as he saw fit.[3]

The loan was not repaid in five years. And Jacob Ruppert did not sell the mortgage. In fact, he held the mortgage to Fenway Park for 13 years.[4] The loan was finally retired on July 29, 1933, by Thomas Yawkey, who had purchased the Red Sox earlier that year from Robert Quinn, who had bought the team from Frazee 10 years before that. Through the last three years of the Frazee ownership, the entirety of the Quinn ownership, and the first few months of the Yawkey era, Fenway Park belonged to Jacob Ruppert. And twice each year during that time, Jacob Ruppert cashed checks for $10,500. Beginning in May of 1925, Ruppert had the option of continuing to cash the checks, or auctioning Fenway Park to the highest bidder. As history shows, he elected to keep the income stream.

Actually, Harry Frazee never owned Fenway Park. Instead, the ballpark was owned by the Fenway Realty Trust, established in September of 1911, when then-Red Sox owner General Charles Taylor transferred the land that would become the site of Fenway Park to the trust and capitalized it with 1,000 shares at $300 each. Taylor and his son, John I. Taylor, owned most of the shares, and arranged for a lease of $30,000 per year between the Red Sox and Fenway Park.[5]

On May 24, 1920, owners of all 1,000 shares of Fenway Realty Trust stock voted and agreed unanimously to approve a $300,000 mortgage that, if foreclosed, would allow for the holder of that mortgage (Ruppert) to sell it. The trustees then turned over all 1,000 shares to the Jacob Ruppert Corporation, wholly owned by Jacob Ruppert, as collateral on the loan.[6] The Trust retained the rental income from the Red Sox, along with the responsibility of paying the property taxes and insurance. Ruppert earned $21,000 per year in interest while holding a mortgage on a very valuable asset – making the loan a solid investment.

To better understand the circumstances surrounding the loan, we need to return to October 1916, when Harry Frazee purchased the Red Sox from Joseph Lannin for $662,000. The price included Lannin's half of the shares in the Fenway Realty Trust. The Taylors held the other half of the shares. The deal involved a note for $262,000 from Frazee to Lannin, with shares in the Fenway Realty Trust held by Lannin as collateral. As a result, Frazee owned the Red Sox, but not Fenway Park, though he would own half of the ballpark when he retired the note.[7]

Three years later, Harry Frazee was strapped for cash. He was simultaneously trying to pay off his note to Lannin, buy out the Taylor interest in Fenway Park, and purchase the Harris Theater on Broadway. Frazee had valuable assets. While he was not necessarily broke, he certainly didn't have enough cash on hand to buy the additional assets he wanted. Thus, the necessity for the loan that was negotiated with Jacob Ruppert in December of 1919 at the same time that the deal for Ruth was finalized.

On May 3, 1920, Frazee retired the note he owed Lannin, securing his share of Fenway Realty Trust stock. That same day, he purchased Taylor's shares of the Trust after nine months of negotiations. He now controlled all of the stock free and clear of any encumbrances and promptly gave up the control as collateral on the loan from Ruppert, which was finalized on May 25.[8]

If the loan had been paid off on the original date five years after the loan, the total interest paid would have been $105,420. In addition to the $10,000 that the Red Sox had agreed to pay the Yankees to help cover Ruth's salary, the total amount of money flowing from Frazee to Ruppert and the Yankees as a result of the Ruth deal was $115,420, or $7,045 more than the Yankees sent to Frazee for Ruth. But the Red Sox weren't done paying yet.

As noted earlier, the loan was not repaid until July of 1933. While the mortgage record does not show how much Yawkey paid to retire the debt, if he paid the entire $300,000, then Ruppert would have received a total of $276,920 in interest payments over the 13-year period of the loan. One reason he may have been willing to hold the mortgage for 13 years was that the 7 percent interest he was receiving was better than he could have earned anywhere else on a similarly risky asset. And, of course, the terms could have been renegotiated to raise the interest rate. There would have been no reason for Ruppert to negotiate a lower interest rate because he controlled the fate of the ballpark as of May 25, 1925, when the original five-year loan was not repaid. It really does not matter why Ruppert held the mortgage for so long. Doing so was a personal financial decision. And the point here is that five years after purchasing Ruth, Frazee had paid more to Ruppert and the Yankees in the Babe Ruth deal than he received. By the time the deal finally closed, Ruppert had actually received nearly three times as much from the owners of the Red Sox as he paid for Ruth, making it the sale of the century, or, as some saw it, the steal of the century.

Notes

1. Michael Haupert, "Babe Ruth: Better than the Dow Jones," *Outside the Lines*, Society for American Baseball Research, Spring 2008: 1, 12-17. Michael Haupert, "The Sultan of Swag: Babe Ruth as a Financial Investment," *Baseball Research Journal* 44 No. 2 (Fall 2015): 100-07.

2. "Ruth Bought by New York Americans for $125,000, Highest Price in Baseball Annals," *New York Times*, January 6, 1920: 16.

3. *Hermann et al Trustees to Jacob Ruppert of New York*, Suffolk County Deeds, May 25, 1920, pp. 4226.49-4226.55.

4. *Jacob Ruppert of New York to Yawkey*, Suffolk County Deeds, July 27, 1933, pp. 5398.234-5398.236.

5. For a thorough history of Fenway Park, see Glenn Stout, *Fenway 1912* (Wilmington, Massachusetts: Mariner Books, 2012).

6. *Hermann et al Trustees to Jacob Ruppert of New York*, Suffolk County Deeds, May 25, 1920, pp. 4226.49-4226.55.

7. James C. O'Leary, "American Leagues Patch Up Quarrels," *Boston Globe*, February 11, 1920: 7.

8. Michael T. Lynch Jr., *Harry Frazee, Ban Johnson and the Feud That Nearly Destroyed the American League* (Jefferson, North Carolina: McFarland & Company, Inc., 2008), 121.

The Mystery of Jackie Mitchell and Babe Ruth

By Leslie Heaphy

Jackie Mitchell with Babe Ruth and Lou Gehrig.
Courtesy of the National Baseball Hall of Fame.

On April 2, 1931 history was made in Chattanooga, Tennessee. That same day a mystery was also born. Seventeen-year-old Jackie Mitchell took the mound against the New York Yankees, striking out Babe Ruth and Lou Gehrig before walking Tony Lazzeri. Mitchell placed her name in the record books with the strikeouts but also became part of an ongoing debate and mystery regarding the circumstances surrounding the game.

Who was Jackie Mitchell? Where did she come from? Did she really strike out the Yankee stars or was it all a publicity hoax?

Born Virne Beatrice Mitchell on August 29, 1913, Mitchell grew up in Memphis, Tennessee. Her mother sold hosiery and her father was an optician. Mitchell was encouraged by her father to take part in sports. Growing up, she played basketball, tennis, and baseball, and swam. As a youngster Mitchell supposedly learned to pitch from one of the family's neighbors, Dazzy Vance. She later told reporters that Vance taught her a drop ball, or sinker. Vance had pitched for the Dodgers, winning the National League MVP in 1924. When she was a teenager, Mitchell's family moved to Chattanooga. Mitchell joined a local baseball school and it was here that the new president of the Chattanooga Lookouts saw her pitching.

Joe Engel signed on as the new president of the Lookouts in 1929 and in 1931 he followed a common practice of minor-league teams arranging exhibition games with major-league clubs. The New York Yankees were returning north after spring training in 1931 and Engel was able to sign a contract for two exhibition games. Shortly after setting up these games, Engel signed Mitchell to a contract, announcing that she would pitch in one of the games. And here is where the real debate begins. Did Engel sign Mitchell for real or was she just a publicity stunt? It was the heart of the Great Depression and teams everywhere were adding special events and exhibitions to make money. Signing Mitchell could certainly be seen in that light.

When Mitchell signed her contract, she became only the second woman to sign an Organized Baseball contract. The first was Lizzie Arlington, who signed to play with the Reading Coal Heavers in 1898. Female baseball players on men's teams were not a common sight. Most women playing baseball were part of the bloomer teams that barnstormed the country from the 1910s through the 1930s. Engel would have certainly seen the opportunity to bring in fans to watch Mitchell pitch, especially against the Yankees. About 4,000 fans were reported in the stands to watch Mitchell get a chance to pitch against Babe Ruth.

Engel had a reputation for pulling off crazy stunts, so the strikeouts could have been staged. Engel raffled off a house to a fan and traded a shortstop for a turkey. He then cooked the turkey and served it to the local reporters. He later sold "stock" to fans to save the ballclub from being sold. He held an elephant hunt in the outfield before a game, offering fans the chance to hunt some papier-mache animals. Engel's willingness to try just about anything to generate publicity has led many researchers and fans to believe the strikeouts were staged. An added fact was that the game was originally supposed to take place on April 1 but was postponed due to cold. The exhibition could have been an April Fool's Day joke.[1]

So what actually took place on April 2, 1931? The Lookouts started Clyde Barfoot against the Yankees but Barfoot never got past the first two batters. He gave up a leadoff double and then a single before Engel called Mitchell in to the game. Mitchell entered the game as a 17-year-old southpaw preparing to pitch to the Sultan of Swat, Babe Ruth. Prior to the game, publicity photos were taken of Mitchell with Ruth and Gehrig. The photos showed a slight young girl in an oversized uniform with a grin on her face and Ruth and Gehrig looking more solemn. They even had her take out a mirror and powder her nose.[2]

After throwing a few warm-up pitches, Mitchell threw two pitches that Ruth swung at and missed. She followed that with a called third strike. Ruth threw his bat in disgust and stormed back to the dugout. Some stories at the time claimed he turned and smiled before he left the field, adding to the idea that the whole thing was staged. Next up was Lou Gehrig and Mitchell struck him out with three pitches as well. She then walked Tony Lazzeri and Engel took her out of the game in favor of bringing back Barfoot. The Lookouts went on to lose, 14-4, making the game less than memorable except for Mitchell's pitching. A few days after the game, Mitchell's contract was voided but she did not leave baseball. She continued to pitch for another Engel team, the Junior Lookouts. After barnstorming the rest of the 1931 season and some of 1932, Mitchell signed with the well-known bearded House of David nine. She was promoted as the famous girl pitcher. After playing with the House of David on and off for a few years, Mitchell retired from baseball in 1937 and went to work for her father. She claimed until the day she died in 1987 that the strikeouts were legitimate. Her own claims added to the debate.[3]

Other ideas that have been proposed to support the legitimacy of the strikeouts include her pitching itself but also Ruth and Gehrig. There were two runners on base when Ruth came up; would he have deliberately struck out to leave the runners stranded? Ruth hit a lot of home runs but he also struck out a great deal, making it believable that Mitchell could have struck him out. Add to that Gehrig's strikeout, which many believed he would never have agreed to stage. Teammate Lefty Gomez later stated in an interview that Yankee manager Joe McCarthy was too competitive to ever stage such strikeouts. Then there was Mitchell herself. She was a southpaw pitcher who had a good sinker/curveball-style pitch. She was also someone they had never faced before. Often pitchers do well the first time they face new hitters but not so much the second time around. She never faced them again since she was taken out of the game.[4]

The publicity before and after the game did not help either. One paper called the stunt a one-time deal. Another said she was a girl with a good changeup pitch but "swings a good lipstick."[5] The local paper took a different approach and talked about her pitching style and how unusual it was. The reporter also stressed her great control as a big asset for her. This reporter seemed to make the case for why she had a chance to strike out The Babe.[6]

So one thing is clear, 17-year-old Jackie Mitchell struck out Babe Ruth and Lou Gehrig on April 2, 1931. Her name went into the record books for that feat but the mystery remains. Were the strikeouts legitimate or staged? Even the film footage that exists cannot solve the debate, since it was too grainy to be any real help.

Sources

In addition to the sources cited in the Notes, the author also consulted:

Aubrecht, Michael. "Jackie Mitchell-The Pride of the Yankees," Baseball-Almanac.com, November 2003. baseball-almanac.com/articles/aubrecht8.shtml.

Cronin, Brian. "Sports Legend Revealed: Did a Female Pitcher Strike Out Babe Ruth and Lou Gehrig?" February 23, 2011.

latimesblogs.latimes.com/sports_blog/2011/02/sports-legend-revealed-did-a-female-pitcher-strike-out-babe-ruth-and-lou-gehrig.html.

Doster, Adam. "The Myth of Jackie Mitchell, the Girl Who Struck Out Ruth and Gehrig," *Daily Beast*, May 18, 2013. thedailybeast.com/the-myth-of-jackie-mitchell-the-girl-who-struck-out-ruth-and-gehrig.

Garau, Annie. "Did This 17-Year-Old Girl Really Strike Out Babe Ruth?" December 18, 2016, updated March 25, 2018. allthatsinteresting.com/jackie-mitchell.

Hiskey, Daven. "There Once Was a 17 Year Old Girl Who Struck Out Babe Ruth and Lou Gehrig Back to Back," *Today I Found Out,* July 12, 2012. todayifoundout.com/index.php/2012/07/there-once-was-a-17-year-old-girl-who-struck-out-babe-ruth-and-lou-gehrig-back-to-back/.

Pickles, Cathy, and Elissa Blattman. "Jackie Mitchell and the Bloomer Girls." June 27, 2017. womenshistory.org/articles/jackie-mitchell-and-bloomer-girls.

Schoenfield, David. "The Girl Who Struck Out Babe Ruth and Lou Gehrig." espn.com/blog/sweetspot/post/_/id/56180/tbt-the-girl-who-struck-out-babe-ruth-and-lou-gehrig.

YouTube Video. youtube.com/watch?v=qeDnHg7nubE.

Notes

[1] Zack Harold, "Jackie Mitchell Couldn't Win," *Lapham's Quarterly*, March 28, 2018. laphamsquarterly.org/roundtable/jackie-mitchell-couldnt-win.

[2] Tony Horwitz, "The Woman Who (Maybe) Struck Out Babe Ruth and Lou Gehrig.," *Smithsonian,* July 2013, smithsonianmag.com/history/the-woman-who-maybe-struck-out-babe-ruth-and-lou-gehrig-4759182/.

[3] Tayla Minsburg, "Overlooked No More: Jackie Mitchell, Who Fanned Two of Baseball's Greats," *New York Times*, November 7, 2018. nytimes.com/2018/11/07/obituaries/jackie-mitchell-overlooked.html; Theresa Vargas, "A Baseball Mystery: Did a Teenage Girl Really Strike Out Babe Ruth and Lou Gehrig?" *Washington Post*, April 5, 2017. washingtonpost.com/news/retropolis/wp/2017/04/05/a-baseball-mystery-did-a-teenage-girl-really-strike-out-babe-ruth-and-lou-gehrig/?utm_term=.9ffa682e1dcb.

[4] Horwitz.

[5] *New York Daily News*, March 30, 1931: 12.

[6] Mary Craig, "Jackie Mitchell: Beyond Babe Ruth," *Beyond the Box Score*, SB Nation, July 27, 2017. beyondtheboxscore.com/2017/7/27/16023858/jackie-mitchell-female-pitcher-babe-ruth-lou-gehrig.

Babe Ruth And Lou Gehrig

By Tara Krieger

Photograph signed to Babe Ruth by Lou Gehrig. *Courtesy of Hunt Auctions.*

Babe Ruth and Lou Gehrig weren't exactly best friends or worst enemies, weren't exactly master and pupil, weren't exactly equals on or off the field. Half a generation apart in age[1] and polar opposites in temperament, they shared a relationship that ranged between avuncular and distant, and the media generally filled in the rest.

Likely even the casual fan reading this article for the first time is aware that the two most feared bats of the Yankees' first great dynasty were a study in contrasts – one craving the spotlight, one hiding from it; one hedonistic, one almost puritanical. As much as Ruth's exploits were exaggerated, Gehrig's were understated. Ruth stayed out on all-night benders, losing track of how many hot dogs and women he'd had. Gehrig made sure to get 10 hours of sleep a night, was said not to touch alcohol or cigarettes (he did in moderation), and couldn't string two sentences together in front of a woman who wasn't his mother or, later, his wife.

Ruth, the established star, led the way during that era that rose during the Roaring Twenties and set during the Depression, and Gehrig, at least in the early going, was content to ride his coattails.

"It's a pretty big shadow," Gehrig said. "It gives me lots of room to spread myself."[2]

When Gehrig joined the Yankees, the lively ball era – in which soiled baseballs were immediately removed from the game, leading to a spike in offensive production – had been in full swing for a few years. But other than the Babe himself, no

American Leaguer had ever hit as many as 40 home runs until 1927.[3] And then Gehrig hit 47 that year to Ruth's immortal 60, and it became clear that celebrity had company.

Over 1,200 home runs socked between them; when Gehrig retired, his 493 dingers were second all-time to Ruth's 714. Over 4,000 runs scored (Ruth, 2,174; Gehrig, 1,888) and 4,200 runs batted in (Ruth 2,214; Gehrig 1,995).[4] Not to mention that they still occupy two of the top three spots in slugging percentage – Ruth, .690 (first); Gehrig, .632 (third)[5] – and are both among the top five in on-base percentage.[6] In that unforgettable 1927 season, they were singlehandedly outhomering whole *teams*.[7] Hard to believe that in the decade they regularly started alongside each other, 1925 to 1934, the Yankees won "only" four pennants and three World Series.

Number three and number four in the batting order – and eventually on the backs of their jerseys – the Home Run Twins; the Caliph of Clout and the Crown Prince; the Sultan of Swat and the Fence Buster; the Bambino and the Slambino. Ruth was a man of a million monikers, but generally the superlatives the sportswriters tried to bestow on Gehrig in the early days didn't stick around very long.[8] At least until writers noticed that Gehrig hadn't taken a day off in years and dubbed him the Iron Horse for his durability. But Gehrig coming into his own as a more unassuming superhero was right around the time that the Behemoth went bust. Shifting power dynamics or personalities opened a rift between the one-time odd couple, one that time and tragedy narrowed, but perhaps never quite closed.

Both the only surviving sons[9] of working-class German stock: Gehrig, from New York City, the son of immigrants; Ruth, from Baltimore, from an insular ethnic community where communicating via the Muttersprache was common around the house. That's about all they had in common.

Young Henry Louis and his domineering mother were a tight-knit duo – a counterbalance to his father, a habitually out-of-work lush. The Gehrigs stressed education and fitness as a means to a better life for their son; Lou lived with his parents until age 30. The Ruths were more dysfunctional, sending young George Herman away to a charity reform school at age 7, and divorcing a few years later. They had both died by the time the Babe was 23, and the writers often styled him an "orphan" (even if he himself did not).

On the pair's barnstorming trip in the fall of 1927, Ruth expressed envy of the parental relationship Gehrig had that he never enjoyed.

"You know, every town we go into, immediately on arrival he writes to his mother and what a wonderful thing it is to have a mother at his age," a misty-eyed Ruth told a reporter then, recalling that he lost his own mother as a "mere tot."[10]

To the extent that Ruth had any parental figures, he found them in the brothers at the St. Mary's Industrial School, in particular Brother Matthias, whom he credited with teaching him how to play ball. Pitching for St. Mary's, he caught the eye of Jack Dunn, the manager of the Baltimore Orioles of the International League, who signed him to his first professional contract in 1914, which ultimately led him to the Boston Red Sox rotation the following season. But his success as a pitcher was ancient history by the time Gehrig's name first appeared in the sports pages.

June 26, 1920 – Ruth, converted into a power-hitting outfielder, had been sold to the New York Yankees that offseason. Just two months into his Yankees career, he had already hit 22 home runs, on the way to nearly doubling the season record he'd set the previous season – from 29 to 54. He didn't go long that day,[11] but a 17-year-old kid dubbed the "Babe Ruth of the High Schools" did.

The baseball team of the now-defunct High School of Commerce in Manhattan had been chosen to travel to Chicago for a promotional intercity championship game against host Lane Technical High School. Gehrig's ninth-inning grand slam at the park now known as Wrigley Field ensured Commerce – and New York City – the 12-6 victory, and the scholastic title.

Newspapers in both cities bubbled with delight that the sandlot slugger had lived up to the hype[12] (albeit repeatedly mangling their subject's name[13]). "The real Babe never poled one more thrilling," wrote James Crusinberry of the *Chicago Tribun*e, who repeatedly referred to him as "'Babe' Gherig."[14]

Gehrig's athletic prowess won him a scholarship to Columbia University, where he both played first base and pitched.[15] His nine home runs in his lone season with the college club are still the stuff of legend – one off Columbia's famed sundial, another hitting the steps of the journalism building, both some 400-plus feet from home plate – and Yankees scout Paul Krichell, upon discovering this prodigious hitter while the team was visiting Rutgers, wired general manager Ed Barrow immediately that he'd "just seen another Babe Ruth."[16]

The year Gehrig broke in with the Yankees, 1923, Ruth won the AL Most Valuable Player and the Yankees inaugurated their eponymous Stadium. The Babe had hit a home run on Opening Day then, the first in the expansive new ballpark, built to accommodate the throngs rushing to see The Bambino. Over 74,000 strong had shown up to see The Babe's three-run blast, christening the area beyond the short right-field porch "Ruthville," and the park "The House That Ruth Built."

The day of that historic home run, some three miles southwest, Gehrig pulled off his own historic feat for Columbia – from the mound. The Lions southpaw had struck out 17 batters against Williams College – still a campus record that as of 2019 has been equaled but not surpassed – and somehow lost the game. A few weeks later, he'd forsake his quest for cap and gown for a cap and uniform.

So it was that the Titan of Terror should meet his sidekick for the first time in the Yankees clubhouse in June 1923. As teammate Waite Hoyt remembered, Yankees trainer Doc Woods had tapped Ruth on the shoulder as he was tying his shoes and introduced the rookie as "Lou Gehrig from Columbia."

"Hiya, keed," said The Babe, addressing Gehrig as he did most acquaintances, names not being his strength.[17]

A short while later, manager Miller Huggins led Gehrig out onto the ballfield and requested that he take batting practice. Gehrig, nervous, grabbed a bat, which happened to be Ruth's 48-ounce model. (Gehrig's bats throughout his career ranged between 35 and 40 ounces.)

Said Hoyt, "Ordinarily, a batter prizes his bat more than he does his watch. In this instance, Ruth could have said, 'Oh, no, kid, that's my good one, grab yourself another stick.' But somehow the Babe didn't protest; it choked in his throat. He said nothing."[18]

After a few misses and false starts, Gehrig found his swing, belting several into Ruthville.

Although Gehrig spent most of the 1923 season at Hartford (and 1924 after that), fans caught their first glimpse of what was to come on September 27, when Gehrig started and batted cleanup behind Ruth for the first time, in Boston.[19] In the first inning, Ruth tripled, and Gehrig drove him in with his first major-league home run, over the right-field fence at Fenway Park. The next day, the duo went a combined 9-for-13 with seven runs and seven RBIs (Ruth, 5-for-6, with two doubles and a home run; Gehrig, 4-for-7 with three doubles), in a 24-4 rout. Ruth and Gehrig would also occupy the middle of the lineup in the Saturday doubleheader that closed out the Red Sox series.

The Yankees had already locked up the pennant at that point, and that fall, Gehrig – ineligible for the postseason because he was called up after September 1 – watched from the bench as Ruth batted .368 (7-for-19) with three home runs en route to the Yankees' first World Series title.

When Gehrig and Ruth next shared the starting nine, on the fateful June 2, 1925, the Yankees were a mess. Floundering in seventh place (of eight), the team was ravaged by age and injury – most notably Ruth, whose personal life finally seemed to be catching up with him. Increasingly at odds with his wife, Helen, and in love with his mistress, Claire – whom he would marry four years later – The Babe had shown up to spring training in St. Petersburg, Florida, out of shape and out of control. His weight had ballooned to at least 256 pounds on his 6-foot-2 frame, and he had little regard to bringing it down, gorging on food and parties and sex and alcohol (yet somehow he managed to bat .447 during the preseason). A bout with the flu didn't help. On April 7, as the Yankees train made its way north, Ruth collapsed on the platform in Asheville, North Carolina, from what became known as "the bellyache heard 'round the world."[20] The official diagnosis was an intestinal attack requiring abdominal surgery, but rumors spread that he had gotten sick from downing too many hot dogs; that he had contracted venereal disease; or, worst of all, as a media outlet in London put it, that he was dead.[21]

Not quite that extreme, but it did keep Ruth out of uniform until June 1. Gehrig, intermittently starting and pinch-hitting in 12 of the Yankees' first 42 games, was batting .167. The day of Ruth's return, he pinch-hit in the ninth and flied out to left in a loss to Washington. The next day, June 2, Huggins decided to shake up the lineup and gave Gehrig the start over regular Wally Pipp, at first base and in the sixth spot in the order.[22] He went 3-for-5 to raise his average almost 75 points. With Ruth batting fourth and going 2-for-4, the Yankees beat the Senators, 8-5. The next time a Yankees box score would appear without the name "Gehrig" was May 2, 1939– so went the unheralded beginning of the Streak of 2,130 games.

As Gehrig hung on Huggins's every word for help en route to a respectable rookie season – .295 (second-highest among teammates), 20 home runs (third), 68 RBIs (second) – Ruth continued to spiral, showing little effort to get in playing shape. On August 29 Huggins finally had it with his troublesome prima donna and suspended him. In the ensuing shower of obscenities between manager and player,[23] Huggins insisted Ruth would not be allowed in uniform again until he at least apologized. A week later, a contrite Ruth swallowed his pride, and Huggins relented. Seemingly reinvigorated, Ruth amassed almost half his offensive statistics for the year in the month of September,[24] but it was too little, too late – for Ruth (.290 average, 25 home runs, 67 RBIs) and for the 69-85 Yankees.

The addition of Gehrig to the batting order added a measure of protection for Ruth in the lineup; pitching around his lefty bat meant facing an equally fearsome left-hander with a runner on base. Gehrig and Ruth would appear in 1,344 regular-season starting lineups together as teammates, in 927 of which Ruth hit third and Gehrig fourth (and another 194 when Gehrig hit third and Ruth fourth). Although intentional walks were not regularly totaled during Ruth's era, Ruth held the career record with 2,062 walks for 66 years – and although he still led the league for seven of the 10 seasons he and Gehrig were regular teammates, he walked somewhat less with Gehrig behind him.[25]

However, they weren't quite there yet in 1926. Ruth put forth another banner year – leading the league in on-base percentage, slugging percentage, runs, RBIs, total bases, and of course home runs (and walks), and the Yankees to another pennant. Gehrig, albeit still developing, led the AL in triples and extra-base hits and spent much of the season batting in front of Ruth. However, in the World Series, which the Yankees lost to the Cardinals, he batted fifth to Ruth's third, with Bob Meusel in between them.[26] Gehrig drove in both runs in the Yankees' Game One victory, including Ruth for the go-ahead in the sixth, and batted .348 for the seven-game set.

But in the span of notable Yankees moments in that fall classic, probably two of the top three belong to The Babe (the third being Cardinals pitcher Grover Cleveland Alexander striking out Tony Lazzeri in Game Seven). Ruth became the first person to hit three home runs in a World Series game, when he kept a promise he'd hit one for injured little Johnny Sylvester. (Less known is that Gehrig sent the boy the ball that made the last out of the Series.)[27] Ruth also caused the last out – and the Yankees' loss – when he was caught stealing in the bottom of the ninth of Game Seven. Gehrig was kneeling in the on-deck circle. Neither Ruth nor Gehrig would ever lose another World Series game as teammates – as the Yankees swept their way to titles in 1927, 1928, and 1932.

The year 1927, in which the team epitomized its "Murderers' Row" nickname[28] and won 110 games, saw a concerned Gehrig heading down to spring training early amid rumors that the team was in the hunt for a right-handed first baseman,[29] and Ruth reporting late after filming a movie, performing on the vaudeville circuit, and holding out for more money. Ruth had demanded as much as $150,000 and settled for three years at $70,000 per. (Gehrig, not yet a household name, was among the first to sign, for $8,000.)

When Ruth finally joined the team, he started slow. It was big news on Opening Day when Ruth removed himself from the lineup for a pinch-hitter, and he was fighting a cold. Two weeks in, he was batting .250 with just one RBI (a home run); Gehrig was hitting .459 and had already driven in 19. Then the weather started to heat up, and so did the Babe. What was less anticipated was that Lou wouldn't cool. Throughout the summer, they traded shot for shot, Ruth going deep, then Gehrig. Whispers abounded about whether the King of Swing or the young usurper would make a run at Ruth's record 59 home runs set in 1921.

Lou Gehrig and Babe Ruth on July 4, 1939 on Lou Gehrig's last day at Yankee Stadium. *Courtesy of the National Baseball Hall of Fame.*

But writers kept it in perspective. "Lou Gehrig isn't another Babe Ruth because there will never be another Babe Ruth," wrote Frank Graham in the *New York Sun*, "No one else has ever hit a baseball as far as the Bambino when he truly leans on it, and doubtless no one else ever will, nor has any other player ever had quite the color of the Babe. Yet Gehrig is the nearest approach to Ruth in modern baseball."[30]

"There was just as much noise when Ruth struck out in the fifth as when Gehrig hit his home run with the bases full in the ninth," wrote Rud Rennie of the *New York Herald Tribune* after a game in May. "They don't pay to see Gehrig hit 'em."[31]

"Gehrig, of course, cannot approach Ruth as a showman and an eccentric," wrote Paul Gallico. "Right now he seems devoted to fishing, devouring pickled eels, and hitting home runs, of which three things the last alone is of interest to the baseball public. For this reason it is a little more difficult to write about Henry Louis than George Herman. Ruth is either planning to cut loose, is cutting loose, or is repenting the last time he cut loose. He is a news story on legs looking for a place to happen. He has not lived a model life, while Henry Louis has, and if Ruth wins the home run race it will come as a great blow to the pure."[32]

Physically, they were a study in contrasts, too. Overindulgence often impeded Ruth's staying in shape, and by 1927 his once tall and leanly athletic frame had developed the famed paunchy midsection that seemed to balance precariously on spindly legs. His face – the upturned nose, the wide grin – was cartoonishly recognizable. Gehrig, with his less distinctive All-American profile, appeared "much more the natural athlete," wrote Robert Edgren of the *New York Evening World*. "His shoulders slope, his neck is long and thick, his arms are like an ordinary man's legs, and his wrists and hands might make him a world's champion knocker-out if he went in for boxing instead of baseball."[33]

Even the way they hit home runs was different.

"When Babe Ruth knocks out a home run he puts everything, from his ankles to his ears, into the clout," Edgren continued. "Babe follows through like a golfer. He uses every flexible muscle in his body, in his legs, and in his long arms.

"Lou Gehrig is a shoulder hitter. He takes a short chop at the ball. He is not a long swinger like Ruth."[34]

"His powerful arms which extend from his more powerful shoulders enable Gehrig to hit to all fields without extra effort," wrote Arthur Mann of the *New York Evening World*. "He is known as a stiff-arm swinger, in contrast to Ruth, who is the pivoting, free-swinging type. Ruth's power comes from the tremendous swing and the fact that his timing is perfect. Gehrig does not swing his bat much. His arms and shoulders are so strong that when the bat meets the all it has about the same momentum as Ruth's."[35]

Fred Lieb of the *New York Post* recalled the press box being divided in 1927 – with Ford Frick, Bill Slocum, and Marsh Hunt rooting for The Babe, and Arthur Mann, Will Wedge, and himself rooting for Gehrig.[36] As for the pair themselves, any rivalry between them for the title appeared at worst good-natured competition. Ruth called Gehrig "one of the finest fellows in the game."[37] Gehrig said of Ruth, "I get more kick out of seeing him hit one than I do from hitting one myself."[38]

As late as September 5, the pair were tied with 44 homers apiece. Then Gehrig's mother was hospitalized with an inflamed goiter. Surgery was required. Lou's bat went cold; he hit just three more.

"I'm so worried about Mom that I can't see straight," Gehrig told Lieb. "If I lost her, I don't know what I'd do."[39]

Ruth, meanwhile, exploded, hitting 16 home runs in the Yankees' final 24 games. The record-breaking 60th came on September 30, 1927, off the Senators' Tom Zachary. "Sixty! Count 'em, sixty! Let's see some other son of a bitch top that!" he famously said.

In the clubhouse after the game, he less famously said, "Will I ever break this again? I don't know and I don't care, but if I don't I know who will. Wait till that bozo over there (pointing to Gehrig) gets waded into them again and they may forget that a guy named Ruth ever lived."[40]

It was preposterous, of course, that "the guy who hit all those home runs the year Ruth broke the record" (as Franklin P. Adams of the *Herald Tribune* put it)[41] would ever erase the memory of The Bambino, particularly with Gehrig's final home run of the season a day later being anticlimactic and all but unsung. But it is a wonder Lou drove in a then-record 173 runs (Ruth held the record previously) when the Babe ensured that the bases were empty at least 60 times before Gehrig even got to bat. And altogether fitting that one of the few career offensive categories in which Gehrig bested Ruth was in RBIs per game (0.92 to 0.88). RBIs are the least heralded of the three traditional Triple Crown categories, not as readily tied to a player's identity as his batting average and generally not as memorable as watching a ball fly 400 feet.

Gehrig also batted .373 (to Ruth's .356), led the league in total bases (447) and doubles (52), and was second to Ruth in slugging percentage (.765). The accomplishments won him the American League Most Valuable Player Award … in part because Ruth did not qualify, as at the time no player could win it more than once.[42]

"If he keeps smackin' 'em, he'll be in the big dough," Ruth said.[43]

Ruth had somewhat of a hand in boosting Gehrig's image. In August Gehrig had parlayed his newfound fame into a contract with Ruth's manager, Christy Walsh. It was Walsh who had booked Ruth's numerous endorsements, organized his offseason exhibition and entertainment schedule, created a trust fund to house his income so The Bambino wouldn't blow it all at once on broads and booze. That offseason, when Ruth embarked on a three-week, 21-city barnstorming tour across America, he took Gehrig with him.

They headed regional teams consisting of semipro, prep-school, or minor-league players, Ruth, the flashy batman with the magnetic personality, wearing the dark Bustin' Babes uniform; Gehrig the shy boy wonder wearing the light Larrupin' Lous. Sometimes they hit home runs; when they couldn't, they took the mound trying to strike each other out. They signed pregame autographs, visited children's homes, were feted by local Elks Clubs. Sometimes they gave speeches over the local airwaves, including a forgettable "comedy" routine (where the only thing worth laughing about was how uncomfortable they were reading lines).[44] Ruth (.616, 61 hits, 20 home runs) was paid $28,281.93 for the trip. Gehrig (.618, 55 hits, 13 home runs) made $9,000

– more than his annual Yankees salary.[45] He planned to give it all to his mother.[46]

Traveling around with Ruth was an education in celebrity. "Ruth taught me how to act while on parade," Gehrig said. "We'd have been to jail more than once if Ruth didn't know how to talk to traffic cops," perhaps a reference to Ruth's penchant for reckless driving.[47]

"You've got to be careful who you talk to and what you say," Ruth told him.[48]

When they met the governor of New Jersey in Trenton, Ruth took the initiative to introduce Gehrig, who demurred. "The kid don't say much," Ruth said.[49]

Gehrig was so stiff, he was frequently the butt of Ruth's jokes, too. Dining in transit, Ruth would ask for "steak a la Gehrig." The incredulous serving staff would make sure they heard him right. "We never had a similar order, Mr. Ruth. Can you tell me how you want this steak?"

At which point, Ruth would deliver the punch line: "Good and thick, that's how I want it. That's steak a la Gehrig."[50]

They both enjoyed card games on road trips and were often bridge partners. Teammate Bill Werber recalled Ruth slowly imbibing whiskey as he played to stay loose. "Ruth would start making bad bids just to aggravate Gehrig," Werber said. It always worked – eventually, the stone-cold sober Gehrig would throw down his cards and stomp off in exasperation. Game over.[51]

Gehrig's reluctance to take risks permeated into his salary negotiations; in spite of Ruth's urging to hold out for what he was worth – when players had little bargaining power in the era of the reserve clause – Gehrig was often too eager to sign what was in front of him and hold onto his job. In contrast to Ruth, who, in spite of never being able to top his desired 100 grand a season, was able to legendarily brag about his Depression-era $80,000 salary being higher than President Hoover's because he "had a better year."

Before 1930, Ruth told Gehrig to hold out with him to give them a stronger position. Gehrig said, "I don't think so," and signed. Ruth biographer Robert Creamer said that "Ruth was always a bit contemptuous of him after that, as he was of Gehrig's spending habits."[52] Teammates used to rib Gehrig about saving the first dollar he ever earned – which may not have been too far off. Later surfacing among Gehrig's things was a postal savings certificate for exactly one dollar dated October 1, 1914, when he was 11 years old.[53]

"Surely Babe was ridiculous when he left a ten dollar tip where fifty cents would have been generous. But Lou's dimes were just as silly," said Claire Ruth.[54]

Still, there were times when Gehrig gladly followed Babe's lead. A particularly raucous celebration on the train back from St. Louis after the Yankees' back-to-back World Series win in 1928 saw Babe and Lou going after people's shirts, culminating with Gehrig crashing through the door of Yankees owner Jacob Ruppert's compartment and fighting with Ruth for the Colonel's lavender pajama top.[55]

They developed their own code for dealing with the public on barnstorming trips – when one of them tired of speaking with fans, he would drag his finger along his sleeve like sharpening a razor – the visitor had become a "barber"; cut him. The other one would then create a diversion to break up the conversation.[56]

They went hunting and fishing together (with an oft-circulated photo showing off their catches – The Babe, naturally, has two fish on the line to Gehrig's one). Gehrig took golf lessons in an attempt to join Ruth in one of his favorite pastimes, until he discovered it was cramping his swing.[57] Ruth became a frequent dinner guest of Mom and Pop Gehrig, who bonded with him because he could converse in their native German. One day he gifted them a Chihuahua, and Mom Gehrig named it Jidge, a corruption of "George," which Ruth's clubhouse and card-playing buddies sometimes used.

Ruth brought his adolescent daughter, Dorothy, in tow so often that she had her own room in the Gehrig house, and considered them her "second family." Searching for "motherly attention," she became close with Mom Gehrig, who looked upon Dorothy as the daughter she never had the opportunity to raise. Dorothy also used to watch Lou shave before he left for the ballpark.

"What young girl wouldn't have had a crush on New York's most eligible bachelor?" Dorothy said.[58]

When Ruth's estranged first wife, Helen, died in a fire in the winter of 1929, Gehrig sent him a letter of "heart-felt sympathy," addressing Ruth as "George." He wrote, "May the Almighty grant you and Dorothy sufficient strength to bear up during your bereavement. Your sincere friend, Lou Gehrig. Key West, Florida, where happiness reigns on a fishing trip I wish you shared."[59]

Meanwhile, on the diamond, Gehrig couldn't even claw himself from Ruth's shadow when he tried. On April 26, 1931, he had a two-run home run called back when teammate Lyn Lary, thinking the ball had been caught, didn't circle the bases. At the end of the season, it cost him sole possession of the home-run title – he and Ruth finished tied with 46 apiece. On June 3, 1932, Gehrig became the first modern player to hit four home runs in a single game (something Ruth would never do) – but had the fortuitous timing to do it the day popular Giants manager John McGraw announced his retirement, costing him top billing on the sports pages. In both the 1928 and 1932 World Series, Gehrig's accomplishments took a backseat to Ruth's singular feats. In the former, Gehrig batted .545 with four home runs; Ruth batted .625 with another three-home-run game. And in the latter, history remembers Ruth's alleged "Called Shot" in Game Three, but mentions less often that Gehrig also hit two home runs in that game (and batted .529 in the Series).[60]

"Let's face it. I'm not a headline guy," Gehrig once said. "I always knew that as long as I was following Babe to the plate I could have gone up there and stood on my head. No one would have noticed the difference. When the Babe was through swinging, whether he hit one or fanned, nobody paid any attention to the next hitter. They all were talking about what The Babe had done."[61]

According to wife Eleanor Gehrig, although Lou was amused that Ruth "could have five affairs in a night," he was annoyed that Ruth could "get away with all the things he did and remain on top." For Lou, living large wasn't the type of fame he wanted.[62]

The "feud" between Gehrig and Ruth is often simplistically attributed to a dispute arising from Mom Gehrig's offhanded comment about Claire Ruth not dressing her stepdaughter, Dorothy, as nicely as her biological daughter, Julia. An offended Claire relayed the remark to her husband, who confronted Gehrig about it. "Tell your mom to mind her own business!" Ruth said. Well! Nobody insulted Lou's mother! And the two supposedly never spoke again.

It wasn't that straightforward, and the cracks were numerous.

Lefty Gomez, a teammate starting in 1930, claimed that much of the Ruth-Gehrig rift was inflated rhetoric. "You keep hearing these stories about Babe and Lou not hitting it off," he recalled.

> "When you consider ballplayers are together from February until October, there are going to be squabbles. But Babe and Lou enemies? Not a chance. Babe was an extrovert in the extreme and Lou was an introvert. Babe threw his money around and Lou counted his pennies. Babe liked the high life and Lou enjoyed the opera and the philharmonic. Babe was glib with the press; Lou found it hard to come up with a snappy quip. There may have been comments here and there that caused temporary chagrin, but Babe and Lou were teammates and friends on and off the field. The press created a feud between Ruth and Gehrig that I never saw. Babe and Lou were both dear friends of mine as well as teammates, and I respected the fact that they lived life their own way. Nothing more, nothing less."[63]

Tension between the two more likely arose from Ruth's decline and ensuing frustration, at the same time as Gehrig found his voice and his identity.

Early signs of frigidity between the pair began to show in 1931, with the hiring of Joe McCarthy to manage. The Babe had thought he would be in line for a managerial position after retired teammate Bob Shawkey had been chosen following Huggins's death in 1929, so he resented the new manager from the beginning. McCarthy could be a disciplinarian – imposing a dress code and more rigorous conditioning requirements – and Gehrig appreciated his high expectations. The childless McCarthy saw Gehrig as the surrogate son he never had. The man-child Ruth, who spurned authority, could not adapt.

One night after losing a hand at bridge, Ruth remarked that he'd "butchered that one just like McCarthy handles his goddamn pitchers!" Gehrig bristled and told Ruth to control his mouth. The next day, he was still fuming; he complained to reporter Stanley Frank that Ruth popped off too "damn much," and that he had a special obligation to respect the game.[64]

By the mid-1930s, Ruth was pushing 40, fed up, and itching to manage a team himself – an opportunity that famously would never come. Old, slow, and out of shape, in 1934, his final season with the Yankees, he took a $17,000 pay cut and had his worst year since he became a full-time hitter (.288, 22 home runs, 84 RBIs), apart from maybe the injury-laden 1925. He started and finished just 31 of the 110 games he played.

Gehrig, meanwhile, won the Triple Crown in 1934 – the first and only season he surpassed Ruth in homers. His marriage Eleanor Twitchell in 1933 had done wonders for his confidence; the more bold Eleanor honed his celebrity, encouraging him to engage with fans and advertisers and to demand from the Yankees what he was worth contractually. His image of clean living and durability, which previously had repelled writers in search of a colorful quote, had shaped him into a team leader; he would be appointed the Yankees' captain in 1935.[65] His obsession with not missing a day of work had turned him into baseball's Iron Man – and he surpassed one-time teammate Everett Scott's record by playing in his 1,308th consecutive game on August 17, 1933.

Gehrig found a way to emerge from Ruth's shadow just as the shadow of Ruth was disappearing. Ruth played a fraction of a season with the Boston Braves in 1935, but he was little more than a sideshow and hung up his spikes by early June. A photo when the Yankees and Braves faced each other during spring training of Ruth and Gehrig perfunctorily shaking hands, exchanging concealed grimaces, tellingly showed how frosty their relationship had become.

The goodwill tour of Japan the previous winter – featuring Ruth, Gehrig, and 13 other American League stars – widened the rift. The pair must have been on speaking terms beforehand, as Ruth lent the stingy Gehrig $5,000 at the outset of the tour to last him until his paycheck.[66] They played alongside each other, and there are few reports of the group being anything but laudable ambassadors for the game[67] – and the Japanese went wild for Ruth.

But on the ship across the Pacific, something went wrong. It happened when Claire Ruth crossed paths one day with Eleanor Gehrig, Lou's wife of about a year. They pooh-poohed whatever bad blood there was between their husbands, and Claire invited Eleanor back to their cabin. The Babe was waiting, and alcohol was involved. Innocent revelry may have been all that occurred.[68] But Lou was worried sick that his new bride had disappeared for several hours, and The Babe was the source of his fury. Gehrig coldly blew off Ruth's peace offering.[69]

Said 18-year-old Julia Ruth to a friend upon passing by Gehrig one day on deck, "Don't stop. The Ruths don't talk to the Gehrigs."[70]

Wrote Eleanor Gehrig, "Their feud, their ridiculous new feud, didn't diminish the team's performance when it came to baseball; we simply went our separate ways, the Ruths and the Gehrigs. … It was silly, it was sad, that their final 'road trip' of any consequence should be queered by champagne, caviar and bruised feelings. But it was, and that's life in the showcase, too."[71]

Ruth gained more of Gehrig's ire when he attacked what Lou nurtured most: the Streak.

"I think Lou's making one of the worst mistakes a ball player can make by trying to keep up that 'iron man' stuff," Ruth told the Associated Press in January 1937. "He's already cut three years off his baseball life with it. He oughta learn to sit on the bench and rest. They're not going to pay off on how many games he's played in a row.

"The next two years will tell Gehrig's fate. When his legs go, they'll go in a hurry."[72]

Incensed, Gehrig responded shortly afterward, careful not to mention Ruth by name. "I don't see why anyone should belittle my record or attack it," he said. "I never belittled anyone else's. I'm not stupid enough to play if my value to the club is endangered. I honestly have to say that I've never been tired on the field."[73]

Clearly, Ruth was bored. Golf kept him busy ("If it wasn't for golf, I'd really miss baseball. I play 240 days out of the 365 now"[74]), and he could continue to pay his expenses simply by being himself – he bragged about the $1,500 he'd made recently appearing on the radio for five minutes. But he was still waiting for that phone call.

"I'm not interested in any business," he said. "I've had all sorts of offers. One week in an office and I'd be dead. I've had a chance to go into the front office of a major league club, but I'm not interested. I need fresh air. If I can't get a major league manager's job, I'll just take it easy. The minors are out."[75]

The closest Ruth got to managing was in 1938, when he coached the Brooklyn Dodgers. General manager Larry MacPhail picked him up on a whim upon seeing the crowds he drew as a spectator at Ebbets Field in June 1938,[76] offering him $15,000 for the balance of the season. There was never any promise that Ruth would succeed current manager Burleigh Grimes, but Brooklyn's dismal 69-80 record and Ruth's inability to get along with Grimes's successor, Leo Durocher, ensured that he wouldn't return.

Meanwhile, Gehrig, having surpassed 2,000 consecutive games, suddenly seemed on the decline. He still hit .295 with 29 home runs and 114 RBIs in 1938, but he went through prolonged slumps, and the ball didn't have the same pop. The next year was even worse, and after a game on April 30, 1939, when teammates congratulated him on fielding a routine groundball at first base, he voluntarily benched himself.

Perhaps his legs *were* starting to go – but not due to exhaustion. The cause was amyotrophic lateral sclerosis. The publicly released statement called it "chronic poliomyelitis," which masked its true effects – ALS is a degenerative neuromuscular disease that no one survives. The media simply reported it meant he was through with baseball.

"Just tell him I'm very sorry – deeply sorry," said The Babe from the clubhouse of the Quaker Ridge Country Club, where he was participating in a golf tournament. "I certainly hope for the best. He certainly had a real career while it lasted."[77]

The Yankees hastily organized a tribute for their fallen captain between games of a doubleheader on July 4, 1939. That was the day Gehrig through his tears proclaimed himself the "luckiest man on the face of the earth."

Dignitaries and former teammates, including Ruth, were invited to pay their respects. Gehrig applauded with the crowd over 61,808 as the Babe strode out in his white suit and took his place among the rest of the 1927 Yankees. "In 1927, Lou was with us, and I say, that that was the best ballclub the Yankees ever had," Ruth jovially addressed the crowd.

The Babe concluded: "What I should think Lou would do – I don't know if the club is gonna consider it or not – but my idea is to let Lou go up into the mountains – I saw a fishing rod here a minute ago – let him go up there and see if he can catch every fish there is." They shook hands; Lou mouthed, "Thank you."

The Babe put his arms around Lou in a giant bear hug – too often this moment gets cited as when their silly feud allegedly ended, but that feels overly simplistic – and the Babe whispered something in Lou's ear that made Gehrig, solemn throughout the ceremonies, crack a rare smile.[78]

The Associated Press claimed Ruth told him, "C'mon kid, C'mon kid. Buck up now. We're with you."[79]

Bill Dickey, Gehrig's best friend on the Yankees, claimed that Ruth and Gehrig were "never friends again" after all that had come between them, and this was clear on Lou Gehrig Day in particular, because "if you look close, Lou never put his arm around the Babe. Lou just never forgave him."

Although his point about who hugged whom is belied by photographic evidence, his overall observation may not be completely out of left field. Gehrig, who stayed on as a nonplaying captain with the team through the end of the season, was photographed with Ruth in the Yankee Stadium dugout during the 1939 World Series (in which the Yankees won their fourth straight championship). But if the pair did meet afterward, it didn't make the papers. Dorothy Ruth Pirone said in her memoir that Ruth did visit Gehrig "often" as his health deteriorated, over Claire's objections.[80] Though Ruth had his own health issues to contend with, having suffered two mild heart attacks within a year.

When Ruth learned of Gehrig's death at age 37 on June 2, 1941, he broke down. "No, no … this is terrible, terrible news. It can't be true," he said. "I knew how ill Lou was, but I think all of us hoped, even against hope, that he would fight his way out.

"Lou was like a son to me. When illness forced him to retire, I was as heartbroken as he was. Believe me when I say his memory should always be kept green as an inspiration to all of us."[81]

"I never knew a fellow who lived a cleaner life," he said in another interview. "He was a clean-living boy, a good baseball player, a great hustler. He was just a grand guy."[82]

Babe and Claire Ruth showed up to pay their respects at the church where Gehrig's body lay in state.[83] Holding back tears, as the Associated Press reported, he "brushed through a hundred fans who had trooped with him to the door of the church and who met him as he came out another door. Even in death, someone remarked, Gehrig shared the spotlight with his famous teammate."[84]

A photo of Ruth standing forlornly beside Gehrig's open coffin made the rounds in the press, but the word was that The Babe showed up visibly drunk at his teammate's wake, angering especially Eleanor Gehrig. "He certainly wasn't wanted by the Gehrigs, as there was friction between them for years," wrote songwriter Fred Fisher, a friend of the family.[85]

Thus, a few months later, when Hollywood wanted to turn Gehrig's life into *Pride of the Yankees*, Eleanor Gehrig objected to Ruth appearing in the picture "in the flesh. Feeling that he would make a further mess of baseball and ruin the beautiful tribute to Lou, who represented the clean side of the sport."[86] Eleanor, still very much in mourning, was afraid of Ruth's gargantuan presence in life consuming her husband's in death.

Christy Walsh believed otherwise: "To tell the life story of Lou Gehrig without some reference to Babe Ruth would be suicide from a box office or the critics' standpoint," he said, assuring Eleanor she'd have control over the nature of Ruth's inclusion.[87] The general compromise was that Ruth would appear only with the Yankees en masse, not by himself. It didn't quite happen that way, but his role was limited enough to a supporting character in a film where Gary Cooper was clearly the star.

To appear in playing shape, Ruth crash-dieted to bring his weight down from around 270 to 223. A car accident, followed by an undisclosed illness that had him hospitalized shortly before shooting began, jeopardized his appearance. But he recovered in time to make it to the set to play a version of himself on the silver screen.

While *Pride of the Yankees* was a box-office success in 1942, *The Babe Ruth Story*, based on Ruth's ghostwritten autobiography with Bob Considine, became a box-office joke. Released while Ruth was dying of cancer in 1948 (he showed up to the premiere doped up on meds and didn't last 20 minutes), the film starring William Bendix was at best hagiographic, at worst –particularly when it tried to evoke the same pathos as the Gehrig story had – a mawkish mess.[88]

Ruth had two "farewells" at Yankee Stadium: the Yankees held a "Babe Ruth Day" on April 27, 1947, and Ruth's cancer-ravaged figure trod out there in his famed number-3 uniform for the ballpark's 25th anniversary on June 13, 1948. The sound bites aren't as immediately recitable – Ruth's tautological "The only real game, I think, in the world is baseball" on the latter date gets the most quoted – but the sentimentality was. That day, which included a pregame contest between retired players, also officially kicked off an annual Yankee Stadium tradition – Old Timers' Day.

Ruth died two months later, on August 16.

Unlike Gehrig, who lay in state in two churches and whose funeral consisted of an under-10-minute ceremony in Riverdale before fewer than 100 intimates, Ruth in death was still attracting mayhem. His body was laid out at Yankee Stadium, where tens of thousands[89] waited hours to catch one last glimpse of The Bambino. His funeral service at historic St. Patrick's Cathedral in Manhattan featured 57 honorary pallbearers, the mayor and governor among them, 44 priests, and a packed house of 6,000.[90]

Less than two miles away from each other in Westchester County sit two adjoining cemeteries, Gate of Heaven, where Babe Ruth is buried, and Kensico, where Gehrig's ashes rest. Fans make the pilgrimages, leaving flowers and all kinds of baseball paraphernalia.[91]

Their enshrinement in Cooperstown also fit their personalities. Ruth was inducted into the Baseball Hall of Fame in 1936 as part of the inaugural class, and was present for much fanfare as the museum opened for business on June 12, 1939. Gehrig, chosen by special election in December 1939, didn't live to see an induction ceremony, which were held every two years at the time.

Their retired numbers – Gehrig first, in 1940, Ruth waiting until 1948 – sit side-by-side in left field at Yankee Stadium today. For years, their monuments also flanked each other as memorials (with Miller Huggins in between them) in fair territory at old Yankee Stadium – Gehrig's erected in July 1941, Ruth's in 1949 – and were moved to Monument Park upon the Stadium's renovation in 1976, and relocation in 2009.

Gehrig's monument says, "A man, a gentleman and a great ballplayer whose amazing record of 2,130 consecutive games should stand for all time." (Cal Ripken Jr. was 19 years away from being born.) Ruth's says simply, "A Great Ball Player, A Great Man, A Great American." Note the dedications, though: Ruth's, "erected by the Yankees and the New York Baseball Writers"; Gehrig's, "a tribute from the Yankee players to their beloved captain and team mate."

Both "great ballplayers," yet who said it was what mattered. Everyone loved The Babe, but the media said it loudest; Gehrig quietly gained respect from those who knew him. Contrasting sentiments on two monuments of the same size.

Notes

1. For much of his life, Ruth believed his birthdate to be February 7, 1894, a year older than he actually was. Gehrig was born on June 19, 1903.

2. Fred Lieb, *Baseball as I Have Known It* (Lincoln and London: University of Nebraska Press, 1996), 176.

3. Two had in the NL: The Cardinals' Rogers Hornsby hit 42 in 1922, and the Phillies' Cy Williams hit 41 in 1923.

4. In spite of extensive research, Ruth's RBI total is sometimes debated, as the RBI was not an "official" stat until 1920. For more research into Ruth's RBI total, see generally sabr.org/research/accurate-rbi-record-babe-ruth.

5. Ted Williams is second, at .634.

6. Baseball-reference.com lists the top five as Williams (.482), Ruth (.474), John McGraw (.466), Billy Hamilton (.455), and Gehrig (.447). As Hamilton and McGraw played largely in the nineteenth century, a case could be made for Gehrig and Ruth actually being in the top three.

7. Ruth's record-setting 60 homers were more than every other team in the American League and all but the Giants and the Cardinals in the National League; Gehrig's 47 round-trippers outdid Boston, Chicago, Cleveland, and Washington in the AL, and three teams in the NL.

8. "Columbia Lou," a reference to where Gehrig went to college, had some staying power, but it wasn't uncommon then for sportswriters to repeatedly pick up on a ballplayer with any background in higher education—"Harvard Eddie" Grant being another notable example.

9. The plague of infant mortality hit both families hard. Gehrig grew up essentially an only child; Ruth had only a younger sister, Mamie, who survived babyhood (and would outlive him).

10. He was actually 17, but Ruth, along with many writers on the circuit, was prone to exaggeration. Jane Leavy, *The Big Fella* (New York: HarperCollins, 2018), 265.

11. Ruth went 2-for-4 with a double that game; the day before – June 25 against Boston – he'd had his fourth two-homer game of the season.

12. The *Chicago Tribune* had singled him out as a player to watch, using the "Babe Ruth" moniker, on June 24, two days before the game took place.

13. The *New York Times* referred to "Gherrig"; the *Chicago Tribune* called him "Gherig"; the *New York Tribune*, "Cherrig."

14. Also: "It was a blow of which any big leaguer would have been proud and was walloped by a boy who hasn't yet started to shave." James Crusinberry, "New York Preps Down Lane Tech in Hitfest, 12-6: Gherig Swats Homer with the Bases Loaded," *Chicago Tribune*, June 27, 1920.

15. The scholarship was actually for football, which Gehrig also played for a season with Columbia.

16. Ray Robinson, *Iron Horse: Lou Gehrig in His Time* (New York: HarperPerennial, 1991), 58.

17. Robinson, 67-68.

18. Robinson, 68. Hoyt also retells the story with Ruth initially protesting, then thinking better of it: "I got others," he said. See Gary Sarnoff, *The First Yankees Dynasty* (Jefferson, North Carolina: McFarland 2014), 50-51.

19. Regular first baseman Wally Pipp had injured his ankle.

20. Interestingly, the column to which such a phrase has been attributed, W.O. McGeehan's "A Demigod Has Indigestion," in the *New York Tribune,* does not quite use that phrase. McGeehan's specific wording is, "It is not remarkable that the stomach ache of Babe Ruth was felt around the world." McGeehan also called Ruth's aliment "the stomach ache of a demigod," and called Ruth "our own national exaggeration." collection. baseballhall.org/PASTIME/demigod-has-indigestion-editorial-1925.

21 See Robert Creamer, *Babe: The Legend Comes to Life* (New York: Simon & Schuster, Pocket Books, 1976), 285-88. Author Jane Leavy also draws attention to reports the wound may have been a fistula, and that genetic intestinal diseases ran in Ruth's family. Leavy, 271.

22 For a debunking of the alleged "headache" that kept Pipp from the lineup that day, see David Mikkelson, "Wally Pipp's Career-Ending 'Headache,'" *Snopes*, August 3, 2003, snopes.com/fact-check/wally-pipp39s-career-ending-39headache39/.

23 The 6-foot-2 Ruth shouted at the 5-foot-6, 140-pound Huggins, "If you were even half my size, I'd punch the shit out of you!" To which Huggins retorted, "If I were half your size, I'd have punched you." Creamer, 292.

24 Before the suspension, Ruth hit .266 with 15 home runs and 36 RBIs over three months; after the suspension, he hit .346 with 10 home runs and 30 RBIs in four *weeks*.

25 Between 1920 and 1924 Ruth tallied .975 walks per game, or .217 per plate appearance; between 1925 and 1934, he had .844 walks per game, or .193 per plate appearance.

26 Meusel had led the AL in home runs and RBIs in 1925.

27 Sarnoff, 121-22.

28 The name was first bestowed on the 1921 squad, thanks to The Babe's 59 home runs and the rest of the starting lineup hitting at least four apiece. G.H. Fleming, *Murderers' Row* (New York: William Morrow & Company, Inc., 1985), 95.

29 Monitor, *New York World*, February 20, 1927, reprinted in Fleming, 38.

30 Frank Graham, *New York Sun*, June 25, 1927, reprinted in Fleming, 229.

31 Rud Rennie, *New York Herald Tribune*, May 8, 1927, reprinted in Fleming, 137.

32 Paul Gallico, *New York Daily News*, September 3, 1927, reprinted in Fleming, 327.

33 Robert Edgren, *New York Evening World*, August 13, 1927, reprinted in Fleming, 303.

34 Ibid.

35 Arthur Mann, *New York Evening World*, June 28, 1927, reprinted in Fleming, 236.

36 Lieb, 174.

37 Richards Vidmer, *New York Times*, August 1, 1927, reprinted in Fleming, 290.

38 Ford C. Frick, *New York Evening Journal*, July 2, 1927, reprinted in Fleming, 250.

39 Lieb, 174-75.

40 Arthur Mann, *New York Evening World*, October 1, 1927, reprinted in Fleming, 359. Mann added, "If the world forgets a guy named Ruth lived, it will be due to universal amnesia."

41 See Jonathan Eig, *Luckiest Man: The Life and Death of Lou Gehrig* (New York: Simon & Schuster, 2005), 103.

42 Using today's metrics, had Ruth been eligible, it's likely he would've edged Gehrig out. He had a higher WAR (12.4 to 11.8), and a higher OPS (1.258 to 1.240), though Gehrig slightly bested him in WPA (8.8 to 8.6). As it was, Gehrig only received seven of the eight first-place votes in 1927 – one went to teammate Tony Lazzeri.

43 Henry L. Farrell, "Babe Ruth Likes Prospects of Home Run Rival, Buster Gehrig," *Long Island Daily Press*, August 18, 1927.

44 "'Babe' and 'Lou' (The Home Run Twins)," Perfect Record Company, 1927, youtube.com/watch?v=6p2WZufrzQk (last visited May 3, 2019).

45 In addition to these sums, Ruth made $3,000 modeling clothing, and the pair split $4,700 in "pickup" money. Leavy, 464.

46 Eig, 117.

47 Leavy, 123.

48 Leavy, 122.

49 Leavy, 87.

50 H.G. Salsinger, "I Remember Babe," in Dan Daniel, *The Real Babe Ruth* (St. Louis: C.C. Spink & Son, 1948), 120-21.

51 Eig, 119.

52 Creamer, 382.

53 Robinson, 58.

54 Creamer, 382.

55 Frederick G. Lieb, "Life of Lou Gehrig," published in *The Sporting News' Baseball Register* (St. Louis: C.C. Spink & Son, 1942), 18.

56 Eig, 117.

57 Dorothy Ruth Pirone with Chris Martens, *My Dad, the Babe: Growing Up with an American Hero* (Boston: Quinlan Press, 1988), 105.

58 Pirone, 107. Dorothy reveals in her book that she was the product of her father's affair with a family friend who she did not know was her mother until the woman was on her deathbed in 1980. As for the Babe's two wives – Helen died before she was 8, and Dorothy had few positive things to say about her relationship with Claire.

59 *Boston Herald*, January 16, 1929, reprinted in Sarnoff, 200.

60 Gehrig is quoted as in awe of Ruth for "calling" his shot ("What do you think of the nerve of that big monkey, calling his shot and getting away with it?"), but also claimed Ruth was actually pointing at Cubs pitcher Charlie Root; from the on-deck circle, he overheard Ruth say, "I'm gonna knock the next pitch down your goddamn throat."

61 lougehrig.com/quotes.

62 Richard Sandomir, *The Pride of the Yankees: Lou Gehrig, Gary Cooper, and the Making of a Classic* (New York, Boston: Hachette Books, 2017), 68.

63 Vernona Gomez and Lawrence Goldstone, *Lefty: An American Odyssey* (New York: Ballantine Books, 2012), 184-85.

64 Robinson, 128.

65 Ruth had been appointed captain of the Yankees for all of five days in 1922. He lost the title after an altercation with an umpire and a fan led to a suspension.

66 Leavy, 413.

67 Creamer, however, mentioned an incident of Ruth getting overly agitated at Gehrig for showing up late to a morning event. Creamer claimed Ruth's reaction caused Philadelphia Athletics manager Connie Mack, who also managed them in Japan, to reconsider his plans to retire and let Ruth take over. Creamer, 383.

68 Rumors of an affair between Babe Ruth and Eleanor Gehrig are unsubstantiated speculation.

69 See Eleanor Gehrig and Joseph Durso, *My Luke and I* (New York: Thomas Y. Crowell Company, 1976), 189-90. June O'Dea Gomez, Lefty's wife, noted in her journal that she spent a night drinking with Claire Ruth and Eleanor Gehrig on the same Japan trip. Whether that was before or after the incident in the Ruths' cabin is unclear. Gomez and Goldstone, 185.

70 Creamer, 383.

71 Gehrig and Durso, 190-91.

72 "Babe Ruth Discusses Gehrig, Dean, The 1937 Pennant Races – and Golf," *New York Times*, January 27, 1937. No one could have any way of knowing how prophetic Ruth's words were – Gehrig had just about two seasons left in him, but playing every day wasn't what brought him down.

73 Robinson, 224. Gehrig would keep his word, voluntarily removing himself from the lineup when he could no longer play.

74 "Babe Ruth Discusses Gehrig, Dean, The 1937 Pennant Races – and Golf."

75 Ibid. Ruth had been offered the job of managing the Yankees' Newark farm club in 1934, but felt it a slap in the face. "Why should I have to go down to the minors first? Cobb and Speaker didn't," he said referring to Hall of Fame player-managers Ty and Tris. See Creamer, 376.

76 The headline that day was Johnny Vander Meer's second of back-to-back no-hitters.

77 Stanley Frank, "Gehrig Has Chronic Infantile Paralysis; Active Career Over," *New York Post*, June 21, 1939. The *Post* indicated Ruth may have found out about Gehrig's predicament the night before and played poorly in the tournament as a result.

78 Depending on which account of the events one reads, the embrace happened either before Gehrig's oratory, as a means of encouragement, or afterward, as a parting shot.

79 "Ruth's 'We're With You, Lou' Keynotes Tribute to Gehrig," Associated Press, *Buffalo Evening News*, July 5, 1939.

80 Dorothy does not say why Claire was against her husband visiting, though Dorothy spends much of her memoir speaking unfavorably of her stepmother. Dorothy also wrongly asserts her father visited Gehrig in the "hospital," when Gehrig was generally homebound as his illness progressed. Pirone, 112.

81 "Babe Ruth Cries When Informed of Death," International News Service, *Syracuse Journal*, June 3, 1941.

82 "Passing of Gehrig Mourned by City," *New York Sun*, June 3, 1941.

83 Eig claims that Babe and Claire Ruth were actually the second mourners – after general manager Ed Barrow and his wife – to arrive, lending credence to the fact that the two had mended fences. Eig, 356.

84 Gayle Talbot (Associated Press), "Final Simple Rites Held for Iron Man of Baseball," *Auburn* (New York) *Citizen Advertiser*, June 3, 1941.

85 Ray Robinson, "Ruth and Gehrig: Friction Between Gods," *New York Times*, June 2, 1991.

86 Sandomir, 67.

87 Sandomir, 66-67.

88 A subsequent effort at a cinematic adaptation of Ruth's life, *The Babe* (1992), went too much in the other direction – with John Goodman portraying Ruth as a fat, angry, gluttonous buffoon – and is largely unwatchable. A television film, *Babe Ruth* (1991), starring Stephen Lang, did an adequate job, but if not for the other two films of its genre being so terrible, would be otherwise unremarkable.

89 Jane Leavy estimates that as many as 77,000 filed past Ruth's coffin. Leavy, 471-72.

90 Seventy-five thousand people were waiting outside as the hearse pulled up. Leavy, 472, 474-75; contrast with Gehrig's funeral where a mere 250 fans stood outside the half-full Christ Episcopal Church in Riverdale. See Associated Press, "Simple Rites Mark Funeral Services for Lou Gehrig," *St. Petersburg Times,* June 5, 1941. news.google.com/newspapers?id=UeNOAAAAIBAJ&sjid=X00DAAAAIBAJ&pg=2384,7032962&dq=gehrig&hl=en.

91 See, e.g.,Corey Kilgannon, "Where Babe Ruth Still Draws Fans (and Liquor, Cigars, and Hot Dogs)," *New York Times*, October 5, 2018, nytimes.com/2018/10/05/nyregion/babe-ruth-grave-yankees-red-sox.html.

Babe Ruth and Ownership: Not a Match Made In Heaven

By Gary Sarnoff

He filled the ballpark with fans who craved to see him hit the long ball. His home runs forever changed the game from scientific baseball to power hitting, and he helped make people forget about the Black Sox scandal. Baseball owners cashed in on his uncanny ability to hit the baseball over the fence, but those owners also knew that having him under contract came with a price. Babe Ruth gave owners many headaches and more than a few gray hairs. He also made life difficult for his managers, umpires, and the commissioner. "He is one of the most selfish and inconsiderate players to ever put on a uniform," said Red Sox owner Harry Frazee.[1] "Ruth has taken more money from the Yankees than I have," said Yankees owner Jacob Ruppert during a salary squabble with Ruth.[2] Jack Dunn, Ruth's first professional baseball manager, once warned him to cool it or go home.

Babe Ruth's disrespect for authority began early in life. His parents, too occupied with their own issues, allowed him to run wild in the streets of Baltimore. With no supervision, he hung with the wrong crowd. Young Ruth stole, chewed tobacco, played hooky, and found other ways to cause trouble. "I learned to fear and hate the coppers and I threw apples and eggs at the truck drivers," he said about his childhood.[3] One time he took a dollar from the till of his father's saloon to buy ice cream for his friends. When his father learned about it, he took his son down to the cellar and gave him a thrashing. The lesson went unlearned, however, and young Ruth continued to steal from the till.

On June 13, 1902, the 7-year-old Ruth was sent across town to live at St. Mary's Industrial School for boys, a Roman Catholic training school for orphans, delinquents, runaways, incorrigibles, and boys who were from broken homes. Ruth was listed as incorrigible. He and the other boys were expected to abide by the rules, and if they failed to do so, they were punished. "These were used on Babe Ruth," a friend of Ruth's was told when guided to a room that had straps hanging from the walls during a tour of the home in later years.[4] "I used to get my discipline the old-fashion way. I knew when I had it coming," Ruth said about his time at St. Mary's.[5] Most of his offenses were due to smoking and chewing tobacco. While at St. Mary's, Ruth met a man, a Xaverian brother who was an authoritative figure and whom Ruth had the utmost respect for. "The greatest man I've ever known," Ruth would say about Brother Mathias, who spoke to the boys in a gentle manner and kept the discipline to the maximum.[6] "He was calm, considerate and gave everyone a fair break," a former resident recalled about Brother Mathias, "but if you ever double-crossed him, you were in big trouble."[7]

Brother Mathias ran the baseball program at St. Mary's, and he assigned every boy to a school team. Ruth excelled in the program to the point where he was placed on the school team, which represented St. Mary's in a league that played against other schools. He became so good that he caught the eye of Jack Dunn, the owner and manager of the Baltimore Orioles of the International League. Amazed that there were professional baseball leagues, Ruth had to ask Dunn to be sure he wasn't dreaming. "You mean you'd pay me?" he asked. Dunn laughed before answering. "Sure, I'll start you out at six-hundred per year." Ruth was awed when hearing this. "You mean six-hundred dollars?" Ruth asked. "That's right," Dunn confirmed.[8] Ruth was also surprised that the Orioles would pay for his meals. "You mean I can eat what I want, and it won't cost me anything?" he asked. "Sure, anything," a teammate confirmed.[9] That was all he needed to hear. Ruth ate and ate, and when he came up for air while devouring his third serving of wheat cakes and ham, he noticed that his teammates were watching in amazement. "I wouldn't have believed it if I hadn't seen it," a teammate said.[10] Dunn, with a wide grin on his face, walked over to Ruth and placed his hand on the rookie's shoulder. "We've got twenty-seven other fellows on this club," Dunn told him, "Leave them some food, will you?"[11]

Ruth traveled with Dunn and the rest of the Orioles to Fayetteville, North Carolina, for spring training in 1914. And it didn't take Ruth long to get into hot water. Dunn had given Ruth $5 to tie him over until he received his first paycheck. Ruth, seeing an elevator for the first time in his life, was fascinated. Like a little boy, he rode up and down the platform, instructing the hotel elevator operator to stop at each floor and open the door so he could poke his head out and look left and right. During a stop, the operator put the elevator in motion while Ruth was still scanning a floor. Luckily, a veteran yelled for Ruth to duck inside in the nick of time. When Dunn learned about the near-mishap and that Ruth had spent most of the $5 to bribe the elevator operator for rides, the manager bawled out the rookie. A few days later, Ruth persuaded a boy to lend him his bicycle. Ruth rode the bike at high speed, barreled around a street corner, and almost collided with Dunn. He then plowed into the back of a wagon and fell heavily to the ground. Ruth climbed to his feet while grinning with embarrassment. "If you want to go home, kid, just keep riding those bikes," Dunn warned.[12]

Ruth had a relationship with Dunn that he would never have with another manager or owner. Dunn had taken over guardianship of Ruth from St. Mary's, who had previously received that role from Ruth's parents. One day Dunn practically took Ruth by the hand as he escorted him from the clubhouse to the pitcher's mound. "Look at Dunnie and his Babe," someone quipped.[13] Some believe that was how George Herman Ruth got his nickname.

In mid-season 1914, with Dunn having financial difficulties, he began to sell his players. One day he called Ruth and two other players into his office to inform them that they were heading to the majors. They had been sold to the Boston Red Sox. Ruth wasn't impressed. Dunn excused the other two players and spoke with Ruth. He told him that the Red Sox were the big leagues and his salary would be increased. Ruth said it wasn't about money. Baltimore was home, the only home he knew. Dunn told Babe he had no choice.

In 1915 Red Sox owner Joe Lannin gave Ruth a $3,500 contract for the season, which made the young ballplayer very happy, for he had never seen that kind of money. "He had no idea whatsoever about money," said Red Sox manager Bill Carrigan. "He was getting $3,500 and that was all the money in the world. He didn't seem to think it would ever run out. He'd buy anything and everything. So, I drew Babe's pay and gave him a little every day. That generally lasted for about five minutes."[14]

After the 1916 season Harry Frazee, a 36-year-old New York theatrical man, bought the Red Sox. In 1917 Frazee came to Ruth's rescue after a dispute with an umpire that threatened to put Ruth on the suspension list. On June 23 Ruth was the Red Sox' starting pitcher against the Washington Senators in Boston. Disagreeing with an umpire's call, and after words were exchanged, Ruth belted the umpire. A heavy fine with a long suspension was certain, but Frazee, said to be a likable guy, sweet-talked American League President Ban Johnson into a reduced fine amount of $100 and a suspension of just 10 days.[15]

In 1918 the Red Sox players persuaded new manager Ed Barrow to put Ruth into the everyday lineup. Barrow, certain the 23-year-old Ruth was on his way to becoming one of the game's best pitchers, hesitated. Through the 1917 season, Ruth had hit nine homers in 361 at-bats, an amount that was almost good enough to lead the American League. Barrow tried it. The experiment was successful, and Ruth's popularity began to grow. Ruth was used in the everyday lineup and took his turn in the starting pitching rotation. The double duty combined with his active night life wore him out to the point where he was hospitalized.

Ruth loved to hit home runs and wanted to be a position player in the everyday lineup. He decided his pitching days were history. Barrow disagreed. The manager knew Ruth was one of the best pitchers in the league and left-handed pitchers were hard to come by. Ruth denied the manager's requests to pitch and kept making excuses to avoid it. He told the manager to stop bugging him. "I'm tired," Ruth said. "If you would get to bed on time, you wouldn't be so tired," said Barrow.[16] In Washington, Ruth swung when instructed to take the pitch. Barrow fined him $500. Ruth responded by leaving and heading back to Baltimore. He got in touch with a shipyard team and agreed to join. Frazee did not know this until he was informed while seated in the grandstand in Philadelphia, watching his Red Sox in action. He told the writers that Ruth had a contract with the Red Sox and could not do this and he would go to court if need be.[17] Knowing Ruth liked and respected Red Sox coach Heinie Wagner, Frazee instructed Wagner to go to Baltimore and fetch Ruth. Wagner did as he was told, visited Ruth and persuaded him to rejoin the Red Sox. When Ruth returned, Barrow gave him a cold shoulder. Upset about being ignored, Ruth blew up. He took off his uniform and said he was quitting for good. Wagner and Frazee and a few others surrounded him, calmed him, and persuaded to him stay. Frazee then spoke with Barrow and persuaded him to forgive. Barrow agreed to waive the fine, and Ruth agreed to pitch.

The year 1919 was the beginning of the end for the Red Sox era of dominance. Frazee began to trade and sell his best players. After winning three pennants and three World Series starting in 1915, the Red Sox fell to 66-71 and finished in sixth place. The Red Sox owner was losing money in his theater business and because of the risky deal he made when he bought the Red Sox for a high cost of $675,000. Two of Frazee's backers had paid half the amount in notes, putting him in a bind from the beginning. The owner became unpopular with the Boston fans and with Ruth, who continuously poked him by complaining that the Red Sox were a lousy outfit.[18]

Yankees manager Miller Muggins knew about Frazee's financial woes. The New York manager, known as the Mite Manager because he stood just 5-feet-4, advised Yankees owners Jacob Ruppert and Tillinghast Huston that Ruth might be available. Confirming that the controversial Boston star could be obtained, the Yankees owners went to work. "Selling Babe Ruth was the only way I could retain the Red Sox," Frazee would later say.[19] The deal cost the owners $100,000, plus a $350,00 loan.

Ruth didn't know anything about it. He had gone to Los Angeles. Huggins traveled west for an unscheduled meeting with his new star. After arriving in town, Huggins headed to the Griffith Park Golf Course and waited by the clubhouse, knowing Ruth would pass by after he completed his golf game. Finally, Ruth appeared, shaking his head after a poor round. He was eager to play another round before sundown, and while heading to the first tee, he met his new manager. Huggins introduced himself and told Ruth he would like to talk with him. Ruth said he didn't have time; he had to go somewhere.

Huggins: "Babe, would you like to play for the New York Yankees?"

Ruth: "Have I been traded?"

Huggins: "[hesitates] … The deal has yet to be finalized."

Ruth: "I like Boston and playing for the Red Sox. But I'll give you my best if traded. Just like I did in Boston."

Huggins: "Babe, you have been a pretty wild boy in Boston. In New York, you'll have to behave."

Ruth: "I already told you I will play the best I can. Let's get down to business. How much are you going to pay me?"

Huggins: "You have two years left on your contract for $10,000 per season."

Ruth: "I want more dough than that."

Huggins: "All right, if you promise to behave yourself, Colonel Ruppert will give you a new contract."[20]

The next time Huggins met Ruth was inside the Yankees team office and with the two owners present. "Huggins' word is the law," one of the owners said. Ruth took a puff from his cigar before responding. "Look at you. Too fat and old to have fun," he told one of the owners. "And as for this shrimp," Ruth said while pointing his thumb at Huggins, "he's half dead right now."[21] Ruth then got up from his chair and left the room while the two owners smiled. They could almost predict the future. They knew they had a great ballplayer with a lot of baggage.

Ruth's first spring training with the Yankees was a party. Jacksonville, Florida, the Yankees' spring-training site, was a festive town, and when Huggins made the mistake of not setting a curfew, Ruth ran wild. "I don't room with Ruth, I room with a suitcase," said Yankees outfielder Ping Bodie when asked his roommate.[22] That changed, however, when Ruth ran into a palm tree while chasing a fly ball, knocking himself out on the play. Huggins responded by issuing a curfew and ordering every player to make an appearance in the hotel dining room every morning before 9 o'clock.

Ruth's safety became a huge concern after the season started. When the team traveled to Washington in early July, Ruth, given extra privileges by the Yankees, was granted permission to drive his four-door sedan rather than take the train with the rest of the team. While driving back to New York after the series, and with his wife and two other passengers in the car, Ruth failed to react in time to a sharp turn in the road. The car spun out of control, tipped over and threw the four from the vehicle. Uninjured, they traveled a half-mile to the nearest farmhouse where they were welcomed to spend the night. The next morning, with the car a wreck, the foursome made their way to nearby Philadelphia. When they came to a newsstand, they noticed the newspaper headlines: "Ruth reported killed in car crash."[23] No wonder why Huggins often wore out the hotel-room rugs by pacing late at night, wondering when Ruth would return after another one of his late-night adventures.

In 1921 the Yankees won their first-ever pennant. After the World Series, another serious problem arose when Ruth decided to make an unauthorized barnstorming trip. Back then, World Series participants were prohibited from going on barnstorming trips for fear it would cheapen the World Series, and it was a rule that Commissioner Kenesaw M. Landis intended to enforce. He called Ruth several times to warn him. Ruth didn't return the message. Ruth finally called Landis to tell him he was going through with the trip. "Oh, you are, are you? That's fine," Landis said angrily into the phone. He then warned, "If you do, it will be the sorriest thing you've ever done in baseball." Landis slammed down the receiver and paced his hotel room while cussing up a storm. "Who does that big monkey think he is?" he said, then paced and cussed some more. "It seems I have to show someone who is running this game."[24]

Sportswriter Fred Lieb was with Landis at the time and heard everything. He decided to warn one of the Yankees owners. Lieb left Landis in his hotel room and taxied to Huston's residence. Huston, who had been drinking with Harry Frazee that evening, was awakened by a knock on his door. When Lieb told him about the conversation, the Yankees co-owner began to worry. If Ruth disobeyed the commissioner, there would be a heavy price to pay. Huston immediately got in touch with Ruth, hoping he could persuade him to change his mind. "Aw, go tell that old guy to jump in the lake," Ruth told Huston.[25] There was no stopping Ruth now.

The Yankees owners thought they could send someone to talk to the commissioner at his office in Chicago and persuade him to impose a milder punishment. Ed Barrow, Ruth's manager in Boston and now the Yankees' business manager, drew the assignment. He received a cool reception in the Windy City. "Well, what do you want?" Landis snapped when Barrow entered his office. "I guess you know what," Barrow said. "Yes, I do," said Landis. The commissioner rose from his chair and escorted Barrow to the office window. They looked down at the street below and saw two kids. "I suppose they are asking each other, 'that big white-haired so-and-so in that office up there is the one keeping Babe Ruth out of the game,'" Landis said. "But tell me, what would you do?" "I'd suspend him, too," Barrow replied.[26] The commissioner suspended Ruth for the first six weeks of the 1922 season and took away his World Series share of $3,362.

Before the 1922 season, Ruth signed a new contract. His two-year contract had expired, and the Yankees made an offer. Ruth declined it. The Yankees upped the amount to $50,000 per season. Ruth again said no. He asked for $52,000 because he wanted to get paid $1,000 a week. The two parties agreed to Ruth's terms and to a four-year contract with an option for a fifth year. He was also rewarded the captaincy of the Yankees, a huge honor in those days.

Ruth served his suspension and played his first game on May 20, at the Polo Grounds. Five days later, after being called out on a close play at second base, he sprang to his feet with a handful of dirt and heaved it in the umpire's face. As expected, the ump ejected Ruth. On his way back to the dugout, Ruth was razzed with hoots and catcalls from the hometown crowd. "Play ball, you bum!" a fan yelled.[27] Ruth raced toward the fan and jumped into the stands. The fan climbed over rows of seats before reaching the top aisle. "Hit that big stiff!" another fan shouted.[28] Ruth retreated and climbed onto the dugout roof. His face red with fury, he issued a challenge for anyone who wanted to fight. That evening, American League President Ban Johnson fined and suspended Ruth for his outburst. He also instructed the Yankees to strip Ruth of his captaincy. In June, Ruth had another altercation with an umpire and was banished from that game. A report went out that night to Ban Johnson, who suspended Ruth for the third time that season. When Ruth heard about the suspension the next day, he confronted the umpire about his report and gave him an earful. Johnson simply added a few more games to the suspension. Later that season, Ruth served another suspension for using some choice words when arguing with an umpire.

Besides his troubles during the season, Ruth struggled at the plate in the Yankees' second straight World Series loss to the Giants. In 1923 he was hungry to have a better year and regain the love of fans who were disappointed over his lost campaign. He enjoyed one of the best seasons (.393, 41 homers), regained the admiration of the fans, and the Yankees won their first World Series. Ruth was happy, Huggins was happy, and Ruppert was happy. This was also the year the majestic Yankee Stadium opened its doors, and due to personal differences, Ruppert bought out Huston to become the sole owner of the New York Yankees.

In 1924 Ruth was having the best season of his career. On August 8 he was hitting .408 with a league-leading 113 runs and 38 homers. And then came a sudden decline. Ruth had gained a lot of weight during the season. He sustained a left shoulder injury that forced him to make an underhand throw to an infielder after fielding every batted ball that came his way. His batting average fell 30 points, he hit just eight more homers during the last seven weeks of the season, and the Yankees fell short of winning a fourth straight pennant.

When Ruth reported for spring training in 1925, he had grown even heavier. In addition, his life had fallen into disarray. His marriage was falling apart and a bookie had exposed him for gambling debts he accumulated through horse racing. "Say it isn't true, Babe," a teammate asked. "Yes, I owe that money," Ruth admitted. "I made those bets last May. I lost seventy-five hundred dollars."[29] It was a difficult spring for Ruth. He and the manager, a man Ruth never liked, continued to squabble. As the team barnstormed through the South to prepare for the season, Ruth became very ill. He continued to travel with the team and play every day until he became so ill that he passed out in the train depot in Asheville. He was rushed to New York City and hospitalized. An examination revealed he had an abdominal abscess and surgery would be required. "That comes as a shock," Huggins said when hearing the news. "We all felt that the big boy would be able to help us in a week. Damn! That's tough luck."[30]

Without Ruth the Yankees got off to a bad start. And with the team losing, Ruppert felt the effect at the gate. Even after Ruth returned on June 1, and "was in no condition to play," opined a writer, the Yankees continued to lose.[31]

Huggins was losing patience with Ruth, who continued to extend his evenings past curfew. One time, while the Yankees were in Chicago, the club hired a detective to trail him. When the report came back, they learned that Ruth had visited six different females at their residences. During one game, Ruth disobeyed his manager twice in a loss to the White Sox. That was the last straw for Huggins. He called Ed Barrow and told the Yankees business manager he wanted to take disciplinary action. "Will you get Ruppert's backing on this?" he asked. "Ruppert's backing is not necessary," replied Barrow, "If that is what you want to do, you have my backing."[32] The next day in St. Louis, Huggins informed Ruth that he was fining him $5,000 and suspending him indefinitely. Ruth responded by cussing and telling the manager he would never play another game for him and would go back to New York and tell Ruppert so. "You don't think he will stand for this, do you?" Ruth asked. "Do as you please," said Huggins.[33]

Ruth traveled to New York (with a friend, Father Joseph Quinn) and, when Ruth arrived, he had a change of heart. He admitted he had overacted and wanted to make his peace with the manager. He went to the Yankees office and spoke with Ruppert. He then headed to Yankee Stadium and spoke with Huggins, thinking he would be forgiven and allowed to play in the day's game. But Huggins told him to sit this one out. "Anything Miller Huggins says goes with me," Ruppert told reporters. "Huggins is running this club, not Babe Ruth. Ruth can quit if he wants to. Huggins can remain manger as long as he wants. As long as he is the manager, his decisions will be backed to the limit."[34]

Ruth entered the 1926 season hungry to regain his stardom. He had a new respect for his manager, reported in tiptop shape, obeyed curfew, and worked hard. Ruth had another great season, and the Yankees returned to the top of the standings. And nobody was happier than his manager. "Babe, I admire a man who can win over a lot of tough opponents, but even more a man who can win over himself," Huggins told him. "That's fine, Hug, do I get the fine back?" asked Ruth. "No," replied the manager.[35]

After the 1926 season, Ruth's contract for $52,000 a year had expired. He made noises about wanting $100,000 a year for the next two seasons. "Either I get it or I don't," he said.[36] He talked about partnering with his trainer, Artie McGovern, in opening more gymnasiums throughout the country. When Ruth arrived in New York after spending time in Los Angeles on his next movie, *Babe Comes Home*, he was greeted by a sign in red letters at Grand Central Station: "Babe Ruth Comes Home."[37] As he walked through the terminal, there were shouts of "Get your one-hundred thousand, Babe! Get your one-hundred thousand!"[38] He waved his hat to the crowd when he appeared at the 42nd Street exit. He was also greeted by reporters who asked if he would settle for anything less than $100,000. "I'll have to see Ruppert," he said. "I hate to quit baseball, but I have other propositions I can earn money at."[39] At 1 o'clock, Ruth arrived at Ruppert's brewery. The two men headed directly to the owner's office and began to negotiate. Ruppert spoke about a multiyear contract, and the more years he mentioned, the lower Ruth went in his demand. When the two men emerged from the office at 1:55 P.M., Ruppert announced an agreement of $70,000 a year for the next three seasons. "It's a gamble," Ruppert admitted, "but I'm convinced that Ruth won't make me sorry."[40] Ruth made the deal pay off by hitting a record 60 homers in 1927 and 54 in 1928. The Yankees won the World Series in both seasons. While heading home from St. Louis after sweeping the Cardinals in 1928, "We were as crazy as a bunch of wild Indians," Ruth said later. "When you win two straight World Series without a loss it calls for something special."[41] Led by Ruth, the Yankees stormed their way through each train car. Ruth punched a hole in every straw hat he found and tore the shirts off the backs of his teammates. But where was Ruppert during all this jubilation? Ruth and a few teammates went in search of him. They hammered on the door of the owner's drawing room. "Go away!" yelled Ruppert. "I have already turned in and want to get some sleep."[42] This was no time to sleep, Ruth insisted. The Babe and a teammate put their shoulders through the door.

Someone reached inside and unlatched the lock. Ruth and his friends tumbled into the room. Noticing Ruppert was wearing an expensive nightshirt, Ruth warned he was going to rip it off. "Don't do it, Mr. Ruth," warned Ruppert. "This is custom-made silk." Ruth said he only wanted a piece of it. "Mr. Ruth, you're suspended," Ruppert said. Riiiiip.[43]

The Yankees finished a distant second in 1929. Worried about his club, Huggins became seriously ill. As the season went on, he wore out to the point that he spent a few days in his hotel room rather than at the ballpark. One day he entered the clubhouse with a red blotch beneath his left eye. Yankees coach Art Fletcher and sportswriter Ford Frick begged him to see a doctor, but he refused. He finally gave in and was advised to check into a hospital. His malady was diagnosed as erysipelas, a skin disease. His facial sore was a mealy carbuncle, but in his case the sore became lethal and poisoned his body. With the manager in their thoughts and prayers, the Yankees traveled to Boston. After the first game of the series, Ruth ventured to Cambridge to appear as a guest speaker at the Catholic Club. He asked the audience to pray for Huggins and ask their friends to do the same. "If prayers can help, that old boy will pull through," Ruth said.[44] The next day at Fenway Park, the Yankees were informed that the manager had succumbed to his illness.

Ruth's three-year contract had expired, and once again he mentioned the amount of $100,000. There was something else on Ruth's mind: Who would manage the Yankees? As he pondered the candidates, a thought had entered his mind: "What's the matter with me?"[45] He informed Ruppert that he wanted the job. "You can't manage yourself," Ruppert replied, "so how are you going to manage the Yankees?"[46] Ruth listed his credentials and was happy to note that Ruppert seemed impressed. The owner told Ruth that he would think it over for the next few days. When he didn't hear anything, Ruth picked up the phone to call Ruppert. Then he noticed the newspaper headlines. Former Yankees pitcher Bob Shawkey had been hired for the job. Ruth was disappointed but kept his good spirit. He phoned Shawkey, congratulated him, and promised to give him his best effort.

Ruth's focus went back to his contract. He was willing to compromise at $85,000 a year. "I'm good for $25,000 per year [in endorsements] even if I quit baseball today," he said.[47] "People are rioting in New York for bread," one of Ruth's friends told him. "They're broke, There's a Depression. You're holding out for $85,000 while they're starving. It makes a bad impression for baseball." Ruth was perplexed. "Why don't people tell me these things?" he said.[48] He signed for $80,000 a year for 1930 and '31.

The 1930 Yankees finished third, and Shawkey was fired after the season. Once again Ruth inquired about the managerial job. Ruppert responded by going over Ruth's mistakes prior to 1926. "Was there any fault in my conduct in 1930 or my efforts to make Shawkey's year a success?" Ruth asked. "You really earned the big money I paid you," said Ruppert.[49] But Ruppert made no promises to Ruth. The owner found his man in former Cubs manager Joe McCarthy and wasted little time in hiring him. "Did they have to go to the National League for a manager?" a disappointed Ruth kept asking.[50]

In 1932 Ruth signed a one-year deal for $75,000. He resented the Yankees new manager, and the manager knew it. McCarthy left Ruth alone, though, and The Babe enjoyed another productive season. The Yankees won another pennant and swept the Cubs in the World Series. In 1933 Ruth's contract was reduced to $52,000. He said, "This was not a salary cut; it was an amputation."[51] Ruth, now slowing down as a player, began to talk more about managing. Supposedly, the Red Sox and White Sox were interested, and possibly the Tigers. But it never happened.

In 1934 the aging Sultan of Swat, now 39, was retiring from games before the ninth inning. The Yankees finished second for the second consecutive season. Still hoping for the managing job, Ruth asked Ruppert if he was happy with McCarthy. "Why yes; aren't you?" replied Ruppert. Ruth said he was not. He insisted the Bronx Bombers could have done better in 1934, which Ruppert didn't like hearing. Ruppert offered Ruth the job of managing the minor-league Newark Bears. That did not please Ruth, who said he deserved to manage in the majors.[52]

A divorce was inevitable. When Ruth's 1935 contract arrived from the Yankees, it was for $1. About that time, Ruth heard from Boston Braves owner Emil Fuchs, who wanted Babe back in Boston. Fuchs offered a job of vice president and assistant manager, in addition to playing duties. Before accepting, Ruth made one last bid to manage the Yankees. He asked Ruppert again if he was happy with McCarthy. The Yankees owner said he was. Ruppert then handed Ruth a paper noting his unconditional release. He had been waived on by the other American League clubs and was free to sign elsewhere. Ruth later said that last experience in dealing with the Yankees owner made him a little sick. It also bothered others around the circuit. "Somebody should have had more compassion when they maneuvered him out of the American League," said Hank Greenberg.[53]

Ruth's 1935 season was unpleasant. He probably should have retired the previous fall, with 708 career home runs. The year got off to a bad start when he learned that Fuchs never told Braves manager Bill McKechnie about Ruth's position as assistant manager. Ruth had hoped that being a manager's assistant would lead to getting a managing job. The Braves, though, had no intention on hiring Ruth to manage. They only wanted his name to help sell tickets. His vice-president duties were confined to attending store openings. His assistant-managing position was limited to letting McKechnie know if he could play that day. On June 2 Ruth called it a career. He officially retired as a player and still had hopes of managing, but the opportunity never came. "Despite his faults, baseball didn't do right by him," said Greenberg.[54]

Notes

1. "Yankees Terms Satisfy Babe Ruth," *New York Times*, January 7, 1920: 22.
2. Tom Meany, *Babe Ruth* (New York: Grosset & Dunlap, 1951), 13.
3. Robert W. Creamer, *Babe* (New York: Fireside, 1992), 29.
4. Leigh Montville, *The Big Bam* (New York: Broadway, 2006), 23.
5. William R. Cobb, *Babe Ruth: Playing the Game* (Mineola, New York: Dover, 2011), 4.
6. Creamer, 37.
7. Creamer, 36.
8. Babe Ruth and Bob Considine, *The Babe Ruth Story* (New York: Penguin, 1992), 10.
9. John Tullius, *I'd Rather be a Yankee* (New York: Macmillan, 1986), 35.
10. Tullius, 34.
11. Tullius, 35.
12. Creamer, 66.
13. Ruth, 15.
14. Creamer, 110-111.
15. Creamer, 138.
16. Creamer, 162.
17. Creamer, 163.
18. Eliot Asinof, *Eight Men Out* (New York: Henry Holt and Company, 1987), 142.
19. Daniel R. Levitt, *Ed Barrow* (Lincoln: University of Nebraska Press, 2008), 163.
20. Montville, 99; Creamer, 211.
21. Jim Reisler, *Babe Ruth* (New York: McGraw-Hill, 2004), 24.
22. Montville, 109.
23. Mike Sowell, *The Pitch That Killed* (New York: Macmillan, 1989), 143-144.
24. J.G. Taylor Spink, *Judge Landis and Twenty-five Years of Baseball* (New York: Thomas C. Crowell, 1947), 104.
25. Spink, 106.
26. Levitt, 294.
27. Marshall Smelser, *The Life that Ruth Built* (Lincoln: University of Nebraska Press, 1975), 244.
28. "Ruth in Row with Umpire and Fan," *New York Times*, May 26, 1922: 1.
29. "Babe Ruth Is Broke?" *St. Petersburg* (Florida) *Evening Independent*, March 11, 1925: 4.
30. Marshall Hunt, "Babe Ruth Under Knife Today," *New York Daily News*, April 15, 1925: 34.
31. James B. Harrison, "Ruth Comes to Yankees Aid, but Senators Win by 5-3," *New York Times*, June 2, 1925: 18.
32. Edward Grant Barrow, *My Fifty Years in Baseball* (New York: Coward-McCann, 1951), 151.
33. Dave Anderson, "Sports of the Times," Miller Huggins file at the National Baseball Hall of Fame.
34. Monitor [George Daily], "Ruppert with Huggins, Even Though Ruth Retires," *New York World*, September 1, 1925: 6.
35. Ruth, 144.
36. "Babe Ruth Insists on $100,000 Salary," *New York Sun*, March 1, 1927: 1.
37. "Babe Ruth to Get $70,000 a Season," *New York Sun*, March 2, 1927: 23.
38. Ibid.
39. Ibid.
40. "Ruth Gets 3 Year Contract: $210,000," *Chicago Tribune*, March 3, 1927: 17.
41. Ruth, 162.
42. Ruth, 163.
43. Montville, 279.
44. "Huggins' Death Shocks Boston," *Boston Post*, September 26, 1929: 23.
45. Ruth, 176.
46. Ira Berkow, *Hank Greenberg* (New York: Times Books, 1989), 88.
47. William B. Mead, *Two Spectacular Seasons* (New York: Macmillan, 1990), 14.
48. Ibid.
49. Ruth, 183.
50. Dave Anderson "Sports of the Times," *New York Times*, July 30, 1974: 27.
51. Creamer, 370.
52. Ruth, 207.
53. Berkow, 88.
54. Ibid.

Babe Ruth and the Boston Braves, Before Opening Day, 1935

By Carolyn Fuchs and Wayne Soini, with Herb Crehan

When George Herman "Babe" Ruth arrived in St Petersburg in 1935 for spring training with the Boston Braves, his illustrious career had come full circle. Twenty-one years earlier the Babe had joined the Red Sox in Boston as an impressionable 19-year-old pitcher. During the intervening years Babe had won 89 games as a pitcher for the Red Sox, set a World Series record for consecutive scoreless innings that would stand for 43 years, and slugged over 700 home runs leading major-league baseball from the Deadball Era to the Lively Ball Era. He had gained international acclaim. There was a candy bar named after him and anything that was too large to describe in words was termed "ruthian." Whatever the opposite of impressionable is, the Babe was it in 1935.

He was also in many ways no longer ruthian. Five years before, at age 35, the Babe had led the American League with 49 home runs. In 1934 his home-run total had fallen to just 22. Babe Ruth's value had tanked as the proverbial "fat and forty" man. Everyone who owned a team knew this and almost every owner concluded against offering a contract to the Babe – all but one – the Judge: Emil Fuchs, owner of the Boston Braves.

Although hoary baseball mythology casts Babe Ruth's 1935 availability to the Boston Braves as the beleaguered Braves owner's last chance to hold onto his team, the opposite is true.

Babe Ruth and Boston Braves executives in a Copley Plaza Hotel room, after signing with the Boston Braves, February 28, 1935. (l to r): Charles F. Adams, Babe Ruth, and Judge Emil Fuchs. *Leslie Jones photo, courtesy of the Boston Public Library.*

The Judge was the Babe's last chance to play ball – or to gain a toehold in management.

The latter was the big draw for Ruth, who had made it known that he wanted to manage. In his excellent biography of Ruth, *The Big Bam*, Leigh Montville recounts a meeting between Babe,

Yankees owner Colonel Jacob Ruppert, and general manager Ed Barrow right after the end of the 1934 season. Montville claims that Ruth asked the two decision-makers if they intended to return manager Joe McCarthy for the 1935 season. When told that they had already decided to bring back McCarthy, Babe is reported to have said, "That's all I wanted to hear," and stormed out of the meeting.[1]

The Judge had not been first in line for the stormer. As Montville further documented, the Philadelphia Athletics' owner-manager, Connie Mack, had resolved to sign Ruth as the manager of the A's for the 1935 season. But Mack made it a point to observe the Babe closely as the 1935 season approached and he quickly realized that Ruth had great difficulty managing himself, let alone a ballclub.[2] When the Yankees formally released the Babe, the owners of every team in both leagues had to sign waivers. They all did, including Connie Mack. Ultimately, nobody wanted the Babe but the Judge.

What then led the Judge to take on the Babe? The short answer is the Judge's unusual personality. He was hot-potato-proof. Unique among owners from the start of his ownership in 1923, he never worried.[3]

By rights the Judge ought to have worried. When he took them over, the Braves were plainly the weaker of Beantown's two clubs. While large populations in New York and Chicago could support two teams – Brooklyn even supported a third in New York – the Judge fought for fans in far smaller Boston. Boston was a city really only big enough for one ballclub. (And not only Boston. As if to prove the fact that they were one-team towns, Philadelphia, St. Louis, and Boston all shed one of their two teams in the mid-1950s. The Judge struggled long and hard against odds that would eventually defeat anybody.)

In part, this did not worry the Judge at first because his day job as a busy New York lawyer supported him and his family in style on Riverside Drive. He did not get into baseball for money. The Judge's initial objective was to enable Christy Mathewson to pursue professional baseball as a team president and owner. He idolized Christy, with whom he'd become close while serving as the lawyer for the New York Giants. He made Christy the president of the Braves. If the team's fortunes improved, Christy could buy out the Judge and become the owner of the Braves. Things did not play out as planned

Given time, the Judge's hopeful plans for Mathewson may have worked out but Christy's health – his lungs had been ruined by exposure to poison gas during World War I – deteriorated too quickly for a fair trial. Mathewson's death in 1925 simultaneously left the Judge mourning a friend and becoming the sole owner of a major-league ballclub.

Babe Ruth and Boston Braves owner Judge Emil Fuchs exchange the newly signed contract for Ruth to play with the Braves
Leslie Jones photo, courtesy of the Boston Public Library.

Rather than sell, the Judge banked on raising the team's morale, record, and dismal standings before he sold the Braves. He set no time limit. The Judge did not close his law office and still fully intended to go back to practicing law full-time in New York as the Twenties spilled over into the Thirties. The Braves improved. For example, the team made $150,000 in 1933, even after the Judge paid himself a salary of $30,000. That was the same season the Braves rose into serious contention for the pennant. Huge Braves Field was sold out for some games, with standing room only. The Braves attracted national attention and some bids came in. Auto baron Henry Ford was moved to offer the Judge one of his spare millions for the team. Incredibly, the Judge declined to sell. Ever optimistic, he was becoming a believer. Like many fans, the Judge preferred "Next year!" The decisive year, the Judge determined, would be 1934. After all, wasn't Henry Ford a good businessman? If so, didn't it make sense to hold on to a good thing? The Judge poured his 1933 profits and a good deal more into his bouncing Braves.

The effort fizzled spectacularly. For the Judge, 1934 had not been so much scary as sad.

"There is nothing more tragic than to be playing to almost empty seats in a ballpark that holds almost 45,000 people," the Judge confided when interviewed in his retirement years.[4]

The Judge had tried everything else to raise revenue. Sunday baseball, Ladies' Days, the Knot Hole Gang, and live radio broadcasts of Braves games were among the Judge's innovations or adaptations. Not every experiment worked. "Music at the Ballpark" proved a sour note when, in 1930, the Judge hired musicians to play before and after games. The bonus of classical and popular pieces drew nobody to Braves Field.[5] Another deal worked out surprisingly – when it failed. The Judge rented Braves Field to the operators of that grand old sports emporium, the Boston Garden. It was to be used for outdoor boxing matches. He sagely negotiated a five-year deal. At $30,000 a summer, after losing money after two seasons, the Garden's field of dreams was on the ropes. The Garden bought out its contract. The imperturbable Judge then scouted for another tenant. In 1934, he toyed with the potential of an offseason greyhound track. Commissioner Kenesaw Mountain Landis, always death on any link between baseball and gambling, squelched the proposal.

Another thing helped. Having taken out large loans (something over $200,000) with Braves stock and his optimism the only collateral, the redoubtable Judge got the National League to guarantee his team's annual rent on Braves Field in 1935. It took a marathon special meeting of owners in December 1934, but it was done. Before mention of the Babe, everything was in place for the Braves to play ball on Opening Day in 1935. With luck in 1935, the Judge would make money as he had in both 1932 and 1933.

The Judge was well aware of the Babe's continuing popularity in Boston. Some 48,000 fans had packed Fenway Park to see, in tears and with cheers, the Babe's last game in Boston. In New York the following month, as the season ended anticlimactically, a mere 2,000 people watched his last at-bat in a Yankees uniform.[6]

Tipped off by Colonel Ruppert of the Babe's availability, the Judge made no effort to sweet-talk the Babe when he called him. He had Colonel Ruppert's okay to speak frankly. The Judge spoke in a "Dutch uncle" manner concerning any move into management. He said that the job of managing was hard, that the Babe would have to master new skills and that the current Braves manager, Bill McKechnie, was a good man to learn from.

The Babe realized that this was the best deal he was going to get from anybody. The Yankees sent him everything but a telegram. The season before, the Babe had his salary cut by $17,000.[7] Nobody else was calling. The Judge represented his only chance at extra innings in the game. The two men agreed and paperwork followed.

The deal solved a big team problem. The Yankees did not have to fire the Babe. He simply left and put on a Braves uniform. Their relief was most clear many years later. The Yankees manager, Joe McCarthy, sat at a dinner in a Boston restaurant in the 1940s, treating Judge Fuchs and his family. McCarthy asked the assembled Fuchs family if any of them knew why he felt so fondly toward the Judge. The Judge's sister, Helen, took a guess. "Because he took Babe Ruth?" she asked. McCarthy smiled and nodded.[8]

Listening only partially as the Judge spoke, the Babe seems in retrospect to have heard the word "manage" and then paid little or no attention to warnings or conditions. That is, he was offered a year as assistant manager, much like an intern watching McKechnie. He might learn and prove himself fit for the job or he might not. Showing obliviousness, the Babe had no questions about that proposal. Instead, he asked for an unprecedented cut of the Braves' exhibition games. Unfazed, the Judge granted him 25 percent.[9] The Babe's appearances would likely bring more fans to those games, perhaps enough to make up for his unheard-of cut.

As for the Judge, he neither had a management problem nor did he want to create one. (If the Judge ever really needed a manager, he could fill in himself. He had managed the team in 1929 by assembling a "Brain Trust" to advise him. And he could spot management talent from afar – he gave Casey Stengel his first manager's job in 1925.) Not unlike most baseball insiders, he did *not* see Babe Ruth as a manager. But, in Babe's best interests, the Judge saw farther out. He concluded that the Babe himself would abandon his unrealistic ambition before very long. The Judge created time, a full season, for the Babe to shadow McKechnie, to observe and to take in what it took to manage. What would happen? Realistically, the Judge expected the Babe to make a transition from player to the front office instead. He gave him, unasked, another job as the team vice president.

"I didn't promise him he would be a manager," the Judge told a sports reporter with more specificity years later than was possible in 1935. "In fact, I told him Bill McKechnie was my friend and suggested that he didn't want to become a manager, that he'd be better off an executive. That's why I made him vice president."[10]

As soon as negotiations by phone between Boston and New York concluded, the Judge wrote up a letter in which he memorialized their conversation and the offer that the Judge was making. The letter is preserved. Its terms were published in newspapers at the time. Anybody who could read knew that the "management" term of the three-year deal was only good for the first year, and that slot was as "assistant manager in 1935."

Thus both acknowledging what the Babe desired as well as preparing him for a potential turn instead to the front office, the Judge gave The Babe a practical contract. He would play, of course, and, if he wished, take a long mental stab at managing. But also, as he carried goodwill with him wherever he went, the gregarious Babe should thrive in a state where he was not only idolized but beloved. As vice president, in a suit rather than a uniform, the Babe would move blocks of ticket by signing baseballs at department stores. He would be the highly visible representative of the team, and a key revenue-producer.

To check out his theory of The Babe's Boston popularity, the Judge invited the Babe to join him on his next trip up to Boston from New York. This train trip to Boston (on February 28, 1935) became big news. It was a much-anticipated photo opportunity but much more: Fans in droves arrived at Back Bay station to catch a glimpse of their favorite player, the legendary Babe.

At Back Bay, adulation moved notches beyond anything the Babe experienced before, even as a winning World Series pitcher for the Red Sox in 1918. Waves of cheers and a seemingly endless, thunderous applause greeted him.

At a hotel banquet that night, a businessman with multiple sports investments, including the Braves, spoke up prophetically. Charles Adams, owner of the Boston Bruins and some of Suffolk Downs, a partner in the Braves who fronted money when the Judge needed it, was on edge about the deal. He plainly trusted the Judge more than he did the Babe. And he had an investment to protect. By 1934, the Judge owed Adams $200,000. Adams was the most clear-minded of the speakers who rose to toast the Babe that night.

Adams warned, "Babe Ruth will become manager of the Braves only when he proves he is capable of filling the post. Current manager Bill McKechnie will be the absolute boss on the field this season."[11]

With a Dutch-uncle phone call, a road map to the front office, and Adams's very public warning, the Babe's baseball career resumed in Boston, where it had begun. But the returning hero, the Babe, really only felt at home now in New York. Strutting about as one of New York's foremost celebrities, he threw himself into a lively social life for obvious reasons: Given physical decline, he lived more for his time off the field.

Curiously, the Judge was hardly less of a New Yorker than the Babe. Although born in Germany, Emil Fuchs grew up to play on the immigrant kids' Settlement House baseball team before World War I. After he became a lawyer, he was the team attorney for the New York Giants and he regularly cheered from the best seats on the Polo Grounds. It was in New York that the Judge got a partnership together to buy the Braves in order to bring Christy Mathewson back into baseball. New York retained a hold. The Judge commuted between New York and Boston for years until he decided to go all in and buy out his partners. He was not a rich man, but the team had never repeated its 1914 miracle and, in the cellar of the league, was to be had cheaply. The Judge loved baseball enough to justify an expensive hobby, even if it would – and it ultimately did – cost him his house.[12]

In 1935, after spring training in St. Petersburg, when the Braves arrived in Boston in mid-April, their first game was at Fenway Park against the Boston Red Sox. The kickoff of the then-annual City Series, exhibition games between the traditional crosstown rivals showcased the Babe's formal return. His first appearance in a Boston Braves uniform, ironically enough at Fenway Park, drew only 11,000 fans. This was an ominous sign just as the regular season neared. What next?

On Opening Day at Braves Field on April 16, 1935, the Boston Braves, now with Babe Ruth, playing against the New York Giants, would start giving the answers.

Notes

1. Leigh Montville, *The Big Bam: The Life and Times of Babe Ruth,* (New York: Doubleday, 2005), 52.

2. Ibid.

3. Judge Fuchs was inclined to be imperturbable. Christy Mathewson noticed that the Judge crossed city streets with uninterrupted steps, even if cars brushed close by him. He wondered aloud how many hours a year the Judge saved by not worrying about being hit. (Anecdote from Robert S. Fuchs, shared orally with Wayne Soini in about 1996.)

4. Cullen Cain, "Giants, Braves Had to Move," *Miami News*, July 12, 1958. (Clipping in the scrapbook in possession of Carolyn Fuchs, granddaughter of Judge Fuchs.)

5. Burt Whitman, "Judge Fuchs Hopes Music at Braves Field Will Strike Responsive Chord with Fans," *Boston Herald*, January 17, 1930.

6. Figures from Allan Wood, "Babe Ruth," sabr.org/bioproj/person/9dcdd01c (accessed June 15, 2018).

7. Ibid.

8. Robert S. Fuchs and Wayne Soini, *Judge Fuchs and the Boston Braves, 1922-35* (Jefferson, North Carolina: McFarland, 1998), 100.

9. Fuchs and Soini, 106, 110. (The Yankees also allowed Ruth to continue to receive his share of exhibition games in 1935.)

10. Tom Monahan, "Mrs. Ruth Hits Yankees, Fuchs, Hub Writers," *Boston Traveler*, March 4, 1959: 28.

11. Fuchs and Soini, 107.

12. The Judge had settled in Jamaica Plain, not far from Boston Mayor Curley's home. When he could not pay the mortgage, the family rented an apartment in the Back Bay neighborhood.

Babe Ruth's National League "Career" Twenty-Eight Games with the 1935 Boston Braves

By Saul Wisnia

The buildup had been tremendous, and for a few days, at least, the hype seemed completely justified.

On April 16, 1935, the Boston Braves hosted the New York Giants in their home opener at Braves Field. The contest featured a matchup of two of the National League's leading power hitters in Boston's Wally Berger and New York's Mel Ott, but all the pregame buzz was about the Braves left fielder batting in front of Berger and making his NL regular-season debut: Babe Ruth.

Ever since the Braves owner, Judge Emil Fuchs, announced the signing of the all-time home-run king in late February, Boston's many daily newspapers had been crammed with stories speculating whether Ruth could help the city's NL franchise improve upon the previous year's fourth-place finish. Even though he had slipped from 41 homers to 34 to 22 in his last three seasons with the Yankees, and hit an un-Ruthian .288 with 84 RBIs in 1934, Fuchs and Braves fans hoped that the Bambino might find a new burst of productivity in the city where his big-league career began as a Red Sox pitcher 20 years earlier.[1] Skeptics pointed to his declining numbers and advancing age – Ruth had turned 40 on February 6 – as reasons to doubt such optimism.[2]

A few days before the opener, the new recruit vowed to make a good showing for Braves manager Bill McKechnie's club. "Wait till that bell rings," Ruth told reporters. "That's when I shall put the pressure on myself, and believe me, I know I am going to play a lot better ball than a whole lot of people think. I am

Boston Braves baserunner Babe Ruth steps on home plate behind Brooklyn Dodgers catcher Al Lopez as Braves teammate Wally Berger (#4) and home plate umpire Dolly Stark look on at Braves Field. *Leslie Jones photo, courtesy of the Boston Public Library.*

not bothered about the hitting. I know when my eye is getting right – and it's just about right now. My legs won't be so bad."[3]

The bell rang on April 16, and Ruth was indeed ready. In the first inning, stepping to the plate with Billy Urbanski on second base and one out, he lined the second pitch from Giants ace Carl Hubbell into right field for a run-scoring single and a 1-0 Boston lead. This quickly grew to 2-0 when Buck Jordan singled to bring The Babe home.

It was still 2-0 in the fifth with Urbanski on second again when Ruth launched a 2-and-2 screwball from Hubbell "20 feet up" into the right-field stands behind Ott, who shrugged his shoulders as it left the big ballpark. The fans cheered wildly again, and McKechnie – who had (justifiable) concerns about Ruth's unexplained contractual role as his "assistant manager" – was caught up in the moment enough to step away from his third-base spot coaching box and grasp the Babe's hand as he passed by on his 709th career regular-season home-run trot (and 16th against NL competition, including World Series play).[4] Always knowing how to play to the crowd, Ruth doffed his cap after crossing the plate.[5]

Hubbell, who had counted Ruth among his record five straight strikeout victims at the previous July's All-Star Game, was haunted by The Babe in more ways than one on this day. In the fifth inning, Hubbell blooped a pitch from Braves pitcher Ed Brandt over third base for what appeared to be a run-scoring single, only to see Ruth come sprinting in from left field to grab the ball with his outstretched glove near the foul line. He then continued running right into the Boston dugout to the delight of an estimated 25,000 chilly fans who included many state and city workers given a half-holiday so they could attend that game.[6]

The final score was 4-2, with Ruth playing a part in all four Boston runs and making the defensive play of the afternoon. His glove work was perhaps the biggest surprise, as newspaper reports from spring training had been filled with accounts of Ruth's struggles in the field. There was even a Johnny Sylvester-like story attached to the game; 14-year-old Bobby Baker, who had "been critically ill all spring," received a baseball autographed by Ruth at his Salem Hospital bedside the day of the opener. Upon hearing of his hero's home run, nurses said, "Bobby's spirits soared" and he vowed to get well.[7]

Fittingly, given Ruth's love of children, a youngster also wound up with the home-run ball. Sergeant Michael Carr of the North End Police Station was working a detail at the game and caught the shot on a bounce in center field. Carr turned down $25 from a fan for the ball, and when he got home, he gave it to his 9-year-old son, George. The other George, Ruth, had autographed it.[8]

(l to r:) Boston Braves Babe Ruth, Wally Berger, and Hal Lee.
Leslie Jones photo, courtesy of the Boston Public Library.

Bill Carrigan, who managed the Red Sox with and against Ruth in earlier years, said that "Babe never hit the ball any harder during the height of his career than he did today."[9] Ruth himself was understandably upbeat; the day after the game, he sat smoking black cigars and told Jimmy Powers of the *New York Daily News,* "Listen, kid, you can tell the world poppa (meaning himself) is happy. I said I might hit forty home runs this summer, didn't I? Well, change that. If I'm lucky I'll hit fifty."[10]

Homer number two came on Easter Sunday, April 21, against the Dodgers. It gave Ruth a .400 batting average for the young season, but he had already struck out six times in 15 at-bats – high by even his free-swinging standards. Brooklyn manager Casey Stengel, convinced that Ruth was still a force, noted, "I played against the Babe in World Series games when he was at his best. He missed quite a few those days and he still does today. But the old Babe was always dangerous with a bat in his hand and he always will be as long as he can walk up to the plate."[11]

Stengel's prediction did not come to pass. When the Braves hit the road, Ruth went 0-for-10 in four games at New York and Brooklyn with four more strikeouts. His average of more than one walk per game in the early going showed the respect pitchers still had for Ruth, but word spread that the Babe's mighty bat now had holes. Hurlers began offering him a steady stream of curveballs, with almost universal success.

Defensively, Ruth's shortcomings were also becoming acute. In a 6-5 loss at the Polo Grounds on April 23, he misjudged a pop fly by Bill Terry in the third inning that fell behind him for an inside-the-park home run, and one inning later booted Gus Mancuso's single into a double.[12] At home vs. the Phillies on April 29, he guessed wrong on a line drive with the bases loaded, resulting in three runs scoring.[13] The Braves managed to win that game, 7-5, but this was becoming the exception rather than the rule. By early May, Boston had fallen into seventh place, ahead of only lowly Philadelphia, and matching the previous year's 78-73 record seemed less likely by the week for McKechnie.

Along with wins on the field, Braves boss Fuchs had hoped that Ruth could bring in big attendance figures at the gate. This was the case on May 5, when 31,200 fans jammed Braves Field to see Boston battle the reigning NL champion Cardinals – with the added attraction of the first-ever matchup between young pitching whiz Dizzy Dean and Ruth. It was strictly a one-sided affair; not only did Babe go hitless with a strikeout in a 7-0 loss, but Dean even beat the Bambino at his own game by hitting a home run and single. The next day, against Pittsburgh, just 2,000 fans showed up as Babe sat things out with a bad head cold.

Rumors were already spreading about Ruth's possible future with the Braves. On April 25 an unattributed story appeared in the *Boston Globe* in which Fuchs denied reports printed in New York papers that Ruth would be succeeding McKechnie as Boston manager within two weeks. "There's absolutely nothing to that story," Fuchs said. "Save for the change of date, it's the same story I've been hearing since Ruth came to the Braves. There was never any truth to it and there's none now."[14]

Whatever the Babe had on his mind, it wasn't helping his game. By May 12 he had gone 10 straight games and 20 at-bats without a hit – dropping his average to .171.[15] He had also missed several contests due to his cold and a sore knee. The rumors of discord between Ruth and McKechnie persisted. Fuchs did his best to deflect them, stating that he hoped both men would "remain with the Boston Braves as long as they live." The owner also showed no public concern over Ruth's slump, stating that "It is my belief … that as soon as the weather conditions are normal, and the physical condition, caused by a cold throughout his system, is improved, he will disprove the prediction of some of the New York writers – that his ability and power in baseball is a thing of the past."[16]

Despite Fuchs's comments, Ruth was losing his enthusiasm as his average and the team's fortunes continued to slide. Still, his loyalty to his fans and his pride won out. "The Babe has intimated several times within the last two weeks that he has felt like quitting the active game," the *Boston Herald* reported in mid-May. "But he said yesterday he would stick it out and give it all he had to further the best interests of the team and of Judge Fuchs." A long road trip loomed for the Braves, with several cities planning "Babe Ruth Day" events that would mean big crowds and a chance for Fuchs to keep the struggling club afloat financially.[17]

Ruth broke a 26-day hitless skein in the opening game of the trip on May 17 at St. Louis, going 1-for-4 with a single. After this game, he denied more rumors – this time reports that he would quit after the road trip. "I'm going to play here tomorrow and keep right on playing as long as I have anything left," he told reporters. "I have a cold but am feeling better and am in good shape."[18]

On May 21 at Chicago, Ruth had his first home run in exactly a month. From there the Braves moved on to Pittsburgh, where in the next two games he was an uninspiring 1-for-8 with a single. His average was now down to .153, and perhaps it was a measure of manager McKechnie's lack of talent that he continued to bat him third in the order. The assistant manager likely had no say in the decision; like the "vice president" title also in his contract, it was clear by now that both designations meant nothing.

There was also no sign that Ruth, or the Braves, would ever emerge from their respective slumps. Boston entered play on Saturday, May 25, in last place with an 8-19 record; after a 2-5 start to their trip, they still had seven more games to go before heading home. They were facing a Pittsburgh team that was eyeing a three-game sweep and would stay in the pennant hunt well into September. Against this uninspiring backdrop, and with all but the most optimistic fans already writing his epitaph, Babe Ruth broke through with his best game since Opening Day – and one of the most awesome displays of pure power in his career.

In the first inning, with one out and Urbanski on second, Ruth faced Pirates right-hander Red Lucas and homered into the right-field stands. In the third, again with one out and one on, he launched a Guy Bush pitch to right, this time an estimated 450 feet into the upper deck. The Braves now led 4-0, but The Babe's big day was far from over. After Pittsburgh came back with four runs in the fourth inning to tie it, Ruth faced Bush again in the fifth and singled in Les Mallon (who had also scored on his second homer). Boston was back in front, 5-4; more precisely, it was Ruth 5, Pittsburgh 4.

Babe's teammates gave up the lead once more, and it was 7-5, Pittsburgh, when he came up for the fourth time in the seventh inning. Bush was still in the game and delivered a fastball to Ruth between the knees and waist. As writer Leigh Montville would describe it, Ruth hit the ball "straight into the air, high, like a pop-up, except it kept carrying, far, far, over the right center-field fence at Forbes Field, bounced in the middle of the street, and rolled into Schenley Park. The estimated distance the ball traveled was well over 500 feet, the longest home run ever hit at Forbes Field."[19]

It was Ruth's fourth hit, third homer, and sixth RBI of the day. The afternoon sent the Babe's average shooting up to .206, but amazingly the Braves still lost, 11-7 – another setback in a last-place season that would eventually bottom out with one of the worst marks (38-115) in major-league history.

Montville and other biographers claim that Ruth's wife, Claire, and friends pleaded with him to quit after this game. It certainly would have been a Hollywood ending, and Hollywood apparently took note. In *The Babe*, a 1992 film that barely outshines the dreadful *Babe Ruth Story*, released in 1948, the title character (played by John Goodman) actually *does* quit after his three-homer day in Pittsburgh in a fictionalized fit of passion that allows Ruth to finish his career and the film on a high note. He realizes he is never going to manage the Braves, and that his best days are behind him, so he literally walks away. The reality was far less dramatic. Knowing that several more National League cities planned to honor him in the weeks ahead and committed to satisfying his fans and fulfilling his contract, Ruth stayed with the club.

His brilliance, however, abandoned him as fast as it had returned. After hitting homers 712, 713, and 714 of his career on May 25, he never had another hit of any kind. He struck out three times in four at-bats the next afternoon – Babe Ruth Day in Cincinnati – and his average dropped below .200 for the final time. He then went 0-for-5 over four contests, although he did manage to walk four times and score twice.

How far had Ruth fallen? In a scene so cruel it almost seems unfathomable, his near-immobility was the subject of scorn in Boston's May 28 game at Cincinnati. Montville describes it: "In the fifth inning, the Reds attacked him in left field. Every batter purposely hit the ball to left in a five-run inning. Ruth, unable to move, was helpless as he tried to field the balls. When the inning ending, he went directly toward the clubhouse, not the dugout, as the fans jeered him."[20]

Thankfully, the worst was over. On May 30, 1935, at Philadelphia, Ruth came up third in the first inning and grounded a Jim Bivin pitch weakly to Dolph Camilli at first base. Then, in the bottom of the first, Ruth removed himself from the game after falling in the outfield and reinjuring his knee. There was no clear indication to the estimated 18,000 fans at the Baker Bowl that they were witnessing history, but for the rest of their lives they could lay claim to seeing George Herman Ruth appear in his final major-league game.[21]

Ruth as a Brave, April 1935.
Leslie Jones photo, courtesy of the Boston Public Library.

A few days later, the news made bold but differing headlines across the country. The *New York Times* perhaps got it best on June 3: "Babe Ruth 'Quits' Braves and Is Dropped by Club." Ruth, sidelined by his bum knee, had been frustrated when Fuchs refused to let him skip a game he wasn't going to play in anyway and attend a party with his wife aboard the ocean liner Normandie. So Ruth quit, was fired by Fuchs, and released by the Boston team, all in one dismal afternoon.

"I do not have to put up with this sort of treatment," the .181 hitter told reporters, "and I will not return to the Braves as long as Fuchs remains in control of the club."[22]

Ruth then got into his car for the drive from Boston back to New York. Fuchs sold the team a few months later, but the Babe never returned – to the Braves or any major-league club as a player. His Hall of Fame career was over, with final batting statistics that would be memorized by generations of fans: *.342 average, 714 home runs, .690 slugging percentage, 2,214 RBIs, 2,174 runs scored.*

It ended sadly, but no player's time in the game was ever more glorious.

Sources

In addition to the sources cited in the Notes, the author used Baseball-Reference.com for box-score, player, team, and season information as well as pitching and batting game logs, and other pertinent material.

Notes

1. Fuchs was also excited about the potential crowds that Ruth would draw. An estimated 48,000 fans had jammed Fenway Park for a doubleheader between the Yankees and Red Sox the previous August, widely speculated to be Babe's last games in Boston as an active player. Since the ballpark had fewer than 35,000 seats, thousands of fans stood on the field in a roped-off area behind the center-field flagpole.

2. Ruth had just found out he was a year younger than he always thought; according to many sources, including *The Big Bam*, by Leigh Montville, the Babe believed he was born on August 6, 1894, until he saw his birth certificate while preparing for an October 1934 trip to Japan. His actual birth date was August 6, 1895.

3. Melvin Webb Jr., "Nothing Wrong with His Wrist, Cronin Assures Globe Writer," *Boston Globe,* April 12, 1935: 27.

4. Interestingly, James Dawson's game story in the *New York Times* stated that it was the 724th home run of Ruth's career without noting that this number combined regular and postseason blasts. Dawson did not hold back his enthusiasm for the day's star, writing that "Ruth was king again with the bludgeoning ash that brought him fame." James Dawson, "Ruth's Home Run Defeats Giants in Boston, 4-2," *New York Times,* April 17, 1935: 29.

5. According to Arthur Siegel's April 17 story in the *Boston Herald*, Ruth also declared the home run as a sixth-anniversary gift to his wife, one day early. "That's one for the old lady," he said after the shot. Arthur Siegel, " "'That's One for the Old Lady,' Says Babe; Rescues Vice-Presidents from Oblivion," *Boston Herald,* April 17, 1935: 28.

6. While the April 16, 1935, attendance was widely noted in Boston newspapers as the largest Opening Day crowd in Braves Field history to that point, it was far below the 40,000 to 50,000 fans that the *Boston Globe, New York Times*, and other papers predicted would attend. The subpar weather liked played a big part. The half-holiday for city and state workers was mentioned in the *Boston Herald's* pregame story by Burt Whitman, and governors from five of the six New England states were also in attendance. April 16 was also declared "Judge Emil Fuchs Day" in Boston, with the Braves owner given a bronze plaque by Massachusetts Governor James Curley that was later displayed at the ballpark permanently. Next-day newspapers at the time reported "nearly 22,000" (*Boston Globe*), or 25,000 (both the *New York Times* and *New York Daily News*).

7. "Curley to 'Babe' to Bobby Erases Sick Boy's Gloom," *Boston Globe,* April 17, 1935: 10.

8. "Boy Has First Home Run Ball Babe Hit in League as Brave," *Boston Globe,* April 19, 1935: 15.

9. Hy Hurwitz, "Bill Carrigan Declares He Never Hit Ball Harder – Crowd Pays Fitting Tribute," *Boston Globe,* April 17, 1935: 28.

10. Jimmy Powers, "Babe Revises H.R. Schedule! He Now Plans to Hit 50!" *New York Daily News,* April 17, 1935: 363.

11. Hy Hurwitz, "Babe No Pushover, Says Casey Stengel," *Boston Globe,* April 20, 1935: 9.

12. Arthur Siegel, "Ruth Hailed by 47,000 in New York as Braves Bow to Giants, 6-5, in 11th," *Boston Herald,* April 24, 1935: 1.

13. James O'Leary, "Braves Beat Phils 7-5, Wilson Injured," *Boston Globe,* April 20, 1935: 20.

14. "Fuchs Denies Ruth Report," *Boston Globe,* April 25, 1935: 25.

15. Ruth's official totals for the hitless stretch, as tallied by the *Boston Globe* on May 13, 1935: 30 plate appearances, 11 walks, 9 strikeouts, 10 balls put in play for outs.

16. "Deny Dissention in Braves Ranks," *Boston Globe,* May 8, 1935: 22.

17. Burt Whitman, "Fuchs Gives Braves Squad Fight Talk," *Boston Herald,* May 15, 1935: 14.

18. Associated Press, "Angry Bambino Denies He Will Quit Playing," May 16, 1935. Appeared in *New York Daily News,* May 17, 1935: 81.

19. Leigh Montville, *The Big Bam: The Life and Times of Babe Ruth* (New York: Doubleday, 2006), 342.

20. Montville, 342-343.

21. In the last 18 games of Ruth's major-league career, the Braves went 3-15. Taking out his 4-for-4, three-homer day at Pittsburgh, he was 3-for-43 in the other 17 contests.

22. Burt Whitman, "Slugger's Plan to Attend Banquet in N.Y. Tonight Led to Break," *Boston Herald,* June 3, 1935: 1.

U.S. Presidents and The Babe

By Curt Smith

In the wake of the 1919-20 Black Sox scandal, baseball got lucky. Luck's name was George Herman Ruth, who entered our vernacular in a long-ball way and chose to never leave. The Babe helped baseball to start earning back its good name. What remains is the legend – a sunny-dark star, the extra-largest size of Everyman, with bumptious couth and whopping strength. In 1969, as Organized Baseball turned 100, "The baseball writers and broadcasters voted Babe Ruth "the Greatest Player Ever"' – columnist George Vecsey wrote – "a title so Twentyish, so circus-posterish, that it was Ruthian in its sweep. The man even had an adjective in his honor."[1] The Babe knew six American presidents, dwarfing most and becoming "the first national superstar," said George Will, "the man who gave us that category."[2]

In a definition of irony, the man who denoted going deep arrived at Fenway Park in 1914 as only a part-time big-league outfielder, hitting .200 with a 2-1 pitching record. A year later, Babe won 18 games and smacked four homers – the American League leader had seven – and hit .315. In 1916 Ruth had nine shutouts, a 23-12 record, and a league-best 1.75 earned-run average. In one game he also got three hits, including a home run. The French statesman Charles M. de Talleyrand once chimed, "This is worse than a crime, it's a blunder."[3] By the mid-'10s, millions thought it both that Babe didn't daily *bat*.

Originally, the Red Sox weren't among them, in 1912 using pitching, defense, and speed to win their first World Series of four in seven years. Next April, newly inaugurated President

Yale baseball captain George H.W. Bush receives the original manuscript of *The Babe Ruth Story* from Babe Ruth, 1948, for donation to the Yale Library. *Official White House photograph.*

Woodrow Wilson saw the Senators play three games in Washington against the defending world titlist. That May 29, Wilson rode back to Griffith Stadium for *another* Red Sox game![4] On October 9, 1915, the president visited Baker Bowl for Game Two of the Red Sox-Philadelphia Phillies World Series with his fiancée, Edith Bolling Galt, a Southern widow and jeweler whom Wilson met after wife Ellen Axson died a year earlier. It marked their public coming-out – also the first president to attend a World Series. Boston won, 2-1, to even the fall classic.[5]

President George H.W. Bush warms up before the 1991 All-Star Game at SkyDome in Toronto. The President had flown with Ted Williams and Joe DiMaggio on Air Force One from D.C. to attend the Game. *Official White House photograph.*

Ruth, 20, barely affected that Series, vainly pinch-hitting but clearly recalling his one time at-bat. In 1928 poet Carl Sandburg asked which of all the presidents was "the best model for boys to follow," Ruth, a Democrat who had grown up largely at the St. Mary's Industrial School for Boys in Baltimore, cast a vote for "Woodrow Wilson … always a great friend of mine."[6] Thin and ascetic, it would be hard to find someone less redolent of Babe. Like Ruth, though, Wilson's DNA included balls and strikes. A page from his boyhood geometry notebook, titled "Base Ball Ground,"[7] shows a hand-scribbled diagram of a baseball diamond. Wilson later became Davidson College's varsity center fielder, scholar and educator, New Jersey governor, and 1913-21 president – the first chief executive Ruth met. (Others, according to historian Michael Beschloss, were Warren Harding, Calvin Coolidge, Herbert Hoover, Franklin D. Roosevelt, and George H.W. Bush. Had Thomas E. Dewey not lost 1948's stunning election to Truman, he would have been lucky 7.)[8]

"Every president wanted him to *hit*!" said Lee Allen, 1959-69 Hall of Fame librarian. "Fans wanted to *see* him hit." At the time, "The Red Sox wanted him to do both."[9] In 1917 he won 24 games and hit .325. In 1918 new skipper Ed Barrow asked Babe if he would like mostly to play left field. He did, batting .300 with a war-curbed league-co-high 11 homers and 13-7 record. Next season pivoted the Red Sox, New York Yankees, and baseball. Ruth's 29 home runs were only one less than the sum of the next three AL sluggers, breaking Ned Williamson's all-time record of 27 in 1884.[10] Babe led the league in RBIs and slugging percentage, homered in each ballpark, and hit a then-record four grand slams.

Even nicknames blared carnival – to wit, Bam, The Bambino (also, Great Bambino), Behemoth of Bust, Caliph of Clout, Colossus of Clout. Goliath of the Grand Slam, Prince of Powders, Sultan of Swat, and Wizard of Whack.[11] "Superstar," indeed. On December 26, 1919, Boston owner and financier Harry Frazee sold Babe to New York for $100,000[12] that he then invested in would-be Broadway hits, including *My Lady Friends* – a farce, like the coming decade's second-division Red Sox. It was the first in a series of deals and sales between the teams that helped New York win its first World Series title in 1923. Of the Yankees' 25 players, 11 had belonged to Boston.[13] The Red Sox won one flag in the next 47 years, often snatching defeat from victory. Meantime, in New York, even then baseball's marquee, Ruth was the first US sports totem to twin his appeal to a presidential incumbent or candidate – "first who dealt with presidents as a celebrity of near-equal magnitude," said Michael Beschloss.[14] It could be hard to tell the star.

In the July 12, 1999, *Sports Illustrated*, Richard Hoffer dubbed Ruth "like rock-and-roll and the Model T … a seminal American invention. Be it his power at the plate, his popularity or his various appetites, the Babe was huge."[15] His first season as a Yankee, Ruth hit 54 homers, topping his old record by 25. That year, 1920, GOP pols wanted him to endorse presidential nominee Warren G. Harding against Democrat James A. Cox. "I'm a Democrat!" boomed Ruth, the party man, before asking how much they were offering. The answer "was … $4,000 in it for Babe and $1,000 for me," New York writer Fred Lieb, trying to arrange the deal, wrote in his 1977 memoir, *Baseball as I Have Known It*.[16] All Ruth had to do was to trek to Harding's Marion, Ohio, home and publicly support him. Talks collapsed, said Lieb, when the Black Sox Scandal erupted, the candidate's staff "cool[ing] off on the whole subject."[17]

Even so, Harding won a landslide on November 2, 1920, bringing baseball DNA to the White House in every form. Born in 1865 in Corsica (now Blooming Grove), Ohio, he moved as a boy to Marion, playing pepper with future National League shortstop Bob Allen. In his 20s Harding owned part of Marion's team, the Diggers, in the Ohio State League[18] and became an ex-officio scout with a pronounced big-league eye. The *Marion Star* newspaper publisher found 1912-26 pitcher Wilbur Cooper, who forged a 216-178 record for Pittsburgh, Detroit, and National League Chicago. Harding's other find was Brooklyn first baseman Jake Daubert, who twice led the NL with a .350 and .329 average.[19] Perhaps the best-ever left-handed pitcher was even named in the then-president's honor. Born in 1921, Warren Spahn had a 363-245 record and a sublime pickoff move. "Once he was said to have picked a runner off first base," said 1950s Braves teammate Ernie Johnson – "and the batter swung."[20]

Harding saw more games at the Senators' Griffith Stadium than any other park – four[21] — but something about the Yankees and New York drew him to the Babe. A decade earlier, the Yankees, outgrowing tiny Hilltop Park, had moved into the Giants' double-decked Polo Grounds in a hollow below Coogan's Bluff. In 1920 Ruth hit .376. Next year, the Yanks won their first flag. In 1922 furious, Jints owner Charles Stoneham raised their rent and in effect kicked the American Leaguers off Manhattan Isle. "They should move to some out-of-the-way place like Queens," huffed Giants skipper John McGraw, presuming no one would ever hear from them again.[22] That year, construction began on a three-deck shrine a quarter-mile from the Polo Grounds across the Harlem River.[23] Lengths were pygmy to the poles (280 and 295 feet at left and right field, respectively) but gaping in the alleys (left-center field, 460 feet, and right-center, 429) and center field (490).[24] Babe was the ultimate pull hitter – perfect for his park.

To Harding, like baseball, Yankee Stadium – a.k.a. The Stadium – straightaway became "The House That Ruth Built." It was also built *for* the Babe. Like Ruth's, Harding's baseball was more intuitive than intellectual, the Ohioan growing up playing more than watching the local team. He knew about the hit and run, sacrifice bunt, and hitting 'em where they ain't. He liked seeing pitcher Walter Johnson's high, hard one, cheering a Honus Wagner triple, and urging us to "strive for production as Babe Ruth strives for home runs."[25] He enjoyed being near jocks, some of their habits being more than faintly similar. Ruth drank at any time available. Harding relished hosting him when the Yankees played in Washington – the teams met there 11 times a year – as much as he enjoyed tossing out the first ball at each Senators home opener. The president liked to inhale bourbon in the Oval Office even as he ardently defended Prohibition![26] His baseball grasp made any conversation about it caring. Yet, like Ruth he was careless about ethics, a fatal flaw.

Almost prophetically, in early 1923 Harding sold the *Marion Star* and wrote a new will. He brooked influenza, a heart condition worsened by stress. Six days after The Stadium opened, he traveled to New York, where on April 24 the baseball lifer told his pitcher, "Walter, I came out to root for Washington." Yanks pitcher Sad Sam Jones then blanked the Senators, 4-0, Ruth homering, in the first shutout in the Big Ballpark in the Bronx.[27] Babe and Harding are shown in a last photo together: the two faces of the National Game.[28] Doubtless they discussed Ruth's next visit to the White House, baseball talk flowing like Prohibition booze. Returning to the capital, Harding began a "voyage of understanding" to rival Franklin Roosevelt's later tours in length and intensity. Speaking daily, he would entrain cross-country, go north to the Alaska Territory, turn south to California, pass through the Panama Canal to Puerto Rico, and return to Washington by the end of August.[29]

On July 26, in British Columbia, Harding became the first US president in office to visit Canada. The next day he spoke to 60,000 at the University of Washington, predicting statehood for Alaska. (It finally happened in 1959.) Weary, Harding "referred to Alaska as Nebraska, dropped his manuscript, and grasped the lectern to keep his balance."[30] He sped through the speech, not waiting for applause, then rushed to San Francisco, where doctors, thinking him better, let their patient sit up in bed. On August 2, wife Florence was apparently reading a magazine story to him. Suddenly her husband began to twist convulsively, then collapsed. His body soon lay in a casket in a cross-country train to DC for services, nine million lining the tracks, shocked by Harding's death at 57 of "a stroke of cerebral apoplexy" – likely a heart attack.[31] He was taken to Marion for burial, then among the most beloved presidents since Lincoln. Ruth penned a handwritten condolence note to Florence, calling himself "a personal friend" of Harding's and thanking "his many kind acts toward individual players."[32]

The day of the funeral, Johnson recalled the prior year when son Walter Jr. played in front of the dugout at Griffith Stadium. Harding nodded the boy over, put him on his lap where he sat for the first inning, and said, "This is a mighty fine boy you have here."[33] Thomas S. Rice, a *Brooklyn Eagle* baseball writer whose interview of the candidate in 1920 had delighted Harding more than any press session of the campaign, evoked how "[Harding] was the sort that gloomed and did not enjoy his supper at the White House if he had seen the Washington team lose. On the contrary, he felt it was a pretty good world, and things could soon come out all right in Europe or elsewhere, if he had seen the Senators win."[34] Unlike the Bambino's Yankees, the Ohioan's second-division team had not spoiled him with success.

John F. Kennedy, throwing out the first ball, 1962, first year at District of Columbia Stadium in Washington. *Official White House photograph.*

President Warren G. Harding shaking hands with
New York Yankee Babe Ruth at Yankee Stadium. April 25, 1923.
Leslie Jones photo, courtesy of the Boston Public Library.

Harding yielded to vice president Calvin Coolidge, described by Senators owner Clark Griffith as "a calculating, unexcitable man who showed nothing."[35] Worse, Coolidge *knew* almost nothing of baseball, yet possessed a politician's sense of appropriation. Numerous photos show Calvin awkwardly posed, about to throw – where and how, he seemed uncertain. Coolidge could be legendarily terse – thus, his moniker, Silent Cal. A woman at a White House dinner gushed, "You must talk to me, Mr. Coolidge. I made a bet today that I could get more than two words out of you." Cal told her: "You lose."[36] Reticence was one thing, frigidity another. How to humanize a man whose body temperature seemed single-digit? If the query troubled aides on the eve of the 1924 election, the answer crystalized as Washington streaked toward an unlikely first flag – tether Coolidge to baseball, then in full flush of popularity. *Use* it to *elect* him.[37]

In late September the Senators returned from a pennant-clinching victory, took a motorcade from Union Station to the White House, and traipsed to the Ellipse, where Lincoln played town ball in the 1860s.[38] There, Cal gave a rousing talk – the kind of speech he had rarely given and after 1924 rarely gave again. "They are a great band, these armored knights of the bat and ball,"[39] Coolidge began, the crowd amazed. Who *was* this suddenly glib and baseball-savvy man? In fact, aiding these and other talks was wife Grace, a former official scorer of her baseball team at the University of Vermont, who knew, unlike Cal, the difference between a Texas Leaguer and a Baltimore Chop. Coolidge adjourned the rally, cheered Washington's only Series title, and rode baseball to a November landslide. He then returned to caring little about it, taking his most telling conversation to the grave. Earlier that year, players of the visiting Yankees had formed a straight line to greet him. At last the Behemoth of Biff came face-to-face with Coolidge. "Mr. Ruth," said the president. Babe wiped his head with a handkerchief and answered, "Hot as hell, ain't it, Prez?"[40]

In 1928 Coolidge declined to seek re-election. Herbert Hoover succeeded him, having played the game since boyhood and for Stanford's freshman team in 1893, challenging the "San Francisco professional team to play us on campus." He continued: "When the score was something like thirty to nothing at the end of the fifth inning and getting dark, we called it off. In time, my colleagues decided I would make a better manager than shortstop,"[41] having dislocated a finger. Hoover took a job promoting Stanford baseball and football as a student in a post now known as "business manager," which helped the prototypal poor boy who made good – born in an Iowa small town, orphaned at age three, and raised by various aunts and uncles – pay his way through college.

Later a.k.a. the Great Humanitarian, Hoover made a fortune in engineering but left in World War I to head the Commission for Belgian Relief and oversee America's wartime food supply. He returned home to become the 1921-29 secretary of commerce, heading flood recovery in 1920s Mississippi. He backed boys' baseball leagues on every level, tossed out the first pitch at an American Legion title game, and signed and gave dozens of baseballs for use as awards to players.[42] A photo shows Hoover opening Washington's sandlot baseball season by throwing out the first ball.[43] "The rigid volunteer rules of right and wrong in sports," he said, "are second only to religious faith in moral training – and baseball is the greatest of American sports." Before their 1970 move to Riverfront Stadium, the Cincinnati Reds displayed his quote on a tablet at Crosley Field.[44]

On one hand, Hoover admired Babe's weaving '20s magic at the bat. "He was a parade all by himself, a burst of dazzle and jingle," Jimmy Cannon wrote, "Santa Claus drinking his whiskey straight and groaning with a bellyache."[45] On the other, Ruth's appetites revolted the pious president to-be: suspended five times, in 1922; again in 1925, for insubordination; overeating [i.e., gonorrhea] that year causing "the stomachache heard 'round the world": the cynosure of all eyes. In 1926 Ruth meant the tying Series run, St. Louis ahead, 3-2, in Game Seven's final frame. A Yankees rally died, Babe out stealing. The next two years, New York won the Classic – truly "Murderers' Row." In Buffalo, Ruth wrestled kids on the field. In Ossining, New York, the convicts team named the Black Sheep played the Yanks in exhibitions at Sing Sing prison, "legend [having] it that Babe hit his longest" blast.[46] On September 30, 1927, he smacked AL homer number 60. Hoover inhaled daily box scores, selective coverage then less cynical than today. Once Bombers pitcher Waite Hoyt drank so much that he entered a hospital to dry out. Papers explained it by dubbing Waite an amnesiac, Babe telegramming his critique: "Read about your case of amnesia. Must be a new brand."⁴⁷

That August 2, a note on the White House press board affirmed Coolidge's decision "not ... to run for re-election in nineteen twenty-eight."⁴⁸ By now, Hoover was so popular that many Democrats wanted to draft him for president. Instead he became 1928 GOP nominee. Hoover was rural, small town, and Protestant. Democrats chose New York Governor Alfred E. Smith – urban, boss-linked, and Catholic. One day, the Bombers' regular lineup, pitcher Waite Hoyt, and batboy posed for a photo, each carrying a bat with a letter attached. Collectively, they read "For Al Smith."⁴⁹ The picture made many papers, an outlier saying that Ruth favored Hoover. This fried the Babe, who made another photo wearing a suit, top hat, and sign reading, "I'm for Al Smith." A few days later at Griffith, Ruth further refused to pose with a photo of the president. "Nothing doing," he reportedly said, repeating support for Smith.⁵⁰ A verbal melee then ensued. RUTH REFUSES TO POSE FOR HOOVER! papers screamed, some vowing to cancel his syndicated column. Later, wrote Michael Beschloss, Babe called the dispute a "misunderstanding" and said posing with Hoover would be an "honor."⁵¹ Soon a picture of the principals surfaced: an armistice, albeit brief.

That October 9, the Yankees won their third Series in six years, beating the Cardinals, 7-3. En route home from St. Louis, Ruth spoke approvingly in Terre Haute, Indiana, from a train, about Smith, whereupon the crowd turned silent.⁵² According to Leigh Montville's 2006 biography, *The Big Bam,* Ruth replied, "The hell with you!"⁵³ Like Smith, Babe was Catholic – to Ruth, the candidate's origins on New York's Lower East Side redolent of his own. "I wasn't fed with a gold spoon when I was a kid," he wrote a Smith campaign official, one Franklin D. Roosevelt. "No poor boy can go any too high in this world to suit me."⁵⁴ In a national radio speech, the Bambino declared "what a wonderful thing it is" that "there is a chance for every boy to get to the top in America."⁵⁵ Nothing kept Hoover from winning an Election Day avalanche: 40 states to Smith's 8, including Al's New York. For Ruth, living well was not solely his best revenge. After the Depression roof fell in, a reporter questioned the propriety of George Herman's $80,000 salary topping Hoover's $75,000 in 1930. "I know," Babe famously said, "but I had a better year than Hoover."⁵⁶

Despite such contempt, Hoover respected Ruth's batting oomph, even as the 1929-31 sans-pennant Yanks marked their driest patch between 1921 and 1964. "I want more runs in baseball," Hoover often said, foretelling FDR. "When you were raised on a sandlot, where the scores ran twenty-three to sixty-one, you yearn for something more than a five to two score." Excitement spiked "when there is someone on base. It reaches ecstasy when somebody makes a run."⁵⁷ How could he not respect a player who 12 times led the AL in going deep or 72 times homered twice in a game – and whose drama peaked as Hoover was about to leave office and Roosevelt was to inherit it? In 1930 New York had dealt popular Mark Koenig to Detroit, which sent him to the Cubs, for whom he hit .353 in 1932 and helped win a pennant. Chicago then denied Koenig a full World Series share, inflaming that year's foe, Koenig's ex-teammate Yanks. The Bombers won the Series' first two games. Before Game Three, Yanks skipper Joe McCarthy and Cubs manager Charlie Grimm posed with FDR, who threw out the first pitch. In the fifth inning, the score tied, 4-4 at Wrigley, starter Charlie Root faced Ruth.

The Cubs righty threw a strike, then ball. The Yankees bayed "Cheapskates," the home dugout responding "Flatfoot" and tossing liniment. Root threw ball two. Babe raised two fingers: a 2-and-2 count. Did he gesture to predict where the next pitch would land? "Ruth most certainly did not call his home run in that game," Root maintained. "I ought to know. I was there."⁵⁸ According to the Yanks' Frank Crosetti, Babe pointed to the Cubs dugout, not the bleachers. "Those Cubs were a bunch of stooges," he said. "They were riding Ruth from the bench."⁵⁹ After the game, Babe told Crosetti, "If the writers want to think that I pointed where I was going to hit the ball, let 'em."⁶⁰ In 1994 Fox TV ran an exposé of the Called Shot. "I asked [his 1956-57 pitching coach Root] if Ruth had called his homer," Braves pitcher Ernie Johnson said. "His eyes narrowed and he said, 'If he [Ruth] had, next time up I'd have stuck the pitch right in his ear.'"⁶¹ Now-Braves skipper Grimm, agreed, telling Ernie, "Boy, Root was mean out there. One time he knocked down three or four guys in a row."⁶² None thought Ruth pointed to the seats – a conclusion Fox TV reached, too.

Elected in 1932, taking 42 states to Hoover's 6, Franklin Roosevelt hosted a 1933 reception at the White House, flinging an arm around Ruth's shoulders in mock complaint about a rarity: being one-upped in public. In 1920, running for vice president,

Babe Ruth at the White House, December 7, 1921. *Courtesy of Library of Congress.*

FDR had been speaking in a hotel lobby when Babe, entering, stole a good part of his audience.⁶³ Before contracting polio, Roosevelt had played baseball eagerly, if not well, as a boy. Later, he became team manager in prep school. As president, he "enjoys himself at a ballgame as much as a kid on Christmas morning," wrote *Baseball Magazine*,⁶⁴ the "kind of fan who 'wants to get plenty of action for my money." FDR admitted to getting "the biggest kick out of the biggest score – a game in which the hitters poke the ball into the far corners of the field, the outfielders scramble, and men run the bases."⁶⁵ A May 7, 1933, Fireside Chat showed FDR's baseball state of mind. "I have no expectation of making a hit every time I come to bat," he said. "What I seek is the highest possible batting average, not only for myself but for the team."⁶⁶

Roosevelt compared a batter sacrificing for the team's good to a citizen sacrificing for the nation's good. Like a play-by-play man, he prized education, interspersing facts and yarns. On May 24, 1935, FDR threw a White House switch to light the first official big-league night game, Dodgers and Reds from Cincinnati's Crosley Field. Ironically, in a game there four days later, Babe "had a lot of difficulty with the left-field terrace," the *Dayton Daily News* wrote, "and once fell down while going after a ball."⁶⁷ Leaving the game, Babe soon retired. In 1939 he attended the formal opening of the National Baseball Hall of Fame and Museum, two years before America entered World War II. After Pearl Harbor, Commissioner Kenesaw Mountain Landis wrote Roosevelt a January 14, 1942, letter, saying, "If you believe we ought to close down for the duration of the war, we are ready to do so immediately. If you feel we ought to continue, we would be delighted to do so. We wait your order."⁶⁸ A day later, FDR read his reply aloud at a White House press conference, saying the national pastime was vital to the national interest. "I honestly feel that it would be best for the country to keep baseball going."⁶⁹

It is impossible to know baseball's fate had Roosevelt not acted. It survived and thrived because he *did*. Baseball remained, as FDR foresaw, "a recreation ... which can be got for very little cost."⁷⁰ Towns formed local teams, gasoline and rubber rationing keeping almost every family close to home. In 1943 broadcaster Mel Allen, serving in the Army, accompanied Ruth to events in the Tri-State New York-Connecticut-New Jersey area. A guest is said to need no introduction. That was *literally* true of Babe, Allen said. "I'm sitting in his Cadillac or hearing him speak at fundraisers [for the USO, American Red Cross, and other service groups] and he's speaking in his outgoing personality like he knew me and his audience for years."⁷¹ It was, Mel mused, "like talking to God." Military personnel played "pickup" games. Ruth threw out the first ball. More night matches were slated as FDR had asked so that "the day shift ... [could] see a game occasionally."⁷² Babe joined Herbert Hoover, among others, to raise money at World War II events for America's allies, including a 1940 Baseball Writers Association of America fundraiser for the Finnish Relief Fund.⁷³ The war made old rivalries seem petty.

In 1944 Ruth endorsed likely history's most famed Might-Have-Been-President. In October, having been asked to again support FDR, he surprisingly said that America needed "a new pitcher in the White House." America's only three-term (soon four) president was "a great man," Babe told reporters, registering to vote for the first time, "but we have got to have a change."⁷⁴ The man Babe had in mind was Governor Thomas E. Dewey, elected New York's governor in 1942, since then having "done a good job" in Albany.⁷⁵ On Election Eve, he and baseball's still-most-titanic name anchored a rally at Madison Square Garden, Ruth saying, "Some people put script in front of some people to say what they want them to say, but I don't have to do that."⁷⁶ Dewey lost, but easily ran FDR the closest of his four presidential primary races. In 1948, heavily favored, the New Yorker lost America's still most luminous political upset to Truman. Years later, I separately asked former Presidents Richard Nixon, Gerald Ford, and George H.W. Bush which person of their lifetime who did *not* become president *should* have. Each chose Dewey.⁷⁷

In 1947 Dewey took both of his sons to the Subway Series between the Yankees and Dodgers.⁷⁸ That year the last president whom the Bambino met led his team to the first collegiate World Series. By then, George H.W. Bush, only 23, had served heroically in World War II, almost lost his life when his plane was shot down over the Pacific, been honorably discharged after 58 combat missions, and enrolled at Yale University, where he had been accepted prior to prewar training.⁷⁹ The young man in a hurry began its accelerated academic program and built a résumé of Delta Kappa Epsilon fraternity; member, Phi Beta Kappa and secret society Skull and Bones; and Yale baseball captain. His yearbook shows Bush, in uniform, with a description: "Captain of championship college baseball team [making the first two (1947-48) College World Series final], while completing college in 2½ years after war service. Phi Beta Kappa – Economics."⁸⁰

The Baseball Quarterly Reviews (BQR), published by the Collegiate Record, compiled statistics on its famed – "infamous," Bush laughed – no-hit, good-field first baseman.⁸¹ It found his batting average lower than previously thought (.224 *v*. .251 listed in 1991 *USA Today*'s *Baseball Weekly*) but his fielding percentage even higher (.983, including a remarkable .993 in Bush's senior year). "He was the only [Yale] man to start every game [76] in that 1946-48 [Yale varsity] period and the only Eli player to achieve that 'iron man' distinction," *BQR* wrote.⁸² If Lou Gehrig was baseball's "Iron Man," Bush was Yale's. Video shows him in his *60s* making a diving stop of a groundball behind first base and making a dazzling putout at the bag. Aptly, his hero was the Bambino's teammate: "Gehrig was steadier, less flamboyant, and more dependable than the Babe," he said, "steadily achieving excellence"[83] – a telling self-portrait.

In June 1948 the *New York Times* recorded Ruth, 53, traveling to New Haven to donate his black-bound manuscript of *The Babe Ruth Story* to the Yale Library, a month before the ill-advised film version, starring William Bendix, was scheduled for release. In a ceremony at Yale Field, Babe gave the book to Yale's captain, whom the *Times* termed "George (Poppy) Bush of Greenwich, [Connecticut]."[84] Some wept. Ruth unsteadily held a cigar stub. At the microphone, a shell of his former 240 pounds, voice spent, Ruth addressed "Captain Bush," saying that his book "has a lot of fun in it, and a lot of laughs, a lot of crying, too."[85] In 1987 Bush wrote his own memoir, *Looking Forward*. "It was obvious that he was dying of cancer [death came August 16]," the future president wrote, "but some of the young, free-spirited 'Babe' was still there, very much alive. 'You know,' he said, winking, 'when you write a book like this, you can't put *everything* in it.'"[86]

Ruth played at Griffith Stadium before five US presidents: Wilson, Harding, Coolidge, Hoover, and FDR. In a sense, he still plays at Cooperstown – a pilgrim to the Hall of Fame struck by the heavy traffic that surrounds Babe's plaque, among the most visited of the more than 300 players, managers, executives, and other honorees. Like vines around baseball's trellis, Ruth intersected even with future presidents he didn't know. In the 1940s, Richard Nixon entered a New York restaurant to ask Babe for an autograph. The Yankees' number 3, of course, complied.[87] His lesson wasn't lost. Later, pre- and post-presidency, Nixon usually spurned luxury boxes for a box seat, sitting among fans, keeping score and signing autographs, saying, "If Ruth can sign, I can sign."[88] Nixon's successor, Gerald Ford, embraced the Babe as vice president in early 1974 as Henry Aaron neared, then tied, Ruth's career home-run record. Hank's first 1974 swing on Opening Day at Cincinnati equaled Babe's Everest 714, Ford cheering lustily, "glad to have been part of history."[89]

Then, on April 8, *another* president-to-be eyed history at Atlanta-Fulton County Stadium. In the fourth inning, Aaron batted. "Sitting on 714. Here's the pitch by [Al] Downing ... swinging ... There's a drive into left-center field!" said Braves voice Milo Hamilton. "That ball is gonna be ... outa here! It's gone! It's 715!" clearing the fence into reliever Tom House's glove. "There's a new home-run champion of all time! And it's Henry Aaron! The fireworks are going! Henry Aaron's coming around third! His teammates are at home plate! Listen to this crowd!"[90] The game was halted to honor Aaron. Then-Georgia Governor Jimmy Carter gave number 44 a special auto tag, HR-715, car to follow.[91]

Strikingly, in a cycle that fused the presidency and baseball, Carter's mother, the beloved Miss Lillian, wrote of never "forget[ting] the experience of seeing Babe Ruth hit two homers in a single game at Yankee Stadium."[92] Each year, when Jimmy was growing up and the family peanut crop was harvested, his parents "would drive 'up north' to spend a week or ten days almost totally immersed in major league baseball," he wrote in *Sharing Good Times*.[93] One year the Carters stayed in Boston for an entire Braves homestand; the next, Washington, to see the Senators; another, New York, the Yankees, in The House That Ruth Built,[94] his thread linking one generation to the next.

In 1998 Babe reemerged in daily conversation as Mark McGwire and Sammy Sosa staged a homerthon that even a later revelation of drug use did not erase. Their Great Race against Ruth's – and Roger Maris's later – single-season mark of 60 and 61 home runs in 154 and 162 games, respectively, spectacularly revived the game. It also renewed an American Original whose legacy astonishes – as Ruthian as any campaign speech and as bipartisan as any prayer.

Sources

I wish to especially thank the former American presidents for the views expressed in this chapter. Grateful appreciation is also made to reprint all play-by-play and color radio text courtesy of John Miley's The Miley Collection. In addition to the sources cited in the Notes, most particularly the Society for American Baseball Research, the author also consulted: Baseball-Reference.com and Retrosheet.org websites' box scores, player, season, and team pages, batting and pitching logs, and other material relevant to this history. FansGraphs.com provided statistical information. In addition to the sources cited in the Notes, the author also consulted:

Books

Ambrose, Stephen E. *Eisenhower: Soldier and President* (New York: Simon and Schuster, 1990).

Benson, Michael. *Ballparks of North America: A Comprehensive Historical Encyclopedia of Baseball Grounds, Yards and Stadiums, 1845 to 1988* (Jefferson, North Carolina: McFarland, 1989).

Bush, George. *All the Bush, George Bush: My Life in Letters* (New York: Scribner, 1999).

Cassuto, Leonard, and Stephen Partridge, eds. *The Cambridge Companion to Baseball* (Cambridge: Cambridge University Press, 2011).

Creamer, Robert W. *Babe: The Legend Comes to Life* (New York: Simon and Schuster, 1974).

Manchester, William. *One Brief Shining Moment* (Boston: Little, Brown, 1983).

Morgan, Ted. *FDR: A Biography* (New York: Simon and Schuster, 1986).

Rickey, Branch, and Robert Riger. *The American Diamond* (New York: Simon and Schuster, 1965).

Ruth, George Herman, with Bob Considine: *The Babe Ruth Story* (New York: Dutton, 1948).

Seymour, Harold. *Baseball: The People's Game* (New York: Oxford University Press, 1990).

Newspapers

The *New York Times* and the *Washington Post* have been a primary source about information about Babe Ruth and the US presidents who knew him. Other key sources include Associated Press, *Baseball Digest*, *SportsBusiness Daily*, the *Boston Globe*, *The Sporting News*, and the *Times of London*.

Magazines/Periodicals

Sports Illustrated, *The Baseball Quarterly Reviews*, and *The Saturday Evening Post*.

Interviews

Lee Allen, with author, June 1967.

Mel Allen, with author, February 1972.

George H.W. Bush, with author, June 2010.

Gerald Ford, with author, May 1994.

Ernie Johnson, with author, May 1986.

Richard Nixon, with author, September 1979.

George Will, with author, April 1989.

Notes

1. George Vecsey, "Babe Ruth," in Gerald Astor, *The Baseball Hall of Fame 50th Anniversary Book* (New York: Prentice Hall, 1988), 141.
2. George Will interview with author, April 1989.
3. thinkexist.com/quotation/this_is_worse_than_a_crime-it-s_a/166660.html.
4. William Mead and Paul Dickson, *Baseball: The Presidents' Game* (Washington: Farragut, 1993), 188.
5. Mead and Dickson, 33, 188.
6. Mead and Dickson, 188.
7. baseballhall.org/discover/polo-grounds-pass-tells-story-of-woodrow-wilson.
8. Michael Beschloss, "Presidents Who Knew the Babe," *New York Times,* April 11, 2015. nytimes.com/2015/04/11/upshot/presidents-who-knew-the-babe.html.
9. Lee Allen interview with author, June 1967.
10. baseball-reference.com/leaders/HR_progress.shtml.
11. biography.com/people/babe-ruth-9468009.
12. Allan Wood, "Babe Ruth," Society for American Baseball Research. sabr.org/bioproj/person/9dcdd01c.
13. "1923 With Regards to Harry." thisgreatgame.com/1923-baseball-history.html.
14. Beschloss.
15. Richard Hoffer, "Our Favorite Athletes. It's Not Nice to Play Favorites but We're Making an Exception Here/ Celebrating Not Necessarily the Greatest but Those Who Brought Us the Greatest Joy," *Sports Illustrated*, July 12, 1999.
16. Beschloss.
17. Ibid.
18. Ibid.
19. Mead and Dickson, 43.
20. Ernie Johnson interview with author, May 1986.
21. Mead and Dickson, 188.
22. baseball-injury-report.com/new-york-yankees/.
23. newyork.yankees.mlb.com/nyy/ballpark/stadium_history.jsp.
24. Philip J. Lowry, *Green Cathedrals* (Reading, Massachusetts: Addison-Wesley, 1992), 61.
25. Beschloss.
26. Luis A. Mendez, "The Roaring Conservative 20s: Harding, Coolidge, and Hoover," *M,* July 31, 2017. medium.com/s/conservative-roots/the-roaring-conservative-20s-harding-coolidge-and-hoover-9c843239c6d3.
27. Mead and Dickson, 44.
28. picclick.com/US-President-WARREN-HARDING-BABE-RUTH-192751296585.html.
29. Jesse Greenspan, "The Unexpected Death of President Harding," The History Channel, August 2, 2013. history.com/news/the-unexpected-death-of-president-harding-90-years-ago.
30. Ibid.
31. Howard Markel, "The Strange Death of Warren Harding," *PBS News Hour,* August 2, 2015. pbs.org/newshour/health/srange-death-warren-harding.
32. Beschloss.
33. Mead and Dickson, 43.
34. Mead and Dickson, 46.

35 Mead and Dickson, 47.
36 washingtonpost.com/archive/entertainment/books/2007/01/21/silent-cal-span-class-bankheadthe- taciturn-coolidges-term-spoke-volumes-about-the-modern-presidencys-pan/61d9fd94-7718-45d7-bd58-0d4f8e68bcb/?utm_terms=.8c3017602d8d.
37 Mead and Dickson, 47.
38 Mead and Dickson, 51.
39 Mead and Dickson, 52.
40 Mead and Dickson, 53.
41 Mead and Dickson, 66.
42 Ibid.
43 Mead and Dickson, 58.
44 Mead and Dickson, 59.
45 quotetab.com/quotes/by-jimmy-cannon#0m50cWbCScgesJzL.97. "Jimmy Cannon Quotations."
46 singsingprisonmuseum.org/quick-facts.html.
47 fpbaseballoutsider.blogspot.com/2014/11
48 encyclopedia.com/people/history/us-history-biographies/calvin-coolidge.
49 Mead and Dickson, 69-70.
50 Beschloss.
51 Ibid.
52 Ibid.
53 penguinrandomhouse.com/books/1164391/the-big-bam-by-leigh-montville/980I-bi7679197151, Leigh Montville, *The Big Bam: The Life and Times of Babe Ruth* (New York: Penguin, 2006), 279.
54 Beschloss.
55 Ibid.
56 baseball-almanac.com/prz_qhh.shtml
57 Mead and Dickson, 59.
58 Gregory H. Wolf, "Charlie Root," Society for American Baseball Research. sabr.org/bioproj/person/22e9a7e7.
59 nytimes.com/2002/02/13/sports/frank-crosetti-91-a-fixture-in-Yankee-pinstripes-is-dead.html.
60 Ibid.
61 Johnson May 1986 interview.
62 Ibid.
63 Beschloss, "Presidents Who Knew the Babe."
64 Mead and Dickson, 71.
65 Ibid.
66 UVA Miller Center, "May 7, 1933: Fireside Chat 2: On Progress During First Two Months. Millercenter.org/the-presidency/presidential-speeches/May-7-1933-fireside-chat-2-progress-during-first-two-months.
67 *Dayton Daily News*, May 29, 1935: 9.
68 Craig Mulder, "President Roosevelt Gives 'Green Light' to Baseball." baseballhall.org/discover/nside-pitch/roosevelt-sendsgreen-light-letter.
69 Mead and Dickson, 78.
70 Mead and Dickson, 79.
71 Mel Allen interview with author, February 1972.
72 Mead and Dickson, 79.
73 Mead and Dickson, 63.
74 Beschloss.
75 Ibid.
76 Ibid.
77 George H.W. Bush, June 2010 interview; Gerald Ford, May 1994 interview; and Richard Nixon, September 1979 interview, each with author.
78 Richard Norton Smith, *Thomas E. Dewey and His Times* (New York: Simon & Schuster, 1982), 457.
79 George H.W. Bush, June 10 interview.
80 Ibid.
81 Ibid.
82 Herm Krabbenhoft, "The Complete Collegiate Record of George H.W. Bush," published in the *Baseball Research Journal* (Fall 2017). sabr.org/research/complete-collegiate-baseball-record-george-hw-bush.
83 Bush June 2010 interview.
84 Beschloss.
85 Ibid.
86 George Bush, *Looking Forward: An Autobiography.* (New York: Doubleday, 1987), 45.
87 Richard Nixon September 1979 interview.
88 Ibid.
89 Gerald Ford May 1994 interview.
90 Play-by-play courtesy of the Miley Collection.
91 Jimmy Carter, *Sharing Good Times.* (New York: Simon and Schuster, 2005), 11.
92 Lillian Carter, *The World Series: A 75th Anniversary*, edited by Joseph L. Reichler (New York: Simon and Schuster, 1978), 79.
93 Jimmy Carter, 8-9.
94 Ibid.

The Babe: In Person and Onscreen

By Rob Edelman

Ever the celebrity, Ruth doffs his cap. *Courtesy of Library of Congress.*

Of any athlete from any sport who does double duty on the big screen and the ballyard/gridiron/basketball court, none has been written about, analyzed, and overanalyzed as much as Babe Ruth. Not Jim Brown. Not Michael Jordan. Not Willie, Mickey, or The Duke.

Upon winning fame as the Sultan of Swat, Babe Ruth often appeared in venues other than ballparks. He was a popular personality in vaudeville, on the radio – and onscreen. So it is no revelation that The Babe would be cast to play himself opposite Gary Cooper's Lou Gehrig in *The Pride of the Yankees* (released in 1942), would clown with Harold Lloyd in a taxi headed to Yankee Stadium in *Speedy* (1928), and would star in features and short films of various types during the 1920s and '30s.

In 1932 The Bambino toplined a series of one-reel Universal photoplays, labeled the "Babe Ruth Baseball Series," which included athletic coaching; among its titles are *Just Pals*, *Perfect Control*, *Fancy Curves*, *Over the Fence*, and *Slide, Babe, Slide*. He was featured in a range of documentaries and instructional films, from 1920's *Over the Fence*, *Play Ball With Babe Ruth*, and *How Babe Ruth Hits a Home Run* to 1939's *Touching All Bases*.[1] However, these titles – with one exception – are bunt singles when compared to the dingers that are The Babe's feature-length films. That one is a one-reeler: *Home Run on the Keys* (1937), in which he offers his "official" take on his celebrated called shot off the Chicago Cubs' Charlie Root in the 1932 World Series.

Home Run on the Keys features The Babe on a hunting trip, and he is shown spending time in a cabin with songwriters Zez Confrey and Byron Gay. Here is his claim:

> Well, I'll tell ya. The papers said it was the longest and the most dramatic home run ever hit at the Cubs park. I'll never forget it. It was a tough Series. Both clubs riding each other. Doing everything to get each other's goat. Well, at this one particular time when I went to bat, Charlie Root was pitching, and the first pitched ball was a called strike. Well, I thought it was outside and didn't like it very much. So the boys over there were given me the 'on ya' 'on ya.' You know what I mean. ... Well, the second pitched ball was another called strike. Well, I didn't like that one either. So, I let it go by. And by that time, they were over there going crazy! Well, I stepped out of the box and I looked over to the bench and then I looked out at center field and I pointed. I said, 'I'm going to hit the next pitched ball right past the flag pole.' Well, the good lord and good luck must have been with me because, I did *exactly* what I said I was going to do. And I'll tell you one thing; that was the best home run I ever hit in my life.[2]

Of course, The Bambino first came to the majors in 1914, but it was not until he arrived in New York in 1920 that his screen career commenced with the production of *Headin' Home*, a low-budget comedy-drama presented by Kessel & Baumann and produced by the Yankee Photo Corporation. While *Headin' Home* is no classic of its era, its historical worth is obvious if only for The Babe's presence. His character may be called "Babe," but there is nothing genuinely biographical here; when the film was produced, his rough upbringing and off-the-field antics were unknown commodities. So depicting Ruth as a humble, stereotypical all-American boy who adores his mother and lives with her and his kid sister in Haverlock, "a little egg and hamlet in the sticks," was a smart marketing ploy. So is showing Babe chopping wood, which he fashions into the baseball bats he employs to smash heroic dingers. He favors peaceful evenings savoring his mom's home cooking, and his innate shyness separates him from the girl he secretly adores: Mildred Tobin (played by Ruth Taylor), the town banker's offspring. During the course of the scenario, Babe belts a game-winning dinger in a local exhibition; saves Mildred from the clenches of a lawbreaker; wins acclaim as a home-run-bashing big-league star; rescues Mildred's brother from a vamp; and returns to Haverlock, where he homers in front of the locals.

As noted on the Turner Classic Movies website, "Just as Babe Ruth was becoming the ballplayer who epitomized the 1920's, *Headin' Home* was the one baseball film that embodied the mass-marketing of the sport. No measly movie palace could house it during its New York premiere. Fight promoter Tex Rickard reportedly paid $35,000 to book the film into Madison Square Garden, where it was screened from September 19 to 26, 1920. *Variety*, the motion-picture trade publication, informed its readers that moviegoers could purchase everything "from Babe Ruth phonographic records to the Babe Ruth song, 'Oh You Babe Ruth,' which was sung and played by Lieut. J. Tim Bryan's Black Devil Band, which accompanied the picture."[3]

For decades, *Headin' Home* existed only in brief excerpts or "complete" films that were shortened and heavily edited. A visually fuzzy VHS tape could be purchased from Grapevine Video, which markets silent films in the public domain. But then professors-film archivists Ted Larson and Rusty Casselton reconstructed an almost complete 16mm version, with a 73-minute running time. Their print was shown in the mid-1990s at a number of venues, from New York's Film Forum (in celebration of The Babe's centennial) to Syracuse's Cinefest (a now-defunct festival of rare vintage films) and the Louisville Bat Museum (at an annual Society for American Baseball Research convention).

Casselton offered a detailed chronicle of the manner in which the restoration evolved. It serves as a textbook example of the rediscovery and restoration of "lost" films:

> In 1993, I received a call from a friend in Arizona about a woman who had a nitrate feature in her front closet. She had inherited the film from her father, and he always told her that it was very special because it starred 'Baby Ruth.' The Arizona print had no title and was brittle from age. The film was distributed on a states rights basis, and this print had been edited to remove references to bootlegging and illegal drinking.

> Ted (Larson) and I started to talk about preserving the film and at that time Bruce Goldstein at the Film Forum was putting together a program for the Babe's 100th birthday. He arranged for *Collector's Sportslook*, a magazine edited by Tucker Smith, to help fund the event and preservation. Now that some of the finances were in place I got serious about the project. ... I ended up tracking down a second nitrate print from a collector in Connecticut. The 'Connecticut' print had an original main title and a total of nine other inserts that had been cut out of the 'Arizona' print. It was, however, missing the last five minutes, and (there were) gaps throughout in the general continuity.

I (was) aware of yet another source for material on the film. Many years ago, a company released in 16mm a very substantial print of the film. There certainly would be no use for that material except for the fact it had one more scene that was still missing from the composite master. I tracked down the negative for that print, but the owner would not cooperate and make the scene available to be incorporated into the restoration print. The scene is near the end of the film, when Babe goes home to visit his sweetheart. The girl's father now accepts Babe and they leave the room. At this point the print cuts and what is missing is a scene with Babe and the father in the basement with a still having a good old time. I guess this leaves the current print as a restoration project in progress. Someday, it will be completed.[4]

If it ever is, neither Casselton nor Larson will be involved as both have since died. However, a different *Headin' Home* restoration – this one a 50-minute-long 35mm print – was shown in April 2006 at New York's Museum of Modern Art in a 12-film program titled "Baseball and American Culture." The *New York Times* dubbed it "a rare, freshly restored silent"[5] and the *New York Daily News* quoted Carl E. Prince, former chairman of the New York University History Department, who organized the series with Charles Silver, a curator in MoMA's Department of Film. "(*Headin' Home*) hasn't been seen in over 80 years," Prince claimed while hyping the program. "It's about home, mother and apple pie – it's just wonderful."[6] It was as if the Larson-Casselton restoration, let alone the Grapevine Video edition, never existed.

A year after the MoMA program, *Headin' Home* was included in *Reel Baseball*, a two-DVD set released by Kino International and consisting of two features (*Headin' Home* and *The Busher*) and 11 shorts released between 1899 and 1926. The version here is the 73-minute Larson-Casselton print.

The Bambino's other silent feature, *Babe Comes Home*, dates from 1927. During its extensive publicity campaign, the film was erroneously hyped as Ruth's screen debut: "On July 1," noted the *New York Times*, "Babe Ruth's first picture, 'Babe Comes Home,' is to be offered at the Longacre Theatre."[7] But unlike *Headin' Home*, *Babe Comes Home* is long-lost. Countless silent films have for one reason or another faded into the mists of history; as each year passes, chances are slim to none that *Babe Comes Home* will reappear after being hidden in the vault of a film archive or in a film collector's attic. However, 13 seconds worth of *Babe Comes Home*-related visuals may be seen on YouTube. Here, The Babe is ever-so-briefly shown having makeup applied and carousing on the set.[8]

Babe Comes Home mirrors the by-then-established view of The Babe as a reveler. Plus, it certainly is of its time as a proud proponent of tobacco usage. In *The American Film Institute Catalog of Feature Films 1921-30*, *Babe Comes Home* is described as a comedy in which Ruth plays "Babe Dugan, star player with the (Los Angeles Angels) baseball team. He chews tobacco and gets his uniform dirtier than any other player. Vernie (played by Anna Q. Nilsson), the laundress who cleans his uniform every week, becomes concerned over his untidiness. Babe calls to apologize for unintentionally striking her with a ball during a game. … On an outing to an amusement park, a roller coaster throws Vernie into Babe's arms; soon they are engaged, and Vernie plans to reform him. Scores of tobacco cubes and spittoons are pre-wedding gifts. And they precipitate a lovers' quarrel. But Babe takes the reform idea seriously, though his game slumps and he is put on the bench. At a crucial moment, Vernie relents and throws him a plug of tobacco; and consequently he delivers a four-base blow."[9]

Cinematically speaking, neither *Headin' Home* nor *Babe Comes Home* would have earned Academy Award nominations (if in fact the Oscars existed at the time of their releases) or landed on critics' 10 Best Films lists. The essence of *Headin' Home* was summed up by the *Brooklyn Daily Eagle*: "Were it not for the fact that Ruth is the star, the film would attract very little attention. … If you are interested in the ball player, there are enough good scenes of the home run hitter in the film to make the picture satisfactory."[10] *Babe Comes Home*, meanwhile, earned mixed reviews. The *Brooklyn Daily Eagle* described it as "not a very good picture," adding, However, (Ruth declared that) he had just loads of fun making it. … Anyway, Babe Ruth is a very, very fine ball player."[11] The *New York Times* labeled it a "broad comedy, and commented, "It's rough-house stuff, but full of fun. … Mr. Ruth himself makes a pleasing screen figure. …"[12]

Added Harold Heffernan, writing about *Babe Comes Home* in the *Detroit News*:

> Babe Ruth has arrived on the screen ... but there is no particular reason for John Barrymore or any of the other noted film thespians to become agitated about the matter. Mr. Ruth is a solid, healthy appearing actor, not especially attractive in comparison to some of our male idols, but probably much better than you ever hoped for. Possibly his long experience with the newsreel cameramen is responsible for his ability to keep his eyes out of the camera lens – something few movie beginners are able to do.
>
> The Bambino, Sultan of Swat, Home Run King or whatever you wish, is the whole show, plus the box office, in 'Babe Comes Home.' Everything is built

around him, over him and under him. The story is rather slim and is liberally padded, but for this type of picture is much better than the average. ... There is a big game for the pennant (at the finale). Babe is in a slump because he has sworn off tobacco chewing. (During) the ninth inning crisis, the girl leans over the box into the playing field and hands Babe a plug of the old stuff, and bang goes the ballgame![13]

The Babe went on to act in two major Hollywood features, both of which differ from *Headin' Home* and *Babe Comes Home* in that he is not the star. Certified screen legends are the headliners – and in both, The Bambino appears in support as himself.

The first is a silent comedy: *Speedy*, starring Harold Lloyd and released in 1928. Here, Lloyd – who joined Charlie Chaplin and Buster Keaton as the premier silent screen clowns – plays Harold "Speedy" Swift, a baseball fan-atic of the first order. Jane Dillon (Ann Christy), his girlfriend, declares that her guy "gets plenty of jobs – but he'll never keep one while his mind is full of baseball." His latest gig is as a cabbie, and he reads in a newspaper that The Bambino will momentarily be autographing baseballs to kids at the City Orphan Asylum. It so happens that Speedy is parked nearby and is determined to gaze at his hero, who is besieged by overzealous fans. Upon realizing that he must head off to his workplace, The Babe hails Speedy's taxi.

The overly-excited cabbie gives The Babe a comedy-laden ride: "Gosh, Babe – this is the proudest moment of my life," he declares while veering through traffic and coming perilously close to other autos and pedestrians. "If I ever want to commit suicide I'll call you," the ballplayer informs the driver. However, The Babe's presence does not end upon arriving at Yankee Stadium, as he invites Speedy into the ballyard to watch the contest. Speedy is overwhelmed with elation as The Bambino homers. He whacks the pate of the fan in front of him, who just so happens to be his new employer. So Speedy's career as a cabbie ends before it begins.

Much can be said about *The Pride of the Yankees*. As it charts the evolving relationship between Lou Gehrig and his beloved Eleanor (Teresa Wright), it is as much a love story as a baseball film. Its content is unabashedly patriotic, and it came to movie houses in July 1942, seven months after Pearl Harbor; Damon Runyon penned the film's preface, in which he labels it "the story of a gentle young man who ... faced death with the same valor and fortitude that has been displayed by thousands of young Americans on far-flung fields of battle. ..."[14]

The Bambino plus Mark Koenig, Bob Meusel, and Bill Dickey play themselves in *The Pride of the Yankees*. And here he is presented as very much the stereotypical, beloved Babe who favors locker-room clowning as much as on-field heroics. Still, the film's center is Larrupin' Lou. If The Sultan of Swat assures a bedridden boy that he will homer in the World Series, which he does, Gehrig is swayed into forecasting that he will belt *two* long balls – which *he* does. Unsurprisingly, the long-standing feud between the two Yankees is nonexistent; however, it is symbolically represented via the repartee between a sportswriter (played by Walter Brennan) and a sarcastic colleague (Dan Duryea).

Typical reviews for *Speedy* and *The Pride of the Yankees* cite The Bambino's presence. Wrote Mordaunt Hall, reviewing *Speedy* in the *New York Times*, "The big Babe does some excellent acting, for if ever a man looked nervous as the vehicle in which he was riding shaved by other cars, it is the illustrious King of Swat."[15] As for *Pride* ..., Time magazine noted that "Babe Ruth is there, playing himself with fidelity and considerable humor. ..."[16]

For indeed, The Bambino was a natural in front of the cameras and might have savored a lengthy career onscreen. But he was not going to embrace Shakespeare, Eugene O'Neill, or George Bernard Shaw. The Three Stooges were more his style and he could have been transformed into Stooge Number Four, with Moe, Larry, and Curly hooking up with The Babe to merrily toss pies in one another's faces.

Notes

1. imdb.com/name/nm0751899/?ref_=nv_sr_1.
2. imdb.com/title/tt0144970/quotes?ref_=tt_ql_trv_4.
3. Rob Edelman, "Silent Baseball Part 1," tcm.com/this-month/article.html?id=180852%7C180854.
4. Casselton's comments first appeared in the SABR 27 Convention Program, which took place in Louisville June 20-23, 1997. Sections were reprinted first in Volume 5, Number 2 of *Base Ball: A Journal of the Early Game* (Fall 2011) and then online in John Thorn's *Our Game*. (ourgame.mlblogs.com/lost-and-found-baseball-part-2-12163c87037b).
5. Terrence Rafferty, "Baseball on the Screen: Some Hits, Many Errors," *New York Times*, April 2, 2006.
6. Julian Kesner, "Bases Loaded: A festival of Baseball Films Steals Home in Time for the Season," *New York Daily News*, April 2, 2006.
7. "Brains and Blondes," *New York Times*. June 26, 1927.
8. youtube.com/watch?v=pSdccXob6bk.
9. *The American Film Institute Catalogue, Feature Films 1921-30* (New York and London: R.R. Bowker Company, 1971).
10. "Ruth's Film Show," *Brooklyn Daily Eagle,* September 20, 1920.
11. Martin Dickstein, "New Films – and Vocafilms," *Brooklyn Daily Eagle*, July 26, 1927.
12. "The Screen," *New York Times*, July 26, 1927.
13. Harold Heffernan, "Babe Comes Home: Babe Ruth, Good Ballplayer," *Detroit News*. May 16, 1927.
14. reelclassics.com/Movies/Yankees/yankees.htm.
15. Mordaunt Hall, "The Screen," *New York Times*, April 7, 1928.
16. "The New Pictures," *Time*, August 3, 1942.

Babe Ruth Characterizations— and Caricatures

By Rob Edelman

Granted, numerous screen biopics have charted the lives of ballplayers from Hall of Famers to major leaguers with unusual, marketable life stories.[1] One legend – Lou Gehrig – has been portrayed twice, in 1942's *The Pride of the Yankees* and *A Love Affair: The Eleanor and Lou Gehrig Story*, a 1977 made-for-television movie. Another – Jackie Robinson – has been featured in two theatrical films (1950's *The Jackie Robinson Story* and 2013's *42*) as well as a host of others, starting with a pair of TV movies (1990's *The Court-Martial of Jackie Robinson* and 1996's *Soul of the Game*).

But what about The Babe? To date, the life of The Sultan of Swat has been charted in three features; he is played by actors as diverse as William Bendix (in 1948's *The Babe Ruth Story*), Stephen Lang (in *Babe Ruth*, a 1991 TV movie), and John Goodman (in 1992's *The Babe*). He appears in 1993's *The Sandlot* (played by Art LaFleur), *A Love Affair: The Eleanor and Lou Gehrig Story* (Ramon Bieri), and *Dempsey*, a 1983 made-for-TV biopic (Michael McManus); in *The Sandlot*, he offers sage advice that any youngster should ponder as he pronounces, "Remember kid, there's heroes and there's legends. Heroes get remembered but legends never die. Follow your heart, kid, and you'll never go wrong." Decades later, Jonathan Winters enacts The Bambino in *The Babe and the Kid*, a seven-minute short from 2009; in 2014's *Henry & Me*, an animated feature, he is voiced by Chazz Palminteri. He has been featured in innumerable documentaries; a typical title is 2013's *I'll Knock a Homer for You: The Timeless Story of Johnny Sylvester and Babe Ruth*. Indeed, The Babe's across-the-decades fame is epitomized in *Whip It*, released in 2009: the tale of a female roller-derby player who nicknames herself "Babe Ruthless."

Bambino portrayals are not limited to the movies. In 1984, *The Babe* – a one-man show featuring Max Gail – came to Broadway; it eventually was taped and shown on ESPN. Here, three stages of Ruth's career are presented: The Babe in his prime; upon his retirement; and at an Old Timers game. But the show failed dismally. "That 'The Babe'... is so wide of the mark, is no small feat," opined Mel Gussow in the *New York Times*. "(It's) an evening of bush league Babe."[2] The production was sent to the showers after eight previews and five performances.[3] Two years later, *The Babe and Libbie Custer*, a dinner-theater vehicle based on a play by Bob Broeg, premiered in St. Louis, with Gilio Gherardini playing The Babe. "I thought maybe the public would accept my fictional meeting between two people who had pulled themselves out of a slump," Broeg declared. As noted in the *St. Louis Post-Dispatch*, "(Broeg) has Ruth talk about the mistakes he has made in his personal life and his career, with engaging candor."[4] But *The Babe and Libbie Custer* never did make it to the Great White Way.[5]

Of primary interest here are the three Babe Ruth biopics, each of which offers a decidedly distinct portrayal of its subject. They depict The Sultan of Swat in relation to the time in which each was produced, combined with the then-prevailing view of its subject. *The Babe Ruth Story*, for example, was scripted and produced when certain insiders were aware that its subject was fatally ill; it came to theaters weeks before his death. Beyond the fact that the film is all-out dreadful cinematically, it is a revisionist biopic that is the equivalent of a 106-minute-long press release. Its story respectfully charts The Babe's life, from his Baltimore youth and time at St. Mary's Industrial School for Boys to his rise with the Red Sox, his switch from pitching to hitting, his arriving in the Bronx, his on-field heroics and records, his aging, and his being inflicted with a nameless fatal malady. Helen, The Babe's first wife, is nowhere to be found. Instead, he is shown to fall deeply in love with Claire (Claire Trevor), his real-life Wife #2; the two first meet when she correctly detects the reason for a pitching slump.

The Babe in this story is a naïve but well-meaning athlete whose good intentions are overridden by poor judgment. He is victimized from the outset: His youthful problems result from his harmlessly belting balls through storefront windows. While at St. Mary's, he is spellbound and compliant. Upon his stardom, he is a friendly kidder; never is he foolhardy or self-absorbed, and never does his behavior cross the line between good-natured joking and outright vulgarity. His issues with Miller Huggins (Fred Lightner) are linked to the skipper's failure to comprehend The Bambino's concern for others; onscreen, Huggins is depicted as an ego-driven squirt who unjustly chastises his ballplayer without learning the facts.

At one point, the ballplayer fails to make the Yankee Stadium starting lineup because he assists a young fan and his injured dog. In a sidesplittingly dreadful sequence, The Babe lines a batting practice pitch which hits the pooch. "Don't let my little dog die!" pleads its freckled, pint-sized owner. So The Bambino whisks the kid and his pet off to a hospital, where its life is spared. "Ah, gee, Babe, you're wonderful!" the boy adoringly tells the Yankee. However, upon returning to the team after missing the game, he is fined and suspended – and is labeled by the media as the "Bad Boy of Baseball." After a couple of gamblers offer him money to throw a game, he belts them both – and finds himself detained for beating up "two innocent bystanders." As he lies dying, he contorts in pain after being casually struck on his back. An elevator operator responds by jesting that The Babe surely has imbibed "one too many."

The onscreen Bambino unfalteringly supports the sport, even after he is duped out of a Boston Braves vice presidency. He responds to a proposal that he sue the Braves by retorting, "That would be like suing the church." And he rejects an offer to manage the Yankees' minor-league Newark franchise solely because it would result in the dismissal of the current skipper. As for The Babe's controversial "called shot" in the 1932 World Series, not only is the feat acknowledged but supposedly happened because he had guaranteed a seriously ill youngster that he would "sock a home run into the centerfield bleachers." While at bat, Claire loudly reminds her husband, "Don't forget Johnny." The Bambino tips his cap and points to the outfield. After taking two strikes, he signals yet again before belting the dinger.

At its worst, the content in *The Babe Ruth Story* is unintentionally comical, never more so than when a crippled boy and his father gaze at The Bambino as he smashes a 600-foot homer during spring training. After a friendly greeting from the ballplayer, the kid miraculously rises to his feet. "They said he'll always be an invalid," his disbelieving father declares. "Spend his life on his back. Now look at him. Just look. Oh, God bless that man. God bless him!"

Conveniently, neither Lou Gehrig nor the infamous Ruth-Gehrig feud appear in *The Babe Ruth Story*. But the Iron Horse is referenced: In a prelude, some youngsters lower their heads upon learning of Gehrig's fate while visiting the Baseball Hall of Fame. This recognition comes off as an awkward add-on, as if to negate the discomfiture of excluding Gehrig from the film's main section.

In the concluding sequences, The Babe is felled by an unnamed illness and, even as he is dying, his self-effacement is overwhelming. While hospitalized, he humbly declares that he receives "so much mail (that it) makes me feel important." He accepts an untried serum that has been tested only on animals. It might speed his passing, but he agrees after being informed that "(if) it works it might help other people."

Another flaw in *The Babe Ruth Story* is the casting of William Bendix. An otherwise fine character actor, Bendix was 42 when he played The Bambino; he was especially miscast in his scenes as a St. Mary's teenager. Robert Creamer, the Babe Ruth biographer, was spot-on when he observed, "For thousands of people, maybe millions, William Bendix in a baseball suit is what Babe Ruth looked like. Which is a terrible shame, because lots of men look like William Bendix, but nobody ever looked like Babe Ruth. Or behaved like him."[6]

Compared with *The Babe Ruth Story*, *The Babe* rates as an all-time-ten-best Hollywood classic. In reality, however, the film is a conventional sports tale that is elevated by the appealing presence of John Goodman and its pleasing production design. The film is hyped for being based on the true events that occurred in the ballplayer's life between 1902 and 1935. It clearly is a post-Production Code biopic[7] in that it emphasizes its subject's famed excesses (as well as his failed first marriage). He is shown to possess a Ruthian carnal craving; he frolics with a 16-year-old, passes time with hookers, and spends an evening with four women in a New Orleans brothel. But his actions are not all sexual. At one juncture, he requests that a woman pull on his finger. She does, and The Bambino noisily passes wind.

During Marriage #1, he and his spouse have sex three times in a single day – and The Bambino is anxious for a fourth tryst. However, Helen (played by Trini Alvarado) is an ordinary young woman who likes animals and loathes The Babe's socializing. Predictably, their union is ill-fated. The Babe sleeps with Wife #2 (Kelly McGillis) prior to his divorce; she is a sophisticate, a Ziegfeld Follies showgirl who is acquainted with Al Capone and is not at all bothered by her husband's lifestyle. She acknowledges and understands this; she loves him, appreciates him better than he appreciates himself, and is a loyal pal even when The Babe is written off as an aging fool.

One intriguing aspect of *The Babe* involves his final three big-league homers, which he belted in a single game at Pittsburgh's Forbes Field while playing for the Boston Braves. The team owner views the aging Bambino as "a circus act, a sideshow," but the homers allow the man who smashed them to leave the field with a special grace. As he exits, he is oh so conveniently met by a grown-up Johnny Sylvester; earlier, the ballplayer dashed off to young Johnny's hospital bed and delivered on a guarantee to smash two homers for the youngster. "I'm gone, Johnny. I'm gone," he tells Sylvester, in a line whose variation actually was uttered to Joe Dugan several weeks before his death.[8]

Unlike *The Babe Ruth Story*, *The Babe* in no way sentimentalizes its hero. Ruth's youth is one of hopelessness and meanness. St. Mary's is presented as a dreary environment, not dissimilar to a juvenile detention facility; he is taunted mercilessly by the other boys and beaten by the Brothers. Later on, he expresses his desire to one day manage the Yankees, but this never occurs as he cannot transcend his reputation for lacking self-restraint. The Babe queries Jacob Ruppert (Bernard Kates), "Ty Cobb is managing. Tris Speaker. Why not Babe Ruth?" The owner tells him, "How can you manage a team when you can't even manage yourself?" Eventually, The Bambino is offered the Newark manager spot, but he refuses because he considers the offer an affront – not out of concern for another man's unemployment.

Additionally, the Ruth-Gehrig friction is acknowledged in *The Babe*. The Bambino senses that the Iron Horse (Michael McGrady) will challenge his status as a living Yankee legend and detests the younger player from his time as a rookie. The Babe even purposefully refers to the first baseman as "Gallagher," perhaps out of jealousy. However, *The Babe* never purports to offer a psychological analysis of its central character. It only presents the events in a man's life, his personal idiosyncrasies, and his achievements and setbacks.

Babe Ruth is the least of the trio, if only because of its made-for-TV status. It premiered several months prior to the theatrical release of *The Babe*, and it differs from *The Babe* and *The Babe Ruth Story* as it spotlights The Bambino's life after his arrival in New York. Additionally, never once is the ballplayer depicted at the bedside of an ailing child.

Stephen Lang, an actor with a lengthy list of stage, film, and TV credits, makes an effective Babe, playing him as an overgrown child who wins acclaim for his athletic feats but fails to embrace maturity. Both his wives are present; plus, Pete Rose is smartly cast in a cameo as – who else? – Ty Cobb! *Babe Ruth* originally was written with John Goodman in mind, but the *Roseanne* star left the project upon being offered *The Babe*.[9] Goodman's choice distinguishes between the high-profile A-list major studio features and the under-publicized TV fare that defined the era.

***

Babe Ruth does not always appear by name onscreen, but his fame and larger-than-life personality have combined to make him fodder for caricature in a range of films. Each reflects the manner in which The Bambino was viewed at specific moments in time.

Slide, Kelly, Slide and *Casey at the Bat* were both released in 1927, near the end of the silent film era, when The Babe already had won fame as a super-celebrity with an over-the-top ego. With a cunning wink at the viewer, the central characters in each exude more than a bit of The Bambino.

Clearly, Jim Kelly (played by William Haines), the protagonist in *Slide, Kelly, Slide*, is Ruthian in his demeanor. He is both a world-class pitcher and home run hitter; at the finale, our previously banished hero tosses a gutsy game and smashes an inside-the-park dinger. Off the field, Kelly is a detestable showoff who boasts that he can hurl two baseballs at once; on his business card, he dubs himself "Jim 'No Hit' Kelly." Plus, he is a trickster with a juvenile sense of humor who passes around exploding cigars and wears a water-squirting carnation. He regularly defies his manager, just as The Bambino battled with Miller Huggins, and thoughtlessly flirts with women. At one juncture, he even practically date-rapes his girlfriend. But he is beloved by the fans, and he loves kids.

The specifics of the plotline also unite fact, fiction, and myth. Kelly's team is the New York Yankees, and Bob Meusel and Tony Lazzeri appear onscreen during spring training. (However, some Yankee links predate the production of *Slide, Kelly, Slide*. One of the Yankees is a catcher by the name of "Pop" Munson [Harry Carey]. Kelly also exhibits a fondness for a ragamuffin [Junior Coghlan] who becomes the team mascot. His name is Mickey Martin, a clever combination of Mickey Mantle and Billy Martin.)

The central character in *Casey at the Bat*, Mike Xavier Aloysious Casey (Wallace Beery), also is a Ruthian parody. The film, set in the 1890s, is a slapstick adaptation of the Ernest Lawrence Thayer poem. Here, Casey is an overly extravagant, none-too-bright small-town junkman who is signed by the "Noo York Giants" and soon becomes "'Home Run' Casey, the man who owns Broadway."

Beery's farcical, larger-than-life performance is the film's centerpiece. His Casey belts massive home runs and also possesses a yen for beer and chorus girls. Upon coming to New York, he would rather swig champagne and ogle Florodora girls parading across a stage than prepare for the next Big Game. Despite his acclaim, Casey is at his core an illiterate hick. He may dress himself in a fancy suit, but its oversized buttons result in his resembling a yokel. And back home, he comes to the plate with a bat in one hand and a pitcher of beer in the other. The country-mile dinger he belts is what lands him a big-league contract.

As in *Slide, Kelly, Slide*, Casey also has a special affinity for children. At one point, he is queried about throwing a big game. "If I'd strike out today," he growls, "every kid in America would know I done it on purpose. Now get out!"

Casey at the Bat and *Slide, Kelly, Slide* are not the lone features with Babe Ruth influences. They stretch across the decades: Even though he is a heavy, one of the characters in *Warming Up* (1928) is McRae (Philo McCullough), a trickster and home-run king who, as noted in *Variety*, is "supposed to be the prototype of Babe Ruth."[10] The Whammer (Joe Don Baker), a slugger who is fanned on three pitches by Roy Hobbs (Robert Redford) in *The Natural* (1984), is a blatant Ruthian inspiration. At the time, writer-producer-director Garry Gross envisioned generating a biopic featuring Baker as The Babe. "I never saw two people who look so much alike," Gross declared.[11] However, the project never came to fruition.

Arguably the gloomiest caricature is found in *Deadline at Dawn* (1946), a murder-mystery. If The Babe is lionized in *The Babe Ruth Story*, here he is depicted as a pathetic drunk named Babe Dooley (Joe Sawyer), a baseball star who stalks the urban byways deep into the night in search of a dame called Edna. "Edna, it's The Babe. Babe Dooley," he yells up at her apartment. "Why don't you open the door for your Babe?" Then he self-pityingly mumbled to himself, "Nobody loves a fat man."

Later on, Dooley returns to Edna's street. "Edna! It's The Babe. Are you home, Edna?" he asks. "It's late. I can't get a drinkie anywhere. Throw down a bottle, will ya?" Two policemen arrive to check the commotion he is causing, and their demeanor changes from brusque to accommodating upon realizing Dooley's identity. "Hey, it's The Babe, Babe Dooley," one declares. His partner chimes in, "Nothin's too good for The Babe," while the first officer asks, "Are we gonna cop the pennant this year, Babe?" But Babe Dooley is obsessed with copping nothing more than his "drinkie." Observes another character (played by Joseph Calleia), "There's a fat ballplayer who some night will die in the streets."

Which depiction is more reflective of the *real* Bambino: Babe Ruth in *The Babe Ruth Story* or Babe Dooley in *Deadline at Dawn*? The answer, perhaps, is somewhere in between. ...

Notes

1. The former includes Dizzy Dean (in 1952's *The Pride of St. Louis*); Grover Cleveland Alexander (1952's *The Winning Team*); Roy Campanella (1974's *It's Good to Be Alive*, a made-for-television movie); and Satchel Paige (1981's *Don't Look Back: The Story of Leroy "Satchel" Paige*, also made-for-TV). Among those in the latter are Monty Stratton (1949's *The Stratton Story*); Jimmy Piersall (1957's *Fear Strikes Out*); Ron LeFlore (1978's *One in a Million: The Ron LeFlore Story*, also a TV movie); Pete Gray (1986's *A Winner Never Quits*, also made-for-TV); Jim Morris (2002's *The Rookie*); and Moe Berg (2018's *The Catcher Was a Spy*).

2. Mel Gussow, "'The Babe' at Princess," *New York Times*, May 18, 1984.

3. ibdb.com/broadway-production/the-babe-4338.

4. "'The Babe and Libbie Custer' Opens," *St. Louis Post-Dispatch*, July 10, 1986.

5. Babe Ruth has been endlessly depicted in art and song, in novels and radio plays. For a thorough list, see James Mote's *Everything Baseball* (New York: Prentice Hall Press, 1989).

6. Shirley Povich, "A Qualified Thumbs-Up for 'The Babe,'" *Washington Post*, May 17, 1992.

7. Further information on the history of the Motion Picture Production Code may be found at: productioncode.dhwritings.com/multipleframes_productioncode.php.

8. Tracy Brown Collins, *Baseball Superstars: Babe Ruth* (New York: Checkmate Books, 2008).

9. Bart Mills, "Stephen Lang Gives The 'Babe' His Best Shot," *Chicago Tribune*, October 6, 1991.

10. *Variety*, June 27, 1928.

11. *Variety*, March 3, 1982.

To the Rescue: Brother Matthias

By Brian (Chip) Martin

During the 1926 season, Babe Ruth played 152 games and launched 47 home runs, while batting .372. He continued to be a headache for general manager Ed Barrow and his diminutive on-field manager Miller Huggins, with whom he clashed about his behavior on and off the field. The Yankees continued to hire private detectives to keep an eye on their star, especially when they were on the road. Late in the 1925 season, a detective reported Ruth was with six different women in Chicago and had patronized the most famous whorehouse in St. Louis.[1] Exasperated, Huggins suspended Babe and fined him $5,000.

From time to time, the Yankees called upon Brother Matthias of St. Mary's to provide fatherly advice to which Babe seemed to respond positively. In June 1926, on their first trip to Chicago, a city whose delights invariably led Babe astray, the Yankees stayed at the Del Prado Hotel and decided once again to call upon Brother Matthias. Their four-game series began June 17 and the city was hopping. The 28th International Eucharistic Congress was being held from June 20 to 24 and the Yankees invited Matthias to attend the event, covering expenses, and hoped he would counsel his former student while he was in town. The Congress, a sort of spiritual Olympics for Catholics, was expected to attract nearly a million attendees for its first time held in the United States. One of the featured events was a pontifical high mass at Soldiers' Field that attracted half a million adherents of the faith.[2]

Brother Matthias with car. *Courtesy of David McDonald.*

One evening, Matthias came to the Del Prado and occupied a chair in the lobby from which he could see the hotel elevator. Ruth soon appeared, with plans for another night on the town, but when he spotted Matthias the two greeted each other warmly. Matthias explained he happened to be in the Windy City for the Congress, but also wanted to see Ruth play. So he learned where the Yankees were staying and wanted to take his former pupil out to dinner. Ruth promptly altered his plans for the night and stayed out with Matthias until nearly 11 p.m.

During their meal, Matthias delivered strong advice to Ruth about his need to clean up his act. It can be easily surmised he told Ruth he was disappointed in what he had been hearing about his off-field activities, the women, the parties, the pursuit of pleasure. Matthias said he hadn't encouraged young Ruth to live a God-centered life only to see him pursue such a hedonistic lifestyle. The boys at St. Mary's worshipped him and they deserved a hero whose behavior they could model. Babe was letting them down. Matthias also suggested Ruth should try to rebuild his relationship with his wife Helen. The papers had been full of stories about his marital woes, but Matthias said divorce was out of the question. The prodigal son listened intently and promised to do better. As Ruth biographer Marshall Smelser put it, "this was the turning point in Ruth's behavior. Certainly he no longer after that time had the reputation for hell-raising that he had before."[3] There would still be lapses. After all, he was Babe Ruth.

There were other times when Matthias lent an ear to the man he addressed only as "George." Babe leaned on him during times of crisis, most notably during his dreadful 1925 season. That year, the Home Run King was hospitalized by a mystery ailment dubbed "The Bellyache Heard Around the World," and later clashed with manager Miller Huggins. At the same time, Ruth's marriage to Helen was in shambles and the newspapers were full of speculation his best days were behind him. Matthias sensed his former pupil needed help. He called Ruth several times from St. Mary's during his darkest hours, offering advice and support and asking if he could somehow help save the troubled marriage.[4]

Matthias, Ruth's surrogate father, always brought him back to earth and the superstar mended his ways, if only for a time. His deep and abiding respect for Matthias saw him purchase his mentor a shiny new Cadillac as a thank-you after one of their "Come to Jesus" sessions. This was in 1922, 1925, or 1926, depending on the source. Biographer Marshall Smelser said the gift came after Babe received one of his first big pay checks from the Yankees in 1922. That date seems to be confirmed by the *Baltimore Sun* which reported in early 1923 that Matthias drove some theatrical performers to St. Joseph's Monastery in

Brother Matthias, who mentored Ruth at the St. Mary's Industrial School for Boys in Baltimore. *Courtesy of David McDonald.*

the Baltimore suburb of Irvington "in an automobile given the latter by 'Babe' Ruth, the baseball player."[5]

Biographer Kal Wagenheim said the extravagant gift was bestowed on Matthias during Babe's dismal 1925 season when he seemed to hit rock bottom as an overweight, ill, and suspended troublemaker. Matthias had called him repeatedly during the crisis, offering his counsel, but Babe wanted to see him in person and invited Matthias to New York. There, the two men engaged in heart-to-heart discussion as they strolled the streets of the city. Babe loved shiny new cars and when he spotted a Cadillac in a Manhattan showroom he was distracted, and asked his towering mentor: "Do you think I ought to buy that

Ruth with wife Helen, presenting gift of car to Brother Matthias (at the wheel); St. Mary's, Baltimore, 1925 or 1926. *Courtesy of David McDonald.*

car?" Matthias replied: "If you can afford it, George." Matthias couldn't believe his eyes the next day when the Cadillac was delivered to his hotel, with a note thanking him "for what you and St. Mary's have done for me."[6] The gift put Matthias in a quandary. When he became a Xaverian Brother, he made a vow of poverty and couldn't own worldly possessions. So the vehicle was registered to the school but Matthias had priority use of it and ferried students to various destinations. In return, they helped him clean and maintain it, learning the basics of auto mechanics. Ever the teacher, Matthias turned his gift into a teaching tool. Ruth biographer Jane Leavy said Ruth bought Matthias a second Cadillac in 1926, shortly after the Chicago visit, but doesn't indicate when the first was given him.[7]

With a recharged and refocused Ruth in their lineup for 1926 and some talented new players, the Yankees claimed the American League pennant but lost the World Series to St. Louis. Babe and his bat were back. But the greatest season for the Yankees and their slugger still lay ahead.

Sources

Research for this article came during preparation of the author's book *The Man Who Made Babe Ruth: Brother Matthias of St. Mary's School*, to be published by McFarland in 2020.

Notes

1. Leigh Montville, *The Big Bam: The Life and Times of Babe Ruth* (New York: Anchor Books, 2006), 207.

2. "Program of the Congress," *Chicago Tribune,* June 14, 1926, 17.

3. Marshall Smelser, *The Life that Ruth Built* (Lincoln: University of Nebraska Press, 1975), 332-333.

4. Kal Wagenheim, *Babe Ruth: His Life and Legend* (Chicago: Olmstead Press, 2001), 147.

5. "White House Talk Explained by Lang," *Baltimore Sun,* March 17, 1924: 4.

6. Joe Winkworth, "I've Been the Sappiest of Saps — Ruth," *The Sporting News*, November 5, 1925: 2.

7. Jane Leavy, *The Big Fella: Babe Ruth and the World He Created* (New York: HarperCollins, 2018), 162.

Babe Ruth: A Man of Simple Faith

By Gabriel B. Costa

In matters of Faith, only The Lord can read one's heart, soul, and mind.

> "We are what we are before God ... no more ... no less"
> — St. Francis of Assisi

However, very often we can get "some sense" of people by their actions. If the person is no longer with us but was a man (as in this case) of renown, we can read what he wrote, listen to what he said, and follow his life's journey from numerous historical sources.

I was born in 1948, the very year Babe Ruth died. I was exactly 3½ months old when the Lord called the Bambino Home.

A few years later, I discovered baseball ... and like many of us, I was obsessed by the game. At about the age of 7 or so, I began hearing about Babe Ruth. ... There seemed to be something magical about that name. For some reason it seemed to fit him perfectly.

Babe Ruth ... every now and then, in the mid-1950s, his picture would appear in the *New York Daily News*. There was usually a welcoming smile on his face, and I could *sense* that his huge torso housed a sentimental and loving heart.

Lou Gehrig and Babe Ruth visit Father Edward J. Flanagan, founder of Boys Town, and young residents of the Nebraska school in 1927.
Knights of Columbus Multimedia Archives/Photo by Ernest Bihler Co.

In addition, every now and then, again in the mid-1950s, a black-and-white film clip of a Ruthian home run would be shown on television. There was something *graceful* about the swing; and the batted ball seemed to trace out a *majestic* arc. And those *Yankee Pinstripes!* And that perfect *Number Three!* The Sultan of Swat was larger than life. ...

When I asked my dad to tell me about Babe Ruth, he told me that he once actually met Ruth – in a freight elevator, of all places. My father was impressed by his massive size, especially his height.

I just *had* to learn more about Babe Ruth. Thus, the odyssey began…

My first *real* contact with Ruth came in 1958. I was watching him on TV one night with my father. Actually, it was William Bendix *playing* Babe Ruth. I remember this Babe Ruth taking an injured dog to a hospital, insisting that the doctors and nurses tend to the dog, even though he was told that the hospital was not where pets could be treated. I also remember a gritty, grimy Sultan of Swat hitting three home runs in his (as it was portrayed) last game, as a member of the Boston Braves, looking so out of place without Yankee pinstripes. Finally, I remember the dying Bambino being wheeled on a gurney, to bravely undergo some experimental medical procedure. I did not want to cry in front of my father, but I knew that the Babe was to die shortly.

That very night, after the movie ended, I decided that I would read *everything* possible about the Maharajah of Mash. I would try to absorb everything I could learn about this man … not just the baseball statistics (math was my favorite subject), but about the *person*, as well.

A year or two later, I met the Babe's widow. Actually, Edward R. Murrow was interviewing her on the TV show "Person to Person." Claire Ruth showed pictures of her deceased husband while telling stories about him and their relationship. And I got to know more about this great man. Mrs. Ruth also told the viewers that they could obtain Ruth's autograph on canceled checks, if they would merely send a request to her. To this day, I *still* do not know why I never took advantage of her kind offer.

Soon after, I read The Babe's autobiography, which he wrote with the assistance of syndicated columnist Bob Considine.[1] The book was published right around the time of Ruth's death and contained dozens of pictures. Although as a young boy I didn't quite understand what "as told to Bob Considine" meant, as I read the book I felt that Ruth's words were directed toward *me*.

After that, it was "off to the races," as far as Babe Ruth was concerned.

I am now (in 2018) 70 years old, and I am still learning about the Sultan of Swat.

I have been very fortunate regarding the Big Bam. Over the years, I met his sister (Mamie), his daughters (Dorothy and Julia), and his granddaughter (Linda). I have been able to discuss Ruth with the likes of former Yankee third baseman and past president of the American League Dr. Bobby Brown, Award-winning cartoonist and journalist Bill Gallo, Hall of Famer Yogi Berra, former major leaguer Rico Brogna, and baseball historian Bill Jenkinson.

There is one simple, short conversation, though, that stands out. It was with a kind gentleman named Raymond Kelly. In 1995 Hofstra University held a four-day commemoration in honor of Babe Ruth's 100th birthday. Ray Kelly, Babe's famed mascot during the Murderers' Row days, was one of the keynote speakers. After Kelly's presentation, I was able to speak privately with Ray and, after having identified myself as a priest, asked him the following question: "Mr. Kelly, was Babe Ruth a good Catholic?" Kelly's answer, as he teared up was, "Yes, Father, he was a good Catholic."

I took the alacrity of his response to be an imprimatur.

Babe Ruth's Catholic upbringing has been well documented. Brother Matthias, C.F.X, a member of a congregation under the patronage of St. Francis Xavier, was assigned to St. Mary's Industrial School in Baltimore, Maryland. The charismatic brother, along with his confreres, provided a moral and religious foundation for Ruth; a basis which would seem to be nearly eclipsed many times in future years, but, in essence, would never, ever be totally eradicated.

For the rest of his life, Ruth he knew he always had a spiritual Home Base at St. Mary's in Baltimore, which, of course, was part of the Universal Catholic Church.

As to Brother Matthias's influence on the future baseball superstar, it is sufficient to recall Ruth's own words about the strapping Xavierian, as recorded in the Babe's autobiography: "It was at St. Mary's that I met and learned to love the greatest man I have ever known. His name was Matthias. …"[2]

(As an interesting aside, there is a tale, not often told, that the Babe actually thought of becoming a Catholic priest. It seems that Brother Matthias, acting as his spiritual director, discerned that Ruth was probably not called to sacred orders. The very image of "Father George Herman Ruth" conjures up many pastoral scenarios, and with God's grace and man's cooperation, all things are possible.)

On this very point, those of us who belong to the Catholic faith strive to live according to a creed which is rooted in certain theological beliefs; two of which are *Sin* and *Conversion*. These designations or categories are intimately connected and are not meant to trivialize the former ("We're all sinners …") or rationalize the latter ("We all need God's help …"). No, the effects of Original Sin are certainly present, and we *struggle* on our pilgrimage to *try* to live a Christian life.

Only God know the depths of our culpability. Some of the greatest saints have struggled with the flesh.

The Babe

> "O Lord, grant me chastity and continence, but not yet."
>
> – St. Augustine

Did The Babe ever resist *anything*? Only God knows. But Ruth certainly seemed to enjoy the pleasures of life in the 1920s ... and then some. As Paul Gallico wrote of Ruth in 1927, "Part of his charm lies in the manner with which he succumbs to every temptation which comes his way."[3]

Yet it would be unfair to concentrate only on Ruth's slavery to the senses. For it has been equally recognized how generous Ruth was with his money and time, especially where poor kids were concerned. The Colossus of Crash himself wrote that he always felt *cleaner* after a visit with children.

To be sure, Ruth made a lot of money. He spent it on himself and on his friends. He was a focal point of the Roaring Twenties for many people. He enjoyed the fruits of his labors. He worked hard; he played hard.

> "He who abhors pleasures is both boorish and ungracious."
>
> – St. Thomas Aquinas

I do not know if Babe Ruth attended Mass every Sunday. I hope he did ... at least every now and then. Perhaps most times, he did not. However, even regarding this most solemn of rites, there is a delightful tale involving, as is decreed on his Hall of Fame plaque, *Baseball's Greatest Drawing Card*.

It seems that the Yankees were on a road trip and Ruth arrived at the hotel early one Sunday morning, presumably after a night of carousing. He made sure all the Yankees who were Catholic were roused out of their beds to accompany him to an early Mass. During the sacred liturgy, as the collection basket was passed around, the Babe put in a $50 bill. When Tony Lazzeri realized what Ruth had done, he said – *non sotto voce* – "What are you doing Babe, paying for last night's sins?"

I don't know if this story is apocryphal, but it seems that both the Babe and Poosh 'em Up Tony were capable of such actions and words. ...

As Ruth aged, he mellowed and gradually slowed down. The 13 years between his retirement from baseball and his death were increasingly disappointing and painful. It was clear that major-league baseball – and especially the Yankees – had no place for the retired Sultan of Swat. For whatever reasons, he was never really considered for a managerial position. His uniform number, 3, was not retired by the Yankees until two months before his death. It was quite a comedown for someone who arguably possessed, at one time, the most recognizable face in the country, if not the planet.

Yes, these were most difficult times for the former King of Clout. But all was not lost. Ruth had an outlet in the game of golf, which allowed him to compete athletically and vent frustrations. He said that without golf, he would have blown up to 300 pounds, in addition to the fear that he would have gone out of his mind.

And he was not alone ... nor would he ever really despair. In addition to his family and friends, Ruth believed that the Church was there for him. And, as he grew older, it became clearer and clearer, that the Church would *always* be there for him.

Babe Ruth's respect for – and reliance upon – the clergy was profound. For example, on many occasions Ruth met the with sainted founder of Boys Town, Father Edward J. Flanagan. One instance was when Ruth, along with Lou Gehrig, visited the Omaha, Nebraska, institution in 1927, while on an extended barnstorming tour.[4] The existence of such a place, led by such a cleric, struck a resonant chord with Ruth, who was, in every sense, a benefactor of this great establishment.

The Rev. Edward J. Quinn, O.S.A., an Augustinian priest, was a friend, adviser and counselor to Ruth on several occasions. Father Quinn was particularly helpful when Ruth and his first wife, Helen, were going through very difficult times. Because of his religious beliefs, the Babe refused to seek a divorce, because the Church did not permit it. (The penalty of excommunication which was in effect in Ruth's time was lifted by Pope Paul VI).

The priests and parishioners of St. Angela Merici in the Bronx benefited from Babe's and Claire's generosity. A plaque in that church commemorates the Ruths' financial support for a new Altar of Sacrifice.

Soon after the end of World War II, Ruth began experiencing a number of physical discomforts, including a raspiness in his throat, severe headaches, and dental problems. Over the next two years, his condition worsened.

During these last two years, the Babe never lost his faith. In fact, it is difficult to imagine that his religious beliefs did *not* deepen or come more and more to the forefront. In his autobiography, Ruth wrote: "I had drifted away from the Church during my harum-scarum early years in the majors. I'd go to Mass now and then and, believe me, I never missed a night without saying my prayers. But I wasn't the Catholic I had been at St. Mary's, especially after Brother Matthias died about the time my baseball career was ending."[5]

As the end was drawing near, surgery was recommended, pretty much as a last-ditch effort to extend The Babe's life. After going to Confession, Ruth received the Body of Christ in the Blessed Sacrament. He added in his book: "Holy Communion gave me additional heart to face a very delicate operation."[6]

On August 16, 1948, the Rev. Thomas Kaufman, O.P., a Dominican priest, was with Ruth during his final moments. "Father Kaufman told a flock of boys waiting beneath Ruth's window that it was a beautiful death."[7] A statue of the Dominican St. Martin de Porres was at his hospital bedside table. St. Martin is the patron saint of the Knights of Columbus, an organization Ruth joined in 1916, when he played with the Boston Red Sox.

Ruth was intuitively aware that the sacraments, which include the Last Rites, are the greatest treasures of the Church. These sources of grace gave The Bambino peace as he entered eternity.

In the final analysis, during the truncated, 53 years that were allotted to him Babe Ruth lived life to the full.

> "I came that they might have life and have it more abundantly."
>
> – John 10:10

Babe Ruth was waked in Yankee Stadium, the House That Ruth Built. Thousands of grievers passed by his bier, to view the deceased Bambino. Those mighty hands, which gripped many a baseball bat, now held a rosary.

His funeral at St. Patrick's Cathedral on the 19th of August was one of the most attended requiems ever witnessed at that ecclesial edifice. There were approximately four dozen members of the clergy present for the celebration of a man who died as he lived: with the simple faith of a child.

And among the mourners who lined the rainy Manhattan streets, were legions of children. After the Mass, boys and girls watched a hearse carry off the remains of the Greatest of All Baseball Players to Gate of Heaven Cemetery in Hawthorne, New York.

Ruth's graveside memorial stands several feet above the ground. Fittingly, on the monument, there is an image of Jesus Christ, with His left arm on the shoulder of a boy.

> "Amen, I say to you, unless you turn and become like children, you will not enter the kingdom of heaven."
>
> – Matthew 18:3

What was Babe Ruth like? He was spontaneous, impetuous, warm, manly, generous, hedonistic, and indomitable. He could laugh and cry at the drop of a hat, so close to the surface were his emotions. He would give you the shirt off his back. He was the greatest hitter ever. He was the most famous athlete of all time. He loved his country. He loved his Church. He loved kids. The man who called *everyone* "Kid!" was the *ultimate* kid. He left an unparalleled legacy. He was real. He was genuine. He gave all he had.

In the depths of his being, even deeper than whatever imperfections he had, Babe Ruth was a giving individual, blessed with a heart of gold.

"Charity covers a multitude of sins." – I Peter 4:8

PRAYER FOR BABE RUTH

MEMORIAL MASS

AUGUST 16, 2009

Loving Father, over sixty years ago today, you called George, your son and servant, to his eternal reward. As with all your creatures, you blessed him with special talents. We thank you for the gift of George, who is known throughout the world as Babe Ruth. He excelled on the baseball diamond with unparalleled prowess and brought joy to millions of people. He was especially loved by children, a love which was reciprocated throughout his life.

Father, we pray that Babe Ruth's example of fair play and athletic courage may inspire generations of professional athletes and the young people who look up to them.

We make this prayer through our Lord Jesus Christ, Who lives and reigns with You in the unity of the Holy Spirit, one God forever and ever. Amen. – *Father Gabriel B. Costa*

(This prayer was requested by Mrs. Linda Ruth Tosetti, Babe Ruth's granddaughter. It appeared on a commemorative card for a Mass celebrating the 61st anniversary of Ruth's death. The Liturgy took place at the Basilica of the National Shrine of the Assumption of the Blessed Virgin Mary, in Baltimore, Maryland.)

Notes

1. Babe Ruth, as told to Bob Considine, *The Babe Ruth Story* (New York: Pocket Books, New York, 1948.

2. *The Babe Ruth Story*, 3.

3. Paul Gallico, *New York Daily News*, September 3, 1927.

4. Jane Leavy, *The Big Fella: Babe Ruth and the World He Created* (New York: Harper Collins, 2018), 197, 218, 449.

5. *The Babe Ruth Story*, 214.

6. Ibid.

7. Leavy, 467

Babe Ruth's Final Legacy to the Kids

By Alan Cohen

"The only real game in the world is baseball. In this game, you have to come up from youth. You've got to start way down at the bottom, if you're going to be successful like those fellows over there (the Yankees lining the field between home and first base)."

– Babe Ruth April 27, 1947 when being honored at Yankee Stadium.

Ruth had taken ill, and throat surgery had kept him out of the public eye for three months. He was most touched by his welcome that day from 14-year-old American Legion ballplayer Larry Cutler, who said, "From all us kids, it's swell to have you back."[1]

During the 1940s Babe Ruth was involved in several national youth all-star games played in New York, and promoted youth baseball through his work with the American Legion. In 1944 Ruth hosted a radio program sponsored by the A.G. Spalding Sporting Goods Company, and on August 5 he hosted the several boys who were in town to play in the Esquire's All-American Boys' Baseball Game. Young Jim Enright of St. Louis asked the Babe how a player could learn to throw a ball harder and faster. Enright was just about the youngest player to participate in any of the games. He had turned 15 on July 21, 1944, making him 15 years and 17 days old on game day. Ruth replied, "Constant

New York Yankee Babe Ruth with four young boys alongside the third base dugout at Fenway Park, ca. 1931-34. *Leslie Jones photo, courtesy of the Boston Public Library.*

practice. Your arm won't come up if you use it only once a week. You must practice hard every day. If you do, I'd say you will be able to throw the ball 20 feet further in a week."[2]

Enright, a second baseman, never played professional baseball. Leonard Cohen of the *New York Post* told his readers that the young man, who had just completed his freshman year of high school, was also a soccer player and dreamed of studying journalism at Notre Dame.³ Joe Fromuth from Reading, Pennsylvania, asked the Babe if he could tell him a joke. Fromuth explained that players run faster from first to second than they do from second to third because there is a "short stop" between second and third. Ruth was amused.⁴

Before the game, held on August 7, Ruth was one of several dignitaries who addressed the crowd of 17,803 spectators. In the pregame festivities, he stepped to the microphone at home plate and said that it mattered little which team won the All-American contest so long as it was played cleanly and hard.⁵ Each of the 29 players who participated in the game received a baseball autographed by The Babe.

Ruth managed the East squad in the Esquire's Game at the Polo Grounds on August 28, 1945. The West squad was managed by Ty Cobb. Future Philadelphia Phillies star Curt Simmons emulated Ruth in the game. After pitching the first four innings, allowing one earned run in the third inning when the West scored four times, he was removed from the mound on the short end of a 4-0 score. Simmons switched to the outfield for the final five innings. In the ninth inning, with one on, he hit the longest drive of the game. His triple to center field drove in a run, and he scored the tying run during a three-run rally as his East team came from behind to win, 5-4. Simmons was chosen the game's MVP. Remembering his experience in New York, Simmons said, "He called everybody kid. But I remember he said, 'Hey kid, you're pitching.' So I got a base hit when I was pitching, and after I pitched he said, 'Go play right field.' So I got to play the whole game, and I hit a triple toward the end of the game, and we ended up winning."⁶

Future major leaguer Bob DiPietro remembered a scene during a pregame practice at the Polo Grounds on August 27, when Ruth was frustrated with one of his players in the batting cage.

Members of the East All-Stars with manager Babe Ruth at the 1945 Esquire's All-American Boys Baseball Game. Seated (and smiling) at Ruth's left shoulder is Burt Stone. In front of Stone is Curtis Simmons from Egypt, Pennsylvania. *Courtesy of Stone's daughter Laurie Kandel*

"He grabbed the bat from one of the players and told the kid, 'Get the hell out of the batting cage. You aren't worth shit as a hitter.' He said, 'Carl (Hubbell), groove a few of 'em here. Let me show them how to hit.' Carl Hubbell was pitching! I look back. Cobb, Ruth, Hubbell, and what did I get? Zip (autographs)! Ruth hit six balls into the stands. It was the damnedest exhibition I'd seen. And he was in a sweat suit. But he had that great swing. Of course, the Polo Grounds, it was very short down both lines, but he hit a good drive to center field. He put on a show; it was great."⁷

In 1946, sportswriter Max Kase of the *New York Journal-American* was instrumental in creating what came to be known as the Hearst Sandlot Classic. In that first year, it was known as the Hearst Diamond Pennant Series. The game featured a team of New York All-Stars against a team of US All-Stars. Early on, Kase enlisted the aid of Babe Ruth, who served as honorary chairman in 1947. Harry Schlacht of the *Journal-American* noted that Ruth "set the spark which kindled a flaming torch in the hearts of the kids of the nation."⁸ The Babe himself stated that "The Hearst papers are doing a grand job in the sandlot program for the youngsters. It keeps the kids off the streets; It keeps them out of mischief; It builds them up physically; It helps them to become better citizens."⁹

On November 26, 1946, Ruth entered French Hospital and over the next 21 months he would rage war against a cancer that would take its toll in the end.

"Fellows, I can't say a lot. But boys, you know how I feel toward the kids. I love 'em and that's why I went as far as I did. They didn't swing the bat for me, but, well, they helped. I'm getting pretty old now, but I'm going to do all I can for them."

– Babe Ruth, April 8, 1947, when he was speaking with the media after accepting a position as a consultant with the American Legion baseball program.¹⁰

On April 27 a crowd of 58,339 fans filled Yankee Stadium for Babe Ruth Day, a day celebrated throughout baseball. The Sultan of Swat had undergone major surgery on his throat on January 6, 1947, and spent 82 days in the hospital. He was but a shell of his former self and barely spoke above a whisper. Nevertheless, during the summer of 1947, Ruth promoted youth baseball, working with the Ford Motor Company to support the American Legion Junior Baseball Tournament. He also took seriously his role as the honorary chairman of the 1947 Hearst Classic.

"The game he graced so well was graced once more by Ruth as it passed another unforgettable milestone with the greatest sandlot game in history."

– Lewis Burton, *New York Journal-American*.[11]

The 1947 Hearst game was played on August 13. In terms of attendance (31,123 fans), future major leaguers (nine), and runs scored by a team (13 by the US All-Stars), the 1947 Hearst game was the best in the 20-year history of the event.

Of course, the icing on the cake at the 1947 game was the appearance by the game's honorary chairman. Ruth took his seat during the bottom of the second inning of the game and received a standing ovation that stopped the game. He was late after accepting a series of engagements that would tire the healthiest of men. First, he visited the bedside of a sick youngster in New Jersey. Then, before heading to the Polo Grounds, he stopped by New York's amateur boxing finals where he signed more than a few autographs.[12] The Babe was interviewed during the slugfest by Jack Conway of the *Boston Daily Record*. Ruth proved himself quite the prognosticator when he said, "I would not hesitate to predict that a least a half-dozen of the 23 boys on the United States All-Stars will be in major league baseball within three or four years."[13]

Ruth was still quite ill with throat cancer and was barely audible, but he asked to speak with the game's MVP. That was Don Ferrarese who had traveled to the game from Oakland, California. Ferrarese was one of the seven US All-Star players to make it to the big leagues. He was on the mound and paused when Ruth arrived in the second inning. One person did not know what all the fuss was about. Pitcher Hy Cohen of the *Journal-American* All-Stars related a couple of memories from that night. Before the Hearst game, Babe Didrikson, the famous female athlete, borrowed Cohen's glove when she gave her pregame exhibition. Cohen's father, who did not know much about baseball, was at the game and seated next to Babe Ruth. He didn't recognize The Bambino.

Ruth was able to travel to spring training in 1948, At a game on March 18, he told Arthur Daley of the *New York Times* that he hoped to be playing golf that summer. Daley wrote:

"Seeing him again, you realize anew the tremendous magnetism of the man and the unshakeable hold he has on public esteem. There never was another like him and there never will be. The fans leap to their collective feet and cheer frenziedly (as they did on August 13, 1947) whenever he enters a ballpark. Small boys, whom the Babe always loved, stare adoringly at him."[14]

Ruth returned from Florida having gained a few much-needed pounds and was planning to depart for California at the end of April to assist in the filming of his biopic, *The Babe Ruth Story*. Before he left for the Coast, his autobiography, written with Bob Considine, was released. These words from the first

Program cover for the 1948 Hearst Sandlot Classic. The game was played in honor of Ruth who died 10 days prior to the game. *Courtesy of Alan Cohen.*

paragraph convey The Babe's never-ending love affair with the young boys who were his adoring fans:

"I was a bad kid. I say that without pride but with a feeling that it is better to say it. Because I live with one great hope in mind: to help kids who now stand where I stood as a boy. If what I have to say here helps even one of them avoid some of my own mistakes, or take heart from such triumphs as I have had, this book will serve its purpose."[15]

On June 5 Ruth traveled to Yale University, where he presented the manuscript of his book to George H.M. Bush, the Elis' captain and first baseman, and the future president.[16] And on June 13 he returned to Yankee Stadium for Old-Timers Day. He donned his old uniform as his number 3 was officially retired at a ceremony marking the 25th anniversary of Yankee Stadium. A week later The Babe joined with Dizzy Dean in St. Louis at a youth baseball clinic before a Browns-Yankees game at Sportsman's Park. But on June 24, Ruth re-entered the hospital.

He emerged briefly on two occasions. On July 13 he traveled to Baltimore, his childhood home, for the annual interfaith charity game, which featured International League rivals Baltimore and Jersey City. When rain caused the festivities to be postponed to the following night, The Babe returned to New York. He was too ill to stay the night. The last time he appeared in public was when he attended the film premiere of his life story on July 26. By then, he was gravely ill.

Baseball lost Babe Ruth on August 16, 1948. He was buried three days later, and the 1948 Hearst game on August 26 was played in his memory. Just before his death, one of the New York area newspapers featured a drawing of The Babe cheering the kids on from his hospital bed. The picture was titled "Your Cheering Section Kid." Joe DiMaggio stepped in as honorary chairman, and each of the players received an autograph from the Yankee Clipper. During the pregame festivities, DiMaggio said, "Babe Ruth was my inspiration. It is one of my great regrets that I came too late to play alongside The Babe." Dick Groat's one vivid memory of his games in New York was standing more than an hour outside in the rain, across from St. Patrick's Cathedral, during Ruth's funeral on August 19, hoping, along with his roommate, Art Ruffing of Pittsburgh, to get a glimpse of Ruth's funeral procession.

Before the game, columnist Bill Corum served as the master of ceremonies and introduced the participants in the Memorial to Babe Ruth. One tribute featured Al Schacht doing his pantomime of The Babe's called shot in the third game of the 1932 World Series, while Robert Merrill brought tears to everyone's eyes with his rendition of "My Buddy."[17] The tributes were many. On hand was New York businessman Johnny Sylvester, who was 11 years old when The Babe made his fabled hospital visit in St. Louis in 1926, promising to hit a home run in the next game of the 1926 World Series – a visit that sportswriters of the day claimed to have saved the young man's life.[18] The Police Athletic League choir sang "Auld Lang Syne" and "Take Me Out to the Ball Game." The St. Vincent's Drum and Bugle Corps from Bayonne, New Jersey, also performed.

Also participating in the pregame festivities were Metropolitan Opera soprano Annamarie Dickey, who sang the National Anthem, National League President Ford Frick, who had chronicled Ruth when he was with the *Journal-American*, and comedian Joe E. Brown.[19]

The 1949 Hearst Classic was held two days after the anniversary of Ruth's death. DiMaggio read a message to youngsters as Ruth was remembered.

To the end, The Babe was devoted to his young fans, and on his deathbed made provision in his will that 10 percent of this estate was bequeathed "to the interests of the kids of America."[20]

Sources

In addition to sources shown in the notes, the author consiulted:

Schumach, Murray. "Babe Ruth, Baseball Idol, Dies at 53 after Lingering Illness," *New York Times*, August 17, 1948: 1.

The author interviewed Don Ferrarese, Billy Harrell, Rudy Regalado, Dick Groat, and Hy Cohen, each of whom played in the 1947 Hearst Sandlot Classic.

Notes

1 "Babe Ruth Receives Tributes on Return to Yankee Stadium," *Baltimore Sun*, April 28, 1947: 17.

2 *The Sporting News*, August 10, 1944: 13.

3 Leonard Cohen. *New York Post*, August 5, 1944: 18.

4 Richard Flannery, *Reading Eagle*, October 18, 1998: D-2.

5 Louis Effrat, *New York Times*, August 8, 1944: 12.

6 Richard Panchyk. *Baseball History for Kids: America at Bat from 1900 to Today, with 19 Activities* (Chicago: Chicago Review Press, 2016), 53.

7 Nick Diunte, "Bob DiPietro" SABR BioProject.

8 Harry H. Schlacht," The Hearst Sandlot Classic – A Living Memorial to Babe Ruth," *New York Journal American*, August 26, 1948 (reprinted in the *Milwaukee Sentinel*, August 26, 1948: 14).

9 Harry Schlacht, "The Spirit of Babe Ruth Lives On," *New York Journal-American*, August 16, 1949: 16.

10 Oscar Fraley, "Broken in Health, Babe Ruth Will Aid Legion Baseball," *Charleston* (South Carolina) *Evening Post*, April 9, 1947: 8.

11 Lewis Burton, "Record Crowd Sees U.S. Sandlotters Win," *New York Journal-American*, August 14, 1947: 24.

12 Edgar C. Greene, "Babe Still 'Do as I Please' Guy,'" *Chicago Herald-American*, August 14, 1947: 24.

13 Jack Conway Jr., "Sandlotters Back; Hail Keany Clout," *Boston Daily Record*, August 15, 1947: 40.

14 Arthur Daley, "Sports of the Times: Mostly About Babe Ruth," *New York Times*, March 19, 1948: 30.

15 Babe Ruth (as told to Bob Considine), *The Babe Ruth Story* (New York: Pocket Books [E.P. Dutton], 1948), 1.

16 John Rendel, "Ruth Gives 'Story' to Yale Library: Babe Presents His Manuscript Before Game in Which Elis Beat Princeton, 14-2," *New York Times*, June 6, 1948: S-1.

17 Tommy Kouzmanoff, *Milwaukee Sentinel*, August 27, 1948: part 2, 3.

18 Al Jonas, "U.S. Aces in Drill: 35,000 Expected at Sandlot Classic," *New York Journal-American*, August 22, 1948: L27.

19 Charlie Poeckel, *Babe and the Kid: The Legendary Story of Babe Ruth and Johnny Sylvester* (Charleston, South Carolina: The History Press, 2007), 132.

20 "Babe Left 'Kids' Share in Estate," *New York Journal-American*, August 23, 1948: 1.

The Babe's Final Personal Appearance

By Steve Smith

In his last personal appearance, Babe Ruth visited Iowa two months before his death to help promote the Junior American Legion Baseball program. Ruth was on tour working for the Ford Motor Company to promote youth baseball.

Ruth flew directly into Sioux City, Iowa, from St. Louis on June 20, 1948. He was accompanied by his wife, Claire, and his publicity man, Clint Mahlke. Ruth had made an appearance at Sportsman's Park in St. Louis the previous day on behalf of Ford. Ruth was greeted in Sioux City by John Hart, president of Spencer (Iowa) Baseball Inc. Hart was the owner of the local Ford dealership and manager of the Spencer semipro baseball club as well as the man who arranged the Babe's appearance.

On the day Ruth flew to Iowa, he'd been suffering from cancer for two years. The sight of an ailing Babe came as a surprise to those who saw him. "It was a shock at first, seeing the gaunt shrunken giant emerge from the plane and walk with that shambling gait to the terminal building at the Sioux City airport," wrote Bill Bryson in the *Des Moines Register*. "... Now he's a tired old man, a man who has been critically ill and who has undergone two delicate neck operations that has left his voice a coarse whisper."[1]

Although Bryson lamented Ruth's illness, he also recognized The Babe as he had been. "Yet he retains that zest, that lust for life, which, with his home runs, made him the most widely known and the best loved individual in the ranks of working sportsmen. The dull glaze of his eyes would give way to a sparkle when anyone mentioned his home run records or, particularly, his early-day pitching that includes an unsurpassed streak of 29 consecutive World Series scoreless innings."

With a Highway Patrol escort, Ruth traveled the 90 miles to Spencer, where the following day there would be a daytime doubleheader of local Junior Legion teams followed by an evening doubleheader which was the playoff of the daytime winners. Ruth was scheduled to appear during the games and would present the championship trophy, which he would personally autograph.

But mother nature did not cooperate, and the afternoon games were rained out. They were rescheduled for that evening with the finals of the tournament the following day. The field was dried out by burning 400 gallons of gasoline. Ruth appeared about 7:45 P.M., arriving on the field in an open car that drove past the stands to a huge ovation. Ruth gave a brief speech to the crowd. He told the estimated crowd of 3,000 to 4,000, "The young players of today are the stars of tomorrow," then thanked those in attendance and retired from the speaker's rostrum.[2]

The next day Ruth flew to Minneapolis, where he held a press conference at the Radisson hotel which was arranged by Ford Motor Company. It was a unique press conference as it was conducted by 11-year-old Johnny Ross of Minneapolis with the regular newspaper reporters looking on. Joe Hendrickson of the *Minneapolis Star* and *Tribune* reported that Johnny was Minneapolis's biggest sports enthusiast even though an illness had deprived him of his eyesight. Although Johnny's questions were basically of the softball variety, Hendrickson reported that "the coldest sportswriter in the business would have had difficulty holding his pencil and pad with a firm grip." The following questions relate the flavor of the interview:

>Johnny: How are you, Babe?
>
>Babe: I don't feel so good. I have a very bad throat and my head aches.
>
>Johnny: Who's your favorite ball team?
>
>Babe: I think I'll have to stick with the Yanks. They'll win the American League pennant.
>
>Johnny: I know they say the time you called your homer was your biggest thrill, but was it?
>
>Babe: Johnny, I think the time I pitched 29 consecutive innings without giving up a run.
>
>Johnny: Would you sooner pitch or play the outfield?
>
>Babe: I'd like to be in there every day. That's how much I like to play.[3]

Hendrickson went on to write, "I must report that the greatest home run hitter of all time was not feeling very good. The rainy weather had irritated his throat, forcing Ruth to speak with a whisper from his chest."

Ruth terminated the interview when Johnny seemed to search for another question by saying, "I think both of us are out of words, Johnny." The Babe posed for pictures, then retired to his room.

Ruth canceled his scheduled appearance in Minneapolis and returned the next day to New York, where he would spend the last weeks of his life in the hospital.

Acknowledgment

Thanks to Ralph Christian for providing much of the research on which this article is based.

Notes

1. Bill Bryson, "Babe Ruth Just a Tired Old Man Now," *Des Moines Register,* June 21, 1948.
2. Russ Ward, "Welcome Mat Is Out for Bambino," *Sioux City Journal,* June 22, 1948.
3. Joe Hendrickson, "Sports Opinions, Interview We Won't Forget," *Minneapolis Morning Tribune,* June 23, 1948.

Even Against HOF Hurlers, Ruth Was King of Swing

By Ed Gruver

Even among Jazz Age giants like Al Jolson and Jack Dempsey, it was Babe Ruth who was the King of Swing.

"I swing as hard as I can, and I try to swing right through the ball," Ruth was quoted as saying. "I swing big, with everything I've got. I hit big or I miss big. I like to live as big as I can."[1]

Ruth roared through the Roaring Twenties, the most famous sports figure in an era that included Dempsey, the ferocious heavyweight champion; gridiron great Red Grange; Notre Dame football coaching legend Knute Rockne; gentleman golfer Bobby Jones; and tennis star Big Bill Tilden.

Ruth rose above them all, his home-run hitting heralding the Lively Ball Era and enthralling everyone from legendary writers Grantland Rice and Damon Runyon to politicos like President Calvin Coolidge and New York Governor Franklin Roosevelt. The Babe's big swing terrorized opposing pitchers, be it regular season, World Series, All-Star Games, or exhibition contests against Negro League and Cuban stars. His home runs were so majestic that no ballpark could contain them, a fact that awed even a Hall of Fame pitcher who was a teammate of The Bambino.

"No one hit home runs the way Babe did," former Yankees ace Lefty Gomez said. "They were something special. They were like homing pigeons. The ball would leave the bat, pause briefly, suddenly gain its bearings then take off for the stands."[2]

There were many outstanding hurlers in Ruth's era, but how did The Sultan of Swat fare against the greatest pitchers of his generation? In his 22-year career, The Babe faced 13 future Hall of Fame pitchers, or 14 depending on which story you believe regarding Ruth hitting against Negro Leagues legend Satchel Paige.

In regular-season play, The Babe batted against Hall of Famers Stan Coveleski, Dizzy Dean, Red Faber, Lefty Grove, Waite Hoyt, Carl Hubbell, Walter Johnson, Ted Lyons, Herb Pennock, and Red Ruffing. His lone All-Star Game matchup with a Hall of Famer came against Hubbell. Ruth's World Series showdowns with HOF pitchers saw him hit against Pete Alexander, Burleigh Grimes, and Jesse Haines.

Coveleski, a tall, lean right-hander, broke into the big leagues in 1912 with Connie Mack's Philadelphia Athletics. He returned to the majors in 1916 with the Cleveland Indians and spent the next 13 seasons in Cleveland and Washington before teaming with Ruth on the Yankees' 1928 World Series squad. Coveleski won 20 or more games in a season five times, including four straight from 1918 to 1921.

He claimed a career-best 24 victories in 1919 and matched it the following season. On May 24, 1918, Coveleski hurled a 19-inning complete-game victory over the Yankees and in 1920 won Game Seven of the World Series for the Indians. Teammate and fellow Hall of Famer Joe Sewell said Coveleski threw a spitball that broke from a hitter's head to the ground and that trying to hit it was like trying to hit a butterfly. Coveleski closed his career with a 215-142 record and a 2.89 earned-run average.

Ruth recorded 86 at-bats against Coveleski and collected 30 hits for a .349 batting average. Among his hits were three home runs, nine doubles, and a triple. Coveleski walked Ruth 37 times and struck him out 10 times.

Ruth's matchups with Dean were heralded but disappointing for The Babe. When The Bambino batted against Dean in 1935, Ruth was 40 years old, overweight, and wearing the uniform of the Boston Braves.

Dean's lifetime record – 150-83 with a 3.02 ERA – scarcely does justice to the skills of the hard-throwing right-hander. A celebrated 30-game winner in 1934, Diz finally got to face The Babe in official at-bats on Sunday, May 5, at Braves Field. A crowd of 30,000 watched the former symbol of the Yankees' Murderers' Row dig in against the ace of the reigning World Series champion Gas House Gang.

Ruth's three plate appearances included an 0-for-2 with a strikeout and walk. Dean won the game, 7-0, and it was he rather than Ruth who homered that afternoon. Ruth and Dean met again on May 19 in St. Louis's Sportsman's Park. The Babe went 0-for-4 with a strikeout as Diz again went the distance, this time in a 7-3 victory. Ruth's batting record against Dean was 0-for-6 with one walk and two strikeouts.

Faber spent his 20-year career with the Chicago White Sox, going 254-213 with a 3.15 ERA from 1914 to 1933. The right-hander won 20 or more games four times, including a career-high 25 in 1921 to highlight a stretch of three straight 20-win seasons. Ruth struggled against Faber, hitting .247 in 158 at-bats. Still, The Babe had his moments, totaling 39 hits and 7 home runs. He worked Faber for 28 walks but fanned 27 times.

Ruth had less difficulty dealing with the greatest left-hander of his era – Grove. The ace of Mack's second Athletics dynasty and later of the Boston Red Sox, Grove was 300-141 with a 3.06 ERA in a 17-year career from 1925 to 1941. He won at least 20 games eight times, including seven straight seasons from 1927 to 1933. The hard thrower peaked in 1931 when he went 31-4 with a 2.06 ERA. Against Grove, Ruth batted .316 with 42 hits in 133 at-bats. He homered nine times. Grove had his say as well, fanning The Bambino 45 times.

Ruth faced several former and future teammates, and three of them – Hoyt, Pennock, and Ruffing – won world championships with him in New York. Hoyt was the right-handed ace of the Yankees' championship squads of 1927-28, winning 45 games in that two-year span. He went 237-182 with a 3.59 ERA in a 21-year career from 1918 to 1938. Ruth's initial at-bats against Hoyt came early in The Babe's career in New York when Hoyt was with the Red Sox in 1920. They opposed each other again in 1930-31 when Hoyt was with Detroit and the Athletics, and finally in 1935 when Hoyt hurled for Pittsburgh.

Nicknamed "Schoolboy," Hoyt was "the man" in the clutch, posting a 1.83 ERA in the World Series and winning six of his 10 decisions. Ruth hit Hoyt hard, batting .563 with nine hits in 16 at-bats, including four homers.

Ruth had less success against Pennock, a reed-thin 160-pounder nicknamed the Squire of Kennett Square after his hometown in Pennsylvania. Pennock proved the perfect complement to Hoyt, serving as the southpaw ace of the dynastic Yankees of the late 1920s. Pennock's career began with the Athletics in 1912, and he teamed with Ruth on the Red Sox from 1915 to 1919 before rejoining him in New York from 1923 to 1933. Pennock closed his career in 1934 with the Red Sox and retired with a 241-162 mark and 3.60 ERA. Like Hoyt, Pennock was a clutch pitcher, posting a 5-0 record and a 1.95 ERA in World Series competition.

In 20 at-bats against Pennock, The Babe rapped five hits for a .250 batting average. He made the most of those hits, four of them going for homers and the fifth one a triple. Ruth walked four times and fanned on three occasions.

Ruffing began his career in 1924 with the Red Sox and teamed with Ruth from 1930 to 1934. His peak years came during the second Yankees dynasty when he won 20 or more games in four straight seasons, 1936-39. He won 273 games in his career, lost 225 and owned an ERA of 3.80.

Ruffing was 7-2 in World Series competition, and Ruth had middling success against the right-hander, hitting .255 with 13 hits in 51 at-bats. He homered three times, drew 11 walks and struck out eight times.

Lyons, whose moniker was Sunday Teddy, enjoyed a 21-year career with the White Sox. From 1923 to 1946 he went 260-230 and fashioned a 3.67 ERA. Lyons won 21 or more games three times and led the league in victories in 1925 and '27. He had less success against Ruth, The Bambino leaving Sunday Teddy with Monday morning blues. In 131 at-bats, Ruth reached the right-hander for 39 hits and seven homers. He doubled five times and tripled twice. Ruth drew 27 walks off Lyons and struck out 17 times.

Ruth's most anticipated and most celebrated matchups may have been with Johnson, the feared and revered Big Train. Renowned for his "radio fastball" – hitters could hear it, couldn't see it – Johnson won 417 games in a 21-year career with the Washington Senators. The Big Train's career numbers are legendary – 12 campaigns with at least 20 wins, including 10 straight from 1910 to 1919. He won 33 games in 1912 and followed with a career-high 36 the following season.

The Babe and Big Train collided in 113 official at-bats. Ruth reached Johnson for 33 hits and a .292 batting average. He slugged eight homers and added eight doubles and two triples. The Big Train blew 25 third strikes past The Bambino.

Baseball's All-Star Game didn't begin until 1933, and Ruth, in the twilight of his career, played in only the first two midsummer classics. He made two plate appearances against Hubbell in 1934. The first began the famous string of strikeouts that saw Hubbell's screwball fan future Hall of Famers Ruth, Gehrig, Jimmie Foxx, Al Simmons, and Joe Cronin in succession. The Bambino batted against King Carl again in the third inning and walked.

After Ruth changed leagues in 1935, he faced Hubbell in regular-season play. On April 16 at Braves Field, Ruth roped an RBI single to right field in the first inning and a two-run home run to right in the fifth to fuel a 4-2 victory. The Babe also struck out to end the second inning. Ruth's homer off Hubbell was his final at-bat against the New York Giants' southpaw. In five plate appearances against Hubbell, who was 253-154 lifetime with a 2.98 ERA, Ruth recorded one homer, a single, walk, and struck out twice.

Until 1969, baseball's postseason consisted of the American and National League champions meeting in the World Series. Ruth's postseason plate appearances against Hall of Famers were limited to facing Alexander, Grimes, and Haines. His first plate appearance against Alexander, a right-hander with a career mark of 373-208 and an ERA of 2.56, came in the ninth inning of Game One of the 1915 World Series.

Ruth, a member of the Red Sox, pinch-hit against Alexander, the Phillies ace who was working on a complete-game victory in Philadelphia's Baker Bowl. Ruth grounded to first for the next to last out of the game. The 3-1 win was the lone victory for the Phillies, who fell to the Red Sox in five games.

Ruth and Alexander renewed acquaintances in Game Two of the 1926 World Series. Ruth was a Yankee by now, Alexander a Cardinal. The Babe went 0-for-4 in a 6-2 St. Louis victory. Ruth was completely handcuffed by the 39-year-old, striking out to end the first inning and failing to get the ball out of the infield the entire afternoon. In Game Six Ruth was 0-for-3 with a walk as Old Pete again went the distance, this time in a 10-2 win. Game Seven saw four future Hall of Famers climb the hill as Haines and Alexander threw for the Cardinals and Hoyt and Pennock for the Yankees. Old Pete trudged out of the bullpen in the seventh and didn't face Ruth until the bottom of the ninth. The Babe worked a two-out walk but was thrown out trying to steal second with Bob Meusel at bat and Lou Gehrig on deck. The caught-stealing ended the game, 3-2, and gave St. Louis the championship.

Ruth also matched up with Haines in three games in the '26 fall classic. A right-hander with a lifetime mark of 210-158 and an ERA of 3.64, Haines hurled the eighth inning in relief in Game One in Yankee Stadium and retired Ruth on a groundout to third. Haines started Game Three in St. Louis and went the route in a 4-0 win. He held The Babe to a 1-for-3 afternoon with a walk. Ruth's lone hit was a single to shallow center to start the fourth. In Game Seven, at Yankee Stadium, Ruth homered off Haines to right-center field in the third inning to give New York a 1-0 lead. Otherwise, he drew four walks off Haines, one intentional.

Two years later, Ruth faced Alexander and Haines in a World Series with a much different ending. Alexander started Game Two in New York, and Ruth walked and scored in the first and singled and scored in the third to help key a 9-3 romp. Haines worked Game Three in St. Louis, and Ruth went 2-for-4 with two singles and two runs scored in a 7-3 victory. Alexander pitched in relief in the fourth and final game. The Babe, in his lone at-bat against Old Pete on that day, helped complete the sweep with a homer to right in the eighth, his record-setting third round-tripper of the afternoon.

Grimes, a stocky right-hander, spent 19 years in the majors with seven teams and compiled a 270-212 record with a 3.53 ERA.

Ruth's appearances against Grimes came in the 1932 World Series, made famous by The Babe's controversial "called shot." Grimes pitched 1⅔ innings of relief in Game One in Yankee Stadium, and Ruth worked a walk to ignite a three-run inning that led to a 12-6 Yankees victory. Grimes didn't pitch again until the ninth inning of the fourth and final game, and he got The Babe to ground out to first.

Baseball was segregated until 1947, so Ruth never faced the great black pitchers of his era in an official game. Ruth was quoted in the *Pittsburgh Courier* in August 1933 as endorsing the quality and showmanship of black players, and he encouraged white fans to watch the "kind of ball that colored performers play." Negro League stars Judy Johnson, Cool Papa Bell, Buck O'Neil, Double Duty Radcliffe, Ray Dandridge, Buck Leonard, Willie Wells, and Monte Irvin returned Ruth's high praise.[3] "We could never seem to get him out no matter what we did," Johnson told baseball historian Bill Jenkinson.[4]

Ruth played in numerous exhibition games against great Cuban and Negro League athletes, but many of the results are lost to history. In 16 documented games in which he faced Negro League pitchers, Babe batted .463, going 25-for-54 with 11 home runs. One such performance came in Trenton, New Jersey, one week after the Yankees swept Pittsburgh in the 1927 World Series. Facing aging fastball legend Dick "Cannonball" Redding, a pitcher some old-timers insisted was greater than Paige, Ruth ripped three consecutive tape-measure home runs.[5]

The story has layers. Trenton promoter George Glasco took Redding aside before the game and reminded him that the fans were there to see Ruth hit home runs, The Babe having smote a record 60 that season. Redding replied that he would heave his pitches "right down the pike." Along with his three homers that day, Ruth also flied out and popped out.[6]

Ruth and Redding were not strangers to each other. They met in the fall of 1920, Babe homering off the Cannonball in a 9-4 loss. In the fall of 1925, Ruth and Redding squared off again. Redding and his Brooklyn Royals led by one run, but Ruth's semipro squad put a runner on in the ninth. With Babe due to bat, Redding's teammates had two words of advice for their pitcher: "Walk Ruth." Redding instead tried to slip his fastball past The Bambino. Royals second baseman Dick Seay said Ruth swung his tree trunk of a bat and launched the Cannonball's offering "into the next county." In the fall of 1926, The Babe batted against Redding once more and stroked three hits, including two doubles, and struck out once in a 3-1 loss.[7]

Whether Ruth ever stepped to the plate against Paige is subject to question. Satchel said several times that he regretted never having pitched to Ruth, whom he referred to as the "big man."[8] Ruth's daughter Julia Ruth Stevens, however, recalled an exhibition game in Brooklyn in which she said Paige got the better of her father. An oft-repeated rumor has Ruth fanning four times against Paige; whether that means in one game or lifetime has never been determined. Buck O'Neil remembered a different outcome during a barnstorming game in Chicago in the late 1930s. He said The Big Bam – as Ruth was sometimes called – hooked his bat into a Paige pitch and pounded a monstrous home run into the trees beyond the center-field wall. The home run was so prodigious – O'Neil estimated it flew 500 feet – that Satchel is said to have stared at The Bambino in wonderment as Ruth rounded the bases.[9] According to the story, Paige was so impressed by Ruth's power that he stood at home plate to shake The Babe's hand. Satchel sent a boy to retrieve the ball so The Bambino could sign it. Whether the Ruth-Paige stories are fact or fiction depends on what one chooses to believe.

What is fact is that Ruth's career marks against Hall of Fame pitchers are exceptional. He went 214-for-632, which translates to a .339 average. Add to that 47 home runs, 149 walks, and 140 strikeouts. Those numbers are strikingly close to his regular-season career averages: .342 batting average, 46 homers, 133 walks, and 86 strikeouts.

What this shows is that even against the greatest pitchers of his generation, Babe Ruth remained the King of Swing.

Notes

1 baberuth.com, Babe Ruth Quotes.

2 Ibid.

3 Bill Jenkinson, "Babe Ruth and the Issue of Race," baberuthcentral.com.

4 Ibid.

5 Ibid.

6 John Holway, "The Cannonball," Society for American Baseball Research, *Baseball Research Journal*, 1980. research.sabr.org/journals/cannonball.

7 Ibid.

8 Satchel Paige and John B. Holway, *Maybe I'll Pitch Forever* (Lincoln: Bison Books, 1993), 57.

9 Jenkinson.

The Babe as a Pitcher

By Pete Palmer

Everybody knows Babe Ruth started out as a pitcher and was quite successful, but how successful? Would he have made the Hall of Fame if he had not shifted to the outfield?

I use a method called player wins, which is calculated from batting, pitching, and fielding stats. These are converted to runs above average and converted to wins above average using 10 runs per win. An average player gets a rating of zero. These are different from pitching wins and losses, although you can get a rough estimate of player wins by taking pitching wins minus losses all over two. For example, in 1917 Ruth had a 24-13 record, which would calculate to (24-13)/2 or 5.5 player wins. His actual rating was 4.9, lower mainly because he had a strong batting team behind him that got credit for some of the pitching wins.

Looking at Ruth's record, you could make a good case that he had the best start of any pitcher through his first four years of at least 100 innings pitched per year in the modern era (from 1893, when the pitching distance was moved to its current value.) Before then, pitchers tended to pitch many more innings and had shorter careers. After not pitching for nine years, Ruth managed two complete-game victories (in 1930 and 1933), with an earned-run average better than the league average.

year	tm lg	w- l	g	ip	era	wins
1914	Bos A	2- 1	4	23	3.91	-0.3
1915	Bos A	18- 8	32	218	2.44	2.8
1916	Bos A	23-12	44	324	1.75	5.7
1917	Bos A	24-13	41	326	2.01	4.9
1918	Bos A	13- 7	20	166	2.22	3.1
1919	Bos A	9- 5	17	133	2.97	1.3
1920	NY A	1- 0	1	4	4.50	-0.1
1921	NY A	2- 0	2	9	9.00	-0.6
1930	NY A	1- 0	1	9	3.00	0.3
1933	NY A	1- 0	1	9	5.00	0.0
10 yrs		94-46	163	1221	2.28	17.1

Ruth was in the process of converting to the outfield in 1918, so I doubled his wins that year in the four-year table, 6.2 instead of 3.1, which made his four-year total 19.6. This table shows all pitchers who had at least 11 wins in their first four years. I also added earlier pitchers who had 20 or more.

name	1st	tm lg	1-4	total	age
Babe Ruth	1915	Bos A	19.6	17.1	20
Wes Ferrell	1929	Cle A	18.2	31.1	21
Bob Lemon	1947	Cle A	17.1	34.2	27
Bob Feller	1937	Cle A	16.3	31.6	19
Joe Wood	1909	Bos A	15.6	21.3	20
Lon Warneke	1932	Chi N	15.6	22.6	23

Player	Year	Team			Age
Tom Seaver	1967	NY N	15.2	49.5	23
Rich Gossage	1975	Chi A	14.9	29.7	24
Dizzy Dean	1932	StL N	14.8	22.3	22
Adam Wainwright	2007	StL N	14.6	21.0	26
Christy Mathewson	1901	NY N	14.5	56.3	21
Ron Guidry	1977	NY A	14.2	20.5	27
Dwight Gooden	1984	NY N	14.1	18.4	20
Mel Parnell	1948	Bos A	13.8	15.5	26
Johan Santana	2000	Min A	13.6	27.9	23
Roger Clemens	1984	Bos A	13.4	73.6	22
Kevin Appier	1990	KC A	12.9	20.3	23
Johnny Antonelli	1953	Mil N	12.5	15.4	23
Frank Tanana	1974	Cal A	12.2	12.8	21
Mike Mussina	1992	Bal A	12.2	36.5	24
Gary Peters	1963	Chi A	12.1	12.7	26
Teddy Higuera	1985	Mil A	12.1	10.8	28
Curt Davis	1934	Phi N	12.0	18.2	31
Vic Willis	1898	Bos N	11.9	20.0	22
Claude Hendrix	1912	Pit N	11.9	14.3	22
Don Drysdale	1957	Bro N	11.9	32.4	21
Ed Reulbach	1905	Chi N	11.8	17.3	23
Bob Gibson	1961	StL N	11.7	45.0	26
Grover Alexander	1911	Phi N	11.6	62.9	25
Remy Kremer	1924	Pit N	11.4	10.6	31
Tex Hughson	1942	Bos A	11.4	10.4	26
Mordecai Brown	1903	StL N	11.3	32.7	27
Jeff Pfeffer	1914	Bro N	11.2	12.2	26
Dazzy Vance	1922	Bro N	11.2	29.2	31
Ned Garver	1948	StL A	11.2	15.2	23
Carlos Zambrano	2002	Chi N	11.2	19.3	21
Mike Garcia	1949	Cle A	11.1	15.7	26
Noodles Hahn	1899	Cin N	11.0	17.0	20
Frank Sullivan	1954	Bos A	11.0	8.2	24
Charley Radbourn	1881	Pro N	23.6	31.6	27
Silver King	1887	StL A	23.5	22.9	19
Bob Caruthers	1885	StL A	23.1	30.0	21
John Clarkson	1885	Chi N	21.2	42.5	23

Looking at the data, the average career totals for these pitchers was about double their initial value, which would mean that 40 wins for a career would be a reasonable projection for Ruth.

The top pitchers based on wins are shown below. Roger Clemens is the only one with 40 or more wins not in the Hall of Fame. As you can see there are plenty of members with a career total in the range of Ruth's four-year record.

Top ranked pitchers

Walter Johnson	89.9	in
Cy Young	77.0	in
Roger Clemens	73.6	
Greg Maddux	64.2	in
Grover Alexander	62.9	in
Mariano Rivera	61.9	in
Lefty Grove	59.1	in
Christy Mathewson	56.3	in
Kid Nichols	56.2	in
Warren Spahn	51.4	in
Pedro Martinez	49.5	in
Tom Seaver	49.5	in
Randy Johnson	49.1	in
Bob Gibson	45.0	in
John Clarkson	42.5	in
Tom Glavine	40.8	in
Carl Hubbell	40.2	in
Clayton Kershaw	39.9	active (2019)
John Smoltz	38.0	in
Ed Walsh	37.6	in
Whitey Ford	37.2	in
Hal Newhouser	37.2	in
Hoyt Wilhelm	37.1	in

pre-1893

The Babe

Amos Rusie	36.7	in	Eppa Rixey	24.2	
Mike Mussina	36.5	in	Al Spalding	23.9	
Jim Palmer	35.0	in	Red Faber	23.4	
Steve Carlton	34.0	in	Addie Joss	23.0	
Bob Lemon	34.0	in	Rollie Fingers	22.7	
Kevin Brown	33.7		Dizzy Dean	22.3	
Bob Caruthers	33.6		Sandy Koufax	22.3	
Ted Lyons	33.5	in	Nolan Ryan	22.2	
Gaylord Perry	32.9	in	Rube Waddell	22.2	
Mordecai Brown	32.7	in	Lefty Gomez	20.1	
Don Drysdale	32.4	in	Vic Willis	20.0	
Curt Schilling	32.1		Early Wynn	19.5	
Zach Greinke	32.0	active (2019)	Joe McGinnity	18.9	
Bert Blyleven	31.8	in	Mickey Welch	18.9	
Carl Mays	31.7		Bruce Sutter	18.5	
Bob Feller	31.6	in	Burleigh Grimes	18.3	
Charley Radbourn	31.5	in	Don Sutton	17.5	
Red Ruffing	31.4	in	Jim Bunning	16.4	
Billy Wagner	31.3		Waite Hoyt	15.7	
Roy Halladay	31.3	in	Chief Bender	14.8	
Wes Ferrell	31.2		Jack Chesbro	11.0	
Dennis Eckersley	30.5	in	Jim Galvin	9.8	
Fergie Jenkins	30.4	in	Catfish Hunter	9.8	
Eddie Plank	30.3	in	Jack Morris	9.3	
Robin Roberts	30.3	in	Jesse Haines	7.3	
Tony Mullane	30.0		Herb Pennock	7.3	
			Rube Marquard	0.5	

Other Hall of Famers

Rich Gossage	29.7
Trevor Hoffman	29.2
Dazzy Vance	29.2
Phil Niekro	29.1
Clark Griffith	28.3
Juan Marichal	27.7
Stan Coveleski	26.0

Thus there is no doubt in my mind that Ruth would have been elected to the Hall of Fame as a pitcher if he had not moved to the outfield. In fact, it would not be hard to imagine that he could have ended up in the top 10 for his career.

Babe Ruth Stealing Home

By Bill Nowlin

Babe Ruth stealing home. *Courtesy of Library of Congress.*

Stealing home plate during a baseball game is one of the most-exciting plays in the sport. Sometimes a steal of home is part of a double steal, and sometimes just a straight steal. It is always unexpected; that's the only way it can work – the pitcher has to be caught unprepared for the possibility. Even with thousands of fans watching the game at a ballpark, very few will likely be watching a baserunner on third base and anticipating that he might attempt to steal home. Umpires, of course, have to be mindful of the possibility.

It is something of a lost art today but was more frequent in days gone by. Ty Cobb is said to have stolen home 54 times, often as part of a double steal. In 1912 alone, he supposedly stole home eight times. A player has stolen home twice in the same game a reported 11 times.[1] One of the most famous steals of home was that executed by Jackie Robinson in Game One of the 1955 World Series against the Yankees.[2]

Some noted basestealers were not known for stealing home. Lou Brock never once stole home, and Rickey Henderson did it only four times. But Babe Ruth reportedly did it 10 times.

You look at old film of The Babe and he comes across as almost the last person you'd expect to see steal any base – second, third, or home. But he is credited with 123 stolen bases over the course of his career. He stole 10 or more bases in a season five times, including in 1930 when he was 35 years old. Ruth even stole second and then third in Game Two of the 1921 World Series.

When did he steal home these 10 times?

It's difficult to pin down data on stolen bases, particularly when ranging back a century or so. One author observed, generally: "The data on stolen bases are a mess. The American League didn't start reliably keeping caught-stealing records until 1920, and the National League not until 1951, thus eliminating a very large number of contenders from our consideration and forcing careful examination of many of the rest."[3]

Retrosheet, in its list of discrepancies regarding Babe Ruth's record, reflects a stolen base in the first game of April 19, 1928,

A time Ruth was out, this time trying to steal third base. August 16, 1925: Ruth out in the fifth inning trying to go from first to third on Lou Gehrig's single. Senators third baseman is Ossie Bluege. Yankees won 3-2. *Courtesy of Library of Congress.*

which is not in the official record. Perhaps Ruth actually had a total of 124 stolen bases? In the course of my research for this article, I discovered what appear to be two stolen bases he was credited with (both from the same game, on May 5, 1920) that may be questionable.[4] I reached out to Retrosheet and asked about these two stolen bases. They had independently come across the same question, and added the two to their list of Babe Ruth discrepancies, to be posted the next time they do an update (which will probably have been done by the time this article appears). Perhaps this all adds up to 122 stolen bases.

Searching for Ruth steals of home plate, I looked up every game in which he was said to have stolen any base – all 124 of them (I looked up the April 19, 1928, one, too), plus four postseason steals. It was easy to rule out many of them as steals of home. Sometimes a newspaper account would straightforwardly report that Ruth had stolen second base. OK, that one gets ruled out. Sometimes he stole a base, but it wasn't clear which base – and yet, since he wasn't credited with a run scored, I tended to think that that probably wasn't a game in which he stole home![5] When the Yankees were shut out, 1-0, on July 28, 1920, we know his stolen base was not a steal of home. Other times, Ruth had one run scored but his home run in that game clearly accounted for the run scored. In the second game on August 15, 1926, the Yankees scored three times and three different Yankees had runs batted in – so we can account for each run. His steal had to have been of second or third.

I was able to rule out a considerable number of games through this approach. Based on contemporary newspaper accounts, I did find the eight steals of home noted here:

August 24, 1918 – Ruth was the starting pitcher against the visiting St. Louis Browns. He won a complete-game 3-1 victory. His steal was the run that made the difference, in a three-run bottom of the second. The next day's *Boston Globe* subhead read: "Ruth Rubs It In, Stealing Home with Third Run."

June 4, 1920 – The Athletics played the Yankees at the Polo Grounds. In the fourth inning, Ruth doubled off the right-field wall, advanced to third on Del Pratt's single along the third-base line, and then the two of them "tried the double steal with such success that Ruth slid in with the run." (June 5 *New York Daily Tribune*)

July 20, 1921 – In Cleveland, the *New York Herald* wrote, "Ruth and (Frank) Baker flashed a double steal in the third which quite discomfited the home folks."

July 28, 1924 – In the top of the fifth inning, in the second game of two at Comiskey Park, Ruth "drew a pass and scored in a double steal with (Bob) Meusel." (*Chicago Tribune*) Ruth had scampered first to third on Meusel's single, then stole home with the 11th run of an eventual 12-10 Yankees win.

September 2, 1924 – With a runner on second and one out in the first inning of the second game of a doubleheader in New York, Ruth was intentionally walked. Wally Pipp singled, driving in the lead runner with Ruth taking third. After Wally Schang fouled out, "Ruth and Pipp then successfully executed a double steal." (*Boston Globe*) Meusel then singled Pipp across. The three runs were all they needed to beat the Babe's former team, the Red Sox.

July 22, 1926 – In this game, Ruth tried to steal home twice. At Yankee Stadium, against the visiting White Sox, Retrosheet reports that he was caught the first time but succeeded the second. The *Chicago Daily News* shows Ruth caught stealing in the bottom of the first inning. In the bottom of the sixth, Ruth had reached base on a force play that retired Lou Gehrig. He took third base on Ben Paschal's single. Paschal then stole second. As Mike Gazella took ball four, both Ruth and Paschal were in motion and were each credited with steals of home and third, respectively. The *Chicago Tribune* wrote that Ruth "stole home, drawing a wild pitch from the pitcher." The pitch was wild enough that Paschal ran around third and scored, too.

June 9, 1927 – Facing relief pitcher Bert Cole, with the Yankees leading 7-3 over Chicago, Ruth tripled over the left fielder's head in the bottom of the eighth. Then Lou Gehrig struck out. Ruth apparently decided to take action. The *New York Times* wrote, "At the first opportunity, the Big Bam lit out for home. Mr. Cole was so unnerved by this unexpected manoeuvre that he threw the ball past his catcher."

July 27, 1931 – Ruth hadn't stolen home in more than four years, but once again the White Sox were the victims. In the bottom of the first, in the second game of a doubleheader, Ben Chapman stole second while Ruth came home on a double steal. Four of the eight listed steals of home were against the White Sox.

As with all baseball statistics, even those almost a century old, there remains the possibility that another researcher will turn up another steal of home, or two, or more. I would welcome hearing information on the subject. Until such time, I feel reasonably confident that Ruth can be credited with eight steals of home plate – which is pretty impressive.

Notes

1. baseball-almanac.com/recbooks/rb_stbah.shtml. This page also provides data on the 38 players who have stolen home 10 or more times in the course of their careers. The only player in the last 50 years to have done so is not a name most would have guessed: Paul Molitor. A note of acknowledgement to Stephen Boren – thanks for encouraging me in my work on this subject.

2. Highlights of the Series, including film of Robinson's steal, may be seen at youtube.com/watch?v=k4EUXTbbsAg. One of the most famous attempted postseason steals was one Babe Ruth failed to execute – in Game Seven of the 1926 World Series, with two outs and the Cardinals leading, 3-2, Ruth was caught trying to steal second base in the bottom of the ninth inning. The game was over, and the World Series was thus over as well. He had stolen second successfully in Game Six. Trying to steal another in the very next game may not have been the wisest decision. Newspaper coverage indicates that he was the one who chose to make the attempt.

3. Mississippi Matt Smith, "Babe Ruth Was the Worst Base Stealer of All Time," at not.fangraphs.com/babe-ruth-was-the-worst-base-stealer-of-all-time/. For a contrary view, see Zachary D. Rymer, "Stealing Home: Or, Why Babe Ruth Is a Better Thief Than Rickey Henderson," BleacherReport.com, August 6, 2010 at bleacherreport.com/articles/430984-stealing-home-or-why-babe-ruth-is-a-better-thief-than-rickey-henderson#slide9.

4. The official records indicated two steals for Ruth in this game. Neither the *New York Times*, *New York Daily News*, nor *Philadelphia Inquirer* reports him stealing any bases. The *Washington Herald* says he stole one. The *Washington Post* says two. But they aren't noted in the game story. There was a play in which he scored from second base, taking third base and then home on a passed ball. Ruth had been on second and Duffy Lewis on first. After the ball got away from the catcher, Val Picinich, the *Post*'s game story said, "Ruth and Lewis broke from their base moorings, but thought better of it. Picinich threw to Judge to get Lewis straggling back to first. As he did so Ruth broke for third, rounded it and watched the Griffs run Lewis up and down between second and third. Finally Babe darted for home, having been allowed too long a lead, and he beat [Frank] Ellerbe's throw."

5. The April 19, 1928, game was at Fenway Park. The steal is reported in the *Boston Herald* box score, but Ruth did not have a run scored in the game. Hence, the *Herald* did not see it as a steal of home. The *Boston Globe* box score was identical in this respect. I went day by day through such newspapers as I could access.

715

by Allan Wood

On April 27, 1969, baseball fans learned that "one of the most hallowed statistics of all sports lore" – Babe Ruth's career total of 714 home runs – would be revised. Leonard Koppett of the *New York Times* reported on a "forgotten" home run hit by Babe Ruth in the summer of 1918. "It turns out," Koppett wrote, "that Ruth hit 715 home runs, not 714, and starting next year the official records will show that."[1]

This surprising announcement came out of the creation of *The Baseball Encyclopedia* – the landmark reference work containing, for the first time ever, "a complete record of every man who ever played in a major league game" – which was published later that year, in August 1969.

Record-keeping for baseball's first four decades was far from meticulous. To make certain that *The Baseball Encyclopedia* contained accurate statistics for the years 1876-1919, researchers working for Information Concepts Incorporated (ICI) combed through miles of microfilm, gathering data game by game.

Questions arose about the statistics for many of those seasons, which had been played under different rules than were in effect for much of the twentieth century. Baseball Commissioner William Eckert formed the Special Baseball Records Committee in early 1968 to address these issues.

Koppett explained the five-man committee's two main purposes: "To evaluate old scoring rules in order to make them logically consistent with existing practices so that the statistics would be

Ruth, hands on bat. *Leslie Jones photo, courtesy of the Boston Public Library.*

truly comparable; and to pass upon outright errors uncovered by the researchers."[2] He also noted: "Since 1920, official league records are in good shape, but before that many games did not have an official scorer, and rules were written and applied inconsistently."[3]

One of the research questions concerned "sudden-death home runs." In its final report, the committee stated, "Before 1920, when the team batting last won the game in the ninth or in an extra inning, the ruling was that the team could not win by more than one run. If a man hit an outside-the-park home run ... he was given credit for a lesser hit [the number of bases necessary to score the winning run] and only the winning run counted."[4]

Only if the bases were empty would the batter get credit for a home run.

In November 1968 the committee ruled unanimously that those game-ending hits should now properly be considered home runs, and that the statistics for the batters, pitchers, and teams should be adjusted accordingly.[5] This was not considered a big deal – until an ICI researcher found the box score of the Red Sox-Indians game played at Fenway Park on July 8, 1918. With the score 0-0 and Amos Strunk on first base in the bottom of the 10th inning, the Boston batter cranked a pitch over the right-field fence. Because three bases were needed to score the winning run, the batter was awarded a triple and the Red Sox celebrated a 1-0 victory. What made this game noteworthy? The batter was Babe Ruth.

"The Colossus of Clouters came up swinging his two heavy, new bats. The crowd yelled loudly and long for a home run. Babe took his stance, made his bid on the very first pitch [from Stan Coveleski], a curve ball, and zowee how it traveled ... up into the realm of eagles, high and higher, far and farther." The baseball landed about three-quarters of the way up the right-field bleachers, "easily the longest hit to that section ever seen."[6]

At ICI's offices in Manhattan's Hotel Pennsylvania, this news caused a huge commotion. Joanne Cotterill, one of the computer programmers, recalled David Neft, who oversaw the *Encyclopedia* project, "roaring all day long. He was so over the top about it. He was thrilled. But he kept saying, 'We can't change that statistic. People have gone to their graves thinking Babe Ruth hit 714 home runs. How could we possibly do this?'"[7]

Nearly 50 years later, Neft was adamant that despite the gravity of changing one of baseball's most iconic numbers, Ruth's home run total should "absolutely" have been changed to 715. "If it had been Joe Smith, they would have approved the change," Neft said. "Clearly, nobody wanted to monkey with Ruth's 714. But why should most of baseball history say that if you hit a walk-off home run, you get credit for a home run, but when Babe Ruth hits one, he gets credit for only the number of bases needed to score the winning run? You have to be consistent. You have to use the same logic for everybody."[8]

A week after the *Times* article appeared, the Special Baseball Records Committee met again and recast its votes. By a 3-to-2 vote, it was decided that Ruth's 715th home run, as well as the other 36 game-winning home runs uncovered by ICI's researchers, should be pushed back down the memory hole.[9] Lee Allen (historian of the Baseball Hall of Fame) and Robert Holbrook (executive assistant to the president of the American League) remained in favor of upholding their earlier decision "in the interest of consistency in the records." However, the other three members – Joseph Reichler (director of public relations of the commissioner's office), David Grote (director of public relations for the National League), and Jack Lang (secretary-treasurer of the Baseball Writers Association of America) – changed their votes.[10]

Reichler noted that he had been out of the country during the November 1968 meeting and someone else from the commissioner's Office had cast his vote. He also claimed the committee "had gone beyond its authority" and should not "tamper with rules which govern baseball records at the time in which these records were made."[11] Lang agreed: "It just doesn't make any sense to go back 50 years and alter rules that were in force then."[12]

However, if Reichler and Lang truly believed that changing rules from 50 years earlier was beyond the committee's mandate, why did they agree to "alter" numerous other old statistics, including games played, hits, batting average, slugging percentage, walks, fielding assists, errors, earned runs, earned-run average, and won-lost decisions?[13] In explaining his opposition to the home-run decision, Reichler said: "When you carry this a little further, what do you want to do about hits that bounced into the stands and were declared homers?" Bill Fleischman of *The Sporting News* answered: "A good question. They now are doubles."[14] That example further undercuts Reichler's explanation, since the committee gave its approval to "tamper" with that rule, as well.

The *New York Times* published an unsigned article the day after the new vote, explaining that the committee believed it had "no right to change, retroactively, a playing rule" in effect in 1918. "All other changes voted on dealt with conventions about scoring, clerical errors, oversights and so forth; but this particular one dealt with actual rules of play, which could not be changed by anyone after the fact."[15]

The rules concerning walk-off home runs – both before and after 1920 – obviously fall under "conventions about scoring," as well as "rules of play." John Thorn, Major League Baseball's official historian since 2011, said "[T]he decision to rescind Ruth's homer was a result of pressures to leave hallowed numbers alone."[16] The committee believed it was better to knowingly retain an incorrect statistic in baseball's official records rather than correctly revise such an iconic number.

Back in July 1918, not long after Ruth's blast crash-landed in the Fenway Park bleachers, there was talk of changing this rule. That season was the first in which Ruth appeared in the Red Sox' everyday lineup, playing either first base or left field when he wasn't pitching, and his exceptional hitting over the first 2½ months of 1918 had become a huge national story.

"Had Strunk been on third yesterday ... 'Babe' would have received credit for only a one-base hit," wrote Melville Webb of the *Boston Globe*. "As the rules now stand the player is discriminated against, and all to no necessary purpose. Nothing is likely to be done about it, but something should be done, even if only in the spirit of fairness. ..."[17]

Five days later, the *Boston Traveler*'s W.C. Spargo called the ruling "an undeserved hardship on the batter." Spargo argued that although a single and a home run are worth the same thing when it comes to a player's batting average, when a batter "drives out a homer that is beyond all question, he should not be cut down by the rules."[18]

American League umpire Billy Evans agreed that the rule should be changed, and he wrote a lengthy article for the *Boston Post* after the 1918 season was over. "The right field bleachers at the Boston grounds are so far from the home plate that you almost need a field glass to get familiar with what is going on. Standing at the home plate with bat in hand, it seems almost impossible to hit the ball into said bleachers. ... If there ever was a real, genuine, sure enough home run, [Ruth's] wallop was the last word. ... [A] batsman who hits the ball over the fence or into the bleachers should be credited with a home run [and] all runners on the bases, as well as the batsman, should be entitled to score."[19]

The rule was changed after the 1919 season. The Rules Committee approved the change, 5 to 1. National League umpire Hank O'Day was the lone holdout, insisting that "there is no way you can score a run after a game is over."

From "Decisions of the Special Baseball Records Committee" Appendix B to The Baseball Encyclopedia (1969)

Here are the 37 instances of a batter hitting an outside-the-park home run and being credited with a lesser hit (1876-1919):

Date	Batter	Team	League	Opponent	Hit
June 17, 1884	Roger Connor	New York	NL	Boston	Single
September 6, 1884	Hardy Richardson	Buffalo	NL	Boston	Triple
April 21, 1885	Fred Mann	Pittsburgh	AA	Louisville	Double
July 30, 1885	Tommy McCarthy	Boston	NL	Detroit	Double
August 20, 1885	Paul Hines	Providence	NL	Boston	Single
June 5, 1890	Sam Thompson	Philadelphia	NL	Brooklyn	Single
June 17, 1890	Mike Griffin	New York	PL	Philadelphia	Double
July 30, 1890	Al McCauley	Philadelphia	NL	Chicago	Triple
May 7, 1891	King Kelly	Cincinnati	AA	Boston	Single
September 13, 1891	George Wood	Philadelphia	AA	Milwaukee	Double (Game 1)
July 7, 1892	Buck Ewing	New York	NL	St. Louis	Single
May 13, 1893	Lou Bierbauer	Pittsburgh	NL	Louisville	Single
August 9, 1893	George Van Haltren	Pittsburgh	NL	Chicago	Double
August 27, 1895	Bill Lange	Chicago	NL	Washington	Single
September 2, 1895	Mike Tiernan	New York	NL	Cleveland	Triple

September 27, 1895	Duke Farrell	New York	NL	Baltimore	Triple
July 27, 1896	Charlie Irwin	Cincinnati	NL	Cleveland	Triple
June 4, 1897	Parke Wilson	New York	NL	Louisville	Double
July 15, 1899	Jimmy Collins	Boston	NL	Pittsburgh	Single
July 24, 1899	Ginger Beaumont	Pittsburgh	NL	Philadelphia	Triple
July 24, 1900	Jimmy Collins	Boston	NL	St. Louis	Single
July 27, 1900	Chick Stahl	Boston	NL	Pittsburgh	Single
May 17, 1901	Bill Coughlin	Washington	AL	Philadelphia	Single
September 1, 1902	Ed Gremminger	Boston	NL	Cincinnati	Double
June 26, 1903	Pat Moran	Boston	NL	Chicago	Triple
September 10, 1904	Roger Bresnahan	New York	NL	Philadelphia	Double
May 5, 1906	Sherry Magee	Philadelphia	NL	Brooklyn	Triple
June 2, 1906	Tim Jordan	Brooklyn	NL	Boston	Double
May 25, 1908	Joe Tinker	Chicago	NL	New York	Double
September 28, 1908	Cy Seymour	New York	NL	Philadelphia	Single
April 23, 1910	Doc Crandall	New York	NL	Brooklyn	Single
August 24, 1911	Tex Erwin	Brooklyn	NL	Chicago	Triple
June 17, 1914	Sherry Magee	Philadelphia	NL	St. Louis	Double
April 19, 1917	Ping Bodie	Philadelphia	AL	Boston	Triple
April 19, 1918	Irish Meusel	Philadelphia	NL	Boston	Triple
July 8, 1918	Babe Ruth	Boston	AL	Cleveland	Triple
July 18, 1918	Frank Baker	New York	AL	Detroit	Single (Game 2)

Notes

1. Leonard Koppett, "Computer Finds Ruth's 715th Homer," *New York Times*, April 27, 1969.
2. Ibid.
3. Ibid.
4. "Decisions of the Special Baseball Records Committee" (Appendix B), *The Baseball Encyclopedia: The Complete and Official Record of Major League Baseball* (New York: The Macmillan Company, 1969), 2329.
5. ICI's researchers eventually found 37 such games between 1876 and 1919.
6. *Boston Herald and Journal*, July 9, 1918.
7. Interview with Allan Wood, August 21, 2014.
8. Interview with Allan Wood, September 3, 2014.
9. At the time, it was Ruth's 21st career home run.
10. Bill Fleischman, "Another Homer for The Babe? Debate Grows Hot, Heavy," *The Sporting News*, May 10, 1969: 8.
11. "Babe's Extra Homer Is Snatched Away," *The Sporting News*, May 17, 1969: 27.
12. Bill Fleischman.
13. "Decisions of the Special Baseball Records Committee," *The Baseball Encyclopedia*, 2328-29. "7. All appearances by a player in an official game shall be counted as a game played. (Before 1912 many pinch-hitters, pinch-runners, and substitutes who did not bat were not credited with a game played. 8. Bases on balls should always be treated as neither a time at bat nor a hit for the batter. (In 1887 bases on balls were scored as hits and in 1876 bases on balls were scored as outs.) ... 10. Bases on balls, wild pitches, passed balls, balks, and hit batsmen shall not be counted as errors. (These items were frequently scored as errors before 1889.) 11. A pitcher shall not be credited with an assist on a strike-out. (Before 1889 pitchers were usually awarded an assist on a strikeout.) 12. Scoring rules governing won and lost decisions by a pitcher did not become official until 1950. It was decided that all pitching decisions during the period 1920-49 shall stand as they are in the official records, but that for the period 1876-1919 the 1950 ruling shall be in effect. ... 13. The present definition on earned runs, as was established in 1969 by the Baseball Scoring Rules Committee, shall be effective from that date on in defining earned runs. Prior to that date, the 1917-68 definition of earned runs shall be applied to the years 1876-1911, and to the American League in 1912. (Before 1912 there was ... a time where bases on balls, hit batsmen, and wild pitches were considered errors in the computation of earned runs.)"
14. Bill Fleischman.
15. "Ruth's Home Runs Restored to 714," *New York Times*, May 6, 1969.
16. Email correspondence with Allan Wood, September 5, 2018. Not every baseball historian agrees on this issue. Jerome Holtzman, official historian from 1999 to 2008, believed changing old rules to conform to the modern game was "an abomination, an absolute falsehood and twisting of the known facts. ... If a walk was a hit in 1887 it should stand as a hit forevermore." From "An Important Change to the Official Record of Major League Baseball," Appendix to *Total Baseball*, 7th edition (Total Sports; 2001), posted on July 24, 2014, by John Thorn to ourgame.mlblogs.com/major-league-baseball-record-keeping-part-2-dd94be2af325. [Accessed April 27, 2019.]
17. Melville Webb Jr., "Rules Should Be Fixed to Cover Hits Like Ruth's," *Boston Globe*, July 9, 1918.
18. W.C. Spargo, "Ruth's Clout Starts Talk of New Rule," *Boston Traveler*, July 13, 1918.
19. Billy Evans, "Bleachers Hit Real Home Run," *Boston Post*, December 22, 1918.

Selected Babe Ruth Ballgames

Babe Ruth Debuts

July 11, 1914: Boston Red Sox 4, Cleveland Naps 3, at Fenway Park

By Joe Schuster

Even before playing an inning of major-league baseball, Babe Ruth was something of a legend.[1]

Partly this came from his on-field accomplishments. At age 19, just before the 1914 season, he joined the International League Baltimore Orioles, signed by owner-manager Jack Dunn after Dunn saw him throw a no-hitter in a 1913 semipro game in Baltimore.[2] Ruth showed up eager for training camp, reportedly one of the first two to arrive,[3] and was spectacular, especially in exhibitions against major-league clubs, showing himself "a sterling southpaw who (was) a terror to the big league clubs."[4]

On March 25 against the Philadelphia Athletics, who'd win the 1914 AL pennant, he pitched "brilliantly" in a complete-game 6-2 victory against a lineup including Eddie Collins and Frank „Home Run" Baker.[5] He also pitched well against the Dodgers, Braves, and Phillies, and continued his effectiveness into the season, shutting out Buffalo 6-0 in his April 22 regular-season debut.[6]

By June, partly because Ruth had a stretch of nine consecutive victories, several major-league teams expressed interest in acquiring him, including at least one from the Federal League.[7]

On July 9 Dunn sold him to the Boston Red Sox, along with Ernie Shore and Ben Egan, for a reported $30,000.[8]

The deal garnered significant attention, some of which furthered the idea of Ruth as legend. The *Baltimore Sun*, profiling him, emphasized his difficult childhood during which his parents had declared him incorrigible and deposited him at St. Mary's Industrial school for delinquents; there, the *Sun* declared, Ruth blossomed into someone "heralded from one end of the country to the other as a wonderful man (whose) whole heart was put into baseball."[9] Announcing the deal, the *Boston Globe* dubbed him "the next (Rube) Waddell."[10]

The team Ruth joined was in sixth place at 39-38 after losing its last five. Its woes stemmed partly from injury and illness. Among others, Joe Wood, who'd won 34 games in 1912, had a sore arm; Heinie Wagner, the team's 1913 shortstop, would miss the season because of rheumatism; an infielder Boston acquired from Detroit, Del Gainer, injured himself almost immediately after arriving; pitcher Rube Foster hurt his knee; and the Red Sox' best hitter, Tris Speaker, was "badly bunged up, though ... sticking it out."[11] Announcing the deal, owner Joseph Lannin said he'd "let no expense stand in the way of putting the Red Sox in the American League race and keeping them there."[12]

Because of the tattered pitching staff, Ruth did not have to wait long to see action, as manager Bill Carrigan started him the day he arrived, a Saturday afternoon contest against the Cleveland Naps, who at 26-49 were the worst team in the majors. Managed by Joe Birmingham, Cleveland featured outfielder Shoeless Joe Jackson (then hitting .333), and shortstop Ray Chapman, who was just beginning to find his way after starting the season late after breaking his leg in the spring.

Opposing Ruth was Willie Mitchell, 24 and in his sixth major-league season, with a 4-9 record and a 3.93 ERA. Mitchell was erratic. Although he would finish second in the league that year in strikeouts with 179, he'd also finish second in walks with 124.

Game day was pleasant; the *Cleveland Plain Dealer* described it as "an ideal summer afternoon (with) an east wind from Boston harbor tempering the heat."[13] The combination of weather and the chance to see Ruth drew 11,087 in paid attendance.[14]

Ruth's day began oddly. He gave up a single to Jack Graney leading off, and a groundout by Terry Turner moved him to second before Jackson singled, but Graney attempted to score on Jackson's hit, was caught in a rundown, and was out at the plate.[15] On that play, Jackson tried for second, but was also thrown out. The Red Sox took the lead in the bottom of the inning. After Olaf Henriksen struck out leading off, Everett Scott singled. He was forced at second by Speaker's grounder. Speaker then stole second, and scored on a triple by Larry Gardner.

Neither team did anything of consequence in the second and third innings, but the second featured Ruth's first major-league at-bat, in which he struck out, though the *Globe* noted that he "received a perfect ovation when he went to the bat, and shaped up like a good batsman."[16]

Cleveland tied it in the top of the fourth: Graney hit a long drive to deep center field that Speaker went after and got his glove on but could not corral, allowing Graney to reach second. The scorer ruled it an error but, the *Plain Dealer* reported, he "was a bit hard on Speaker. … (He) just reached it after a long run and most everybody in the press box regarded it as awfully close to a two-base hit."[17] Turner sacrificed Graney to third, and he scored on Jackson's second single of the day.

Boston went back on top with a pair of two-out runs in the bottom of the inning. Gardner singled leading off and advanced to third on a sacrifice by Hal Janvrin and a groundout by Wally Rehg. Steve Yerkes walked and stole second. When catcher Steve O'Neill's throw sailed into center field, Gardner scored. Carrigan (who was also the team's starting catcher) followed with a double, driving in Yerkes, before Ruth ended the inning by flying out to Jackson in right.

The lead held until the seventh, when Cleveland tied the score on three singles: Jay Kirke led off with one and moved to second on another by Chapman. Nemo Leibold sacrificed, moving both to second and third, respectively, and they scored on a single by O'Neill. Ruth got out of the inning when Mitchell grounded to short for a double play.

That was the end of Ruth's day. Duffy Lewis pinch-hit for him leading off the bottom of the seventh and grounded a roller to Kirke at first. When Kirke threw to Mitchell covering, the ball eluded the pitcher, letting Lewis reach second. After Henriksen flied out, Scott bounced back to Mitchell, who, instead of throwing to first for the out, went after Lewis, who was caught between second and third. Lewis managed to stay in a rundown long enough for Scott to advance to second. He came in on Speaker's single. The inning ended with Speaker being caught trying to steal.

To relieve Ruth, Carrigan brought in Dutch Leonard, who was having the best year of his career (he would lead the league with a microscopic 0.96 ERA while going 19-5). He set down the last six Naps in order, striking out four, picking up his first save on the season, and giving Ruth his first major-league victory. Ruth's final line: seven innings, eight hits, three runs (two earned), no walks, and one strikeout. Despite his faltering in the seventh and although noting that he could improve, the *Globe* praised him: "(He) proved a natural ballplayer and went through his act like a veteran of many wars. He has a natural delivery, fine control and a curve ball that bothers the batsmen."[18] Mitchell, the losing hurler, pitched at least as well as Ruth, going the distance and surrendering four runs (three earned) on eight hits and two walks, while striking out five.

Five days later, Ruth got his second start, this time against Detroit. He lasted three innings, allowing two earned runs on three hits and a walk, striking out one, and taking the loss. After he spent the next month on the bench without getting into a game, Boston sent him to the minors on August 18.

While his arrival was ballyhooed by long, laudatory newspaper articles, his departure was noted by almost a journalistic whisper, a single sentence on the bottom of the page in the August 18 edition of the *Globe*: "'Babe' Ruth, the 'Southpaw' pitcher who came to Boston from Baltimore, has been released to the Providence club of the International League."[19]

He may have arrived in the majors described as a legend, but it would take some time before he would actually be one.

Sources

In addition to the sources cited in the Notes, the author also relied on Baseball Reference for statistics, as well as the Society for American Baseball Research's Biography Project for background information.

Notes

1. See, for example, C. Starr Matthews, "The Rise of Babe Ruth," *Baltimore Sun*, July 10, 1914: 5, and J.C. O'Leary, "Three New Men for the Red Sox," *Boston Globe*, July 10, 1914: 1.
2. O'Leary.
3. "Orioles to Leave for Camp Tonight," *Baltimore Evening Sun*, March 2, 1914: 8.
4. "Giants in the Final Exhibition Game," *Baltimore Evening Sun*, April 13, 1914: 2.
5. Jesse A. Linthicum, "Birds Beat Athletics," *Baltimore Sun*, March 26, 1914: 5.
6. "Ruth Scores Shutout," *Baltimore Sun*, April 23, 1914: 11.
7. "Federal League After Babe Ruth," *Baltimore Evening Sun*, June 5, 1914: 8.
8. O'Leary.
9. Matthews.
10. O'Leary.
11. O'Leary.
12. Ibid.
13. "Red Sox Hits and Naps' Errors Give Boston Game," *Cleveland Plain Dealer*, July 12, 1914: II-1.
14. Ibid.
15. Play-by-play detail comes from the *Boston Globe* and *Cleveland Plain Dealer* accounts of the game.
16. T.H. Murnane, "Ruth Leads Red Sox to Victory, *Boston Globe*, July 12, 1914: 11.
17. "Features," *Cleveland Plain Dealer*, July 12, 1914: 1B.
18. Murnane.
19. "Ruth Goes to Providence," *Boston Globe*, August 18, 1914: 6.

A Sign of So Many Swats to Come: Ruth Doubles for First Big-League Hit as Red Sox Rout Yankees

October 2, 1914: Boston Red Sox 11, New York Yankees 5, at Fenway Park

By Mark S. Sternman

Even after the game, the 1,500 people who watched a meaningless late-season contest between the Red Sox and the Yankees in the last week of the 1914 American League season would have had no idea that they had witnessed a historic hit by a rookie off a reliever nearing the end of his career.

In the midst of a seven-year run that saw Boston win four championships, the Red Sox had the much stronger of the two clubs led by the superstar center fielder Tris Speaker. The Gray Eagle enjoyed a 22-year career in the AL and played a career-high 158 games in 1914, including this contest.

New York, by contrast, lacked boldface names in both the batting order and pitching rotation. Before the season, Yankee fans might have pointed to the Peerless Leader, Frank Chance, as a reason for optimism, but with 20 games to go in the team's fourth straight nonwinning campaign, Chance resigned. His replacement, the 23-year-old Roger Peckinpaugh, became the youngest skipper in the history of the majors when he took over as player-manager.

To face Boston, Peckinpaugh tapped Carroll Brown, "the best pitcher that ever promenaded the boardwalk at Atlantic City,"[1] thus earning him the splendid sobriquet Boardwalk in place of his more pedestrian birth name. Red Sox player-manager Bill Carrigan countered with rookie southpaw George Ruth, who made his third start for Boston after splitting his first two decisions in July.

The game served as a microcosm of the season for the two teams. The Red Sox took a 2-0 lead in the first thanks to a double by Olaf Henriksen, Speaker's 18th triple of the year,[2] and a single by Dick Hoblitzell, who enjoyed a perfect 4-for-4 day at the plate.

Boston extended its lead in the fourth. Catcher Hick Cady singled, Henriksen walked, Hal Janvrin doubled, Duffy Lewis tripled, and Hoblitzell doubled.

Trailing 6-0, the Yankees finally broke through against Ruth in the sixth thanks to an error by first baseman Janvrin, Peckinpaugh's single, and a two-run double by the former Boston backstop Les Nunamaker.[3] Even here, New York played poor baseball. Down by four runs, catcher Nunamaker should have held at second with a two-bagger rather than trying to take an extra base against the excellent outfield arm of Lewis. Lewis's peg, one of his 22 assists as a left fielder in 1914, cut down Nunamaker, keeping the Red Sox lead at 6-2.

The Yankees would draw no closer. In the bottom of the same frame, Henriksen and Janvrin both walked, and Roy Hartzell's error on Speaker's fly loaded the bases. Lewis's fly ball scored one run and Hoblitzell's double plated two more. Brown had given up nine runs (eight earned), the most he had yielded since a September 13, 1912, game against Cleveland. Boston now led 9-2.

King Cole replaced Brown. As Brown had pitched for the pennant-winning 1913 A's and had won 30 games for the Athletics in 1912-1913, Cole had toiled for the pennant-winning 1910 Cubs and captured 38 games in 1910-1911.

Ruth had gone hitless in his two-plus games for the Red Sox before facing Cole in the seventh. The Babe doubled for the first of his career 2,873 hits and 506 doubles. The "smashing two-ply drive"[4] preceded a single by Henriksen and a fly by Janvrin, which enabled Ruth to score the first of his 2,174 career runs and put the Red Sox up 10-2. As of 2018, Ruth had still scored the fourth-most runs in major-league history. In a neat coincidence, Hank Aaron also finished his career with 2,174 runs scored.

Cruising along with a big lead and perhaps tired by his labor on the bases, Ruth eased up. New York scored a run in the eighth on two singles, a walk, and a fly ball. Boston got the run back in the bottom half on a walk, an error, and a single to go up 11-3. In the ninth, the speedy Fritz Maisel smacked an inside-the-park homer, one of three such clouts he would hit as a Yankee.[5] Doc Cook walked. Down 11-4, he stole second base and third base. Today, an official scorer would deem these two plays defensive indifference, but in 1914 Cook got credit for two meaningless steals.[6] Birdie Cree doubled in Cook to make the final score 11-5 and give Ruth the second of his 94 wins on the mound.

The Cole-Ruth confrontation that transformed the game from meaningless to memorable highlighted two hurlers who had more similarities than the casual baseball fan might assume. Superficially, both pitchers with four-letter last names more commonly went by four-letter nicknames rather than their given names (Leonard for Cole and George for Ruth). Both pitched for the Yankees under Hall of Fame managers (Cole for Chance,[7] and Ruth for Miller Huggins and Joe McCarthy). Both won 20 games as pitchers with league-leading ERAs under 2 for pennant winners (Cole went 20-4 with a 1.80 ERA for the 1910 Cubs; Ruth went 23-12 with a 1.75 ERA for the 1916 Red Sox).

Both died young, Cole at the age of 29, and Ruth at 53. Deadball Era baseball fans could hardly have imagined that years after his hit off Cole, the Boston rookie hurler Ruth would go on to become the Sultan of Swat for New York.

Ruth hit a then-record 54 homers in his first season with the Yankees in 1920, playing regularly alongside two of the more prominent players in this 1914 game. Duffy Lewis had preceded Ruth by one year, going from Boston to New York in time for the 1919 season.[8] Alone among his 1914 New York teammates, Peckinpaugh remained with the Yankees and still held down the shortstop position through 1921.

In the first postseason game in franchise history, that year, Peckinpaugh played shortstop and batted second, one slot in front of Ruth, who played left field. The Yankees have the most storied World Series record of any team, a history that began on October 5, 1921, against the New York Giants with a leadoff single by Elmer Miller, a sacrifice by Peckinpaugh, and an RBI single by Ruth that gave the Yanks a 1-0 lead in a game that would end 3-0. Although the Giants would go on to win the 1921 World Series, the echoes of a double Ruth hit in 1914 would resound for generations of Bronx Bombers.

Notes

1. "Athletics Helpless before Caldwell," *New York Times*, April 18, 1914.

2. Speaker finished third in the AL with 18 triples behind his teammate Larry Gardner, who hit 19, and the remarkable Sam Crawford, who, at the age of 34, hit a career-best 26 triples. Crawford holds the all-time record with 309 career triples.

3. Nunamaker averaged fewer than 10 extra-base hits per season, but had at least three of them against Ruth. "On April 25, [1916,] he clobbered Red Sox ace Babe Ruth for a double, a triple, and two singles…" Tony Bunting, "Les Nunamaker," sabr.org/bioproj/person/790ea82d (accessed May 23, 2018).

4. T.H. Murnane, "Highlanders Out of Running from Start," *Boston Globe*, October 3, 1914: 7. A correspondent for a New York paper made a simple reference to "Ruth's double" rather than describing the hit in any detail. "Red Sox Pound Yankee Pitchers," *New York Times*, October 3, 1914.

5. Mitchell S. Soivenski, *New York Yankees Home Runs* (Jefferson, North Carolina: McFarland & Company, Inc., 2013), 283. Maisel also got his 69th stolen base of the season in this game. His 1914 total of 74 stolen bases remained the Yankee record until Rickey Henderson stole 80 in 1985. Henderson subsequently stole 87 bases for the Yankees in 1986 and 93 in 1988. Maisel's 1914 total remained fourth best in franchise history at the end of the 2018 season.

6. Cook needed the scoring generosity. He finished the 1914 season with 26 steals, which appears impressive absent the context that he was caught stealing 32 times. Both Cook and Eddie Murphy of the A's finished with the league-worst mark in this category, but Murphy at least had 10 more stolen bases than Cook did.

7. "Frank Chance always considered Cole a great pitcher, when he was in condition, and when the Peerless Leader came … to manage the Yankees one of his first official acts was to bring Cole back from the minors." "Pitcher 'King' Cole Dead," *New York Times*, January 7, 1916.

8. "A story Lewis loved telling in later years was about the time he pinch-hit for Babe Ruth. On July 11, 1914, Ruth made his major-league debut, hurling a 4-3 victory over the Cleveland Indians. Lewis hit for Ruth in the seventh inning and singled, helping to give his young teammate the victory." Mark Armour, "Duffy Lewis," sabr.org/bioproj/person/5f9f3a44 (accessed May 23, 2018).

Red Sox Pitcher Babe Ruth Hits First Career Home Run But Suffers Loss to Yankees in 13th Inning

May 6, 1915: New York Yankees 4, Boston Red Sox 3 (13 innings), at Polo Grounds

by Mike Huber

Boston Red Sox pitcher Babe Ruth, later nicknamed the Sultan of Swat, started his home run career in a game on May 6, 1915, against his future team, the New York Yankees. A crowd of approximately 5,000 visited the Polo Grounds for an American League match-up between the Red Sox and the Yankees. Coincidentally on this same date, in the National League, the New York Giants were playing the Boston Braves at Fenway Park.

According to the *Boston Globe*, "the Sox defense wobbled sufficiently to give the Yanks a decided advantage in the early innings."[1] Six errors were made in the game, with four of them by the visiting Red Sox, at critical times in the game. They would

Babe Ruth and three of his 1915 Red Sox teammates. *Courtesy of Library of Congress.*

have a decided effect on the game's outcome, as the Yankees fought the Red Sox "tooth and nail for thirteen innings."[2]

Ruth was making his third start (and fourth appearance) of the season for the Red Sox. In his previous outings, he was 1-0 with a 5.02 earned run average. At the plate, though, he had picked up two hits in seven at-bats, good for a .286 batting average. The *New York Times* affirmed that "the big left-handed pitcher, Babe Ruth, was all that a pitcher is supposed to be, and some more."[3] The Yankees countered with Jack Warhop, a 5-foot-9 right-hander also making his third start. Warhop was 0-2 with a 6.19 ERA in the young season. After 15 games, Boston was in fifth place in the American League. New York was only 1 1/2 games behind league-leading Detroit.

The game moved steadily for the first two frames. In the third inning, "Ruth, who impressed the onlookers as being a hitter of the first rank, swatted a low ball into the upper tier of the right-field grandstand and trotted about the bases to slow music."[4] Boston had the lead and Ruth was pitching through the New York lineup, prompting the *Globe* to print, "This run looked as tall as the Woolworth Building."[5]

New York tied the score in the fifth, without the assistance of a base hit. Instead, Boston infielders Heinie Wagner and Mike McNally each made fielding errors and a force out off the bat of Luke Boone brought home Doc Cook with the equalizer. Through seven innings and despite allowing the one run, the 20-year-old Ruth had only allowed one hit, a single to Hugh High in the very first inning.

Boston regained the lead in the top of the seventh inning. Bill Carrigan stroked a double to left, and he came around to score on Wagner's timely "long single to the same territory."[6] Cook and Boone both singled in the Yankees' half of the seventh, but Boone overran his base and "was caught by a quick throw from [right fielder Harry] Hooper."[7]

In Boston's next at-bat, Duffy Lewis and Everett Scott each stroked doubles to give the Red Sox a 3-1 edge. Again from the *Boston Globe*: "The Sox seemed to feel that the victory had been padlocked, but they reckoned without Mr. Unexpected Error."[8] Fritz Maisel singled in the New York eighth. When he attempted to steal second, Boston catcher Carrigan threw the ball into center field, allowing Maisel to advance to third. Maisel then scored when Roy Hartzell grounded out to first. Instead of having a comfortable advantage going into the final frame, the Red Sox had struggled, but, according to the *New York Times*, "The Bostons looked like sure enough winners up to the ninth inning."[9] However, the lead did not last. The New Yorkers managed to tie the game in the bottom of the ninth. Ruth retired Wally Pipp on a grounder to first, but then he hit Cook with a pitch, and the speedy Cook then stole second.[10] After Roger Peckinpaugh sent a high fly to Dick Hoblitzell in short right field for the second out, "Daniel Boone set off some fireworks with a two-base shot to centre which scored Doc Cook with the tying run,"[11] sending the game into extra innings. It was each team's first extra-inning affair of the season.

Yankees starter Warhop had been replaced in the top of the ninth by Cy Pieh. Pieh got through that inning and the tenth without incident, but Boston threatened in the 11th, getting runners on second and third with just one out. Pieh then struck out the next two batters. New York also put two men on with two outs in the bottom of the 11th, but Ruth pitched his way out of it, retiring Les Nunamaker on a fly ball to right.

At the end of 12 rounds, Ruth was still on the mound. He then "weakened a bit in the 13th, yielding two successive singles, which, with a steal, gave the much coveted run to the Yankees."[12] High started it off for the Yankees with a single and the theft of second. Ruth struck out Pipp, but then "Cook grounded his single to right and High romped home with the game."[13]

For the day, Ruth was 3-for-5 at the plate, including his first home run of the season, raising his batting average to .417. Wagner and Lewis each contributed three hits to Boston's 12-hit attack. Ruth eventually hit four home runs in 42 games in 1915, and his quartet of over-the-wall hits led the Red Sox.[14] The Babe's .315 seasonal batting average was second on the Sox only to teammate Tris Speaker (.322), but Ruth's slugging percentage (.576) and OPS (.952) led the Boston regular players (fellow pitcher Vean Gregg did bat .350 (7-for-20), but he only had 20 at-bats for the season, compared to Ruth's 92).

Despite the loss, Boston went on to win 101 games in 1915, edging out the Tigers for the pennant. The Yankees finished in the fifth spot, 32 1/2 games back. In earning the loss, Ruth had yielded 10 hits and three walks, striking out three. Pieh picked up his first win of the season. While Ruth was just beginning his amazing career as a pitcher and slugger, both Warhop and Pieh did not play in the majors after the 1915 season.

Ruth's first major-league home run came in his 10th major-league game. His next round-tripper came on June 2, in a contest against the Yankees, again played at the Polo Grounds. In that game, he pitched another complete game and earned a 7-1 victory. In fact, Ruth belted three of his four home runs in 1915 against the Yankees. For the season, his pitching record against New York was 4-2, with a 1.91 ERA. In his career with the Red Sox, Ruth hit 12 home runs against the Yankees.

Twenty years after this contest, on May 30, 1935, Ruth played his last game. He had hit a total of 714 career home runs, with

The Babe

Notes

1. "Red Sox Lose to Yanks in 13th," *Boston Globe*, May 7, 1915: 9.
2. "New York Clubs Defeat Boston's Two Teams: High and Cook Spill Red Sox in 13th," *New York Times*, May 7, 1915: 11.
3. Ibid.
4. *Boston Globe*.
5. Ibid.
6. Ibid.
7. Ibid.
8. Ibid.
9. *New York Times*.
10. Cook stole 29 bases in 1915; this amount was second on the Yankees behind Maisel's 51 swipes.
11. *New York Times*.
12. *Boston Globe*.
13. *New York Times*.
14. Ruth hit four home runs in 1915 on a Boston squad that only produced a grand total of 14 homers.

Babe Ruth Replaced While Throwing a No-Hitter

May 20, 1916: Boston Red Sox 3, St. Louis Browns 1, at Fenway Park

By Bill Nowlin

Young Babe Ruth, 21, gave out plenty of free passes on this Saturday afternoon. He walked seven Browns batters in six innings of work. The lefty didn't allow a hit, though, and got some help from his St. Louis counterparts, who allowed eight bases on balls.

Ruth improved his won-lost mark in the young season to 5-2. Maybe he was a bit rusty. The Babe had last pitched 10 days earlier, a complete-game 6-2 loss to Cleveland.

Boston entered the game 13-15; the St. Louis Browns were 11-16 and had knocked off the Red Sox, 7-1 and 5-1, in the two previous games. The reigning world champion Red Sox were struggling some in the 1916 campaign.

The game was originally scheduled to start at 3 P.M. but was delayed until 4:09 due to a heavy rain shower. A band concert and a "boy soprano" entertained the 5,232 patrons until groundskeeper Jerome Kelley and his crew were able to put the field into playing shape.[1]

Photograph shows George Herman "Babe" Ruth, Ernest G. "Ernie" Shore, George "Rube" Foster, and Dellos "Del" Gainer, facing front, wearing Boston Red Sox baseball team uniforms, sitting on a low wall in front of a dugout. *Courtesy of Library of Congress.*

St. Louis went ahead in the top of the fourth inning. Ruth walked left fielder Burt Shotton and shortstop Ernie Johnson, and both advanced a base on a sacrifice by George Sisler. Ruth got Ward Miller to hit a grounder that second baseman Jack Barry fielded and fired home to the catcher for an out. Johnson took third on the play. Miller and Johnson then executed a double steal, Johnson scoring. After that, Ruth retired the side. He still hadn't given up a hit, but the Red Sox were down 1-0.

At the risk of repetition, perhaps we can pause and enjoy the *Boston Herald*'s description of how the Browns scored their run. The writing was exceptionally florid, even by the standards of the day: "After Catcher Thomas had been banished, and Agnew stepped in, George Sisler suicided his pals along. On Miller's smack to Barry, Shotton was torpedoed at the saucer, Johnson meantime trotting to third. Then the two Browns started a double pilfer. Agnew pegged to Janny [Hal Janvrin], who was so busy chasing Miller that he forgot all about the chap on third, who naturally took advantage and scored."[2]

The Red Sox scored twice in the bottom of the fourth. First, they loaded the bases on a single, a walk, and another single. Browns starter Dave Davenport then walked Hal Janvrin on four pitches, forcing in the tying run. Catcher Sam Agnew hit a sacrifice fly to left field that scored Tillie Walker and ended the day for Davenport, one of four pitchers the Browns used during this low-scoring game. Reliever Jim Park prevented any more runs from scoring. In fact, he didn't allow a hit in his 2⅔ innings of work.

Ruth got through the fifth inning without allowing a hit and had even nicely picked off Sisler in the first inning. He ran into control problems in the sixth. It should be mentioned here that although Ruth doled out seven walks in the game, the *Boston Globe* suggested that he might not have been completely at fault. Early in the game, the newspaper said, "the big portsider was getting much the worst of it from Umpire Nallin on balls and strikes. Babe thought so and so did 'Ginger' Thomas, the latter giving such vent to his disgust that Nallin banished him, but not before the Red Sox catcher had thrown his mask at Nallin's feet and let loose a little more conversation."[3] Agnew had taken his place. Later in the game, the Red Sox used a third catcher, Hick Cady. The *Boston Herald* noted that both teams had differences with plate umpire Dick Nallin. By game's end, there were 17 walks in the game, eight by Browns pitchers and nine by the Red Sox.

Despite the challenging state of the field, the game featured two great catches by Red Sox right fielder Harry Hooper, one saving the Sox in the sixth, and the other in the seventh, quashing another rally.

Ruth gave up three walks to fill the bases with Browns in the top of the sixth. There were two outs when the Babe was "mercifully derricked,"[4] still without having given up a hit. Red Sox manager Bill Carrigan brought in Carl Mays to pitch to Del Pratt, who hit a ball deep to right that Hooper hauled in for the final out of the inning. Or, as the *Globe* put it, "Modest Harry, after a long chase, pulled down Pratt's drive."[5]

In the seventh, the Browns put runners on first and second with one out. Pinch-hitter Babe Borton hit "what looked to be a sure triple" (*Globe*). Hooper, though, made a spectacular catch and threw to Barry at second base for the third out after both St. Louis baserunners had confidently taken off, looking to give the Browns a 3-2 lead. The *Herald* described the play: "Through the spike-scarred marshes of right field, Harry Hooper splashed and plashed in the murky gloom. … Skimming over a puddle with the grace of a swallow, Harry stuck up his hands. He snatched the hurtling baseball out of murk. He turned and pegged the baseball in to Jack Barry."[6] Hooper's catch was, writer Flatley remarked, "one of the greatest he or anybody else ever made."

The Red Sox held their 2-1 lead before adding one more run in the bottom of the seventh. Agnew walked and Carl Mays singled up the middle. Carrigan had Mike McNally pinch-run for Agnew. Hooper flied out to left. Barry singled over the shortstop, but McNally needed to hold. The bases were loaded with one out. Duffy Lewis hit the ball hard to Johnson at shortstop, and Johnson threw home, nabbing McNally. Tom McCabe, the fourth St. Louis pitcher of the day, walked Dick Hoblitzell, forcing in Mays with the insurance run.

There were the 17 walks in the game, and, ultimately, just two hits for the Browns and six for the Red Sox. The Browns left seven runners on base, and the Red Sox stranded nine. Given the playing conditions, it was remarkable that no team committed an error. The game was played in 2 hours and 16 minutes.

At the plate, Ruth went 0-for-2 and his average in the still-young season was just .071. He finished the campaign with a .272 average and had three home runs, one short of the four he had hit in 1915, to that point his career high.

His pitching record for 1916 was 23-12, with a league-leading 1.75 earned-run average, in part built on nine shutouts, which also led the league. The Red Sox recovered from their slow start and won a second straight World Series championship, this time knocking off the Brooklyn Robins in five games.

Sources

In addition to the sources cited in the Notes, the author also relied on Baseball-Reference.com and Retrosheet.org.

Notes

1. "Red Sox Break Spell, Beating Browns 3-1," *Boston Globe*, May 21, 1916: 15.
2. N.J. Flatley, "Hooper's Great Catch Saved Day for the Red Sox," *Boston Herald*, May 21, 1916: 22.
3. "Red Sox Break Spell, Beating Browns 3-1."
4. N.J. Flatley.
5. "Red Sox Break Spell, Beating Browns 3-1."
6. N.J. Flatley.

Red-Hot Ruth On a Tear Against the Browns

June 13, 1916: Boston Red Sox 5, St. Louis Browns 3, at Sportsman's Park, St. Louis

By James Forr

He was just 21 and only in his second full season but Babe Ruth was already proving to be a man who could do the undoable.

As a rookie in 1915 he won 18 games for the World Series champion Boston Red Sox. He did pretty well at his side job as a hitter, too, finishing in the top 10 in the American League in home runs – in fewer than 100 at-bats. The young man was arguably "the hardest hitting pitcher in captivity," as one sportswriter put it.[1]

In slight contrast, Ruth's 1916 season was off to a nice start but was lacking in supernatural feats. He was pitching well but at the plate he flailed away fruitlessly, as most pitchers do. That is, until a mid-June offensive outburst – capped by a brilliant day against the St. Louis Browns – served notice to baseball that, for Ruth, almost anything was possible.

With the season nearly one-third complete, the standings were all topsy-turvy. The Indians and Yankees, who finished 44½ and 32½ games out respectively in 1915, stood atop the AL while the Red Sox, Tigers, and White Sox – the top three teams from a year earlier – were sandwiched in the middle of pack, hovering around .500. Boston's trade of a disgruntled Tris Speaker to Cleveland before the start of the season set off some of those seismic shifts. "When Speaker was sold by the Red Sox many cried that Boston had lost the most important cog in its flag winning machine," wrote J.J. Alcock in the *Chicago Tribune* in late May. "The season is too young to draw a definite line on the present strength of the Red Sox. But the effect of Speaker's addition to the Cleveland team is already a known quantity."[2]

While the rest of the league was in tumult, it was business as usual for the Browns. They came in 21-26 and appeared to be on their way to their typical 90-loss season. That would change. Manager Fielder Jones, in his first year taking over for Branch Rickey, would turn things around and steer his club to a winning record – the only time that happened for the Browns between 1909 and 1920.

Ruth was the starting pitcher on this partly cloudy, 80-degree afternoon at Sportsman's Park. He entered the game 8-3 with a 1.90 ERA and shutouts in three of his last five starts. He was building upon the promise he had shown as a rookie and now was maturing into one of the truly premier pitchers in the league.

Taking the ball for St. Louis was Dave Davenport, a foul-tempered, hard-drinking, 6-foot-6 right-hander from the Louisiana bayou. He came to the Browns from the Federal League's St.

Louis Terriers, where he led all major leaguers with 392⅔ innings pitched in 1915. With the exception of Grover Alexander, no other pitcher in baseball came within 50 innings of him. This was his 12th start and 21st appearance as a member of the Browns and thus far it had not gone well. He was 2-5 with a subpar ERA of 3.35 in a time when runs were hard to come by.

Boston got to Davenport quickly. With Mike McNally on second and one away, Duffy Lewis drew a walk as the pitch got past catcher Harry Chapman, allowing McNally to sprint to third. Doc Hoblitzell's grounder to second forced Lewis, but his aggressive slide prevented a double play and enabled McNally to score the first run of the afternoon.

Ruth cruised through the first two innings before stepping in to lead off the top of the third. Boston's sluggish season was attributable in small part to Ruth's own struggles at the plate. He entered June batting .171 with no home runs and just two extra-base hits in 38 plate appearances. However, over the last few games he had begun to crank it up. He went 3-for-3 in a loss to Detroit on June 9, including a majestic home run deep into the bleacher seats at Navin Field. The *Detroit Free Press* marveled, "There have been a lot of pokes into the 25-cent section since the park was built but none ever [landed] so close to the flagpole."[3] On June 10, in the first game of the Browns series, manager Bill Carrigan called upon Ruth to pinch-hit but, for reasons lost to time, called him back to the dugout with a 1-and-1 count. On June 12 the Babe's three-run pinch-hit homer was all the offense the Red Sox could muster in a 4-3 loss.

Now Ruth faced Davenport. St. Louis center fielder Armando Marsans and right fielder Ward Miller were playing back almost against the fence, but it wasn't deep enough, as Ruth lifted a Davenport offering into the seats for a 2-0 lead. It was Ruth's third homer in his last five plate appearances and it tied him for second place in the AL in home runs. (In fact, only 12 American Leaguers would hit more than three home runs all year.)

Harry Hooper followed with a walk, went to second on McNally's sacrifice, crossed over to third on Lewis's infield single, and then one out later came in to score when Tillie Walker drew a bases on balls and the pitch again eluded poor Chapman, who hurt his hand trying to make the stop. With that, Fielder Jones swapped in a new battery – pitcher Ernie Koob and catcher Hank Severeid.

In the fourth, after Hal Janvrin singled, Ruth slashed a base hit to right field, his sixth hit in his last six at-bats. Janvrin scooted around to third as Miller cut down Ruth trying to stretch it into a double. Hooper's single plated Janvrin to make it 4-0.

As good a pitcher as Ruth was, he could get a little wild sometimes and control would be his undoing on this day. He walked three men through the first five innings before it all fell apart in the sixth. He opened the inning with walks to Miller and George Sisler. After Del Pratt struck out, Marsans singled to right to load the bases and then Ruth walked Ernie Johnson to force in a run. Carrigan called to the bullpen for Ernie Shore, who retired the next two batters to prevent any further damage. Boston got that run back right away on McNally's RBI single in the seventh, and the score was 5-1.

Almost exactly a year later Shore would etch his name into baseball lore when he worked nine perfect innings in relief of Ruth, who was ejected for clobbering an umpire after a leadoff walk. Shore was far from perfect against the Browns but he muddled through. Back-to-back walks to lead off the bottom of the seventh turned into two more St. Louis runs. In the ninth Miller rapped a single to lead off but third baseman Larry Gardner made a leaping stab of Sisler's sizzling liner and turned it into a double play to put a damper on the home crowd's hopes. Shore retired Pratt to end the game and sew up a 5-3 victory.

Ruth also was hit by a pitch in this game, meaning he had reached base safely in 11 of his last 12 plate appearances. His OPS stood at .916, which would mark his statistical peak for 1916. These June home runs would be Ruth's only three of the season and, in fact, 1916 proved to be one of the least impressive offensive years of his career. But he did iron out his wildness to finish 23-12 with a league-best 1.75 ERA as the Red Sox pulled it together and stormed to their second consecutive World Series title.

Sources

In addition to the newspaper sources cited in the Notes, the author used Baseball-Reference.com and Retrosheet.org.

The author also reviewed the following newspaper articles for play-by-play and other information:

Martin, Edward F. "Scott's Drive Wins for Red Sox in 10th," *Boston Sunday Globe*, June 11, 1916.

Martin, Edward F. "Shore Brings Red Sox to Victory," *Boston Globe*, June 14, 1916.

O'Connor, W.J. "Browns' Attacking Methods Fail With Men On; Lack of Daring Makes Contest Dull," *St. Louis Post-Dispatch*, June 14, 1916.

Shannon, Paul H. "Browns Beaten by Red Sox 5-3," *Boston Post*, June 14, 1916.

Notes

1 Paul H. Shannon, "Red Sox Divide With the Browns," *Boston Post*, August 11, 1915.

2 J.J. Alcock, "Pep of Speaker Pushes Indians Into Top Place," *Chicago Tribune,* May 21, 1916.

3 E.A. Batchelor, "Burns Hero of Another Tiger Win," *Detroit Free Press*, June 10, 1916.

Ruth Outlasts Johnson in 13 Innings

August 15, 1916: Boston Red Sox 1, Washington Senators 0 (13 innings), at Fenway Park, Boston

By Jack Zerby

Clark Griffith was prescient. At the end of the 1914 season, with the Philadelphia A's advancing to represent the American League in the World Series, the Washington Senators manager told reporters, "The best ball club in the game today will not take part in the coming world's series."[1] He gave that distinction to the Boston Red Sox, a team that had finished 8½ games behind Philadelphia, but 10½ in front of his own 81-73 Senators. "The changes that have made the Red Sox such a wonderful ball club were not made until the American League race had ceased to be a race," Griffith said. "With recent acquisitions the Red Sox are clearly the best balanced ball club in the game today."[2]

Griffith especially liked the Boston pitching staff, singling out Ernie Shore, who had gone 10-2 with a 2.00 ERA after being acquired from the Baltimore Orioles of the International League on July 9, 1914. The skipper did not mention another Baltimore pitcher who arrived in the same transaction, Babe Ruth. The lefty had also debuted with Boston in 1914.[3]

Legendary Boston baseball writer Tim Murnane saw promise in Ruth as the Red Sox trained in Hot Springs, Arkansas, in 1915. Starting on the mound for the backups against the regulars, Ruth went "three splendid innings" before a fourth-inning uprising. In his only at-bat he smashed "a savage wallop" home run off Carl Mays that was "fully enjoyed by the crowd."[4] Ruth, 20, then settled into the Red Sox' 1915 pitching rotation, going 18-8 in 217⅔ innings. Boston fulfilled Griffith's prediction by winning 101 games and the American League pennant before dispatching the Philadelphia Phillies in five games in the 1915 World Series.

The Red Sox enjoyed such solid pitching that Ruth appeared in that Series only as a pinch-hitter.[5] But his manager, Bill Carrigan, had no doubt about Ruth's mound ability during spring training in 1916. "Ruth will be one of the very best pitchers in the league this year," Carrigan said. "He is stronger than ever. He was fit and capable to pitch in the world's series, but we had three other men all ready and fit."[6]

True to prediction, the 21-year-old Ruth rolled off four straight wins to open the 1916 season. By July 18 he was 14-5, but then took losses in four of his next five decisions. His only win in that string was a two-hit shutout at Detroit on July 31. After Ruth was hit hard at St. Louis on August 4, he pinch-hit unsuccessfully once and otherwise sat idle until August 12, when he was Carrigan's starting pitcher for the opener of a three-game series at Fenway Park with Griffith's visiting seventh-place Senators. Although Ruth yielded only one run in seven innings and Boston won, 2-1, Dutch Leonard got the win in relief against Walter Johnson, who also appeared in relief.[7]

That midsummer of 1916 saw the Red Sox in a tight race for their second consecutive AL pennant. The August 12 win left them two games ahead of the Chicago White Sox in a closely bunched top four, but three days later they were only a game and a half in front of the second-place Cleveland Indians.

The Senators were still in town for the final game of the series the following Tuesday, August 15. Ruth once again got the ball,[8] this time against Johnson, and if the weekday crowd of 5,467[9] sought a classic pitchers' duel, they got it.

Hometown baseball writers had begun referring to the Red Sox as "the champions," but Paul Shannon of the *Boston Post* gave Johnson, 28, his due: "Seldom has Johnson been seen on better advantage, and not once on this long and dubious trip away from home had he pitched such ball."[10]

Jack Barry seemed to get Boston off to a good start with a one-out double in the bottom of the first, but advanced only to third base. In the third, right fielder Sam Rice lost Ruth's fly ball in the sun – it was a two-base error, but like Barry, Ruth only got to third. Meanwhile, Ruth was in a "bad hole" as early as the Washington second inning, when it took "a fine catch off [George] McBride" by Harry Hooper in right field to close out the half-inning with runners on second and third.[11] A walk to Duffy Lewis and a sacrifice advanced a runner to second base in the Boston fourth, but Tillie Walker couldn't deliver; the game remained scoreless.

Johnson failed to help himself in the Washington fifth. Eddie Ainsmith doubled off the scoreboard to open the half-inning, and McBride bunted him to third. With one out and Ainsmith on third, Johnson popped out. Ruth got Ray Morgan to end the threat.

The Senators came right back against Ruth in their half of the sixth. With two outs and Rice on first base, "[Howie] Shanks dropped a Texas leaguer in right. Rice went to third, and when Hooper's throw got by [third baseman Larry] Gardner, he tried to score."[12] Gardner recovered the ball in foul territory and gunned Rice down at the plate – the *Boston Post* deemed this "Washington's most promising chance to score" in the game, featuring the play in the first of four frames of a page-width sports cartoon accompanying its game story.[13]

Gardner singled for Boston's third hit off Johnson in the seventh and reached second base on a sacrifice, but nothing further developed. Neither team threatened in the eighth, either. Red Sox catcher Pinch Thomas helped Ruth out of mild trouble in the ninth by nailing Danny Moeller[14] on an attempted steal of second base to abruptly end the inning as Shanks struck out.[15]

Boston roused the home fans in the bottom of the ninth when Gardner tripled to left-center with two outs and Chick Shorten pinch-hit for Everett Scott. Shorten, though, tapped back to Johnson; the game went into extra innings still scoreless.

The Senators ran into another out at home plate in the 10th as Ainsmith tried to score from second base on Johnson's groundball to Hal Janvrin, who had replaced Scott at shortstop. Janvrin relayed to Barry at second for a force out, and Barry's throw home completed a snazzy 6-4-2 double play. Boston got runners to second and third with two out in the 11th but Johnson retired Gardner. Ruth "hit a ball almost into the center field seats"[16] in the 12th that Clyde Milan ran down; it was deep enough to advance Janvrin to third base with two outs.[17] Johnson again prevailed, getting Hooper on a popup.

Sharp defense helped Ruth pitch around an error and his own balk in the Washington 13th as first baseman Dick Hoblitzell snagged Rip Williams's would-be extra-base hit and threw to Janvrin to double Ray Morgan off second base.

And although it had been Ruth – pitching in and out of trouble and rescued by timely defense –who had looked the most vulnerable as the innings unfolded, it was Johnson who finally yielded. The Big Train gave up only four hits through 12 innings,[18] but Barry reached him to open the Boston 13th with an infield single off Johnson's hand.[19] Lewis and Hoblitzell made outs, but Barry hustled to third on a single to center field by Walker. Gardner, who hadn't been able to deliver in the 11th, then drilled the third single of the half-inning up the middle to score Barry and close out the epic for Ruth, 1-0.[20]

Ruth bumped his season record to 16-9[21] with the win and bested Johnson again, 2-1, when the two matched up in Washington on September 9. They were at it yet again just three days later in Washington. But this time Johnson exacted some revenge – Ruth left the game after 8⅔ innings, while Johnson persevered; the Senators got him a 4-2 win in 10 innings over Shore, pitching in relief.

The Red Sox went on to win the American League pennant by two games over the White Sox and met the Brooklyn Robins in the World Series. They once again prevailed, four games to one, for their second consecutive title, amply fulfilling Clark Griffith's "best ball club" prediction at the end of the 1914 season. And this time Ruth did get a turn on the mound. Showing the same kind of endurance he had on August 15 against Johnson, he gave up a run to Brooklyn in the first inning of Game Two,[22] then shut the Robins down for the next 13 innings as the Red Sox won, 2-1, in the bottom of the 14th inning.[23]

Sources

In addition to the sources cited in the Notes, I used the Baseball-Reference.com and Retrosheet.org websites for their respective box scores of this game as well as player, team, and season pages and batting and pitching logs. All cited newspaper items were accessed at Newspapers.com.

Notes

1 Unattributed wire report, "Red Sox Best Club in Game," *Great Falls* (Montana) *Tribune,* October 3, 1914: 9.

2 Ibid.

3 Ruth, age 19, made his debut with Boston on July 11, 1914. He started against Cleveland at Fenway Park and went seven innings in a 4-3 Red Sox win. Three days later, also against Cleveland at Fenway, Shore pitched a complete-game 2-1 win in his own debut. Ruth started again on July 16 against Detroit, was gone after three innings, and was sent to Providence of the International League until he was recalled for two more appearances in October. Ruth pitched 23 innings for the Red Sox in 1914; Shore pitched 139⅔ in his partial season.

4 T.H. Murnane, "Sox Get Seven in Their Fourth," *Boston Globe*, March 24, 1915: 7, 23.

5 Ruth grounded out against Grover Cleveland Alexander in the ninth inning of Game One. The Phillies won, 3-1, taking their only victory in the Series.

6 "Carrigan Expects Much of Babe Ruth This Year," *Baltimore Sun*, March 12, 1916: 28. The Red Sox used only Rube Foster, Dutch Leonard, and Shore on the mound in the 1915 Series.

7 Walter Johnson, "The Big Train," pitched for Washington from 1907 through 1927. A true workhorse even for the era, he pitched 369⅔ innings in 1916 in 48 games, with 38 starts and 36 complete games, posting a 25-20 record for a 76-77 team. He led the American League in innings pitched for four consecutive seasons (1913-16). Johnson was a member of the inaugural Baseball Hall of Fame class selected in 1936 and inducted in 1939.

8 But it wasn't from Carrigan. The manager was away from the team attending to family duties and "[was] not able to be on deck for a couple of days." "Bill Carrigan's Father-in-Law Dead," *Boston Post,* August 16, 1916: 10.

9 Washington-Boston AL box score, *Boston Post*, August 16, 1916: 10.

10 Paul H. Shannon, "Red Sox Beat Out Johnson," *Boston Post,* August 16, 1916: 1, 10. The Washington road trip had begun on July 25 in Detroit and moved on through Cleveland, Chicago, and St. Louis before the Senators arrived in Boston. Going into the August 15 game, Johnson had pitched in six games on the trip, with a 2-4 record.

11 Shannon.

12 Ibid.

13 Page-width, four-frame, sports cartoon signed "Scott," *Boston Post*, August 16, 1916: 10.

14 Moeller had pinch-hit for Sam Rice and reached base on a force out.

15 Shannon.

16 Ibid.

17 The Milan catch warranted the third frame in the *Post's* sports cartoon.

18 "Ruth Outpitches Johnson," *New York Times,* August 16, 1916: 8.

19 Ibid.

20 The *Boston Post* box score that accompanies Paul Shannon's game story, cited in Note 9, notes "one out when winning run was scored." Shannon's game story, which accounts for two outs (by Duffy Lewis and Hoblitzell) between Barry's single and the single by Walker that moved Barry to third and brought up Gardner, is correct, given the Boston batting order and the fact that Gardner had the only run batted in in the game. The box score printed with the *New York Times* item cited in Note 18 correctly states that there were two outs when the winning run scored.

21 The 21-year-old Ruth led the 1916 American League in ERA (1.75), games started (40), and shutouts (9).

22 The first-inning run came on an inside-the-park home run by Hy Myers with two outs. Ruth drove in his own tying run in the third inning on a groundout to second base that scored Everett Scott, who had tripled.

23 The Red Sox played their home games in both the 1915 and 1916 World Series at Braves Field rather than Fenway Park, taking advantage of the National League ballpark's greater seating capacity. Glenn Stout, *Fenway 1912: The Birth of a Ballpark* (Boston: Mariner Books, 2011), 340. The attendance on a Monday afternoon for Game Two of the 1916 Series at Braves Field was 47,373. As noted, this regular-season Tuesday matchup between Ruth and Johnson had attracted 5,467 to Fenway Park, which, from its opening in 1912 until extensive renovation between the 1933 and 1934 seasons, had a seating capacity of approximately 27,000. (Fenway Park entry, Ballparks of Baseball.com, accessed April 6, 2018).

Red Sox Win Game Two on a Loaned Diamond; Babe Ruth Goes the Distance in 14

October 9, 1916: Boston Red Sox 2, Brooklyn Robins 1 (14 innings), at Braves Field, Boston
Game Two of the 1916 World Series

By Cecilia Tan and Bill Nowlin

For the second year in a row, Boston won the pennant in 1916, by just two games over the Chicago White Sox and four over the Detroit Tigers. As in 1915, the Red Sox' World Series home games were played at Braves Field, but this time Boston faced the Brooklyn Robins (later, Dodgers).

The Red Sox presented a similar but not identical team to that of the previous year. Bill Carrigan remained as manager, but Tris Speaker was traded away, and Smoky Joe Wood was injured. George Herman Ruth emerged as the ace on the pitching staff (23-12, 1.75 ERA), while Dutch Leonard and Carl Mays each won 18 games. All in all, the staff ERA was 2.48, slightly worse than the 2.39 of the previous year. Team batting was off marginally, too – the 1915 team average was .260 (.336 OBP) while in 1916 it dipped to .248 (.317 OBP), decent numbers in the era of the dead ball. Run production dropped from 668 runs to 548. Still, the Red Sox had done what they needed to do; they won the pennant.

This was an over-confident team, and there was talk in the papers about the Sox sweeping Brooklyn.

Game One opened in Boston, with Ernie Shore against Rube Marquard (who'd opposed the Red Sox in the 1912 Series for the Giants, but was now pitching for Brooklyn). The game turned into a 6-5 win when the Red Sox managed to shut down a four-run rally in the top of the ninth before the Robins could tie the game.

Game Two pitted Red Sox ace Ruth against Sherry Smith, both southpaws. Ruth's 1.75 ERA had led the American League. Smith was 14-10, with a 2.34 ERA. Brooklyn batted first and didn't wait long to put a run on the board. After Ruth retired the first two Robins, center fielder Hi Myers drove a ball between Tillie Walker in center and Harry Hooper in right, sparking a Keystone Kops moment. Hooper dove but the ball rolled all the way to the fence and Walker fell trying to field the rebound. Myers legged all the way around the bases for an inside-the-park home run.

Brooklyn's moundsman Smith doubled to right field with one out in the top of the third, and was waved toward third, but Hooper threw the ball to Walker, the cutoff man; the center fielder fired a strike to third and cut down Smith. The score remained 1-0, Brooklyn.

Boston tried to answer in its half of the inning. Everett "Deacon" Scott led off with a triple to the cement wall in right field. He had to hold at third on Pinch Thomas's grounder to George Cutshaw at second. Ruth grounded to Cutshaw, too, but this time the second baseman bobbled the ball. Though Ruth was thrown out on the play, Scott scored to even things at 1-1. After that, both teams put men into scoring position at times but neither brought them home. In the fifth Brooklyn's shortstop Ivy Olson was accused of tripping Pinch Thomas as he rounded second and the umpire awarded Thomas third base on interference. But Thomas languished there when Ruth struck out.

In the eighth Brooklyn again feinted. Harry "Mike" Mowrey singled, moved to second on a sacrifice, and moved up when Otto Miller singled. But Walker fired so fast to the plate that Mowrey had to stop at third, Miller taking second on the throw. With runners at second and third, and just one out, the pitcher Smith grounded to short and Scott luckily caught Mowrey in a rundown between third and home, Ruth making the tag. Jimmy Johnston hit a high bounder and Ruth leapt up to grab it, threw to first, and snuffed the threat.

The score remained tied as Boston came to bat in the bottom of the ninth. Hal Janvrin doubled to lead off for a promising start. Jimmy Walsh, pinch-hitting for Walker, managed only a comebacker. Smith fielded the ball and tossed to Mowrey to cut down the lead runner, but Mowrey dropped the ball and Janny was safe. With runners on first and third and no one out, the crowd was on the edge of their seats. Even a fly ball could score Janvrin. Dick Hoblitzell got that fly to center, but Myers' throw home erased Janvrin, two outs on one play. After an intentional walk to Duffy Lewis, Larry Gardner fouled out to send the game into extra innings, still tied 1-1.

The Red Sox escaped a couple of potential problems in the top of the 10th as a deflected grounder was converted into an out and a walk went for naught, and looked once again to push across that one crucial run. Scott singled to lead off and Thomas moved him up with a sacrifice. Ruth swung hard three times, and missed three times for the second out. Hooper hit a ball down the third-base line; as it went off his glove, Mowrey knew Hooper had it beat but feigned a throw to first. The decoy worked and Scott overran third. Olson scooted over from shortstop and took Mowrey's throw, nabbing Scott as he tried to get back to the bag. The scorer credited Hooper with a single, but the side was retired.

Neither team had particularly good chances in the 11th or 12th inning, and the sky was growing dark. If the game were called because of darkness, it would go into the scorebook as a tie. Neither team wanted to waste a great pitching performance, but they were running out of time.

So to the 13th. Brooklyn's first batter, Mowrey, reached base when Gardner's throw pulled Hoblitzell off the bag. The Robins sacrificed to move Mowrey to second, but Miller popped up to the catcher for out number two. Smith, still pitching for Brooklyn, almost dropped one into short left but Lewis made a "phenomenal" catch and the Sox were out of the 13th. Tim Murnane of the *Boston Globe* felt sure that Lewis had saved a run: "Tearing along as if it was a case of life or death, he made one final reach while twisting his neck like a seagull and managed to reach and hold the ball." The game had been characterized throughout by exceptional fielding for both teams. Smith quickly retired all three of Boston's batters, and the game entered the 14th inning.

Babe Ruth had not given up a hit since the eighth inning. He set Brooklyn down again 1-2-3 in the top of the 14th. The Sox came up in the bottom half and Smith walked Hoblitzell, the fourth time in the game that Hobby had worked a walk. Lewis sacrificed the walking man to second, first-pitch bunting. A hit now could win the game. Larry Gardner was due up, but he was 0-for-5 and Carrigan decided to try something different. He put the speedy Mike McNally in to run for Hobby and sent up "Sheriff" Del Gainer (a .254 hitter in 1916) to pinch-hit for Gardner (.308 in the regular season, and 1-for-4 in Game One, and reached on an error). Despite his overall better numbers, Gardner was 1-for-9 in the Series at this point and had struggled against the left-handed Smith. The switch paid off. Gainer singled, a low liner to left, and Zack Wheat had to play it on one hop and hope the throw home could beat McNally. Not a chance. McNally burned around the bases and crossed the plate. The Red Sox had their second run and the game.

No other World Series game before or after has gone to 14 innings. After Myers' freak inside-the-park home run back in the first inning, Babe Ruth had held the National League champions scoreless and earned the complete-game victory.

The Series would be over in five games. Game Three saw Brooklyn take one from the Red Sox 4-3, but the Red Sox handled the Robins by a 6-2 score in Game Four (Larry Gardner's three-run inside-the-park homer in the second inning being the decisive blow). They won the World Series, their fourth, the second in a row, and the third in five years, with a 4-1 triumph the next day, Ernie Shore allowing just three hits and picking up his second win.

A lengthy *Globe* editorial rhapsodized about how the Athens of America followed in the Greek tradition of the Olympics being justly proud of the manly prowess of its sons. Carrigan, who had caught Game Four, gone 2-for-3, and managed the club, was dubbed "another Ivanhoe, less brutal and more civilized, less romantic than Scott's fictional hero, but more skillful."[1] The confidence the Sox had carried into the Series had been justified.

Sources

The authors relied on Baseball-reference.com, and Retrosheet.org, in addition to contemporary newspaper accounts of the game.

This article appeared in *Braves Field: Memorable Moments at Boston's Lost Diamond* (SABR, 2015), edited by Bill Nowlin and Bob Brady. An earlier version of this article was published in *The 50 Greatest Red Sox Games* by Cecilia Tan and Bill Nowlin and appears here by permission from Riverdale Avenue Books.

Notes

1 "Boston Triumphant," *Boston Globe*, October 13, 1916: 12.

The Babe Makes His First Start As A Position Player

May 6, 1918: New York Yankees 10, Boston Red Sox 3, at the Polo Grounds

By Glen Sparks

Boston Red Sox manager Ed Barrow scoffed at the very idea. Turn Babe Ruth, one of baseball's top pitchers, into an everyday player? Just to let him hit some home runs and revel in the glory? Barrow imagined the wisecracks that would certainly follow. "I'd be the laughingstock of baseball if I changed the best lefthander in the game into an outfielder," Barrow said early in the 1918 campaign.[1]

No one doubted that Ruth could handle his duties on the mound. He won 24 games in 1917 and led the American League with 35 complete games in 38 starts. One year earlier, the left-hander had won 23 times and topped the circuit in ERA (1.75) and shutouts (nine).

He also pummeled baseballs when he stepped into the batter's box. In his rookie campaign of 1915, Ruth – besides posting an 18-8 won-lost record – knocked four home runs in just 92 at-bats. Braggo Roth topped the AL with seven homers. Roth, who split time with the Chicago White Sox and Cleveland In-

Ruth with the Red Sox. *Courtesy of Library of Congress.*

dians, went to bat 384 times. Babe hit three home runs in 1916 and two in 1917 over a combined 259 at-bats.

Barrow put Ruth at first base and right field during some spring-training games in 1918. Babe hit two home runs in one game against the Brooklyn Dodgers. He blasted five over the fence during batting practice when the same two teams met a few days later at Camp Pike, an Army post in Arkansas. The soldiers on hand enjoyed the show; Barrow did not. Baseballs cost money, and the Babe was losing them. Writers and fans came to expect these dynamic clouts. "Babe Ruth was not able to make any home runs," a sportswriter noted after one game.[2]

The Red Sox began the regular season on April 15 at home against the Philadelphia Athletics. Ruth drew the Opening Day assignment and knocked a two-run single as Boston won, 7-1. He occasionally pinch-hit in the early going but did not play in the field except as a pitcher. Ruth hit his first home run of the campaign on May 4 in a 5-4 loss to the Yankees at the Polo Grounds. Ruth gave up all five runs. Even so, "Had all of Ruth's mates played with the same vigor in all departments, especially hitting, that he did, the Sox would have triumphed. Babe's hitting was really the feature of the game. He walloped a homer into upper tier of the grandstand in the seventh inning when (Everett) Scott was roosting on first."[3]

Two days later, on May 6, 1918, again against the Yankees, Barrow penciled in Ruth's name at first base. The regular at that position for Boston, Dick Hoblitzell, had fallen into a dreadful slump and injured a finger. Barrow, at least for now, could forget all that "laughingstock" business.

Babe had never started a regular-season game at any position except pitcher. Barrow put him in the sixth spot in the batting order. The Red Sox' record stood at 12-5 going into the contest; the Yankees' at 8-8. Boston's submarine-style right-hander Carl Mays faced New York lefty George Mogridge.

Boston broke out on top with three runs in the fourth. Wally Schang led off with a double but was thrown out at third after Stuffy McInnis laid down a "pretty bunt, leaving practically no opportunity for a play at first."[4] That brought up Ruth, "the sensational hitting pitcher for the Bostons,"[5] who blasted a two-run homer into the right-field stands. W.C. Macbeth in the *New York Tribune,* wrote that Ruth "lined one into the upper right tier some fifty feet fair, that shot on a line like a rifle bullet sand knocked the back out of the seat."[6] Yankees owner Jake Ruppert and Red Sox owner Harry Frazee were seated together at the game. Ruppert offered $150,000 for Ruth just moments after the round-tripper sailed over the fence. It was a joke, and the two men laughed.[7] Scott followed Ruth by rattling a double off the left-field wall. He raced home on Sam Agnew's single to make the score 3-0.

New York tied the game in the bottom half of the frame "because of a lot of bush league errors that completely unnerved Carl Mays."[8] Home Run Baker (acquired from Philadelphia before the 1916 season) led off with a base hit, and Pratt drew a walk. Wally Pipp's single loaded the bases. Ping Bodie "whistled"[9] a hit to left that scored Baker, while Schang uncorked a wild throw that brought home Pratt. An error by Agnew allowed Pipp to score.

The Yankees added three more runs in the fifth. Roger Peckinpaugh singled, and then Harry Hooper muffed a flyball off the bat of Baker. Pipp reached base on a wild pitch that scored Peckinpaugh. Bodie singled to bring home Baker and Pipp. That ended the day for Mays, who gave up six runs. Just two were earned. Sad Sam Jones entered the game and got the final two outs of the inning.

Following a scoreless sixth, New York put up another three-spot in the seventh. Baker and Truck Hannah singled. Pipp and Bodie followed with doubles. The Yankees added a solo run in the eighth to make the final score 10-3. Pipp, Bodie, and Baker each had three hits in the game. Bodie drove in five runs.

Mogridge, meanwhile, gave up only the three runs in the fourth. He scattered 10 hits and improved his won-lost record to 4-1, while Mays fell to 3-2. Besides hitting a home run, Ruth added a single and went 2-for-4. He raised his batting average to a robust .450. Already, some newspaper writers were suggesting that pitchers surrender to Ruth's powerful swing. "The best way to keep Babe Ruth from breaking up a ball game is to walk him and take a chance on the next batsman," wrote the *Paterson* (New Jersey) *Morning Call.*[10] Another writer put it this way: "As a rule, a pitcher at bat holds little interest for the fans, but when Babe Ruth steps to the plate the crowd is disappointed if the Red Sox twirler doesn't hit the ball a mile."[11]

The next day, in a 7-2 loss to the Washington Senators, first baseman Ruth hit another homer, his third in three games. A *Boston Globe* writer acknowledged that "Ruth's big ambition is to be an everyday member of the ball club."[12] Even so, while the Red Sox could use Babe's bat, "it's not likely that Barrow will use Ruth except as an emergency regular, but the Babe's work yesterday suggests that the future holds much in store for him."[13] Barrow still envisioned Ruth as a pitcher. He and his phenom went 'round and 'round. Sometimes, Ruth begged off his mound duties. He complained that his wrist hurt too much to pitch. Barrow didn't believe him. All the while, Ruth insisted "I like to pitch."[14]

"My main objection is that pitching keeps you out of so many games," Ruth continued. "I like to be in there every day." Given a choice, Ruth wanted to play only first base. No one gave him that choice. "I don't think a man can pitch in his regular turn, and play some other positions and keep the pace year after year," he said. "I can do it this season all right. I'm young and strong and don't mind the work, but I wouldn't guarantee to do it for many seasons."[15]

Ruth excelled while doing double duty in 1918, a season cut short due to America's entry into World War I. He appeared in 95 games, 20 of them as a pitcher. The 23-year-old finished with a 13-7 won-lost record and a 2.22 ERA. In the other contests, he pinch-hit, played first base, or saw action in the outfield. Babe hit 11 home runs, "despite the soggy ball,"[16] and tied for the league lead with the Athletics' Tillie Walker. The Red Sox won the World Series against the Chicago Cubs. Ruth hit just .200 (1-for-5) and failed to go deep. On the mound, he went 2-0 in two starts with a 1.06 ERA.

After the season columnist W.G. Evans asked, "Who was the sensation of 1918 in major league circles?" This was a year when Ty Cobb batted .382 and Walter Johnson posted a 1.27 ERA. "My answer without hesitation," Evans wrote, "would be 'Babe' Ruth of the Boson Red Sox." Ruth was, according to Evans, "a great pitcher," but – maybe – an even more talented batsman. "He always was dangerous at the bat in season's [*sic*] past," Evans wrote, "but not until 1918 did Babe Ruth realize that he was a great slugger."[17]

Notes

1. Robert Creamer, *Babe: The Legend Comes to Life* (New York: Simon & Schuster, 1974), 152.
2. Creamer, 151.
3. "Babe's Hitting All Right, but Yanks Bunch on Him," *Boston Globe*, May 5, 1918: 15.
4. W.J. Macbeth, "Ping Bodie Brings Glory to Yankee Escutcheon," *New York Tribune*, May 7, 1918.
5. Frederick G. Lieb, "Murderers' Row Batters Red Sox," *New York Herald*, May 7, 1918: 13.
6. Macbeth.
7. Leigh Montville, *The Big Bam: The Life and Times of Babe Ruth* (New York: Doubleday, 2006), 69.
8. Macbeth.
9. Ibid.
10. "Baseball Gossip from Major Leagues," *Paterson* (New Jersey) *Morning Call*, May 7, 1918: 3.
11. "Baseball Gossip," *Wichita Daily Eagle*, May 7, 1918: 7.
12. "Live Tips and Topics." *Boston Globe*, May 7, 1918: 3.
13. Ibid.
14. Montville, 74.
15. Ibid.
16. Babe Ruth and Bob Considine, *The Babe Ruth Story* (New York: Signet, 1992), 51.
17. W.G. Evans, "Babe Ruth Is Great Sensation of Year in Major Leagues," *Lincoln* (Nebraska) *Star,* November 17, 1918: 7.

Babe Ruth Tosses Shutout as Patriotism Prevails in Opening of Fall Classic

September 5, 1918: Boston Red Sox 1, Chicago Cubs 0, at Comiskey Park
Game One of the World Series

By Michael Huber

With the war in Europe still underway, the 1918 World Series began. A meager yet patriotic crowd of 19,274 fans was on hand, "the smallest that has witnessed the diamond classic in many years."[1] The minds of the spectators were clearly on the overseas conflict, yet they came to see "an unusually brilliant exhibition of baseball."[2] The first game had originally been scheduled for September 4, but rain had caused a delay. Further, the venue was moved from the Cubs' home ballpark of Weeghman Park (currently Wrigley Field) to Comiskey Park, "because it held more fans."[3] Many "believed that the Weeghman machine would win without allowing the American League club a single victory."[4]

For the Red Sox, Joe Bush had been warming up to take the mound, but Boston skipper Ed Barrow surprised the Cubs as "the Baltimore mauler [Babe Ruth] was named for the task."[5]

The Cubs countered with their ace, Hippo Vaughn. In a battle of southpaws, "these two giants fought it out all the way"[6] in a classic pitcher's duel.

Chicago threatened in the opening frame, "with victory within their grasp."[7] With two outs, Les Mann singled and motored to third when Dode Paskert hit a Texas leaguer to left field (Paskert advanced to second on the throw to third). Ruth then walked Fred Merkle to load the bases. With the game possibly depending "on his next offering, Ruth served up a low, fast ball to [Charlie] Pick, at the same time waving his outfielders back toward the bleachers."[8] Pick lifted the ball high into left, but George Whiteman made the catch to end the inning.

The Babe

Babe Ruth during the 1918 World Series. *Courtesy of Tim Reid @ LTRIIIDesigns*

They may have taken Ruth's pitching for granted, but the Cubs feared Ruth's bat. When Ruth hit the first ball in batting practice "into the right field bleachers, the crowd roared with appreciation."[9] And as the Babe strode to the plate in the top of the third inning, "Max Flack simply turned about and marched about forty paces toward the right wall,"[10] while the crowd cheered, expecting some action. Ruth sent a deep line drive to right center, and "the Cubs rooters groaned the moment their tympanums registered the sound of the bat and ball contact. It seemed a potential home run, but, as was the case throughout the afternoon with both sides, the high wind blowing directly against the batter, held back the swat and dropped it right into the mitt of the centerfielder" Paskert, who had stumbled at first, recovered quickly, and ran down the ball for a long out. In his two other at-bats, Ruth fanned and "struck out in such a manner that the crowd tee-heed audibly."[11] Throughout the game, the Cubs "successfully stifled the perilous home-run bat of Ruth, but they overlooked the menace of his pitching arm."[12]

Boston "did all of its stick execution in the first four innings, getting one hit in each of the first three, then grouping two for the winning tally in the fourth."[13] In the fourth, Vaughn allowed a leadoff walk to Dave Shean. Amos Strunk tried to bunt Shean to second but popped up the ball and Vaughn caught it. Whiteman did advance Shean to second, when he looped a single over short, bringing up Stuffy McInnis, "a notorious left-field hitter."[14] McInnis took Vaughn's first offering for a ball, "but the second pitch came across to suit him and he dropped a rather indifferent rap into left field along the foul line. Proper preliminary coaching would have placed [Cubs left fielder] Mann directly in line for an easy catch on this ball and a resulting out, with no score."[15] Instead, this proved to be the game-winner. The *New York Times* reported that the "one lone run grew larger as the pitchers battled along, both displaying an impenetrable mysticism of curves."[16]

The Cubs presented another opportunity in the sixth inning. With one down, "Paskert stung a hit to centre and Merkle slapped one to the same baliwick, and Ruth was becoming plainly worried."[17] Boston's Barrow waved to the bullpen and Bush started warming up again. Pick rolled a sacrifice down the first-base line and both runners advance. When Ruth got Charlie Deal to fly out to left, the threat ended.

And then, something happened during the seventh inning stretch that was "far different from any incident that has ever occurred in the history of baseball. As the crowd ... stood up to take their afternoon yawn,"[18] a band from the Navy training station just north of Chicago began to play "The Star Spangled Banner." This was the first time the song was played at a World Series game. "The yawns were checked and heads were bared as the ball players turned quickly and faced the music."[19] A few in the crowd began singing, then more joined in, until "a great volume of melody rolled across the field."[20] The crowd then "exploded into thunderous applause,"[21] and the beginning of a new tradition was being witnessed. "Certainly the outpouring of sentiment, enthusiasm, and patriotism at the 1918 World Series went a long way to making the (song) the national anthem," wrote John Thorn, the official historian of Major League Baseball.[22] It would be another 13 years before President Hoover officially designated the song as America's national anthem.[23] From the *New York Times*: "If the greatest reason for playing this world's series this year was to give the boys overseas something to talk about besides war, this game today will serve the purpose."[24]

The Cubs made one last attempt in the bottom of the ninth. With two outs, Deal dragged a bunt down the third-base line and beat the throw from Thomas for a single. Bill McCabe came on as a pinch-runner. Then Bill Killefer "took one last grand slam at the ball and shot a high ballooner between right and centre fields," but Hooper raced to the ball for the final out of the game. The Red Sox, behind Ruth's pitching, had won 1-0.

Several accounts of the game mentioned how few occasions there were for the fans to cheer. The *Chicago Tribune* commented, "From the ball player's standpoint it was a great game, because of its proximity to perfection. From the rooter's view point it was tame and monotonous because there were so few tense moments."[25] Further, "the crowd present sat through the entire game, all primed to burst forth when the proper time came. But it never came, because Ruth never allowed an attack to go far enough to do damage."[26] Ruth allowed six hits and one walk in the win, striking out four. Vaughn yielded only five hits, all singles. He struck out six and walked three. Neither team made an error, and perhaps the difference came down to the Red Sox getting one hit with men in scoring position (1-for-7) while the Cubs were 0-for-5.

Sources

In addition to the sources mentioned in the notes, the author consulted baseball-reference.com and retrosheet.org.

Notes

1. "Red Sox Beat Cubs in Initial Battle of World's Series," *New York Times*, September 6, 1918: 14.
2. Ibid.
3. Don Babwin (Associated Press), "1918 World Series key in US love affair with national anthem," found online at *bostonglobe.com/sports/redsox/2017/07/03/world-series-key-love-affair-with-national-anthem/J4XmvKVNXp69P4EQEU8piK/story.html*. Accessed September 2017. Weeghman Park was the home of the Federal League's Chicago Whales in 1914 and Chicago Chi-Feds in 1915. The Cubs started playing there in 1916 and have stayed. The name was changed to Cubs Park in 1920 and then to Wrigley Field in 1926.
4. John E. Wray, "Vaughn's Defeat in World Series Opener Puts Bruins on Defensive in Pitching," *St. Louis Post-Dispatch*, September 6, 1918: 20.
5. *New York Times*.
6. "Sox Take First Game at Chicago," *Burlington Free Press*, September 6, 1918: 1.
7. *New York Times*.
8. *Burlington Free Press*.
9. Edward F. Martin, "McInnis' Smash Beats Cubs, 1-0," *Boston Globe*, September 6, 1918: 4.
10. James Crusinberry, "All Primed to Yell, But Precise Hurling Gives Fan No Chance," *Chicago Tribune*, September 6, 1918: 9.
11. Wray.
12. *New York Times*.
13. I.E. Sanborn, "Red Sox Grab First World's Series Battle From Cubs, 1-0," *Chicago Tribune*, September 6, 1918: 9.
14. "Crowd Present Seemed to Take Little Interest in Work of Rival Athletes," *St. Louis Post-Dispatch*, September 6, 1918: 20.
15. Ibid.
16. *New York Times*.
17. Ibid.
18. Ibid.
19. Ibid.
20. Ibid.
21. Ibid.
22. Babwin.
23. Ibid.
24. *New York Times*.
25. Sanborn.
26. Crusinberry.

Ruth Hits Six Home Runs in Six At-Bats

April 18, 1919: Boston Red Sox 12, Baltimore Orioles 3, at Oriole Park

By Jimmy Keenan

Babe Ruth put on a home-run show in his hometown on April 18, 1919. The Boston Red Sox pitcher-outfielder swatted four round-trippers in four at-bats during a chilly, one-sided exhibition game against the Baltimore Orioles.

The Babe had begun to make his grand transition from top-flight left-handed pitcher to full-time outfielder and slugger. In 1918 he tied Philadelphia Athletics outfielder Tillie Walker for the major-league lead in homers with 11. (Ruth went to bat almost 100 fewer times than Walker.)

It was a hectic time in the baseball world. Because of US involvement in World War I, teams played abbreviated schedules in 1918. The Red Sox defeated the Chicago Cubs in the World Series, which was held in early September. When the war ended two months later, players who were in the military or had taken stateside jobs to support the war effort flocked back to their teams.

Red Sox owner Harry Frazee made several offseason moves while handling contract negotiations with many of his star

Babe Ruth, bat in hand 1919. *Courtesy of Library of Congress.*

players who were holding out for more money. Those holdouts included Ruth, who, in addition to his work with the bat, went 13-7 with a 2.22 ERA on the mound in 1918.

On March 18, 1919, Red Sox manager Ed Barrow and 10 of his players boarded the steamer Arapahoe in New York Harbor. When the ship docked at Jacksonville, Florida, Barrow and his party traveled by rail to Tampa for the start of spring training. Another contingent of Red Sox skipped the scenic trip down the Eastern Seaboard and took the train directly to Tampa.

The remaining unsigned men – including the Babe – stayed at home, while shortstop Everett Scott reported to camp without a contract.

On March 22 Frazee and Ruth finally came to an agreement. The national newspapers reported that the Bambino had inked a three-year deal worth $27,000. The other Red Sox holdouts soon followed suit, Scott being the last to sign.

After a few weeks in Florida, including a game in which Ruth blasted what is believed to be the longest home run ever hit in Tampa, the Red Sox headed northward.[1] One scheduled stop was at Richmond, where the Red Sox and Baltimore Orioles were slated to play a three-game series at Boulevard Park. From there, both clubs would travel to Baltimore for two more games at Oriole Park. The Richmond promoters belatedly called off the games with Baltimore, choosing instead to showcase local ballclubs against the reigning World Series champs.

When the games in Richmond were canceled, Orioles owner-manager Jack Dunn contacted Harry Frazee about scheduling a third game in Baltimore. Dunn had purchased the Baltimore franchise from owner Ned Hanlon in 1909 for a reported $35,000. Dunn signed George Herman Ruth, a standout pitcher for St. Mary's Industrial School, to his first professional contract in February of 1914. Later that season, Dunn's team began losing money because of stiff competition at the box office from Baltimore's Federal League franchise. To remain fiscally solvent, Dunn began selling off his star players. He sent Ruth to the Red Sox, along with Ben Egan and Ernie Shore.

Frazee and Dunn agreed to play an additional game in Baltimore on April 17, the day before the series was originally scheduled to start. But Frazee didn't inform anyone from the Boston organization about the change in plans. That afternoon a few hundred people, braving the unseasonably cold weather, showed up at Oriole Park. Regrettably for these diehard fans, the Boston club was not at the ballpark or even in Baltimore for that matter. Regarding the mixup, the *Baltimore Sun* wrote, "It is believed that Frazee forgot to notify Barrow of the change regarding yesterday which caused the manager to remain in Richmond instead of coming to this city yesterday morning."[2]

The Red Sox left Richmond by train on the evening of April 17, arriving at the railway station in Baltimore at 1:30 the next morning. Later that afternoon, Boston and Baltimore took the field at Oriole Park in front of 2,000 wind-chilled fans.

Dunn gave the starting assignment to Allen "Lefty" Herbert, while Barrow went with southpaw Herb Pennock.[3]

Veteran infielder Jack Barry started off the Boston offense by doubling in the opening inning. Amos Strunk followed with a single, Barry holding at third. Walks to Ruth and Ossie Vitt pushed across a run before Herbert worked his way out of trouble. The Orioles countered with a run in the bottom of the first. Merwin Jacobson lashed an opposite-field single, then advanced to third on a wild pitch and passed ball. Jacobson came home on Johnny Honig's base hit up the middle.

Neither club scored in the second. In the third, Ruth's two-run homer, along with Everett Scott's sacrifice fly, bumped up the score to 4-1. Left-hander Sam Hersperger replaced Herbert on the mound during this inning.

Baltimore scored two runs in the bottom of the third. Fritz Maisel led off with a single to center. After a passed ball allowed Maisel to advance to second, Jacobson reached first base on an error by Scott at short. Max Bishop followed with a walk to load the bases. After Honig struck out, Joe Boley swatted a single to right that plated two runs.

Hersperger, who once struck out 21 batters in a game against the Gallaudet University Reserves, began having control issues in the fourth. Dunn replaced him with Harry Frank. In his first at-bat against the new pitcher, Ruth smacked a towering blast over the fence in right-center field. The *Baltimore Sun* observed, "This was the real drive of the day. It went between two houses fronting on Greenmount Avenue and the rest of its travels were not reported at a late hour last night."[4] When the dust cleared, the Red Sox had padded their lead to the tune of 7-3.

Sam Jones relieved Pennock in the sixth and held the Orioles scoreless for the remainder of the contest. Frank, meanwhile, finished out the game for Baltimore and allowed five more Red Sox runs. Ruth remained locked in, cranking a solo home run over the right-field wall in the seventh and another in the ninth. When the last out was recorded, the scoreboard read Boston 12, Baltimore 3.

Ruth, who patrolled left field and batted fifth, went 4-for-4 with four homers and two walks. In regard to Ruth's power display, the *Baltimore Sun* wrote, "Yes, Johnny Honig and Merwin Jacobson practically sat on the wall surrounding Oriole Park yesterday, but four times Babe Ruth, the greatest clouter baseball ever has known, drove the white rocket far over their heads thus equaling the batting record established years ago by big Ed Delahanty."[5]

Center fielder Strunk contributed four hits for Boston. Honig, Jacobson, and Sumpter Clarke collected two hits each for Baltimore. The following afternoon, the two teams squared off again at Oriole Park on another raw day in front of 3,000 hardy souls. Ruth pitched the first four innings, at one point retiring 10 consecutive batters before giving up a run. In keeping with his hot hitting from the previous day, the Babe belted homers in his first two plate appearances.

Former Philadelphia Athletics right-hander Rube Parnham was Ruth's first victim. Babe launched one of Parnham's offerings high over a candy advertisement sign on the right-field fence. Reporters covering the game noted that Ruth hit a pitch that was at least three inches outside. New York native Bert Lewis relieved Parnham in the fourth and lasted only a third of an inning before being replaced by left-hander Rudy Kneisch.

The Bambino's second blast of the day came off Kneisch, the ball soaring high over the wall in right field. Kneisch gained some redemption by fanning Ruth in the slugger's third and final at-bat of the game. Veteran submarine pitcher Carl Mays took over for Ruth in the fifth, allowing one run over the next five frames. The lopsided affair ended with Boston up 16-2. The following day, the *Baltimore Sun* noted that Ruth had compiled 18 round-trippers since the start of the spring exhibition games.

When asked by a reporter about hitting six home runs in front of his hometown fans, the Babe replied, "I was afraid some of my old neighbors didn't believe all that they've read in the papers about me. This was my chance to show them what I could do."[6]

Ruth's heavy hitting would carry over into the regular season. The future Sultan of Swat ushered in the live ball era with a major-league leading 29 home runs. The Babe's new mark eclipsed the old record of 27 set by the Chicago White Stockings' Ned Williamson in 1884.

Sources

In addition to the sources cited in the Notes, the author consulted Baseball-reference.com and the *Baltimore American, Harrisburg Telegraph, New York Sun, New York Tribune, Richmond Times-Dispatch, Washington Herald,* and *Washington Post*.

Keenan, Jimmy. "Jack Dunn," SABR BioProject, at sabr.org/bioproj/person/e1addacb.

Lowry, Philip. *Green Cathedrals* (New York: Walker Publishing, 2006).

Montville, Leigh. *The Big Bam*: *The Life and Times of Babe Ruth* (New York: Doubleday Publishing, 2006).

Russo, Frank. *The Cooperstown Chronicles: Baseball's Colorful Characters, Unusual Lives, and Strange Demises* (Lanham, Maryland: Rowman and Littlefield Publishers, 2014), 98-99.

Steinberg, Steve, and Lyle Spatz. *The Colonel and The Hug*: *The Partnership that Changed the New York Yankees* (Lincoln: University of Nebraska Press, 2015).

Thanks to the Enoch Pratt Library of Baltimore.

Notes

1   On the home run in Tampa, see roadsideamerica.com/story/14158.

2   "To Open Series Today," *Baltimore Sun*, April 18, 1919: 9.

3   Herbert had been a standout at Mount St. Joseph High School in Baltimore and St. John's College in Annapolis before signing with the Orioles. Pennock had started his big-league career with the Philadelphia Athletics in 1912 and was acquired on waivers by Boston in 1915. Pennock rejoined the Red Sox in March of 1919 after his discharge from the Navy.

4   C. Starr Mathews, "Equals World's Record," *Baltimore Sun*, April 19, 1919: 10.

5   Ibid.

6   Allan Wood, *Babe Ruth and the 1918 Red Sox* (Bloomington, Indiana: iUniverse publishing, 2000), 349.

Babe Ruth's First Grand Slam

May 20, 1919: Boston Red Sox 6, St. Louis Browns 4, at Sportsman's Park, St. Louis

By Skip Nipper

When Boston's 1918 World Series championship season was over, Babe Ruth asked for more money through his new agent, Johnny Igoe, demanding a two-year contract at $15,000 a year. Red Sox owner Harry Frazee, in economic survival mode, responded with an emphatic no.

Negotiations included Frazee's offer of $8,500 after Igoe insisted on a three-year deal for Babe at $10,000 a year. Ruth said he did not want to both pitch and play left field, that he only wanted to play left and be in the lineup each day.

When Red Sox manager Ed Barrow was asked what he thought, he made it clear who would be in charge of the ballclub on the field: "If Ruth plays for the Red Sox in 1919, he will probably pitch and pinch-hit."[1]

Barrow was wrong; Babe would pitch in only 17 games. He would have a breakout year in his final season with Boston before being sold to the Yankees.

Ruth finally signed a contract with Frazee in Boston on March 21, a three-year deal at $10,000 a year, and immediately reported to Tampa, Florida, where Barrow was holding training camp.

In the first game of spring training, on April 4 against the New York Giants, Ruth hit a towering drive to right center that reportedly traveled 579 feet. The club headed north with the Giants before Boston played a two-game series in Ruth's hometown, Baltimore, against the Orioles.

He was spectacular. In the first game, on April 18, Babe hit four home runs.

"Ruth, only a short while ago unknown to all save his schoolmates at St. Mary's, among whom he was an idol, proved conclusively to about 2,000 spectators who braced the wintry winds that Harry Frazee has the greatest bargain in the United States," wrote a sportswriter for the *Baltimore Sun*. "Of course, the Red Sox, world's champions all, won, but everyone expected that. The score, which was 12 to 3, really made no difference. The fans went to the ball yard to see if Ruth could hit one over the fence. They got their money's worth many times over."[2]

The next day Ruth was the starting pitcher and was at the plate three times. After slugging two more round-trippers, he was struck out by Orioles lefty Rudy Kneisch on three pitches and

Barrow called on Carl Mays in relief with the score 12-1 in favor of Boston.

In the two games Babe finished 6-for-9 from the plate, all six hits home runs.

No matter how Ruth had performed on the field, Barrow had become suspicious of the young slugger's inclination toward all-night partying. After the third game of the new season on April 28 in Washington, he waited for Ruth in the lobby of the Raleigh Hotel until 4 in the morning before giving up on catching his star's appearance.

A hotel porter reported to Barrow at 6 A.M. that Ruth had finally come to the hotel, and Barrow confronted Babe, who was fully dressed and smoking a pipe in bed with his covers pulled up to his chin.

"I'll see you at the ballpark," Barrow said.

Before that day's game Ruth challenged his manager, and though the confrontation was averted, it appears that it had some effect on his performance over the next few weeks. His batting average dropped from .316 on May 1 to a low of .180 on May 26, and he had only 11 hits for the season before getting two on May 27 that raised his average to .203.

Ruth's first pitching performance came on May 3 at Fenway Park against the Yankees and resulted in a complete-game 3-2 victory. Babe had a double and an RBI. On May 15 he was called on in relief of Joe Bush early in the game against the White Sox in Chicago on and gained his second win as Stuffy McInnis drove in Jack Barry with the winning run in the top of the 12th inning.

Either still in Barrow's doghouse or simply kept out of the lineup due to his weak hitting during a three-game set in Chicago (he had one hit in 11 plate appearances), Ruth pinch-hit for Sad Sam Jones in the eighth inning on May 17 in St. Louis. A paltry roller resulted in an out and catcalls by the fans rang out as St. Louis won, 2-1.[3] Ruth did not play in the next day's game, another victory for the Browns, 4-3.

With the Red Sox' record 8-8 and four losses in the last five games, Barrow named Babe the starting pitcher on May 20 against the Browns. Sportswriter Melville Webb offered his advice to Boston's manager.

"It looks now as if 'Babe' Ruth would be the fellow relied on to pull out at least one game in the series with the Browns. As time has passed, it has been more and more apparent that the value the club is to get out of 'Babe' is in the pitcher's box. He was held in the game regularly until he failed to hit in form consistent with a regular berth, and the way to get full value on his pitching was for Ed Barrow to stipulate that Ruth make the flinging game strictly his business, for a time at least."[4]

Babe took his 2-0 record to the mound against Dave Davenport, who was in his final months in the big leagues. St. Louis manager Jimmy Burke pinned hopes on the 6-foot-6, 220-pound right-hander to continue the Browns' five-game winning streak.

Ruth won his own cause by smashing Davenport's first pitch for a home run with two out in the second inning after two runs had scored and Boston loaded the bases. Frank Gilhooley, Barry, and Amos Strunk preceded Ruth across the plate.

"One fast ball, pitched waist high to 'Babe' Ruth cost Dave Davenport a victory over the Boston Red Sox in the concluding game of the series at Sportsman's Park this afternoon and shattered the winning streak of the Browns," the *Boston Globe* wrote. "The fast ball served up to Ruth by Davenport came in that inning with two runs across the plate, the bases full and two out. 'Babe' swung hard and dropped the ball far on the other side of the right field bleacher wall for a home run, scoring three men ahead of him with what proved to be the decisive runs.

"That one titanic smash ended the offensive activities of the burly Bostonian for the day and he consumed the remainder of the game trying to reduce the hitting of the Browns to a minimum."[5]

Ruth gave up nine hits and four runs, walking four and allowing a run to score on a balk.

Ruth "pitched none too strongly, but the insurmountable barrier that his home placed in the path of the Browns proved too much for them to overcome," the *Globe* wrote.[6]

A final newspaper mention of Ruth came in the form of an anecdote: " 'One swallow doesn't make a drunkard' is an axiom with Dave Davenport, but the tall right-hander admits that one pitched ball to 'Babe' Ruth makes a ball game."[7]

The grand slam was Babe's first and he would add three more to set the Red Sox' single-season record. He hit 15 more grand slams in his career. Interestingly, none were hit in Fenway Park but nine in Yankee Stadium.

Organized Baseball's first grand slam was hit by Charley Gould of the Boston Red Stockings in an 1871 National Association game, and Roger Connor hit what is accepted as the first major-league grand slam on September 10, 1881, for the Troy Trojans. Neither was a match for Babe Ruth's total of 16, even though the first line of Connor's obituary called him "The Babe Ruth of the '80s" when he died in 1931.[8]

Ruth's first grand slam was the 22nd home run of his career and he was on his way to finishing the season with an unheard-of home-run total of 29. The Bambino was off and running toward an amazing career of 714 homers to become an icon in the history of baseball.

Ruth's grand slams

Date	Opponent	Location	Pitcher
With Boston			
May 20, 1919	St. Louis Browns	St. Louis	Dave Davenport
June 30, 1919 (1)	New York Yankees	New York	Bob Shawkey
July 18, 1919	Cleveland Indians	Cleveland	Fritz Coumbe
August 23, 1919	Detroit Tigers	Detroit	Hooks Dauss
With New York			
July 6, 1922 (1)	Cleveland Indians	New York	Duster Mails
September 24, 1925	Chicago White Sox	New York	Sarge Connally
September 25, 1926 (1)	St. Louis Browns	St. Louis	Elam Vangilder
September 27, 1927	Philadelphia Athletics	New York	Lefty Grove
September 29, 1927	Washington Senators	New York	Paul Hopkins
July 3, 1929	Boston Red Sox	New York	Red Ruffing
August 6, 1929 (2)	Washington Senators	New York	Bobby Burke
August 7, 1929 (1)	Philadelphia Athletics	Philadelphia	Howard Ehmke
September 27, 1930	Philadelphia Athletics	Philadelphia	George Earnshaw
August 20, 1931	St. Louis Browns	St. Louis	Wally Hebert
May 21, 1932 (1)	Washington Senators	New York	Lloyd Brown
June 24, 1934	Chicago White Sox	New York	Sad Sam Jones

Sources

In addition to the sources cited in the Notes, the author consulted Baseball-Almanac.com, Baseball-Reference.com, Baseballhall.org, Newspapers.com, Retrosheet.org, and Sabr.org, and the following:

Barthel, Thomas. *Babe Ruth and the Creation of the Celebrity Athlete* (Jefferson, North Carolina: McFarland, 2018).

Stewart, Wayne. *Babe Ruth: A Biography* (Westport, Connecticut: Greenwood, 2006).

Notes

1. Robert W. Creamer, *Babe: The Legend Comes to Life* (New York: Simon and Schuster, 1974), 186-187.
2. C. Starr Matthews, "Equals World's Record," *Baltimore Sun*, April 19, 1919: 10.
3. "Red Sox Dazzled by Gallia's Shoots," *Boston Globe*, May 18, 1919: 17.
4. Melvin E. Webb Jr., "Red Sox Must Work Hard to Break Even," *Boston Globe*, May 20, 1919: 10.
5. "Bases Loaded, Ruth Clouts Over Fence," *Boston Globe*, May 21, 1919: 9.
6. Ibid.
7. Ibid.
8. National Baseball Hall of Fame, "Roger Connor," baseballhall.org/hall-of-famers/connor-roger. Accessed April 17, 2019.

Athletics Prevail Despite a Pair of Long Balls by Babe Ruth

July 5, 1919: Philadelphia Athletics 8, Boston Red Sox 6 (second game of doubleheader), at Fenway Park, Boston

By Rock Hoffman

When it comes to the home run, Babe Ruth, of course, is a man of many firsts but a personal first for him came on July 5, 1919, at Fenway Park in Boston when The Bambino had the first of what would be 72 multi-home-run games (which as of 2019 was still the major-league record). On that day, Ruth hit a pair of round-trippers in the second game of a doubleheader against the Philadelphia Athletics. Unfortunately for the Red Sox – and The Babe – they came in a losing effort, as Connie Mack's team won the game, 8-6 in 10 innings, to sweep the twin bill.

In 1919 the Red Sox were coming off what would be their final World Series win of the twentieth century but they struggled to a sixth-place finish with a mark of 66-71. The Athletics were in the midst of a seven-year run of last-place finishes. The victories on this day accounted for two of just 36 wins they would accumulate for the season, against 104 defeats.

One day after Christmas in 1919, the Red Sox gave the New York Yankees a gift by selling Ruth to them, but before he left the Hub, the Babe would have a season for the ages – the first of many – with the bat in his hands. He clubbed 29 homers in 1919 to break the single-season home-run record. The number was one more than the major-league team average as he out-homered 10 of the 15 other teams. He also led the American League in runs, on-base percentage, slugging percentage, and RBIs (although runs batted in were was not yet an official statistic). His slash line was .322/.456/.657 in his first season as a full-time player in the field. He started 111 games (106 in left field and 5 at first base) easily surpassing his starts in 1918 when made 57 in the outfield and 13 at first. He did pitch in 1919, taking the mound 17 times with 15 starts, compiling a 9-5 mark with a 2.97 ERA; he struck out 30 batters while walking 58 in 133⅓ innings. For the remainder of his career, Ruth would toe the rubber just five more times, for a total of 31 innings.

The games on July 5 were played in record-breaking heat. The temperature reached 101 degrees at 2:30 in the afternoon, making it the hottest July 5 on record[1] (another mark that still stands). The Athletics won game one, 5-3, by scoring three runs in the ninth inning. Ruth was hitless in five plate appearances but walked twice.

In the second game – a makeup of a May 9 rainout – the Red Sox jumped out to an early lead. With one out in the bottom of the first, Harry Hooper's double to left knocked in Ossie Vitt, who had reached via a walk. Next, Ruth hit the ball to third baseman Fred Thomas, who tagged out Hooper, but threw wildly to first. The error allowed The Babe to get to second, and he scored from there on a single to center field by Roxy Walters after Stuffy McInnis walked.

Poor defense cost the Red Sox the lead in the sixth as they made three errors that allowed the A's to plate four runs. However, it did set the stage for eighth-inning heroics by Ruth, who had failed to reach base in his two previous at-bats. With Hooper on first base after walking, The Bambino swatted a liner into the right-field seats. Ruth's drive was described by *Boston Globe* writer James C. O'Leary as "screeching,"[2] and it tied the score at 4-4.

Some two-out lightning in the ninth put Mack's squad back on top. Cy Perkins singled, then pitcher Jing Johnson helped himself with a double to right that scored his catcher.

In the Red Sox half of the ninth, Everett Scott got a leadoff single and after Red Shannon bunted him to second, Mike McNally came in to pinch-run. Wally Schang pinch-hit for starting pitcher Bill James and while Schang was at the plate, Johnson threw a wild pitch.

O'Leary wrote that after the ball hit the plate, it climbed the screen and "before it rolled back McNally was over the plate."[3]

In the 10th, Boston was undone again by poor fielding. Sad Sam Jones was now on the hill and he retired the first two men he faced but Amos Strunk walked. First baseman George Burns hit a liner to center near the flagpole and Strunk trotted home to give Philadelphia a 6-5 advantage. The Red Sox would have been out of the inning but Shannon made his second error of the game when he threw the ball away on a grounder by Merlin Kopp; Burns scored and Kopp provided additional insurance when he scored on a single by Joe Dugan.

Those extra two runs meant that the two-out solo home run Ruth hit over the scoreboard in left field in the bottom of the inning was basically meaningless as far as the game was concerned as McInnis, the next batter, made the final out.

As for Ruth, it was his ninth homer of the season and the 29th of his career. Johnson gave up both in this game; he was the 20th pitcher to be victimized by The Sultan of Swat and the eighth to allow more than one.

Sources

In addition to the sources cited in the Notes, the author consulted Baseball-reference.com, Retrosheet.org, Baseball-almanac.com, and Weather.gov.

Notes

1 "Break in Torrid Wave Promised," *Boston Globe,* July 6, 1919: 16.

2 James C. O'Leary, "Mackmen Fight Way to Double Triumph," *Boston Globe,* July 6, 1919: 15.

3 Ibid.

Babe's Blast Ties American League Record as Boston Goes Down Swinging

July 29, 1919: Detroit Tigers 10, Boston Red Sox 8, at Fenway Park

By Nathan Bierma

There was no highly hyped home-run chase in 1919. That's one of the many things Babe Ruth put on the baseball map.

First, he raised the home run to an art form and a focal point, after decades of 90-feet-at-a-time offense in the Deadball Era. Then, when Ruth slammed 60 home runs in 1927, every subsequent slugger would be measured against that mighty stick, with the press breathlessly comparing each challenger's pace against the Babe day by day.

But in 1919, the home run was still more of an afterthought, and so was the American League record for home runs in a season. It was held by Ralph "Socks" Seybold, who clubbed 16 circuits for the Philadelphia Athletics in 1902. So as Babe Ruth took the field at Fenway Park for a series-opening game with the Detroit Tigers, sitting on 15 home runs, his chances of matching Seybold came with little fanfare and little suspense. After all, it was only July.

In fact, Babe's subsequent feat did not appear in the headline of the game report in the *Detroit Free Press*, and did not warrant mention until the seventh paragraph.[1]

Instead, the focus going into the game, which matched Hughie Jennings' third-place Tigers (48-37) against Ed Barrow's sixth-place Red Sox (37-46), was on the pitchers, who were not expected to allow the shootout that was about to unfold. After all, Dutch Leonard and Paul Musser had matched up exactly one week before at Navin Field in Detroit, with the Tigers pulling out a narrow 2-1 win. Musser, whom the *Boston Globe* called the "strike-out king of the Western League,"[2] had just been called up and was solid in his Red Sox debut, striking out seven but getting stuck with the loss.

Early on in the rematch, it looked as if another pitchers' duel might be in store.

"Musser started like a thoroughbred from a barrier, striking out his first two batters," the *Free Press* reported.³ Ty Cobb flared a single into center field, but cut the inning short when he "strayed too far off the bag and was run down."⁴

Boston took the lead in the bottom of the inning on a base hit by Braggo Roth that scored Harry Hooper, and Musser preserved it in the second. A walk to Harry Heilmann was his only mistake, and that was erased when, as the *Free Press* said, "Harry died stealing."⁵

But the Tigers pounced on Musser in the third inning, overcoming his oral output of "saliva that he decorated the pill with," according to the *Free Press*, and giving Musser "a beating that he isn't apt to cherish."⁶

Third baseman Bob Jones led off with a walk and moved to second on a sacrifice by catcher Eddie Ainsmith. After Leonard was retired, Donie Bush and Ralph Young banged back-to-back singles, pushing across Jones and then Bush. The Tigers took the lead, 2-1.

Detroit poured on the pressure in the fourth. Bobby Veach singled to center and then made it to second on a steal attempt that would have fallen short before second sacker Red Shannon dropped what the *Globe* called "Schang's perfect throw."⁷ Chick Shorten reached on an error by former Tiger Ossie Vitt at third, and Shorten and Veach marched home when Ainsmith, "catching one of Musser's heaves where he wanted it, clubbed over Roth's head for three bases," the *Free Press* said.⁸ Then Leonard joined the attack with a single to score Ainsmith before the Tigers were finally silenced, having claimed a 5-1 lead.

In the bottom of the inning, Boston turned to Babe Ruth. The left fielder came up with one out and bashed a double, then advanced to third on a wild pitch to catcher Wally Schang, who drew a walk. Del Gainer knocked a grounder to third, where Jones "made a great stop on Gainer's drive, but threw wild to second," sending Schang to third and Gainer to second while Ruth made it home.⁹ Schang scored on Shannon's groundout, and then, with two outs, Everett Scott bunted and made it to first to get Gainer home. After an eventful fourth inning, it was a competitive game again, with the Red Sox trailing only 5-4.

But not for long. Young walked and would have scored on a deep drive by Cobb, only to have Hooper make the defensive play of the game, a running catch followed by a crash into the wall. "With momentum enough to have carried it three feet further the ball would have landed in the bleachers for a home run," the *Globe* said, but Cobb couldn't even settle for an extra-base hit after Hooper's heroics.¹⁰ Then Veach doubled home Young, Heilmann singled to shift Veach to third, Shorten hit a sacrifice fly to complete Veach's trip, and Jones pelted a base hit to score Heilmann and open up an 8-4 Tigers lead.

Ruth would mount an answer once more. With two out and one on, he belted a double to move Hooper to third, and both men reached where they started on a base hit by Schang. The Red Sox were back within striking distance, trailing 8-6 after seven innings.

Ray Caldwell began his third inning of work in the top of the ninth inning. He had taken over for Musser, who was lifted for a pinch-hitter in the sixth inning. Caldwell had known Fenway Park from the very beginning; he was the first opposing pitcher in the park's opener in 1912, with the Highlanders.¹¹

Now, after two scoreless frames, Caldwell gave the Tigers the breathing room they would end up needing. He walked Young, who was forced out on a fielder's choice by Cobb, then surrendered three straight singles to score two runs and let Detroit reach double digits. The Red Sox moved to the bottom of the ninth trailing 10-6.

Leonard retired Hooper and Vitt on fly balls, bringing up Roth with Ruth on deck. For some reason, Leonard elected to walk Roth and face the Babe.

"It would be interesting to know just what Leonard had in mind by deliberately passing Roth and bringing Ruth to bat in the ninth," the *Globe* puzzled.¹²

It was a big mistake. "The first ball he sent up was a high, fast one, which Ruth met fair, and sent into the centre field bleachers."¹³

"Ball and bat met, and the apple sailed among the fans," the *Free Press* ruefully reported.¹⁴

It was home-run number 16 for Ruth, tying Seybold. Once again, Ruth had single-handedly made the game close. But his blast was Boston's last gasp, and the Red Sox lost 10-8.

With the win the Tigers moved into second place, taking advantage of losses by Chicago and Cleveland, which split a doubleheader.

Every Tiger tallied at least one hit. Veach, whom the *Free Press* identified as "the left gardener in the Jungle clan," finished with "a regular field day" of three hits.¹⁵

"The Bengals grouped 12 robust wallops for 10 honest trips around the route of bases," the *Free Press* crowed. "The contest was typical of the Tigers when they measure a victim for the morgue, and attend the obsequies."¹⁶

Fittingly, despite all the offense, it was characteristic of the pre-1920 variety, with Ruth's final shot being the only ball to clear the fence.

But Babe was on the brink of changing the game of baseball. The imminence of a new record was clear, as Ruth still had two months left in the season to beat Seybold and make a run at Ned Williamson's major-league record of 27 round trippers for the Chicago White Stockings in 1884.[17]

"Nothing but a world's record for home runs by Ruth will now satisfy the Boston fans," the *Globe* said, "and his chances of setting one are pretty good."

But the *Globe* figured that history had already been made. After all, it pointed out, Williamson's mark was "made in small parks which cannot be compared with those of the present day, and which makes Ruth's performances all the more remarkable."

Notes

1. Harry Bullion, "Paul Musser Finds Tigers Bad Seconds," *Detroit Free Press*, July 30, 1919: 12.
2. James O'Leary, "Ruth Gets His 16th Home Run of Season," *Boston Globe*, July 30, 1919: 6.
3. Bullion, "Paul Musser Finds Tigers Bad Seconds."
4. Ibid.
5. Ibid.
6. Ibid.
7. O'Leary, "Ruth Gets His 16th Home Run."
8. Bullion, "Paul Musser Finds Tigers Bad Seconds."
9. O'Leary, "Ruth Gets His 16th Home Run."
10. Ibid.
11. He would soon make more history: The Red Sox would release him before he made another appearance with them. In his first game with Cleveland, he would get struck by lightning on the mound, only to rise and finish a complete game. Then, his 1919 campaign having lacked sufficient excitement, he would throw a no-hitter in September.
12. O'Leary, "Ruth Gets His 16th Home Run."
13. Ibid.
14. Bullion, "Paul Musser Finds Tigers Bad Seconds."
15. Ibid.
16. Ibid.
17. He would finish with 29, then bash 54 in his first year with the Yankees in 1920.

The Babe's Walk-Off Round-Tripper Ties Season Home-Run Record

September 20, 1919: Boston 4, Chicago White Sox 3 (game one of doubleheader), at Fenway Park

By Gregory H. Wolf

For 35 seasons, Ned Williamson of the Chicago Cubs held the major-league record for home runs in a season. In 1884, when pitchers tossed from a 4-foot-by-6-foot box, the front of which was located 50 feet from home plate, Williamson walloped 27 round-trippers, during a season in which he and three of his teammates, Fred Pfeffer (25), Abner Dalrymple (22), and Cap Anson (21), became the first big leaguers to hit at least 20 round-trippers in a season. Only four additional players clouted at least 20 in one season until 1919, when Babe Ruth emerged as the greatest slugger in the history of the sport.[1]

After winning the World Series in 1916 and 1918, the Boston Red Sox slogged through a disappointing campaign in 1919. Skipper Ed Barrow's squad was in fifth-place (63-67), 22½ games behind their opponent, skipper Kid Gleason's eventual pennant-winning Chicago White Sox (87-46), as they prepared for a Saturday afternoon twin bill and final home contests of the season.

Despite the ominous late morning skies, a crowd estimated by sportswriter Burt Whitman of the *Boston Herald* to be 30,000 strong packed Fenway Park for a special occasion, Babe Ruth Day.[2] Fans were lined several deep in the outfield and cordoned off by rope while order was maintained by soldiers of the state guard. The celebration was sponsored by the Pere Marquette Council of the Knights of Columbus, a Catholic fraternal organization and mutual benefit society. Ruth himself was a member of the Council. An estimated 5,000 society members from throughout Massachusetts were on hand to cheer on their most famous representative.

Toeing the rubber for the Red Sox was none other than The Babe himself. The 24-year-old was once regarded as one of the best left-handed pitchers in baseball, winning 20 or more games in 1916 and 1917, leading the AL in ERA in 1916 (1.75), and owning a 3-0 record in the World Series, including a record 29⅔ consecutive scoreless innings (a record he held until Whitey Ford broke it in 1961). Despite his hurling successes, Ruth's home-run prowess was transforming baseball. In 1918 he transitioned into a legitimate two-way player, making 19 starts on the mound and a combined 70 in the field (left field, center, and first base) and led the AL with 11 home runs. Ruth's offensive juggernaut and assault on batting records in 1919 caught the attention of the nation, in need of distraction after the end of World War I. He was making his 15th start on the mound, though just third since the end of July, and sported a 9-5 slate (2.95 ERA). Few fans probably cared if Ruth's curves were snapping; they paid admission to see him take his mighty swings. The Babe began the day leading the big leagues in home runs (26), RBIs (108), slugging (.650), and on-base-percentage (.457).

The Red Sox got on the board first, in the bottom of the first inning against White Sox starter Lefty Williams, who had emerged this season as one of the best southpaws in the league. He was 23-9 and was coming off a sparkling two-hit shutout nine days earlier against the Washington Senators in the nation's capital. With two outs, the normally accurate Williams issued consecutive free passes to Braggo Roth and Ruth. Wally Shang followed with a hard grounder to shortstop Swede Risberg, who saved a run by knocking down the ball behind second, according to sportswriter I.E. Sanborn in the *Chicago Tribune*.[3] With the bases jammed, Stuffy McInnis lined a single to left to drive in two runs. The Red Sox tallied their third run on an attempted double steal. When Chicago catcher Ray Schalk threw to Risberg to nab McInnis, Schang broke for home and scored while McInnis was caught in a rundown and eventually tagged out.

Despite the rough first, Williams pitched "air tight" ball, opined Sanborn, permitting just two baserunners, both singles, from the second inning through the eighth.[4]

Ruth sent the Fenway crowd in a frenzied round of applause by striking out three batters in the third while working around a walk and single. The White Sox broke through in the fourth, led by Buck Weaver's leadoff double and Shoeless Joe Jackson's run-scoring single. Happy Felsch singled, and Ruth's errant throw to throw shortstop Everett Scott enabled both runners to move up a station. Chick Gandil's deep fly brought home Jackson. "The Gleasons wrecked themselves by poor baserunning," lamented Sanborn.[5] With Ruth laboring, Felsch was caught stealing third. Risberg followed with a single, then was picked off first by Ruth to end the frame.

Ruth was greeted by what Whitman described as a "rude display of power" in the sixth.[6] Weaver smashed a one-out double off the left-field fence and Shoeless Joe, en route to battling .351, beat out a single. Felsch's two-bagger drove in Weaver to tie the game, 3-3, and force Ruth from the mound. In came reliever Allen Russell, a midseason acquisition from the New York Yankees, while Ruth moved to left field, replacing Bill Lamar. Baserunning blunders, coupled with some heads-up defensive plays, kept the score tied. Shortstop Scott fielded Gandil's bounder up the middle and fired a strike to Schang to erase Jackson at the plate. With Risberg at bat, the White Sox' double steal backfired when Schang's rocket to third sacker Ossie Vitt easily beat a sliding Felsch for the final out.

Russell, a spitballing right-hander and the unsung hero of the game, tossed 3⅔ scoreless innings, walking one and fanning four. His strong performance set the stage for The Babe's heroics.

In the bottom of the ninth, Ruth strolled to the plate after Roth had been called out on strikes for the first out. Williams was cautious and threw a pitch "high and fast and on the outside," noted Whitman, adding that "they are afraid to pitch them close to Ruth, for fear that he will smack them over the right field bleacher."[7] It didn't matter. Ruth connected, sending the orb "clean over the left field fence," wrote Whitman, as the crowd burst into a euphoric yell.[8] A svelte Ruth circled the bases for the winning-run, 4-3, in a fairy-tale setting.

"Never will we forget the setting of that 27th circuit crash by the Colossus," gushed Whitman.[9]

Ruth's round-tripper tied Williamson for the most in a single season, but the excitement was far from over. During the short intermission between games of the doubleheader, the festivities honoring Ruth took place at home plate. The local council of

"The World's champion home-run slugger has entered the cigar manufacturing business and is learning it, as he learned baseball, from start to finish. He'll do in any box pitcher's box, batter's box or cigar box. Watch his smoke!" October 30, 1919. *Courtesy of Library of Congress.*

the Knight of Columbus presented Ruth with $600 in US Treasury bonds and a diamond-studded insignia, and also a box of cigars for his teammates. Ruth's wife, Helen, was presented a decorated travel bag.

To cap off what proved to be his last home game as a member of the Red Sox, Ruth supplied more heroics in the second game. [Ruth was sold to the Yankees in the offseason]. With the score tied, 4-4, Ruth smashed a double to deep right-center field, clearing the row of fans in the outfield and bouncing off the bleacher wall, according to the *Herald*.[10] Ruth thought it was a home run, as did other players, and a mini-protest erupted. Umpire Billy Evans finally ruled firmly that the ball was hit into the group of spectators and Ruth was permitted only a double.

Ruth subsequently scored the winning run on Mike McNally's grounder, which Risberg misplayed.

Sources

In addition to the sources cited in the Notes, the author also accessed Retrosheet.org, Baseball-Reference.com, and SABR.org.

Notes

1. Those four players were Sam Thompson (20 in 1889), Buck Freeman (25 in 1899), Frank Schulte (21 in 1911), and Gavvy Cravath (24 in 1915).
2. Burt Whitman, "Clouts of Mighty Babe Ruth Twice Tumble White Sox," *Boston Herald*, September 21, 1919: Sport 1.
3. I.E. Sanborn, "Boston Impedes Sox Dash to Flag by Winning Pair," *Chicago Tribune*, September 21, 1909: 17.
4. Ibid.
5. Ibid.
6. Whitman.
7. Ibid.
8. Ibid.
9. Ibid.
10. Ibid.

Babe Ruth Passes Ned Williamson's Homer Mark

September 24, 1919: New York Yankees 2, Boston Red Sox 1, at the Polo Grounds

By Glen Sparks

Babe Ruth wanted more money. The star pitcher and home-run hitter for the Boston Red Sox made $7,500 in 1918. He hoped to double that figure the following season. Ruth and Red Sox owner Harry Frazee, a theatrical producer, talked over a deal, the Babe deciding to hold out for top dollar. Both sides haggled even as spring training began in Florida. Finally, Ruth agreed to a three-year contract worth $10,000 per season. He had asked for more, but it was still a nice raise.

Ruth planned to give up his mound duties. "I'll win more games playing every day in the outfield than I will pitching every fourth day," he told reporters.[1] The left-hander had established himself as one of the game's top hurlers, compiling a career won-lost mark of 80-41 with a 2.09 ERA. He topped the American League with a 1.75 ERA in 1916. Red Sox manager Ed Barrow still wanted Ruth to pitch. The two had argued about this several times during 1918 when Ruth tied for the AL lead with 11 homers and went 13-7 on the mound. "If Ruth plays for the Red Sox in 1919," Barrow said during Babe's holdout, "he will probably pitch and pinch-hit."[2]

Another thing: Ruth stayed out late. Very late. Sometimes the entire night. Barrow insisted that the young ballplayer get some sleep. Stop breaking curfew, Barrow barked at The Babe. The skipper even talked hotel porters into turning snitch. "When he comes in tonight, you come to my room and tell me," Barrow said. "Wake me up."[3]

One early morning, not long after Ruth rejoined the team, Barrow confronted his ballplayer. A fight nearly broke out. The two men argued and argued. After another incident, Barrow suspended The Babe. Finally, he pleaded with the 24-year-old wunderkind, a man not quite an orphan as a child, but close enough. "I know you had it tough as a kid," Barrow said. "But don't you think it's time you straightened out and started leading a decent life now?"[4] The Babe, contrite, agreed.

Barrow made Ruth happy during spring training. Babe roamed the outfield and batted cleanup. He hit pitches as far as some had ever seen. He smashed one ball "more than 500 feet," according to a reporter.[5] Or, said some, "more than 600 feet."[6] Barrow said the ball traveled 579 feet.[7]

On opening day, Ruth smacked a home run and then fell into a terrific slump. His batting average dropped to .180 after he went 0-for-3 on May 26. Then he got hot. Ruth batted .385 in June and hit four home runs. He ripped nine more in July and passed Ralph "Socks" Seybold to claim the American League record. Seybold hit 16 home runs for the 1902 Philadelphia Athletics.

Ruth added seven more homers in August. He also knocked "Cactus" Gavvy Cravath out of the record books. Cravath, one the early players to come out of Southern California, set the "modern era" mark (post-1900) after hitting 24 home runs while playing for the 1915 Philadelphia Phillies. Next up, the Washington Senators' Buck Freeman, who established the pre-1900 record of 25 in 1899. Or so, most baseball experts believed. "This was considered the ultimate goal."[8] A diligent researcher discovered that Edward "Ned" Williamson once enjoyed an even bigger year than Freeman.

A compact (5-feet-11, 210 pounds), mustachioed infielder, Williamson knocked 27 home runs for the Chicago White Stockings of 1884. It didn't hurt that Williamson played home games at Lake Front Park, one of baseball's great bandboxes. The right-field fence stood just 215 feet from home plate, a cheap pop fly away. (Williamson, who died in 1894 from dropsy at the age of 36, set the single-season mark for doubles in 1883. Tip O'Neill of the St. Louis Browns broke that mark in 1887 when he recorded 52 two-base hits.)

Ruth, who "pitched in a regular turn in different stretches during the season,"[9] in addition to playing left field and a little first base, tied Williamson's mark on September 20 against the Chicago White Sox at Fenway Park. He broke the record four days later in the second game of a doubleheader against the New York Yankees. Boston won the first game, 4-0, at the Polo Grounds. Ruth went hitless in three at-bats, walked once and scored a run. The Yankees played "a listless game," according to the *New York Times*.[10] Sad Sam Jones hurled the shutout despite giving up five hits and walking nine batters. "Sam Jones was unable to control his sharp curve," the *Boston Globe* reported, "and it broke before it reached the plate, with the result that (catcher) Wally Schang was hopping around like a headless chicken."[11] The fifth-place Red Sox upped their record to 66-67; the third-place Yankees dropped to 74-59.

Nineteen-year-old Waite Hoyt started for Boston in the second game against 28-year-old Bob Shawkey. New York went ahead 1-0 in the second inning on Wally Pipp's single, a double by Del Pratt, and a run-scoring single by Duffy Lewis. Ruth lined out in his first at-bat and jogged to first after receiving an intentional walk in his second plate appearance. He "slammed" a Shawkey pitch in his third at-bat and should have gotten a triple. "But Ruth forgot to touch second base in his haste to get around and was declared out at the keystone sack."[12]

Boston trailed 1-0 in the ninth inning when Ruth once again stepped to the plate. "He was the first man up, and his huge frame was shaking with anxiety to swing his bat on something tangible," W.O. McGeehan wrote in the *New York Tribune*.[13] The *Times* reported, "Ruth stood firmly on his sturdy legs like the Colossus of Rhodes."[14] Shawkey's first pitch sailed "high and wide" and Ruth let it go by. Babe swung at the next offering, a big, slow curveball. He met the pitch and drove it deep and out of the ballpark. The *Daily News*, which called Ruth "the Boston Tarzan," described the record-breaking home run as "a wonder," adding, "It sailed far and high over the right-field stand. It was one of the longest hits ever seen at the Polo Grounds, if not the longest."[15] The *New York Times* agreed. "Ruth's glorious smash yesterday was the longest drive ever made at the Polo Grounds."[16]

The *Boston Globe* reported that "the 6,000 enthusiasts (at the Polo Grounds) who had watched the struggle arose and cheered the wonderful feat." Ruth's homer was, the *Globe* exclaimed, "unquestionably the most sensational batting achievement ever seen on the Polo Grounds." After the ball "soared upward like the flight of a hawk," it left the park and landed in Manhattan Field, "where it was retrieved by a little boy who disappeared with the trophy."[17]

Ruth's homer tied the game, 1-1. New York did not score in the bottom of the ninth. Hoyt and Shawkey continued battling in the extra innings. Ruth came to bat more time, in the 12th. He drove another Shawkey pitch into the air. "It looked as though it would climb into the 25-cent seats, but it fell inside and (Chick) Fewster (playing in center field) got it."[18] In the 13th, Pipp and Pratt combined again to produce a Yankee run. Pipp led off with a triple against Hoyt and sprinted home on Pratt's fly ball to Ruth in left field. The game lasted 4½ hours.[19]

Losing pitcher Hoyt (4-6 for the season so far) threw a "remarkable game,"[20] giving up five hits and none over one nine-inning stretch. On the other hand, "the Sox were hitting Shawkey (19-11) hard and often, and only the sharpest kind of fielding kept them from scoring at several stages of the play."[21]

Writers devoted most of their attention to Ruth. The *Daily News* declared him an "absolute monarch of major-league four-base clouters."[22] The *Boston Globe*, mentioning the recent controversy surrounding Freeman and Williamson, noted that Ruth "established a world's home-run record beyond all question, and one which may never be equaled."[23]

Sources

In addition to the sources cited in the Notes, the author used Baseball-Reference.com for player and team information.

Notes

1. Robert Creamer, *Babe: The Legend Comes to Life* (New York: Simon and Schuster, 1974), 187.
2. Ibid.
3. Creamer, 193.
4. Creamer, 195.
5. Creamer, 190.
6. Ibid.
7. Ibid.
8. Creamer, 201.
9. Leigh Montville, *The Big Bam* (New York: Doubleday, 2006), 89. Ruth went 9-5 with a 2.97 ERA in 1919. He threw 133⅓ innings. He pitched in only five more games in his career after 1919.
10. "Ruth Wallops Out His 28th Home Run," *New York Times*, September 25, 1919: 10.
11. "Ruth's 28th Homer Ties Count in Second," *Boston Globe*, September 25, 1919: 10.
12. Ibid.
13. W.O. McGeehan, "Babe Ruth Hits 28th Homer, Ball Clearing Roof of Stand," *New York Tribune*, September 25, 1919: 16.
14. "Ruth Wallops Out His 28th Home Run."
15. "Yankees Battle Thirteen Rounds for Even Break," *Daily News* (New York), September 25, 1919: 19.
16. "Ruth Wallops Out His 28th Home Run."
17. "Ruth's 28th Homer Ties Count in Second."
18. Ibid.
19. Ibid.
20. Ibid.
21. Ibid.
22. "Yankees Battle Thirteen Rounds for Even Break."
23. "Ruth Now Champion Home Run Swatter," *Boston Globe*, September 25, 1919: 10.

Babe Ruth's First Yankee Home Run is a "Colossal Clout" Against Red Sox

May 1, 1920: New York Yankees 6, Boston Red Sox 0, at Polo Grounds

by Mike Huber

As the second month of the 1920 season opened, the New York Yankees routed the Boston Red Sox at the Polo Grounds, 6-0, behind Babe Ruth's first home run as a New Yorker. The first-place Red Sox, coming into this contest with a record of 10-2-1, had beaten the Yankees (4-7) in their four previous meetings of the season. A crowd of 12,000 was on hand for the Sunday afternoon contest.[1] New York manager Miller Huggins sent Bob Shawkey to the mound to oppose Boston's Herb Pennock.

The Yankees scored in the bottom of the first. Aaron Ward drew a leadoff walk and moved to second base on a sacrifice by Roger Peckinpaugh. Wally Pipp's single to right plated Ward and gave Shawkey all the support he would need. However, the Yankees were not finished. In the fourth, Ruth slammed a double off of the right-field wall to start the inning. Duffy Lewis grounded out to first, advancing Ruth to third. Del Pratt then hit a ground ball to Boston's shortstop Everett Scott, who fired to first baseman Stuffy McInnis for the second out of the inning. Ruth "started down the third base line with the swing of Scott's arm and crossed the plate before McInnis could get the ball to [Roxy] Walters at the plate."[2] New York increased its lead to 2-0.

Throughout the early part of the game, a few of the Yankees were protesting the umpires' calls. Pitchers Carl Mays, Ernie Shore and Lefty O'Doul[3] all were heckling umpires Bill Dinneen and Dick Nallin. By the fifth inning, the bickering reached a level where the umpires stopped play, had a small conference and ejected all three of the Yankees players, sending them "from the bench to the Siberia of the club house,"[4] as the fans "yelled in soprano, alto, bass and baritone against the high-handed demonstration of the law of the diamond."[5] Pop bottles and papers were tossed onto the field.

In the sixth inning with one out, Ruth, the two-time reigning home run champion, "lambasted a home run high over the right field grand stand into Manhattan Field."[6] Babe's first home run of the season as a New York Yankee was labeled a "sockdolager."[7] According to *Dictionary.com*, a sockdolager is defined as "a heavy, finishing blow,"[8] which is fitting as the ball cleared the roof in right field and virtually sealed the home team's victory. In fact, the blow "seemed to dishearten the Sox."[9] The *New York Times* reported that "the ball flitted out of sight between the third and fourth flagstaffs on the top of the stand. Ruth smashed it over the same place when he broke the world's home run record last season."[10] The only other batter besides Ruth who had hit a ball over the right field grand stand was Joe Jackson in 1913. Lewis followed Ruth with a back-to-back blast, as he "belted the pellet into the left field stand."[11] The *Boston Globe* reported, "Hardly had the ovation to Ruth simmered when Duffy Lewis, another former Red Sox player, brought another wave of enthusiasm by smashing the spheroid into the left-field bleachers for another four-base clout."[12] The two home runs were on consecutive Pennock pitches, both "knee-high."[13]

The Yankees added to their advantage in the seventh frame "with a brace of markers."[14] Harry Harper relieved Pennock to start the inning and walked both Muddy Ruel and Shawkey. Ward lifted a fly ball out to center, allowing Ruel to scamper to third. Boston manager Ed Barrow made the call to the bullpen and brought in Gary Fortune. Peckinpaugh greeted the third Boston hurler with an RBI single, sending Shawkey to third base. Pipp walked and Ruth rolled a grounder to first which enabled Shawkey to score. Harper was charged with the two runs in one-third of an inning pitched, but "every pitcher that Barrow sent to the mound was bombarded in heartless manner."[15]

The game lasted two hours and five minutes and the fans went home talking about Ruth's colossal clout they had witnessed. According to the *Boston Globe*, "a good time was had by all, save the Sox."[16] With the 6-0 final score, Boston was "certainly slaughtered to make a Yankee holiday, and the chief cause of the jubilation was the fact that the great Babe Ruth found his batting eye."[17] In addition to the four-bagger, Ruth had a double, two runs batted in and two runs scored in his four plate appearances. Ruel and Ping Bodie each had two hits for New York as well.

Shawkey limited the Red Sox hitters to just four hits, all singles, in the shut-out. A total of 16 Boston batters made fly ball outs. For the Red Sox, only Harry Hooper reached second base, after he had singled in the top of the ninth. Shawkey issued one free pass and struck out four. He raised his record to 1-3 and lowered his ERA to 1.56. Pennock earned his first loss of the season. New York batters touched him for eight hits, including the two home runs, and four earned runs in six innings.

The Yankees won three of five against Boston in this series. At the end of May, the Yankees swept four more games from the Red Sox, causing them to drop from first place, and Boston never recovered, ending the 1920 campaign in fifth place with a record of 72-81-1. After losing the first four meetings of the year against Boston, New York finished the season with a 13-9 mark against the Red Sox. Unfortunately, their season record of 95-59 was only good for third place in the American League, three games behind the pennant-winning Cleveland Indians and a game back of the Chicago White Sox.

Ruth homered the next night as well, and he went on to smack 12 homers in the month of May. Ten of his record-breaking 54 round-trippers in 1920 came against his old club, the Red Sox. He broke his 1919 record of 29 homers before the month of July was finished and became the first player to hit 30, 40 and 50 home runs in a single season.

Sources

In addition to the sources mentioned in the Notes, the author consulted baseball-reference.com and retrosheet.org. The author sincerely thanks Ms. Lisa Tuite of the *Boston Globe* for providing newspaper accounts.

Notes

1 The *Boston Globe* reported that the crowd was 15,000.

2 *New York Times*.

3 In 1920, O'Doul appeared in two games for the Yankees as a relief pitcher and in one game playing centerfield. In ten other games, he was used as a pinch-hitter and did not play the field.

4 *New York Times*.

5 Ibid.

6 Ibid.

7 Ibid.

8 dictionary.com/browse/sockdolager. Accessed August 2017.

9 "Ruth and Lewis Clout Homers as Yankees Win," *Boston Globe*, May 2, 1920: 16.

10 *New York Times*.

11 "Ruth Makes His First Homer And Yankees Beat Red Sox," *Brooklyn Daily Eagle*, May 2, 1920: 67.

12 *Boston Globe*.

13 *Brooklyn Daily Eagle*.

14 Ibid.

15 *Boston Globe*.

16 Ibid.

17 Ibid.

Bambino Homers on Babe Ruth Day at the Polo Grounds

July 9, 1920: New York Yankees 9, Detroit Tigers 3, at the Polo Grounds

By Stew Thornley

New York's American League team, known as the Highlanders in the earliest years before morphing into the Yankees, was mostly moribund in its first decade and a half. Only twice, in 1904 and 1906, did it even challenge for the flag. The Yanks finished third in 1919, 7½ games behind the pennant-winning Chicago White Sox and 4 behind the second-place Cleveland Indians.

The Yankees battled these teams again in 1920, but this time their arsenal employed a new weapon. They had purchased a pitcher-turned-hitter, Babe Ruth, who had set the single-season home-run record of 29 with the Boston Red Sox just months earlier.

Playing half his games at the homer-friendly Polo Grounds, Ruth was transforming baseball and attracting fans to see him; the Yankees more than doubled their home attendance from 1919. Ruth was also on a tear to shatter his not-even-a-year-old home-run record.

In early July the Yankees made a road trip to Philadelphia and Washington. Ruth used his own car to get to the cities, and the Yankees concluded with a 17-0 win over the Washington Senators on July 6, putting them in first place by one game over Cleveland.

The team headed home to start a series against the Detroit Tigers. For the journey from Washington to New York, Ruth was accompanied in his car by his wife, Helen, teammates Fred Hofmann and Frank Gleich, and coach Charley O'Leary. In the early hours of Wednesday, July 7, the group was outside Wawa, Pennsylvania, west of Philadelphia, when the car went off the road and overturned.

Reports vary as to whether the occupants were thrown from the car or pinned underneath. The *Philadelphia Inquirer* reported, "By a herculean effort, Ruth tilted the car sufficiently to permit his wife to crawl from beneath. Then the three ball players crawled out and then raised the motor high enough to permit Ruth to be pulled from beneath it." The party went to a nearby farmhouse, then walked a mile to Wawa, took a 5:34 A.M. train to Philadelphia and, from there, another train to New York. As for the car, it was towed away with Ruth giving instructions to sell it.[1]

The Yankees had the day off on July 7, leaving time for Ruth's banged-up knee to heal as the team prepared for the beginning of a 21-game homestand. While the knee ached, Ruth was hampered more by a sore left wrist, which he hurt while sliding in the Washington series.

Another injured star, an opponent, drove in the winning run in the Yankees' first game back home. On July 8 Ty Cobb pinch-hit and singled in the ninth to lead Detroit past New York and knock the Yankees out of first place. It was Cobb's first time up since he hurt his knee on June 6.

The Knights of Columbus honored Ruth, one of their own, before the July 9 game. Ruth had become a Knight – with the Pere Marquette Council in South Boston – while he was with the Red Sox.[2] It wasn't unusual for Knights councils in New York, and perhaps elsewhere, to honor him. For this Babe Ruth Day in New York, a local council presented him with a diamond-studded watch fob while the Knights of Columbus band played.[3]

The game began at 3:30 with 37-year-old Jack Quinn[4] on the mound for the Yankees. The only baserunner he allowed through the first two innings came on a throwing error by third baseman Bob Meusel. However, in the third, Detroit shortstop Donie Bush squeezed home Eddie Ainsmith to give the Tigers a 1-0 lead.

In the bottom of the inning, Red Oldham retired Quinn but then walked Chick Fewster and hit Sammy Vick with a pitch. Wally Pipp hit a grounder behind second base. Shortstop Bush fielded it and tried to step on second in time to force Vick, but umpire George Hildebrand called the runner safe.[5] Bush argued and pushed Hildebrand, but somehow didn't get ejected. However, second baseman Ralph Young was tossed out when he kicked his glove into center field.

Bob Jones took Young's spot at second as Ruth stepped in with the bases loaded and one out. Ruth hit a line drive to right that handcuffed Harry Heilmann, who dropped the ball. Heilmann recovered in time to throw to Bush and force Pipp at second, while Fewster came in from third to tie the game. The official scorer determined that Heilmann would have been charged with an error had he not forced out Pipp, so Ruth did not get a hit. The scorer also judged that had Heilmann caught the ball, Fewster could have tagged and scored. As a result, under the scoring rules, Ruth was credited with a sacrifice.[6]

Meusel was the next batter, and he pounded a three-run homer into the lower stands in right field that broke the tie and put the Yankees ahead 4-1. The lead went to 5-1 in the fourth as Fewster singled in Del Pratt, and Ruth led off the fifth.

Ruth hit the ball even harder than in his previous at-bat and this time did it with more lift, sailing it into the upper deck in right. William B. Hanna in *The Sun and New York Herald* described the home runs in this way: "The Babe and Meusel were knocking them out of their seats. There is more truth than metaphor in that statement. The Babe spilled a home run against a pillar in the upper stand and had the fans up there dodging, and Meusel made them scatter in the third inning, when he lifted a homer into the lower stand."[7]

The home run was Ruth's 25th of the season, putting him within four of the major-league record he had set the year before. As he came around the bases, he tipped his hat toward the stands where the Knights of Columbus were seated.[8]

Meusel wasn't done yet. The Yankees put a run across in the sixth with Pipp on second and Ruth, having walked, on first when Meusel drove a double to right-center, scoring both runners and completing the New York scoring.

The Yankees threatened in the eighth despite losing two runners on the bases, Fewster when he was caught stealing and Pipp when he was thrown out trying to stretch a single. Vick stood on third when Ruth came up, and the fans hoped for another home run. The Sultan of Swat hit a shot that went over the right-field roof but not before the wind blew it foul. He then grounded out.

New York took a 9-1 lead into the ninth, but Quinn had some trouble getting the final three outs. Bobby Veach led off by reaching base when Fewster made a low throw to first on his grounder. Heilmann tripled to score Veach, although he also hurt his ankle on the play and was replaced by pinch-runner Larry Woodall, who came home on a groundout by Babe Ellison.

Babe Pinelli got on with a bunt single and went to second when Quinn threw the ball away. The Tigers were down to their number-eight hitter, and Polo Grounds fans began clamoring for Cobb. However, Ainsmith hit for himself and grounded out. Once more the calls went out for a pinch-hitting appearance by Cobb, but instead Ira Flagstead came up for Oldham and grounded out to end the game.

"Old Jack Quinn, who is maturing gracefully, which same his pitching proves, slid and sped the ball past the couchant Tigers with such effect that they had little chance to win," wrote Hanna in the *Sun and Herald* of the right-hander's performance.[9]

The Yankees stayed a half-game out of first as Cleveland also won. They battled in a three-way race with the Indians and White Sox and stood atop the league for a few days in mid-September.

New York dropped out of first after being swept in a three-game series with the White Sox, and finished in third place, three games behind Cleveland and one behind Chicago. Ruth broke his own record with a seemingly insurmountable 54 home runs.

But as the Roaring Twenties would demonstrate, nothing would be insurmountable for Ruth, the Yankees, and baseball.

Notes

1   "Babe Ruth Hurt When Auto Upset," *Philadelphia Inquirer,* July 8, 1920: 16.

2   Michael O'Loughlin, "For Babe Ruth, Catholicism Was a Lifelong Pursuit," *Crux,* February 5, 2016, cruxnow.com/faith/2016/02/05/for-babe-ruth-catholicism-was-a-lifelong-pursuit.

3   "Ruth Makes 25th and Yankees Win," *New York Times,* July 10, 1920: 8.

4   In his biography of Jack Quinn at sabr.org/bioproj/person/cf88d73c, Charles F. Faber discusses the uncertainty of Quinn's age, especially during his career. Faber says the most likely birth date is July 5, 1883, for Quinn, who pitched beyond his 50th birthday.

5   Newspaper accounts vary on whether Vick beat Bush to the base or whether Bush missed the base.

6   Ruth had hit a sacrifice fly under the rules, although sacrifices and sacrifice flies were not then distinguished in separate categories.

7   William B. Hanna, "Meusel's Batting Helps in Winning," *The Sun and New York Herald,* July 10, 1920: 5.

8   Robert W. Creamer, *Babe: The Legend Comes to Life* (New York: Simon and Schuster, 1974), 232.

9   Hanna.

Babe Ruth Knocks Two Home Runs to Move Record over 30

July 19, 1920: Chicago White Sox 8, New York Yankees 5 (second game of doubleheader), at Polo Grounds, New York

By Tim Rask

With two months left in the 1920 season, the New York Yankees and the Chicago White Sox were both in the thick of the American League pennant race. The Yankees began the day in second place, 1½ games behind the front-running Cleveland Indians. The defending AL champion White Sox lurked in third place, 5½ games off the pace.

The Yankees and White Sox were in the middle of a six-game series on Monday, July 19. The series included two doubleheaders on July 19 and 20 to make up for weather postponements during Chicago's previous visit to New York in May. The Yankees had taken the first two games of the series over the weekend, but the bigger story was that Babe Ruth had not hit any home runs, his last circuit clout having come against the Browns' Bill Burwell on July 15.

The Monday doubleheader between the Yankees and White Sox attracted a packed house to the Polo Grounds,[1] although the pennant race was a secondary concern to many of the fans. The "two games were mere incidents. They were waiting for the breaking of the world's record, so they could say that they were there when the Colossus of Swat swung and hid the achievements of the Ansons, the Delahantys, the Brouthers[es], the Freemans and all the others further in the dim mists."[2]

The Yankee faithful had some anxious moments prior to the game when a localized burst of rain showers struck northern Manhattan about a half-hour before the scheduled 1:30 P.M. starting time, and it appeared that the two teams might be able to squeeze in only a single contest that afternoon. After assessing the state of the grounds, Yankees manager Miller Huggins determined that the doubleheader could begin at 2:00 P.M.

The Yankees won the first game, 8-2, behind the stellar pitching of Bob Shawkey, who made his first start since suffering an injury in St. Louis on June 23. Ruth, however, disappointed the crowd by failing to homer in the Yankees victory.

In the second game, the Yankees sent left-hander Herb Thormahlen to the mound to oppose the White Sox' diminutive southpaw Dickey Kerr. The throng at the Polo Grounds was again frustrated as Kerr walked Ruth in the scoreless first inning and the wait for home run number 30 continued.

The White Sox scored the game's first run in the second with their own slugging star, Shoeless Joe Jackson, clouting a home run into the right-field stands. "This made some of the spectators a little impatient," reported W.O. McGeehan of the *New York Tribune*. "They began to inquire when the Babe would give them a home run for their price of admission."[3]

Ruth finally rewarded the patience of Yankees rooters when he came up again in the bottom of the fourth inning. After a single by first baseman Wally Pipp led off the inning, Babe put the Yankees on the board. Kerr tried to sneak a curveball past the big slugger and "there was a resounding smack as bat met ball and the noise from the stand swelled in volume before the ball started its descent. Every last fan knew that this was the much awaited punch. Nemo Leibold, playing a deep right field for the Wizard of Wallop, backed until his shoulders rubbed against the fence of the right field bleachers and then he gazed upward as the ball sailed over his head. It wasn't the longest hit Ruth has made into this section, but it was longer than any other ball player ever has hit at the Polo Grounds."[4] Baseball scribe William Hanna commented, "It was a drive worthy of the creation of a new record and of the longest and hardest hitter since time was."[5]

The Bambino reveled in his home run and egged on the raucous crowd, according to the *New York Times*. "While the fans howled in glee, tossed hats around the stand in reckless abandon and made the big stand a mass of waving arms, Ruth completed his journey to the plate and then beamed back with a smile that spurred the crowd on to great exertion, if that were possible. Doffing his cap, the conventional response which usually stills a cheering crowd of fans, had no effect here. Several times on his way to the bench Ruth bowed his acknowledgments, but the din continued after he disappeared in the dugout. His march to the left field at the close of the inning was the signal for another outburst, and the applause was renewed when he came in after the White Sox had been retired in the fourth inning."[6]

Then Yankees tacked on another run in the bottom of the sixth when Roger Peckinpaugh led off the inning with a single and was plated by a triple from second baseman Del Pratt. Ruth was unable to score Pratt from third, as Kerr got a measure of revenge by striking out the slugger, but the home team still held a 3-1 lead going into the seventh and seemed well on its way to sweeping the doubleheader.

Things began to turn south for Yankees starter Thormahlen in the top of the seventh. He opened by walking Hap Felsch, then gave up a single to right field by Shano Collins. Swede Risberg promptly drove in Felsch with a single. One out later, Risberg stole second base, and with men on second and third, Dickey Kerr hit a grounder to third, but catcher Truck Hannah dropped the throw from third sacker Aaron Ward, allowing Collins to score the tying run. A double-steal attempt fizzled when Risberg was called out but Nemo Leibold extended the inning with a scratch single past Ward and Eddie Collins followed by singling home Kerr with the go-ahead run.

The White Sox used "small ball" tactics again in the eighth inning to great success and broke the game open with an assist from some more Yankee miscues. Singles from Jackson, Felsch, and Shano Collins loaded the bases to start the inning, prompting Miller Huggins to summon Ernie Shore from the bullpen to try to put out the fire. Shore uncorked a wild pitch that allowed Shoeless Joe to score Chicago's fifth run. One out later, Shore misplayed Ray Schalk's bunt when the pitcher's "feet became entangled, throwing him for a big loss."[7] The result was Schalk safe at first with Felsch scoring on the play. Kerr laid down a sacrifice bunt, and a double steal scored Collins when Hannah's attempt to nail Schalk at second base went to center field. Leibold singled home Schalk to cap the four-run inning and the White Sox held an 8-3 lead.

The Yankees' Roger Peckinpaugh responded with a leadoff homer in the bottom of the frame, although "the assassins of Murderers Row did not follow him"[8] and the Yankees went into the ninth trailing 8-4.

Ruth's final chance at individual glory game in the bottom of the ninth, and Babe cracked a solo shot into the lower tier of right-field stands for his 31st homer of the season "although the homer only added to the string of the Babe and did not take the Yanks anywhere." The *Times* described an almost melancholy scene, reporting "there was no joy for Babe as he jogged around the bases and back to the bench on the second homer. It arrived when the Yanks were defeated, and that always serves to take interest out of the circuit hits for Ruth, much as the fans revel in such performances, whether the Yanks are winning or losing."[9]

The Yankees would continue to experience plenty of wins in 1920, and Babe would continue to raise the bar for the season's home-run record. The team remained in a three-way pennant chase with Cleveland and Chicago until the end of the season, and eventually finish third behind the Indians and White Sox. Babe took the home-run mark past 40, then 50, finally finishing the season with 54.

W.O. McGeehan of the *Tribune* reported that The Babe's 30th home run earned Ruth a film contract worth $100,000,[10] and indeed Ruth would make his movie debut that fall in the silent film *Headin' Home*. Babe was well on his way to becoming an American pop-culture icon.

The Chicago White Sox went on to become icons of a sort as well. Late in the following season, reports would link them with gamblers and a conspiracy to throw the 1919 World Series. Eight members of the club would go down in history as the Black Sox.

Sources

In addition to the sources cited in the Notes, the author also consulted Baseball-Reference.com, Retrosheet.org, and the following:

Crusinberry, James. "Ruth Breaks His Record Twice as Sox Split Even, *Chicago Tribune*, July 20, 1920: 5.

Hanna, William. "Ruth Hits Two More Home Runs, Increasing His Total to Thirty-One and Setting a New High Record, *The Sun* and *New York Herald*, July 20, 1920: 11.

Somerville, Charles. "Ruth Gets Two Homers, Breaking World's Record, but Yanks Lose Game," *New York Evening World,* July 20, 1920: 19.

Notes

1. Reports of the attendance vary. Retrosheet and Baseball Reference box scores cite 20,000, while contemporary newspapers pegged the attendance higher. The *Chicago Tribune* reported 25,000, the *New York Tribune* 26,000, the *Sun and New York Herald* 27,000, and the *New York Times*, 28,000.

2. W.O. McGeehan, "Ruth Breaks Home Run Record, Wins $100,000 Film Contract," *New York Herald*, July 20, 1920.

3. Ibid.

4. "Babe Sets Record, Then Adds Another," *New York Times*, July 20, 1920: 8.

5. McGeehan.

6. "Babe Sets Record, Then Adds Another."

7. McGeehan.

8. Ibid.

9. "Babe Sets Record, Then Adds Another."

10. McGeehan. Jane Leavy reports that the contract was for $50,000 and, further, "He got $15,000 up front and got stiffed for the rest when the producers went belly-up." Jane Leavy, *The Big Fella* (New York: Harper, 2018), 228, 229.

Ruth Smacks 50th HR

September 24, 1920: Washington Senators 3, New York Yankees 1 (first game of doubleheader), at Polo Grounds V

By Paul Hofmann

When Babe Ruth was traded to the New York Yankees by Boston Red Sox owner Harry Frazee in January 1920, he was already the most feared slugger in the game. He led the American League in home runs for the first time in 1918 with 11 and in 1919 he established a new single-season record for home runs with 29, surpassing the 35-year-old record of 27 held by Ned Williamson.[1] After breaking Williamson's record, Ruth began to publicly express his home-run goal for the 1920 season: "A half-century."[2]

When Ruth first announced he would hit 50 home runs, "wise baseball men tapped themselves on the head, winked an eye and said that Babe was cookoo in the attic."[3] Only two short years earlier, the idea of anyone hitting 50 home runs in a single major-league baseball season was as unfathomable as sending a man to the moon. But this was the start of the Roaring Twenties, a decade of innovation in America, and Ruth was singlehandedly ushering in the Live Ball Era.

With seven games to play, and no remaining games against the front-running Indians, the Yankees were in need of some help as they clung to their slim pennant hopes. They entered the game in third place with a 90-57 record, 2½ games behind the first-place Cleveland Indians and two games behind the Chicago White Sox, who were grabbing headlines as the plot to fix the

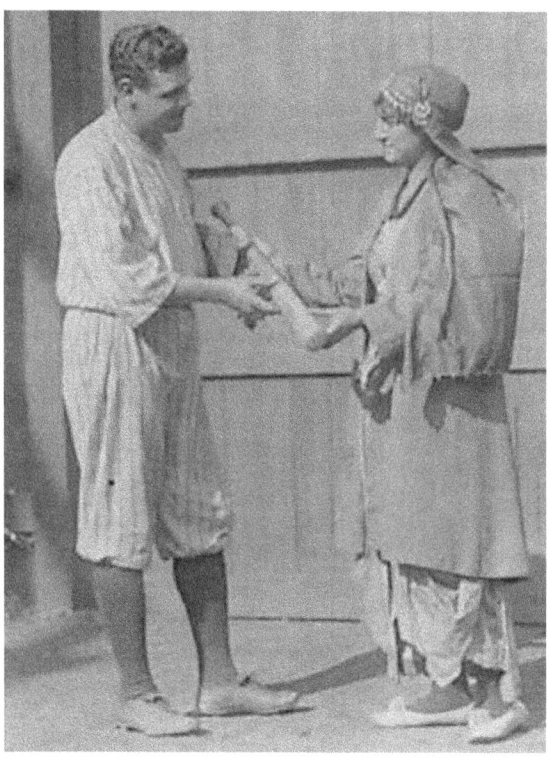

Ruth presented his 50th home run bat to Ms. Nouvart Dzeron Koshkarian, a representative of the Near East Relief Fund. *Courtesy of Hratch Harry Hannessian and the Armenian Genocide Museum.*

1919 World Series was made public for the first time that same day in testimony given to a Cook County, Illinois, Grand Jury.[4] Meanwhile, the Senators were 62-78, 27 games off the pace and looking ahead toward the next season.

The Friday afternoon opener featured a pitching matchup between the Yankees' 28-year-old veteran Carl Mays and the Senators' 29-year-old rookie José Acosta. Mays, a five-time 20-game winner with 207 career victories, is best remembered for his role in major-league baseball's only on-field fatality. A little more than six weeks earlier, on August 16, 1920, Mays had thrown the pitch that led to the death of Cleveland shortstop Ray Chapman. The 5-foot-11 right-hander with the submarine delivery entered the game with a record of 25-10 and a 3.15 ERA. Acosta, a right-handed hurler from Cuba, was making just the fifth start of his career. The 5-foot-6, 135-pound Acosta had been with the Senators since July and was 3-4 with a 4.72 ERA.

Ruth's prediction of 50 was no longer a remote possibility; he had 49 home runs.

An unseasonably warm September afternoon welcomed 28,000 fans who flocked to the Polo Grounds for the primary purpose of seeing Ruth hit his 50th home run, and maybe another, and the secondary purpose of watching the Yankees play a doubleheader against the Senators.[5] The large crowd included the band from the St. Mary's School of Industrial Arts in Baltimore, where Ruth grew up from the time he was 6 until he was 19, when he left to join the International League's Baltimore Orioles. The throng also included members of the Brooklyn Dodgers and New York Giants, who had an offday, and a large contingent of Cuban fans who turned out in support of Acosta.[6] The temperature was nearly 80 degrees when the Yankees ran onto the field for the opener and continued and rise to a high of 83, 19 degrees higher than the 64-degree average for Upper Manhattan that time of year.

Mays and the Yankees got off to a shaky start in the top of the first. Joe Judge opened the inning when his hit bounded over the head of Ruth in center field for a triple.[7] Bucky Harris followed with a walk. With runners at the corners and no one down, Sam Rice doubled to right to score Judge. Harris, attempting to score on the play, was thrown out at the plate when Aaron Ward relayed the throw from right fielder Bob Meusel to Truck Hannah. Right fielder Braggo Roth followed with a single to advance Rice to third. Rice came in to score when Yankees catcher Hannah wildly sailed his throw into center field while trying to catch Roth attempting to steal second. Things seemed to be unraveling on the Yankees before Mays pulled himself together and fanned left fielder Howie Shanks to end the inning.

All things considered, Mays and the Yankees were fortunate to get out of the inning trailing only 2-0.

After Acosta retired Ward to start the bottom of the first, a short delay temporarily interrupted the building excitement. With Wally Pipp at the plate, a foul tip caught home-plate umpire Tommy Connolly on the leg and delayed the game for five minutes while he "hopped around on one leg like a stork."[8] After Pipp was retired, the crowd began to buzz in anticipation as Ruth strode to the plate.

The Bambino didn't keep the fans in suspense very long. The count was three balls and two strikes when Ruth straightened out one of "Senor Acosta's shoots" and delivered his 50th home run of the season.[9] It was a typically majestic Ruthian blast that ricocheted off the grandstand roof in right field and bounced toward the infield, sending the fans into hysteria. The crowd gave Babe a tremendous ovation as he traveled over the plate "smiling a smile as broad as his massive shoulders and raising his cap to the populace."[10] The long awaited 50th home run had come to pass and the crowd celebrated an occasion of human achievement – the accomplishment of something once thought impossible.

After Ruth's blast, Acosta "closed like a clam."[11] Despite walking six batters, the diminutive Senators pitcher limited the Yankees to three additional hits. Duffy Lewis opened the bottom of the second with a single over short, but he was forced at second before Roger Peckinpaugh and Hannah fouled out to Judge at first to end the inning. The left-handed-hitting Mays singled over first to lead off the third, but was cut down when he attempted to stretch the hit into a double. Lewis collected his second hit of the day with a single in the ninth. The Yankees, unable to come up with a big hit, stranded seven baserunners. The victory moved Acosta to 4-4.

The Senators added a run in the sixth. Harris singled to center and when Ruth inexplicably threw the ball to Pipp at first, Harris alertly advanced to second. Rice attempted to sacrifice Harris to third, but by the time Mays fielded the bunt and tossed the ball to Ward, the Senators second baseman had safely beaten the throw. Roth delivered his second RBI of the day when he sent a fly ball to deep left that allowed Harris to trot home with the game's final run.

Mays went the distance and gave up three runs, all earned, on eight hits. He walked one and struck out five as he dropped to 25-11 for the season. Three days later he tossed a six-hit shutout against the A's at Philadelphia to end his season at 26-11.

Ruth had three attempts to extend his home run record to 51. In the fourth inning he grounded to Judge, who threw to Acosta covering first. The Yankees center fielder walked in the sixth and later grounded out to Harris at second base in the eighth. Number 51 would have to wait, for now.

The loss, coupled with the Indians' 2-0 shutout of the White Sox, dropped the Yankees 3½ games behind the Indians. With only six games remaining on the schedule, the afternoon's nightcap was a must-win for Ruth and the Yankees. They did win the game, 2-1, scoring the winning run in the bottom of the ninth inning. Ruth was 4-for-4 in the game, and hit his 51st home run – a solo shot – off Jim Shaw in the first inning. The Yankees didn't score again until the bottom of the ninth, but got their win, 2-1.

Ruth, who himself was abandoned as a child, had a lifelong love for children and his commitment to help disadvantaged children around the world was well documented. After the game Ruth gifted his 50th-home-run bat to Nouvart Dzeron Koshkarian, a noted Armenian singer and artist and representative of the Near East Relief Fund.[12] The bat was to be auctioned off to benefit the Armenian orphans who had survived the Armenian Genocide of 1915.[13]

Sources

In addition to the sources cited in the Notes, the author also relied on Baseball-reference.com and Retrosheet.org.

Notes

1. Williamson's 27 home runs in 1884 were largely attributed to the fact that Chicago played its home games in White Stocking Park (a.k.a. Lake Front Park). In 1884 the park's dimensions were 180 feet down the line to left, 280 to left-center, 300 to dead center field, 252 to right-center, and 196 down the line to right. The right-handed-hitting Williamson hit 25 of his 27 home runs at White Stocking Park and never hit more than nine home runs in any other season.

2. Jacob Pomrenke, "Two of a Kind," National Baseball Hall of Fame, Retrieved from baseballhall.org/discover-more/stories/baseball-history/ruth-back-to-back-records.

3. "Ruth Crashes Out Homers 50 and 51: Mauling Monarch Passes Half-Century Mark," *New York Times*, September 25, 1920: 9.

4. "Grand Jury Hears World Series Plot," *New York Times*, September 25, 1920: 9.

5. Ajax, "Babe Ruth's Record Now 51; Yankees Get Even Break," *Daily News* (New York), September 25, 1920: 36.

6. "Curves and Bingles," *New York Times*, September 25, 1920: 9.

7. Multiple contemporary newspaper accounts of the game credit Judge with a triple in the first inning. While researching this game, the author discovered three unique box scores with only one crediting Judge with a triple. Play-by-play data for this game is unavailable on Retrosheet.org and Baseball-Reference.com.

8. "Curves and Bingles."

9. W.O. McGeehan, "Babe's 50th Fails to Win, But His 51st Turns Trick," *New York Tribune*, September 25, 1920: 10.

10. "Ruth Crashes Out Homers 50 and 51."

11. Ibid.

12. Nouvart Dzeron Koshikarian was born in the province of Harpoot, Armenia. At an early age, she was brought to the United States by her parents, who had been forced to flee Turkish persecution. A successful professional painter in her adult life, she abandoned her career and devoted her time to spreading awareness about the atrocities that had occurred against the Armenian people.

13. "Curves and Bingles."

...and then 51

September 24, 1920: New York Yankees 2, Washington Senators 1 (second game of doubleheader), at Polo Grounds V

By Paul Hofmann

With Babe Ruth's 50th home run of the year in the record books, newspaper accounts of the game celebrated the accomplishment in a manner that suggested it might be a once-in-a-lifetime event. The *Chicago Tribune* wrote, "Such batting as Babe Ruth has done this season never before has been accomplished. Perhaps it never will be accomplished again – if Babe Ruth does not do it."[1] The *New York Times* opined, "Babe Ruth placed himself upon a pedestal in the baseball world from which no landlord living can evict him."[2]

Indeed, in less than a full season with the New York Yankees, the 25-year-old Ruth was well on his way to becoming America's first sports superstar. Tommy Henrich, an all-star outfielder with the New York Yankees, was a 7-year-old in Massillon, Ohio, in 1920. Henrich later recalled the New York phenomenon that captivated a nation, "Babe Ruth went to the Yankees, (in) 1920. And now, no radio, no nothing you still heard of Babe Ruth."[3]

Accolades aside, the season was not yet over. The Yankees had yet to be mathematically eliminated and there was another game to play that afternoon and six games remaining in the season. This also meant that there were six more games in which Ruth could add to his jaw-dropping home-run total.

Ruth Hit Two Homers, Pitches, Strikes Out Cobb and Sets Record

"Ruth Hit Two Homers..." headline: *Buffalo Commercial,* June 14, 1921: 6.

After a sloppy performance in which they dropped the first game of the doubleheader, 3-1, to the Senators earlier in the afternoon, the Yankees now found themselves 3½ games behind the front-running Cleveland Indians. In a nutshell, the Yankees were in a must-win situation as they entered the nightcap.

The Yankees turned to rookie right-hander Rip Collins to keep the season alive. Collins had enjoyed an excellent season in which he had been used as often in relief as he was as a starter. He entered the game with a record of 13-8 and a 3.34 ERA. The Senators countered with veteran right-hander Jim Shaw. Perhaps suffering from the newly imposed major-league ban on trick pitches like his sailer, Shaw got off to a 0-4 season start with an ERA above 9.00 and did not post a victory until June 20.[4] He pitched better during the second half of the season and entered the game 10-16 with a 4.41 ERA.

The game started with Collins throwing a scoreless frame in the top of the first. Just as was the case in the opener, Ruth came to the plate in the bottom of the inning with the bases empty and two down. And, just as he did in the opener, Ruth delivered a home run, walloping a Shaw offering "high over the head of Robert Roth into the right field bleachers about midway of the yellow cigarette sign."[5] The home run was Ruth's ninth first-inning homer of the year and his second of the season off Shaw.[6] Ruth had victimized Shaw on August 14 at Griffith Stadium in Washington.

Ruth's 51st home run of the season was the 100h home run of his major-league career. Given that the career record for home runs at this time was 138 by Roger Connor, the speed at which Ruth reached 100 was awe-inspiring. The *New York Times* put the Bambino's feat into context as follows: "This is remarkable when it is considered that most of the time he has been a pitcher. Hans Wagner played ball for twenty-one years before he made 100 home runs."[7] The *Daily News* noted, "In the middle of the season the odds were 10 to 1 and longer that Babe would not boost his home run total over fifty."[8]

Collins, "wilder than a Texas steer,"[9] lasted just three innings, scattering three hits and walking two, and retired after he turned his ankle while attempting to field an infield dribbler off the bat of Sam Rice. Tom Connelly, making his major-league debut and only appearance of the season, batted for Collins in the bottom of the third before Miller Huggins summoned left-hander Herb Thormahlen from the bullpen to start the fourth.[10]

The Senators broke through against Thormahlen in the top of the sixth. Roth led off the inning with a single to left and was sacrificed to second by Frank Ellerbee. Thormahlen walked Howie Shanks and Frank O'Rourke followed with a single that appeared to be a tailor-made double-play ball but went through Aaron Ward at third to score Roth. Just when it appeared that the Senators were poised to take the lead, Patsy Gharrity abruptly ended the uprising by hitting into an inning-ending double play.

The Yankees threatened again in the bottom of the sixth. With two outs and one on, Ruth singled to right. Second baseman Del Pratt followed with a single to short and Duffy Lewis walked to load the bases. Bob Meusel was at plate when Ruth "took the situation into his own hands and tried to steal home."[11] Ruth was out at the plate. It was the second time he had been caught stealing in the game. He was also thrown out trying to steal second after he singled in the fourth inning.

The game remained tied 1-1 until Ruth opened the bottom of the ninth with a double that landed just inside the right-field foul line. Undeterred after being caught stealing twice earlier in the game, Ruth took a big lead off second and enticed Gharrity to attempt to pick him off. The ball sailed into center field and Ruth galloped to third. Pratt followed with his third hit of the day, a single to left-center, scoring Ruth with the game-winning run.

Ruth finished the game 4-for-4 with two singles, a double, a home run, and two runs scored. He factored into all three Yankees runs in the two games and went 5-for-8 with two home runs, two RBIs, and three runs scored in the doubleheader. The three runs he scored in the two games extended his single-season American League record for runs scored to 154.[12]

Seated in the left-field stands was the band from St. Mary's Industrial School in Baltimore, who were there as Ruth's guests. In 1919 a fire destroyed much of the old Victorian-style campus that Ruth called home for the better part of 12 years. Now a nationally known sports superstar, Ruth received permission from the Yankees to take the St. Mary's School band along on road trips to several major-league ballparks around the Northeast, in an attempt to help them raise money to replace the main school building.[13]

After the game Ruth revealed how happy he was to have hit his 50th and 51st home runs with the band in attendance. Just six years removed from his days at St. Mary's, Ruth said, "This was the greatest day I ever lived, for the brothers from my old school at Baltimore."[14]

The victory trimmed the Indians' lead over the third-place Yankees to three games. However, Ruth and his teammates would get no closer. The Yankees finished the season 95-59, three games behind the American League champion Indians and one behind the second-place White Sox.

Sources

In addition to the sources cited in the Notes, the author also relied on Baseball-reference.com and Retrosheet.org.

Notes

1. Ray Pearson, "Dempsey, Ruth, Man O' War Lead World of Sport: Such a Galaxy of Stars Unknown in One Year," *Chicago Tribune*, September 26, 1926: 18.

2. "Ruth Crashes Out Homers 50 and 51: Mauling Monarch Passes Half-Century Mark and Sends Fans Into Hysteria," *New York Times*, September 25, 1920: 9.

3. Fay Vincent, *The Only Game in Town* (New York: Simon & Schuster, 2006), 59.

4. Bill Lamb, "Jim Shaw," SABR BioProject. Retrieved from sabr.org/bioproj/person/5f888acd.

5. William Hanna, "Yankees Break Even With Senators Before 25,000," *New York Herald*, September 25, 1920: 13.

6. "Babe Has Soaked 'Em for a Hundred Homers," *New York Herald*, September 25, 1920: 13.

7. "Curves and Bingles," *New York Times*, September 25, 1920: 9.

8. W.O. McGeehan, "Babe's 50th Fails to Win, but His 51st Turns Trick," *New York Tribune*, September 25, 1920: 10.

9. Ibid.

10. According to Bill Nowlin, baseball databases list Herb Thormahlen as Hank, but in the several thousand news stories mentioning Thormahlen, never once was he identified as Hank. Bill Nowlin, "Herb Thomahlen, "SABR BioProject. Retrieved from sabr.org/bioproj/person/5d7570fd.

11. "Ruth Crashes Out Homers 50 and 51."

12. The previous single-season American League record for runs scored was held by Ty Cobb, who scored 147 runs in 1911.

13. Richard Sandomir, "A Fight to Save the House That Ruth Built," *New York Times*, April 17, 2010: SP2.

14. Babe Ruth, "Greatest Day of All Is What Ruth Thinks After Hitting No. 51," *Chicago Tribune*, September 25, 1920: 13.

Ruth Hits Number 54

September 29, 1920: New York Yankees 7, Philadelphia Athletics 3, at Shibe Park, Philadelphia (game one of doubleheader)

By James Forr

Babe Ruth was hammering the final stamp onto one of baseball's most remarkable seasons but hardly anyone was paying attention.

The newspaper headlines on September 29, 1920, trumpeted the indictment of eight Chicago White Sox players on charges of conspiring to fix the 1919 World Series. Even in the *New York Times* the scandal was on the front page while the only hint of what the Yankees were up to was a small note in agate at the bottom of the standings: "New York at Philadelphia (2 Games)." It was one of the few times the Babe took second billing.

It didn't help that the doubleheader was meaningless as far as the AL race went. After purchasing Ruth from the Boston Red Sox in December, the already ascendant Yankees appeared to have added the missing piece that finally would put them over the top. "Given anything like an even break, the Yankees should win the American League pennant this season," predicted Weed Dickinson in the *Washington Post*. "[N]o alibi will satisfy New York fans if the Yanks do not come through."[1] Ruth's new teammates Del Pratt and Bob Shawkey boldly declared that they, too, saw an AL flag in the Yankees' immediate future.

Things didn't work out, although that certainly wasn't Ruth's fault. He entered the day with a nearly incomprehensible total of 53 home runs. He broke his own single-season record of 29, set the previous season, on July 19. Unfortunately for the Yankees, the rest of the offense was undistinguished and, ultimately, not quite good enough. Arriving at Shibe Park for these final two games of the season, New York found itself in third place, 3½ games behind Cleveland and mathematically eliminated from contention.

It seemed as if the Athletics had been mathematically eliminated since February. They hadn't enjoyed a winning season since 1914 and wouldn't again until 1925. Most of those years in the wilderness were ugly ones and this was no exception: They came into the day 47-101, 47½ games out of first. Their pitchers had nothing to be ashamed of. Philadelphia's team ERA was a tick above the league average and although Ruth destroyed everyone in 1920, the Athletics sort of held him in check, relatively speaking. He hit fewer home runs against them – five – than against any other team.

So, the pitching was fine. The problem was everything else. The Athletics were the worst defensive team in baseball, by far – as evinced by the eight errors they committed in this doubleheader. Their inability to catch the ball was matched by their hapless attempts to hit it. Philadelphia's team OPS of .641 was more than

50 points lower than anyone else in the American League. It was one of the weakest offenses the major leagues have ever seen.

The *Philadelphia Inquirer* estimated that 15,000 people were on hand for the doubleheader. Baseball-Reference.com lists the attendance at 7,000. Either way, the Athletics averaged fewer than 4,000 a game that season, so it appears that the chance to witness the spectacle that was Babe Ruth drew a lot of fans who normally would have spent their Wednesday afternoon in the office or at their workbench.

They watched the home team break on top in the first inning against the Yankees' outstanding rookie, Rip Collins. With one down, Charlie High tripled and later scored on Cy Perkins' single, but New York answered moments later when Sammy Vick's two-out triple plated Pratt to make it 1-1. The Athletics recaptured the lead in the bottom of the second on Jimmy Dykes' single to center, which knocked in Tillie Walker. Philadelphia had a chance for a big inning after High's infield hit loaded the bases but Collins struck out Ivy Griffin and retired Perkins on a grounder to snuff out the threat.

Leads were all too few for the Athletics in 1920 and "they hung on to that slim lead like grim death," as the *New York Times* put it.[2] But Philadelphia hadn't lost 101 games by accident. It was almost inevitable they would lose their grip – and so they did in the fifth.

Speedy Bob Meusel sparked the rally by legging out a squibber between short and third. He was erased at second on a force play before Truck Hannah, playing in his final major-league game, slapped one to second baseman Dykes, who booted it. After Collins struck out, Aaron Ward lashed Slim Harriss's offering for a single, which scored Vick and tied the game, 2-2. Wally Pipp reached on another error, which gave Ruth a shot with the bases loaded but Harriss struck him out to end the inning.

The game got away from Philadelphia in the top of the sixth. The trouble started right away when shortstop Chick Galloway threw wildly to first on Pratt's groundball. The Yankees took the lead on run-scoring singles by Meusel and Hannah and added insurance when Vick stole home on the front end of a double steal. Harriss exited for a pinch-hitter moments later, down 5-2, although three of the runs charged to him were unearned. A writer in the *Philadelphia Inquirer* was beside himself at how Harriss's teammates had done him wrong. "Five errors of commission were committed by our infielders, while several other examples of slow fielding, particularly on the part of … Galloway, were scored as base hits when anything approximately a big league brand of ball would have retired the batsmen and saved two or three of the alien tallies."[3]

Walker, who finished third in the AL in home runs with 17, led off the Athletics' eighth with a solo shot to cut the lead to 5-3. In the ninth, Ruth brought an 0-for-4 to the plate with two outs and Ward at first following another error. He faced reliever Dave Keefe. Keefe had only four fingers on his pitching hand thanks to a childhood confrontation with a corn crusher, but for whatever inconvenience the injury caused him in daily life, it did help him develop a pretty nasty forkball that got him to the big leagues. That was of no consequence to Ruth, who drove Keefe's first pitch over the right-field wall for his 54th home run of the season and a 7-3 Yankees lead, which is how the game ended after Collins retired the side in the bottom of the ninth.

According to the *Inquirer*, a pedestrian returned the home-run ball to an Athletics employee, who gave it to Ruth, who planned to autograph it and sell it at an auction to benefit St. Mary's Industrial Home for Boys in Baltimore, the orphanage where he was raised. St. Mary's had suffered a devastating fire the previous year and the funds were intended to help with the reconstruction efforts.

(Ruth and Keefe crossed paths again with quite different results during a wartime fundraising effort at Shibe Park in 1944. Keefe was the Athletics' batting-practice pitcher and his job was to groove a few pitches so that Ruth, nine years into his retirement, could blast them over the fence and delight the crowd. Instead, Keefe was so wild that Ruth hardly could make any contact at all. He tweaked his knee lunging after one of Keefe's off-target pitches and hobbled back to the dugout homerless.)[4]

The Yankees won the second game, 9-4. Ruth didn't homer but did go 3-for-5 with a double to cap what was possibly his greatest statistical season. He ended with a batting average of .376 and 135 RBIs to go with his 54 home runs. He had more home runs than all but one other major-league team. His slugging percentage of .847 and OPS of 1.379 were major-league records until Barry Bonds came along more than 80 years later.

That still wasn't enough for some skeptics. A commentator in *The Sporting News* suggested that Ruth's magnificent season might be a fluke. "Whether Ruth can equal this mark in 1921 is a doubtful question," the writer warned. "His great hitting will no longer be a novelty."[5] Indeed, Ruth did not match his 54-homer outburst in 1921 – instead, he hit 59. That was a precursor to his 60 home runs during the Yankees' mythical 1927 season.

The year turned out to be somewhat disappointing for New York. Nevertheless, the predictions of the previous winter soon came true. Beyond the horizon lay seven pennants and four world championships over the next 12 years of Ruth's reign. The journey had begun.

Sources

In addition to the newspaper sources cited in the Notes, the author used Baseball-Reference.com and Retrosheet.org.

The author also reviewed the following newspaper articles for play-by-play and other information:

"Double Victory Won by Yankees," *New York Herald*, September 30, 1920: 13.

"Yankees Will Win Flag With Ruth, Says Pratt," *Washington Post*, February 9, 1920: 9.

"Yanks Buy Babe Ruth for $125,000," *New York Times*, January 6, 1920: 16.

Notes

1. Weed Dickinson, "Yanks' Strength in New Material," *Washington Post*, March 16, 1920: 12.

2. "Yankees Wind Up by Winning Two," *New York Times*, September 30, 1920: 20.

3. Jim Nasium, "Another Home Run on Last Day of Year," *Philadelphia Inquirer*, September 30, 1920: 14.

4. Tom Simon, "Dave Keefe," SABR Baseball Biography Project, sabr.org/bioproj/person/9e77592f, accessed June 26, 2018.

5. "Men on the Inside Knew It Would Come Out," *The Sporting News*, October 7, 1920: 1.

Ruth's Yanks Knock Out Cobb's Tigers

June 13, 1921: New York Yankees 13, Detroit Tigers 8, at the Polo Grounds

By T.S. Flynn

Led by player-manager Ty Cobb, the third-place Tigers met the second-place Yankees for a four-game series in mid-June of 1921 at the Polo Grounds, hoping to leapfrog Babe Ruth and Co. in the American League standings. Only two games separated the teams, while the first-place Cleveland Indians led New York by just 2½ games. The 34-year-old Cobb was on his way to 197 hits in his 17th big-league season. He'd finish with a .389 BA and 1.048 OPS in 128 games. But by 1921 the Deadball Era's offensive approach that Cobb epitomized had given way to a new era personified by the brash young Babe. The 25-year-old swatted 54 home runs and compiled a 1.379 OPS in 1920, his first year as a Yankee. The new Baseball King had arrived, but the Georgia Peach wouldn't abdicate without a fight.

On the afternoon of Saturday, June 11, the Tigers took control in the seventh inning, scoring three runs to take a 6-3 lead. But the Detroit advantage lasted only until Ruth came to bat with two outs and two on in the bottom of the frame. His 18th home run of the season knotted the score, and the Yankees won on a Roger Peckinpaugh walk-off single. The next day, before the second game in the series, "a photographer asked Babe if he'd pose for a picture with the Peach and Ruth refused in some unkind way, so the photographer, nothing else to do, repeated to Cobb what Ruth had said and the dispositions of both were set aflame."[1] Tempers continued to flare after the game began. With one out in the top of the second inning, Detroit first baseman Lu Blue and Yankees catcher Wally Schang argued over a pitch that had been called a ball. Schang tossed his mask and faced off with Blue. "Both teams poured off the benches like smoke out of the funnels of a trans-Atlantic liner," wrote Harry Bullion. "All of the trainers and groundskeepers figured in the melee and while Cobb was endeavoring to pacify Blue and Schang's mates tried to console him, Ruth took the occasion to renew hostilities with the Georgian and there were two jobs for the peace-makers."[2] Order was restored and play resumed. (Blue struck out.)

An inning later, the Tigers scored a pair of runs, and Detroit led until the bottom of the fifth, an explosive half-inning that featured an argument between shortstop Donie Bush and umpire Bill Dinneen. Bush insisted he had tagged out Schang on an infield play. When Dinneen disagreed, Bush "playfully" punched the arbiter in the stomach and jaw.[3] The next batter, Peckinpaugh, cleared the bases with a triple. "As Peck reached third, Bush resumed his attack on Dinneen and was chased from the game."[4] Ruth smacked his 19th home run of the year, "a sirocco-like devastator into the right field stand."[5] By time the dust finally settled, the Yankees had sent 12 batters to the plate and collected nine hits. Schang and Bob Shawkey each knocked two singles in the frame. As the Yankees trotted to their positions to defend their 8-2 lead, Cobb and Ruth faced off again, barking at each other behind the mound. In the eighth inning, the Tigers clawed back, tying the game, 8-8. But the Yankees answered in the bottom of the frame with six hits, including a Ruth double, scoring four runs and taking a 12-8 lead that proved to be the final tally. The Yankees had won the first two rounds against the Tigers and remained in second place. Meanwhile, the Washington Senators moved into third and Detroit dropped to fourth.

Prior to the game on Monday, June 13, Ruth approached Yankees manager Miller Huggins "with an offer to go into the box and save Carl Mays for another day. Huggins pounced on the suggestion, and when the crowd gathered to see the third downfall of the Tigers, there was the Babe, as large as life, warming up, while even the Tigers stood about popeyed."[6] Ruth took to the mound for just the second time as a Yankee – the first had been on June 1, 1920, when he went four innings in a victory over Washington. Given the intensity of the previous two games, it's likely Ruth requested the start primarily for the opportunity to challenge Cobb from a distance of 60 feet 6 inches.

Batting third, Cobb earned a one-out walk in the top of the first inning, the second free pass allowed by Ruth. But the Bambino escaped the stanza without surrendering a run. The Yanks manufactured a first-inning run on Wally Pipp's sacrifice fly. They extended the lead to 3-0 in the second on the strength of a two-run inside-the-park home run off the bat of Chicken Hawks. In the third Cobb flied out and the Tigers left two on base for the second time in three innings. Ruth led off the bottom of the third with a towering fly ball into the upper deck in right field, his 20th homer of the season. Bob Meusel doubled and Frank "Home Run" Baker followed with an eponymous round-tripper. Schang, who had hit safely in four of five at-bats the previous game, faced Tigers starter Howard Ehmke, who unleashed a rising fastball. At the last instant, Schang raised his arm to protect his face and the ball struck his wrist. He was assisted off the field in great pain and delivered to a local hospital where, to great surprise, x-rays revealed no fractured bones.

When the Tigers came to bat in the fourth inning, they found themselves in a 6-0 hole. The score held until the fifth inning. Ralph Young doubled and scored on an error. Ruth struck out Cobb, but three more runs followed the strikeout. Ruth had contained Cobb, but the Tigers were back in the game, 6-4. As had happened in the previous two games, the Tigers' rally prodded the Yankees' offense into action. New York scored four runs on four hits in the bottom of the fifth and the lead swelled again to six runs, 10-4. After Ruth surrendered a single and a walk to open the sixth inning, Huggins sent him to center field and called on Mays to take the ball. He retired the side without surrendering a run. The teams traded runs in the bottom of the sixth and the top of the seventh.

When Ruth strode to the plate in the bottom of the seventh with two outs and Peckinpaugh on second base, the Yankees led 11-5. The Babe delivered a knockout blow. His 21st home run sailed 480 feet, into the center-field seats – the first time anyone had accomplished the feat at the Polo Grounds. "The ball fell into the exit stairway of the bleachers and then down under the benches, where a mob of boys had a free for all for the prized memento," noted the *Herald*'s Dan Daniel.[7] The clout was Ruth's second of the day and, more noteworthy, his fifth in four days, also a first. The Tigers gamely clawed and scratched two runs in the eighth and one in the ninth to narrow the gap, but they went down in defeat for the third straight day, this time by 13-8. Ruth had set records with his bat and silenced Cobb with his pitching, striking out the Peach once and holding him hitless in three plate appearances.

But the Yankees and Ruth weren't finished. They completed the sweep on Tuesday, 9-6, behind another pair of Ruth home runs, "giving him three home runs in three at bats and seven in five games. The first shot almost cleared the distant left-field bleachers. The second blast went to virtually the same spot in the center-field bleachers, perhaps even a little farther than the previous day's home run had reached."[8] Ruth finished the series with six home runs, and a total of eight hits in 12 at-bats. Cobb went 7-for-18 in the 4 games. The Tigers left New York reeling and lost their next five games, effectively dropping from contention. The Yankees remained in second place for much of the season, before overtaking the Indians down the stretch to win the American League pennant.

Notes

1. Harry Bullion, "Stormy Contest Is Won by Yanks, 12-8," *Detroit Free Press*, June 13, 1921: 9.
2. Ibid.
3. Ibid.
4. Daniel, "Ruth Hits 19th Homer, but Peck Is Star of Victory," *New York Herald*, June 13, 1921: 8.
5. Ibid.
6. Daniel, "Pitcher Ruth Hits Brace of Homers," *New York Herald*, June 14, 1921: 12.
7. Ibid.
8. Lyle Spatz and Steve Steinberg, *1921: The Yankees, the Giants, and the Battle for Baseball Supremacy in New York* (Lincoln: University of Nebraska Press, 2010), 155.

Ruth's 138th Career Home Run Ties Roger Connor's Big-League Record

July 15, 1921: New York Yankees 7, St. Louis Browns 2, at Sportsman's Park

By Gregory H. Wolf

It was a "mastodonic thrust," according to the *New York Times*.[1] With his mighty stroke of the bat, the Yankees' Babe Ruth smashed a towering shot that sailed over the right-center-field bleachers in Sportsman's Park in St. Louis. It was the Sultan of Swat's 35th home run of the 1921 season and newspapers from around the country excitedly compared his home-run pace to the previous season, when Ruth belted 54 round-trippers, more than each of the other seven AL teams, in his first season with the New York Yankees. Conspicuously absent from accounts of Ruth's home run in the Gateway City was a more important milestone: It tied the major-league record for most career round-trippers in big-league history.

Babe Ruth's assault on home-run records began in 1919 when the former two-time 20-game-winning southpaw pitcher reduced his pitching load (166⅓ innings) to start 106 games in the outfield for the Boston Red Sox. That season he belted 29 round-trippers to break the Chicago Cubs' Ned Williamson's 35-year old record of 27, set in 1884. Sold to the Yankees a day after Christmas in 1919, Ruth with his prodigious power redefined baseball and signaled the end of the Deadball Era. In the second game of a twin bill on September 24, 1920, the Bambino walloped the 100th home run in his career, becoming the 11th big leaguer to reach the century mark. The leader in home runs with 138 was Roger Connor, described by SABR's Bill Lamb as "baseball's first great slugger," but who was also "[u]nderappreciated in his late-19th-century heyday and largely forgotten for decades thereafter."[2] For 25 years, beginning in 1895, Connor held the record, until the Babe's ascent as the most transformative figure in baseball history.

The Babe

Ruth getting in some fielding practice before a game, 1921.
Courtesy of Library of Congress.

The Yankees and Browns were well-rested as they headed to Sportsman's Park on St. Louis's north side to conclude a series on Friday, July 15, as rain had canceled the previous day's game. Skipper Miller Huggins's second-place Yankees (49-31), on the second stop of a 15-game, four-city road swing, had pennant aspirations and were trailing the Cleveland Indians by three games. Manager Lee Fohl's sixth-place Brownies (35-47) were reeling, having lost nine of their last 13 contests and were in the middle of a 26-game homestand.

Toeing the rubber for each team was a young, relatively untried right-hander. The Browns' 25-year-old Elam Vangilder, with a 7-11 career slate (3-3 thus far in 1921), faced off against Brooklyn native Waite Hoyt. The much-ballyhooed 21-year-old, known as the "School Boy," had struggled since he debuted in 1918 and was playing for his third big-league team. His 9-7 slate in his first campaign for the Yankees evened his career record, 19-19.

On a gorgeous afternoon with temperatures rising to the high 80s, about 10,000 spectators, according to the *St. Louis Star and Times*, piled into Sportsman's Park for a respite with the national pastime and a special celebration.[3] Browns star and fan favorite Jack Tobin was honored in a pregame ceremony. The right fielder, who had collected 202 hits in 1920 (the first of four straight seasons with at least 200 safeties) and batted .341, was presented a luxurious Essex automobile and then driven around the park and along the outfield wall.[4]

The Browns got on the board first, aided by a fluke hit. Ken Williams led off the second with a double. According to the *Star and Times*, the next batter, Baby Doll Jacobson, tried to avoid a wild pitch by Hoyt, but the ball hit his bat and "trickled" down the right-field line, through first baseman Wally Pipp's legs for an error.[5] Williams scored easily and Jacobson reached second, where he was stranded.

Easily the major leagues' highest-scoring team, the Yankees tied the game in the fourth and took the lead the following inning. Hoyt's single drove in Pipp, who had led off with a double, for the Yankees first tally. In the fifth, Roger Peckinpaugh led off with a double followed by Ruth's walk, which elicited a round of boos directed at their own hurler, noted the *Star and Times*.[6] After Home Run Baker sacrificed both runners up a station, Bob Meusel slapped a Texas Leaguer into shallow right to drive in a run. Praised by the *Times* as the "altitudinous guardian of the primary corner," Pipp followed with his second two-bagger, driving in both Ruth and Meusel, but he was cut down trying to stretch the hit into a triple.[7]

The Yankees' juggernaut against Vangilder continued in the sixth. Peckinpaugh lined a two-out single to left to drive in Wally Schang, who had led off the frame with a walk. To the plate stepped hot-hitting Ruth, who entered the game with 10 home runs in his previous 62 at-bats in 17 games. For the season thus far, the Bambino's stat line (.372/34/87) looked like something from a computer game almost a century later; his slugging (.860) and on-base-percentage (.508) were even more awe-inspiring. Ruth sent the crowd into a euphoric frenzy by clouting a deep blast, which was "still climbing when it went out of the park," noted the *Times*, as it sailed over the wall and onto Grand Avenue.[8] Ruth's clout, continued the paper, was one of the longest he had ever hit in the park and it "crashed into a lamp post and demolished it."[9] Relievers Bill Bayne and Bugs Bennett hurled the final three frames for the Browns, permitting just one hit.

While the Yankees pounded the Browns, Hoyt set down the Brownies with ease. The brazen youngster "palmed fast ones that blinded them, curves that fooled them and slow ones that made fools of them," gushed the *Times*.[10] After holding the Browns hitless from the fourth through eighth innings, Hoyt yielded his sixth and last hit of the game, a leadoff single by Frank Ellerbe in the ninth. Baker's wild throw on George Sisler's grounder sailed over Pipp's head, giving the Browns another run. It was the Yankees' third error of the game. Sisler eventually scored on Jacobson's sacrifice fly; all three Browns runs were unearned. Hoyt completed the game in 2 hours and 33 minutes by retiring Pat Collins to give the Yankees a 7-3 victory.

A few hours after the game, the Yankees were in a Pullman coach on their way to the Motor City for a quartet of games with the Detroit Tigers. In the third of those contests, on July 18, Ruth hit his 36th home run of the season and passed Connor to become the major-league leader in career home runs with 139. For the next 14 seasons, Ruth added to his home-run record, retiring with 714 after the 1935 season.

Sources

In addition to the sources cited in the Notes, the author also accessed Retrosheet.org, Baseball-Reference.com, SABR.org, and *The Sporting News* archive via Paper of Record.

Notes

1 "Babe Ruth Hits No. 35; Yanks Gain in Race," *New York Times*, July 16, 1921: 8.

2 Bill Lamb, "Roger Connor," SABR BioProject, sabr.org/bioproj/person/4ef2cfff.

3 "Ruth Raps 3th[h] Home Run Clout in Sixth Session," *St. Louis Star and Times*, July 15, 1921: 13.

4 Ibid.

5 Ibid. The game account from the *Star and Times* provides a play-by-play account of the game. Neither BaseballReference.com nor Retrosheet has play-by-play information.

6 Ibid.

7 "Babe Ruth Hits No. 35; Yanks Gain in Race."

8 "Ruth Adds to His Home Run Hoard as Yankees Win – Storm Keeps Giants and Dodgers Idle," *New York Times*, July 16, 1921: 8.

9 "Babe Ruth Hits No. 35; Yanks Gain in Race."

10 Ibid.

Babe Ruth's 560-ft Homer Against Tigers Sets Career Record

July 18, 1921: New York Yankees 10, Detroit Tigers 1, at Navin Field

by Mike Huber

It was the bottom of the eighth inning in a summer contest at Detroit's Navin Field when Babe Ruth sent a Bert Cole pitch over the fence at the deepest part of the stadium. The historic shot officially measured a distance of 560 feet, giving Ruth his 36th home run of the season and 139th of his career.[1] The Herculean blast set a new major-league record for most home runs in a career, surpassing Roger Connor, whose mark of 138 career four-baggers had stood since 1897.[2] It also was Ruth's longest home run of his career (to this date). The Yankees defeated the Tigers 10-1, but the score was not relevant; Ruth's clobbering of a baseball, sending it farther than anyone had in the past, provided the approximately 3,000 fans with "something to talk about in front of the family hearth."[3]

Coming into the contest, New York was riding a six-game winning streak, and had won 14 of their last 17, but the Yankees began the day one game behind the Cleveland Indians in the standings. Detroit was sliding, having lost four in a row and stood 13 games back of Cleveland. Carl Mays, New York's "blond U-boat artist"[4] (so named because of his submarine-style pitching), started for the Yankees. For the Tigers, "Manager Cobb entrusted Howard Ehmke with the task of checking the march of the visitors."[5]

The Yankees scored early and often. In the top of the first, Chick Fewster and Roger Peckinpaugh both singled to left field. Ehmke then walked Ruth intentionally to load 'em up with no outs. That brought up Frank Baker, who hit a sacrifice fly to left, bringing in Fewster. Wally Pipp followed with a single to left, and Peckinpaugh scored run number two. In the second, Wally Schang walked, moved to second on a ground out, to third on a passed ball, and to home on a Fewster single.

The Tigers pegged their lone run in the bottom half of the second. Bobby Veach led off and hit a fly which dropped into short right field between second baseman Aaron Ward, right fielder Bob Meusel and first baseman Pipp, and Veach scooted to second for a double. He scored on a single to center by Lu Blue.

The Yankees wasted no time in the third to answer that run. Pipp launched a one-out homer to the bleachers in right-center field.[6] Then New York manufactured a run on a single by Ward, a fielder's choice, sacrifice fly and an RBI single by Fewster. The

Babe Ruth, 1921, always ready to pose for a photograph, especially with children. *Courtesy of Library of Congress.*

visitors added three more tallies in the sixth. Fewster singled and was bunted to second by Peckinpaugh. Ruth drew another walk. Baker lined an RBI single into center field. Meusel then stroked a triple to center field, driving in Peckinpaugh and Ruth. The Yankees led 8-1.

Entering the eighth inning, Cobb brought Cole on to face the Yankees bats. Ehmke had allowed eight runs (five earned) on 10 hits and six walks. Peckinpaugh reached on an error by Ira Flagstead, bringing the historic moment to bear. Ruth had walked in all four previous at-bats. With a count of one-and-one, Ruth "found one to his liking"[7] and put such force into the ball that it "disappeared from view at the spot where the wooden fence at the far end of the center field bleachers connect with the concrete walls at the corner of Cherry and Trumbull avenues."[8] According to the *New York Times*, "the Detroit statisticians aver that it is 560 feet from the plate to the point where the ball soared out of sight over the centre field barrier, and they brought out the old surveying rod and sextant to prove the contention."[9] That could mean that ball actually traveled *farther* than 560 feet to the spot where it landed. Prior to this blast, Ruth's longest home run was a ball he hit at the Polo Grounds that was officially measured at 460 feet.[10]

Ruth came to bat one more time, in the top of the ninth inning, and this time, Cole struck out the Bambino to end the inning. The final score was New York 10, Detroit 1.

Fewster led the Yankees with a 4-for-6 day at the plate, and Pipp was 3-for-5 with a home run and two RBIs. He also anchored three double plays at first base for the Yankees. Ruth's line was a mere 1-for-2 with two runs scored and two driven in, but he also had four walks, which helped his on-base percentage. The home run increased his slugging percentage to a whopping .849!

Mays encountered little difficulty in the game and was only "solved for six safeties"[11] by the Tigers hitters (five singles and the double by Veach). He allowed only four hits after the second inning, cruised to a complete game victory, and improved his record to 15-5. Ehmke's mission on the mound was "just the reverse, in that he seemed extremely liberal with the safeties." The Yankees had 13 hits in the game, 10 off of Ehmke in seven innings. In addition, "the Tigers introduced a quartet of 'boots',"[12] which accounted for four unearned runs. Coincidentally, the final score of 10-1 matched the outcome of the Yankees-Tigers season series to this point.[13]

Ruth of course continued to add to his home run total. He hit 23 more round trippers in 1921, setting a new season high mark of 59, breaking his own record of 54 (set in 1920). His career total continued to increase over the next 14 seasons, finally settling on the magic number of 714 in 1935. That record stood until 1974, when Hank Aaron hit his #715. Ruth owned the career home run record for 53 seasons.

Sources

In addition to the sources mentioned in the notes, the author consulted baseball-reference.com and retrosheet.org.

Notes

1 See baseball-reference.com:8080/players/event_hr.cgi?id=ruthba01&t=b for a log of Ruth's 714 career home runs.

2 Connor claimed ownership of the career total record in 1895, after he hit his 123rd home run. He finished the season with 126. He hit 11 additional homers in 1896 and one more, his last, in 1897, to set the mark of 138. It lasted 24 years.

3 "Speeding Yankees Run Down a Tiger," *New York Times*, July 19, 1921: 11.

4 Ibid.

5 Harry Bullion, "Yanks, Win, 10 to 1; Ruth's Blow Record," *Detroit Free Press*, July 19, 1921: 12.

6 According to the *New York Times*, the homer landed in the right field bleachers, but the *Detroit Free Press* claims it landed in the bleachers in center.

7 *New York Times*.

8 Bullion.

9 *New York Times*.

10 "Ruth Hits His Longest Homer; Yanks Win, 10-1," *Chicago Tribune*, July 19, 1921: 10.

11 Bullion.

12 Ibid.

13 New York won 17 of 22 games against Detroit in 1921.

#55

September 15, 1921: New York Yankees 10, St. Louis Browns 6 (game one of doubleheader), at Polo Grounds, New York

By Paul E. Doutrich

It came on a full count. A fastball a little bit up in the zone, right in his wheelhouse. From the instant it left the bat there was no doubt that it was bound for the right-field stands. The only question was whether it would end up in the bleachers or in the upper deck. It landed in the upper deck. A towering rainbow shot. Not his longest, but easily long enough. As he trotted around the bases The Babe had a satisfied smile on his face.[1] He had once again done what many said he could not do. He had hit his 55th home run of the season. He broke the record that he had set the previous season. It was the third year in a row that he had rewritten the home-run record book.

The blast came at an opportune time for the Yankees. Through four innings, they were down a run to the St. Louis Browns. Until the third inning the only New York hit was a first-inning leadoff single by center fielder Elmer Miller. After walking the next hitter, Roger Peckinpaugh, Browns pitcher Bill Bayne set down the next six Yankees he faced. Carl Mays did even better, retiring all six St. Louis hitters who came to the plate.

That all changed in the third. Wally Gerber, the Browns shortstop, led off with a single and was sacrificed to second. Pitcher Bayne walked and Jack Tobin smacked a double to left, driving in the game's first run. Bayne scored the second run when Frank Ellerbe grounded out to first. Another run scored on George Sisler's single to right. The St. Louis star first baseman then stole second, went to third on an error by Yankees catcher Wally Schang, and scored the Browns' fourth run on a single by Ken Williams.

Down by four, the Yankees immediately mounted an assault of their own. Atoning a bit for his costly error, Schang opened with a single. Pitcher Mays, one of the best hitting pitchers in the American League, shot one to center. Miller laid down a run-scoring bunt single to keep the rally alive. Bayne then struck out Peckinpaugh and got Ruth on a popout to shortstop. However, the three-run lead disappeared instantly when Bob Meusel launched one into the left-field stands.

The Browns regained the lead in the fourth. Second baseman Marty McManus hit a two-out double that scored the Browns' hulking center fielder, Bill "Baby Doll" Jacobson, who had led off with a single. This time the Yankees were unable to match the Browns' run.

The Browns went in order in the fifth, setting the stage for Ruth's record-breaking blast. Miller led off the Yankees' half of the inning with his third hit of the game, a double. Peckinpaugh flied to right, bringing Ruth to the plate. Bayne had "reveled in a chuckle" after punching Ruth out on three swinging strikes in the first.[2] The Browns pitcher added a bit of insult to injury in the third. He "had taken the dangerous liberty of laughing at the Babe" after Ruth popped to shortstop.[3] In the fifth, as he so often did, "Babe the Ruthless" had the last laugh.[4]

Even before the ball landed, hats began raining down on the field. The "hurricane of straw hats" continued as Ruth circled the bases.[5] Old battered straw hats mixed with brand-new ones swirling down onto the field. The Babe took his time trotting around the bases. It had been six anxious days since he had hit number 54 and he wanted to savor the moment. Waiting at home plate was the diminutive Yankee mascot, Eddie Bennett. As soon as Ruth stepped on the plate, little Eddie leaped up on to his back and there he stayed as the Babe walked into the dugout.

Ruth's race to a new home-run record began even before the season started. "You can tell the world I'll smash out more than 54 homers this year. ... That's what the fans want and the Babe isn't going to disappoint them."[6] Baseball fans everywhere followed the journey and eagerly awaited the record-breaker. To keep them updated the *New York Daily News* included a "How Babe Ruth Batted Yesterday" column.

The "Batterin' Bambino" began his assault in the third game of the season with a shot against Philadelphia.[7] By May 1, the date when he had hit his first homer a year earlier, he was already nine games ahead of the pace. Midway through the season, he had stretched his lead to 11 games. In addition to the number of home runs, he included record distances. On July 18 in Detroit he hit what was considered the longest ball ever hit, 565 feet.[8] A week later, in an exhibition game against Cincinnati, he hit "two magnificent wallops. Both of them were record-breakers for Redland Field."[9]

Meanwhile, after a brief delay to clear the hats off the playing field, the two teams got back to work. Bayne gave up another single but allowed no more runs in the inning. The first batter to face Mays in the sixth, left fielder Ken Williams, tied the game with the third home run of the afternoon. Despite an error by Peckinpaugh, Mays was able to get out of the inning with no additional problems. Bayne matched his Yankee counterpart.

Bill Bayne was a diminutive southpaw who depended on guile and control. On a Browns staff that included 27-game winner Urban Shocker, he was used primarily in relief. However, in a rare start four weeks earlier, he had brilliantly shut out the Yankees, giving up only four hits and striking out 10, including Ruth twice. Since then he had four more starts, winning three of them. On his way to his best major-league season, he would finish with 11 wins. This was not one of them.

The Yankees unloaded on Bayne in the seventh. Miller led off with his fourth hit, a home run. Two walks, including one to Ruth, a bunt single, errors by Bayne and McManus, and Wally Pipp's single pushed four Yankee runs across the plate and ended Bayne's day.

Though Ruth was the story of the game, it was center fielder Elmer Miller who was having a career day. In early August he had been reacquired from the St. Paul Saints, where he had spent the previous two seasons. Since his acquisition he had been the Yankees' regular center fielder and leadoff hitter. His four hits in the opening game brought his batting average to the .300 mark. It was the third of four times he got four hits in a game. There were also four times in which he scored three runs in a game. For a player who hit only 16 home runs during his seven-year major-league career, any game that he knocked one out of the park was notable.

Now up by four runs, submariner Carl Mays cruised through the last two innings. It was not one of his better performances, but it was good enough. This was his 25th of 27 wins in the best season of his 15-year career. Of course, the day's big story was the fifth-inning blast by The Babe. He added four more before the season ended, setting a mark that he would top six years later.

In the second game of the afternoon, the Yankees clobbered the Browns 13-5. Ruth started the show with a first-inning triple that scored Miller. Three more runs crossed the plate before the Yankees hitters were done. Two innings later, Ruth and his mates added five more, effectively ending the game. Wally Pipp put a cap on the day with a home run in the sixth.

The only concern in the second game came in the seventh inning. With the Yankees safely up by eight runs, Ruth came up limping after dropping a bunt single down the third-base line. Manager Miller Huggins feared his slugger had pulled a groin muscle and might be on the bench at least for the next couple of days. That was not to be. The next afternoon Ruth was back patrolling right field and hammered his 56th of the year.

As the 25,000 fans, some of them without their hats, left the Polo Grounds, most were satisfied that they had seen history made. They were also relieved that the Yankees, who came into the day a half-game ahead of Cleveland for the American League lead, had been able to keep pace with the Indians, who had swept the Philadelphia Athletics.

Sources

In addition to the sources cited in the Notes, the author also relied upon Baseball-Reference.com and Retrosheet.org.

Notes

1. "Batterin' Babe Hits Out No. 55 at Polo Grounds," *New York Daily News,* September 16, 1921: 24.

2. Daniel, "Babe Ruth Betters His Record with Fifty-fifth Homer: Yankees Win Twice," *New York Herald*, September 16, 1921: 12.

3. Ibid.

4. Charles A. Taylor, "Yanks Capture Two in a Row and Hold Lead," *New York Tribune*, September 16, 1921: 14.

5. Daniel.

6. Dean Snyder, "Babe Ruth Promises New Home Run Record in '21," *Olean* (New York) *Times Herald,* April 4, 1921: 17.

7. Jack Veiock, "'Round the Sport Circle," *Buffalo Enquirer*, September 1, 1921: 7.

8. Harry Bullion, "Yanks Win, 10 to 1: Ruth's Blow Record," *Detroit Free Press*, July 19, 1921: 12.

9. Jack Ryder, "Ruth Hits Two Homers at Redland Field," *Cincinnati Enquirer*, July 21, 1921: 8.

An Injured Babe Wallops His First World Series Home Run While Shufflin' Phil Steals the Show

October 9, 1921: New York Giants 4, New York Yankees 2, at the Polo Grounds
Game Four of the World Series

By Gregory H. Wolf

On Sunday, October 9, 1921, the sporting world was obsessed with one question: Would Babe Ruth play in Game Four of the World Series?

Three days earlier, the Yankees slugger seriously injured his left forearm, gashing it below the elbow while sliding into third base in the eighth inning of his team's second consecutive 3-0 victory over the New York Giants. The next day, the Babe played despite the pain, but aggravated the injury attempting a steal in the Giants' 13-5 thrashing. That evening, the wound became infected, necessitating Dr. George D. Stewart to lance and drain it, rendering the game's biggest star and gate draw unavailable for Game Four, scheduled for Saturday at the Polo Grounds, the home park for both clubs. But the Sultan of Swat and the Bronx Bombers caught a break. Inclement weather postponed the game; however, Yankees skipper Miller Huggins wasn't sure when Ruth would return. "It is difficult to figure just how long it will take for such a wound to heal sufficiently enough to permit the arm to be subjected to the rigors of throwing and batting," he said.[1] Many sportswriters predicted that Ruth would miss the rest of the fall classic.

As the first of 36,372 spectators poured into the Polo Grounds for Game Four, it appeared as if Ruth would not play. His designated replacement in left field, Chick Fewster, took BP and shagged fly balls. About 30 minutes before the 2 P.M. start time, Babe "burst heroically" onto the field, gushed New York sportswriter James Whittaker in the *Daily News*.[2] "[I]t is more and more apparent," Whittaker continued, "that Mr. Ruth is superior to the common vicissitudes of our national pastime."

The 26-year-old Ruth was indeed a larger-than-life figure. His home-run blasts had transformed the sport and signaled the end of the Deadball Era. He was coming off an unfathomable campaign, his second with the Yankees after his acquisition from the Boston Red Sox, setting new records for home runs (59) and RBIs (168). Ruth was no stranger to baseball's biggest stage, either. He helped the Red Sox to World Series championships in 1916 and 1918, tossing three complete-game victories, yielding three earned runs in 31 innings. If the Bambino had a weak spot on his already otherworldly resume, it might have been his hitting in the World Series. He was just 3-for-18, though he had knocked in six runs, but he was still searching for his elusive first home run.

As a light mist gave way to sunny skies, Game Four commenced under ideal conditions and featured the pitching matchup from the opening game. Each team alternated as host, so it was the Yankees' turn to take the field first and right-hander Carl Mays toed the rubber. The 29-year-old submariner, whose throwing style the *New York Times* chided as "uncouth," had led the AL with 27 victories, the fourth time in five seasons he won at last 20 games, and owned a 134-74 career slate.[3] Nationally syndicated sportswriter Westbrook Pegler noted that Mays "specialized in a ball that starts about where Achilles got shot and climbs a wobbly course up to the plate."[4] Like Ruth, the Yankees had obtained Mays from the Red Sox, albeit during the 1919 season. And like Ruth, he had excelled on the mound in the World Series, tossing two complete-game victories in the '18 Series and shutting out the Giants on five hits in Game One of this Series. He breezed through the first five innings of this game, holding the NL's highest-scoring offense hitless.

On the slab for skipper John "Little Napoleon" McGraw was 31-year-old journeyman Shufflin' Phil Douglas. Playing for his fifth team, Douglas was coming off a sturdy campaign with a career-best 15 wins yet sported a losing lifetime slate (83-89) in parts of eight seasons. He was nicked for five hits and three runs over eight frames in Game One and was tagged with the loss but looked sharp early in this contest. The Yankees, who had set a new American League record for runs scored (948) in the twentieth century, managed just two innocuous singles (one by Ruth) through four frames. Wally Pipp led off the fifth with a single and moved up a station on Aaron Ward's sacrifice bunt, but was then caught off base on Mike McNally's sharp grounder to third base. Wally Schang sent a shot to deep left field. According to scribe W.J. MacBeth in the *New York Tribune*, the clout appeared to be the first home run of the Series, but "missed landing in the bleachers by inches" and caromed off the wall for an RBI triple.[5]

With mounting tension produced by the pitchers' duel, Mays surrendered his first hit, a single to George Burns, with two outs in sixth, and another one in the seventh. Douglas, who had tied for the NL lead with three shutouts, kept pace. The notorious spitballer subdued the high-flying Yankees with an assortment of offerings, described by the *Times* as a "slow dipping curve, a fast ball with a leap, a fast drop and an outside curve that grazed the corners of the plate."[6]

The turning point of the game, indeed the entire best-of-nine World Series, was the fateful eighth inning. "In that space of a quarter hour or so," opined the *Times*, "the Giants rose in their might, swept over the powerless Mays with the same fury that they swept over lesser pitchers on Friday [in Game Three], and rescued a game that seemed well-nigh lost."[7] The Giants' Irish Meusel (whose brother Bob was star for the Yankees) led off the frame with a blast into the left-center-field gap that rolled to the wall for a triple. Johnny Rawlings, an "obscure and unsung" journeyman, wrote the *Times*, singled to right to drive in Meusel for the tying run.[8] Up stepped slow-footed Frank Snyder, who had been robbed of a hit two innings earlier by third baseman Mike McNally's "marvelous one-hand catch" on the run (according to the *Tribune*).[9] On McGraw's orders, Snyder executed a perfect sacrifice bunt down the first-base line. Mays had an easy play on the ball; however, "instead of stopping it, he sprawled in the ground," reported the *Times*, and the ball rolled away.[10] Douglas followed with another sacrifice bunt to move up both runners. Burns doubled to left, driving in Rawlings and Snyder and giving the Giants the lead, 3-1.

After a scoreless eighth, the Giants tacked on a run when Irish Meusel's one-out single drove home High Pockets Kelly, who had doubled.

Trailing 4-1, the Bombers had three outs to mount a comeback against Douglas, who had scattered six hits and quietly and unexpectedly emerged as an unlikely hero of the game. His "spitter broke in such baffling fashion," gushed sportswriter Edward F. Ballinger, "and his control was so perfect that the Yankees were at their wits end."[11] With one out in the frame, Ruth caught what sportswriter Jack Lawrence of the *Tribune* described as a "low-breaking spitter" with a mighty thud of the bat.[12] According to the *Times*, the "ball shot on a fairly high arch toward right field, leaped through the opening between the grandstand and bleaches and disappeared," for the Babe's first home run in World Series play.[13] The crowd, which was equally divided between Giants and Yankees fans, erupted into a "tumultuous salvo," noted Lawrence, as Ruth round the bases. The normally jovial slugger "trotted disgustedly around the bases and failed to loft his cap to the applause of the crowd," wrote syndicated columnist William Slavens McNutt.[14] Ruth, perhaps perturbed that his clout lacked a flair for the dramatic, would have plenty of additional chances to enjoy a home-run trot in the World Series: He belted 15 Series round-trippers in his career, though not another one in 1921. Unfazed, Douglas retired Bob Meusel on a popup to the catcher, and then fielded Pipp's grounder and raced first to end the game in 1 hour and 38 minutes.

"[T]he biggest halo of all should go to Shufflin' Phil Douglas whose long arms and round shoulders contained enough power to keep even Huggins's great sluggers at a distance," glowed one report.[15] He didn't issue a walk and fanned eight (including five swinging), the most strikeouts in a World Series game since the Cincinnati Reds' Hod Eller punched out nine Chicago White Sox in a 5-0 shutout in Game Five of the 1919 series.

The game "confounded all the prophets," wrote the *Times*.[16] Ruth wasn't expected to play, yet did and blasted a round-tripper. Mays mowed down the Giants with ease, destined for another shutout, yet lost the game. More than anything, the victory suddenly and dramatically shifted the momentum. "The Giants started the series apprehensive and uncertain," opined the *Times*. "Now they know their power."[17] The World Series had been reduced to the best-of-five and a test of wills: McGraw's small ball vs. Huggins's bashers.

Sources

In addition to the sources cited in the Notes, the author also accessed Retrosheet.org, Baseball-Reference.com, SABR.org, and *The Sporting News* archive via Paper of Record.

Notes

1   "Ruth Out, Probably for Series, as Rain Prevents 4th Game," *New York Times*, October 9, 1921: 1.

2   James Whittaker, "Ruth Earns a Pass for Rest of Series," *Daily News* (New York), October 10, 1921: 3.

3   "Ruth's Appearance Fooled Dopesters," *New York Times*, October 10, 1921: 16.

4   Westbrook Pegler (United News), "Battle for Three Out of Next Five Games Starts," *Pittsburgh Post*, October 10, 1921: 8.

5   W.J. MacBeth, "Carl Mays's Magic Spell Fails When Giants Get Eyes on Ball," *New York Tribune*, October 10, 1921: 11.

6   "Ruth Gets a Homer but Giants Win, 4-2; World's Series Tied," *New York Times*, October 10, 1921: 1.

7   Ibid.

8   Ibid.

9   MacBeth.

10 "Ruth Gets a Homer but Giants Win, 4-2; World's Series Tied."

11 Edward F. Ballinger, "Ruth Disregards Order to Remain Out of Struggle," *Pittsburgh Post*, October 10, 1921: 8.

12 Jack Lawrence, "Salvo of Hits Ends Pitching Duel in Favor of McGraw Men," *New York Tribune*, October 10, 1921: 11.

13 "Ruth Gets a Homer but Giants Win, 4-2; World's Series Tied."

14 William Slaven McNutt (United News), "Giants' Strong Man Overcomes Weaker Opponents and Wins," *Pittsburgh Post*, October 10, 1921: 8.

15 "Ruth Gets a Homer but Giants Win, 4-2; World's Series Tied."

16 "Ruth's Appearance Fooled Dopesters."

17 "Ruth Gets a Homer but Giants Win, 4-2; World's Series Tied."

Yankees Win 3-1 and Regain Series Lead

October 10, 1921: New York Yankees 3, New York Giants 1, at the Polo Grounds
Game Five of the 1921 World Series

By Kevin Larkin

In 1921, for the first time in the brief history of the modern World Series, all the games were played at one venue, in this case the Polo Grounds in New York. The same two teams played in the World Series in 1922, again with all the games at the Polo Grounds. The same two teams squared off for a third year in a row in 1923, but by then the Yankees had their own ballpark, Yankee Stadium. The third and final time the World Series was played in one ballpark was in 1944 when the St. Louis Browns met the St. Louis Cardinals; all six games were played at Sportsman's Park.

After the Giants' 4-2 victory in Game Four, the best-of-nine 1921 Series was tied at two games apiece. The Giants were the home team for Game Five. Yankees manager Miller Huggins named Waite Hoyt as his starter. Giants manager John McGraw selected left-hander Art Nehf to pitch; Nehf had lost Game Two 3-0 to Hoyt, who had pitched a two-hit shutout. Carl Mays had shut out the Giants in Game One by the same 3-0 score.

The Giants had come back strongly, however, with a 13-5 victory in Game Three and a 4-2 win in Game Four. The bleachers were filled (attendance was 35,758) long before umpire Cy Rigler yelled for them to play ball.[2] The back-to-back wins in the prior two games had dampened the enthusiasm of Yankees fans.[3]

As for Yankees star Babe Ruth, he was nursing a cut on his throwing arm that had become infected.[4] In the two games after the injury, he had gone 3-for-7, including a ninth-inning home run in Game Four that gave the Yankees their final run in the 4-2 loss to the Giants. Ruth had a great 1921 season, perhaps one of the greatest of all time. He hit 59 home runs, scored 177 runs, had 168 runs batted in, and walked 145 times, all American League-leading figures. Ruth also led the league in on-base percentage (.512) and slugging percentage (.846) while hitting for a .378 average, third best in the league behind Harry Heilmann (.394) and Ty Cobb (.389).

In the top of the first inning Ruth was Nehf's first strikeout victim and the final out of the inning. The Giants scored a run in the bottom of the first after an error by shortstop Roger Peckinpaugh that allowed George Burns to reach base safely. Frankie Frisch singled and Ross Youngs walked to load the bases and George "High Pockets" Kelly singled in Burns with the game's first run. The Yankees scored once in the top of the third to tie the game.

Ruth led off the top of the fourth inning but crossed up the entire Giants infield with a bunt down the third-base line, and while the play was close at first base, umpire George Moriarty ruled that Ruth had beaten the throw from Nehf.[5]

Grantland Rice wrote: "Right fielder Bob Meusel then laced a double to left-center field which sent Ruth scurrying around the bases. Few in attendance expected Ruth to reach third base, but with a new burst of speed he rounded third base and sped towards the plate like a pachyderm running on greyhound legs."[6]

The Babe scored. Wally Pipp grounded out to second baseman Johnny Rawlings for the first out of the inning. Yankee second sacker Aaron Ward flied out to George Burns in center field and Meusel beat the throw from Burns to Earl Smith for the Yankees' second run of the inning and third run of the game. Burns made a fancy catch of Mike McNally's fly ball to prevent any more scoring.[7]

Ruth's burst of speed was nearly his undoing. He got to the bench and was near collapse as his teammates began to try to get him well enough to keep playing. The game was held up for several minutes until Ruth was finally ready to return to his position in left field; his shaky walk to left field cast some doubts as to his condition.[8]

The bunt must have been a surprise for McGraw's Giants; for the past three seasons Ruth had set a new record for home runs: 29 in 1919, 54 in 1920, and 59 in 1921.

Hoyt retired the Giants easily in the bottom of the fourth inning after issuing a walk to leadoff batter Earl Smith. Smith was caught stealing and Hoyt then struck out Nehf and Burns. For the rest of the game Hoyt allowed just four more hits, a sixth-inning single by High Pockets Kelly, singles by Ross Youngs and Kelly in the bottom of the eighth, and a leadoff double by Rawlings in the ninth. Hoyt then bore done, getting Earl Smith to pop out and striking out Frank Snyder and Burns to end the game.

From the fifth inning on, Nehf was just as good as Hoyt, allowing just a fifth-inning double to Elmer Miller and an eighth-inning single by Roger Peckinpaugh. But after the fourth there was no more scoring by either team and the Yankees were 3-1 winners and now had a three-games-to-two advantage. Hoyt got the win.

The Yankees' winning and taking the Series lead was not the big story. Nor was the big story Babe Ruth's bunt in the fourth inning the big story. Monday night after the game, Dr. George King, the Babe's personal physician, conducted a physical of the Yankee slugger at the Ruths' residence in the Hotel Ansonia.[9]

King reported that he had ordered Ruth not to play the next day. He said, "Ruth's injured arm is in such condition that he would be taking chances of further injury, possibly of a serious nature if he were to take part in tomorrow's contest."[10] Sportswriters asked King whether his order would be extended should the Series go the full nine games.[11] He responded, "It is possible that the injury may take a turn for the better sooner than expected or that the Series will be strung out for a time. In either event Ruth might be able to get into the game before it is over. But as things stand tonight his chances of playing are none too bright."[12]

The Yankees and their fans had to wait nervously to see if the Babe would be available for any more games in the Series. Ruth was unable to play in either Game Six or Game Seven, both of which were won by the Giants, 8-5 and 2-1 respectively. With the Giants then holding a four-games-to-three edge, a Giants win in Game Eight would clinch the Series for them.

The Yankees had lost Game Seven by just the one run. The absence of the American League RBI champion hurt them at the plate. Game Eight was another Nehf vs. Hoyt matchup. The Giants scored a unearned run in the top of the first. It was the only run scored for the first eight innings. In the bottom of the ninth, with the Yankees still down 1-0, Ruth led off, pinch-hitting for Wally Pipp. He grounded out to first base unassisted. Aaron Ward walked, but Home Run Baker hit into a double play and the Giants won the 1921 World Series.

Sources

In addition to the game story and box-score sources cited in the Notes, the author consulted the Baseball-Reference.com and Retrosheet.org websites.

Notes

1. Headline from the *New York Tribune,* October 11, 1921: 1.
2. Robert Boyd, "Giants Beaten by the Yankees 3-1: Ruth Faints as He Scores: But Stays In Game," *New York Evening World,* October 10, 1921: 1.
3. Ibid.
4. Allen Wood, "Babe Ruth," SABR Biography Project, sabr.org, accessed March 26, 2018.
5. "The Game by Innings," *New York Times,* October 11, 1921: 15.
6. Grantland Rice, "Yankees Triumph Over Giants in Fifth Game by 3 to 1 Score," *New York Tribune,* October 11, 1921: 12.
7. "The Game by Innings."
8. "Ruth Near Collapse After His Bunt Wins for Yankees, 3 to 1" *New York Times,* October 11, 1921: 1.
9. "Ruth Out of Game by Doctor's Orders," *New York Times,* October 11, 1921: 1.
10. Ibid.
11. Ibid.
12. Ibid.

Ruth's Ejection Costs Him Yankees Captaincy

May 25, 1922: New York Yankees 6, Washington Senators 4, at the Polo Grounds, New York

By Mike Lynch

When the 1922 season began on April 12, the New York Yankees were without the star and face of the franchise Babe Ruth and slugger Bob Meusel, both of whom were suspended for six weeks after brazenly defying Commissioner Kenesaw Mountain Landis's order not to barnstorm after the 1921 World Series.[1] Landis had told Ruth in no uncertain terms that ignoring him would be "the sorriest thing you've ever done in baseball."[2] But Ruth was adamant and headed to Buffalo, where the tour was to begin. There was money to be made and the Bambino wasn't about to let Landis rain on his parade. But rain the commissioner did.[3]

Ruth and Meusel wouldn't debut until May 20, but the team weathered the storm with aplomb and after a 12-4 drubbing of the Cleveland Indians on May 19, the Yankees had a record of 22-11 and held a two-game lead over the second-place St. Louis Browns. Opinions about Ruth's return varied. The *Boston Globe* wrote on May 20, "On this day the exile of the King of Swat expires, and the fans are crowding at the gates or waiting expectantly for news, confident that the Babe will knock one, perhaps two, out of the lot."[4] But the *Philadelphia Inquirer* was less enthusiastic, calling Ruth and Meusel "spoiled darlings of the fickle public."[5]

The Yankees celebrated Ruth's return by naming him captain of the team.[6] But by the time the May 25 game against the Washington Senators rolled around, fans had turned on Ruth. He went 0-for-4 with a strikeout in his first game and was hitting an anemic .095 after a 5-3 loss to Washington on May 24. The locals derisively cheered when Ruth made two routine catches in the outfield against the Browns on May 22 and he responded with a contemptuous doff of his cap.

The *New York Herald* also took a swipe at Ruth after a 0-for-5 day against Walter Johnson, who pitched the Senators to a win over the Yankees on May 24. Light-slugging future Hall of Famer Sam Rice hit his first home run of the season, prompting the *Herald* to tease, "It begins to look as though almost anybody can hit a home run but the Babe. Nobody loves a fat man."[7]

The catcalls heaped on him from the stands on May 25 finally became too much and Ruth snapped.

At 24-14, the Yankees held a 1½-game lead over the Browns going into their tilt with the Senators at the Polo Grounds in New York. Yankees skipper Miller Huggins sent 22-year-old right-hander Waite Hoyt to the mound to face 33-year-old journeyman Tom Phillips. Hoyt was 5-2 with a 2.84 ERA and had tossed 10 innings against the Browns only four days earlier in a 6-5 victory over St. Louis. Phillips was 2-6 with an abysmal 4.66 ERA and had only seven more major-league appearances ahead of him before landing back in the minors.

As he had in his first five games, Ruth was playing left field and batting third and Meusel was in his usual right-field spot and batting fifth behind third baseman Frank "Home Run" Baker. Only two batters in, Rice smacked an inside-the-park homer to left field to give the Senators a 1-0 lead. But the Yankees took a 2-1 lead in the bottom of the first. Whitey Witt led off with a walk, Aaron Ward singled on a bunt to put runners at first and second, and Ruth laid down a sacrifice to put runners at second and third. Baker shot a single to center and both runners scored, giving New York a one-run lead.

The second inning was relatively quiet but it was in the third that Ruth made a spectacle of himself and drew the ire of an umpire, and many in attendance. With one out, Ruth stepped to the plate and poled a hit to center that Rice fumbled, prompting Ruth to try to extend his single into a double. Rice threw the slugger out at second in a close play. Ruth came up with a handful of dirt and hurled it at umpire George Hildebrand.

"[Ruth] leaped to his feet with the quickness of a cat and he brought up with him a handful of dirt," reported the *New York Times*, "which he threw in the direction of the umpire. From the grandstand it seemed that the dust spattered over Hildebrand's face and neck. Some of it seeped down inside his collar and the rest fell on his arm and on the front of his blue uniform."[8]

As Ruth walked off the field, many in the crowd jeered and hooted.[9] Ruth returned the favor and mockingly doffed his cap as he headed to the dugout. At this, a fan yelled, "You goddamned big bum, why don't you play ball?"[10] With a crowd of only 10,000 on hand, Ruth had an easy time picking out the heckler. Ruth climbed onto the dugout roof and went into the stands, but the heckler had already distanced himself from his seat and was out of harm's way.

Ruth was slowed by fans and someone in the crowd yelled, "Hit the big stiff!" Rather than continue his pursuit, the slugger returned to the dugout roof and challenged anyone and everyone to a brawl. "Come on down and fight! Anyone who wants to fight," he shouted, "come down on the field!"[11] As he exited the Polo Grounds, the catcalls grew louder.

Elmer Miller replaced Ruth in left field and went 0-for-2 with a strikeout. Fortunately for the Yankees, an equally-struggling Meusel, who was hitting only .100 going into the game, caught fire and blasted two home runs to lead them to a 6-4 win and a two-game lead over St. Louis. His first homer was a long drive into the left-field bleachers in the fourth inning that gave the Yankees a 4-1 lead. His second came in the eighth against Jim Brillheart, a line drive into the left-field seats that gave New York an insurance run in the 6-4 win.

The Senators made a game of it in the sixth when Joe Judge slammed a three-run homer into the upper deck in right field to tie the game at 4-4. But the Yankees responded immediately and broke the tie in the bottom of the inning on Wally Pipp's single to center followed by Everett Scott's double to left that gave New York a 5-4 lead.

American League President Ban Johnson announced that Ruth would be suspended until he had a chance to investigate his incident with Hildebrand. But Ruth missed only one game, was fined $200, and was stripped of his captaincy. His tenure had lasted all of six days.[12]

Sources

In addition to the sources cited in the Notes, the author also accessed Retrosheet.org, Baseball-Reference.com, and SABR.org.

Notes

1 Pitchers Tom Sheehan and Bill Piercy were also suspended but Sheehan spent the 1922 season with the Double-A St. Paul Saints and Piercy had been traded to the Boston Red Sox on December 20, 1921.

2 Robert Creamer, *Babe: The Legend Comes to Life* (New York: Simon & Schuster, 1974), 246.

3 In addition to the suspension, Landis also fined the players an amount equal to their World Series share. Consequences for the Yankees could have been even more severe had pitcher Carl Mays and catcher Wally Schang accompanied Ruth as originally planned. They wisely backed out and helped the Yankees win their second straight pennant.

4 "Back in the Game," *Boston Globe*, May 20, 1922: 6.

5 "Judge Landis as 'Babe' Ruth's Friend," *Philadelphia Inquirer*, May 20, 1922: 12.

6 Some claim that Ruth was named captain in the winter of 1921-1922, but others, including Ruth's SABR biographer Allan Wood, say the designation came on May 20. sabr.org/bioproj/person/9dcdd01c

7 W.O. McGeehan, "Opportunity Raps Often, Not So Ruth," *New York Herald*, May 25, 1922: 13. Sam Rice would go on to hit only 34 home runs in a 20-year career that saw him bat .322 in 9,269 at-bats and fall 13 hits shy of 3,000.

8 "Ruth in Row With Umpire and Fan at Polo Grounds," *New York Times*, May 26, 1922: 1. Both Hildebrand and Ruth insisted afterward that the dirt didn't end up in the umpire's face, but landed on his sleeve.

9 Ibid.

10 Creamer, *Babe*: 258.

11 Ibid.

12 "Ruth Is in Line-Up in To-Day's Game, But Not Captain," *New York Evening World*, March 27, 1922: 5. Senators owner Clark Griffith appealed to Ban Johnson to not suspend Ruth for more than a game because he desperately needed the gate receipts that Ruth would bring in over the last two games of a five-game series. Johnson was sympathetic to Ruth and chalked up the latter's outburst, at least publicly, to his lengthy suspension at the start of the season, which caused him to lose his "batting eye" and endure criticism from fans. "Ruth plainly did not possess the mental strength and stability to brave this sudden reversal of public adoration," Johnson announced to the press. "It served to warp his playing ability, and for days he has been nervous and irritable."

Yankee Stadium Grand Opening Hints at Franchise's Dynastic Future

April 18, 1923: New York Yankees 4, Boston Red Sox 1, at Yankee Stadium

By Frederick C. Bush

In 1913 the New York Highlanders were renamed the Yankees and moved from Hilltop Park into the Polo Grounds, the home field of the National League's New York Giants. Two years later, the franchise was under the new co-ownership of Jacob Ruppert and Tillinghast L'Hommedieu Huston, who initiated the team's transformation into an American League powerhouse by purchasing Babe Ruth from the Boston Red Sox in December 1919. The Big Bam's prodigious home-run output eventually resulted in the tenant Yankees outdrawing the landlord Giants in their own home park.

As a result, John McGraw, the Giants' manager, minority owner, and noted hater of the American League, could no longer abide the Yankees. It was not enough for him that he had led the Giants to consecutive World Series triumphs over his despised rivals in 1921 and 1922, including holding the vaunted Sultan of Swat to a .188 batting average with no home runs in a four-game sweep in the latter Series. He wanted the Yankees gone and persuaded majority owner Horace Stoneham to banish them in the hope that the team would falter and fold. When McGraw found out that the Yankees' new stadium would be built in the Bronx, right across the Harlem River from the Polo Grounds, he gleefully crowed, "They are going up to Goatville. And before long they will be lost sight of. A New York team should be based on Manhattan Island."[1]

Although McGraw was an innovator who had a long, successful career in baseball, his assessment of the Yankees' new home and the team's future could not have been more in error. The $2.5 million structure was situated on a 10-acre plot, and it took 500 workmen 11 months to complete "the first ballpark to be referred to as a stadium" just in time for opening day of

74,200 SEE YANKEES OPEN NEW STADIUM; RUTH HITS HOME RUN

Record Baseball Crowd Cheers as Slugger's Drive Beats Red Sox, 4 to 1.

25,000 ARE TURNED AWAY

Gates to $2,500,000 Arena Are Closed Half an Hour Before Start of Game.

MANY NOTABLES ATTEND

Governor Smith Throws Out First Ball—Shawkey, In Great Form, Allows Only Three Hits.

the 1923 season.[2] In light of its size and price tag, the *New York Times* rhapsodized:

Down on the Potomac, close by the National Capitol, they are thinking about erecting an impressive monument to the national game of baseball. But in the busy borough of the Bronx ... the real monument to baseball will be unveiled this afternoon – the new Yankee Stadium ... comprising in its broad reaches of concrete and steel the last word in baseball arenas.[3]

Everyone who was someone, along with a host of anyones – more than 25,000 of whom were unable to gain admission to the sold-out stadium – wanted to be part of the grand opening on April 18, 1923. The Yankees gave the official attendance that day as 74,200, but later amended that number to 62,200.[4] The list of dignitaries present included Baseball Commissioner Kenesaw Mountain Landis, New York Governor Al Smith, and New York City Mayor John Hylan.

John Philip Sousa directed the Seventh Regiment Band as it marched to the center-field flagpole, where New York manager Miller Huggins and Boston skipper Frank Chance raised the American flag and the Yankees' 1922 pennant as the band played "The Star-Spangled Banner." After Governor Smith threw the ceremonial first ball to Yankees catcher Wally Schang, it was time to play ball. New York hurler Bob Shawkey threw the first pitch in Yankee Stadium history, a ball high and inside, to Schang with Chick Fewster at bat for Boston.

Another notable moment took place in the top of the second inning, when Red Sox first baseman George Burns got the first hit in stadium history. Burns then attempted to garner the first stolen base of the day, but he was gunned down at second base by Schang. Second baseman Aaron Ward made the first base hit for the home team when he singled in the third. After the game Burns received a box of cigars and Ward received 50 "ropes" [cigars] for their landmark hits.[5]

Ruth, whose popularity had made this new stadium both possible and necessary, naturally provided the day's biggest thrill as the Yankees scored all four of their runs in the third inning. Shawkey and Whitey Witt had reached base on consecutive singles, and Joe Dugan followed with a base hit of his own to drive in the first run. The next batter to step to the plate, with runners at first and third, was The Bambino.

Ruth was seeking redemption after a miserable 1922 season in which he had batted .315 with 35 homers after hitting .378 and clouting 59 round-trippers in 1921; there was also the cloud of that .188 World Series performance hanging over his head. Ruth knew "[t]he talk was that he was boozing it up a lot and couldn't be managed, and maybe he was through."[6] He had spent the offseason walking the straight and narrow and working his way back into playing shape. In spite of his efforts, he had not performed well in spring-training exhibition games, and he told his teammates, as they left the clubhouse on Opening Day, "I'd give a year off my life to hit one today."[7]

Ruth now had his second opportunity of the day to deliver the desired blow. He fouled off Red Sox pitcher Howard Ehmke's first pitch, took a ball, hit another pitch foul, and watched ball two go by. Then Ehmke left a letter-high curveball over the plate that Ruth ripped several rows up into the bleachers for a three-run blast that gave the Yankees a 4-0 lead. As he crossed home plate, Ruth "lifted his Kelley and smiled from ear to ear as he faced the multitude and made those graceful bows rehearsed so many times in his great season of 1921."[8]

Ever the showman, and often a bit of a huckster, Ruth afterward asserted that his blast had been forecast earlier in the week. He claimed that Hendrik Willem van Loon, author of *The Story of Mankind*, had given him a silver dollar for good luck and had promised him, "You'll get a homer in the third inning with two on base."[9] The fact that the certainty expressed in this story did not exactly jibe with Ruth's willingness to sacrifice a year of his life for an Opening Day homer did not faze The Big Bam.

Ruth's clout was the climax of the game, though the Yankees did threaten to score again in the fourth inning. Bob Meusel led off the frame with a double, but Ehmke fielded Schang's bunt and nailed Meusel at third base. After Ward struck out, Everett Scott, playing in his 987th consecutive game, delivered a double of his own.[10] Schang tried to score from first base but was gunned down at home on a nice play from right fielder Shano Collins to first baseman Burns, who fired the relay throw to catcher Al DeVormer.

The Red Sox scored their lone run in the top of the seventh inning when Shawkey walked Burns and Norm McMillan drove him in with a triple. It was the only hiccup of the afternoon for Shawkey, who pitched a complete-game three-hitter to earn the first win in Yankee Stadium history.

The final noteworthy event occurred in the ninth inning, with Burns batting for Boston, when fans from the bleachers scaled the outfield wall and surrounded Ruth in right field. Home-plate umpire Tom Connolly stopped the game but soon realized "the futility of trying to clear the outskirts. Accordingly, Ruth had plenty of comrades in right when the game closed."[11]

The Yankees emerged victorious in their 1923 debut, and everyone seemed certain that Ruth was back on track. However, the *New York Times* summarized the importance of the day by stating, "But the game, after all, was only an incident of a busy afternoon. The stadium was the thing. For the Yankee owners it was the realization of a dream long cherished. For the fans it was something which they had never seen before in baseball."[12] Perhaps to the chagrin of McGraw and Stoneham, the *Times* added, "The Yankees' new home, besides being beautiful and majestic, is practical. It was emptied yesterday of its 74,000 in quicker time than the Polo Grounds ever was."[13]

After slugging his Opening Day home run, Ruth had referred to his offseason training regimen and abstinence from his vices, saying, "I guess there must be something in that old gag about virtue being its own reward."[14] By the end of the 1923 season, the tenants of the new "beautiful, majestic, and practical" baseball cathedral called Yankee Stadium would be World Series champions for the first time after defeating the denizens of their previous home, McGraw's Giants, in six games. Ruth batted .393 and led the league with 41 homers in the regular season. He redeemed himself in the World Series as well by battering Giants pitching for a .368 average and three home runs. It was indeed quite a reward.

Notes

1 Harvey Frommer, "Remembering the First Game at Yankee Stadium April 18, 1923," travel-watch.com/remembering1stgameatyankeestad1.htm, accessed May 18, 2018.

2 Ibid.

3 "Yanks' New Stadium to Be Opened Today: Record Crowd Expected to Witness Dedication of $2,500,000 Baseball Arena," *New York Times*, April 18, 1923: 17.

4 Robert Weintraub, *The House That Ruth Built: A New Stadium, the First Yankees Championship, and the Redemption of 1923* (New York: Little, Brown and Company, 2011), 17-18. According to Weintraub, a boxing match was held at Yankee Stadium in May for which 10,000 extra seats were placed on the field. The total number of tickets printed for the match was 70,000, which indicated that the current capacity for baseball games was approximately 60,000. Yankees business manager Ed Barrow then admitted that he had added standing-room fans to his original estimate and amended his Opening Day figure to 62,200. Weintraub writes that even this figure is "probably still exaggerated, but [it was] nevertheless by far the largest crowd in the sport's history,"

5 Ed Cunningham, "Echoes from That Babe Ruth Swat," *Boston Herald*, April 19, 1923: 14.

6 John Durant, "April 1923: First Day at Yankee Stadium," si.com/vault/1963/04/22/602983/april-1923-first-day-at-yankee-stadium, accessed May 18, 2018.

7 Weintraub, 27.

8 "The Paying Colonels Draw Dividend When King George Whacks," *Boston Herald*, April 19, 1923: 14.

9 "Ruth Says Van Loon Predicted Home Run," *Springfield* (Massachusetts) *Republican*, April 19, 1923: 6.

10 Everett Scott played in a major-league record 1,307 consecutive games between June 20, 1916, and May 5, 1925. His record would eventually be broken by another Yankees player, a rookie who had debuted in 1923 but had played in only 13 games and had been left off the team's playoff roster. Lou Gehrig would eventually shatter Scott's record by playing in 2,130 consecutive games.

11 Cunningham, "Echoes from That Babe Ruth Swat."

12 "74,200 See Yankees Open New Stadium; Ruth Hits Home Run," *New York Times*, April 19, 1923: 1.

13 "74,200 See Yankees Open New Stadium: 15.

14 "Ruth Says Van Loon Predicted Home Run."

Babe Hit the Wall, and the Wall Won

July 5, 1924: New York Yankees 2, Washington Senators 0 (first game of doubleheader), at Griffith Stadium, Washington, D.C.

By Chad Osborne

Babe Ruth feared the worst when he played right field in Washington's Griffith Stadium. The unsightly concrete barrier that separated the playing field from the seats and spectators seemed especially menacing and dangerous. "Babe says he's been afraid that he was going to bump into that wall in the Washington Park ever since he began playing right field." [1]

His fear became reality in early July of 1924, when his New York Yankees played the Senators in the first game of a doubleheader at the D.C. ballpark.

Picture the scene …

Lying on the grass, in front of the concrete wall with concerned onlookers draped over it, was one of the best-known baseball players – if not individuals – in the country. Ruth lay motionless as a medical trainer, having just poured icy water on his face, tried to revive him, to no avail.

Ruth's teammates and opponents gathered around. Others, too, joined the scene. One was a photographer who snapped

Photo shows baseball player Babe Ruth knocked unconscious, after he ran into a concrete wall at Griffith Stadium, Washington, D.C., while trying to catch a foul ball on July 5, 1924. *Source: Flickr Commons project, 2009 and New York Times, July 6, 1924.*

a now-famous black and white photograph that captures the dramatic spectacle.

We see, through the photograph, Ruth lying on the ground unconscious, his body straddling the chalky right-field foul line. The charismatic and gregarious Bambino, the world's greatest ballplayer, had moments earlier sprinted full steam ahead and slammed his body into that concrete wall and knocked himself out cold.

Ruth, normally the irresistible force *and* the immovable object, had met his match and his fear had become reality. The Sultan of Swat had been swatted.

The Bambino's Yankees were in the nation's capital on Saturday, July 5, 1924, for a second day of doubleheaders with the Senators. They had swept a twin bill on Friday, Independence Day, 4-2 and 2-0, to move to within two games of the American League-leading Washington club. Two wins on Saturday would tie the two teams for first place.

The great Walter Johnson was on the mound for the Senators. He had won 10 games already this season, but the Yankees came out swinging and got to the 18-year veteran early in the contest. Leadoff hitter Whitey Witt "bounded a high single" [2] over the reach of the 6-foot-1 Johnson's head, and Ruth smacked a double to right-center that moved Witt to third. The next batter, Bob Meusel, delivered a long sacrifice fly to the Senators' Sam Rice in right field that scored Witt to give the Yankees a 1-0 advantage.

Herb Pennock took his 8-6 record to the mound for the Yankees and kept the bats of the league-leading Senators quiet. Washington's Wid Matthews recorded the first of his two hits in the first inning, but player-manager Bucky Harris erased Matthews from the basepaths by hitting into a double play. The *New York Times* speculated that Harris's failure at bat might have been caused by embarrassment after he was presented with a large bouquet of red roses at the plate just before he was to hit. [3]

In the fourth, Matthews reached first on an infield hit after slapping a pitch that ricocheted off Pennock's glove. The center fielder reached second on a sacrifice by Harris and advanced to third as left fielder Goose Goslin grounded out.

With two outs and Matthews standing on third, left-handed-batting Joe Judge walked to the plate. Pennock had retired Judge once already in the game, but this time the first baseman struck a pitch that came within a few feet of being a home run and would have given the Senators the lead.

Judge smoked Pennock's pitch and sent it cruising down the right-field line. Ruth, patrolling right field, sprinted to his left and homed in on the flying spheroid, hoping to record an out and send the Senators back to the dugout without a run.

As the ball dropped foul into the crowd, "The Babe ran into the pavilion parapet with the full force of his body, and dropped unconscious to the grass," the *New York Times* reported.

Yankees trainer Doc Woods, carrying a "little black bag" and a bucket of cold water, ran to assist Ruth. Uniformed police officers also hurried to the Babe's aid and held back some members of curious and anxious crowd, most of whom were young black men sitting in a section reserved for African-American spectators. Several photographers were there to document the scene. [4]

"At first it was thought that Ruth had been knocked out by a blow from the concrete on his chin, but it was soon discovered that he had been knocked out by a jolt in the solar plexus," the *New York Times* reported, adding, "His left leg was also hurt at the hip."

Ruth was unconscious for five minutes, according to the *Washington Post*. [5] When he came to, Ruth insisted that he stay in the game despite New York manager Miller Huggins's contrary suggestion.

The Babe, who had spent an hour that morning swatting autographed baseballs to citizen soldiers at Camp Meade, Maryland,[6] batted in the top of the sixth and hit a Johnson pitch off the center-field wall for a double. He moved to third when the next hitter, Meusel, grounded out. Ruth scored a batter later when Wally Pipp slapped a single to center.

The 25,000 "highly excited Washington fans" [7] – a 16-year-old Buck Leonard, future star of the Homestead Grays, may have been among those [8] – cheered Ruth, who galloped around the bases with a noticeable limp from his too-close encounter with the wall an inning and a half earlier. The crowd was "the largest gathering of fans to take in a local game," *Washington Post* wrote. [9]

The Bambino batted once more in the game, accepting a free pass to first from Johnson. Ruth finished the game with three hits in as many at-bats. His teammate Witt also had three hits, and collectively the Yankees punched 10 base knocks off Johnson for a 2-0 win.

The victory meant New York had climbed to within a single game of the Senators, and it gave the Yankees a chance to even the race in the second game.

Ruth, however, still shaken from the collision, was no help at the plate in the nightcap. He finished 0-for-3, and "swung with evident pain." [10] He did lay down a successful bunt in the first that helped the Yankees score twice for a quick lead. The

Senators, however, rallied for four in the bottom of the frame, and got two more in the fourth and one in the eighth for an easy 7-2 triumph.

After the final out of the second game that Saturday, Ruth was diagnosed with a bruised pelvic bone. It hampered him for days, but it did not hinder his performance.

The next day, the Bambino went 3-for-4 and hit his 22nd home run of the season in a 7-4 win as the Yankees concluded the series in Washington. The Yankees had an offday Monday and traveled back to New York, giving Ruth a much-needed rest. The defending World Series champions hosted the Chicago White Sox for a Tuesday doubleheader in the Bronx. Ruth was a combined 3-for-5 in the games, in which the two teams split wins.

His hip was examined once more.

"Two x-rays were made of the side after Tuesday's game, but they failed to show any broken or fractured bones," wrote the *Times*.

Ruth's play at the plate didn't suffer, but he did. Huggins gave the Bambino the day off from starting on Wednesday, and the *New York Times* reported "Ruth, who is too badly crippled to play, is worried over the condition of his side."[11]

On Wednesday against the White Sox, Huggins sent Ruth to the plate "limping and glowering," and he belted a pinch-hit single that scored two runs.[12] The timely hit, however, "failed to cheer him up," the *New York Times* reported of Ruth, who immediately yielded to a pinch runner.

Notes

1 "Yanks Rally in 9th Fails; Sox Win, 8-6," *New York Times*, July 10, 1924: 16.

2 Ibid.

3 Ibid.

4 Ibid.

5 Frank H. Young, "Nationals Salvage Split of Doubleheader as Ruth Crashes Into Wall," *Washington Post*, July 6, 1924.

6 "Yanks Break Even and Fail to Advance," *New York Times*, July 6, 1924: 24.

7 Ibid.

8 Brad Snyder, *Beyond the Shadow of the Senators: The Untold Story of the Homestead Grays and the Integration of Baseball* (New York: McGraw-Hill, 2004), 15.

9 "Nationals Salvage Split."

10 "Yanks Break Even and Fail to Advance."

11 "Caught at the Plate," *New York Times*, July 10, 1924: 16.

12 "Yanks Rally in 9th Fails; Sox Win, 8-6," *New York Times*, July 10, 1924: 16.

Babe Ruth Returns from "Bellyache Heard 'Round the World"

June 1, 1925: Washington Senators 5, New York Yankees 3, at Yankee Stadium

By Josh Berk

Babe Ruth got a huge cheer when he stepped onto the field at Yankee Stadium on June 1, 1925 – a well-deserved ovation considering that just a few months ago he was dead. The announcement of his demise was wildly inaccurate, of course, but it was right there in black and white in newspapers around the world. One Scottish paper ran the headline BASEBALL FANS GET SHOCK: IDOL OF THE CROWDS REPORTED DEAD.[1] Similar reports appeared in papers in London, Belfast, and elsewhere. The *New York Times* noted the next day that the false story had begun in Canada for unknown reasons and "spread with almost incredible rapidity."[2]

While the report of his demise was an exaggeration to say the least (and no doubt a surprise to Ruth), the diagnosis of Dr. Edward King was quite serious. Babe had persistent high fevers all during spring training and collapsed in a train station in Asheville, North Carolina, after a preseason game.[3] He had to be hospitalized and operated on. Some reports said it was influenza but this wasn't a consensus opinion. There were whispers that he'd never play again and that "the true nature of his illness was being kept secret."[4] Sportswriter W.O. McGeehan penned the lasting story that Ruth's ailment was the result of eating a dozen hot dogs and a legend was born. The incident became known as "the bellyache heard round the world."[5]

The hot-dog story was pure fiction, an example of the colorful writing of the time, made believable by the true gluttonous personality of The Babe. There were alternate theories, including the suggestion that it wasn't his stomach but something lower.[6] The rumor persists that the team was spinning a kid-friendly hot-dog theory to cover up a sexually transmitted disease. However believable this also sounds (see: Babe's gluttonous personality), it's not true.

Ruth went under the knife to treat an abscess; he had a scar and it took weeks to recover – not treatment consistent with venereal disease.[7] If there was an attempt to hide the truth, it was probably because Babe's prodigious alcohol consumption was at least partially to blame – an awkward fact during the era of prohibition. Babe was a heavy imbiber, there was a lack of quality control in moonshine, and alcohol poisoning was common. Although never confirmed as the cause of Ruth's abscess and intestinal issues, all that homemade booze certainly did not help.

The newspapers and fans anxiously followed Ruth's stay in New York's St. Vincent Hospital; he was at the height of his fame in 1925. He was the game's – and probably the country's – biggest star. Original estimates from the Yankees predicted he'd be back in uniform in May. As the month went on, it was clear he wasn't ready. Revised estimates predicted the middle of June. A May 27 report said he was discharged from the hospital, but that he remained "a delicate if interesting invalid."[8] He appeared far from a return.

But Ruth must have grown restless, a condition not improved by watching the Yankees – who came in second the year before and expected to compete for the pennant – plummet in the standings. It was suddenly announced that he would be in the lineup on June 1 to face the Washington Senators. Perhaps because of the late notice, it wasn't a packed house but a small crowd of about 10,000 who braved a brutal New York heat wave to come to Yankee Stadium to cheer his return.[9]

The Senators were 26-15 (second place) while the Yankees languished without Babe at a nearly opposite mark of 15-25 (next to last). Yankees fans were happy to see him though some observers felt he "really ought not to be in the contest" and was "still a sick man."[10] Recently unearthed footage from the game shows him running at less than full strength, and looking thin, but still taking his trademark violent hacks at pitch after pitch.[11]

The starting pitcher for the Senators was the great Walter Johnson. It was his 19th season in the majors and the Big Train was still rolling. He led the league in wins, winning percentage, ERA, and shutouts the previous year. He was off to a strong 1925 as well, with a 7-2 record entering play despite having been hit hard his previous two starts. Starting for the Yankees was Sad Sam Jones, who gave up a leadoff double to Sam Rice (no mood given) to begin the game. Rice was stranded as Jones retired the next three hitters.

Johnson cruised through his half of the first and there was little excitement until Babe, batting fourth, stepped in to lead off the bottom of the second. Making his first plate appearance in the team's 41st game of the year, he had to feel some rust. Johnson got him to tap weakly to the mound.

The score remained tied thanks in part to a nice play by the Yankees' Earle Combs to rob Joe Harris of extra bases in the top of the third. In the top of the fourth, the Senators plated one, then the Yankees got one right back in their half. It was nearly a much bigger inning for New York as Ruth hammered a shot to deep right with Combs on first. The blast brought the crowd to its feet, but the ball veered foul by "just a foot or two."[12] Babe ended up walking. The next batter, Bob Meusel, hit a fly to deep center field that went past Rice for a double. Combs scored, but Ruth was thrown out at the plate, and it wasn't close. It wasn't pretty either. He reportedly "staggered,"[13] then "landed with a thud, flat on his waistline – out by a foot."[14] It was noted that if he was able to run at full speed he likely would have scored standing up.

Despite his limited mobility, Babe was the star on defense in the fifth inning. There were two runners on when Joe Judge hit one in the gap in right-center. Ruth sprinted up the small hill that served as the warning track in Yankee Stadium. He leaped, snagged the fly, and though he tumbled to the ground, the ball remained in his glove. Center fielder Combs had to "help the fallen gladiator to his feet," but the side was retired and the game remained tied, 1-1.[15]

The second physically painful play of the game and the brutal heat made it a tough day to return from a long absence. Yankees manager Miller Huggins sent Babe to the bench after the sixth for Bobby Veach. In the seventh the Senators cracked it open, scoring three runs. The big blow was a two-run triple by Goose Goslin. This gave Johnson a 4-1 lead, but he tired in the bottom of eighth, loading the bases on a double and two walks. Firpo Marberry came on in relief and retired the side without allowing a run to score, striking out Meusel on three pitches to end the inning. Notably, the second out of that inning was made by young Lou Gehrig, who had pinch-hit for Pee-Wee Wanninger. Wanninger, a light-hitting shortstop, was known for the fact that as a rookie he ended original iron man Everett Scott's consecutive-game streak, a major-league record of 1,307 games some believed would never be topped.[16] Yankees reliable first baseman Wally Pipp went 1-for-4 in the game. His average was .244, down from past years, and manager Huggins was considering a youth movement. He contemplated giving Gehrig – "the kid" – an extended look.[17]

In the top of the ninth, Washington leadoff man and star-of-the-game Rice got a one-out triple for his fifth hit of the day. The Yankees trailed 5-1 in the ninth when replacement shortstop Ernie Johnson hit a surprise two-run home run to right, cutting the lead to two. Johnson was followed by pinch-hitter Whitey Witt, who walked, bringing third baseman Joe Dugan to the plate. Jumping Joe represented the tying run and no doubt was the man Huggins wanted to see in this spot. Dugan was hot, with 44 hits in the month of May (30 games) and 21 hits in his last 12 games. Facing Marberry with the game on the line, he got good wood on the ball but hit it right at Senators second baseman Bucky Harris for the final out. The Babe was no doubt a little sore, physically, as well as disappointed in the way the game turned out, a 5-3 loss. But the big man showed that there was plenty of baseball left in him. He was very much alive, back, and hungry for more.

Notes

1. "Baseball Fans Get Shock: Idol of the Crowds Reported Dead." *Dundee* (Scotland) *Evening Telegraph*, April 9, 1925.

2. "Washington Is Stirred: Early Morning Reports of Ruth's Death Arouse Capital," *New York Times*, April 10, 1925: 6.

3. Bill Ballew, "The Babe & The Bellyache: Babe Ruth, Asheville & McCormick Field | Asheville Tourists McCormick Field," MiLB.com, undated. milb.com/content/page.jsp?sid=t573&ymd=20070425&content_id=232912&vkey=team1.

4. Dave Anderson and Alec Baldwin, *The New York Times Story of the Yankees: 1903 – Present* (New York: Black Dog & Leventhal, 2017), 59.

5. Kal Wagenheim, *Babe Ruth: His Life and Legend* (New York: Praeger Publishers, 1974), 135.

6. Robert W. Creamer. *Babe: The Legend Comes to Life* (New York: Simon & Schuster, 1992), 289.

7. Ibid.

8. "Ruth Is Discharged from Hospital," *New York Times*, May 27, 1925: 19.

9. James R. Harrison, "Ruth Back in Game but Yankees Lose 5-3," *New York Times*, June 2, 1925: 18.

10. "Babe Ruth Still a Sick Man, but His Spirit Is Unimpaired," *Washington Evening Star,* June 2, 1925: 30.

11. Mike Axisa, "VIDEO: Rare Footage of Babe Ruth and Lou Gehrig from 1925," CBSSports.com, CBS Sports, June 2, 2015, cbssports.com/mlb/news/video-rare-footage-of-babe-ruth-and-lou-gehrig-from-1925/.

12. Harrison: 8.

13. "Babe Ruth Still a Sick Man, But His Spirit Is Unimpaired."

14. Harrison: 8.

15. Ibid.

16. Ray Birch, "Everett Scott," https://sabr.org/bioproj/person/365591cd.

17. John Eisenberg, *The Streak: Lou Gehrig, Cal Ripken Jr., and Baseball's Most Historic Record* (Boston: Houghton Mifflin Harcourt, 2017), 6.

Babe Ruth Beats White Sox with Extra-inning Walkoff Grand Slam

September 24, 1925: New York Yankees 6, Chicago White Sox 5, at Yankee Stadium

by Mike Huber

In adding to his legend, Babe Ruth drove a pitch into the Yankee Stadium's right-field bleachers to steal a victory away from the Chicago White Sox. The White Sox had scored three runs in the top of the 10th, believing they had the game in the bag, but Ruth's walkoff grand slam in the bottom of the 10th meant otherwise. This prompted the *New York Times* to print, "Ruth is stranger than fiction."[1]

Two teams far removed from the postseason play were finishing the 1925 season. Eddie Collins' Chicago team was in fifth place, while the Yankees were even lower, in seventh position in the American League standings. This was game number 149 for each club. Red Faber was called on to keep the New Yorkers in check, and he did so, until he was injured in the ninth inning. For the home team, manager Miller Huggins called on Ben Shields to start, a lefty who would give the Chicago batters "quite a fight for nine innings."[2]

Shields had faced the White Sox two days earlier, after having been called up from the Richmond Colts of the Virginia League (Class-B ball). Rookie Hank Johnson had started that game for New York and Shields came on in relief to pitch the ninth, facing six batters, walking three but allowing no runs. In this game, the 22-year-old left-hander was making his first career start in the major leagues. Faber was making his start number 31 of the season for Chicago.

The game amounted to a pitcher's duel for the regulation innings. The Yankees "helped themselves to a lead in the second,"[3] when Bob Meusel tripled and scored when Lou Gehrig drove him home with a sacrifice fly. An inning later, a second run was scored by New York, on a comedy of errors caused by "wild throws by

[Ray] Schalk and [Johnny] Mostil."4 Earle Combs had forced Shields at second. Combs then stole second and went to third on a bad throw by catcher Schalk. Center fielder Mostil threw to third baseman Willie Kamm to get Combs, but the "bad fling past Kamm"5 enabled Combs to score.

The White Sox notched solo tallies in the sixth and seventh innings. Doubles by Roy Elsh and Earl Sheely accounted to the first run, and Kamm's triple in the seventh led to run number two, when he scored on an out by Ike Davis. When the ninth inning was complete, the score was 2-2.

In the top of the first extra frame, the White Sox "has amassed what looked like a comfortable lead of three runs."6 Shields had labored in the first nine innings, but in the tenth, he lost his control. He walked leadoff batter Schalk. He then hit Faber "with such a cruel swat on the left elbow that the red-haired spitballer had to leave the game."7 Dickey Kerr entered as a pinch-runner. Mostil singled to center, driving in Schalk. Kerr motored to third on the hit. Elsh then dribbled a grounder to first and beat it out for a single, with Kerr crossing the plate and Mostil advancing to third base. Sheely then grounded to short for an out, but it allowed Mostil to score the third White Sox run of the inning.

Sarge Connally entered the game in relief of the ailing Faber. Connally was used by manager Eddie Collins as a long reliever during much of the season. He retired Benny Bengough for the first out in the bottom of the tenth. Wally Pipp pinch-hit for Shields and worked a walk. Combs and Mark Koenig both singled to left. With the bases loaded, the stage was set for Ruth to be the hero. The first two pitches were balls. The next was sent high and foul into the stands. Then came ball three, so Connally offered a chest-high fastball and the "ball sailed away to parts remote,"8 landing in the right-field bleachers for a walkoff grand slam. The crowd erupted and stormed the field, crowding the base lines, forcing Ruth to "fight his way through a cheering mob before he touched the plate and won the game."9 The final score was 6-5 in favor of the Yankees.

Ruth finished the game with a 2-for-5 line and the four runs batted in. This was his sixth career grand slam and seventh career game that he had won for the Yankees with a walkoff home run, but it was the first time he had slammed a walkoff victory.10 Teammate Bob Meusel was 4-for-4 with three singles and a triple. Shields pitched a complete game, earning his first victory of the season and his first victory as a New York Yankee.

Ruth had only played in 98 games in 1925, and all of his offensive numbers were down. Coming into this game, Ruth's batting average of .283 was 95 points below that of the 1924 season. He had only hit 20 home runs and had just over half as many runs batted in as the previous year.. He had played one-third of his games in left field, away from his usual right field spot. Yet on this day, according to the *Chicago Tribune*, "Ruth's star hasn't set as yet."11

Sources

In addition to the sources mentioned in the notes, the author consulted baseball-reference.com and retrosheet.org.

Notes

1 James B. Harrison, "Ruth's Homer Wins; Clears Bags in 10th," *New York Times*, September 25, 1925: 16.

2 Irving Vaughan, "Ruth's Homer in 10th, with 3 on, Beats Sox, 6 to 5," *Chicago Tribune*, September 25, 1925: 21.

3 Ibid.

4 Ibid.

5 Harrison.

6 Vaughan.

7 Harrison.

8 Vaughan.

9 Harrison.

10 See baseball-reference.com:8080/players/event_hr.cgi?id=ruthba01&t=b for a log of Ruth's 714 career home runs.

11 Vaughan.

Babe Ruth First to Hit Three Homers in World Series Game

October 6, 1926: New York Yankees 10, St. Louis Cardinals 5, at Sportsman's Park

Game Four of the World Series

By Mark S. Sternman

The American League home-run leader with 47 in 1926, Babe Ruth had hit only four in his first 25 World Series games. Then he gave "the greatest exhibition of batting a World's Series ever saw"[1] and become the first player to hit a trio of homers in a postseason game as the Yankees evened the 1926 World Series at two games apiece with a 10-5 triumph over the Cardinals.

New York had scored only four times in the first 26 innings of the Series. "We hope to get going today," said Yankees manager Miller Huggins. "Our bats can't be tied indefinitely. The boys are bound to get some hits out of their system."[2]

In the first three games St. Louis received excellent starts from Bill Sherdel, Pete Alexander, and Jesse Haines. Game Four starter Flint Rhem, who had a career record of 10-15 entering the season only to lead the National League with 20 wins in 1926, began strongly by fanning Earle Combs and Mark Koenig. But

Babe Ruth during the 1926 World Series. *Courtesy of National Baseball Hall of Fame.*

Ruth put New York on top, 1-0, with a blast "a mile high [that] seemed a mile long. It went away out over the pavilion and came down among the mass of fans in Grand Avenue, who couldn't get into the park and stood out there listening to the cheering."[3]

Following Ruth, cleanup hitter Bob Meusel walked, but when he tried to score from first base on a single to right by Lou Gehrig, a throw from Billy Southworth to Rogers Hornsby to Bob O'Farrell cut him down at home.

New York starter Waite Hoyt went 16-12 in the regular season. He was facing the Cardinals for the first time since tossing a scoreless inning against them in his big-league debut as a member of the Giants in 1918. Hoyt's reacquaintance with the Cardinals quickly turned sour as St. Louis tied the game thanks to a trio of singles by Taylor Douthit, Southworth, and player-manager Hornsby. With men at second and third, Hoyt avoided further damage when he fanned Chick Hafey to end the frame.

Tony Lazzeri doubled off Rhem to start the second but, in more adventures in bad New York baserunning, fell victim to a Douthit-to-Tommy-Thevenow-to-Les-Bell relay while trying to stretch his hit into a triple. On a nice play, Bell "made a desperate drive to lay the ball on the sliding Yankee."[4] The last three New York batters had homered, walked, singled, and doubled, but the Yankees had just one run to show for all of these productive plate appearances.

Hoyt set down the Cardinals in order in the bottom of the second, and Rhem again retired Combs and Koenig in the top of the third to face Ruth with two outs and nobody on base. "Rhem threw Ruth a slow ball … as big as a derby hat, but the motion was deceptive and the Babe had started a quick swing when he saw that he was shooting too soon. Then, so quickly that you could barely perceive the motion, he pulled back again and took a long, slow swipe. ... He banged the baseball … over the roof of the right field pavilion close to the middle of the park."[5] New York led 2-1, a score that would hold until the top of the fourth inning.

With one out in that frame, Rhem walked Lazzeri. Next Joe Dugan lifted one to shallow left-center. As sportswriter Grantland Rice described the scene, "Both Douthit and Hafey started for the ball. They were traveling at top speed after the manner of two taxicabs attempting to cross the street from opposite directions when the collision took place. One had just reached the ball when the other struck him with the force of a tornado."[6] Dugan got credit for a double, and Lazzeri raced home with the third Yankee run. Hank Severeid singled, but Douthit got his second outfield assist in three innings by throwing out Dugan at home.

Down 3-1, St. Louis rallied in the bottom of the fourth. With one out, Hafey singled and O'Farrell reached on a Koenig error. In his postgame analysis, Huggins said, "Koenig … tried to do too much: He was trying to scoop the ball and throw it with the one motion, overeager to make the kill."[7]

Thevenow doubled to score Hafey and cut the Yankees' lead to 3-2. Specs Toporcer batted for Rhem and hit a sacrifice fly to tie the game, and then Douthit doubled in Thevenow to give the Cardinals a lead for the first time, 4-3. All three St. Louis runs in the inning were unearned. Southworth followed with a single to left, and Douthit tried to score. According to the radio broadcaster, "Ruth relayed it home with a perfect throw, a gorgeous throw and gets Douthit trying to come in from second base. Babe Ruth nor no other man ever made a better throw than that. … Babe shot it like an arrow and Severeid did not have to move for it."[8]

Art Reinhart relieved Rhem but failed to retire a batter. Combs walked and Koenig doubled him in to knot the game, 4-4. Reinhart walked Ruth and Meusel to load the bases, and threw two balls to Gehrig. "Here was the point where Hornsby should have acted," wrote the *New York Times's* James Harrison. "He had Herman Bell warmed up, and it was no secret that Reinhart was now in the clouds. The left-hander steadied a little, but [after] the count was two and two, he walked Gehrig, forcing Koenig in and sending New York ahead" with a 5-4 lead.[9] Hi Bell came in with the bases loaded and none out. A Lazzeri sacrifice fly and a Dugan squib to the catcher gave the Yankees two more runs to make the score 7-4.

New York expanded on its lead in the top of the sixth. Bell gave up a single to Combs and fanned Koenig before yielding Ruth's third homer of the game, this time to deep center field, to extend the Yankee lead to 9-4. The 39-year-old Alexander, in his 16th season in the majors, wrote, "It was one of the longest, if not the longest drive I have seen since I have been in baseball."[10]

After the game, in response to an assertion that the blast had gone almost 600 feet, the slugger admired his own prodigious feat. "Boy, that was a darling," Ruth proudly exclaimed.[11]

Meusel followed with a single, but Southworth earned his second assist of the game, matching Douthit, by throwing out Meusel trying to stretch the hit into a double. That saved a run as Gehrig followed with a double before Lazzeri popped to short.

O'Farrell and Thevenow gave the Cardinals a good start with singles to start the bottom of the sixth, but Hoyt escaped unscathed.

New York tallied its final run in the top of the seventh thanks to a Severeid single, Hoyt's sacrifice, and a double by Combs.

Wild Bill Hallahan, a back-of-the-bullpen reliever who walked more than five batters per nine innings in 1926 but who would become a frontline starter for St. Louis in the 1930s and the NL starter in the first All-Star game, in 1933, lived up to his nickname by walking the bases loaded in the top of the eighth, an inning that also featured the lone sacrifice bunt of Gehrig's

34-game World Series career. Severeid fouled to Les Bell at third, however, to strand a trio of Yankees.

St. Louis still trailed 10-4 going into the bottom of the ninth. Hornsby reached on a one-out single, advanced to second on Jim Bottomley's grounder, and scored on a two-out single by Les Bell. But Hoyt secured the 10-5 win by getting Hafey to pop to Severeid. According to Brooklyn manager Wilbert Robinson, Hoyt's "good control of a high fast one and a low curve made half of them of no value to the Cardinals."[12]

The Yankees had relied on heavy hitting to compensate for losing four runners on the bases. New York would ultimately fall to the Cardinals in Game Seven on another aggressive baserunning adventure that failed – when Ruth was caught stealing to end the game.

Notes

1   "Ruth's Great Exhibition," *The Sporting News*, October 14, 1926.

2   William F. Allen, "Crowd at Game Today Likely to Set New Record," *St. Louis Post-Dispatch*, October 6, 1926 (evening edition).

3   James Crusinberry, "Ruth Gets 3 Homers; Yanks Win, 10-5," *Chicago Tribune*, October 7, 1926.

4   J. Roy Stockton, "Yankees 3, Cardinals 1 (3½ Innings); Ruth Hits Two Home Runs," *St. Louis Post-Dispatch*, October 6, 1926 (evening edition).

5   Westbrook Pegler, "Finders Is Keepers When the Babe Swings the Bat," *Chicago Tribune*, October 7, 1926.

6   Grantland Rice, "Cardinals Crushed as Babe Ruth Smashes Three Mighty Home Runs," *Boston Globe*, October 7, 1926: 12; "Douthit played out the game, but the next day was stiff and sore, and Hornsby advised him to stay on the side lines" for the rest of the Series. "Alexander Joins Immortals in Cardinals' Series Triumph," *The Sporting News*, October 14, 1926.

7   "'I Told You So!' Huggins Chortles," *New York Times*, October 7, 1926.

8   "Radio Description of Fourth Game," *New York Times*, October 7, 1926.

9   James R. Harrison, "Ruth Hits 3 Homers and Yanks Win 10-5; Series Even Again," *New York Times*, October 7, 1926.

10 Grover C. Alexander, "Alexander Takes Hat off to Babe," *Boston Globe*, October 7, 1926: 12.

11 Associated Press, "Spirit of Cards Broken by Yank Attack: Huggins," *Chicago Tribune*, October 7, 1926.

12 Wilbert Robinson, "Ruth Really Great, Robinson Declares," *New York Times*, October 7, 1926.

The Babe's World Series Gamble

October 10, 1926: St. Louis Cardinals 3, New York Yankees 2, at Yankee Stadium

Game Seven of the World Series

By Paul E. Doutrich

Rogers Hornsby tags out Babe Ruth for the final out of the 1926 World Series. *Courtesy of the National Baseball Hall of Fame.*

The seventh game of the 1926 World Series between the St. Louis Cardinals and the New York Yankees was played on a cold, damp day in New York City. Rain had fallen during the night and a steady drizzle continued throughout the morning threatening a postponement. However, about noon the rain stopped and conditions improved enough to go ahead with the game as planned. When the first pitch was thrown two hours later 38,093 eager baseball devotees, a sm all crowd by Yankee Stadium standards, had pushed through the turnstiles.

On the mound for the Yankees that day was Waite Hoyt. At times during the season he had pitched excellently. On other occasions he had a difficult time lasting more than a few innings. Meanwhile the Cardinals sent their ace, Jesse "Pop" Haines, to the mound. Haines had missed several weeks early in the season with an injury but finished the campaign with a fine 13-4 record.

Hoyt got off to a good start allowing only two hits through the first three innings. Haines's start was less impressive. When he came to the plate in the first inning, all eyes were on Babe Ruth. Cardinals pitchers had been instructed by player-manager Rogers Hornsby to pitch around the Babe. Haines did, walking Ruth. Bob Meusel followed with a single but the Yankees were unable to score. Haines gave up another two hits in the second but avoided more trouble when catcher Bob O'Farrell gunned down "Jumpin'" Joe Dugan as he attempted to steal second. Despite the Cardinal "Ruth strategy," in the third the Bambino walloped a two-out shot into the right-field bleachers scoring the game's first run.

Down a run in the fourth, the Cardinals — with considerable help from the Yankees defense — mounted an attack of their own. "Sunny" Jim Bottomley got it started with a one-out single to left. Third baseman Les Bell followed with what looked like an inning-ending double-play ball but shortstop Mark Koenig let the ball bounce off his glove. Chick Hafey followed with a sharp single to left, loading the bases. O'Farrell then lifted a routine fly ball to the outfield. Left fielder Meusel positioned himself under the ball, reached up to make the catch, but let the ball plunk off his glove. Bottomley scampered home with the tying run. With the bases still loaded, shortstop Tommy Thevenow punched a pitch into right field scoring two more runs. Hoyt then struck out Haines and got Wattie Holm to ground one to shortstop. This time Koenig made the play ending the inning but the Cardinals had scored three unearned runs.

Haines got through the fourth allowing only a walk to Lou Gehrig. In the fifth the Yankees put two more men on base via a single by Earle Combs and another walk to Ruth but failed to score. The Cardinal hurler's struggle continued in the sixth when the Yankees scored a second run on hits by Dugan and Hank Severeid.

The Yankees' half of the seventh proved to be three outs for the ages. It started with a single by Combs, a sacrifice bunt by Koenig, and a four-pitch walk by Ruth. Meusel then bounced one to third baseman Bell who got the force out at second. Clearly struggling, Haines's next four pitches to Gehrig were alarmingly far out of the strike zone. Concerned, Hornsby called time and trotted from second in to talk to his ace. Five days earlier in Game Three a throw-back from his catcher had smashed the tip of the index finger on Haines's pitching hand. The next day the finger was swollen, badly bruised, and the nail was bloody. Hornsby knew about the freak accident and checked on Haines between innings. Each time Haines had assured his manager that he was all right. Finally in the seventh Haines admitted he could go no further.

For Hornsby the question became who to call in to relieve. The only member of the Cardinals staff that seemed unavailable was Grover Cleveland Alexander, who had pitched a complete game the previous day winning for the second time in the Series. Once one of the best pitchers in the game, "Old Pete" was in the twilight of his illustrious career. He was also a confirmed alcoholic and everyone assumed that he had celebrated his previous day's big win by drinking into the early morning hours. Clearly he would not be ready to face the Yankees again.

Standing amidst gloomy late afternoon shadows that darkened the cavernous stadium, Hornsby knew exactly who he wanted on the mound and waved to the bullpen. Through the cold, misty fog that had descended upon the field all eyes strained to see his choice. After a minute or so the hushed fans watched as the gate to the Cardinals bullpen opened and the grey silhouette of a solitary figure emerged onto the playing field. The new pitcher appeared a bit stooped. He was wearing a red Cardinals sweater and had his cap tilted a bit to one side. As he slowly ambled across the outfield grass he touched gloves with left-fielder Holm and a few seconds later did the same with shortstop Thevenow. By the time he reached Hornsby at the edge on the infield the whispers that had been circulating throughout the stadium became a low roar. "It's Alexander…'Alex the Great'!" "Does Hornsby really want 'Old Alex'?"

Reporters after the game claimed that when he took the ball from Hornsby, Alexander was well lubricated and suffering from a long night of drinking. The truth is that Alexander was completely lucid and in control of himself. After Game Six Hornsby had told him to limit his celebrations because he might have to pitch in relief the next afternoon in Game Seven. Alex abided by his manager's instructions.

Waiting at the plate was young Tony Lazzeri, who had smacked 18 homers and driven in 117 runs during the season. Alexander told his manager that he planned to set Lazzeri up with inside fastballs and then break a curve or two over the outside part of the plate. Hornsby, who would have told any other pitcher how to pitch, instead simply nodded and gave Alexander the ball.

With Combs on third, Meusel on second, and Gehrig on first Alexander started Lazzeri off as planned, a fastball high and inside for ball one. Working quickly and with no windup the wily veteran brought the next pitch, another fastball, down across the inside corner of the plate for a strike. He took a little off the third offering but delivered it close to the same spot as the previous pitch. As Alexander had predicted he would, Lazzeri swung hard at the pitch lifting it deep down the left-field line. Hornsby at second watched, fearing the worst. The Yankees bench jumped on to the dugout steps as the ball climbed toward the left-field bleachers. All 38,093 in the stands leapt to their feet, most of them certain that the young slugger had knocked one out of the park. And then as it sped toward the fence the ball began to bend just a bit to the left. It returned to earth well beyond the fence but a few feet in foul territory — nothing more than a long second strike. On the mound Alexander, as calm as ever, ended the drama just as he had promised: a tantalizing curve low and outside. Lazzeri took the bait. He swung hard but completely missed the ball. The immediate Yankees threat was over but there were still two innings to play.

Herb Pennock, who had replaced Hoyt an inning earlier, gave up two hits in the eighth but the Cardinals were unable to score. In the bottom half of the inning Alexander set down the side in order. Pennock did the same in the top of the ninth.

As he took the mound in the bottom of the ninth, Alexander knew that Babe Ruth was the third scheduled Yankee hitter. Two quick outs later, Ruth came to the plate. Alexander started the Bambino with the first strike Ruth had seen since his third-inning home run. A ball and a foul second strike left the Cardinals one pitch away from their first world championship but the next three pitches all missed the plate and Ruth, for the fourth time in the game, walked to first.

With Ruth on first, Meusel came to the plate with a chance to redeem himself for his crucial 4th inning error. The Yankees left fielder was the only hitter who had consistently given Alexander problems. In the seven times the two had faced each other during the Series Meusel had three hits including a double and a triple the previous day. As Alex released his first pitch to Meusel, a strike, Ruth made his bet. He inexplicably took off for second. O'Farrell gunned a perfect strike to second. Hornsby tagged out the sliding Ruth. The slugger had lost his bet and the Cardinals had won their first world championship.[1]

Sources

Doutrich, Paul E., *The Cardinals and the Yankees, 1926: A Classic Season and St. Louis in Seven* (Jefferson, North Carolina: McFarland & Company, Inc., Publishers, 2011).

Notes

1 After the game Ruth explained that he took off on his own. He figured that as well as Alexander was pitching he wanted to be in scoring position in case Meusel got a hit. It is the only time a World Series has ended with a runner caught stealing.

Ruth and the Roof

August 16, 1927: New York Yankees 8, Chicago White Sox 1, at Comiskey Park, Chicago

By John Gabcik

During the 1926 American League season, there were a handful of instances where the capacity of Comiskey Park in Chicago was exceeded by the demands of the public, usually when the New York Yankees came to town.[1] In these situations, the excess attendees were allowed onto the playing field and rather ineffectively roped off from the action. These situations bruised the sensitivities of White Sox owner Charles Comiskey, who decided to open his pocketbook, and build a second deck atop the outfield stands. Comiskey hired noted Chicago architect Zachary Taylor Davis to make the improvements. The old wooden stands would be removed; the new, modern double-deck structure would be built with concrete and steel, and cost $600,000.

The additional seating would increase the park's capacity from 28,000 to 52,000. This was an amazonian leap in optimism, considering that the franchise had topped 800,000 in a season only twice in its 26-year history. The roof above the second tier would be 75 feet above the playing surface, offering shelter to the fans, but giving the park a cavernous, enclosed look. "Well, nobody is going to hit the ball over those stands," Comiskey chirped.[2]

Was Comiskey's statement an offhand remark, or was it a challenge? He certainly wasn't speaking to his own hitters. The 1926 White Sox had hit only 32 home runs as a team. Outfielder Bibb Falk, with 12 homers in 1922, was the only active White Sox player who had ever hit more than 10 in a season. But with Babe Ruth of the Yankees, this was a much different story. The Sultan of Swat, at age 32, was still in his prime, having cranked out 47 homers the previous season, many of them prodigious clouts. Including the 60 homers he would hit in 1927, he had 358 more round-trippers left in his tank.

On Tuesday, August 16, 1927, the New York Yankees came to Chicago to start a four-game series with the White Sox. An estimated 20,000 fans were in the seats, an especially good gate for a Tuesday, or most any day, at Comiskey Park in the 1920s. There was nothing "crucial" about the game. New York was running away from the rest of the league, playing .705 ball with a 79-33 record. The Washington Senators were the nearest competitor, 13 games back. The White Sox were ensconced in fifth place, 25½ games out.

But the game was the undercard. Lou Gehrig, eight years younger than Ruth, was coming into his own as a slugger. Gehrig had already amassed 38 home runs this season, two more than Ruth. The public was keenly aware both that Gehrig might top Ruth for the season, and that the two men together were likely to set a number of marvelous records. And then there was that roof, staring them in the face.

The Yankees' pitching opponent on this day was Alphonse "Tommy" Thomas, a 5-foot-10, 175-pound righty noted for a fastball that worked the corners of the plate.[3] Thomas had been acquired by the White Sox from the International League's Baltimore Orioles for $15,000 after the 1925 season.[4] Now he was establishing himself as a major component of the White Sox staff. Thomas was coming off a tough 2-1, 10-inning loss at Cleveland five days earlier. Nonetheless, he was having a good season with a 14-11 record and a 2.95 ERA. Although two of the current White Sox moundsmen, Red Faber and Ted Lyons, were future Hall of Famers, Thomas, in 1927, may have been the most effective of the bunch.[5] Thomas would end the season with a 19-16 record, a team-leading 40 starts, and a 2.98 ERA.

Despite Thomas's general success in 1927, he was not solving the Yankees' batters all that well. Thomas had faced the Yankees twice and lost both games, dropping a 4-1 decision on June 7, then losing again, 3-2, on July 24. In both games, Thomas's undoing was the home-run ball. On June 7 Gehrig, Pat Collins, and Ruth had gone deep, Ruth's blast to deep center being his 18th of the season. And in the July game, the Babe had smacked his 31st, this time to right.

The game itself had little intrigue after three innings. Earle Combs' triple and a double by Bob Meusel, the first of his four hits in the game, led to two runs for the Yankees in the top of the first. Ruth got on base with a walk, but later was tagged out at the plate on a fielder's choice. The White Sox tried to retaliate in their half, loading the bases with one out on a hit batter, a walk, and a single. When White Sox left fielder Bibb Falk flied to left, Ray Flaskamper tried to score from third, but Ruth, this time the aggressor, gunned him down at the plate – an inning-ending double play.

The Yankees were at it again in the third: Ruth walked, Gehrig doubled, and both came home on a pair of fly balls, making the score 4-0. With Yankees star pitcher Herb Pennock firing off the mound against a weak White Sox offense, there was little doubt, or surprise, about the game's outcome. But the game itself was not what had brought out all those fans on a weekday afternoon.

Both pitchers sailed through the fourth inning, but Thomas had the heart of the Yankees order to face again in the top of the fifth. Ruth led off the inning, having already walked in his first two at-bats, but this time Thomas threw him a pitch he liked, a high fastball.[6] The ball flew off the bat, heading well above Comiskey's insurmountable roof in right field. It cleared the outfield wall, 360 feet from home plate, then the roof, landed in a parking lot, and bounced off, eastwardly, toward what today is the Dan Ryan Expressway. Thomas retained enough composure to deliver a called third strike to Gehrig, and got through the rest of the inning without further damage. And Ruth now had 37 homers, only one fewer than his teammate, Gehrig.

When catcher Moe Berg led off the White Sox fifth with a double, Chicago manager Ray Schalk saw it as a propitious time to remove Thomas from the game for a pinch-hitter, Bernie Neis, who grounded out.[7] The inning came to a close with Berg still parked on second. Bert Cole came in to pitch the last four innings for the home team, giving up three more runs in the eighth but no homers. The White Sox strung together three hits in the seventh to score a token run, making the final score 8-1. The Yankees plodded on, taking the next two games, before Chicago won the finale on Friday, 3-2. Ruth homered again in the Wednesday game, Gehrig in the loss on Friday. The Yankees left town with Gehrig maintaining his one-homer lead over Ruth, 39-38.

But Gehrig's power binge was about to stall out; he hit only two more homers in August, then six in September, finishing with 47. Ruth, meanwhile, hit five more round-trippers in August, then went ballistic with his record 17 homers in September, to finish at 60. The two teammates – Ruth and Gehrig – had hit a record 107 homers in a season that lasted until 1961 when two other Yankees, Mickey Mantle and Roger Maris, combined for 115.

And then there was that roof. Comiskey's edifice remained unsullied again until May 4, 1929, when Lou Gehrig homered off Urban Faber. Over the next 20-plus years, other American League sluggers – Jimmie Foxx, Hank Greenberg, and Ted Williams – also recorded "roof shots," but it was not until April 25, 1951, that a White Sox player, first baseman Eddie Robinson, was successful in topping the structure.

The last game at Comiskey Park was played on September 30, 1990. In its 64-year history, the roof had been violated 22 times by White Sox batters, 14 times by opponents.[8] Ron Kittle, with seven roof shots, and Greg Luzinski with four – all in the mid-1980s – were the most prolific White Sox sluggers to reach the roof.[9] Ted Williams and Jimmie Foxx were out-of-towners who found the roof twice.

Interestingly, for both Babe Ruth and Lou Gehrig, the roof shot was a one-and-done. Both men, but especially Ruth, would seem to have been capable of reaching the roof multiple times – but chose not to. It was as if these men were saying to Comiskey,

"Okay, Charley, you have your roof, we made our point; now let's get on with the game."

Sources

In addition to the sources cited in the Notes, the author also relied on Baseball-Reference.com and Retrosheet.org.

Notes

1. Estimated attendances from Baseball-Reference.com box scores show five 1926 Comiskey Park games with attendances of 30,000 or more, including the June 20 game with New York, when 40,000 showed up.

2. Michael Benson, *Ballparks of North America* (Jefferson, North Carolina: McFarland and Co., 1981), 91.

3. Bill James and Rob Neyer, *The Neyer/James Guide to Pitchers* (New York: Fireside Books, 2004), 402-403.

4. Jimmy Keenan, "Tommy Thomas," SABR Biography Project, sabr.org.

5. Baseball-Reference.com lists Thomas as the third-highest American League player in Wins Above Replacement with 8.0, trailing only Ruth (12.4), Gehrig (11.8), and teammate Ted Lyons (8.1).

6. John G. Robertson, *The Babe Chases 60* (Jefferson, North Carolina: McFarland and Company, 1999), 103.

7. Thomas continued to have great difficulty with Ruth throughout his career. Ruth batted .458 against Thomas with a 1.529 OPS, including 10 home runs. Other pitchers gave up even more homers to Ruth, Rube Walberg leading the list with 14.

8. It should be noted that a "roof shot" includes any home run that made it onto the roof, not necessarily beyond it. Assuming that each of the upper deck's 20 rows was 2½ feet deep, considering both the seat and the foot space, the back edge of the roof would be at least 50 feet beyond the front. That Ruth's drive completely cleared the roof on the fly puts it in a stratum well beyond many other recorded "roof shots."

9. Richard C. Lindberg, *Total White Sox* (Philadelphia: Temple University Press, 2006), 635-636. The book notes that home plate at the stadium had been moved eight feet closer to the outfield wall during the Kittle-Luzinski era.

Babe Ruth Hits Grand Slam in Two Consecutive Games

September 29, 1927: New York Yankees 15, Washington Senators 4, at Yankee Stadium

By Thomas J. Brown Jr.

Babe Ruth was on fire. He had already hit 14 home runs in September 1927, the most recent one being a grand slam on the 27th. No one had hit that many in a single month. His most recent blast was the first grand slam he hit all season and just the ninth of his career. It not only gave the Yankees a 6-1 lead but it was one of just six home runs given up by Lefty Grove that season.

The Yankees had the day off on September 28 before the Washington Senators arrived in New York to play the final three games of the season. The Senators' 84-66 record was good enough for third place, 22½ games behind first-place New York. The Yankees had rolled over the American League, winning 107 games with three more games remaining.

Urban Shocker started for the Yankees. He was enjoying his best season since coming to the Yankees in 1925. Shocker entered the game with a 17-6 record and a 2.94 ERA. He gave up consecutive singles to Bucky Harris and Babe Ganzel in the first before retiring the next two batters to get out of the inning.

Horace "Hod" Lisenbee took the mound for the Senators. He was a rookie who was having a great year. He entered the game with an 18-8 record, which would turn out to the best season of his career and the only winning one.

Lisenbee retired Earle Combs and Mark Koenig on infield groundouts in the bottom of the first. Ruth stepped to the plate. With the count 0-and-2, Lisenbee "was quite craftily trying to curve over [a] third one when Ruth stuck that one in the right-field bleachers. It was a low winging drive that went up only a few rows."[1]

But it went far enough to be Ruth's 58th home run of the season. It was just the sixth round-tripper Lisenbee had surrendered all season. One of the previous five was by Ruth. That home run, on July 3, was also a solo blast in the first inning.

Ruth gave the Yankees the lead, but the Senators bounced back and took the lead in the second. Ossie Bluege reached first on an error by shortstop Koenig. Bobby Reeves hit Shocker's next pitch over the left-field wall for two-run homer and the Senators were ahead, 2-1.

Their lead didn't last long. The Yankees jumped all over Lisenbee in the bottom of the second. Tony Lazzeri drew a leadoff walk and Joe Dugan singled. Pat Collins followed with a double that scored Lazzeri. Shocker's bunt down the first-base line scored Dugan. Combs flied out for the second out but Koenig singled and Ruth tripled to right-center. (It might have been a home run if he had pulled it a little more.) Ruth scored on Lisenbee's wild pitch, and Lou Gehrig walked.

When Lisenbee gave up a double to Bob Meusel, Senators player-manager Harris went to his bullpen. Firpo Marberry relieved and gave up a single to Lazzeri, who got to second on right fielder Sam Rice's throw home trying to get Meusel at the plate. Lazzeri stole third base but Marberry struck out Dugan for the final out. The Yankees led 8-2.

Marberry got the Yankees out in order in the third but the Yankees struck again in the fourth for three more runs. Koenig hit a leadoff single and Ruth flied out to center field. Koenig moved to third on a single by Gehrig. Koenig and Gehrig scored when Meusel doubled. On Lazzeri's second single of the game, Meusel scored. Marberry got out of the inning when Dugan hit a line drive to shortstop Reeves, who doubled Lazzeri off first. The Yankees' lead climbed to 11-2.

Shocker pitched two more scoreless innings before he was replaced by Dutch Ruether. Ruether got the first two outs in the fifth before giving up a single to Harris. Ganzel then hit Ruether's first pitch deep into the left-field corner for an inside-the-park home run. Ruether yielded three consecutive singles after Ganzel's home run, but the Senators failed to score and were left trailing 11-4 when Bluege grounded out.

Right-hander Paul Hopkins took over pitching duties in the fifth for the Senators. It was his major-league debut. After graduating from Colgate University in May, he pitched in 23 games for the New Haven Profs (Eastern League) before being called up to the Senators in September. Most fans at Yankee Stadium must have wondered: Who was this young player taking the mound?

Hopkins gave up a leadoff single to Collins. Ruether reached first and Collins was safe at second when shortstop Reeves couldn't handle the throw from the pitcher. On Combs's single to left, Collins was thrown out trying to score. But Koenig's single loaded the bases.

Ruth approached the plate. Hopkins watched him. He remembered being "a little nervous, but I wasn't scared. I always thought I could get anybody out."[2] "Muddy Ruel, [my] catcher, came out and said, 'I think we better throw curves as much as possible, and if it gets to a 3-and-2 count throw a slow curve, because Babe will be looking for a fastball.'"[3]

Following Ruel's instructions, Hopkins pitched carefully to Ruth. The count reached 3-and-2 and Hopkins threw a curve. Hopkins remembered years later, "It was so slow that Ruth started to swing and then hesitated, hitched on it and brought the bat back. And then he swung, breaking his wrists as he came through it. What a great eye he had! He hit it at the right second – put everything behind it. I can still hear the crack of the bat. I can still see the swing."[4]

The *New York Times* described it this way: "The ball landed halfway up the right field bleacher[s] and though there were hardly 7,500 eyewitnesses present, the roar they sent up could hardly have been drowned out had the spacious stands been packed to capacity."[5] The home run widened the Yankees' lead to 15-4.

After Ruth's home run, Hopkins struck out Gehrig. Then he gave up a triple to Meusel, who was called out at home when he tried to stretch the hit into an inside-the-park homer. Hopkins returned to the dugout and cried.[6]

Hopkins stayed on the mound and finished the game with three scoreless innings. Ruth almost hit a third home run on his final turn at bat, in the seventh. Right fielder Red Barnes caught the ball with his back to the wall. "Just a foot or two more of distance on this one and a new record would already be established," John Drebinger of the *New York Times* wrote.[7]

After Ruether gave up the home run in the fifth, he pitched two scoreless innings. He was replaced by Bob Shawkey in the eighth. Shawkey got the side out in order in the final two innings. He struck out three of the six Senators he faced and allowed just two balls out of the infield on the way to his third save of the year.

Ruth tied his 1921 record of 59 home runs with the two round-trippers. After his 1921 accomplishment, many sportswriters felt that the record would never be equaled. Ruth did it six years later. As always, Ruth did in his own inimitable style, doffing his cap to the fans and shaking Gehrig's hand as he returned to the dugout.

Sources

In addition to the sources cited in the Notes, the author used Baseball-Reference.com and Retrosheet.org for box-score, player, team, and season information as well as pitching and batting game logs, and other pertinent material.

Notes

1. John Drebinger, "Ruth Hits 2, Equals 1921 Homer Record," *New York Times*, September 30, 1927: 18.

2. William Nack, "The Colossus," *Sports Illustrated*, August 24, 1998. si.com/vault/1998/08/24/247910/the-colossus-in-the-late-summer-of-1927-babe-ruth-who-died-50-years-ago-this-week-went-on-a-historic-home-run-hitting-spree-to-set-the-record-that-would-seal-his-immortality.

3. Jack Cavanaugh, "A 3-2 Pitch That Was No. 59," *New York Times*, September 24, 1995: CN1.

4. Bill Bryson, *One Summer* (New York: Doubleday, 2013), 458.

5. Drebinger.

6. Nack.

7. Drebinger.

Babe Ruth Hits Record 60th Home Run

September 30, 1927: New York Yankees 4, Washington Senators 2, at Yankee Stadium

By Kevin Larkin

Baseball history is filled with accounts of memorable home runs. The Los Angeles Dodgers' Kirk Gibson, for one, knocked a one-legged homer in Game One of the 1988 World Series against the Oakland A's. The Pittsburgh Pirates' Bill Mazeroski hit a dramatic round-tripper in Game Seven of the 1960 fall classic to beat the New York Yankees. Bobby Thomson ripped his "Shot Heard Round the World" in Game Three of the 1951 National League playoffs, leading the New York Giants over the Brooklyn Dodgers.

Decades before those epic clouts came another great home run, hit September 30, 1927, at Yankee Stadium in the Bronx, New York. Yankees slugger Babe Ruth belted his 60th home run of the season, breaking the record of 59 he set in 1921.[1]

While it was a happy day for many given the magnitude of Ruth's accomplishment, it was also a sad day for some. Baseball said goodbye to one of the greatest pitchers of all-time, Walter Johnson.[2] The legendary Big Train was retiring after 21 seasons with the Washington Senators.

On the mound for the Yankees (who were in first place by a whopping 18½ games) that day was right-hander George Pipgras, sporting a record of 10-3. The Senators (who were in third place and trailed the Yankees by 23½ games) countered with left-hander Tom Zachary, who had a record of 8-12. Both lineups were loaded with talent. The Senators featured Sam Rice, Bucky Harris, Goose Goslin, and Joe Judge. Of course, the Yankees boasted a lineup famously referred to as "Murderers' Row."[3] Earle Combs led off, followed by Mark Koenig, Babe Ruth, Lou Gehrig, Bob Meusel, and Tony Lazzeri in the two-through-six spots. The Yankees had clinched the pennant early in the month and were getting ready to face the Pittsburgh Pirates in Game One of the World Series on October 5.

It was a relatively easy first inning for Pipgras as he quickly got a groundout and a fly out. Babe Ganzel singled, but Goslin popped out to Koenig at shortstop for the third out. In the Yankees' half of the first, Combs flied out to left field and Koenig grounded out. Ruth drew a walk but was stranded after Gehrig's groundout.

Through the first three innings, the game was scoreless. Each team had managed just one hit. Things heated up offensively in the fourth inning. Goslin singled with one out for Washington, advanced to second base on Judge's groundout to first and scored on Muddy Ruel's single. Ruel then stole second and went home on Ossie Bluege's base hit to make the score 2-0. Bluege stole second base but was left stranded when Grant Gillis grounded out.

New York came back with a run of its own in the bottom of the fourth. Ruth led off with a single, followed by a base hit from Gehrig. Ruth advanced to third on the hit, while Gehrig went to second on the throw to third. Meusel hit a fly ball that scored Ruth and sent Gehrig to third. Lazzeri lined into a double play to end the frame.

Goslin and Judge flied out to begin the Washington sixth. Ruel walked and made it to third after a pickoff attempt by Pipgras and subsequent error by Gehrig. Ossie Bluege walked, but Gillis flied out to end the inning. The Yankees tied the game, 2-2, in the bottom of the sixth inning. Ruth singled to right field with two outs and advanced to second on Gehrig's single. Meusel followed with an RBI hit to score Ruth. Lazzeri popped out to end the rally.

Herb Pennock, the Yankees' ace left-hander, replaced Pipgras on the mound to open the seventh. He got Zachary to fly out and then gave up a double to Sam Rice. Bucky Harris walked, putting runners on first and second base. Ganzel grounded out, advancing Rice to third and Harris to second. Harris was then picked off second base for the third out.

New York went down in order in the bottom of the seventh with Joe Dugan fouling out, Benny Bengough popping out, and Pennock flying out to left field.

Pennock, in turn, retired the Senators in order in the eighth. Goslin and Judge grounded out, and Ruel flied out to left field. The game was getting late.

Combs grounded out to third base to open the New York eighth. Mark Koenig tripled[4] and up to the plate stepped the Bambino, Babe Ruth. In Ruth's time with the Yankees, he had hit 366 home runs.[5] Now, he was ready to blast another record-breaker.

With his slugging prowess, Ruth had changed the way the game of baseball was played. He broke the single-season home-run mark in three straight seasons, in 1919 (29), 1920 (54), and 1921 (59). Babe had moved into first place on the all-time homer list in 1921 with No. 139.[6]

Zachary delivered a low fastball[7] that Ruth sent into the right-field stands for number 60 on the year. It was also number 17 for the month of September and it gave the Yankees a 4-2 lead.[8] Gehrig flied out to right field, and Meusel flied out to center field. The Yankees took their lead into the top of the ninth inning.

Pennock got Bluege to fly out to left field, and then Gillis grounded out. The Senators were down to their last out. With Zachary due up, player-manager Bucky Harris sent in Walter Johnson to pinch-hit. The Big Train was a career .235 batter. In what would be Johnson's last appearance in uniform as a player, he flied out to Ruth in right field. (Johnson had made his last appearance as a pitcher on September 22. He started against the St. Louis Browns and gave up nine hits and six runs in just 3⅓ innings.)

Johnson subsequently asked for his release from the Senators. He still had the arm to pitch, but had lost the power generated from his legs.[9] During spring training Johnson had suffered a broken ankle while pitching batting practice.[10] While he somewhat recovered, the injury reduced the power generated from his legs. Despite his arm remaining sound, Johnson realized the end was at hand. "The leg I broke bothers me a lot, and not where it was broken. You see, when the legs are bad and you lose the old ‹zip› on the ball, you find pitching a lot harder and you find you are not effective."[11] The Big Train went just 5-6 with a 5.10 ERA in his final season.

Certainly, for baseball fans of all ages and eras, September 30, 1927, was a day to remember.

Sources

In addition to the game story and the box-score sources cited in the Notes, the author consulted the Baseball-Reference.com and Retrosheet.org websites.

Notes

1 "Ruth Breaks Record: Yanks Win," *Portsmouth Daily Times,* October 1, 1927: 12.

2 Johnson would end his career with 417 wins, 110 shutouts, and 3,509 strikeouts.

3 http://thenewmurderersrow.com.

4 "Record-Making Homer Breaks 2-2 Deadlock in the Eighth Inning; Babe Also Scores Three Runs," *Bridgeport Telegram* (Bridgeport, Connecticut), October 1, 1927: 31.

5 "8,000 Fans Thrilled as Bambino Leans on Ball Hurled By Tom Zachary," *Appleton Post Crescent* (Appleton, Wisconsin), October 1, 1927: 12.

6 Cliff Corcoran, "99 Cool Facts about Babe Ruth," http://si.com http://www.si.com/mlb/strike-zone/2013/07/12.

7 "Babe Ruth Cracks His 60th Home Run," *Lincoln Evening Journal* (Lincoln, Nebraska), October 1, 1927: 9.

8 Ruth's 17 home runs in September set a new record for most home runs hit in one month.

9 *Evening Journal*, Wilmington Delaware May 13, 1926: 18.

10 Henry W. Thomas, *Walter Johnson: Baseball's Big Train* (Washington: Phenom Press, 1995), 292.

11 Ibid., 299.

The Sultan of Swat Smacks Three Homers to Sink the Cardinals

October 9, 1928: New York Yankees 7, St. Louis Cardinals 3, at Sportsman's Park

Game Four of the World Series

By Richard Cuicchi

Not even the all-powerful Kenesaw Mountain Landis could predict the future. At 11:00 A.M. on October 8, with a steady rain falling, the commissioner decided to postpone Game Four of the 1928 World Series. When the skies had cleared by 1:00 P.M., Landis looked a bit foolish and many fans were understandably upset.[1] In reality, the Cardinals could have used the extra day of rest to regroup, as the gloomy weather matched their demoralized disposition after they suffered their third consecutive loss to the New York Yankees the day before.

On the other hand, Yankees manager Miller Huggins had to warn his players against "making whoopee" because of their commanding lead over the Cardinals.[2] Any overconfidence would have been well-founded, because the Yankees had overmatched the favored Cardinals in the first three games. Yankees pitchers stifled the Cardinals' offense, while Lou Gehrig was terrorizing St. Louis pitching. But Babe Ruth would steal the limelight in the final game.

The Cardinals sported their new game uniforms for Game Four before a home crowd of 37,331. The Redbirds had been prevented from wearing them in Game Three because many of them didn't fit.[3] However, the new uniforms and an extra day of rest didn't help the Cardinals alter their fortunes, as the Yankees swept them in the Series for their second consecutive championship.[4]

Huggins tapped Waite Hoyt for his second starting assignment of the Series. The 29-year-old right-hander had limited the Cardinals to one run on three hits in Game One. He was opposed by lefty Bill "Wee Willie" Sherdel, a 21-game winner who had taken the loss in Game One, giving him three consecutive World Series losses to the Yankees since 1926.

In the first inning Ruth grounded into a double play, which would be his only significant blemish that day. The Cardinals didn't score in the bottom of the first even though they got two runners on base via a double and a walk.

The Cardinals were able to draw first blood in the bottom of the third inning. Ernie Orsatti, who started in center field in place of the struggling Taylor Douthit, doubled to center field. Andy High advanced Orsatti to third when he beat out a bunt, and Frankie Frisch followed with a sacrifice fly to center field that scored Orsatti.

The Yankees responded in the top of the fourth inning with a solo home run by Ruth over the right-field pavilion roof. Gehrig followed with a walk and Tony Lazzeri singled, but Sherdel got out of the inning without further damage.

Hoyt gave up another run in the bottom of the fourth inning on two costly errors by the Yankees. Earl Smith led off with a single to right field. Rabbit Maranville hit a potential double-play ball to second base. Lazzeri flipped to shortstop Mark Koenig to force Smith but Koenig's relay was off-target and Maranville advanced to second base. With Orsatti batting, Hoyt threw wildly on a pickoff attempt at second, which allowed Maranville to score and the Cardinals to regain the lead, 2-1.

The Yankees threatened again in the fifth and sixth innings, but were unable to score, leaving a total of five runners on base.

With one out in the top of the seventh inning, Sherdel got two strikes on Ruth. When Ruth turned to argue the second strike call, Cardinals catcher Earl Smith promptly whipped the ball back to Sherdel, who then abruptly threw an apparent third-strike pitch to Ruth. However, umpire Cy Pfirman quickly declared a "no pitch." Cardinals manager Bill McKechnie and his players argued the umpire's decision, but to no avail. After Ruth and Sherdel exchanged heated words, Ruth got his revenge, belting his second home run of the game to tie it.[5] Gehrig immediately followed with another homer, his fourth of the Series, to give New York a 3-2 lead.

Up to that point, Sherdel had kept the Yankees in check. After the game, baseball pundits argued that perhaps he had become unnerved by the umpire's call. Official scorers commented that Sherdel had actually made a legal pitch – his feet were on the rubber when he retrieved the ball from the catcher and took a windup, while Ruth was still standing in the batter's box. However, before the Series a conference between the umpires and the teams decided that use of the "quick return" (also known as quick pitch) would not be allowed, even though the National League had permitted it during the regular season.[6]

After the back-to-back home runs, Bob Meusel singled, chasing Sherdel. Pete Alexander came on in relief but couldn't quell the rally. The Yankees scored two more runs – one more charged to Sherdel and one to Alexander. The Yankees had forged a 5-2 lead they would never relinquish.

In the top of the eighth inning, the Yankees scored two meaningless runs, since the Cardinals were already a deflated team. However, the manner in which the Yankees scored put an exclamation point on the way they had dominated the Cardinals in the Series. Cedric Durst, who replaced Ben Paschal in center field at the top of the inning, hit a leadoff home run off Alexander. Then, in his fifth at-bat, Ruth put another layer of icing on the cake for the Yankees when he hit his third home run of the game. Ruth had previously performed this feat against the Cardinals in Game Four of the 1926 World Series.

The Cardinals scored once more in the bottom of the ninth inning before Ruth caught the final out of the game in dramatic fashion: a running catch of Frankie Frisch's foul fly to left field. Forgetting a gimpy knee that had plagued him during the Series, Ruth chased the ball down near the edge of the extra box seats that lined the playing field and speared it among fans whose papers and scorecards went flying. He ran to the dugout with the ball raised high in the air, while fans screamed for him to toss them a souvenir. The exuberant Ruth kept the ball, taking it to the clubhouse, where he exclaimed as he brandished it, "There's the ball that says it's all over!"[7]

The final score was 7-3. Hoyt pitched a complete game, yielding 11 hits and three walks while striking out eight. He put runners on base in six of his nine innings. Suffering his second loss of the Series, the hard-luck Sherdel also gave up 11 hits and three walks, while yielding four earned runs in 6⅓ innings.

The Yankees' sweep of the Cardinals was a surprise in some quarters. The Cardinals had been favored because numerous Yankees were banged up, including Herb Pennock (arm), Earle Combs (wrist), Lazzeri (shoulder), Gehrig (beaned in the final game of the season), and Ruth (knee). Furthermore, the Cardinals' confidence going into the Series was high, since they had defeated the Yankees in the 1926 World Series.[8]

McKechnie allowed his pitchers to throw to Ruth during the Series, contrary to the strategy Cardinals manager Rogers Hornsby employed in 1926 when St. Louis walked Ruth 11 times. Ruth walked only once in 1928, and he capitalized on the pitches in the strike zone with a then-World Series record .625 batting average.[9]

The Cardinals' skipper offered no excuses for his team's collapse. He remarked in his guest column in the *St. Louis Post-Dispatch* on October 11, "What other explanation of the rout can there be? Here was a team of healthy athletes opposed to a club supposed to be crippled from Ruth to the clubhouse boy. The crippled team comes on the field and makes the healthy club look like a collection of misfits."[10]

Understandably, Ruth received most of the national attention in the World Series for his three round-trippers in Game Four. James Harrison proclaimed in the *New York Times*, "If there is any lingering doubt, if anywhere in this broad land there were misguided souls who believe that Babe Ruth was not the greatest living ballplayer, they should have seen him today.[11]

Yet Gehrig arguably had a better overall Series. His four home runs and .545 batting average were momentous, too. His slugging percentage of 1.727 and OPS of 2.433 remain World Series records. Even Ruth himself declared Gehrig the hero of the Series. "(Gehrig) getting on base safely in nine consecutive times at bat deserves all the honors. … We think he's the greatest coming player in the business. Watch him and see."[12]

There were no good numbers on the Cardinals' side. They batted .206 as a team while their pitchers racked up an ERA of 6.09. (Alexander's ERA, over five innings, was 19.80.)

The defeat of the Cardinals was the third World Series victory for the Yankees and they were on their way to becoming one of the most storied major-league franchises.[13]

Sources

In addition to the sources mentioned in the Notes, the author also consulted:

Baseball-Reference.com.

Cantor, George. *Inside Sports World Series Factbook* (Detroit: Visible Ink Press, 1996).

Creamer, Robert W. *Babe: The Legend Comes to Life* (New York: Simon and Schuster, 1974).

Gallagher, Mark. *The Yankee Encyclopedia 6th Edition* (Champaign, Illinois: Sports Publishing LLC, 2003).

Krueger, Joseph J. *Baseball's Greatest Drama* (Milwaukee: Joseph J. Krueger, 1945).

Notes

1 "Cardinal Plumage Droops in Listless Trio of Lost Games," *The Sporting News*, October 11, 1928:1.

2 Leigh Montville, *The Big Bam* (New York: Doubleday, 2006), 276.

3 "Gossip of the Game," *The Sporting News*, October 11, 1928: 5.

4 The Yankees had defeated the Pittsburgh Pirates in four straight games in the 1927 World Series.

5 Montville, 277.

6 J. Roy Stockton, "Ruth's Three Home Runs Enable Yanks to Sweep Series," *St. Louis Post-Dispatch*, October 10, 1928: 22.

7 Montville, 277.

8 Montville, 275.

9 John Devaney and Burt Goldblatt, *The World Series: A Complete Pictorial History* (Chicago: Rand McNally & Company, 1981), 121.

10 William McKechnie, "It Had to Be, All McKechnie Can Say of Rout," *St. Louis Post-Dispatch*, October 11, 1928: 28.

11 Montville, 276.

12 Babe Ruth, "We Say It With Base Hits; That's All – Babe Ruth," *St. Louis Post-Dispatch*, October 10, 1928: 22.

13 As of 2016 the Yankees had won a record 27 World Series championships.

Bambino on Fire

August 7, 1929:
New York Yankees 13, Philadelphia A's 1
(first game of doubleheader), at Shibe Park

by Thomas E. Schott

In this first game of a twin bill in the dog days of August 1929, both teams were coming off doubleheaders the previous day. The visiting Yankees had split their pair of games with the Washington Senators, while the Philadelphia A's had done the same with the St. Louis Browns on their home grounds at Shibe Park. In fact, the A's were now beginning the team's third doubleheader in a row, the vagaries of the season requiring that they play two consecutive doubleheaders against St. Louis and then the one with the Yankees.

To describe Philadelphia as frenzied that day is understatement. An estimated 46,000 fans jammed the park. From lines that formed in the early morning hours, the 36,000 paid seats had been filled an hour before the game; an additional 10,000 fans forced their way inside, some 200 climbing over the right-field wall and the barbed-wire constraints atop it. "Forty thousand wild, howling, happy baseball fans jammed every square inch of Shibe Park, every girder, every cornice, every railing," while 1,000 perched on the roof over the left-field pavilion. Behind the right-field wall, those who managed to secure seats on the rooftop of dwellings for the whole block along Twentieth Street were the lucky ones, even at the grossly inflated price of $10. For outside the ballpark and on surrounding streets, bedlam ruled; another estimated 40,000 "even wilder" people surged about.[1] These were record numbers both inside and outside the ballpark.

Understandably, the police were sorely pressed what with the overwhelming numbers and the periodic eruption of "several small sized riots" during the games. Mounted and afoot, they freely wielded their nightsticks, although there's no report of any arrests. At one point, the cops had to call in 135 reserves. In a classic instance of drollness, one reporter characterized the crowd outside as "unreasonable," adding, "It wanted to see the game. It would stand quiet for a while until some ear-splitting roar from the inside would herald a great play or a tense moment and then there was no law and order."[2]

That commodity was scarce inside the stadium, also where the "spirit of Moon Mullins prevailed." The rivals split the doubleheader "to the accompaniment of a series of personal brawls on the playing field, sporadic slugging parties in the stands and a pop bottle shower for the finale." The umpires had to suspend play in the ninth inning of the first game to clear the baseline of "missiles" thrown at Lou Gehrig. "Pillows, bottles, and taunting insults" dogged the Yankees, especially Babe Ruth in left and catcher Bill Dickey during the second game, in which the A's would salvage a split in the twin bill via a three-run outburst in the bottom of the eighth to win, 4-2.[3]

The Yankees dominated game one immediately, and before 30 minutes had passed, they had scored 10 runs to their opponents' one. Three Yankee tallies came in the first. Tony Lazzeri's bases-loaded single scored two, and Dickey's masterful bunt down the third-base line scored The Babe, who had walked and moved to third on Bob Meusel's fly to right. (As it turned out, Mickey Cochrane's home run into the left-field stands in the bottom half of the inning kept the A's from being shut out and was the only home-team run of the game.) The roof caved in on A's hurler Howard Ehmke in the top of the second. After fanning his counterpart, right-hander George Pipgras, to start the inning, he put the next three hitters on. This brought Ruth to the plate, and he promptly parked a titanic home run, "one of his copyrighted hoists," over the right-field scoreboard onto Twentieth Street.[4] It was his league-leading 28th of the year, his third home run in two games, and his second grand slam in two consecutive games.

The Bronx Bombers had come into Philly hot. Just the day before, in their doubleheader split against Washington, they scored 17 runs in "some very impressive tuning up" for the A's series. In the second game against the Senators, which the Yankees won 8-0, the Bambino crushed a pair of homers – "how that big fat fellow paddled the onion," burbled one New York sportswriter – something Ruth would do twice more in this month of August 1929 and 72 times in his illustrious career, still the major-league record.[5] One of his homers against the Senators came with the bases loaded. And it contributed mightily to his seven RBIs, the most he ever accumulated in a game, and which he did three other times in his career.[6]

And the Yankees still weren't finished with the A's in this first game of their series. With seven runs already in for the visitors and with only one down in the top of the second, the hapless Ehmke followed up his disastrous gopher ball to Ruth by plunking Tony Lazzeri with a pitch. His day was over: Right-hander Bill Shores replaced him, induced Meusel to pop out, and then surrendered a double to Dickey. Whereupon shortstop Mark Koenig, who averaged a little over two homers a year, sent the ball deep into the right-field stands for another three Yankee runs. Yankees pitcher Pipgras continued cruising his way to a seven-hit complete-game victory, while his teammates touched the third Philly hurler, southpaw Ossie Orwoll, for two more unearned runs on Meusel's round-tripper in the sixth, and another on Lazzeri's solo shot in the top of the ninth.

The 34-year-old Ruth went on to lead the league in home runs (46) for the fourth consecutive time (he would do it again the next two seasons) and in OPS+ with 193 on his way to a storied career. And despite this drubbing, the Mackmen, as the Philly press dubbed them, were never seriously deterred from their dominance of the league. The 1929 A's, one of baseball history's most powerful teams, had played this game (and several others) without two of their stars: third baseman Jimmy Dykes and second-sacker Max Bishop. And by the close of the series, they still occupied the catbird's seat as season's end began creeping into sight. The Yankees had gained no ground on them at all. The A's led the American League by 11 games over these hated rivals at this point, and they would stretch their lead to a crushing 18 games over these same second-place Yankees by season's end.

Notes

1. "40,000 Wild Fans See A's and Yanks Split Twin Bill," *Philadelphia Inquirer*, August 8, 1929: 1; William E. Brandt, "Yanks and Athletics Divide Before 46,000; Ruth Hits 28th; Giants Lose, 4-3," *New York Times*, August 8, 1929: 19. The rooftop sitters paid $10 for vantage points that usually went for $1.

2. Jimmy Powers, "Yanks-A's in Stand-Off," *New York Daily News*, August 8, 1929: 34; James C. Isaminger, "40,000 See Earnshaw Capture 2d to Give Mackmen Even Break," *Philadelphia Inquirer*, August 8, 1929: 18.

3. Powers, "Yanks-A's in Stand-Off." Moon Mullins starred in a cartoon of the same name that ran from 1923-91. A would-be prizefighter, he was an amiable roughneck with a taste for fighting, gambling, and other lowlife activities.

4. Isaminger. Ehmke gave up 13 home runs to Ruth in his career. Only two other pitchers gave up more, fellow Athletic Rube Walberg (16) and Detroit righty Hooks Dauss (14).

5. Brandt."

6. Jimmy Powers, "Lefty Heimach Hurls 8-0 Shutout After 13-9 Slugging Bee," *New York Daily News*, August 7, 1929: 116.

Ruth Hits 500th Home Run

August 11, 1929: Cleveland Indians 6, New York Yankees 5, at League Park, Cleveland

By Chad Osborne

A solid klop must have filled Jake Geiser's ears when a baseball ricocheted off a doorstep on Cleveland's Lexington Avenue and rolled toward the New Philadelphia, Ohio, resident's feet.

Geiser, waiting to board a bus to his home about 90 miles south of the city, was standing just beyond the tall right-field fence at Cleveland's League Park. He most likely heard, too, the roar of the overflow ballpark crowd of more than 25,000 people just as The Sultan of Swat cocked his bat over his left shoulder and swung fiercely, launching the baseball toward the street.[1]

As Geiser was about to depart from Cleveland that Sunday afternoon after visiting relatives in the city, Babe Ruth stepped to the plate in the top of the second inning with 499 career home runs tallied on his stat sheet. Ruth had been hitting homers at a torrid pace; he had four in his last five games. The Babe seemed to find League Park particularly accommodating, having slugged many moonshots there since he first deposited one over the fence at the ballpark on June 5, 1918, as a member of the Boston Red Sox.

As the Bambino settled at the plate – it was his first at-bat of the game – Cleveland pitcher Willis Hudlin threw a high fastball "which left home plate much higher and ten times faster than it arrived," reported *New York Times* writer William Brandt. "It soared over the right-field fence near the foul line, and was the first run of the afternoon."[2]

According to the page one, above-the-fold article in the next day's *Cleveland Plain Dealer*, Ruth called his shot before the game. In his story, Gordon Cobbledick wrote about an exchange the Yankees slugger had with the ballpark's security chief, H. Clay Folger. "Listen," said The Babe, "I'm going to hit number 500 today and I tell you what I wish you'd do. I wish you'd find the kid who gets the ball and bring him to me. I'd kinda like to save that one."[3]

Geiser was no kid. Brandt wrote in the *Times* that he was 46 years old. As for respecting the Babe's wishes and returning the ball, the *Times* simply reported that he, the "ball retriever," was brought back to the ballpark and escorted to the Yankees dugout.[4] The *Plain Dealer*, sticking with the kid theme, provided a more elaborate tale of how Geiser reached and met the Babe.

"Folger and his men immediately went into action," Cobbledick reported. "This and that urchin they interviewed and at length they found one who said: 'A fella got it. I think he went in to the ball park.'"

The Cleveland newspaper wrote that Folger rushed back to the ballpark, and soon "there entered a young man with a suspicious looking bulge at his right-hand coat pocket."

There, the *Plain Dealer* reported, Folger offered to exchange a "brand new one [baseball] with the Babe's autograph on it" for the 500th-home-run ball.

We learn from Cobbledick's side of the story that Geiser was accompanied by an unidentified friend, who may have been trying to score a better deal for his pal by piping up with, "Oh, yeah? Maybe my friend would like to save it, too."

At that moment, everyone involved headed to the Yankees dugout to meet the Babe.

Once there, Ruth asked the ball retriever his name. His reply, according to the *Plain Dealer*: "I'm Jake Geiser," said the youth. "I came up from New Philadelphia, Ohio, to see the game."[5]

From that point, the *Plain Dealer* and *New York Times* stories mostly agree. Ruth hands an autographed ball – the *Times* reported it was two balls – to either a young or a 46-year-old Geiser, and an unautographed $20 bill. *The Sporting News*, perhaps gleaning information from the Cleveland reports, did not list Geiser's name or age, but referend to him as "youngster" and "boy" in its August 15, 1929, edition.[6]

The *Times* reported that Geiser delayed his bus trip back to New Philadelphia to stick around at League Park – often called Dunn Field, for former owner Jim Dunn – in hopes of seeing Ruth hit another shot toward Lexington Avenue. After "watching Ruth miss the fence on three subsequent efforts, and asserting that Ruth's 600th homer is not likely to happen here this week, he left for his home tonight, richer by $20 to say nothing of the two baseballs."

So much had happened on and off the field, but so much more was yet to be played out. After Ruth hit his milestone home run in the second – it was his 30th of the season – Lou Gehrig came to bat in the fourth with the bases empty. As Cobbledick wrote in a separate story for the next day's *Plain Dealer*, the Yankees first baseman hit "another slow ball floating lazily up toward the plate, bashed into approximately the same spot where his more illustrious mate's had landed."[7]

Lou Gehrig's 27th home run of the year gave the "terrible men of Gotham" a 2-0 lead.[8]

Going into the game, Cleveland already had won nine games against the Yankees throughout the season. The Roger Peckinpaugh-managed team was 55-51 and sat in fourth place, a distant 22 games out of first place. They had lost three in a row, including the series opener to the Yankees, the defending World Series champions.

Down early in the contest, Peckinpaugh's men rallied in the bottom of the fourth. The Indians up to this point had managed just a couple of harmless singles off Yankees lefty hurler Ed Wells.

Rookie left-handed hitter Earl Averill, who for the previous three seasons had played for the Pacific Coast League's San Francisco Seals, sparked the Cleveland rally by squaring his bat, dropping a bunt toward first base, and running to the bag safely. It was one of three hits in the game for the center fielder. First baseman Lew Fonseca singled up the middle to put runners on first and second. Bibb Falk's sacrifice advanced each runner 90 feet closer to home.

"This set the stage for Johnny Hodapp and he came through with a single that scored Averill and Fonseca. Then he moved up on [Ray] Gardner's infield out and when Luke Sewell slid a single into left he disregarded Coach Howard Shanks' instructions to stop at third and came racing in ahead of [Bob] Meusel's bad throw with the run that put the Tribe in the lead."[9]

The Indians led 3-2 after four. The Yankees rebounded for a run in the top of the fifth to tie the game, but Cleveland got its own tally in the bottom half of the frame.

Bob Meusel's bases-loaded, two-run double notched more Yankees runs on the League Park scoreboard, putting the New Yorkers ahead, 5-4.

The Indians donned their rally caps, figuratively speaking, once again in the bottom half of the sixth when Yankees second baseman Tony Lazzeri muffed a throw that should have retired the side runless. The Indians scored two runs, and Wells retired to the seclusion of the showers."[10] He exited in the sixth having been knocked around for 12 hits and six runs – four of those were earned. Righty Roy Sherid took Wells's place on the mound and allowed only one hit.

Willis Hudlin recorded the win for Cleveland, his 12th of the season, "making him the first Indians flinger to accomplish a dozen wins."[11]

The win moved Cleveland into sole possession of third place in the American League. The Yankees remained 10½ games behind the league-leading Philadelphia Athletics, who lost 9-8 in 11 innings that day in Detroit.

Ruth's second-inning blast made him the first player in big-league history to hit 500 home runs. Rogers Hornsby, with 263 home runs, was the Bambino's closest competitor. The veteran outfielder had collected 249 career homers as of August 11, 1929, the day Ruth paddled a Willis Hudlin pitch over the 40-foot-high concrete and steel right-field wall that thumped off a doorstep on Lexington Avenue and rolled unsuspectedly toward the footsteps of a traveler from New Philadelphia, Ohio.

Sources

In addition to the sources cited in the Notes, the author also consulted Baseball-Reference.com and Restrosheet.org.

Notes

1. William E. Brandt, "Ruth Hits His 500th Major League Homer, but Yankees Lose," *New York Times*, August 12, 1929.
2. Brandt.
3. Gordon Cobbledick, "Ruth Rides 500th Homer, but Tribe Trips Yanks, 6 to 5," *Cleveland Plain Dealer,* August 12, 1929.
4. Brandt.
5. Cobbledick
6. "Ruth's 500th Homer Costs Him $20 Bill," *The Sporting News*, August 15, 1929: 1.
7. Cobbledick.
8. Ibid.
9. Ibid.
10. Brandt.
11. Cobbledick.

The Babe Calls His Shot... Or Does He?

October 1, 1932: New York Yankees 7, Chicago Cubs 5, at Wrigley Field

(Game Three of the World Series)

By Gary Sarnoff

Ruth crosses Wrigley Field's home plate after his famous World Series home run, October 1, 1932. *Courtesy of Library of Congress.*

"Keep up the pepper, boys!" Chicago manager Charlie Grimm told his team in the clubhouse after the Chicago Cubs' 7-5 loss to the New York Yankees in Game Three of the 1932 World Series to put the Cubs at a three-games-to-none disadvantage.[1]

"You can't take it away from that pair; they can hit," said Cubs losing pitcher Charlie Root, who had served up two home runs apiece to Babe Ruth and Lou Gehrig in the game.[2] "If I had to do it all over again I'd pitch the same way."[3]

"It was a change of pace ball, low and outside," Root said of the second home run he had yielded to Ruth. "If it had been a fastball I wouldn't have been surprised. But he picked it out and sent on the line to center field. That convinced me of the power he has in his swings."[4]

"We'll be going home tomorrow," Babe Ruth bellowed in the joyous New York clubhouse, referring to his expectation of his team winning the next day to wrap up the 1932 World Series.[5]

"Well I picked a couple of 'em out today anyhow," Ruth continued, "and I seldom get more fun out of doing it. They've got some pretty good bench jockeys on that Cubs bench. But I think I had the last laugh."[6]

Before the October 1, 1932 game Ruth stepped into the batter's box for his turn during batting practice on a warm Indian summer day, with the temperature reaching an unseasonable 78 degrees. As one might expect, Ruth put on a good show by hammering a half-dozen baseballs over the fences, "and he knew he had the trick for the day," wrote sportswriter Westbrook Pegler, who also told his readers, "I'm telling you that before the game began the Babe knew he was going to hit one or more home runs."[7]

After slamming the last practice pitch into the far distance, "(H)e waddled toward the Cubs dugout, his large and a man jiggling in spite of his rubber corsets, and yelled, 'You mugs are not going to see Yankee Stadium any more this year. The World Series is going to be over Sunday afternoon, four straight.'"[8]

He then turned to a group of autograph seekers along the third-base barrier to inform them: "Did you hear what I told them? I told them over there? I told them that they ain't going back to New York. We lick 'em here, today and tomorrow."[9]

"The Babe is on fire," Lou Gehrig said as he laughed. "He ought to hit one today; maybe a couple."[10] Then the Yankees first baseman, having a poor turn in his batting practice session, focused on himself. "I'm not catching them right, but I know what's the trouble. I'm catching them on the end of the club. I ought to catch them about four inches down to make 'em ride."[11]

Cubs starting pitcher Charlie Root drew the assignment to tame the Yankees in Game Three. A 15-game winner in 1932, he was currently hot, with four wins during the last month of the season. He seemed to start off right by getting New York's first batter, Earle Combs, to ground one to the shortstop. However, Cubs shortstop Billy Jurges threw the ball away, allowing Combs to take second. Then Root walked the next batter, bringing up Ruth for his first at-bat with runners on first and second.

A salvo of boos greeted Ruth as he paced his way to the plate. Several lemons, thrown from the stands, landed on the field and rolled by Ruth's feet. He stepped up to the plate and readied himself as he looked out at the Cubs pitcher. Root made his pitch and, "With a step forward, a lurch of his massive shoulders and sweep of his celebrated bat, Ruth drove the ball high into temporary bleachers that had been erected beyond the right field fence. Upward and onward the ball flew, a white streak outlined against the bright blue sky."[12]

The top of the first concluded with a 3-0 Yankees lead. When the Yankees took the field in the bottom of the inning, Ruth was greeted by booing from the left-field bleachers. A fan threw a lemon that hit Ruth on the leg. "With graphic gestures, old Mr. Ruth called on them for fair play."[13]

The Cubs scored one in their half of the first inning against New York's starting pitcher, George Pipgras. In the top of the second, Ruth came to the plate with a runner on first and two outs. He got hold of a Root pitch and backed Cubs right fielder Kiki Cuyler up against the screen fence in right. Cuyler made the catch to retire Ruth.

In the top of the third, the score still 3-1, Gehrig came up for his second at-bat. Hoping to fool the Yankees first baseman, Root threw a change-of-pace pitch. Gehrig connected and sent the ball for a long ride into the right-field bleachers. "It wasn't as far as Ruth's, and it came with nobody on the bases, but it was just as effective in throwing fear into the hearts of the Cubs."[14]

The Cubs, who were not going to go down without a fight, rallied for three runs to tie the game, 4-4, after four innings. In the top of the fifth Ruth led off. "As Ruth came to the plate, swinging three bats over his shoulder, a concerted shout of derision broke in the stands. There was a bellowing of boos, hisses, and jeers. There were cries of encouragement for the pitcher, and from the Cubs dugout came a storm of abuse directed at the Babe."[15]

"Ruth, grinning in the face of the hostile greeting, laughed back at the Cubs and took his place, supremely confident."[16]

In the Cubs dugout pitchers Guy Bush and Bob Smith, both seated at the top of the dugout steps, were the loudest among the Cubs.

Root's first pitch sailed by Ruth for a called strike. He responded by holding up one finger as he looked into the Cubs dugout to indicate strike one. "Wait, Mug; I'm going to hit one out of the yard," he shouted.[17] Guy Bush responded by inching up the steps and yelling more insults. Then after two balls, Ruth let another one go by for strike two. Ruth held up two fingers and told the Cubs, "That's only two strikes, boys. I still have one coming."[18] Bush again responded while scooting closer to the point where he was now sitting on the grass at the edge before the Cubs dugout.

"Then, with a warning gesture of his hand to Bush, he sent the signal for the customers to see, as if to say, 'Now this is the one, look.'"[19]

With a count of two balls and two strikes, Root threw his change-of-pace pitch. Ruth swung and "there was a resounding report like the explosion of a gun. The ball soared on a line to center field. Johnny Moore (Cubs center fielder) raced back then stopped and stared."[20]

The ball sailed over the center-field fence, passed a flagpole, and dropped into the street. Ruth rounded the bases, and after he passed second base, he slowed down to deliver a message to Bush and the Cubs in the Chicago dugout. "The Yankees spilled out of the dugout and danced with glee. They moved forward to shake Ruth's hand and pat him on the back."[21]

As the Yankees continued to talk about Ruth's home run, Gehrig hit a high curveball and sent it for a ride into the right-field bleachers for his second homer of the game. The score was now 6-4 in favor of the Yankees.

In the bottom of the ninth, with the Yankees nursing a two-run lead, a runner on first and Rollie Hemsley at the plate for the Cubs, Guy Bush, who was warming up in the left-field bullpen, shouted advice for the Yankees left fielder. "Say Babe, don't you know that Hemsley is a left-field hitter? You better come over close to the foul line."[22]

"Well, if that's true, I will," responded Ruth, who then walked to his right until he was 12 feet from the left-field foul line. "Is this the right spot?" asked Ruth.[23]

Bush assured him that it was.

Hemsley struck out, the next batter grounded out, and then Cubs third baseman Woody English grounded out to end the game. "Well, I'll see you tomorrow, Joe," Ruth told Bush, and then jogged toward the infield.[24]

An angry look then came across Bush's features: not because Ruth called him by the wrong name. He tried his best, but he was unable to get Ruth's goat that day.

Sources

In addition to the sources cited in the Notes, the author also consulted Baseball-Reference.com and Retrosheet.org.

Notes

1 Irving Vaughan, "Cubs Agree You Can't Fool Two Yank Sluggers," *Chicago Tribune*, October 2, 1932: section 2, 1.

2 Ibid.

3 Ibid.

4 Ibid.

5 Edgar Munzel, "Ruth Begs for One Season in Wrigley Field," *Chicago Herald-American*, October 2, 1932: section 2, 2.

6 Ibid.

7 Westbrook Pegler, "Gehrig Hit 'Em," *Chicago Tribune*, Ocotber 2, 1932: section 2, 1.

8 Ibid.

9 Ibid.

10 Ibid.

11 Pegler, section 2, 3.

12 Richards Vidmer, "Yankee Home Runs Crush Cubs, 7-5, Ruth and Gehrig Smashing Two Apiece in Third Straight World Series victory," *New York Herald-Tribune*, October 2, 1932: Section 3, 1.

13 Pegler.

14 Vidmer.

15 Ibid.

16 Ibid.

17 Pegler.

18 Vaughan.

19 Ibid.

20 Ibid.

21 Vidmer.

22 Vaughan.

23 Ibid.

24 Ibid.

A Dream Realized

July 6, 1933: American League 4 National League 2, at Comiskey Park

By Lyle Spatz

In 1933, Chicago was celebrating its centennial by hosting a World's Fair, entitled *A Century of Progress Exposition*. Fair officials asked the local sports editors to think of an athletic event that would attract fans to Chicago from around the country.

Arch Ward, sports editor of the *Chicago Tribune*, suggested a baseball game to be played at Comiskey Park matching the best players in the American League against the best players in the National League. Labeling it "the game of the century," he was certain it would be a success. Fan interest was sure to be high, but to make it even more so, he would have the fans select the players. But before any announcement of such a game could be made, Ward had to ascertain if his dream was feasible. The first person he consulted was American League President Will Harridge.

Ward was prepared to drop the whole scheme if he could not get Harridge's approval. To Ward's delight, Harridge not only approved, he promised to recommend it to the eight American League club owners. The following day, Ward explained the plan to William E. Veeck, president of the Chicago Cubs. Veeck loved the idea and promised to lobby for the game with the other National League owners. A call by Ward to National League President John Heydler also elicited a promise to discuss the proposed game with those owners.

On May 9, at a special meeting in Cleveland, the American League owners enthusiastically voted in favor of the game and chose July 6 as the date. However, a few days later, Ward received a telegram from Heydler informing him that three NL owners – the Giants' Charles Stoneham, the Braves' Charles Adams, and the Cardinals' Sam Breadon – had turned down the idea.

Breadon based his opposition on the fear that any future games, as this one was doing, would be forced to donate the proceeds to charity. Stoneham and Adams opposed the idea because of the selected date. The Giants and Braves were scheduled to play a doubleheader in Boston on July 5, making it impossible for any chosen players to be in Chicago in time to play on July 6.

Breadon dropped his opposition after Ward convinced him that other cities, including St. Louis, could benefit by hosting a future All-Star Game. The only obstacle remaining was the July 5 Giants-Braves doubleheader. After National League owners persuaded Heydler to postpone that doubleheader, a contract was signed by Ward, representing the *Tribune*, Heydler, and Harridge.

Editors at the *Tribune* had thought it unlikely other newspapers would do anything to help publicize a rival newspaper, yet all 55 Ward had asked to join in, accepted. In a gesture of cooperation, they even volunteered to help in the polling. The idea captured the imagination of fans everywhere, who then took the opportunity to vote for the players they most wanted to see.

Chicago White Sox outfielder Al Simmons, tied with Washington manager-shortstop Joe Cronin for the league lead in batting, got the most votes, 346,291. Philadelphia Phillies outfielder Chuck Klein, the National League's leading hitter, was also its leading vote-getter, with 342,283.

The final rosters, 18 players per league, were determined by a combination of the fans' votes and the selections of the respective managers. The players would not be paid for participating, but would benefit indirectly by the net receipts of $46,506 the game raised for the Association of Professional Baseball Players of America.

The two most honored managers in the game, one from each league, were selected to lead their respective teams. John McGraw had stepped down in June 1932 after 30 years at the helm of the New York Giants, but the National League called him out of retirement to manage this one game. The Americans gave the managerial honors to Connie Mack, who had led the Athletics since the league's birth.

The regular season would resume the following day, although the owners had agreed that if the All-Star Game was rained out, they would cancel the next day's schedule and play it then. That precaution proved unnecessary; the weather was perfect and though the country was struggling through the worst economic crisis in its history, every seat was filled.

For all sections of the park, patrons had been allowed to buy only four tickets, and there was no standing room. All seats were priced the same as for regular-season games at Comiskey Park, and because they played the game under "World Series rules," no spectators would be allowed on the field. The crowd of 47,595, conducted itself in an exemplary manner, as if each fan knew he was witnessing something special.

The American League stars won the game, 4-2, but both sides offered strong pitching, solid hitting, and near-flawless defense. Yankees first baseman Lou Gehrig's drop of Philadelphia Phillies shortstop Dick Bartell's foul pop in the fifth inning was the game's only error.

Babe Ruth, 38 years old and nearing the end of his career, provided the AL's margin of victory with the first home run in All-Star competition, a third-inning two-run blast. It came off National League starter Bill Hallahan of St. Louis and increased the American League's lead to 3-0.

Five days before the game, McGraw and Mack had announced that the starting pitchers would be Carl Hubbell of the Giants and Lefty Grove of the A's, the game's two best left-handers. But both managers changed their minds on game day, although both stayed with left-handers: McGraw went with Hallahan (10-4), while Mack chose the Yankees' Lefty Gomez (9-6).

Current Giants manager Bill Terry captained the National Leaguers, who had the words "NATIONAL LEAGUE" on the fronts of their gray road uniforms with an "NL" emblazoned on their caps. Tigers second baseman Charlie Gehringer captained the Americans, each of whom wore his regular home uniform.

To help familiarize themselves with the other league, both teams used the other's ball during batting practice to acclimate themselves to the different constructions. An American League ball, reputed to be livelier, would be used for the first 4½ innings, before the teams switched to the thicker-covered National League ball.

At 1:15 P.M., home-plate umpire Bill Dinneen of the American League called "Play Ball!" and Cardinals third baseman Pepper Martin stepped in as the first All-Star batter. Gomez retired him on a groundball to shortstop Cronin, and the "dream game" had become a reality. In the second inning, the American Leaguers scored the first All-Star run, helped along by the wildness of Hallahan, who not for nothing was known as "Wild Bill."[1] After walking White Sox third baseman Jimmy Dykes and Cronin, he yielded a two-out single to Gomez, a historically weak batter, that scored Dykes.

When Hallahan walked Gehrig following Ruth's third-inning home run, McGraw replaced him with Cubs right-hander Lon Warneke. Meanwhile, Gomez held the National Leaguers scoreless in his three innings, as did Washington's Alvin Crowder in the fourth and fifth. The Nationals finally broke through in the sixth. Warneke hit a one-out triple, a long fly down the right-field line that was poorly handled by Ruth, and scored as Martin was grounding out. Frankie Frisch, manager-second baseman of the Cardinals, followed with a home run to cut the AL's lead to 3-2.

Warneke had already pitched three full innings, and had raced around the bases in the top of the sixth; nevertheless, McGraw sent him out to pitch the home half of the inning. The American Leaguers quickly got a run back on a single by Cronin, a sacrifice by Rick Ferrell, and a single by Cleveland's Earl Averill, batting for Crowder. Ferrell, the Red Sox' lone representative, caught the entire game, despite having finished third in the voting behind the Yankees' Bill Dickey and Philadelphia's Mickey Cochrane, both of whom were injured.

Hubbell and Grove came on in the seventh. Hubbell, who had shut out the Cardinals, 1-0, in 18 innings four days earlier, pitched two innings, blanking the American Leaguers on one hit. Grove pitched the final three innings for the AL, also allowing no runs, though the National Leaguers threatened in both the seventh and the eighth.

They had runners on second and third in the seventh, with just one out, but Grove struck out the Cubs' Gabby Hartnett and got Hartnett's Chicago teammate, Woody English, on a fly ball. Then in the eighth, with two out and Frisch, who had singled, on first, Hafey hit what would have been a game-tying home run in a park less spacious than Comiskey. Ruth ran it down and caught it with his back pressed to the right-field wall. Grove retired the National Leaguers one-two-three in the ninth, and the "game of the century" was over.

McGraw went to the winners' locker room to congratulate Mack, his longtime rival, and Ruth, whom he had often denigrated in the past.

Both managers said they hoped the game would be repeated annually.

Adapted from the author's article on the 1933 All-Star Game that appeared in *The Midsummer Classic: The Complete History of Baseball's All-Star Game*.

Sources

The author also accessed Retrosheet.org, Baseball-Reference.com, and SABR.org.

Notes

1 Hallahan walked five in his two-plus innings, which remain the most walks given up by a pitcher in one All-Star Game.

Lefty Ruth All Right in Final Mound Appearance

October 1, 1933: New York Yankees 6, Boston Red Sox 5, at Yankee Stadium

By Ed Gruver

For all of his tremendous success in the batter's box, Babe Ruth felt just as at home on the pitcher's mound.

"As soon as I got out there I felt a strange relationship with the pitcher's mound," Ruth said. "It was as if I'd been born out there. Pitching just felt like the most natural thing in the world."[1]

Ruth's record on the mound is indeed impressive. In 163 mound appearances from 1914 to 1933 he went 94-46 for a .671 win percentage. A southpaw, Ruth won 23 games in 1916 when he led the American League with a 1.75 earned-run average and won a career-high 24 the following season while also leading the league in complete games with 35. He fashioned a career 2.28 ERA over 163 mound appearances and threw 107 complete games.

Ruth was also undefeated in three World Series appearances for the Boston Red Sox in 1916 and 1918, and strung together a consecutive scoreless-innings streak that stretched to 29⅔ innings. Ruth's mark stood until another Yankees legend, Whitey Ford, set a new standard in 1961. If The Sultan of Swat hadn't made baseball's Hall of Fame for his hitting, he almost certainly would have claimed a place in Cooperstown for his pitching.

By 1933, his next to last season in Yankees pinstripes, The Babe was winding down his unparalleled career. He was 38 years old, hadn't made a mound appearance since the season finale three years earlier and hadn't pitched regularly since 1919, his final season with the Red Sox.

Ruth hurled a complete-game victory over a depleted Red Sox squad on September 28, 1930, ending a nine-year hiatus from the mound. The Yankees were a distant third to Connie Mack's powerful Philadelphia Athletics, who were in the process of claiming the second of three straight American League pennants. The Yankees-Red Sox series at season's end was so insignificant that New York's rookie manager, Bob Shawkey, excused his three top pitchers, Red Ruffing, Herb Pennock, and George Pipgras, and starting catcher Bill Dickey from making the trip.

Ruth had hurled exhibition games through the years but those occasional offseason outings hardly prepared him to pitch again in the majors. Ruth, being the incredible player that he was, climbed the hill at Braves Field. No longer the lean lefty who starred for the Red Sox in the Teens, the portly Ruth still succeeded in turning back the clock to his years as a dominant hurler.

In his only appearance as a Yankees pitcher outside of New York, The Babe blanked Boston for the first five innings in an eventual 9-3 win. He yielded 11 hits, struck out three – Ruth was never a strikeout pitcher, even in his prime – and started two double plays by twice snaring what the *New York Times* described as a "smash hot off the bat."[2]

The *Brooklyn Daily Eagle* wrote that Ruth displayed "both speed and puzzling curves."[3]

The Associated Press noted that six of the Red Sox' hits came in the final two innings when Ruth was reportedly just lobbing the ball and coasting behind a comfortable lead.

Interestingly, the game was played at Braves Field rather the Red Sox' home of Fenway Park, due to Sunday laws that prohibited the use of Fenway Park because of its close proximity to a church.[4]

The crowd, numbered at just 12,000, was reported by the *New York Times* to be "visibly and audibly impressed" by the Babe's mound performance.[5]

As strange it may have seen for fans to see Ruth toeing the rubber, it must have been equally odd to see Lou Gehrig occupying Ruth's position in left field. The celebrated Iron Man, in the midst of a streak that reached 2,130 games before his fatal illness forced him to rest, had long anchored the Yankees infield at first base and had not played the outfield since 1925.

Ruth returned to the mound one final time, in the final game of the 1933 season. The Red Sox were once again Ruth's opponent, but the venue this time was Yankee Stadium. In his 20th major-league season, The Babe had grown increasingly overweight and out of shape. Once again the Yankees were out of contention, finishing second to Washington, so Ruth volunteered to pitch the final game. To get ready for his first mound appearance in three years, The Babe tossed batting practice for several weeks.

In order to attract fans to the Stadium, the Yankees advertised that a fungo-hitting contest would be held to highlight pregame festivities. To the delight of many in the announced crowd of 25,000, many of whom felt Ruth might be making his final appearance in pinstripes, The Bambino as he was also known, won the event with a 395-foot blast. James P. Dawson's story on the game in the *Times* said Yankees trainer Doc Painter soothed the Babe's aching left arm between innings with "diligent rubbing."[6]

Ruth struggled but persevered. Just as he had done in Fenway Park in 1930, The Babe shut out the Red Sox for the first five innings. He surrendered four runs in the sixth but survived and went the distance in a 6-5 victory. His pitching line for the game read 12 hits, 5 earned runs, 3 walks, and zero strikeouts. Batting from his accustomed third spot in the order, The Bambino helped his cause by hammering a home run in the fifth inning, his 34th homer of the season. He also walked and scored.

Ruth was a fast worker on the mound; his complete game clocked in at just 1:38.

Yet he acknowledged in the aftermath that he was exhausted.

"I lost eight pounds in that game," he said. "No regular pitching job for me. The outfield has it licked. About one game a month is all I want to pitch. I've got a sore arm and a headache."[7]

With Dickey having been given the day off, Ruth's catcher for the game was a husky youngster named Joe Glenn. Dickey's understudy noted that despite not having pitched in three years, The Babe maintained his Ruthian image, warming up on the sidelines and striding to the mound as if he had been pitching all season.

"He knew how to operate," Glenn told writer Joe Lawler.[8]

Glenn remembered Ruth having good command that day.

"He pitched better than a lot of guys who were pitching in the major leagues," Glenn said.[9]

Glenn recalled Ruth having an average fastball, and also throwing a curve and change of pace. The Babe had good control of his pitches, Glenn added, and had pitching savvy.

Ruth received rubdowns and ice water between innings, allowing him to close out a game few expected him to finish. Glenn said no one figured on Ruth pitching nine innings. The thinking was to let Babe start the game to draw people to the ballpark. While Ruth said the effort exhausted him, Glenn thought The Babe finished the game without any problem.

"He looked good," Glenn told Lawler. "Like a regular pitcher, not like a guy who was wild, throwing the ball in the dirt."[10]

What pulled Ruth through was his previous experience as a pitcher, said Glenn. Ruth knew most of the Boston batters and was aware of their strengths and weaknesses. Ruth was a heads-up ballplayer, Glenn said, and on top of that The Babe was an ironman who could do things the average player would fall down trying to do. Ruth's teammate Joe Dugan said once that to understand The Babe you had to understand this: Ruth wasn't human.[11]

Ruth never again climbed a major-league mound, closing his pitching career in pinstripes with five wins in five appearances and two complete-game victories. He finished with a flourish, a fitting finale for one of the greats of the game.

Notes

1. baberuth.com, Babe Ruth Quotes.
2. Ken Schlager, "Babe Ruth Called His Shot, from the Mound," *New York Times*, August 16, 2008.
3. " 'Pitcher Babe' Would Rather Stay in Field," *Brooklyn Daily Eagle,* October 2, 1933.
4. Frank Jackson, "Babe Ruth, the New York Pitcher," *Hardball Times*, September 10, 2012.
5. Schlager.
6. Ibid.
7. " 'Pitcher Babe' Would Rather Stay in Field."
8. Joe Lawler, "Today's Battery: Ruth and Glenn," SABR, *Baseball Research Journal*, 1978: 8-11.
9. Ibid.
10. Ibid.
11. baberuth.com, Babe Ruth Quotes.

The Babe Bashes 700th Career Home Run

July 13, 1934: New York Yankees 4, Detroit Tigers 2, at Navin Field, Detroit

By Kevin Larkin

Ruth hits the deck at Fenway Park, 1934. Catcher is Boston's Rick Ferrell.
Leslie Jones photo, courtesy of the Boston Public Library.

Babe Ruth spent 15 years of his 22-year major-league career with the New York Yankees. His career began in 1914 with the Boston Red Sox, where he was a standout pitcher until the end of the 1919 season. His contract was then sold to the Yankees in 1920. After the 1934 season, the Yankees and Boston Braves arranged a deal for the 40-year-old Ruth to go to Boston in various capacities, one of them as "assistant manager."[1]

In his 15 years with the Yankees, Ruth had hit 659 home runs, with many milestones. He slugged 60 homers in 1927, the last one coming off Tom Zachary of the Washington Senators on September 30. The Babe hit his 500th career home run off Willis Hudlin of the Cleveland Indians on August 11, 1929, and his 600th off George Blaeholder of the St. Louis Browns on August 21, 1931.

Ruth mashed career home run No. 700 on July 13, 1934, off Tommy Bridges of the Detroit Tigers. On that notable day, the Yankees sent Red Ruffing to the mound to face Bridges. Both Bridges and Ruffing had identical 4-2 records in their last six games. Ruffing would finish the year with 19 wins and 11 losses; he also pitched in the All-Star Game. Bridges finished the year with a record of 22 wins and 11 losses and a league-leading 35 games started, and was an American League All-Star selection, though he didn't get into the game.

In 1933, Ruth had batted .288, hit 22 home runs, and had 84 RBIs. Teammate Lou Gehrig outplayed the Babe, winning the AL Triple Crown with a .363 batting average, 49 home runs, and 166 RBIs. Yankee catcher Bill Dickey had a solid season as well, hitting 12 home runs, driving in 72 runs, and batting .322 with his second consecutive All-Star game selection.

Detroit was also loaded with talent in 1934 and went on to its first American League pennant since 1909, although they lost the World Series to the St. Louis Cardinals in seven games. The Tiger lineup had hitters like Goose Goslin, Charlie Gehringer, Hank Greenberg, and player-manager Mickey Cochrane, all of whom were later elected to the National Baseball Hall of Fame.[2]

As Bridges and Ruffing got down to work that Friday the 13th afternoon in front of the crowd at Navin Field, the Tigers were a scant half-game ahead of New York in the American League standings.

There was no scoring in either the first or the second innings, although the Yankees came close in the top of the second. Gehrig and Ben Chapman singled to lead off the frame. Dickey's line drive to right field was turned into a double play when Gehrig was caught off second. Chapman stole second and Frank Crosetti walked. Bridges threw a wild pitch that advanced Chapman to third and Crosetti to second. Bridges ended the threat when he got Don Heffner to fly out to center.

Gehrig left the game with one out in the bottom of the second, plagued by lumbago.[3] Third baseman Jack Saltzgaver replaced Gehrig at first, Frankie Crosetti moved from shortstop to third and newcomer Red Rolfe went in to play shortstop, batting in Gehrig's cleanup spot in the lineup. The Iron Horse's lumbago created serious doubt as to whether his consecutive-game streak, now at 1,426, could continue.[4]

The Tigers got runners to second and third with one out in the bottom of the second on a double by Greenberg and a single and stolen base by Cochrane, but Marv Owen popped out to second and Bridges grounded to shortstop.

Ruffing struck out to begin the Yankees' third. Earle Combs singled to center field and Saltzgaver struck out. Ruth hit next and drove a Bridges pitch well into the right-field bleachers for his 14th home run of the season, No. 700 of his career, giving the Yankees a 2-0 lead.[5]

(To put Ruth's accomplishment in perspective, when he got his 700th, the next four career home-run leaders were his teammate Gehrig, with 323; Jimmie Foxx, with 248; Al Simmons, with 235; and Mel Ott, with 197.)

In the bottom of the third inning the Tigers made the score 2-1 when Jo-Jo White scored on a high fly to second base by Gehringer.[6]

The game remained 2-1 Yankees, despite scoring chances by the Yankees in the fourth inning and the Tigers in the sixth inning. In the Yankees' fourth, Dickey led off with a single but was picked off first. Heffner singled to center with two outs and advanced to second on a wild pitch, but was left there when Ruffing flied out. As for Detroit in the sixth inning, Billy Rogell hit a one-out single. He advanced to second on a groundout and Cochrane walked. But both were left on base when Owen struck out.

New York came to bat in the bottom of the eighth inning still leading 2-1. Ruth walked with one out, and Rolfe's single sent him to second base. Rolfe was picked off first base, but Chapman drew a two-out walk. Bill Dickey's double to center scored Ruth and Chapman, and it was now 4-1 in favor of the Yankees.

Detroit made it 4-2 in the bottom of the eighth inning when Greenberg's triple scored Rogell. Ruffing retired the Tigers in order in the ninth.

Ruth hit eight more home runs as a Yankee after this game, with his final pinstripes round-tripper run coming on September 29, 1934, against the Washington Senators' Syd Cohen in an 8-5 Senators victory. His first home run in the National League came off the Giants' Carl Hubbell on April 16, 1935; in a 4-2 Braves win on Opening Day. His final home run, one of three he hit that day, was off Guy Bush May 25, 1925, in an 11-7 Braves' loss to the Pirates at Forbes Field.[7]

Gehrig, meanwhile, managed to preserve his consecutive games streak the next day with the help of some creative lineup-juggling. He was penciled in at shortstop and led off the game against the Tigers with a single to right. He was immediately replaced by pinch-runner Rolfe, who also took Gehrig's place at shortstop. The following day, the Iron Horse returned to the lineup full-time. He bashed three doubles, but the Yankees fell to the Tigers, 8-3.

Sources

In addition to the sources cited in the Notes, the author consulted the Baseball-Reference.com and Retrosheet.org websites, Robert Creamer's *Babe: The Legend Comes to Life* (New York: Simon & Schuster, 1992), and Leigh Montville's *The Big Bam: The Life and Times of Babe Ruth* (New York: Doubleday, 2006

Notes

1. Jack Zerby, "Ruth Smashes 3 Homers in Final Hurrah," SABR Games Project, sabr.org, accessed March 1, 2017.

2. Baseballhall.org, Hall of Fame Explorer, accessed March 8, 2017.

3. "Even Lumbago Can't Keep Lou Out of Lineup," *Brooklyn Daily Eagle*, July 14, 1934: 8.

4. James Dawson, "Ruth Hits 700th As Yankees Score 4-2," *New York Times*, July 14, 1934: 8.

5. Ibid.

6. "Ruth Again," *Burlington Free Press* (Burlington, Vermont), July 14, 1934: 13.

7. Allan Wood, "Babe Ruth," SABR Biography Project, sabr.org, accessed February 15, 2017; Zerby, "Ruth . . ."

Ruth Smashes Three Homers in Final Hurrah

May 25, 1935: Pittsburgh Pirates 11, Boston Braves 7, at Forbes Field, Pittsburgh

By Jack Zerby

The bedraggled Boston Braves were already in their familiar abode—the National League cellar—at 8-19 and 11 games out when they played their 28th game of the 1935 season. It was a Saturday afternoon at Pittsburgh's bucolic Forbes Field, where a local newspaper, the *Sun-Telegraph,* had invited "hundreds of boy and girl guests"[1] to cheer on their home-standing Pirates.

And by happenstance, those guests also had the opportunity to also see a living baseball legend, new to the National League. The Braves had Babe Ruth, a free agent acquired at a high-mileage age 40 by Boston's owner and erstwhile manager[2] Judge Emil E. Fuchs[3] when the Yankees cast the legend adrift on February 26. Although the Braves already had a "new Babe Ruth," as writers tabbed popular slugger Wally Berger[4], "the Judge liked to take on long-shot comeback players,"[5] and Ruth became "a very big frog in a very small pond" when Fuchs signed him.[6] It was a return of sorts. The Babe had departed Boston 15 years earlier, when Red Sox owner-theater impresario Harry Frazee sold his contract to the Yankees.

The Yankees had scorned Ruth in 1935 spring training by re-assigning his uniform number and using his locker for firewood as prelude to release.[7] Fuchs brought him to Boston in the announced triple capacities of player, second vice president, and assistant manager,[8] but the VP and assistant managerial posts were public relations fluff. Ruth's playing days were essentially over, but after banishment by the Yankees, taking his celebrity back to Boston seemed a better option than retirement.

As the early season progressed, his new pond tended to engulf the overweight, weak-legged Babe. He had lifted spirits and made Fuchs look like a genius with an Opening Day home run at Braves Field against Giants ace Carl Hubbell on April 16. But through May 24 he was hitting just .153 with three home runs and five RBIs, three of which had come in the opener.

Ruth's curiosity value had resulted in his starting 22 of the team's first 27 games, generally in left field, although manager Bill McKechnie often lifted him for a pinch-runner or defensive replacement. This day in Pittsburgh, however, McKechnie had the Babe starting in his time-honored right-field position, slotted third in the batting order in front of steady producer Berger.

Pirate manager Pie Traynor started Red Lucas. The righty was in trouble before all of the recorded 10,000 in attendance, including the young *Sun-Telegraph* guests, had settled into their seats on a chilly Saturday afternoon. Boston shortstop Billy Urbanski walked and advanced to second on a sacrifice by second baseman Les Mallon, bringing up Ruth, slugging a paltry .305. But the Babe, seeing yet another new National League pitcher, responded with some of his old-time pizazz and methodically lofted career home run No. 712 into the right-field stands to give the Braves a quick 2-0 edge. After Berger and first baseman Randy Moore both singled, Traynor yanked Lucas in favor of National League veteran Guy Bush, now toiling for Pittsburgh after 12 seasons with the Cubs. Bush induced a double-play grounder off the bat of left fielder Hal "Sheriff" Lee to end the inning.

Huck Betts, only two years Ruth's junior at 38, was the Boston starter. He survived two hits and an error to hold Pittsburgh scoreless in the first, and then notched a perfect one, two, three second inning.

Ruth batted for the second time in the Braves' third. Facing Bush, who had hit him with a pitch in Game Four of the 1932 World Series—with Ruth and the Yankees on the way to a demoralizing sweep of the Cubs—he belatedly retaliated with another homer to right. The shot, career No. 713, plated Urbanski again and upped the Braves' lead to 4-0.

Betts cruised through the third, but his 4-0 lead dissolved into a 4-4 deadlock in the Pittsburgh fourth on RBI hits by Gus Suhr and Tommy Thevenow and Earl Grace's sacrifice fly.

Still in a groove, Ruth added another RBI with a punched, opposite-field single off Bush in the fifth to put the Braves back on top, 5-4.[9] Pittsburgh responded in the bottom of the inning with three runs on four hits, including an inside-the-park home run by second baseman Pep Young. The rally chased Betts as McKechnie needed Ben Cantwell to record the third out. The Pirates now led 7-5.

With that score intact and Bush still pitching, Ruth came up for the fourth time in the top of the seventh with one out and the bases empty. By now the crowd[10] was solidly on the Bambino's side and rooted enthusiastically for more of his old magic. The Babe obliged, dramatically. Career home run No. 714 came on a 3-1 count and bettered his two more mundane earlier efforts, majestically clearing Forbes Field's right field roof—for the first time in the ballpark's 26-year history.[11] "The way he smacked it, you knew it was gone. The crowd just roared," Paul Warhola, brother of iconic Pittsburgh pop artist Andy Warhol, remembered.[12] "He was fat and old but he still had that great swing," was sportswriter Robert W. Creamer's retrospective take.[13]

After rounding the bases in a truncated 1935 version of his classic trot, Babe saluted the fans with a tipped cap, and then excused himself from the game. Sole access to the visiting clubhouse was through the Pittsburgh dugout. En route, he briefly plopped himself down at the end of the bench and told rookie Pirates pitcher Mace Brown, "Boy, that last one felt good!"[14]

No. 714 had closed the gap to a run and the Braves tied the score, 7-7, later in the inning.[15] But Cantwell faltered in the seventh, allowing three runs. Larry Benton pitched the eighth for Boston, yielding another run. Waite Hoyt, who had been the Babe's teammate with the Yankees from 1921 through 1930, finished up for the Pirates and was the winning pitcher in their 11-7 victory.

It's sometimes reported that this memorable game was the Babe's last. It truly was his "last hurrah," but he went on to play in five more games, without a hit in 13 plate appearances. Throughout May, Fuchs, Ruth, and McKechnie had come to the conclusion that Ruth's retirement, sooner rather than later, was in the mutual best interest. He made it official in early June after batting once in the first game of a doubleheader[16] in Philadelphia on May 30—the same day his May 25 feats were noted without fanfare in a routine, agate-type, *Sporting News* "Highlights of the Week" column.[17]

Two weeks later that paper, widely known as the "Bible of Baseball," editorialized: "If the Babe saw the hand writing on the wall, as he indicated that he did, it is too bad that he did not announce his retirement the day after he made three home runs in one game in Pittsburgh, so he could have gone out in a blaze of glory, instead of waiting to make his departure along a trail of unpleasantness."[18]

Sources

In addition to the sources cited in the Notes, the author used the Baseball-Reference.com and Retrosheet.org websites for box scores, play-by-play details, and player and team pages and logs.

Notes

1. Photo cutline, *Pittsburgh Sun-Telegraph*, May 26, 1935: 17.

2. Robert S. Fuchs and Wayne Soini, *Judge Fuchs and the Boston* Braves (Jefferson, North Carolina: McFarland & Co., 1998), 68. Fuchs owned the Braves from 1923 through 1935 and out of frugality assumed the field managerial reins as well for the 1929 season. The team finished eighth, at 56-98. For 1930, Fuchs plucked future Hall of Fame manager Bill McKechnie away from Cardinals' owner Sam Breadon. Ibid., 83-84. McKechnie had managed the 1925 Pirates to a World Series victory. He was still at the Braves' helm in 1935.

3. "He served briefly as a real judge [in New York City], but the name was his ever after." Ibid., 11.

4. Ibid., 84-85. The Braves acquired Berger from the Pacific Coast League Los Angeles Angels in late 1929. He hit 38 home runs and drove in 119 runs in his rookie 1930 season, kept slugging, and capably anchored center field to earn the acclaim of Braves fans with little else to cheer about.

5. Ibid., 102.

6. Ibid., 103-04.

7. Alan Wood, "Babe Ruth," SABR Baseball Biography Project, https://sabr.org/bioproj/person/9dcdd01c, accessed June 5, 2019.

8. Fuchs., 110-11.

9. "Babe Needed One More to Tie Record," *Pittsburgh Press*, May 25, 1935: 15.

10. "It was far from a sellout," recalled A. J. Marucci, a then-15-year-old Pittsburgh fan who saw the game from the bleachers. Robert Dvorchak, "Ruthian Moment for Fans," *Pittsburgh Post-Gazette*, May 25, 2010: 29, 32.

11. David Cicotello and Angelo J. Louisa, eds., *Forbes Field* (Jefferson North Carolina: McFarland & Co., 2007), 2, 42.

12. Dvorchak, noting that Warhola, 12 years old, was selling newspapers in the ballpark that day.

13. Dvorchak, quoting Creamer's book *Babe: The Legend Comes To Life* (New York: Simon & Schuster, 1974).

14. Dvorchak, quoting Tom Foreman's 1995 interview with Mace Brown for the Associated Press. Tom Foreman, AP, "Babe's Last 3 HRs Were Rookie's Top Thrill," *Detroit Free Press*, May 24, 1995: 37.

15. When Ruth left the game, he was 4-for-4 and had driven in all six Boston runs.

16. "The big Bambino limped out into left field to start the first game, batted once and played one inning and then retired to the clubhouse to pet his creaking joints." Stan Baumgartner, "Phils Take Two," *Philadelphia Inquirer*, May 31, 1935: 15.

17. *The Sporting News*, May 30, 1935: 5.

18. Unattributed editorial, "The Babe Strikes Out, *The Sporting News*, June 13, 1935: 4.

Babe Ruth Plays His Last Game

May 30, 1935: Philadelphia Phillies 11, Boston Braves 6 at Baker Bowl, Philadelphia

By Thomas J. Brown Jr.

Babe Ruth was released by the New York Yankees at the end of the 1934 season. He still wanted to get hired as a manager and so he signed with the Boston Braves. His job titles were vice-president, assistant manager, and left fielder. Ruth hoped that he would be named manager if the Braves skipper Bill McKechnie left.[1] The Braves were a franchise in need of a savior and they were anticipating that Ruth's presence in the lineup would fill the ballpark.

Ruth hit three home runs in a losing effort against the Pittsburgh Pirates on May 25. After that slugging performance, he went hitless in the next four games. He started three of those games in left field and pinch-hit in another one. Ruth pulled a muscle while playing outfield on May 26, Babe Ruth Day in Cincinnati. He pinch-hit the following day but started in left field in the final game of the series.

In that game, Ruth endured possibly the worst experience of his career. Every Reds batter purposely hit the ball to left field in the fifth inning. Ruth, hampered by his muscle strain, was unable to field the balls and the Reds scored five runs. When the inning finally ended, Ruth went to the clubhouse, not the dugout, as the fans heckled him.[2] On the way, he picked up a small boy and hugged him before leaving the field.[3]

When the Braves arrived in Philadelphia on May 29, the Phillies celebrated Babe Ruth Day. Ruth was presented with a floral bouquet as the crowd cheered him.[4] Ruth walked twice during the game as he helped the Braves snap out of an six-game losing streak. But he was hitting just .188 when the Braves arrived in Philadelphia and his batting average continued to drop when he failed to get a hit in two at-bats that afternoon.

The Braves hoped to notch another win when they took the field for the first game of doubleheader on May 30. Jim Bivin started for the Phillies. Although he did not give up a run in the first, he did surrender runs in four of the next five innings before he left the game with the Phillies down 5-4.

Ruth was penciled in as the starting left fielder for the game. In the first inning, he grounded out to Dolph Camilli at first. Unknown to everyone in attendance, it was the last time that Babe would stand in the batter's box as a major leaguer.

When the Braves took the field, Ruth took his place in left field. He continued to struggle defensively. First, a ball dropped in front of him when he couldn't run in to catch it. When Lou Chiozza hit a fly ball to left field, Ruth failed to catch it. The ball rolled past him to the wall. Ruth finally caught up to the ball and threw it to the relay man, third baseman Pinkey Whitney. Whitney relayed the ball to home and Chiozza was thrown out as he tried to make an inside-the-park home run. Ruth was credited with an assist on the play, his last one, but the Phillies had jumped out to a 3-0 lead.

As the Braves left the field after the third out, Ruth did not join them. He left through the center-field fence where the clubhouse was located. As he slowly trotted off the field, the 18,000 fans who had shown up gave him one last standing ovation.[5] No one at the Baker Bowl suspected that Ruth would announce his retirement three days later.

Fred Frankhouse started for the . He lost his last outing after winning three games in a row for the . He was looking to rebound from his previous loss where he pitched seven innings and gave up four runs. The Phillies jumped on Frankhouse for three runs in the bottom of the first. But he settled down and gave up only one more run until the eighth when things fell apart for him.

The Braves nibbled at the Phillies lead over the next six innings. They scored one run in the second. Les Mallon singled and then landed on third when Whitney doubled. He scored on an error by Chiozza. They scored another run in the third when Wally Berger homered.

Although the Phillies scored another run in the fourth inning, the Braves tied the game in the fifth. Hal Lee, who had replaced Ruth in left field, singled. Then Randy Moore homered and suddenly the score was 4-4.

The Braves grabbed the lead in the sixth when they scored a run. Boston added another run in the seventh. Orville Jorgens was now pitching for the Phillies. He walked Moore who moved into scoring position on a sacrifice by Mallon. Moore scored when Whitney hit a deep single to left field. With the score 6-4, it looked like the Braves might win their second consecutive game. But the Phillies bats came back alive in the bottom of the eighth inning.

First Frankhouse walked Camilli. Then Mickey Haslin singled to center. When the center fielder couldn't handle the ball, Camilli ended up on third and Haslin was standing on second. Chiozza singled both runners home. Al Todd hit the ball to Frankhouse, forcing Chiozza out at second. Then Johnny Vergez hit a ground ball to the shortstop who threw the ball wild as he tried to get the force out on Todd. Todd ended up on third. Jimmie Wilson then laid down a perfect squeeze bunt to score Todd.

Ethan Allen hit the ball to Billy Urbanski at short. Urbanski threw to Mallon to get the lead runner but then Mallon threw the ball into the dugout when he tried to turn the double play. Vergez scored and Allen ended up on second. George Watkins doubled in Allen. Frankhouse then walked Moore and gave up a single to Camilli to score Watkins.

Frankhouse struggled to get the third out. After Watkins scored, Braves manager Bill McKechnie finally removed him for Ben Cantwell. Cantwell gave up a double to Haslin to score Moore. Cantwell walked Chiozza to load the bases before getting Todd to fly out to center for the elusive third out. By the time that the inning ended, the Phillies scored seven runs and grabbed the lead 11-6.

The Braves had run out of steam. They managed one hit against Curt Davis who was brought in to save the game in the ninth. But that was all that they could muster. They not only lost the game but were pummeled by the Phillies in the second game of the doubleheader, 9-3.

Ruth did not know it at the time but he would never play another major-league game. After the Braves returned to Boston, he told Judge Emil Fuchs, the Boston Braves owner, that he couldn't play. Ruth said that his knee was going to need some rest. Yet he was willing to play in an exhibition game in Bridgeport, Connecticut to fulfill a promise that he had made. Fuchs was angry and refused to let Ruth play in the game. Ruth quit and Fuchs told him that he was fired.[6]

Ruth and his wife Claire packed their car and drove back to New York. Claire said later that Ruth cried during the drive back to their home. On June 4, 1935, Ruth called a press conference and told reporters that he was finished with the Boston Braves. He vented his anger at Fuchs, saying "[h]e would double-cross a hot cross bun."[7]

The baseball world had lost a legend. The newspapers of the day expressed sadness that Ruth's time had passed. The *Milwaukee Journal* wrote that "a truly great figure in the field of sports passes rather forlornly, and we are sorry. We guess that there is no way to beat this inevitable anti-climax to a brilliant sports career."[8]

Jake Wade in the *Charlotte Observer* said Ruth was "the finest slugger that baseball has ever known, the most powerful drawing card in the history of the game. [His] gestures to the kids, his tolerance to old people and young people…made life happier and gayer for thousands."[9]

The *New York Times* wrote that the presidents of several major-league teams stated that no teams were interested in giving Ruth any more chances. "To put it bluntly, the magnates are convinced that Ruth has outlived his usefulness as a player and that he has not shown any real capacity to justify giving him a trial as a club manager."[10]

Although there rumors persisted throughout the season that he would be back in Boston or with some other team, Ruth never played again. The only offer that he received was from a minor-league team in Palatka, Florida.[11] Ruth's career ended with ground ball and a slow walk off the field in Philadelphia.

Sources

In addition to the sources cited in the Notes, the author used Baseball-Reference.com and Retrosheet.org for box score, player, team, and season information as well as pitching and batting game logs, and other pertinent material.

Notes

1. David Hill, "Braves History: Babe Ruth Makes Final Appearance," Fox Sports.com, January 30, 2017.
2. The clubhouse at Crosley Field was located behind the left-field wall.
3. Leigh Montville, *The Big Bam: The Life and Times of Babe Ruth* (New York: Doubleday and Co., 2006), 342.
4. Robert Creamer, *Babe: The Legend Comes to Life* (New York: Simon and Schuster, 1974), 398.
5. Cory Collins, "Babe Ruth played his last game 80 years ago today — in a different world," *Sporting News.com*, May 30, 2015.
6. Montville, 343.
7. Montville, 344.
8. "The Passing of Babe Ruth," *Milwaukee Journal*, June 4, 1935: 10.
9. Jake Wade, "Jake Wade's Sport Parade," *Charlotte Observer*, June 4, 1935: Sec. 2, p.5.
10. "No Place Open in the Majors for Ruth, Club Poll Reveals," *New York Times*, June 4, 1935: 27.
11. Montville, 344.

From Boston to Bushwick: The Big Bam Takes One Last Bow in 1935

By Frederick C. Bush

Babe Ruth's glorious major-league career abruptly ended after a doubleheader on May 30, 1935, at the Baker Bowl in Philadelphia. Baseball's Sultan of Swat was batting just .181 with six home runs for the Boston Braves when he called it quits. Thus, it probably surprised many fans that the Big Bam was playing October baseball later that year in Gotham, just as he had done so often during his years with the Yankees. Ruth handled first base for the Brooklyn Bay Parkways, a semipro team, as they played the Brooklyn Bushwicks on October 13 at Dexter Park in Queens.[1] Ruth socked a home run off Bushwicks pitcher Dazzy Vance in a 3-2 loss before a crowd of 14,500.[2] Vance, a seven-time NL strikeout king for the Brooklyn Robins, engaged in some theatrical hubris against the 12-time AL home-run champion by calling in his outfielders when Ruth came to bat in the sixth inning. The Bambino answered by knocking "a 320-foot blow that cleared the right field wall with plenty to spare."[3] The four-bagger was his only hit of the day, but the game proved he could still "bust 'em over the fence and make the turnstiles click."[4] In the field, Ruth recorded 11 putouts at first and committed one error.

An earlier visit with the Bushwicks. Babe Ruth and Lou Gehrig dressed in cowboy gear with Ruth astride the front hood of an automobile outfitted with longhorn steer horns at Dexter Park in Brooklyn. Several players from the Brooklyn Bushwicks semipro team (far left) look on. October 12, 1927. *Leslie Jones photo, courtesy of the Boston Public Library.*

Fans still loved watching Ruth. After his first appearance at Dexter Park, they "insisted that the greatest slugger of all time return to the Woodhaven ballpark once more before retiring for the winter."[5] The Babe obliged on October 20, this time as a member of the Long Island City Springfields. In the second inning, Ruth hit another Vance offering over the wall, but this time the ball landed foul by inches. The Bambino ended up with a single and two walks, although "he appeared lively and fielded perfectly" at first base in the Springfields' 6-5 victory.[6]

After the game, Ruth said something over the park's public-address system "that brought tears to the eyes of even hardened fans that were included in the crowd of 15,000."[7] He told the crowd that his days as an active player were done, and he "hurried from the park" into retirement.[8]

Dazzy Vance of the Bushwicks in 1935 with Babe Ruth (wearing the uniform from the 1934 tour of Japan). *Courtesy of Tom Barthel.*

Notes

1. Dexter Park was located in the Woodhaven neighborhood in Queens, which was just across the county line from Brooklyn. Originally, the Brooklyn Bushwicks had rented different parks to be their home field; once they made the permanent move to Dexter Park, team owner Max Rosner opted to keep Brooklyn in his squad's name, perhaps due to its familiarity to fans.

2. "The Babe Busts One Off Dazzy Vance as Bushwicks Win First," *Brooklyn Daily Eagle*, October 14, 1935: 26. The *Daily Eagle* reported the crowd as 14,500, though most news reports gave the attendance as 16,500. The official capacity of Dexter Park in the 1930s was 15,400; however a crowd as large as 20,000 was reported for a 1933 game that featured Carl Hubbell. (See covehurst.net/ddyte/brooklyn/dexter.html for more information about Dexter Park.)

3. "Vance Calls in Outfielders, Babe Hits Over Fence," *New Orleans Times-Picayune*, October 14, 1935: 12.

4. "The Babe Busts One Off Dazzy Vance."

5. "Vance and Babe Will Lock Horns: Bambino and Dazzy Again Grab Bushwick Spotlight Sunday," *New York Amsterdam News*, October 19, 1935: 12.

6. "Ruth Emphasizes Fact He's Through as Active Player," *New Orleans Times-Picayune*, October 21, 1935: 12.

7. "Ruth Tells Fans He Is Hanging Up His Glove Forever: Babe Makes Farewell Speech After Playing Final Game of Career," *Brooklyn Daily Eagle*, October 21, 1935: 20.

8. Ibid.

Ruth Makes His Coaching Debut for the Dodgers

June 19, 1938: Brooklyn Dodgers 6, Chicago Cubs 2 (first game of doubleheader), at Ebbets Field

By Glen Sparks

Fans at Ebbets Field cheered when Babe Ruth – decked out in Dodger blue – trotted to the third-base coach's box on Sunday, June 19, 1938, in the first game of a doubleheader. Baseball's home-run king had agreed the previous day to join the Brooklyn staff. Dodgers general manager Larry MacPhail signed him to a $15,000 deal for the remainder of the season.

Ruth, who retired as a player early in the 1935 season, said his golf game could wait. "Y'know, I didn't realize how much I'd miss this until I got this job," Ruth said. "Of course, golf is great. This will sure knock blazes out of my game, but it can't match this stuff."[1]

Coach Ruth took a round of batting practice before the game began. Fans roared with every swing. Afterward, the Sultan of Swat slapped his prodigious belly and smiled. "Gosh, it sure is good to be back," he told reporters. "But I'm not in shape. Stood up there and hit for five minutes and felt like I'd been doing it all week."[2]

Brooklyn Dodgers coach Babe Ruth leaning on the dugout railing at Braves Field, 1938. *Leslie Jones photo, courtesy of the Boston Public Library.*

Rumors swirled that the Dodgers wanted Ruth to eventually replace manager Burleigh Grimes, the former pitcher who won 270 games in a 19-year mound career, much of it spent with Brooklyn. Grimes compiled a 62-91 won-lost mark in 1937 as a rookie skipper. On the morning of Ruth's first day as coach, Brooklyn's record stood at 22-31, good for seventh place in the National League. The Babe dismissed any idea that he coveted Grimes's job.

"Right this minute, I haven't a thought about a manager's position," Ruth said. "I signed as coach for the Dodgers for the rest of this season. I don't even know what's going to happen next year."[3] Furthermore, he said, "Burleigh Grimes is the manager. Sure, I'd like to be a manger, here or somewhere else, but I guess I gotta wait awhile."[4]

Ruth settled into the coach's box on a warm day in Flatbush with 28,000 fans at the ballpark. Tot Pressnell, a 31-year-old rookie right-hander, started for Brooklyn against 30-year-old Larry French, a left-hander in his 10th big-league season. Pressnell featured a knuckleball, which he developed while toiling several years in the minor leagues. French, a three-time 18-game winner, threw a screwball.

Chicago jumped on top with two runs in the opening frame. Stan Hack singled and advanced to second base on Phil Cavarretta's sacrifice bunt. Carl Reynolds followed by knocking a two-run homer, his first round-tripper of the year.

The game stayed 2-0 until the Dodgers put together a fifth-inning rally. French walked Pressnell and loaded the bases by allowing singles to Kiki Cuyler and Buddy Hassett. Hard-hitting catcher Babe Phelps knocked a two-run base hit over second baseman Billy Herman's head. That ended the day for French, who gave way to veteran relief pitcher Jack Russell. It did not stop the Brooklyn scoring. Dolph Camilli ripped an RBI single, bringing home Hassett and giving the Dodgers a 3-2 lead.

Brooklyn added two more runs in the sixth inning. Pressnell led off by hitting a single, once again helping his own cause. Cuyler doubled to center, putting runners on second and third. Johnny Hudson, batting for Pete Coscarart, rapped a comebacker to Russell, who froze the runners and threw to first baseman Ripper Collins for the out. He then left the game in favor of reliever Bob Logan.

Hassett flied out to left field off Logan, but not deep enough for Pressnell to score. With Phelps up, Logan unleashed a pitch that slipped through catcher Gabby Harnett's legs. Pressnell sprinted home on the passed ball. Phelps whacked a two-out hit to the right-field wall, scoring Cuyler. The Dodgers now led 5-2.

Reliever Al Epperly started the seventh inning for Chicago. Camilli lined a double to right field against the new pitcher and scored on Leo Durocher's single. Brooklyn and Pressnell kept the Cubs scoreless after that two-run first and won 6-2. Pressnell threw a complete game and evened his won-loss record at 5-5.

He gave up nine hits, struck out three, and walked two. French, who lasted just 4⅓ innings. dropped to 4-9. He allowed six hits and five walks, while not fanning a single Brooklyn batter. The Dodgers advanced to 23-31, while the Cubs dropped to 31-25.

Mostly, Ruth clapped and cheered on the Brooklyn players. He did some real coaching in the fifth inning. When Pressnell rounded third, a "wild throw"[5] skipped past Cubs first baseman Collins and crashed into the grandstand. The ball, though, quickly bounced back. "As it did," according to a *Chicago Tribune* reporter, "Ruth wheeled and held Pressnell at third. He saved a run, for Collins' throw to Gabby Hartnett at the plate was fast and true."[6]

In the weeks after his coaching debut (Chicago won the second game of the June 19 twin bill, 4-3), Ruth kept taking pregame swings in the batting cage, and another rumor began circulating. Maybe the Babe could swat some homers in a real game. Grimes, though, shot down any talk of a Ruthian comeback. "He can't see," said the 44-year-old former spitballer, retired as a player since 1934. "If he can hit, I can still pitch." Years later, Grimes said, "Sometimes, he couldn't see pitches. … I knew he had trouble when I threw batting practice. So, we used to have Merv Shea, a catcher, throw to him. Shea just sort of flipped his arm when he threw, and it was easy to follow the ball. But you put him in a game? He might have been killed."[7]

Baseball's Sultan of Swat also signed autographs and made numerous visits to hospitals and orphanages. He played in 10 exhibition games, mostly in small towns. Some young pitchers wanted nothing more than to strike out a baseball legend, even a 43-year-old retired one with a big gut and bad eyesight. "It's a wonder I didn't get skulled," Ruth wrote in his autobiography, *The Babe Ruth Story*, essentially agreeing with Grimes's comment.[8]

Ruth coached both third base and first base. Most players liked the fabled slugger, who cracked jokes, told stories, and called left-handed pitcher Vito Tamulis "Tomatoes." "When he spoke, everyone listened, all but Durocher," Grimes said many years later.[9] The acrimony between Ruth and Durocher went back many years. The two were teammates for a few seasons with the Yankees when Ruth called the young, light-hitting Durocher "the All-American out." Leo, in turn, annoyed some Yankee veterans with his nonstop yapping. When the two were reunited in Brooklyn, they nearly came to blows. Durocher screamed that Ruth couldn't remember the signs that were given from the dugout. The Babe took offense. Ruth biographer Robert Creamer shrugged off the charge. Ruth could relay signs, Creamer wrote. Simply put, "He (Ruth) tended to ignore" them.[10] The Dodgers trudged through the 1938 season and finished 69-80, in seventh place and 18½ games out of first place. As many expected,

Brooklyn Dodger Babe Ruth coaching first base at Braves Field. 1938.
Leslie Jones photo, courtesy of the Boston Public Library.

MacPhail fired Grimes in October and hired Durocher as the new skipper. That move pretty much ended Ruth's coaching tenure in Flatbush. "I knew I wouldn't return to the Dodgers," he wrote in his autobiography.[11]

The Babe went back to playing golf, drinking, and living life large. Leigh Montville wrote a biography of Ruth, *The Big Bam: The Life and Times of Babe Ruth*, published in 2006. He devoted just a small section to the retired home-run king's managerial ambitions. Why didn't any team take a chance and sign Ruth as a manager? Maybe Ruth's wild lifestyle during his younger days still bothered some front-office people, Montville supposed. Maybe some owners thought Ruth couldn't handle the mental side of the job. He forgot people's names all the time, Montville pointed out. Or maybe Ruth commanded too large a presence. Ego-laden owners might not like that. Anyway, Ruth didn't hustle to get a job, Montville wrote, and he didn't take a minor-league post. "Managing baseball, unlike playing baseball, is a political job," Montville wrote. "He was not a political person. He was Babe Ruth, dammit. … He waited. The call never came."[12]

Creamer argued that Ruth boasted baseball smarts, players respected him, and he talked a good, colorful game to reporters. "He may not have been a success," Creamer wrote. "Most managers are not. But he should have been given a chance."[13]

Sources

In addition to the sources cited in the Notes, the author also consulted baseball-reference.com.

Notes

1 Associated Press, "Crowd Cheers for Babe Ruth," *Rhinelander* (Wisconsin) *Daily News,* June 20, 1938: 5.

2 Ibid.

3 Sid Feder (Associated Press), "Question of Manager's Post Not Worrying Ruth at Present," *Ottawa* (Ontario) *Citizen,* June 20, 1938: 13.

4 Drew Middleton (Associated Press), "Babe Ruth Happy to Be Back as a Baseball Coach," *Oshkosh* (Wisconsin) *Northwestern,* June 20, 1938: 12.

5 Associated Press, "Babe Saves Run for Brooklyn; Gets Big Hand," *Chicago Tribune*, June 20, 1938: 15

6 Ibid.

7 Robert W. Creamer, *Babe: The Legend Comes to Life* (New York: Simon and Schuster, 1974), 413.

8 Babe Ruth and Bob Considine, *The Babe Ruth Story* (New York: Signet, 1948), 217.

9 Creamer, 413.

10 Creamer, 411.

11 Ruth and Considine, 218.

12 Leigh Montville, *The Big Bam: The Life and Times of Babe Ruth* (New York: Doubleday. 2006), 349.

13 Creamer, 404.

Lou Gehrig Appreciation Day: Ruth and Gehrig End Feud

July 4, 1939: Game One — Washington Senators 3, New York Yankees 2; Game Two — New York Yankees 11, Washington Sena

By Paul Hofmann

Though both men were amazingly talented on the field, the Yankees' Home Run Twins couldn't have been any more different. Babe Ruth was a brash and boorish free spirit who had a casual and often defiant way of dealing with authority. He was also fun-loving and charismatic, with an ego that craved the spotlight. By contrast, Lou Gehrig was modest and reserved, avoiding public attention. He was the consummate company man. Given these differences, it seemed unlikely that a Ruth-Gehrig relationship beyond the playing field, locker room, and Pullman car would have developed.[1] However, a relationship between the two developed and from the very beginning it was complicated.

In the early years, Ruth was a mentor whom Gehrig idolized. Columbia Lou never believed that he could be Ruth's equal. "The only real home run hitter that has ever lived," Gehrig once said in reference to Ruth. "I'm fortunate to be even close to him."[2] The two developed a close relationship. Sharing confidences, eating, traveling and barnstorming together, playing cards, swapping batting tips, fishing and golfing together, Ruth and Gehrig should have grown closer with the passing years.[3]

Instead they grew apart and the relationship entered a period of estrangement, when both men refused to speak to each other. The relationship came full circle on July 4, 1939, when Ruth ended their long antagonism by impulsively putting his arm around Gehrig and hugging him during a ceremony to honor his estranged friend.[4]

The Independence Day doubleheader pitted the sixth-place Washington Senators, who entered play with a 28-42 record, 24½ games off the pace, and the three-time defending World Series champion New York Yankees, who were 51-16, 12½ games clear of the second-place Boston Red Sox. The games were overshadowed by the ceremony that took place between games. It was Lou Gehrig Appreciation Day and 61,808 fans jammed the House that Ruth Built to pay homage to the ailing Yankees star, who was dying from amyotrophic lateral sclerosis (ALS).[5]

While Gehrig dressed in the clubhouse, some of his old teammates dropped in to say hello, including Mark Koenig, Wally Schang, Herb Pennock, Wally Pipp, Bob Shawkey, Benny Bengough,

George Pipgras. Tony Lazzeri, Earle Combs, Joe Dugan, Waite Hoyt, Bob Meusel, Everett Scott, and Wally Pipp, who faded away as the Yankees' first baseman the day Gehrig took the job back in 1925.[6] Ruth had yet to arrive and everyone wondered whether the Bambino would show up.

In the opener, the Senators scored two first-inning runs in support of right-hander Dutch Leonard (8-2), who limited the Yankees to six hits and helped his own cause with a sixth-inning RBI single. Right-hander Monte Pearson (7-2) suffered the loss for Yankees, who managed a single run in the third and another in the ninth on a one-out home run by right fielder George Selkirk as the Senators hung on for a 3-2 victory.

Ruth arrived in plenty of time for the ceremony wearing a cream-colored suit and looking tanned and rested. By the late 1930s Ruth had ballooned to 270 pounds and was beginning to experience some health problems of his own.[7]

Between games, a group of microphones were set up behind home plate for the ceremony. Sid Mercer, dean of beat reporters covering the Yankees, served as emcee for the event. New York Mayor Fiorello La Guardia officially extended the city's appreciation of the service Gehrig had given to his hometown. The mayor praised Gehrig as "the greatest prototype of good sportsmanship and citizenship."[8] Postmaster General James Farley, also in attendance, concluded his remarks with "for generations to come, boys who play baseball will point with pride to your record."[9]

Ruth then took a turn at the microphone. Though their relationship had been troubled, Ruth never held a grudge and seemed happy to be reunited with his old friend. In his own blustering style, Ruth gave his unqualified opinion that the 1927 Yankees were better than the 1939 edition. Summarizing his belief, Ruth said, "In 1927 Lou was with us, and I say that was the greatest ball club the Yankees ever had.[10] The Sultan of Swat continued, "Anyway, that's my opinion and while Lazzeri here pointed out to me that there are only about 13 or 14 of us here, my answer is, shucks, we only need nine to beat 'em."[11]

Mercer then introduced Gehrig to the huge throng in attendance and millions listening on radios across the country. Head bowed, Gehrig stood silent until he privately whispered something to Mercer, who returned to the microphone and told the crowd and listening audience, "Lou has asked me to thank you all for him. He is too moved to speak."[12] The response to Mercer's remark were chants of "We want Gehrig!" throughout the ballpark.[13]

As the chants continued, Gehrig took a handkerchief from his pocket, wiped away his tears and moved toward the microphones once again. Head bowed, he spoke slowly and evenly as he delivered the most memorable farewell speech in baseball history.

"Fans, for the past two weeks you have been reading about the bad break I got. Yet today I consider myself the luckiest man on the face of this earth. I have been in ballparks for seventeen years and have never received anything but kindness and encouragement from you fans.

"Look at these grand men. Which of you wouldn't consider it the highlight of his career just to associate with them for even one day? Sure, I'm lucky. Who wouldn't consider it an honor to have known Jacob Ruppert? Also, the builder of baseball's greatest empire, Ed Barrow? To have spent six years with that wonderful little fellow, Miller Huggins? Then to have spent the next nine years with that outstanding leader, that smart student of psychology, the best manager in baseball today, Joe McCarthy? Sure, I'm lucky.

"When the New York Giants, a team you would give your right arm to beat, and vice versa, sends you a gift – that's something. When everybody down to the groundskeepers and those boys in white coats remember you with trophies – that's something. When you have a wonderful mother-in-law who takes sides with you in squabbles with her own daughter – that's something. When you have a father and a mother who work all their lives so you can have an education and build your body – it's a blessing. When you have a wife who has been a tower of strength and shown more courage than you dreamed existed – that's the finest I know.

"So I close in saying that I may have had a tough break, but I have an awful lot to live for."[14]

Ruth was moved to tears by Gehrig's 277-word speech. The Babe went over to shake his old friend's hand but hugged him instead – ending the long-standing and petty feud between them. It was the first time Gehrig cracked a smile all day. As they embraced, a tearful Ruth couldn't have imagined he would be facing a similar crowd under very similar circumstances less than a decade later.

After the ceremony, Gehrig returned to the clubhouse, where he saw right-hander Steve Sundra, who was slated to start the nightcap for the Yankees. Gehrig went to Sundra and said, "Big Steve, win the second game for me, will ya?"[15]

Sundra (5-0) delivered a six-hit complete game and the Yankees scored six runs in the first three innings off Venezuelan rookie right-hander Alex Carrasquel (4-6) on their way to an 11-1 victory. Selkirk paced the Yankees' hitting attack with three hits, including a home run, while second baseman Joe Gordon drove in four for the Yankees. Right fielder Taffy Wright accounted for the Senators' lone run with a second-inning home run.

On June 2, 1941, Gehrig died at his home. Upon hearing the news of Gehrig's passing, Ruth and his wife, Claire, were among the first to go to the Gehrig house to console Eleanor Gehrig.[16]

Sources

In addition to the sources cited in the Notes, the author also consulted Baseball-Reference.com and Retrosheet.org

Notes

1. Jonathan Eig. *Luckiest Man: The Life and Death of Lou Gehrig* (New York: Simon & Schuster, 2005), 97.
2. Eig, 100.
3. Ray Robinson, "Ruth and Gehrig: Friction Between Gods," *New York Times*, June 2, 1991: 394.
4. Robert Creamer, *Babe: The Legend Comes to Life* (New York: Simon & Schuster, 1974), 415.
5. Amyotrophic lateral sclerosis, commonly known as ALS or Lou Gehrig's disease, is an incurable fatal neuromuscular disease. The disease attacks nerve cells in the brain and spinal cord. Motor neurons, which control the movement of voluntary muscles, deteriorate and eventually die. When the motor neurons die, the brain can no longer initiate and control muscle movement. Because muscles no longer receive the messages they need in order to function, they gradually weaken and deteriorate, resulting in paralysis.
6. John Drebinger, "61,808 Fans Roar Tribute to Gehrig: Chief Figure at the Stadium and Old-Time Yankees who Gathered in His Honor," *New York Times*, July 5, 1939: 21.
7. Ruth experienced the first of two heart attacks while playing golf in 1939.
8. Ibid.
9. Ibid.
10. Eig, 315.
11. Drebinger.
12. Rosaleen Doherty, "Wife Brave, Lou Shaken as 61,000 Cheer Gehrig," *Daily News* (New York), July 5, 1939: 120.
13. Ibid.
14. "Farewell Speech," lougehrig.com/.
15. ' Pages Out of the Past," *Atlantic City Evening Union,* January 18, 1952, as cited by David Skelton, "Steve Sundra," SABR BioProject, sabr.org/bioproj/person/3c2f6fad.
16. James Lincoln Ray, "Lou Gehrig," SABR BioProject, sabr.org/bioproj/person/ccdffd4c

Babe Ruth Day

April 27, 1947: Washington Senators 1, New York Yankees 0, at Yankee Stadium

By Joe Schuster

Two days before Thanksgiving 1946, Babe Ruth went to New York's French Hospital, complaining of headaches.[1] Initially, doctors diagnosed a sinus condition but in January determined that he needed surgery and he underwent a "serious" procedure.[2] News stories at the time were vague about the pain's cause; the hospital said only, "One of the main arteries on the left side of the neck was ligated. Post-operative condition satisfactory."[3] The truth was that Ruth had cancer, a tumor on a carotid artery, and surgery was able to remove only part of it.[4]

For weeks, Americans fretted over him. In late January *The Sporting News* devoted two pages to fans' concern, describing their letters and gifts, and reporting that droves made pilgrimages to the hospital.[5] During his stay, which ended February 15, he received 26,835 letters and telegrams.[6]

On February 3, Baseball Commissioner A.B. "Happy" Chandler visited the star, and was stunned at Ruth's deterioration. The *New York Times* reported both men wept during the meeting, adding that Chandler said, "Babe, you are Mr. Baseball. I'm going to say a little prayer for you ... and may you get well soon."[7] For Ruth's part, he was unable to respond: "Ruth, thinned by his long hospital siege, turned his head slightly and wept. He pointed to his toothpick arms, but was too choked up to speak."[8]

A number of Ruth's supporters, including Chicago's Emory Perry, called on Chandler and suggested that Opening Day in every ballpark be declared "Babe Ruth Day" on an annual basis, with proceeds going to a planned Babe Ruth Foundation.[9]

Not long after Ruth's discharge, Chandler announced that major-league baseball would honor him: "All Americans ... have been concerned ... over the illness of one of baseball's most beloved figures. ... In order that (everyone) might have an opportunity to unite in a ... prayer for his early recovery, Sunday, April 27, has been designated as 'Babe Ruth Day.'"[10]

The Sporting News noted that the festivities represented only the second time in history that every major-league city simultaneously honored a single player; the first player was Harry Wright, whom baseball honored in April 1896 after Wright died the previous October.[11] The intention for the Wright event was to raise funds for a gravesite monument; however, Chandler said that the Ruth festivities were meant merely to honor him and were not an event to raise money.[12]

The plan was that the center of the day's activities would be, fittingly, Yankee Stadium, and that other clubs would hold "appropriate ceremonies."[13] Roughly two weeks after Chandler's announcement, George M. Trautman, president of National Association of Professional Baseball Leagues, announced that every minor-league team with a game on April 27 would also celebrate Ruth.[14] As it turned out, Japan also honored him that day, in ceremonies in Tokyo and Osaka.[15]

That Sunday afternoon brought pleasant weather to New York, with temperatures in the mid-60s at the time of the ceremony. The park was full, as 58,339 fans turned out, by far the Yankees' largest attendance in the young season. (While they drew larger crowds later that year, the total was roughly 20,000 higher than Opening Day's 39,344, previously the team's biggest 1947 crowd.) In every major-league ballpark hosting a game that day, the attendance was the high-water mark on the season to that point, save in Brooklyn.

Although Chandler had said the event was not intended to raise money, Ruth nonetheless received lavish gifts. Ford Motor Company gave him a $5,000 Lincoln, the Yankees gave him "a check to help tide him over (during) the illness he hadn't licked yet," and baseball announced it would create a foundation in Ruth's name to promote youth programs.[16]

The 10-minute ceremony, which featured a half-dozen speakers, was heavy on talk of Ruth's devotion to youth, beginning with the invocation by Cardinal Francis Spellman, who had originally said he would be unable to attend but came after Ruth asked him. After blessing Ruth, Spellman praised him as "a manly leader of youths in America." When Chandler stood to speak, the crowd booed him, largely because he'd suspended Dodgers manager Leo Durocher for the season because Durocher had allegedly associated with known gamblers. Chandler concluded his remarks by saying, "[T]he spirit of Babe Ruth ... will be with us as we build a new generation capable of protecting our heritage as a free people." To introduce Ruth, the Yankees tapped a "freckled 13-year-old" Legion ballplayer named Larry Cutler, who said, in part, "From all of us kids, Babe, it's swell to have you back."[17] Cutler later played baseball at City College of New York before spending three season in the minors with the White Sox and Pirates organizations.[18] He was an all-star twice, in 1955 with Dubuque in the Mississippi-Ohio Valley League, and again with Dubuque in 1957 in the Midwest League.[19]

When Ruth stood to speak, his weakness was evident: it took two friends to support him on his walk to the microphone.[20] The crowd greeted him "with such thunder from their throats as the home run king had never heard in his moments of greatest glory."[21] Speaking in a hoarse whisper, Ruth thanked them and devoted the majority of his ad-libbed remarks to talking about the importance of youth beginning to play the sport at an early age if they were going to master it.[22] Then, helped off the field, he went beneath the stands to recover from his effort, having "a few trying moments" before settling into a box beside the Yankees dugout to watch the game.[23]

The contest, which the *New York Daily News* described as "an afterthought" in the context of the day, matched the 7-3 Yankees with the 3-4 Washington Senators, two teams on opposite tracks.[24] The Yankees were about to begin a run of six pennants in seven years, while the Senators were in the second of six consecutive years of sub-.500 ball.

Almost as if the players were reluctant to upstage the sport's greatest hero, the game itself was a quiet one, with the Yankees the only team to make much noise until the eighth. Through the seventh, the Senators managed only three hits and two walks off Yankees starter Spud Chandler, while New York threatened to break through against Washington's Sid Hudson several times but failed.[25] With two on and two out in the first, Charlie Keller hit a fly to deep center but Stan Spence ran it down. Again in the third, New York put two on, but Hudson closed them out on two infield popouts; they loaded the bases in the fourth with two outs, but again failed as Bobby Brown "rapped" to first.[26] After a one-out walk to Joe DiMaggio in the fifth, Tommy Henrich hit a ball to the wall in right, but it fell short and Buddy Lewis caught it.

Chandler finally broke in eighth. Hudson led off with a pop that dropped into right, advanced to second on Joe Grace's sacrifice, then scored the game's only run on a "a half-hit one bagger" in short left-center by Lewis. The Yankees managed but one more single, in the eighth, as Hudson advanced his season's record to 2-0 with the 1-0 shutout; his line: no runs, eight hits, three walks, six strikeouts. Chandler gave up only the one run, on seven hits and three walks, and fanned four, falling to 1-2.

Ruth was not there for the end: He had left after the seventh.[27] He made one more visit to the Stadium, roughly 14 months later, when he came for a second ceremony, the retirement of his iconic number 3 jersey.[28] He died on August 16, 1948.

Notes

1. "Nation's Fans Root for Ruth After Surgery," *The Sporting News*, January 15, 1947: 6.
2. Ibid.
3. Ibid.
4. Robert Creamer, *Babe: The Legend Comes to Life* (New York: Simon and Schuster, 1992), 418.
5. Dan Daniel, "Nation's Cheers Speed Ruth's Recovery," *The Sporting News*, January 29, 1947: 5.
6. Bob Considine, "Hank Gets Secret of Homer-Hitting from Babe," *The Sporting News*, March 5, 1947: 4.
7. "Chandler Calls On Ruth, Both Break Into Tears," *New York Times*, February 4, 1947: 27.
8. Ibid.
9. Jane Leavy, *The Big Fella* (New York: Harper, 2018), 444.
10. "Chandler Sets Date to Honor Babe Ruth," *New York Times*, March 9, 1947: S1.
11. "Ruth First to Be Given Day by All Majors in 51 Years," *The Sporting News*, March 26, 1947: 2.
12. Ibid.
13. "Chandler Sets Date."
14. "Minors Observe Same 'Ruth Day,'" *New York Daily News*, March 22, 1947: 18.
15. "Japan's Fans Honor Ruth," *New York Times*, April 28, 1947: 29.
16. Hy Turkin, "Ruth Whispers His Gratitude to Cheering Fans," *New York Daily News*, April 28, 1947: 3. Unless noted otherwise, details of the Babe Ruth Day festivities come from this story.
17. Dan Daniel, "58,339 Cheer Homer King in Yank Stadium Ceremony," *The Sporting News*, May 7, 1947: 5.
18. "Cutler Half of DP Pair," *City College Observation Post*, April 13, 1954: 4. See also Cutler's page on Baseball Reference.
19. Jamie Selko, *Minor League All-Star Teams 1922-1962* (Jefferson North Carolina: McFarland & Company, 2007), 426, 458.
20. Shirley Povich, "Babe's Shoulders Squared by Thunderous Reception," *The Sporting News*, May 7, 1947: 5.
21. Hy Turkin, "Ruth Whispers Thanks, Fans Roar Affection," *New York Daily News*, April 28, 1947: C3.
22. Ibid.
23. Louis Effrat, "58,339 Acclaim Babe Ruth in Rare Tribute at Stadium," *New York Times*, April 28, 1947: 1.
24. Turkin.
25. Game details come from Baseball Reference as well as Joe Trimble; "Yanks Fail the Babe, Bowing to Nats, 1-0," *New York Daily News* April 28, 1947: C17.
26. Effrat.
27. Daniel, "58,339 Cheer Homer King."
28. Allan Wood, "Babe Ruth," SABR Baseball Biography Project, sabr.org/bioproj/person/9dcdd01c, accessed March 1, 2019.

Babe Ruth Make Final Visit to Yankee Stadium

June 13, 1948: New York Yankees 5, Cleveland Indians 3, at Yankee Stadium

By Glen Sparks

New Yorkers awoke to a dismal morning on June 13, 1948. Raindrops fell in spurts from low, gray clouds. A chill, unusual for late spring, filled the air. Players gathered in the clubhouse at Yankee Stadium. Where was Babe Ruth?

The Yankees had scheduled a celebration on this day to mark the stadium's 25th anniversary and retire Ruth's uniform number 3. Team owner Jacob Ruppert held a banquet at his brewery the night before to honor the World Series champion 1923 squad. Ruth, who hit 41 home runs and batted .393 for that year's version of Murderers' Row, felt too ill to attend.

Finally, he shuffled into the Yankee Stadium clubhouse, where for so many seasons he told jokes and bawdy stories to teammates and where he regaled newspaper reporters about his home-run exploits. He – the Sultan of Swat – smacked 714 homers during his incredible career, far more than anyone else. He led the majors in home runs 12 times. On this day, Ruth walked slowly, wore a heavy wool overcoat, and looked noticeably thinner than he did in his playing days. Ruth's nurse, Frank Dulaney, helped remove the overcoat. Dulaney also helped Ruth put on the Yankee uniform one last time. The Babe, 53 years old, was dying from cancer.

The time neared for Ruth to take the field. Dulaney cautioned him to stay in the dugout runway. "It's too damp here," Dulaney said.[1] Ruth returned to the clubhouse and rested. He tired easily. Public-address announcer Mel Allen rang out the names of the Yankee old-timers. The crowd applauded for former third baseman Joe Dugan, first baseman Wally Pipp, and the others. Some players already had died. The great first baseman Lou Gehrig, the man who replaced Pipp at that position for New York, passed away in 1941 at the age of 37. Pitcher Urban Shocker died in 1928, just 13 days shy of his 38th birthday. Manager Miller Huggins, second baseman Tony Lazzeri, and many others also were gone. Calls of taps rang out at the stadium. "The ceremonies were maudlin," Leigh Montville wrote in his 2006 Ruth biography *The Big Bam*.[2]

At last Allen called out the Babe's name at the House That Ruth Built, a synonym for Yankee Stadium and a name inspired by the great slugger's longball exploits. Ruth left his topcoat behind, and the Indians' Eddie Robinson handed him a bat to use as a cane. Babe moved ever so slowly toward his former teammates.[3] The nearly 50,000 fans in attendance roared with appreciation, of course, So did all the Yankees, the ones from 1923 as well as the current squad. Cleveland Indians players cheered from the opposing dugout. W.C. Heinz wrote that Ruth "walked out into the cauldron of sound he must have known better than any other man."[4]

New York City Mayor William O'Dwyer spoke for a few minutes. He apologized for the foul weather and then welcomed the entire Yankees team on this silver anniversary day, but especially "Babe Ruth, the hero of all our baseball days."[5] Ruth himself spoke for just a few minutes. The inoperable nasopharyngeal cancer made his voice horse, and it hurt him to talk.[6] "I am proud I hit the first home run here in 1923," Ruth said. "It was marvelous to see 13 of 14 players who were my teammates going back 25 years. I'm telling you it makes me proud and happy to be here."[7]

Nat Fein, a 33-year-old photographer from the *New York Herald-Tribune,* watched the ceremony. Ruth, frail but still with a thick head of hair, held tightly to his makeshift cane in one hand and a Yankees cap in the other. He stood on the third-base line. "He looked tired, very tired," Fein said of Ruth. "The power that had been his in his youth and manhood were slowly ebbing away."[8] Photographers jockeyed for position along the first-base line near home plate. Yankees players stood just a few feet away.

Fein slipped behind Ruth. The number 3 stood out on the back of the great player's uniform. Fein knelt in the same fashion as the other photographers. He wanted to capture Ruth from a low angle. "The number 3 was the thing I was interested in," Fein said many years later. "I felt the only way to tell the story of Babe retiring was from the back."[9] Fein, holding a Speed Graphic news camera, did not use a flash on this dark day. He shot his photo at f5.6 and 1/25 shutter speed[10] to achieve depth and detail. Then Babe walked off the field. He met Dugan a few minutes later at a makeshift bar in the locker room. "I'm gone, Joe," Babe said.[11]

A two-inning exhibition matchup followed the ceremony. Ruth, who always said he wanted to manage a big-league ballclub but never got the chance, was supposed to serve as skipper of the New York exhibition squad. Too ill, he skipped the affair and left the ballpark.

The actual game pitted a red-hot Indians team, with a 31-13 won-lost record, against a 27-21 Yankees squad. Cleveland had won eight of its previous nine games and built a 3½-game lead in the American League over the second-place Philadelphia Athletics. New York sat in third place, six games out of first.

Fireballer Bob Feller started for Cleveland. Junkball artist Eddie Lopat, a native New Yorker, took the mound for New York. The Indians mounted a scoring chance in the third inning. Feller reached on an error by Yankees third baseman Billy Johnson to lead off the frame, advanced to second on Allie Clark's one-out single and made it to third on a fielder's choice. With two out, Eddie Robinson popped up to end the threat. Feller, meanwhile, allowed two walks and a Johnny Lindell single through the first three innings.

The Indians went ahead 1-0 in the fourth inning. Joe Gordon led off with a double and scored on Wally Judnich's one-out single. Maybe that was all the 29-year-old Feller, already a five-time 20-game winner, would need that day. He put away the Yankees in order in the fourth inning and allowed two hits but no runs in the fifth.

New York finally pushed across two runs in the bottom of the sixth. Joe DiMaggio tripled with one out and jogged home on Yogi Berra's sixth home run of the season. Feller also gave up a two-out single to George McQuinn but fanned Phil Rizzuto.

Indians player-manager Lou Boudreau pulled Feller after six innings. Rapid Robert gave up two runs, six hits and two walks. He struck out four Yankees batters. Rookie left-hander Gene Bearden pitched a scoreless seventh inning but ran into trouble in the eighth. DiMaggio led off with his second triple of the game. Berra popped out and Billy Johnson struck out before McQuinn reached on an error that brought home a run. The next batter, Rizzuto, knocked a two-run homer to make the score 5-1, Yankees.

Lopat, who toiled for several years in the minors and finally made it to the majors as a 26-year-old rookie in 1944, nearly threw a complete game. Manager Bucky Harris summoned lefty Joe Page out of the bullpen with two out in the ninth. Lopat had walked Judnich to start the inning. Jim Hegan followed by hitting a home run. Joe Tipton grounded out and Bob Kennedy popped out. Allie Clark's two-out single kept Cleveland's hopes alive; Boudreau walked to put runners on first and second. That ended the day for Steady Eddie. Page fanned Eddie Robinson to get the final out and gain his eighth save of the season. Lopat improved his record to 3-5, while Feller dropped to 5-6.

The next day, newspapers reported on both Ruth and the game. The *New York Daily News* offered a straightforward recount of the action. Hy Turkin wrote that "Feller scattered three harmless singles over the first five rounds, but in the sixth he lost the edge on his fast one and the ball came off Yank bats with more speed than he served it."[12] About Ruth, Joe Trimble wrote "As he stood out there (on the Yankee Stadium field), he was as magnificent as ever – the top showman of them all."[13]

Ruth never returned to Yankee Stadium. He spent much of the next few months in a hospital and died on August 16. Nat Fein's photograph, which appeared on Page 1 of the *Herald-Tribune* on June 14, won a Pulitzer Prize. *Life* magazine in 1999 described the photo, titled "The Babe Bows Out," as "one of the greatest pictures of the 20th century."[14] Fein, who died in 2000 at age 86, once said, "I didn't think it was a great shot." Even so, he added that it "got the feeling"[15] of that sad moment.

Sources

In addition to the sources cited in the Notes, the author also consulted Baseball-Reference.com.

Notes

1. Robert W. Creamer, *Babe: The Legend Comes to Life*. (New York: Simon & Shuster, 1974), 422.
2. Leigh Montville, *The Big Bam: The Life and Times of Babe Ruth* (New York: Doubleday, 2006), 363.
3. The bat that Ruth used belonged to Bob Feller. Feller explained: "Babe Ruth came walking down what was the common runway, because in those days the clubhouses were in the same runway, the third-base runway. Babe came in, and he kind of stumbled a little bit. We went up the steps, and Eddie Robinson, our first baseman, grabbed a bat –it happened to be my bat – and gave it to Babe." The bat was also a Babe Ruth model. Julia Ruth Stevens and Bill Gilbert, *Babe Ruth: Remembering the Bambino in Stories, Photos & Memorabilia* (New York: Stewart, Tabori and Chang, 2008), 159.
4. Creamer, 422.
5. Joe Trimble, "Number 3 Brings Down House That Ruth Built," *New York Daily News*, June 14, 1948: C17.
6. Jane Leavy devotes considerable space to his cancer and forms of treatment. Jane Leavy, *The Big Fella* (New York: Harper, 2018), 442-449.
7. Montville, 364.
8. Flickr flickr.com/photos/nostri-imago/4999513923/.
9. lens.blogs.nytimes.com/2010/10/06/timeless-babe-ruth-retires/.
10. iconicphotos.wordpress.com/2009/06/01/babe-ruth-bows-out/.
11. Creamer, 423.
12. Hy Turkin, "Yanks Nip Tribe, 5-3, Yogi, Phil, Hegan HR," *New York Daily News*, June 14, 1948: C17.
13. Trimble: C17.
14. *Sports Collectors Daily,* sportscollectorsdaily.com/famous-babe-ruth-photo-stands-test-of-time/.
15. Richard Goldstein, "Nat Fein, 86, Pulitzer Winner for Picture of Ruth's Final Bow," *New York Times*, September 29, 2000. nytimes.com/2000/09/29/sports/nat-fein-86-pulitzer-winner-for-picture-of-ruth-s-final-bow.html.

Contributors

Josh Berk is an author of books for children and teens including the *Lenny and the Mikes* series of baseball mysteries. He lives in Bethlehem, Pennsylvania, and is the Executive Director of the Bethlehem Area Public Library. His favorite team is the Phillies and his favorite baseball player is his son Elliot.

Nathan Bierma is a SABR member and SABR Games Project contributor living in Grand Rapids, Michigan. His writing has appeared in the *Chicago Tribune*, *Chicago Sports Review*, and *Detroit Free Press*, and in SABR's recent books on the greatest games at Wrigley Field and Comiskey Park. He is the author of *The Eclectic Encyclopedia of English: Language at Its Most Enigmatic, Ephemeral, and Egregious*. His website is www.nathanbierma.com.

Thomas J. Brown Jr. is a lifelong Mets fan who became a Durham Bulls fan after moving to North Carolina in the early 1980s. He was a national board-certified high-school science teacher for 34 years before retiring in 2016. Tom still volunteers with the ELL students at his former high school, serving as a mentor to those students and the teachers who are now working with them. He also provides support and guidance for his former ELL students when they embark on different career paths after graduation. Tom has been a member of SABR since 1995 when he learned about the organization during a visit to Cooperstown on his honeymoon. He has become active in the organization since his retirement and has written numerous biographies and game stories, mostly about the New York Mets. Tom also enjoys traveling as much as possible with his wife and has visited major-league and minor-league baseball parks across the country. He also loves to cook and makes all the meals at his house while writing about those meals on his blog, Cooking and My Family.

In his younger years, **Frederick C. (Rick) Bush** wondered why a poor diet and questionable habits had not led him to sports stardom as they had done for Babe Ruth. Eventually, he realized it was because he lacked the Big Bam's otherworldly athletic talent. Rick turned to writing and has contributed to almost two dozen SABR books as well as the Biography and Games Project websites. He and Bill Nowlin have co-edited two SABR books about the Negro Leagues, *Bittersweet Goodbye* and the forthcoming *The Eagles Take Flight*, and are working on a third volume about the 1935 Pittsburgh Crawfords. Rick lives with his wife, Michelle, and their three sons – Michael, Andrew, and Daniel – in Cypress, Texas, and he teaches English at Wharton County Junior College in Sugar Land, Texas.

Alan Cohen serves as Vice President-Treasurer of the Connecticut Smoky Joe Wood Chapter and is datacaster for the Hartford Yard Goats, the Double-A affiliate of the Rockies. His biographies, game stories and essays have appeared in more than 40 SABR publications. His work on youth ballgames awakened an interest in the role of Babe Ruth in these games. Alan has continued to expand his research into the Hearst Sandlot Classic (1946-1965), which launched the careers of 88 major-league players, and had Babe Ruth as its honorary chairman in 1947. He has four children and six grandchildren and resides in Connecticut with wife Frances, their cat Morty, and their dog Buddy.

Father Gabriel B. Costa is a Catholic priest on an extended academic leave from Seton Hall University. He is currently a Mathematics professor at the United States Military Academy, where he also functions as a chaplain.

Herb Crehan is one day younger than Rico Petrocelli and attended his first Red Sox game in 1952—a doubleheader against the St. Louis Browns! He is in his 24th season as a contributing writer for *Red Sox Magazine*, the team's official program. He has interviewed over 140 former Red Sox players during his 24 seasons of writing the series, "Native and Adopted Sons of New England's Team." He publishes and maintains the website www.bostonbaseballhistory.com and he has been a member of SABR since 1995.

Reynaldo Cruz Díaz is the founder and head editor of the Cuban-based magazine *Universo Béisbol*, which is hosted in MLBlogs. He is a language graduate of the University of Holguin, in his hometown, and has been leading the aforementioned magazine since March 2010. A SABR member since the summer of 2014, he writes, translates, and photographs baseball and was in the first row of the Barack Obama game in Havana, shooting from the Tampa Bay Rays dugout. In spite of the rich history of Cuban baseball, his favorite player happens to be no other than Ichiro Suzuki, whom he hopes to meet and interview. A retro-ballpark lover, he views Fenway Park, Wrigley Field, Koshien Stadium, and Estadio Palmar de Junco as the can't-miss places in baseball.

Richard Cuicchi joined SABR in 1983 and is an active member of the Schott-Pelican Chapter.

Since his retirement as an information technology executive, Richard authored *Family Ties: A Comprehensive Collection of Facts and Trivia about Baseball's Relatives*. He has contributed to numerous SABR BioProject and Games publications. He does freelance writing and blogging about a variety of baseball topics on his website TheTenthInning.com. Richard lives in New Orleans with his wife, Mary.

Paul E. Doutrich is professor emeritus at York College of Pennsylvania where he taught American history for 30 years. He now lives in Brewster, Massachusetts. Among the courses he taught was one titled "Baseball History." He has written scholarly articles and contributed to several anthologies about the Revolutionary era and has written a book about Jacksonian America. He has also curated several museum exhibits. His recent scholarship has focused on baseball history. He has contributed numerous manuscripts to various SABR publications and is the author of *The Cardinals and the Yankees, 1926: A Classical Season and St. Louis in Seven.*

Rob Edelman is the author of *Great Baseball Films* and *Baseball on the Web* (which Amazon.com cited as a Top 10 Internet book) and was a frequent contributor to *Base Ball: A Journal of the Early Game*. He offered film commentary on WAMC Northeast Public Radio and was a longtime Contributing Editor of *Leonard Maltin's Movie Guide* and other Maltin publications. With his wife, Audrey Kupferberg, he co-authored *Meet the Mertzes,* a double biography of Vivian Vance and super-baseball fan William Frawley, and *Matthau: A Life*. His byline has appeared in *Total Baseball, The Total Baseball Catalog, Baseball and American Culture: Across the Diamond, NINE: A Journal of Baseball History and Culture, The National Pastime: A Review of Baseball History, The Baseball Research Journal,* and histories of the 1918 Boston Red Sox, 1947 Brooklyn Dodgers, 1947 New York Yankees, and 1960 Pittsburgh Pirates. He wrote a baseball film essay for the Kino International DVD *Reel Baseball: Baseball Films from the Silent Era, 1899-1926*; was interviewed on several documentaries on the director's cut DVD of *The Natural*; was the keynote speaker at the 23rd Annual NINE Spring Training Conference; and before his death in 2019 taught film history courses at the University at Albany (SUNY).

A former archaeologist with a Ph.D. from Brown University, **Robert K. Fitts** left academics behind to follow his passion - Japanese Baseball. His articles have appeared in numerous magazines and websites, including *Nine*, the *Baseball Research Journal*, the *National Pastime, Sports Collectors Digest*, and on MLB.com. He is the author of five books on Japanese baseball: *Mashi: The Unfulfilled Baseball Dreams of Masanori Murakami, the First Japanese Major Leaguer* (University of Nebraska Press, 2015); *Banzai Babe Ruth* (University of Nebraska Press, 2012); *Wally Yonamine: The Man Who Changed Japanese Baseball* (University of Nebraska Press, 2008); and *Remembering Japanese Baseball: An Oral History of the Game* (Southern Illinois University Press, 2005). Fitts is the founder of SABR's Asian Baseball Committee and recipient of the society's 2013 Seymour Medal, 2019 McFarland-SABR Baseball Research Award, 2012 Doug Pappas Award, and the 2006 Sporting News- SABR Research Award. He has also been a finalist for the Casey Award and a silver medalist at the Independent Publish Book Awards. His next book, *Issei Baseball: The Story of the First Japanese American Ballplayers* will be published by the University of Nebraska in 2020.

T.S. Flynn is an educator and writer in Minneapolis. His articles on Oil Can Boyd, J.R. Richard, the 1921 World Series, and the 1925 World Series have appeared in SABR books. He has written short fiction, essays, articles, and reviews for a variety of publications, including *Hobart, The Classical*, and the *Peoria Journal Star.*

James Forr is past winner of the McFarland-SABR Baseball Research Award and co-author (along with David Proctor) of *Pie Traynor: A Baseball Biography*, which was a finalist for the 2010 CASEY Award. He lives in Columbia, Missouri.

Carolyn R. Fuchs, M.Ed, has baseball in her blood. She in the granddaughter of the late Judge Emil Fuchs. Her dad Robert Fuchs wrote a book about the Judge and the Boston Braves. Carolyn heard first-hand from her father Robert about the Judge. She is a member of the Boston Braves Historic Society and continues to write and support articles about the Braves during the Judge Fuchs era. She provides the silver tray annually at the Boston Baseball Writers Association where the last award of the evening is the Judge Emil Fuchs Award for "long and meritorious service to baseball" presented to a recipient selected by the baseball writers.

John Gabcik (1943-2019) was born and raised in Chicago, and had been following the White Sox since 1952. He and his wife, Edie, retired from the Chicago area to Brevard, North Carolina, in 2007. John joined SABR in 2009 and wrote biographies and game stories, concentrating on under-appreciated White Sox pitchers and other personalities. He also helped Retrosheet develop game play-by-play recreations.

John passed away in Brevard on August 2, 2019, from complications of recurring cancer.

Ed Gruver is the author of seven books and a contributing writer to SABR's Games Project and several online sports sites.

Mike Haupert is Professor of Economics at the University of Wisconsin-La Crosse and co-chair of the SABR Business of Baseball Committee.

Leslie Heaphy is an Associate Professor of History at Kent State University at Stark, Vice President of the SABR Board, and chair of the SABR Women in Baseball Committee.

Rock Hoffman has been a SABR member since 1995, he co-hosts *Sports Page*, a sports talk radio show Saturday at 10 PM on WRDV-FM (WRDV.org) in suburban Philadelphia. He's active in the Connie Mack Chapter by helping at local meetings and running the chapter Facebook site. He was a member of the local organizing committee for the 2013 SABR National Convention in Philadelphia and volunteers to judge oral and poster presentations at the national conventions. He enjoys disc golf and American Civil War history. His home in Ardsley, Pennsylvania, is a Ruthian clout from the final resting place of Hall of Fame pitcher Charles Albert "Chief" Bender. Previously, he contributed to the SABR books *When Pops Led the Family: The 1979 Pittsburgh Pirates* and *Moments of Joy and Heartbreak: 66 Significant Episodes in the History of the Pittsburgh Pirates.*

Paul Hofmann, a SABR member since 2002, is the Associate Vice President for International Affairs at Sacramento State University and frequent contributor to SABR publications. Paul is a native of Detroit, Michigan and lifelong Detroit Tigers fan. He currently resides in Folsom, California.

Hot Springs Historic Trail Research Team

"The Home Runs That Changed Everything" was researched and written collectively by the Hot Springs Historic Baseball Trail Research Team. All are members of SABR, and all were founding members of the Hot Springs Historic Baseball Trail, under the direction of Hot Springs civic leader, Steve Arrison. Additionally, all also served as historical advisors, and appeared in, Larry Foley's 2015 Emmy Award winning film documentary, *The First Boys of Spring*. These "Trailmen" are:

Mark Blaeuer
Mark toiled in the field (and labs) of archeology for years. As a ranger for two decades at Hot Springs National Park, he is deeply familiar with park history. He is also an accomplished poet, whose work, including translations, can be found in 80-plus journals. A devoted researcher, he is the country's leading scholar on African-American baseball history in Hot Springs. Mark is the author of *Didn't All the Indians Come Here? Separating Fact from Fiction at Hot Springs National Park* (2007), *Fragments of a Nocturne* (2014), and *Baseball in Hot Springs* (2016).

Mike Dugan
Mike was born and raised in Hot Springs. His Irish ancestors came to town in 1870 and settled on Whittington Avenue, less than a hundred yards from the site which later became the national epicenter of major-league spring training. Mike served as Sports Information Director at Henderson State University before becoming a business and community leader in Hot Springs. Henderson has honored Mike with its "H" Award as Outstanding Alumni and inducted him into its Reddie Athletic Hall of Honor. A member of SABR since 1992 on the Dead Ball Era and College Baseball committees, Mike has been a major, long-time, and multifaceted, contributor to baseball history in Hot Springs. He even portrayed Royal Rooter leader, Michael T. McGreevy, in *The First Boys of Spring*! Nuf Ced!

Don Duren

Don is the great-great-great grandson of Arkansas pioneer Granville Whittington. He grew up playing baseball on the historic diamonds of Hot Springs, including where Babe Ruth played, at Majestic Park and Whittington Field. Following decades of groundbreaking, exhaustive research, he authored *Boiling Out at the Springs: A History of Major League Baseball Spring Training at Hot Springs, Arkansas* (2015); *Bathers Baseball: A History of Minor League Baseball at the Arkansas Spa* (2011); and *Lon Warneke: The Arkansas Hummingbird* (2014). Don now resides outside of Dallas, Texas, working as Christian minister.

Bill Jenkinson
Bill Jenkinson is a renowned baseball scholar, known internationally for his groundbreaking research of major-league baseball's most significant sluggers and long-distance home runs. He is the world's leading authority on Babe Ruth's batting prowess, "the Babe Ruth of Babe Ruth historians," as he has been referred to by media, colleagues, and fans. Bill has served as a consultant to the National Baseball Hall of Fame, Major League Baseball, SABR, ESPN, and the Babe Ruth Museum. He has appeared on numerous television and radio broadcasts and has been quoted in nearly every major newspaper in America, as well as by *Time*, *Newsweek*, and *Sports Illustrated*, and many other leading magazines. Bill's books on baseball include *The Year Babe Ruth Hit 104 Home Runs: Recrowning Baseball's Greatest Slugger* (2007), *Baseball's Ultimate Power: Ranking the All-Time Greatest Home Run Hitters* (2010), and *Babe Ruth: Against All Odds, World's Mightiest Slugger* (2014). Bill is the world's leading authority and archivist of historic, long-distance home runs, including The Babe's game-changing home runs of 1918 in Hot Springs. Bill was a primary designer of the Hot Springs Historic Baseball Trail.

Tim Reid
Tim Reid, together with his cousin and colleague Bob Ward, founded the St. Petersburg and National committees to commemorate Babe Ruth. Teamed with other historians, they have very extensively researched and noted Babe Ruth's Ruthian contributions to baseball and American culture. Thanks especially to Bill Jenkinson, and to several members of the Ruth Family, the Committee to Commemorate Babe Ruth's research and commemorations has significantly contributed to baseball history. Tim also writes baseball tribute songs on occasion, including "Babe Ruth, King of 'Em All," and "Take Me Out to the Ball Fields of Old Hot Springs." Tim is currently researching early twentieth-century baseball in Baja California, including Babe Ruth's Prohibition-Era adventures in the Mexican state.

Mike Huber is a Professor of Mathematics at Muhlenberg College in Allentown, Pennsylvania. He enjoys researching and writing about rare events in baseball, and he joined SABR in 1996 after teaching his first sabermetrics course, which included many discussions about the dominance of Babe Ruth.

Jimmy Keenan has been a SABR member since 2001. His grandfather, Jimmy Lyston, and four other family members were all professional baseball players. A frequent contributor to SABR publications, Keenan is the author of the following books: *The Lystons: A Story of One Baltimore Family & Our National Pastime*; *The Life, Times and Tragic Death of Pitcher Win Mercer*; and *The Lyston Brothers: A Journey Through 19th Century Baseball*. Keenan is a 2010 inductee into the Oldtimers Baseball Association of Maryland's Hall of Fame and a 2012 inductee into the Baltimore's Boys of Summer Hall of Fame.

Tara Krieger has regaled in telling stories about Babe Ruth and Lou Gehrig since her ninth grade English teacher let her do a term paper on the 1927 Yankees. Although her current day job is as an attorney for the City of New York, she has previously been on staff as a sportswriter for *Newsday* and as an editorial producer with MLB Advanced Media. With SABR, where she has been an active member of the Casey Stengel chapter since 2005, she is an editor and contributor to BioProject and has participated in the publication of several SABR books, including *Van Lingle Mungo*, *The Miracle Has Landed*, *Bridging Two Dynasties*, *Go-Go to Glory*, *Minnesotans in Baseball*, *No-Hitters*, and *Met-rospectives*.

Kevin Larkin retired after 24 years as a police officer in his hometown of Great Barrington, Massachusetts. He has always been a baseball fan and has been going to minor league and major league baseball games since he was five years old. He has authored two books on baseball: *Baseball in the Bay State (*a history of baseball in the Commonwealth of Massachusetts) and *Gehrig: Game by Game* (an account of all of the major league baseball games played by his hero, Lou Gehrig. He has also co-authored *Baseball in the Berkshires: A County's Common Bond* along with James Tom Daly, James Overmyer and Larry Moore. The book details a history of baseball in Berkshire County, where Larkin grew up. He has written numerous articles for SABR and recently had published on Legends On Deck, a list of who Larkin thinks are the top 100 Black Baseball/Negro League baseball players. He does fact checking and hyperlinking for SABR, as well as writing biographies and game accounts, and according to him, is living the dream of writing and researching about the great sport of baseball.

Jane Leavy is the author of three *New York Times* bestsellers: *The Big Fella, Babe Ruth and the World He Created*; *The Last Boy, Mickey Mantle and the End of America's Childhood*; and *Sandy Koufax, A Lefty's Legacy.* In 2019, *The Big Fella* earned her SABR's Seymour Medal, presented annually to the best book of baseball history or biography. She was also a finalist for the National Book Critics Circle Award for Biography and the PEN/ESPN Award for Literary Sports Writing. A former staff writer for the *Washington Post*, she grew up on Long Island where she pitched briefly and poorly in little league for the Blue Jays of Roslyn Heights. She lives in Washington, DC and Truro, Massachusetts.

Len Levin sometimes likes to imagine how his beloved Red Sox might have fared had the Babe stayed with them. Pipe dreams. Len is a retired newspaper editor (*Providence Journal*) who nowadays edits the decisions of the Rhode Island Supreme Court and also is the copy editor for many SABR publications, including this one.

SABR member and Massachusetts native **Mike Lynch** is the founder of Seamheads.com and author of five books, including *Harry Frazee, Ban Johnson and the Feud That Nearly Destroyed the American League*, which was named a finalist for the 2009 Larry Ritter Award and nominated for a Seymour Medal. His most recent work includes a three-book series called *Baseball's Untold History* and several articles that have appeared in SABR books and on The National Pastime Museum's website. He lives in Roslindale, Massachusetts, with the love of his life and their cats, Jiggs and Pepper.

Brian "Chip" Martin is a retired journalist from London, Ontario. He is a member of SABR, member of selection committee for Canadian Baseball Hall of Fame, and founding director of Centre For Canadian Baseball Research, as well as the author of eight books to date, which will include the forthcoming *The Man Who Made Babe Ruth: Brother Matthias of St. Mary's School* (coming from McFarland in 2020.)

David McDonald is a writer, filmmaker and broadcaster who grew up watching Rocky Nelson, Sam Jethroe, and Mike Goliat at Maple Leaf Stadium in Toronto. He lives in Ottawa, Ontario.

Skip Nipper is the author of *Baseball in Nashville* (2007, Arcadia Publishing), is a member of SABR's Grantland Rice-Fred Russell (Nashville) chapter and serves as secretary of the Old Timers Baseball Association of Nashville. He has contributed biographies to several SABR books and publishes Nashville baseball history at baseballinnashville.com. A graduate of Memphis State University, he and his wife Sheila reside in Mt. Juliet, Tennessee. Together they have seven children and 17 grandchildren, a dog, Ellie, and a cat, Stell. They all love baseball.

In writing the afterword for *Ted Williams' Hit List*, the book by noted authors Ted Williams and Jim Prime, **Bill Nowlin** once tried very hard to prove that Ted Williams was statistically a better hitter than Babe Ruth. It was a tough chore and not all that convincing. The only way to accomplish that was to compare their strikeout frequency. A ground ball might advance a baserunner or drive in a run; a strikeout itself never adds any value. Ruth struck out 15.8% of the time; Williams only struck out 9.2% of the time. By assigning sufficient negatives to Ruth… As noted, it was not that convincing. They were both pretty good, Ruth second only to Williams in on-base percentage and Williams second only to Ruth in career slugging percentage. And both began with the Boston Red Sox.

Chad Osborne is a public relations writer at Radford University in Virginia and has worked in higher education for 20 years. In 2006, he created The Rainout Blog, where he writes about baseball and inclement weather. Chad regularly attends Bristol Pirates (Appalachian League) games with his wife, Tina; daughter, Gracie; and son, Ty. They live in Marion, Virginia, two miles from the site of where Nolan Ryan made his first professional pitch. Chad serves as chair of SABR's Baseball and the Media Research Committee.

Pete Palmer is the co-author with John Thorn of *The Hidden Game of Baseball* and co-editor with Gary Gillette of the *Barnes and Noble ESPN Baseball Encyclopedia* (five editions). Pete worked as a consultant to Sports Information Center, the official statisticians for the American League from 1976 to 1987. Pete introduced on-base average as an official statistic for the

American League in 1979 and invented on-base plus slugging (OPS), now universally used as a good measure of batting strength. He won the SABR Bob Davids Award in 1989 and was selected by the SABR in 2010 as a charter member of the Henry Chadwick Award. Pete was given a lifetime achievement award by SABR in 2018. Pete also edited with John Thorn seven editions of *Total Baseball.* He previously edited four editions of the *Barnes Official Encyclopedia of Baseball* (1974-79). A member of SABR since 1973, Pete was also the editor of

Who's Who in Baseball, which celebrated its 101st and last year in 2016.

Tim Rask is the outgoing "Umpire-in-Chief" of SABR's Field of Dreams (Iowa) regional chapter. The longtime Iowa City resident is relocating to Eau Claire, Wisconsin. Eau Claire was the first minor-league stop for a young Henry Aaron, who would go on to break Babe Ruth's career home-run record.

Carl Riechers retired from United Parcel Service in 2012 after 35 years of service. With more free time, he became a SABR member that same year. Born and raised in the suburbs of St.

Louis, he became a big fan of the Cardinals. He and his wife Janet have three children and are the proud grandparents of two.

Harry Rothgerber, a SABR member since 1983, has led the Pee Wee Reese Chapter for 20 years. A former member of the national SABR Board of Directors, he served as co-chair of the successful 1997 national convention in Louisville, Kentucky. Harry collects books by and about Babe Ruth, and his own work *Young Babe Ruth* was published by McFarland in 1999. An attorney by profession, he works as a prosecutor and writer and lives in Louisville with his wife of 50 years, Helen.

Gary A. Sarnoff has been an active SABR member since 1994. A member of the Bob Davids Chapter, he has contributed to SABR's BioProject and Games Project, to the annual *National Pastime* publication, is a member of the SABR Negro Leagues committee, and is the chairman of the Ron Gabriel Committee. In addition, he has authored two baseball books: *The Wrecking Crew of '33* and *The First Yankees Dynasty*. He currently resides in Alexandria, Virginia.

Tom Schott holds a Ph.D. in American history (LSU, 1978) and is a retired historian for the Air Force and Special Operations Command. He currently reads, writes, plays chess, and freelance edits to stay busy.

Joe Schuster is the author of a novel, *The Might Have Been*, a finalist for the 2013 CASEY Award for the best book about baseball. He has also written two titles for the Gemma Open Door series of books for adult literacy programs, *One Season in the Sun*, about ballplayers who had major-league careers lasting a few weeks or less, and *Jackie Robinson*. A regular contributor to the official publications of the St. Louis Cardinals, he has also written for a number of SABR books, including *Wrigley Field: The Friendly Confines at Clark and Addison, 20-Game Losers, Sportsman's Park in St. Louis*, and *Sweet '60: The 1960 Pittsburgh Pirates,* among others. He lives outside St. Louis, is married, and is the father of five rabid Redbird fans.

Curt Smith's essay on Babe Ruth and U.S. presidents links two subjects that since boyhood have gripped his heart—baseball and politics. As speechwriter to George H.W. Bush, he wrote more addresses than anyone else for the 41st president in his 1989-93 term and beyond, including Bush's "Just War" speech, address on the 50th anniversary of Pearl Harbor at the USS *Arizona* memorial site in 1991, and eulogy to Ronald Reagan in 2004. Smith also frequently spoke to another baseball-loving president, Richard Nixon, who had been offered the post of commissioner in 1965. Born and raised in Upstate New York, Smith grew up a Yankees fan, idolizing Ruth, Maris, and Mantle. In the 1960s, the then-teen and future author of 17 books, most recently *The Presidents and the Pastime,* Gate House Media Columnist, and Senior Lecturer in English at the University of Rochester saw the light, becoming a fan of Babe's first team, the Red Sox. He still enjoys trips to his mother's native home, Worcester, Massachusetts, every other sentence asking, "How about those *Sawx?*"

Steve Smith is a retired CPA who has been a SABR member since 2000. His primary passion is researching the baseball history of his hometown, Keokuk, Iowa. He spends his winters in Englewood, Florida, near the Tampa Bay Rays spring training site in Port Charlotte.

Wayne Soini, a lifelong history buff, holds a master's degree in History from the University of Massachusetts Boston. Prior to publishing two historical novels, *Nixon in Love* and *Germany Surrenders!* in 2015, Soini coauthored a local sports history book with Robert Fuchs, *Judge Fuchs and the Boston Braves* (McFarland, 1998), *Gloucester's Sea Serpent* (History Press, 2010) and *Porter's Secret*.

Glen Sparks has contributed to several SABR books and is working on a full-length biography of Hall of Fame shortstop Pee Wee Reese. A veteran of the Santa Monica, California, Little League program, he majored in journalism at the University of Missouri and lives in St. Louis with his wife, Pam.

Lyle Spatz joined SABR in 1973. He was chairman of the Baseball Records Committee from 1991 to 2016.

Mark S. Sternman has traveled a reverse Ruth route by growing up in New York before moving to Boston. He has attended games at all three Yankee Stadium iterations. Sternman heartily recommends *The House That Ruth Built: A New Stadium, the First Yankees Championship, and the Redemption of 1923* by his grade-school friend and longtime pal Robert Weintraub.

Cecilia Tan is such a Ruth aficionado she once spent 10 days traipsing through the Carolinas, Georgia, and Florida, visiting sites where Ruth hit home runs. She has served as SABR's Publications Director since 2011 and has previously written for Baseball Prospectus, *Yankees Magazine, Gotham Baseball, Yankees Annual,* and many other publications. She is the author of *The 50 Greatest Yankees Games* and co-author *The 50 Greatest Red Sox Games*. Her baseball blog, one of the oldest on the Internet, is at WhyILikeBaseball.com.

Stew Thornley has been a SABR member since 1979 and has written or edited two books on the Polo Grounds.

Saul Wisnia has authored, coauthored, or contributed to numerous books on Boston and general baseball history, including *Fenway Park: The Centennial, Miracle at Fenway: The Inside Story of the Boston Red Sox 2004 Championship Season*, and *Son* of Havana: A Baseball Journey from Cuba to the Big Leagues and Back* (with Luis Tiant). He is a former sports and news correspondent for *The Washington Post* and feature writer for *The Boston Herald* whose essays have appeared in *Sports Illustrated, Boston Globe, Boston Magazine,* and *Red Sox Magazine.* For the past 20 years, he has chronicled the special relationship between the Red Sox and young cancer patients as senior publications editor-writer at Dana-Farber Cancer Institute. Wisnia lives in his native Newton, Massachusetts, 5.7 miles from Fenway Park.

Gregory H. Wolf was born in Pittsburgh, but now resides in the Chicagoland area with his wife, Margaret, and daughter, Gabriela. A professor of German studies and holder of the Dennis and Jean Bauman Endowed Chair in the Humanities at North Central College in Naperville, Illinois, he has edited nine books for SABR. He is currently working on projects about Comiskey Park in Chicago, Shibe Park in Philadelphia, and the 1982 Milwaukee Brewers. As of January 2017, he serves as co-director of SABR's BioProject, which you can follow on Facebook and Twitter.

Allan Wood is the author of *Babe Ruth and the 1918 Red Sox* and *Don't Let Us Win Tonight: An Oral History of the 2004 Boston Red Sox's Impossible Playoff Run"* (with Bill Nowlin). He has been writing "The Joy of Sox" blog since 2003 and has contributed to eight SABR books. Born and raised in Vermont, Allan enjoyed 2004 while living in New York City. He now lives on Vancouver Island, British Columbia, with his partner Laura Kaminker and their three dogs.

Jack Zerby enjoys researching baseball from the Ruth era and the classic sports writing that made it come alive for fans. The games he wrote about here are interesting bookends for the Babe's career. Jack grew up watching the Pirates play in Forbes Field in the '50s and well remembers the right-field roof Babe cleared on that memorable day in 1935. Jack is a retired attorney and estates/trusts administrator, a SABR member since 1994, and active in the BioProject and Games Project. He and his wife Diana, a professional violinist, live in Brevard in western North Carolina.

Society for American Baseball Research
Cronkite School at ASU
555 N. Central Ave. #416, Phoenix, AZ 85004
602.496.1460 (phone)
SABR.org

Become a SABR member today!

If you're interested in baseball — writing about it, reading about it, talking about it — there's a place for you in the Society for American Baseball Research.

SABR memberships are available on annual, multi-year, or monthly subscription basis. Annual and monthly subscription memberships auto-renew for your convenience. Young Professional memberships are for ages 30 and under. Senior memberships are for ages 65 and older. Student memberships are available to currently enrolled middle/high school or full-time college/university students. Monthly subscription members receive SABR publications electronically and are eligible for SABR event discounts after 12 months.

Here's a list of some of the key benefits you'll receive as a SABR member:

- Receive two editions (spring and fall) of the *Baseball Research Journal*, our flagship publication
- Receive expanded e-book edition of *The National Pastime*, our annual convention journal
- 8-10 new e-books published by the SABR Digital Library, all FREE to members
- "This Week in SABR" e-newsletter, sent to members every Friday
- Join dozens of research committees, from Statistical Analysis to Women in Baseball.
- Join one of 70+ regional chapters in the U.S., Canada, Latin America, and abroad
- Participate in online discussion groups
- Ask and answer baseball research questions on the SABR-L e-mail listserv
- Complete archives of *The Sporting News* dating back to 1886 and other research resources
- Promote your research in "This Week in SABR"
- Diamond Dollars Case Competition
- Yoseloff Scholarships
- Discounts on SABR national conferences, including the SABR National Convention, the SABR Analytics Conference, Jerry Malloy Negro League Conference, Frederick Ivor-Campbell 19th Century Conference, and the Arizona Fall League Experience
- Publish your research in peer-reviewed SABR journals
- Collaborate with SABR researchers and experts
- Contribute to Baseball Biography Project or the SABR Games Project
- List your new book in the SABR Bookshelf
- Lead a SABR research committee or chapter
- Networking opportunities at SABR Analytics Conference
- Meet baseball authors and historians at SABR events and chapter meetings
- 50% discounts on paperback versions of SABR e-books
- Discounts with other partners in the baseball community
- SABR research awards

We hope you'll join the most passionate international community of baseball fans at SABR! Check us out online at SABR.org/join.

SABR MEMBERSHIP FORM

	Standard	Senior	Young Pro.	Student
Annual:	❏ $65	❏ $45	❏ $45	❏ $25
3 Year:	❏ $175	❏ $129	❏ $129	
5 Year:	❏ $249			
Monthly:	❏ $6.95	❏ $4.95	❏ $4.95	

(International members wishing to be mailed the Baseball Research Journal should add $10/yr for Canada/Mexico or $19/yr for overseas locations.)

Participate in Our Donor Program!
Support the preservation of baseball research. Designate your gift toward:
❏ General Fund ❏ Endowment Fund ❏ Research Resources ❏ _____
❏ I want to maximize the impact of my gift; do not send any donor premiums
❏ I would like this gift to remain anonymous.

Note: Any donation not designated will be placed in the General Fund.
SABR is a 501 (c) (3) not-for-profit organization & donations are tax-deductible to the extent allowed by law.

Name _____

E-mail* _____

Address _____

City _____ ST _____ ZIP _____

Phone _____ Birthday _____

* Your e-mail address on file ensures you will receive the most recent SABR news.

Dues $ _____
Donation $ _____
Amount Enclosed $ _____

Do you work for a matching grant corporation? Call (602) 496-1460 for details.

If you wish to pay by credit card, please contact the SABR office at (602) 496-1460 or sign up securely online at SABR.org/join. We accept Visa, Mastercard & Discover.

Do you wish to receive the *Baseball Research Journal* electronically? ❏ Yes ❏ No
Our e-books are available in PDF, Kindle, or EPUB (iBooks, iPad, Nook) formats.

Mail to: SABR, Cronkite School at ASU, 555 N. Central Ave. #416, Phoenix, AZ 85004

Friends of SABR

You can become a Friend of SABR by giving as little as $10 per month or by making a one-time gift of $1,000 or more. When you do so, you will be inducted into a community of passionate baseball fans dedicated to supporting SABR's work.

Friends of SABR receive the following benefits:
- ✓ Annual Friends of SABR Commemorative Lapel Pin
- ✓ Recognition in This Week in SABR, SABR.org, and the SABR Annual Report
- ✓ Access to the SABR Annual Convention VIP donor event
- ✓ Invitations to exclusive Friends of SABR events

SABR On-Deck Circle - $10/month, $30/month, $50/month

Get in the SABR On-Deck Circle, and help SABR become the essential community for the world of baseball. Your support will build capacity around all things SABR, including publications, website content, podcast development, and community growth.

A monthly gift is deducted from your bank account or charged to a credit card until you tell us to stop. No more email, mail, or phone reminders.

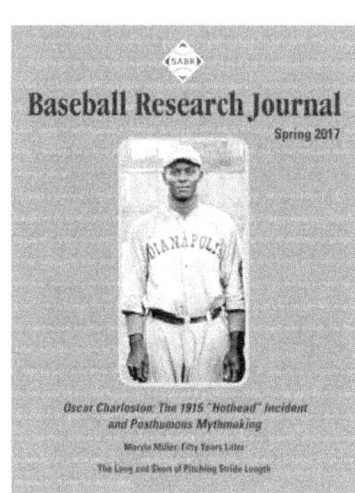
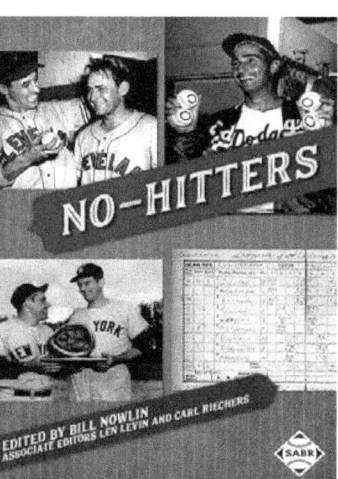

Join the SABR On-Deck Circle

Payment Info: _____ Visa _____ Mastercard   ○ $10/month

Name on Card: _____   ○ $30/month

Card #: _____   ○ $50/month

Exp. Date: _____ Security Code: _____   ○ Other amount _____

Signature: _____

Go to sabr.org/donate to make your gift online

SABR BioProject Team Books

In 2002, the Society for American Baseball Research launched an effort to write and publish biographies of every player, manager, and individual who has made a contribution to baseball. Over the past decade, the BioProject Committee has produced over 6,000 biographical articles. Many have been part of efforts to create theme- or team-oriented books, spearheaded by chapters or other committees of SABR.

THE 1986 BOSTON RED SOX:
THERE WAS MORE THAN GAME SIX
One of a two-book series on the rivals that met in the 1986 World Series, the Boston Red Sox and the New York Mets, including biographies of every player, coach, broadcaster, and other important figures in the top organizations in baseball that year. .
Edited by Leslie Heaphy and Bill Nowlin
$19.95 paperback (ISBN 978-1-943816-19-4)
$9.99 ebook (ISBN 978-1-943816-18-7)
8.5"X11", 420 pages, over 200 photos

THE 1986 NEW YORK METS:
THERE WAS MORE THAN GAME SIX
The other book in the "rivalry" set from the 1986 World Series. This book re-tells the story of that year's classic World Series and this is the story of each of the players, coaches, managers, and broadcasters, their lives in baseball and the way the 1986 season fit into their lives.
Edited by Leslie Heaphy and Bill Nowlin
$19.95 paperback (ISBN 978-1-943816-13-2)
$9.99 ebook (ISBN 978-1-943816-12-5)
8.5"X11", 392 pages, over 100 photos

SCANDAL ON THE SOUTH SIDE:
THE 1919 CHICAGO WHITE SOX
The Black Sox Scandal isn't the only story worth telling about the 1919 Chicago White Sox. The team roster included three future Hall of Famers, a 20-year-old spitballer who would win 300 games in the minors, and even a batboy who later became a celebrity with the "Murderers' Row" New York Yankees. All of their stories are included in Scandal on the South Side with a timeline of the 1919 season.
Edited by Jacob Pomrenke
$19.95 paperback (ISBN 978-1-933599-95-3)
$9.99 ebook (ISBN 978-1-933599-94-6)
8.5"x11", 324 pages, 55 historic photos

WINNING ON THE NORTH SIDE
THE 1929 CHICAGO CUBS
Celebrate the 1929 Chicago Cubs, one of the most exciting teams in baseball history. Future Hall of Famers Hack Wilson, '29 NL MVP Rogers Hornsby, and Kiki Cuyler, along with Riggs Stephenson formed one of the most potent quartets in baseball history. The magical season came to an ignominious end in the World Series and helped craft the future "lovable loser" image of the team.
Edited by Gregory H. Wolf
$19.95 paperback (ISBN 978-1-933599-89-2)
$9.99 ebook (ISBN 978-1-933599-88-5)
8.5"x11", 314 pages, 59 photos

DETROIT THE UNCONQUERABLE:
THE 1935 WORLD CHAMPION TIGERS
Biographies of every player, coach, and broadcaster involved with the 1935 World Champion Detroit Tigers baseball team, written by members of the Society for American Baseball Research. Also includes a season in review and other articles about the 1935 team. Hank Greenberg, Mickey Cochrane, Charlie Gehringer, Schoolboy Rowe, and more.
Edited by Scott Ferkovich
$19.95 paperback (ISBN 9978-1-933599-78-6)
$9.99 ebook (ISBN 978-1-933599-79-3)
8.5"X11", 230 pages, 52 photos

THE TEAM THAT TIME WON'T FORGET:
THE 1951 NEW YORK GIANTS
Because of Bobby Thomson's dramatic "Shot Heard 'Round the World" in the bottom of the ninth of the decisive playoff game against the Brooklyn Dodgers, the team will forever be in baseball public's consciousness. Includes a foreword by Giants outfielder Monte Irvin.
Edited by Bill Nowlin and C. Paul Rogers III
$19.95 paperback (ISBN 978-1-933599-99-1)
$9.99 ebook (ISBN 978-1-933599-98-4)
8.5"X11", 282 pages, 47 photos

A PENNANT FOR THE TWIN CITIES:
THE 1965 MINNESOTA TWINS
This volume celebrates the 1965 Minnesota Twins, who captured the American League pennant in just their fifth season in the Twin Cities. Led by an All-Star cast, from Harmon Killebrew, Tony Oliva, Zoilo Versalles, and Mudcat Grant to Bob Allison, Jim Kaat, Earl Battey, and Jim Perry, the Twins won 102 games, but bowed to the Los Angeles Dodgers and Sandy Koufax in Game Seven
Edited by Gregory H. Wolf
$19.95 paperback (ISBN 978-1-943816-09-5)
$9.99 ebook (ISBN 978-1-943816-08-8)
8.5"X11", 405 pages, over 80 photos

MUSTACHES AND MAYHEM: CHARLIE O'S THREE TIME CHAMPIONS:
THE OAKLAND ATHLETICS: 1972-74
The Oakland Athletics captured major league baseball's crown each year from 1972 through 1974. Led by future Hall of Famers Reggie Jackson, Catfish Hunter and Rollie Fingers, the Athletics were a largely homegrown group who came of age together. Biographies of every player, coach, manager, and broadcaster (and mascot) from 1972 through 1974 are included, along with season recaps.
Edited by Chip Greene
$29.95 paperback (ISBN 978-1-943816-07-1)
$9.99 ebook (ISBN 978-1-943816-06-4)
8.5"X11", 600 pages, almost 100 photos

SABR Members can purchase each book at a significant discount (often 50% off) and receive the ebook edtions free as a member benefit. Each book is available in a trade paperback edition as well as ebooks suitable for reading on a home computer or Nook, Kindle, or iPad/tablet.
To learn more about becoming a member of SABR, visit the website: sabr.org/join

The SABR Digital Library

The Society for American Baseball Research, the top baseball research organization in the world, disseminates some of the best in baseball history, analysis, and biography through our publishing programs. The SABR Digital Library contains a mix of books old and new, and focuses on a tandem program of paperback and ebook publication, making these materials widely available for both on digital devices and as traditional printed books.

Greatest Games Books

TIGERS BY THE TALE:
GREAT GAMES AT MICHIGAN AND TRUMBULL
For over 100 years, Michigan and Trumbull was the scene of some of the most exciting baseball ever. This book portrays 50 classic games at the corner, spanning the earliest days of Bennett Park until Tiger Stadium's final closing act. From Ty Cobb to Mickey Cochrane, Hank Greenberg to Al Kaline, and Willie Horton to Alan Trammell.
Edited by Scott Ferkovich
$12.95 paperback (ISBN 978-1-943816-21-7)
$6.99 ebook (ISBN 978-1-943816-20-0)
8.5"x11", 160 pages, 22 photos

FROM THE BRAVES TO THE BREWERS: GREAT GAMES AND HISTORY AT MILWAUKEE'S COUNTY STADIUM
The National Pastime provides in-depth articles focused on the geographic region where the national SABR convention is taking place annually. The SABR 45 convention took place in Chicago, and here are 45 articles on baseball in and around the bat-and-ball crazed Windy City: 25 that appeared in the souvenir book of the convention plus another 20 articles available in ebook only.
Edited by Gregory H. Wolf
$19.95 paperback (ISBN 978-1-943816-23-1)
$9.99 ebook (ISBN 978-1-943816-22-4)
8.5"X11", 290 pages, 58 photos

BRAVES FIELD:
MEMORABLE MOMENTS AT BOSTON'S LOST DIAMOND
From its opening on August 18, 1915, to the sudden departure of the Boston Braves to Milwaukee before the 1953 baseball season, Braves Field was home to Boston's National League baseball club and also hosted many other events: from NFL football to championship boxing. The most memorable moments to occur in Braves Field history are portrayed here.
Edited by Bill Nowlin and Bob Brady
$19.95 paperback (ISBN 978-1-933599-93-9)
$9.99 ebook (ISBN 978-1-933599-92-2)
8.5"X11", 282 pages, 182 photos

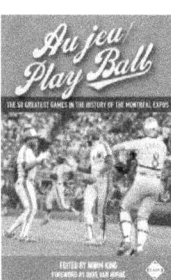

AU JEU/PLAY BALL: THE 50 GREATEST GAMES IN THE HISTORY OF THE MONTREAL EXPOS
The 50 greatest games in Montreal Expos history. The games described here recount the exploits of the many great players who wore Expos uniforms over the years—Bill Stoneman, Gary Carter, Andre Dawson, Steve Rogers, Pedro Martinez, from the earliest days of the franchise, to the glory years of 1979-1981, the what-might-have-been years of the early 1990s, and the sad, final days.and others.
Edited by Norm King
$12.95 paperback (ISBN 978-1-943816-15-6)
$5.99 ebook (ISBN978-1-943816-14-9)
8.5"x11", 162 pages, 50 photos

Original SABR Research

CALLING THE GAME:
BASEBALL BROADCASTING FROM 1920 TO THE PRESENT
An exhaustive, meticulously researched history of bringing the national pastime out of the ballparks and into living rooms via the airwaves. Every play-by-play announcer, color commentator, and ex-ballplayer, every broadcast deal, radio station, and TV network. Plus a foreword by "Voice of the Chicago Cubs" Pat Hughes, and an afterword by Jacques Doucet, the "Voice of the Montreal Expos" 1972-2004.
by Stuart Shea
$24.95 paperback (ISBN 978-1-933599-40-3)
$9.99 ebook (ISBN 978-1-933599-41-0)
7"X10", 712 pages, 40 photos

BioProject Books

WHO'S ON FIRST:
REPLACEMENT PLAYERS IN WORLD WAR II
During World War II, 533 players made the major league debuts. More than 60% of the players in the 1941 Opening Day lineups departed for the service and were replaced by first-timers and oldsters. Hod Lisenbee was 46. POW Bert Shepard had an artificial leg, and Pete Gray had only one arm. The 1944 St. Louis Browns had 13 players classified 4-F. These are their stories.
Edited by Marc Z Aaron and Bill Nowlin
$19.95 paperback (ISBN 978-1-933599-91-5)
$9.99 ebook (ISBN 978-1-933599-90-8)
8.5"X11", 422 pages, 67 photos

VAN LINGLE MUNGO:
THE MAN, THE SONG, THE PLAYERS
40 baseball players with intriguing names have been named in renditions of Dave Frishberg's classic 1969 song, Van Lingle Mungo. This book presents biographies of all 40 players and additional information about one of the greatest baseball novelty songs of all time.
Edited by Bill Nowlin
$19.95 paperback (ISBN 978-1-933599-76-2)
$9.99 ebook (ISBN 978-1-933599-77-9)
8.5"X11", 278 pages, 46 photos

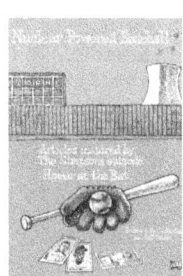

NUCLEAR POWERED BASEBALL
Nuclear Powered Baseball tells the stories of each player—past and present—featured in the classic Simpsons episode "Homer at the Bat." Wade Boggs, Ken Griffey Jr., Ozzie Smith, Nap Lajoie, Don Mattingly, and many more. We've also included a few very entertaining takes on the now-famous episode from prominent baseball writers Jonah Keri, Joe Posnanski, Erik Malinowski, and Bradley Woodrum.
Edited by Emily Hawks and Bill Nowlin
$19.95 paperback (ISBN 978-1-943816-11-8)
$9.99 ebook (ISBN 978-1-943816-10-1)
8.5"X11", 250 pages

SABR Members can purchase each book at a significant discount (often 50% off) and receive the ebook edtions free as a member benefit. Each book is available in a trade paperback edition as well as ebooks suitable for reading on a home computer or Nook, Kindle, or iPad/tablet.
To learn more about becoming a member of SABR, visit the website: sabr.org/join

SABR BioProject Books

In 2002, the Society for American Baseball Research launched an effort to write and publish biographies of every player, manager, and individual who has made a contribution to baseball. Over the past decade, the BioProject Committee has produced over 2,200 biographical articles. Many have been part of efforts to create theme- or team-oriented books, spearheaded by chapters or other committees of SABR.

THE YEAR OF THE BLUE SNOW:
THE 1964 PHILADELPHIA PHILLIES
Catcher Gus Triandos dubbed the Philadelphia Phillies' 1964 season "the year of the blue snow," a rare thing that happens once in a great while. This book sheds light on lingering questions about the 1964 season—but any book about a team is really about the players. This work offers life stories of all the players and others (managers, coaches, owners, and broadcasters) associated with this star-crossed team, as well as essays of analysis and history.
Edited by Mel Marmer and Bill Nowlin
$19.95 paperback (ISBN 978-1-933599-51-9)
$9.99 ebook (ISBN 978-1-933599-52-6)
8.5"X11", 356 PAGES, over 70 photos

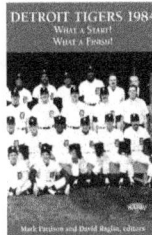

DETROIT TIGERS 1984:
WHAT A START! WHAT A FINISH!
The 1984 Detroit tigers roared out of the gate, winning their first nine games of the season and compiling an eye-popping 35-5 record after the campaign's first 40 games—still the best start ever for any team in major league history. This book brings together biographical profiles of every Tiger from that magical season, plus those of field management, top executives, the broadcasters—even venerable Tiger Stadium and the city itself.
Edited by Mark Pattison and David Raglin
$19.95 paperback (ISBN 978-1-933599-44-1)
$9.99 ebook (ISBN 978-1-933599-45-8)
8.5"x11", 250 pages (Over 230,000 words!)

SWEET '60: THE 1960 PITTSBURGH PIRATES
A portrait of the 1960 team which pulled off one of the biggest upsets of the last 60 years. When Bill Mazeroski's home run left the park to win in Game Seven of the World Series, beating the New York Yankees, David had toppled Goliath. It was a blow that awakened a generation, one that millions of people saw on television, one of TV's first iconic World Series moments.
Edited by Clifton Blue Parker and Bill Nowlin
$19.95 paperback (ISBN 978-1-933599-48-9)
$9.99 ebook (ISBN 978-1-933599-49-6)
8.5"X11", 340 pages, 75 photos

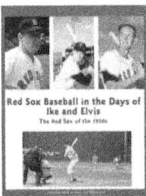

RED SOX BASEBALL IN THE DAYS OF IKE AND ELVIS: THE RED SOX OF THE 1950s
Although the Red Sox spent most of the 1950s far out of contention, the team was filled with fascinating players who captured the heart of their fans. In *Red Sox Baseball*, members of SABR present 46 biographies on players such as Ted Williams and Pumpsie Green as well as season-by-season recaps.
Edited by Mark Armour and Bill Nowlin
$19.95 paperback (ISBN 978-1-933599-24-3)
$9.99 ebook (ISBN 978-1-933599-34-2)
8.5"X11", 372 PAGES, over 100 photos

THE MIRACLE BRAVES OF 1914
BOSTON'S ORIGINAL WORST-TO-FIRST CHAMPIONS
Long before the Red Sox "Impossible Dream" season, Boston's now nearly forgotten "other" team, the 1914 Boston Braves, performed a baseball "miracle" that resounds to this very day. The "Miracle Braves" were Boston's first "worst-to-first" winners of the World Series. Refusing to throw in the towel at the midseason mark, George Stallings engineered a remarkable second-half climb in the standings all the way to first place.
Edited by Bill Nowlin
$19.95 paperback (ISBN 978-1-933599-69-4)
$9.99 ebook (ISBN 978-1-933599-70-0)
8.5"X11", 392 PAGES, over 100 photos

THAR'S JOY IN BRAVELAND!
THE 1957 MILWAUKEE BRAVES
Few teams in baseball history have captured the hearts of their fans like the Milwaukee Braves of the 1950s. During the Braves' 13-year tenure in Milwaukee (1953-1965), they had a winning record every season, won two consecutive NL pennants (1957 and 1958), lost two more in the final week of the season (1956 and 1959), and set big-league attendance records along the way.
Edited by Gregory H. Wolf
$19.95 paperback (ISBN 978-1-933599-71-7)
$9.99 ebook (ISBN 978-1-933599-72-4)
8.5"x11", 330 pages, over 60 photos

NEW CENTURY, NEW TEAM:
THE 1901 BOSTON AMERICANS
The team now known as the Boston Red Sox played its first season in 1901. Boston had a well-established National League team, but the American League went head-to-head with the N.L. in Chicago, Philadelphia, and Boston. Chicago won the American League pennant and Boston finished second, only four games behind.
Edited by Bill Nowlin
$19.95 paperback (ISBN 978-1-933599-58-8)
$9.99 ebook (ISBN 978-1-933599-59-5)
8.5"X11", 268 pages, over 125 photos

CAN HE PLAY?
A LOOK AT BASEBALL SCOUTS AND THEIR PROFESSION
They dig through tons of coal to find a single diamond. Here in the world of scouts, we meet the "King of Weeds," a Ph.D. we call "Baseball's Renaissance Man," a husband-and-wife team, pioneering Latin scouts, and a Japanese-American interned during World War II who became a successful scout—and many, many more.
Edited by Jim Sandoval and Bill Nowlin
$19.95 paperback (ISBN 978-1-933599-23-6)
$9.99 ebook (ISBN 978-1-933599-25-0)
8.5"X11", 200 PAGES, over 100 photos

SABR Members can purchase each book at a significant discount (often 50% off) and receive the ebook editions free as a member benefit. Each book is available in a trade paperback edition as well as ebooks suitable for reading on a home computer or Nook, Kindle, or iPad/tablet.
To learn more about becoming a member of SABR, visit the website: sabr.org/join

www.ingramcontent.com/pod-product-compliance
Lightning Source LLC
Chambersburg PA
CBHW081152070526
44583CB00021B/2806